D0231042

The **AA** **KEY**Guide
Rome

Contents

KEY TO SYMBOLS

✚ Map reference
☎ Telephone number
🕐 Opening times
✋ Admission prices
Ⓜ Underground station
🚌 Bus or tram number
🚆 Train station
Tours
📖 Guidebook
🍴 Restaurant
☕ Café
🍸 Bar
🏬 Shop
🚻 Toilets
① Number of rooms
🅿 Parking
❄ Air conditioning
🏊 Swimming pool
🏋 Gym
❓ Other useful information

How to Use this Book

Understanding Rome is an introduction to the city, its geography, economy and people. **Living Rome** gives an insight into the city today, while **The Story of Rome** takes you through its past.

For detailed advice on getting to Rome—and getting around once you are there—turn to **On the Move**. For useful practical information, from weather forecasts to emergency services, turn to **Planning**.

Rome's key attractions are listed alphabetically in **The Sights** and are located on the maps on pages 56–59. The key sightseeing areas are described on pages 60–64 and are circled in blue on the map on the inside front cover.

Turn to **What to Do** for information on shops, entertainment, nightlife, sport, health and beauty, children's activities, and festivals and events. Entries are listed by these themes, then alphabetically. Shops are located on the maps on pages 152–155 and theatres on the maps on pages 176–179. The top shopping areas are described on pages 157–160 and circled in green on the map on the inside front cover.

Out and About offers four walks around Rome and four excursions that encourage you to explore further afield.

Eating and Staying gives you selected restaurants and hotels, listed alphabetically. Restaurants are located on the maps on pages 228–231 and hotels on the maps on pages 258–261.

Map references refer to the locator maps within the book or the street atlas at the end. For example, Basilica di San Pietro has the grid reference 56 B4, indicating the page on which the map is found (56) and the grid square in which the basilica sits (B4). Grid squares remain the same whatever page the map is on.

UNDERSTANDING ROME

Rome is the world's greatest historical city, its staggering monuments, museums, galleries and architectural treasures spanning almost 3,000 years. Nowhere else will you find such a surfeit of artistic riches, from the grandiose ruins of imperial Rome to the glories of the Vatican, and from sculptural masterpieces of the baroque to the golden age of the Renaissance. But although history has left a considerable legacy, it is not the legacy of a modern capital city and Rome sometimes strains to live up to its contemporary role. Traffic and pollution can be a problem, as can the pressure imposed by many millions of visitors on an already overburdened infrastructure. But Rome has survived three millennia, and today, as monuments are restored and problems confronted, its time-worn face is slowly adapting to the needs of one more in a long line of new centuries.

LAYOUT OF THE CITY

Rome belongs to no single historical period, but is a patchwork of ancient, medieval and modern sights. At the same time, it is small enough to explore on foot, with all but a handful of its main sights being in, or close to, the place where it all started—the Foro Romano. To the north of the Forum lies Piazza Venezia, heart of the more modern city, linked by roads that strike off to the four points of the compass: Via dei Fori Imperiali leads south, back past the Forum to the Colosseo; Via IV Novembre heads east towards a mostly newer 19th-century quarter; Via del Corso strikes north to Piazza del Popolo, passing close to Piazza di Spagna and the shopping streets around Via Condotti; and Via Corso Vittorio Emanuele II runs west towards St. Peter's and Vatican City. This last street also bisects the *centro storico*, or historic heart, the area where most of the sights are, including two of the city's most captivating squares: Piazza Campo dei Fiori and Piazza Navona. This area is bounded to the west by the curve of the River Tiber, across which lies St. Peter's, and, to the south, the more traditional Trastevere area, known today for its restaurants and nightlife. Farther south still is the nightlife district of Testaccio.

CLIMATE

Rome has a marked Mediterranean climate, characterized by summers that are hot and dry, with possible thunderstorms (especially in July and August) and temperatures up to 38°C (100°F). Winters are short and mild, with temperatures that average 14°C (58°F) and rarely fall below freezing. Spring (late March–end May) is usually brief and autumn (September–end November) long: Both can be prone to spells of heavy rain or humid weather. October and November are the wettest months.

THE ECONOMY

Rome may be the Italian capital, but it is far from being its economic fulcrum. It lacks the financial clout of Milan, the heavy manufacturing base of Turin or the international maritime reach of Genoa. Most jobs are in the service sector, in particular those parts of it that provide for the city's millions of visitors. The state is also a big employer, with many jobs in local and national government. Office workers outnumber industrial workers by about six to one. Manufacturing firms are mainly small-scale family concerns, economic mainstays that help counter what might otherwise be a debilitating unemployment problem.

THE SEVEN HILLS OF ROME

According to tradition, Rome was built on seven hills, but 3,000 years of occupation and urban planning means that it is difficult to see the contours of the ancient city. Look closely, however, and the hills are still there, playing host to all manner of historically important sites.

Legend has it that the **Palatine Hill** was the site of Romulus' ancient city. In the middle of the group, it became the seat of power and the residential district of choice, and gave us the word 'palace' after the elegant houses of the patrician classes who built on its summit. Today, you can see the remains of temples and palaces on the hill, as well as the Orti Farnesiani—the 16th-century gardens of the Farnese family. To the northwest is the **Capitoline Hill,** once a fortified stronghold and later, following the building of the Temple of Jupiter, a religious hub. The Capitoline has two summits: the Arx, where a temple to Juno was built, and where the church of Santa Maria in Aracoeli stands today; and the Asylum, where Romulus allowed refugees from other towns to stay,

Ancient ruins on the Palatine Hill (left and middle), and the medieval piazza on the Capitoline (right)

and which is now Piazza del Campidoglio. North of the Capitoline is the **Quirinal Hill,** which, during the imperial age, was the largest residential area. Here is the Palazzo del Quirinale, home of the popes from 1573, then the official residence of the king until Italy's unification in 1870. It is now the seat of the president of the republic. Just to the south lies the **Viminal Hill,** the smallest of the seven, running towards Termini station. Farther south again is the largest of all the hills, the **Esquiline Hill,** where Nero built his Domus Aurea, the Golden House. Below this and to the east of the Palatine is the **Caelian Hill,** stretching across the city from the Colosseo to San Giovanni in Laterano. The **Aventine Hill,** the most southerly of all the seven hills, is divided from the Palatine by the Circo Massimo. It was traditionally the home of the working classes.

POLITICS

Italy's politics are largely Rome's politics, the city having been a political hub for millennia: head of an empire that once covered much of the known world, the headquarters of the Roman Catholic Church for almost 2,000 years, and—more recently—the seat of Italy's national government. It has been capital of a united Italy since 1870 and of the present Italian republic since 1946, when the monarchy was abolished by popular referendum. The two houses of the Italian parliament are here, the Senate (in the Palazzo Madama) and Chamber of Deputies (in the Palazzo Montecitorio); members of both houses are elected for five years. The city's Palazzo del Quirinale is home to the Italian president, elected by both houses and regional representatives for seven years. Most power, however, is wielded by the prime minister, who is usually the leader of the party with a majority of seats in the Chamber of Deputies. The present prime minister is controversial media-magnate Silvio Berlusconi. Much day-to-day administrative business in the city is carried out by the Comune di Roma, or city council, which has its headquarters in the Palazzo Senatorio in Piazza del Campidoglio on the Capitoline Hill.

SOCIETY

Rome sits on a social and economic faultline, with the more prosperous and more dynamic Italy to the north and the more traditional and generally less wealthy Italy to the south. As such, its inhabitants exhibit a variety of traits, from the lingering Mediterranean habits of the siesta and a generally laid-back attitude to life, to a more northern European sensibility that finds expression in obvious displays of material well-being and the increased all-day opening of shops and offices. Rome's inhabitants also share the largely liberal values of Italians as a whole, values that can come as a surprise to those who still see Italy as a country hidebound by religion and history. Divorce and abortion, for example, have been legal for decades, while one of Europe's lowest birth rates belies the notion of Italians in thrall to the Church. Indeed, while most Romans are Catholics, fewer than 10 per cent regularly attend church services. To speak of Romans these days, however, is not only to speak of the familiar Fellini-esque stereotypes, as the last decade has seen the arrival of many thousands of immigrants, notably from the Philippines and Eastern Europe, an influx that is slowly changing the face of the city.

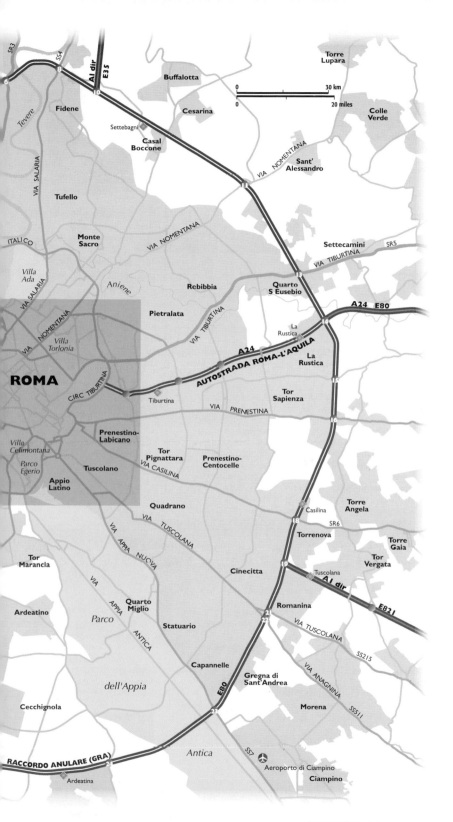

SR3

SS4

Al dir

E35

6

8

10

Torre
Lupara

0   30 km

0   20 miles

Buffalotta

Fidene

Cesarina

Colle
Verde

Tevere

Settebagni

Casal
Boccone

VIA NOMENTANA

Sant'
Alessandro

VIA SALARIA

Tufello

ITALICO

Monte
Sacro

VIA NOMENTANA

Settecamini

SR5

VIA TIBURTINA

Villa
Ada

Aniene

Rebibbia

Quarto
S Eusebio

VIA SALARIA

A24 E80

VIA NOMENTANA

Pietralata

VIA TIBURTINA

La
Rustica

14

VIA

Villa
Torlonia

A24

La
Rustica

ROMA

CIRC TIBURTINA

AUTOSTRADA ROMA-L'AQUILA

15

Tiburtina

Tor
Sapienza

VIA PRENESTINA

16

Villa
Celimontana

Prenestino-
Labicano

Tor
Pignattara

Prenestino-
Centocelle

Parco
Egerio

VIA CASILINA

Tuscolano

Appio
Latino

Quadrano

Casilina

Torre
Angela

18

VIA TUSCOLANA

SR6

Torrenova

Torre
Gaia

VIA APPIA NUOVA

Cinecitta

19

Tuscolana

Al dir

Tor
Vergata

E821

Tor
Marancia

VIA

APPIA

Quarto
Miglio

Romanina

21

23

VIA TUSCOLANA

Ardeatino

Parco

Statuario

ANTICA

VIA ANAGNINA

SS215

Capannelle

Gregna di
Sant'Andrea

Morena

SS511

dell'Appia

E80

Cecchignola

22

23

Antica

RACCORDO ANULARE (GRA)

24

Aeroporto di Ciampino

Ardeatina

Ciampino

BEST ROMAN MONUMENTS

Castel Sant'Angelo (▷ 73): This imperial mausoleum sits grandly by the banks of the Tiber.

Colonna di Marco Aurelio (▷ 78): Magnificent third-century AD bas-reliefs cover this massive column.

Colosseo (▷ 74–77): Its partially ruined state hardly dents the impact of this vast amphitheatre.

Foro Romano (▷ 84–89): The focal point of the Roman Empire for almost a thousand years.

Pantheon (▷ 120–121): Hadrian's temple is Rome's best-preserved ancient monument.

Detail of Ponte Sant'Angelo, leading to Castel Sant'Angelo (above)

The Tempio di Saturno in the Foro Romano (left)

BEST PAINTINGS AND SCULPTURES

Bernini's *St. Teresa* (▷ 137): This statue, in Santa Maria della Vittoria, has been called one of the most erotic in Italy.

Gaul and His Wife Committing Suicide (▷ 112–113): One of the most dramatic statues of the Classical age, at Palazzo Altemps.

Laocoön (▷ 109): A virtuoso Classical sculpture and the highlight of the Musei Vaticani's extensive sculpture collection.

Marcus Aurelius (▷ 100 and 118): Either the original in Musei Capitolini or the copy in Piazza del Campidoglio.

Michelangelo's *Pietà* (▷ 68–69): Now behind glass in St. Peter's following a vandal's attack.

Paolina Borghese (▷ 93): Canova's statue in the Museo e Galleria Borghese leaves little to the imagination.

Raphael's *Transfiguration* (▷ 108): In the Vatican's Pinacoteca, long considered the city's most sublime painting.

San Luigi dei Francesi (▷ 133): An otherwise modest church, made exceptional by a trio of paintings by Caravaggio.

Stanze di Raffaello (▷ 106): Four rooms in the Musei Vaticani with stunning allegorical frescoes by Raphael.

Villa Farnesina (▷ 146): Surprisingly few people visit this Trastevere villa, which has an exceptional series of frescoes by Raphael and Baldassare Peruzzi.

Michelangelo's Pietà in the Basilica di San Pietro

BEST SHOPS

Castroni (▷ 167): Stands out even in Rome, which has more than its share of good delicatessens.

La Città del Sole (▷ 174): A long-established store crammed with educational and high-quality toys.

Coin (▷ 164): A popular department store and Rome's best bet for one-stop shopping.

Frette (▷ 170): Internationally recognized for fine Italian linens and sleepwear.

Giorgio Sermoneta (▷ 169): Gloves, gloves and more gloves.

Spazio Sette (▷ 171): A vast and tempting range of furnishings, gadgets and other items for the home.

Volpetti (▷ 168): Rome's best deli is worth a trip if you want to buy food to take home.

There is no shortage of shopping opportunities in Rome (above). If you like your nightlife late and loud, head for Alibi (below)

BEST BARS AND CLUBS

Alibi (▷ 186): One of the longest-established of the Testaccio clubs, with a delightful summer terrace.

Gilda (▷ 190): If you must see and be seen, this has for many years been the place to come in central Rome.

Jonathan's Angels (▷ 188): Quirky to a fault, this eccentrically decorated bar is popular with locals and visitors.

Piper Club (▷ 190): Piper was trendy before the word was coined, and decades later it's still popular.

BEST PLACES TO EAT

Alberto Ciarla (▷ 232): The best place to eat fish and seafood in Rome—but at a price.

Il Convivio (▷ 238): Creative regional cuisine served in spacious modern surroundings.

Da Agusto (▷ 239): Trastevere used to be the home of the simple trattoria; this is the best of the handful that survive.

Dai Tre Amici (▷ 240): All the bustle and old-fashioned fittings you could want from a traditional Roman restaurant.

Der Pallaro (▷ 241): This trattoria seems to have been around for ever, and offers a reliable Roman home cooking.

Pizzeria La Montecarlo (▷ 248): Simple, inexpensive food with good service.

Pizzeria Popi Popi (▷ 248): A long-established pizzeria in Trastevere, with outside tables in summer.

Roof Garden 'Les Etoiles' (▷ 250): Fine food, with a sensational view of St. Peter's.

Pizza al fresco

BEST CAFÉS

Antico Caffè della Pace (▷ 233): One of Rome's prettiest bars, and a lovely place to sit, indoors or out.

Bar Capitolina (▷ 234): This bar has few rivals when it comes to views of ancient Rome.

Café di Marzio (▷ 237): One of two good cafés in Piazza Santa Maria in Trastevere (the other is Café dell'Arancia ▷ 237).

Antico Caffè della Pace

Sant'Eustachio il Caffè (▷ 251): Rivals the nearby Tazza d'Oro (see below) for the quality of its coffee, but has the bonus of somewhere to sit.

Tazza d'Oro (▷ 252): Join the queues at this café for what many Romans consider the city's best cup of coffee.

BEST LUXURY HOTELS

Grand Hotel de la Minerve (▷ 266): An excellent position close to the Pantheon.

Hassler (▷ 266): The traditional luxury hotel of choice for visiting film stars and other VIPs.

Hotel de Russie (▷ 267): This is by far the best of Rome's modern hotels, a blend of the classic and the contemporary.

Lord Byron Hotel (▷ 268): An art deco villa in leafy, out-of-town Parioli, away from the bustle of the city.

Raphael (▷ 271): More intimate than many of the city's luxury hotels, with romantic rooms behind an ivy-covered façade.

The roof terrace of the Raphael hotel (right)

TOP EXPERIENCES

Don't miss the Palatine Hill when you visit the Foro Romano. It's a leafy retreat with pretty gardens and sweeping views of the ancient city (▷ 110–111).

Walk up the Gianicolo Hill, and stroll along the ridge (Passeggiata del Gianicolo) that overlooks Rome. (▷ 90)

Visit Campo dei Fiori in the morning, partly to take in one of the city's quainter squares, but also to enjoy the sights, smells and sounds of one of Rome's best markets (▷ 122–123).

When it starts to rain, don't dive for just any available cover, but head for the Pantheon, where the water pouring through the deliberately left hole in the dome is one of the city's most evocative sights (▷ 120–121).

Join the Romans walking along the Via Appia Antica (▷ 146)—the road is traffic-free on Sundays and public holidays.

It's not just the traffic that causes problems for scooter riders

Drink coffee in the Piazza Navona. Although you pay a premium to sit at a café table in the square (left), it's worth it to watch the constant parade of people, and to admire Bernini's famous central fountain (▷ 124–125).

Climb to the top of the dome at Basilica di San Pietro (▷ 70–71). The views from the top, over the Vatican gardens and back into the city, are stunning.

Eat an ice cream in Piazza Navona (▷ 124–125): Tre Scalini makes the best *tartufi* in the city, or try a poison apple—ice cream, coated in chocolate, with an alcoholic filling.

Enjoying an ice cream

Making a wish at the Fontana di Trevi (left)

Throw a coin into the Fontana di Trevi (▷ 80–81): Throw the first coin backwards, over your shoulder, into the fountain and make a wish to come back to Rome; a second coin makes the wish come true.

The Villa Borghese (▷ 146) is popular at weekends with families. If you want to do more than relax, take a walk through the park (▷ 208–209) or visit the Museo Nazionale Etrusco at Villa Giulia (▷ 147).

Mingle with the *bel mondo* on the world-famous shopping avenue, Via dei Condotti (▷ 157), where you'll find all the top fashion names: Armani, Fendi, Gucci, Max Mara, Valentino, Versace and (on Via Bocca di Leone, cutting across Via Condotti) Yves Sant Laurent.

Window shopping in the Via dei Condotti (left).
The floodlit Colosseo (below)

View the outside of the Colosseo and Foro Romano on a summer evening, when they're floodlit (▷ 74–77 and 84–89).

Living Rome

Life goes on for modern Romans in the shadow of their ancestors (above)

Keeping the city clean (top left) and policed (left) is a full-time job, but older *romani* take time to relax in the sun (above)

Life in

Ruins

It's not always easy living with 3,000 years of history. Monuments tend to get in the way, and the Forum occupies a prime piece of *centro storico* (historic centre) real estate. But Romans have grown used to the challenge. Writer and historian Georgina Masson summed up the way Rome lives with its past when she called the city a palimpsest: a sheet of parchment used over and over again, with the new text written over the faded original or squeezed in between the lines. Rome is just such a sheet of parchment, except that it has many more overwritings than other cities, and far fewer rubbings-out. This reuse is seen in single buildings—as in the Teatro di Marcello, a Renaissance palace grafted onto a first-century BC theatre— but it is also seen in the ground plan of the city: Piazza Navona curves to follow an ancient racetrack, and public parks mark out the boundaries of former private estates.

Rome's archaeology

A celebrated scene from Fellini's *Roma* shows workers who are drilling a new metro line suddenly breaking through into a room decorated with spectacular Classical frescoes, which begin to fade as soon as they come into contact with the atmosphere. The wealth of archaeological remains is one of the main reasons why Rome has only two metro lines, neither of which goes through the heart of the *centro storico*. The new C line, which has been on the drawing board for decades, will bridge the gap, and planners intend to make the most of this underground wealth, rather than hide it. Stations will allow access to previously hidden archaeological sites, like the Teatro di Pompeo, and some tunnels may be lined with clear acrylic sheet to allow glimpses of illuminated ruins.

Rome's abundance of public drinking fountains fascinates visitors (right)

As the city's streets are so crowded, it makes sense to drive a small car, like the Fiat 500 (below)

The ancient aqueducts, like this one along Via Appia Antica (below), brought water into Rome

A detail from the fountain in Piazza della Rotonda (left)

Look for the city's motto, *senatus populusque romanus,* on statues, but also on rubbish bins and drain covers (below left)

Romans en masse

Romans are good at high-density living. It breeds habits that may appear rude to those from more sedate cultures, but that are often determined by sheer force of numbers. Queuing three or four abreast is often the only way not to spill out of the door and down the street, but you can be sure that everyone in the queue knows exactly who came in after them (in doctors' waiting rooms, new arrivals will always ask, 'Chi è l'ultimo?'—'Who's last?'). The same goes for parking, which is all to do with making the most of the available space—even if this means parking facing into the edge of the road (a feat that the archetypal Roman car, the Fiat 500, is uniquely designed to perform).

Acqua potabile

Between 312BC and AD206, 11 aqueducts were built to provide classical Rome with fresh water. These feats of engineering passed both overland (well-preserved sections of the Acquedotto Claudio can still be seen on the road to Ciampino airport) and underground, bringing more than a million cubic metres (35 million cubic feet) of water a day into the capital. Despite the fact that most of Rome's modern water supply is guaranteed by a huge underground reservoir called the Peschiera, inaugurated in 1949, three of the old aqueducts (the Acqua Marcia, the Appio–Alessandrino and the Vergine) are still in use, though the routes they follow are slightly different now. Many older Romans can still be seen filling up bottles from certain single-aqueduct fountains: They swear it tastes better than the water that comes out of the taps.

Living Latin

There have been a number of attempts by Roman politicians and power brokers down through the ages to co-opt the Glory That Was Rome. In 1347, rabble-rouser Cola da Rienzo persuaded the citizens to revolt against their aristocratic bosses and establish the Senate once more on the Capitoline (this new republic lasted precisely six months). Even the popes got in on the act, giving themselves the high-sounding Latin title Pontifex Maximus (chief priest). And Mussolini pushed the Roman parallels for all he was worth, adopting the Roman *fascio littorio* (a ceremonial bundle of sticks) as his party symbol. Today, Rome's city council continues the tradition, inscribing its motto SPQR (*senatus populusque romanus*—the Senate and the Roman people) on everything from trams to drain covers.

Auditiorium moved

Inaugurated in December 2002, the Auditorium is the biggest new building project to have been unveiled in Rome for a number of years. Designed by Italian architectural superstar Renzo Piano—whose career was launched as Richard Rogers' partner on the Centre Georges Pompidou in Paris—this three-hall city of music is the new home of Rome's premier Santa Cecilia classical music academy and orchestra. But the €140-million complex risked not being built at all when remains of a huge Roman villa were discovered on the site. In the end, the whole project was simply shifted around on its axis to create room for the archaeological area, which has now become an added visitor attraction, complete with small museum.

Mother Teresa is one of many modern-day candidates for canonization (below left).
The Vatican is still a place of pilgrimage (left), and the Pope says weekly public Masses (bottom left).
The new pope meets with his cardinals (below)

Vatican Life

News of the death of Pope John Paul II in April 2005 (▷ 40) was broadcast to crowds of devoted followers that had gathered in Piazza San Pietro. They had been closely watching for clues regarding the Pope's progress, such as the closing of the shutters in his bedroom. The strong sense of the Pope's final hours being an experience shared by Romans and people around the world as well as those inside the Vatican walls owed a great deal to his personal qualities and achievements. It showed that Romans were far from indifferent to the mini-state in their midst. Similarly the Vatican went out of its way to keep the devoted informed. The Holy See is a well-oiled para-governmental organization, whose 4,000 employees serve 950 million Catholics worldwide. Like any such organization, it has public areas—such as Basilica di San Pietro and the Musei Vaticani—and strictly private sections, hidden behind the imposing Leonine Walls. This is where the various ministries of the Vatican State are housed; but there are also more mundane necessities, like the tax-free Vatican supermarket and filling station.

The conclave

The conclave, or the election of a new pope, is one of the world's most mysterious ballots. It's strictly one cardinal one vote, though the Holy Spirit is allowed (indeed expected) to influence the outcome. Following the pontiff's death, the cardinals are locked into the conclave area, which comprises the Sistine Chapel and some adjoining rooms. Voting takes place twice a day until a successful candidate emerges. At the end of each session, the voting slips are burned. In the event of a deadlock, the slips are mixed with wet straw to produce a plume of black smoke. When a pope is finally chosen—usually after several days—a plume of white smoke (*la fumata bianca*) rises from the chapel.

Religious merchandise (left and below), including souvenirs of the late Pope John Paul II, is widely available. The Swiss Guard (far left) still wear uniforms designed by Michelangelo

Newly elected Pope Benedict XVI greets the crowd in Piazza San Pietro

The papal paper

One of the most constant aspects of Vatican life is its daily newspaper, *L'Osservatore Romano*, distributed in Vatican City and 129 other countries worldwide. First published on 1 July 1861, its original aim was to bolster and defend the Papal States, which had lost power and territory following the proclamation of the Kingdom of Italy. One of its founding articles declared its intention 'to reveal and to refute the calumnies unleashed against Rome and the Roman pontificate'. For years, many articles were written in closely worded Latin. The first weekly edition in English appeared in 1968. Ultra-serious in tone and content, the paper has been called 'the pope's own paper'. A recent issue promised a photo story on 'A day in the "vacation life" of Pope Benedict XVI' and a feature on St. Alphonsus and the Eucharist.

The Vatican online

The Vatican may be a male-dominated organization, but one branch at least is in female hands. Sister Judith Zoebelein, an American Franciscan nun, is the mind behind the Holy See's website. Brought over in 1991 to expand the Vatican's rudimentary computer network, she soon became involved in setting up the website (www.vatican.va), which was launched in earnest over Easter 1997. The three computers that initially handled the Internet traffic were called Michael, Gabriel and Raphael, after the three archangels. After a million hits in the first three days, contacts settled to their present average of 50,000 per day. Available in six languages, the Vatican website gives access to over 25,000 Holy See documents, including some in the Vatican Secret Archives.

Working for God

The Holy See's 600 clerical staff and 3,300 lay workers may not be paid global corporate rates, but staff loyalty is boosted by a range of tax breaks and other perks, which include free health care and subsidized rents. Vatican workers pay around a third less for fuel than they would across the border in overpriced Italy—which explains the popularity of Vatican City's two fuel pumps. The employees-only Vatican supermarket also offers substantial savings, though the patchy selection of items on offer can recall Eastern Europe before the fall of the Wall. The only part of the complex that is open to outsiders is the Vatican pharmacy, which stocks certain medicines that are unavailable in Italy (a doctor's prescription is required).

John Paul II—the saintmaker

The late Pope John Paul II created more saints than any other pope in history, and more than all the popes of the previous four centuries. As of March 2003, the tally stood at 465. The Polish Pope also smoothed the road to sainthood, reducing the interval between the death of the candidate and the initiation of the lengthy process from 30 years to just 5. The first step, beatification, is a courtroom-style 'cause' in which the prosecuting attorney—the original 'devil's advocate'—argues against the person's holiness. Full canonization requires two proven miracles to take place after beatification, after direct appeals to the purported saint through prayer. Even for those on the 'fast track' to sainthood, like Mother Teresa of Calcutta, the full process will take a minimum of 15 years.

Art isn't confined to Rome's museums (above). Taking your pizza away can save on cost (left), as can drinking your coffee at the bar (below)

Insider's Rome

Sometimes it's not the obvious things that strike you about a city. It might be a detail, like the scent of cherry blossom in spring, the leisurely walking pace, or the way Italian banks seem geared towards keeping people out. In Rome, for example, the Colosseo is a top tourist priority—but so is crossing the road in one piece. At first this might seem a vain hope, as cars and Vespas are often reluctant to stop even for those waiting at crossings. The local technique seems to be to stride out purposefully, all the while staring the oncoming driver or motorcyclist firmly in the eye. Roman drivers, after all, have no desire to mow down pedestrians: It messes up their car and makes them late (or, rather, later) for appointments. A little inside knowledge also helps make sense of other local stimuli, from soccer graffiti to stray cats; and mastering Roman habits, such as not drinking cappuccino after lunch and not leaving tips of more than five per cent, will do wonders for your self-esteem, though hard-up waiters may be less impressed.

Caffè culture

Coffee is a serious business in Rome and has little to do with the Americanized genre peddled in London or Seattle by lookalike chains. To do *caffè* as the Romans do, a few rules are in order. First, opt for tradition over variety: Mochacchino is unheard of, as is any form of flavoured coffee. Second, respect the time of day: Cappuccino is a breakfast drink, and no Roman would dream of ordering it after lunch or dinner. Third, learn the terminology: If you want an espresso, just ask for *un caffè*; if you want a little more water, it's *un caffè lungo*; if you just want a coffee stain in the bottom of the cup, ask for *un caffè ristretto*.

Locals find the best way to get around the city is by scooter or on foot, while the feline population finds another use for cars (below left)

The cat ladies

Visitors to Rome are often surprised, and sometimes shocked, by the number of stray cats that roam around the city's archaeological sites. There are large communities in the Forum, in the sunken Area Sacra in the middle of busy Largo Argentina, around Caius Cestius' Pyramide and in the adjacent Cimitero Protestante, where Keats and Shelley are buried. But although they are not as well groomed as pampered single-owner apartment cats, these strays are in fact well looked after. An army of voluntary *gattare* (cat ladies) feed the cats, report illnesses or deaths to the city council vet, and provide extra comforts such as wooden cat houses.

Giallorossi or *biancocelesti*?

Rome has two Serie A (premier league) soccer teams: Roma and Lazio. They share the 85,000-capacity Stadio Olimpico, scheduling home matches on alternate Sundays (stadium time-shares are common in Italian soccer: AC Milan and Inter have the same arrangement in Milan, Juventus and Torino in Turin). Roma have fared better in recent years, coming second in the premier league in 2002 and 2004. Both teams are often referred to by the colours they wear: Roma are the *giallorossi* (yellow-and-reds), while Lazio are the *biancocelesti* (white-and-light-blues). Roma supporters are concentrated in the city itself, and tend to be more leftist (soccer, like everything else in Italy, is politicized), while Lazio supporters hail more from the hinterland, and mostly veer to the right.

The *motorini* invasion

As anyone who has tried to cross Piazza Venezia during the rush hour can testify, Rome has been invaded by motorcycles and *motorini* (light, 50cc mopeds and scooters) in the last 15 years. It now has a staggering 600,000 motorized two-wheelers: that's one for every five inhabitants, more than any other city in the world. Rome's balmy climate is one reason for the boom, but it's also connected to the fact that going by scooter can more than halve journey times across the city, and it makes it a lot easier to find a parking space. All two-wheelers are now supposed to have catalytic exhausts, though there are still plenty of unmodified Vespas buzzing around.

Faith in the future

It was not only in ancient times that Romans put their faith in soothsayers and augurs. Around 100,000 Romans visit one of the capital's estimated 1,700 *maghi*, or magicians, every year. Some come for help with unrequited love affairs, others because they believe that enemies have put the *malocchio* (evil eye) on them. With names like Zorzi and Osiris, these modern soothsayers have websites and advertise on buses. Their customers range from professional types to housewives, and even Fellini used to consult a Turinese *mago* called Rol. In the Lazio region as a whole, the annual turnover of these tarot-readers, palm-readers and crystal-ball-gazers is estimated at over €75 million.

Standing guard outside Palazzo Madama (left), seat of the Senate, Rome's upper house

The Palazzo Montecitorio (below), which houses the Chamber of Deputies, the lower house

Controversial prime minister, Silvio Berlusconi

People, Money and Power

Romans are quick to complain whenever the city's place as the nation's capital—and as the spiritual home of one of the world's largest religions—causes them any grief. Hold-ups resulting from anti-government demonstrations or motorcades ferrying heads of state to and from the airport are frequent, and are part of any self-respecting *romano's* repertoire of excuses for being late. But the city benefits from its special status, too; major events like the 1990 World Cup and the Jubilee Year in 2000 saw a huge influx of funds to the capital, which is looking better now than it has for a number of years. The Eternal City has a diversified economy, based on small-scale trade and service concerns; tourism and, more recently, IT are two important sectors. As a consequence, Rome has been largely immune to the post-industrial shake-ups affecting northern cities such as Milan and Turin, where heavy industry accounts for a larger slice of the cake. On the political front, Rome is currently split—acrimoniously at times—between the centre-left loyalties of the city and provincial councils, and the centre-right orientation of both the Lazio region (of which Rome is the capital) and the national government, to which the city plays host.

Silvio Berlusconi

In a country where politicians often have a short shelf life, prime minister Silvio Berlusconi has proved to be a remarkable exception. He began his career in property in 1962, moving into television in the 1980s, and buying the soccer team AC Milan in 1986. In 1993, he founded the centre-right Forza Italia party, the springboard from which he became prime minister a year later. His first term lasted just seven months, and opponents highlighted the potential conflicts of interest arising from his political and business interests. The criticisms didn't prevent him becoming prime minister for a second term in May 2001. Nor have other accusations cramped his style. Mr Berlusconi may be controversial, but in Italian politics he's that rarest of creatures—a survivor.

Whether at work or play, Romans like to dress well

Small families are now more common in modern-day Rome (right)

A modern-day melting pot

It was only in 1976 that Italy became a net importer of people: For over a century, Italians were more used to being immigrants than receiving them. Romans have had plenty of experience of outsiders: In the 25 years following the unification of Italy in 1870, the city's population doubled. Today's immigrants, though, come not from Abruzzo or Campania but from the Philippines, Romania and Poland (in that order), plus a host of other developing and developed countries. There are established African and Asian communities around Piazza Vittorio, near the station, where it is not unusual to see impromptu cricket matches in the park in the summer. Integration has been slow; most Romans still use *la filippina* as a synonym for the cleaning lady.

The Roman art of getting by

The *arte di arrangiarsi*—the old Roman knack of muddling through and of turning even the least promising situation to some advantage—extends to matters of finance and employment. The classic example is the *portiere condominiale*, the porter who, in the more well-heeled areas of the city, sits in a tiny booth at the entrance to an apartment block, screening visitors and taking messages. The *portiere*, who generally lives with his family in the basement apartment, earns a subsistence wage, collected via a tax levied on the apartments' owners. But this is supplemented by a whole range of other activities: procuring documents, doing the shopping, watering plants, taking calls from lovers—all of which carry extra fees.

Mamma's children

These days, the image of a prosperous, pasta-serving *mamma* surrounded by dozens of kids is way off the mark. Italy has one of the world's lowest birth rates, at 9.1 per 1,000 inhabitants, and one of the lowest fertility rates, with 1.2 children born per adult woman (compared with 1.7 for the UK and 2.0 for the US). But *mamma* still exercises a strong influence on the few kids she does have: At the last count, 56 per cent of 25- to 29-year-olds still lived at home, and the number is increasing. According to Italian statistical institute Eurispes, the two figures are connected: 'Young people are getting married less, and until they do marry they prefer to live at home.'

Rome's mayor, Walter Veltroni

Walter Veltroni

Roman mayor Walter Veltroni took over city hall in May 2001, inheriting the job from fellow left-wing politician Francesco Rutelli. His main achievement so far has been to persuade the national government to channel €300 million into city funds. But he's a smart cookie and should make his mark by pushing through the long-awaited new *piano regolatore*, the first Rome town-planning blueprint for 40 years, which aims to put an end to the unregulated building that plagues the capital. The next mayoral elections take place in 2006.

Raphael's frescoes in the Musei Vaticani dwarf visitors (above), while a statue at the Palazzo dello Sport at the EUR watches over a runner (left)

Wealthy families sponsored much of the building work, and their emblems, like the Barberini bees (right), can often be picked out

Art and
Architecture

Rome is too full of life and noise and theatre to allow itself to become a museum. But this is all to the benefit of the tuned-in visitor. Caravaggio's striking *chiaroscuro* canvases in the churches of San Luigi dei Francesi or Santa Maria del Popolo are likely to seem forced and artificial until, emerging into a Roman summer evening, you see how the golden light really does slant in sideways, leaving dark pools of shadow. Bernini's baroque creations, like the Four Rivers fountain in Piazza Navona, translate the city's love of theatre and spectacle into a concerto of stone and water. To uncover Rome's artistic jewels, a little patience is needed. Alongside top attractions like the Sistine Chapel are lesser-known treats such as the church of Santi Quattro Coronati, with its medieval cloister, and that of Santa Prassede, with its Byzantine mosaics. There are quirky architectural one-offs, such as Bramante's *tempietto* (miniature temple) in the church of San Pietro in Montorio, and a few unexpected modern classics, including Mazzoni's Termini station and Libera's Marmorata post office.

Pietro Cavallini

Few visitors realize that one of Italy's great medieval frescoes is not in Tuscany but in Rome. In its nascent realism, Pietro Cavallini's late 13th-century *Last Judgement* in the church of Santa Cecilia is a clear anticipation of the Renaissance. Late, great Italian art critic Federico Zeri (1921–1998) went so far as to suggest that Cavallini, rather than Giotto, may have been responsible for the St. Francis cycle in the Upper Basilica at Assisi; and a recent book by Zeri disciple Bruno Zanardi lends support to the claim by demonstrating the clear stylistic analogies between the Santa Cecilia frescoes and the Upper Basilica cycle. The jury is still out—so catch Cavallini before he becomes a household name.

Stazione Termini (right).
Bernini's Fontana dei Fiume (below).
The Colosseo, illuminated at night (below right)

Outside Fiumicino airport (far right, middle) and the Musei Capitolini's courtyard (far right, bottom)

The perfect blue

Renaissance painters, and their patrons, observed a rigid hierarchy of hues. It is easy for us today to appreciate the value of the silver and gold pigments that enriched the altarpieces of the Middle Ages, and that derived directly from the precious metals themselves. But few modern observers realize that ultramarine blue was just as valuable: Extracted from lapis lazuli, it was a costly Arabian import. Contracts would stipulate the grade to be used, in order to prevent its replacement with the inferior German blue (a copper carbonate). Without lapis lazuli, the deep blue firmament that provides the luminous backdrop of Michelangelo's *Last Judgement*, on the altar wall of the Sistine Chapel, would by now have faded to grey.

Fascist architecture

Mussolini may have made those trains run on time, but it was architecture, rather than punctuality, that he bequeathed to the Romans. Fascism is kept alive today only by a fringe of far-right nostalgics, but the clean, sharp, marble-faced buildings that encapsulated the regime's dreams of a Brave New World are still standing, in silent reproach to the lack of identity and vision of their postwar counterparts. Leading examples are the Foro Italico, built between 1928 and 1935 to host the Olympic Games; the model suburb of EUR to the south of the city, which includes Adalberto Libera's groundbreaking Palazzo dei Congressi; and Termini station, with its soaring cantilevered roof, completed after the war to a 1930s design by Angiolo Mazzoni.

Private wealth makes public art

In terms of masterpieces per square metre, Rome does not have a gallery to compare with the Ufizzi in Florence or the Accademia in Venice. But what it does have is a wealth of private collections that have remained substantially intact. The Museo e Galleria Borghese, the Palazzo-Galleria Doria Pamphilj and the Ludovisi collection in Palazzo Altemps are fascinating because of the personalities that lie behind them and the way they illuminate the history of taste. The Ludovisis, for instance, thought nothing of asking baroque sculptors such as Alessandro Algardi to 'improve' the classical statues they owned. Meanwhile, Scipione Borghese's mixture of hedonism and seriousness comes through in his eclectic collection, which veers from the religious piety of Raphael's *Deposition* to the worldly eroticism of Correggio's *Danaë*.

The rarity of new buildings

Compared to London, Paris or Berlin, Rome has little contemporary architecture of any breadth or vision. Red tape is one problem; so is the sheer lack of sites in a city where nothing is ever knocked down. Well, almost nothing. Of the handful of new projects that represent Rome's long-awaited architectural reawakening, the most controversial is the new casing for the Ara Pacis monument, designed by American architect Richard Meier. Until recently this graceful classical altar, brought to light in the 1930s, was housed in a fascist-era pavilion, which was demolished to prepare the ground for Meier's boxy white Ara Pacis Museum. The ensuing political row blocked work on the project and is likely to keep this masterpiece of Roman art out of bounds to visitors for quite some time.

Gregory Peck recognized Audrey Hepburn's star quality when they appeared together in *Roman Holiday* (left): He insisted her name was put above the film title

Marcello Mastroianni and Sophia Loren (above) starred together in over a dozen films.
Alberto Sordi (right)

Hollywood on the Tiber

Rome has always seen itself as one big movie set. Much of the city's theatre is spontaneous: Rows erupt, jokes are cracked—Romans love playing to the gallery. It's no surprise, then, if this talent for spectacle should take more organized forms, and the natural medium for this instinct is cinema. The golden age of Roman film was in the 1950s and 1960s, when low-budget swords-and-sandals movies, many shot in the historic Cinecittà studios, alternated with intense neo-realist classics such as De Sica's *Umberto D* or Pasolini's *Accattone*, shot on location in the depressed inner suburbs. And then there were the Americans, attracted by low labour costs. Today, you can rent a Vespa to re-enact *Roman Holiday* (though helmets are now compulsory) or mime the chariot race from *Ben Hur* in the Circo Massimo. But don't attempt a *Dolce Vita*-style dip in the Trevi Fountain: The resident policeman's main job these days is to foil any would-be Anitas and Marcellos.

Federico Fellini

Albertone

When actor Alberto Sordi died in February 2003, a quarter of a million Romans turned out for his funeral. In almost 200 films, 'Albertone' (Big Alberto) had become a screen icon.

But Sordi was no action hero. With his *faccia da mammone* (mummy's-boy face), he embodied a new type of Italian of the postwar generation: Outwardly modern and besotted with American values (as in *Un Americano a Roma*, 1954) but in reality profoundly Italian; outwardly the Don Giovanni (as in Fellini's *I Vitelloni*, 1953) but in reality ill at ease with women. Later in life, Sordi became an unofficial Roman elder statesman; he was even made mayor for a day on his 80th birthday.

Anthony Minghella (far right) filmed parts of *The Talented Mr. Ripley* (1999) on location in Rome

Cameron Diaz (below far right) with Martin Scorsese on the set of *Gangs of New York* (2002). The actress was nominated for a Golden Globe for the role of Jenny Everdeane

Anita Ekberg (right) in *La Dolce Vita* (1960), the film that introduced the word *paparazzi* into general use

Cinecittà

It was not until the 1930s that Rome emerged as the capital of Italian cinema ahead of two early contenders, Turin and Florence. Inaugurated by Mussolini in 1937, the Cinecittà studios covered what had been until then a huge area of farmland on the Via Tuscolana. The studios worked flat out until the wartime lull, then returned to health in the 1950s on the back of a string of American productions, from *Roman Holiday* (1952) to *Cleopatra* (1963). Meanwhile, Federico Fellini (far left), who claimed that the real world never matched the heightened reality of a studio set, was weaving his cinematic fantasies in Studio 5. The 1970s and 1980s saw a drastic decline in Cinecittà's fortunes, with TV productions outnumbering films.

The not-so-sweet life

Perhaps the most iconic Italian film of all time, Federico Fellini's *La Dolce Vita* was shot in Rome between March and September 1959. It was not an easy birth: The film's original producer, Dino De Laurentiis, pulled out at the last moment, alarmed by the 'chaotic' script and Fellini's refusal to replace Marcello Mastroianni with Paul Newman. Shooting was equally eventful. The famous Trevi Fountain sequence was shot on a freezing night in March, with Anita Ekberg shivering in her backless ball dress. Ever the entertainer, Fellini turned his megaphone to the crowd and said:

'Where would you find another like her? I've made her do things a circus horse wouldn't do. And now I'm throwing her into the water.'

The return of the Americans

The Americans are back. Although the days when Rome was known as 'Hollywood on the Tiber' are long gone, when stars such as Cary Grant, Ava Gardner, Charlton Heston and Elizabeth Taylor kept the paparazzi of the Via Veneto snap-happy, the 1990s saw a significant return of big-budget international productions to the competitively priced Cinecittà studios. First came two Sylvester Stallone vehicles, *Cliffhanger* and *Daylight*; interior scenes of *The Portrait of a Lady* and *The Talented Mr Ripley* were also shot here. Then, in the autumn of 2000, the heavy artillery moved in, when Martin Scorsese built a replica of 1860s New York on the studio backlot for *Gangs of New York*. With Leonardo DiCaprio and Cameron Diaz in town, it was paparazzi paradise once again.

Italian cinema

It's not quite true that nothing has happened in Italian cinema since those glorious art house days of Fellini, Pasolini, Antonioni and Bertolucci. But it's an understandable assumption, as few contemporary Italian films are distributed abroad, and those that are tend to languish in cineclub ghettos. The exception to the rule is Roberto Benigni, whose Oscar-winning *La Vita è Bella* (*Life Is Beautiful*) was a huge international hit. But Benigni is not really representative of the new Italian cinema, which is at its most incisive in the films of Roman auteur Nanni Moretti (*The Son's Room*, 2001), veteran political filmmaker Marco Bellocchio (*The Divinity Lesson*, 2002), and the emotional tangles of young Turk (literally, as he was born in Istanbul) Ferzan Özpetek (*Ignorant Fairies*, 2002).

From head to toe, and everywhere in between, if it's stylish, you can buy it in Rome

La Bella Figura

Roman style

Understand *bella figura* and you're halfway to understanding the Romans. *Bella figura* is a little bit presence, a little bit self-respect and a little bit being careful not to let the side down. It's what *carabinieri* motorcycle cops are communicating when they lean against their Moto Guzzis in jodhpurs and wraparound shades; it's what makes kids from the depressed outer suburbs dress up on Saturday night as if they were in Beverly Hills. The opposite is *brutta figura*, to show oneself up. In Rome, it's not so much what you've got, it's what you project.

If style is all about care for one's appearance, an instinct for what looks good and the ability to project self-confidence, most Romans have it in bagfuls. All three qualities can be observed during the evening *passeggiata*. Though not as strong a tradition as it is in other towns farther south, the custom of walking up and down observing others who are also walking up and down reaches critical mass along Via del Corso on Fridays and Saturdays between 5pm and 8pm. But if style is interpreted in the more Northern European sense of originality and standing out from the crowd, many Romans would fail to qualify. Roman style tends to be fairly conformist, opting for the prevailing designer uniform rather than going out on a customized limb. In fashion terms, Rome is more provincial, but also more relaxed, than Milan, Italy's *capitale della moda*. The only big designer to have made his power base in the city is Valentino, though the Fendi siblings and a few mavericks such as Roberto Cappucci are a strong supporting act.

Valentino

Though he hails from Voghera in the north of Italy, Valentino long ago adopted the Eternal City as the hub of his fashion empire. Valentino Garavani, as he was christened in 1932, moved to Rome in 1959 after a stint as an apprentice in the couture houses of Paris. It was the White Collection in 1967 that really made his name and before long he was dressing such divas as Jackie Kennedy and Elizabeth Taylor. His Roman headquarters is at Rampa Mignanelli, just behind the Spanish Steps, where the *alta moda* (haute couture) collections are presented in January and July.

Valentino has been leading Italian fashion since the 1960s

The Story of Rome

Early Rome

All civilizations have their creation myths, like the tale of Romulus and Remus. We know for certain that tribes had colonized the Seven Hills of Rome by 1000BC, between the Etruscans to the north and the Greeks to the south. The Etruscans soon dominated the city and brought with them much of what we regard as typically Roman: irrigation, temple-building, gladiatorial displays and togas. Their aristocratic rule was oppressive, and the last of the kings was driven out in 509BC. The following republic was a system of power-sharing among noble families, but rights for commoners were gradually won, set out in the Twelve Tables in 450BC and displayed in the Forum.

Over the next two centuries the Romans conquered Italy and moved inexorably beyond. They defeated the Carthaginians so, by the end of the Third Punic War in 146BC, the Roman Empire comprised Italy, the western Mediterranean and Asia Minor. Strict warrior values had created it, but the aristocracy appropriated land and wealth, leaving soldiers and peasants almost nothing. Attempts at reform from the top, led by the Gracchi brothers, and from the bottom in the form of slave revolts, achieved nothing. By 100BC the rulers of Rome had become violent, selfish and dictatorial.

Via Appia Antica was built in 312BC and is still paved with its original basalt cobbles

Romulus and Remus

The legend goes that Romulus and Remus were the twin sons of Mars and a vestal virgin. Left to die on the banks of the Tiber, they were cared for by a she-wolf and fed by a wood-pecker. The brothers grew up to be robbers and wandered with a band of men. Romulus took possession of the Palatine Hill and founded Rome on 21 April 753BC. Remus set up his rival kingdom on the Aventino. Eventually, Romulus killed Remus and his power grew. The legend rings true in one respect: the gaining of imperial power through violence and murder within the family, which was to become a familiar pattern in Roman history.

The she-wolf is the symbol of Rome.

735BC

By the second century BC, the Roman Empire was expanding

The theft of the Sabine Women

Romulus' fledgling state needed women, so he decided to steal some. In 750BC, he invited the nearby Sabine tribe to attend a ceremony in honour of a newly discovered holy altar to the god Concus. The Sabines came peacefully, and Romulus and his armed men simply ran away with their women, 683 of them if legend is true. Strangely enough, after a few skirmishes both sides agreed to avoid a ruinous war and co-operate. Romulus, with typical Roman pragmatism, then ruled over the Seven Hills jointly with the Sabine chief, Titus Tatius. This joint rule system entered Roman government: Consuls often worked in pairs, as did many of the other officers of state.

The rape of Lucretia

According to tradition, in 509BC Sextus Tarquinius, the son of the Etruscan king, went to visit Lucretia and her husband, Collatinus, one night, and they fell to discussing virtuous wives. Lucretia, a true Roman matron, was strict and irreproachable, and Tarquinius, aroused by this, determined to seduce her. He came back when she was alone, threatened her and then raped her. With her honour gone, Lucretia committed suicide after telling her husband what had happened. This act represented everything that was wrong with the corrupt Etruscan monarchy, which was plundering the country and trampling on Roman virtues, so Collatinus and his powerful friends rose up in revolt. The people of Rome supported them, the King was forced into exile and the republic was established.

Giambologna's statue *Rape of the Sabine Women* (left)

The Capitoline geese

In 390BC, an army of Gauls surrounded Rome. The smaller Roman army withdrew and evacuated the city except for the Capitoline Hill, where the soldiers were besieged. One night a former consul, Marcus Manlius, woke to hear the honking of a gaggle of geese, which the starving soldiers had not eaten because they were sacred to Juno. Manlius looked over the wall in time to see the shield of a Gaulish soldier who was about to climb over. He knocked him back, and a volley of stones and javelins from the other soldiers sent the Gauls crashing down the hill to their deaths. The Capitoline Hill never was taken, but the Gauls stayed in Rome for seven more months, and left only when they got a hefty ransom.

The Gracchi brothers

The tribune Tiberius Gracchus attempted to break up the great estates of the rich and distribute the land to the poor, especially former soldiers, who were wandering the country. The Senate, composed of the owners of great estates, was horrified to see public support for Tiberius and hired a band of thugs to kill him. He was beaten to death with a chair leg outside the Capitoline temple, and 300 supporters were thrown into the Tiber. In 120BC his brother Sempronius met the same fate over the same issue, and 3,000 followers were murdered. These acts of shocking violence by the very men supposed to uphold the law set the scene for the fall of the republic 60 years later.

100BC

OMAN EMPIRE

Most of what is known about the Etruscans comes from their pottery and artwork (left)

The Palatine Hill is rich with archaeological remains (above)

Honking geese warned of a surprise attack by the Gauls (left)

Brutality and Dictatorship

Riot, unrest and civil war in the first century BC led to the emergence of the army and the rise of ruthless dictators as the guarantors of public order, gladly supported by the Senate. The brutal rule of Sulla was followed by the first triumvirate in 70BC, composed of Pompey, Crassus and Julius Caesar. They resisted all attempts by the Senate, somewhat belatedly, to regain democratic power. The triumvirs eventually turned on each other. In 49BC Julius Caesar crossed the Rubicon from his territories of Gaul and took control of Rome; by the following year he was sole ruler of the empire. Caesar was an autocrat who demanded total obedience: The republic was finally at an end. The Senate nevertheless rallied its forces, albeit for the last time, and a group of conspirators murdered the dictator in 44BC. What followed was a contest for power between the impulsive, emotional Mark Antony and the icy, calculating Octavian. Antony was absent from Rome for long periods during his spectacular love affair with the queen of Egypt, Cleopatra, while Octavian built up his military base in the western part of the empire. After moving against Antony and defeating him at the Battle of Actium in 31BC, Octavian secured the empire for himself to become the first emperor, Augustus.

100BC

Marius and Sulla

Gaius Marius, the son of a farmer, and Lucius Cornelius Sulla, an aristocrat, played out the murderous rivalry that Romulus and Remus had set as the Roman pattern. The men had once been comrades, but, as the republic was about to collapse, Marius, seven times consul, wanted to break the power of the Senate; Sulla was determined to oppose him. Marius massacred the Senate and thousands of aristocrats in 87BC. After Marius' death, Sulla murdered his foe's army. He formed a dictatorship and paraded through the streets protected by a vicious force of 10,000 slaves, the Cornelii. When Sulla abruptly stepped down and retired to the country, he left Rome brutalized and the Senate ripe for overthrow.

Gaius Marius (top left) and Lucius Cornelius Sulla (left)

Julius Caesar ignored warnings to 'beware the ides of March' (below)

Spartacus

There were three slave revolts between 140BC and 70BC. Life rested on the caprice of the master: 'Lighten a ship by throwing out the slaves, not the horses,' Cicero said, while the philosopher Seneca thought slavery the worst shame of the empire. Spartacus, possibly a deserter, was a slave in the gladiator barracks in Capua in 73BC, when he escaped with 70 other gladiators and weapons from the kitchens. They hid on the slopes of Vesuvius and were soon joined by other escaped slaves and gladiators. Spartacus wanted to lead his men to freedom across the Alps, but his followers sought to plunder the surrounding countryside, attracting punitive action from Rome. For two years Spartacus' army (120,000 strong at its peak) managed to defeat all the forces the Roman senate sent to deal with it. Eventually, in 71BC, his forces were defeated at Brindisi, and 6,000 slaves were crucified along the Appian Way. Spartacus died in battle and his body was never found.

Cicero

Cicero was Rome's best lawyer, a respected author with political skills that made him consul in 63BC, a position usually reserved for the aristocracy. These were violent times—killing was state policy—and he spent much time on murder trials. In 80BC the young Cicero made his reputation defending Sextius Roscius for the murder of his father. In a barnstorming speech he described the horrible punishment for this: being tied up in a sack and thrown into the sea. Then Cicero dared to suggest that a servant of Sulla, the dictator of Rome, was the real murderer, since he wanted the Roscius estates. Sensationally, the jury believed him, Roscius was acquitted and the young lawyer was on his way.

The assassination of Julius Caesar

Julius Caesar was dictator of Rome. 'Regard what I say as law,' he declared. When the Senate, gritting its teeth, knelt before him, Caesar stayed seated. In the atmosphere of brutality and murder that he had used himself, the arrogant dictator's fate was sealed. A group of conspirators planned his murder for 15 March 44BC in the Senate. Caesar seemed not to fear assassination, taking no great precautions, and the night before he died said he wanted a quick and unexpected death. He ignored all warnings. The conspirators stabbed him 23 times, and a strange detail is recorded: He put his toga around his head, then drew the bottom around his thighs to preserve his modesty. He knew he was going to fall.

Antony and Cleopatra

In 41BC Mark Antony, joint ruler of the empire, became captivated by Cleopatra during her spectacular entrance to Tarsus, on a bejewelled ship with silver oars, dressed in cloth of gold. Antony left his wife, and he and Cleopatra were crowned as semi-divine rulers of Egypt. Rome was outraged: Antony had abandoned his country and ideals. His co-ruler, Octavian, declared war and met Antony's navy at Actium in 31BC. The battle went to Octavian, and Cleopatra sailed away. Antony had to choose. He still had his armies and his wealth: Rome might still be his. Nevertheless, he sailed after Cleopatra and lost everything. They committed suicide together the next year.

Cicero was a great lawyer and statesman, but later fell from grace

Mark Antony's obsession with Cleopatra lost him the city of Rome. The pair later died in a joint suicide pact (left)

27BC

The Ponte Fabricio, built in 62BC, is the oldest bridge in Rome

The Early Emperors

The 41 years of Emperor Augustus' rule (27BC–AD14) were looked back on as the Golden Age by the Romans. He halted expansionist wars, set up a government bureaucracy and transformed the face of Rome itself. Too shrewd to accept the title of emperor—he was called 'First Citizen'—Augustus held all major posts in government, the army and religion for life, while leaving the forms of the republic intact. The glory of his reign notwithstanding, it set the scene for the breath-taking excesses that followed: Tiberius, Caligula and Nero were known for lust, perversion and cruelty. A well-ordered bureaucracy ensured the empire almost ran itself: Germanicus easily suppressed revolts in Germany (AD14–16), and great public buildings rose throughout Italy. However, Tiberius (AD14–37), fearing conspiracy, invoked laws to suppress any opposition; Caligula (AD37–41) despised the Senate so much that he planned to turn the empire into an autocracy. Fear and oppression seeped into government, and the emperors depended on the Praetorian Guard to terrorize opponents. Claudius (AD41–54) bribed the Praetorians well, but the reckless actions of his successor, Nero (AD54–68), antagonized the Senate and lost him the army's support. Nero fled the city and committed suicide in AD68.

Augustus

The first emperor, Augustus (previously know as Octavian; ruled 27BC–AD14), lived in a modest villa by the Palatine, but he made the city splendid, saying, 'I found Rome built of brick; I leave it clothed in marble.' This was not personal vanity; Rome had to be grand in the eyes of the world and orderly for its citizens. A hundred public buildings were raised; *insulae*, tenements for the poor, were limited in height to 25m (80ft). The city was divided into 250 precincts, each with its own police force and fire brigade—the poor made do with wood, not marble, and Rome was forever in flames. To deal with this, Augustus' architect, Agrippa, created a remarkable system of six aqueducts, which brought in over a billion litres (220 million gallons) of water a day.

27BC

Augustus, whose Golden Age saw the arts flourish (left)

The great fire of Rome in AD64 was reputed to have been started by Nero (below)

The original Pantheon was built in 27BC, but the inscription on the front is all that remains of that building (above)

Caligula

The notorious Caligula (ruled AD37–41) suffered a traumatic childhood and probably had some kind of mental illness. His appearance—tall, thin, bald and hollow-eyed— was truly frightening. Stories about his private life are outdone only by his amazing extravagance. He sailed along the coast in jewel-studded galleys fitted with baths and dining rooms. He offered dinner guests titbits made of gold. Mountains were levelled and plains raised for his public buildings, all at high speed since everything was done under threat of death. He showered people in the streets with gold and liked rolling around on heaps of it. The coffers were soon empty. In one year, it is estimated, he spent 3 billion sesterces, the entire revenue of Tiberius' 23-year reign.

Claudius

It was easy to make fun of Claudius (ruled AD41–54) in his lifetime. He stammered and trembled, gave way to screaming anger, and stuffed himself with so much food and drink he often fell asleep in the middle of a banquet. His mother called him a monster whom Nature had begun but failed to complete, and he was regularly the focus of practical jokes. As often happens, the embittered, humiliated man retreated to the world of books and learning. He made himself a formidable scholar. Pliny regarded Claudius as one of the greatest minds in the empire. Claudius wrote a treatise on dicing, a study of the Roman alphabet and a 20-volume Etruscan history whose loss is a tragedy for historians.

Nero

Nero (ruled AD54–68) wanted to be a great actor and athlete. Progressing from private theatricals, he made his debut in Naples during an earthquake, warbling to his lyre and dressed in garish wig and robes. He entered competitions and, naturally, won. During a tour of Greece, he won 1,808 prizes, including one for a race when he'd fallen out of his chariot and been knocked senseless. Contemporaries giggled over his awful acting, but he was probably just mediocre. The doors were locked when he performed and the audience, bored to tears, endured endless applause and encores. More seriously, the Senate abhorred Nero's neglect of government business and rose against him. Deluded to the end, he fled Rome crying, 'What a loss I shall be to the arts!'

St. Peter in Rome

Peter probably visited Rome in the AD50s and it's almost certain that he died there during the persecution of the Christians begun by Nero around AD64. Some of those martyrs were torn to pieces by animals, others smeared with pitch and burned as human torches in the Circus of Nero to illuminate night-time races. According to early Church tradition, Peter was crucified upside-down at his own request, feeling unworthy to be killed in the same way as Christ. In AD324, Constantine built a church on the site of the Circus of Nero, which was subsequently replaced by Julius II's basilica that we see today. In the crypt of the great basilica is a place that tradition glorifies as St. Peter's grave.

Nero is best remembered for his debauchery and extravagance (right)

AD 72

The gladiatorial games were noted for their brutality, with the emperor deciding if the fallen gladiator should live or die (far left)

This obelisk, now in Piazza del Popolo, was brought from ancient Egypt by Augustus (left)

The Height of the Empire

For nearly two centuries, the citizens of Rome enjoyed peace and wealth. The five 'good emperors' of the Antonine dynasty—Nerva, Trajan, Hadrian, Antoninus and Marcus Aurelius (ruled AD81–180)—worked with the Senate, and the empire expanded to its greatest limits. Soon, though, its very size proved its undoing. A huge army of approximately half a million men, composed of many different nationalities, could not easily be controlled. The army started to dictate policy, and local commanders were often made emperor without ever seeing Rome. In AD193 the Praetorian Guard put the empire up for sale—the winner lasted 66 days in power. In all, some 50 emperors came and went in the period up to the beginning of the rule of Diocletian in AD286.

The enormous territories in the east meant Rome no longer occupied its central role. Recognizing that the empire was ready to collapse under its own weight, Diocletian divided it into the Western and Eastern empires, under two rulers, which brought some respite from political tension. Diocletian then tackled a much greater force for change, the Christians. He persecuted them ruthlessly, but the conversions went on and the Church continued to grow and develop, with converts increasingly coming from all ranks of society.

The Colosseum

The ruins of the Colosseo, built AD79–96, dominate the city today, much as the games once held in it dominated Roman life. Their equivalent today is the hugely expensive blockbuster movie with its pampered stars, but there the similarity ends. A successful gladiator might be adored by the whole city, but, as Seneca said, 'this was a serious business—pure murder.' The games themselves probably evolved from Etruscan funeral games, and this echo of the underworld never left them. At the games of Trajan in AD107, for example, 80,000 people watched 10,000 men fight to the death over a period of four months. As they became an instrument of social control, more frequent games with greater cruelty kept the populace quiet.

The Colosseo (left. Porta Pia, built in AD271–75, was or of the main gates in the Aurelian Walls (below)

AD 72

Triumphal arches, like this one dedicated to Titus, were built to celebrate military victories (below)

Trajan

During Trajan's reign (ruled AD98–117) the *Pax Romana* (Roman Peace) extended over a huge empire, from Scotland to Portugal, over the Sahara to the borders of Persia, and into Germany. Trajan expanded the empire to its limits, his armies following the routes of Alexander the Great. Trajan was a typical mixture of Roman brutality and magnanimity. The Dacians (modern-day Transylvanians) were completely subdued by him. Their gold was taken to Rome and thousands of men and women brought there as slaves and gladiators. Yet Trajan forbade the persecution of Christians, causing the governor of Bithynia, worried about that troublesome group, to write that 'they create the worst kind of precedent and are out of keeping with the spirit of the age.'

Hadrian

Hadrian (ruled AD117–138) spent most of his time journeying through the empire and usually left a building or two behind him. In Britain, he constructed a wall across the north to keep out marauding tribes. In Egypt, an entire city, Antinopolis, was raised in memory of his friend, Antinous. Two buildings in Rome express the opposites in his personality, the cool-headed administrator and the imperial master. The Pantheon is a masterpiece of design—classical, deceptively simple, perfectly symmetrical, the work of the man who revised the codes of tax and the law. His tomb, on the other hand, turned out to be an immense piece of unsubtle grandeur, so vast that medieval Romans used it as a fortress. It's now within Castel Sant'Angelo.

The feasts of Elegabalus

Even by Roman standards, Elegabalus (ruled AD218–221) is astonishing. He was a teenage Syrian covered in make-up, jewels and silk, and the tales of his luxury are astounding. He liked to swim in pools stained yellow with saffron, and to walk on roses and lilies. At his feasts guests lay on couches of solid silver; one evening the food was blue, the next it was green. He liked to eat peacocks' tongues, then suddenly would demand nightingales' tongues instead. Once, 600 ostrich heads were served and guests ate their brains. Not surprisingly, the guests often fell asleep in a stupor. Elegabalus' idea of fun was then to lock them in the hall, and send in tame bears and lions to wake them up.

Rome without an emperor

In AD300, over a thousand years after Romulus occupied the Palatine Hill, the emperors left Rome. The vast city was a rich brew of contrasting nationalities, from Arabs to Britons and Turks. The emperor himself might be African or Spanish, but he had always respected Rome as the focal point of the world: Diocletian had no such scruples. He came from Dalamatia, toured the empire as all the emperors had done, and it's likely that he did not even see Rome until he was almost 60. He didn't like the excess and corruption, and found Milan to the north and Nicomedia to the east far more practical as capitals. They were built up swiftly and soon became as grand as the Eternal City itself.

Trajan was a popular emperor, despite spending most of his reign abroad (below left)

Hadrian (left) built his mausoleum north of the Tiber. Today, it is in the Castel Sant'Angelo (right)

305

Piazza Navona's racetrack shape (left) follows the lines of Domitian's AD86 Stadium

Emperor Aurelius built the city's fortification walls in AD271 (above)

SPQR
IMP·CAESARI·NERVAE·F
TRAIANO
OPTIMO·PRINCIPI
ANNO·XI
A·FASCIBVS·RENOVATIS

Christian Rome

Christianity became the state religion under Diocletian's successor, Constantine (AD306–37). Although he moved the capital to Byzantium, Rome became the empire's spiritual hub. Increasingly, the western borders were under threat from Goths and Vandals. The city was sacked several times and in AD476 the last Roman emperor, Romulus Augustulus, was deposed. During centuries of war between the Byzantine Empire and the Goths, the popes acquired territory known as the Papal States and the authority to crown the Holy Roman Emperor. The emperor of Germany claimed rights over the election of the pope, and only under Innocent III (1198–1216) did papal power finally become independent.

Throughout this turmoil Rome shrank to a provincial town. In AD546, reduced to rubble by the Goths, it was deserted for weeks. The papacy alone ensured Rome's survival, but its very wealth and power sparked such feuding that the popes fled to France from 1307 to 1377. The demagogue Cola di Rienzo set up a republic based on ancient principles during this period, but it soon collapsed. The return of the papacy was marred by the Great Schism of the West, when popes and antipopes fought for control of the Church, each backed by half of Europe. Only in 1417 did the Vatican gain its position as the residence of the true pope.

The conversion of Constantine

No one is sure when Constantine converted to Christianity. Was it at the vision of a flaming cross in the sky in AD312, or at his deathbed baptism in AD337? Despite being the son of St. Helena, who found the True Cross, did he genuinely convert at all? What mattered was that a spirit of Christianity began to pervade the empire. A master who mistreated his slaves was punished, children were protected from abusive parents, prisoners no longer fought in gladiatorial displays, which were denounced by Constantine as 'bloody spectacles'. Much money was spent on erecting churches, many at sites linked with events of the New Testament. Constantine himself gave up imperial power, and the honour of being high priest of the state religion now went to the Bishop of Rome.

AD305

Constantine (right). This 12th-century mosaic, from the church of San Clemente, is a wonderful example of Byzantine art (below right)

Pope Gregory the Great (left) was a particularly pious man, who founded several monasteries

The Arch of Constantine, from which this detail comes, was built to commemorate his defeat of the last pagan emperor, Maxentius, in 312 (above)

The sack of Rome

The Goths, being driven out of their own lands by invading Huns in AD370, moved south into Greece and then, in AD400, under their leader Alaric, attacked Italy. The Italians begged Alaric to stop, but he told them of a voice urging him on: 'It says to me, "Go to Rome and make that city desolate."' The day came when he besieged the city itself. Alaric told ambassadors from the city to give him all their gold, silver and slaves. Horrified, they asked what he would leave them. 'Your lives,' he replied. The Goths stripped Rome of everything in four days and left behind a traumatised city, which had been inviolate for 800 years.

Visigoth leader Alaric (below)

Pope Gregory the Great

Gregory I combined the grandeur of his position with the simplicity of a true Christian, eating sparingly and giving money to the poor. His revision of the Mass introduced Gregorian chant. He sent St. Augustine to England to convert the Anglo-Saxons ('not Angles but angels'). Gregory became pope in AD590, a testing time: Rome was gripped by plague (the previous pope had died of it). He arranged penitential processions in Rome to ask for God's mercy. On his procession near the Tiber, he had a vision of an angel in the sky sheathing a bloody sword; from that moment the plague ended. The building beneath the vision, Hadrian's Tomb, was renamed Castel Sant'Angelo. On his death, Gregory was made a saint by popular acclamation.

The mosaic of Mary Enthroned (right), in the church of Santa Maria in Trastevere

Charlemagne, Holy Roman Emperor

Pope Leo III was attacked by jealous rivals who wanted the wealth of the papacy for themselves; he also needed to separate the Church from the influence of the Byzantine Empire. He was fortunate to find his saviour in Charlemagne, king of the Franks, a truly great leader, enlightened and energetic. Charlemagne arrived in Rome and Leo was reconciled with his enemies. They then played out a little charade: Charlemagne, who happened to be wearing splendid robes, went to St. Peter's on Christmas Day AD800 to attend Mass. Suddenly, the Pope drew out a crown, put it on the amazed King's head and declared him Holy Roman Emperor. Rome now had a worthy successor to the likes of Trajan and Hadrian.

Charlemagne's coronation as Holy Roman Emperor marked the revival of the Western Empire (below right)

The Popes leave Rome

The medieval Church was cursed by its wealth and power. Everyday corruption was so great, and papal elections themselves so violent, that the popes were driven out. For almost 70 years from the beginning of the 14th century, the papacy resided in Avignon, in the south of France. For a while the popes were safe, but the greed of King Philip of France (which lay behind his original invitation) soon infected the Court of Avignon, giving robbers much to plunder. The poet Petrarch, a man of immense public influence, pleaded with the popes to come back to their traditional home. Finally, it was a young mystic, Catherine of Siena, who succeeded in convincing Gregory XI to return to Rome in 1377.

1417

The Renaissance and the
Baroque

The papacy dominated Rome completely. Clement VII, trying to lessen the power of the Habsburg emperor by a treaty with France, drew down on himself the terrifying Sack of Rome in 1527. After this, the energy of the papacy was taken up with the Counter-Reformation. Paul III (1534–39) approved a new order, the Jesuits, whose members pledged their services to the pope and tackled heresy. Papal wealth continued to attract the Roman nobility. Some were monsters, like Roderigo Borgia (Pope Alexander VI, 1492–1503); others were great patrons of the arts, such as Urban VIII (Maffeo Barberini, 1623–44), who issued a directive for public building.

Rome's glory was the baroque. Even so, Julius II (1503–13) brought the Renaissance masters to the city and commissioned Rome's great Renaissance artist, Bramante, to rebuild St. Peter's in 1506. In the 17th century the flamboyant baroque architecture of Bernini and Borromini filled the city, and much of the Gothic and Romanesque disappeared. Sometimes, building materials from ancient monuments were used. The papal coffers were emptying fast, and Rome's influence and importance all but vanished in the 18th century. As the century ended, Napoleon annexed the Papal States to the French Empire and forced Pope Pius VII to come to France as a virtual prisoner.

The Sistine Chapel

Julius II and Michelangelo were both strong-willed men who secretly enjoyed their tempestuous relationship. When Julius sent envoys to arrest the artist, who had left Rome in a huff, Michelangelo returned with a rope around his neck, a childish symbol of imprisonment. In 1508 Julius commissioned Michelangelo to decorate the ceiling of the Sistine Chapel. He wanted a pattern of circles and squares bordered by the Twelve Apostles. Michelangelo retorted he would paint anything he liked. Wisely, Julius let him alone, fully understanding the nature of his genius. However, after four years of painting, it was only when Julius threatened to hurl the man off his scaffold that Michelangelo showed off his masterpiece, one of the greatest frescoes in the world.

1506

Despite protesting that he was a sculptor and not a painter, Michelangelo (above) designed and painted the ceiling of the Sistine Chapel (left)

Crowning of the Virgin by Filippo Lippi and assistants used the newly discovered principles of perspective (right)

Charles V and the sack of Rome

The armies of the Habsburg emperor Charles V, in his war against the French, fought on Italian soil and entered Rome in May 1527. It was the last of the sackings of the city and in some ways the worst: 20,000 German, Spanish and Italian soldiers occupied Rome and stayed for nearly a year. Their leader died in the assault, and the troops ran out of control, raping, murdering and burning every day. The Pope escaped into Castel Sant'Angelo. Many of the Germans were Protestants and delighted in smashing all evidence of Catholicism, including countless artworks. Rome was left in ruins and the population fell to 30,000. This catastrophe could well have brought about the end of the Renaissance.

The trial of Galileo

In 1633 Galileo was charged with 'grave suspicion of heresy' and summoned to Rome for trial by the Inquisition. His bold advocacy of Copernican theory—that the earth revolved around the sun—provoked Church authorities, who interpreted Scripture as saying the opposite. As the 69-year-old Galileo was ill, his patrons, the Medicis, attempted to have the trial held in Florence, but the Pope insisted on Rome. Galileo was interrogated four times, finally under threat of torture, and recanted. He was found guilty and sentenced to unlimited imprisonment. However, the Church was not harsh. The Pope, once Galileo's patron, let him leave Rome for house arrest, and many of the prelates secretly supported him. He was allowed to work and write for the rest of his life. He died in 1642.

Roman baroque: Borromini and Bernini

If the Renaissance belonged to Florence, then the baroque belonged to Rome. Its two greatest practitioners, Gian Lorenzo Bernini (1598–1680) and Francesco Borromini (1599–1667), loathed each other with that ancient Roman fratricidal passion. Bernini, aristocratic and urbane, produced sophisticated work; Borromini, plebeian and hot-tempered, was wild and untamed. Borromini's genius led him to create beautiful churches in the cramped spaces of Rome. Bernini, never a trained architect, produced flamboyant sculptures of angels, tritons and saints. It all ended tragically. Old and frustrated, Borromini committed suicide; Bernini went smoothly on, blackening his rival's name.

The Grand Tour

Wealthy young Englishmen of the 18th century were expected to travel to France and Italy as clumsy youths and to come back as polished gentlemen. The tours could last four years, and Rome was the high spot, for various reasons: 'Look, listen, learn—and buy' was one of them. Young lords with money to burn returned with paintings, sculptures, coins and anything else the dealers could sell. More tellingly, Britain was conscious of her growing empire, and where better to educate her young men in ruling it than Rome, the blueprint of all empires? The young John Northall, an 18th-century traveller, wrote in 1752, 'One is confronted by emperors, consuls, generals...a cast of almost 2,000 years backwards, and the past becomes present.'

Bernini's fountains and statues, like the Fontana dei Fiumi (left) in Piazza Navona, and Borromini's churches, including Sant'Ivo alla Sapienza (right), characterize baroque Rome

1797

The colonnade and piazza of St. Peter's (above) were designed in 1656 by Bernini, as was most of the interior (left). The floor plan, however, remains Michelangelo's

From Risorgimento to world war

For centuries, Italy had been a collection of states under the control of foreign nations. The shock of Napoleon's occupations was felt across Europe, not only by the Papal States, annexed by the French between 1797 and 1814. A wave of nationalism swept the Continent; Germany was unified, as was Italy eventually. Rome kept out of the great movement of this Risorgimento (resurgence). The papacy was unwilling to give up its political power. Even when Garibaldi and Cavour united the country in 1860, the Pope held off until he was forced to join in 1870. Rome became the capital and administrative hub of the new country. Immense government buildings went up and boulevards cut through the city. Papal political power vanished completely and the popes withdrew until the onset of fascism in the 1920s, when Mussolini finally recognized the Vatican State. The fascists had great dreams for Rome as the capital of a new empire, but many of these had to be postponed with the onset of the war. Mussolini was overthrown in 1943 and Rome was ruled directly by the Germans. As the war ended, Rome was threatened with massive destruction during the Allies' battle for control. Then the Germans suddenly left—Hitler had declared Rome an 'open city'.

Napoleon and Pius VII

'Being master of Italy, I considered myself master of Rome,' Napoleon announced in his memoirs. He didn't like opposition and decided that the Pope should cease to have any political power. Moreover, since France ruled most of Europe, it made sense to the Emperor for the Pope to establish himself in Paris. Pius VII was told to come to Paris for Napoleon's coronation in 1804. He was treated rudely by the Emperor, and the Romans, outraged, felt a new affection for a pope they previously hadn't much liked. Napoleon consolidated his power ruthlessly, Rome was declared second capital of the empire and his son was made king of Rome in 1811.

1797

The Lateran Pact (below), signed in 1929, on behalf of the King and the Pope, recognized the Vatican as an independent state

Revolution in Rome

The year of revolution in Europe came in 1848 as people called for more freedoms. For a few months Rome experienced a social experiment, a kind of welfare state that anticipated modern systems by a hundred years. Republicans drove Pope Pius IX out in the autumn. Pius allowed a free press and granted amnesty to all political opponents, but would not support a war for the unification of Italy. The romantic revolutionary Giuseppe Mazzini became part of the triumvirate of Rome and for three months ruled as an idealist socialist. He pardoned his enemies, introduced progressive taxation and rehoused the poor. It was not to last. The French restored the Pope in 1849, and Mazzini fled the country.

The capital of Italy

After 1860, when Italy was united, it lacked its true capital. The new king of Italy, Vittorio Emanuele II, had been king of Piedmont and lived in Turin. The Pope refused to recognize unification and was protected by French troops. In 1870, when Garibaldi finally occupied Rome, the Pope, like the emperors of the collapsing empire, fled from his territories into St. Peter's, declaring himself 'the prisoner of the Vatican'. Garibaldi passed the Law of Guarantees, promising to defend the Pope and granting him a pension. The Pope retaliated with *Non Expedit*, forbidding Italians from participating in the new state. This had little effect, and the king occupied the Pope's residence, the Quirinale Palace, when Rome was declared the official capital in 1871.

The march on Rome

Italy could not be ruled without Rome, and in his bid for power, Mussolini's dramatic march on the city in 1922 was more a piece of theatre than political warfare. Although Mussolini controlled large forces throughout Italy and reviewed 40,000 soldiers in Naples on 24 October, he could not have fought a civil war. Four days later a fascist army of 16,000 surrounded Rome. Since most of them had arrived by train and were poorly organized, they presented no great threat to the city. The royal army was well run and equipped, and up until the evening of the 27th the King seemed determined to resist Mussolini. However, fearing civil war, the King relented and the fascists entered Rome. Mussolini was soon declared prime minister.

The Lateran Pact

Almost 60 years had passed since Garibaldi had occupied the papal territories. The Lateran Pact of 1929, which became part of the constitution of the republic, settled the differences between the Vatican and the kingdom of Italy. The Pope became head of an independent state measuring 43ha (106 acres) and received 2 billion lire compensation for the loss of all lands in 1870. The pact established Catholicism as the state religion of Italy and made it a required subject in all schools. In return, the papacy recognized the unification of the country. At the time, public imagery showed the pope, the monarch and the dictator as the three pillars of the state. Today, only the papacy survives.

Giuseppe Garibaldi meets King Vittorio Emanuele II (far left). Pope Pius VII (middle). Early nationalist Giuseppe Mazzini (left)

When Mussolini's Blackshirts marched on Rome in October 1922 (left), they met little opposition from the King

1945

Garibaldi was a popular leader, and there are many monuments dedicated to him (left)

Dominating Piazza Venezia is the monument to Vittorio Emanuele II, the first king of unified Italy (below)

Postwar Rome

The new republic of Italy enjoyed a postwar boom. For a few years in the 1950s, Rome became the hub of fashion and hedonism, summed up in Fellini's film *La Dolce Vita,* made in 1960, the same year Rome hosted the Olympics. The 1970s were marred by terrorism from both extreme Right and Left. One of the worst acts, the kidnap and murder of Prime Minister Aldo Moro, took place in Rome in 1978. Protests and demonstrations eventually led to the election of a communist city government in 1976, which did much to improve housing and a chronic transportation problem. Further to this, plans for the new millennium, *Roma Capitale*, extended the metro and improved the bus system.

The Treaty of Rome

The Treaty of Rome was signed on 25 March 1957 by six European nations, thereby creating what would become the European Union (EU). Echoes down the centuries are strong: Much of the EU today comprises the vassal states of the former Roman Empire, and the inclusion of Turkey would see the ancient territories reunited after a split of 1,700 years.

A new constitution

A referendum in 1946 voted against the monarchy. The King's ties with Mussolini and his flight from Rome when German troops attacked after the fall of the fascists made him unpopular, and the new constitution aimed to prevent a return of either the monarchy or fascism. Parliament elects a president, who then nominates a prime minister for parliament's approval. In 1946, Luigi Einaudi was elected as the first president. He took up residence in the Quirinale Palace, home of popes and then the king, almost 2,000 years after Julius Caesar destroyed the Republic of Rome.

A new pope

April 2005 was an extraordinary month in the life of the Roman Catholic Church. On 2 April, Pope John Paul II died after serving 26 years as head of the world's 1.1 billion Roman Catholics. The news was received by huge crowds keeping vigil in Piazza San Pietro. Millions of pilgrims subsequently flocked to the Vatican to say their final farewell to the pope, and to attend the emotional open-air service held in Piazza San Pietro, which accompanied his solemn funeral in the splendour of Basilica di San Pietro. The election of his successor then gripped the attention of the world's media for several weeks, until on 24 April, Cardinal Joseph Ratzinger, a 78-year-old German, took the name Pope Benedict XVI, and was installed as the new pontiff in an open-air Mass in Piazza San Pietro.

Murdered prime minister Aldo Moro (far left). Pope Benedict XVI (left)

1945 to the present

The Treaty of Rome, signed on 25 March 1957, was the first step towards creating the European Union (below)

Italian President Giovanni Gronchi (front row, second from left) opened the 1960 Olympic Games (right)

On the Move

ARRIVING

Arriving by Air

Rome has two airports: Fiumicino (officially Aeroporto Leonardo da Vinci) and Ciampino (Aeroporto G. B. Pastine).

Fiumicino, 36km (22 miles) southwest of the city, has been Rome's main gateway since 1961, and over the past 40 years it has been refurbished and extended into the Mediterranean's largest airport. On average, its four runways handle more than 30 flights an hour. It is the destination of most scheduled international and domestic flights with Air Canada, Alitalia, British Airways, Cathay Pacific, Continental Airlines, Delta, Japan Airlines, Lufthansa and Qantas. The airport has three terminals, plus a satellite, which is linked by an automated shuttle, the Sky Bridge. Terminal A handles domestic flights, Terminal B handles international and some domestic flights and

Terminal C (including the satellite) handles international flights only. The airport is open 24 hours.

In the arrivals areas *(arrivi)* of terminals B and C there are ATMs *(bancomats)*, foreign exchange facilities *(cambio)*, toilets and public phones. Coffee and light refreshments are available, as is limited shopping (newspapers, magazines and sweets). Not all of these facilities are open 24 hours.

The best way to get to the city centre from Fiumicino is by fast train. The Leonardo Express runs from just outside the airport to Termini station *(stazione)*. The service runs every 30 minutes between 6.37am and 11.37pm, takes around half an hour and costs €9.50 one way. There are other, more frequent trains

(treni) that stop at Tiburtina, Tuscolana, Ostiense and Trastevere (but not Termini). These smaller stations are usually not as convenient for visitors as Termini. These services operate from 5.57am to 11.27pm and cost €5 one way. Outside of these times a night bus runs between the airport, Termini station and Tiburtina station. There are four buses through the night (1.15, 2.15, 3.30 and 5am), which leave from near the international arrivals area. The journey costs €5 one way, and you can buy your ticket *(biglietto)* on the bus.

Rome's congested streets mean that travelling by taxi into the city can take longer than by train. The 36km (22-mile) taxi ride takes anything from

GETTING TO CENTRAL ROME FROM THE AIRPORT		
AIRPORT	**FIUMICINO (FCO)**	**CIAMPINO (CIA)**
	Aeroporto Leonardo da Vinci (Fiumicino) Via dell'Aeroporto di Fiumicino 320, 00050 Fiumicino (Roma) Tel 06 65951 (switchboard)	**Aeroporto G.B. Pastine (Ciampino)** Via Appia Nuova, 00040 Tel 06 794941
TAXI	€40 plus	€35 plus
TRAINS	Fast train, around 30 minutes—€9.50 Stopping train, 50 minutes—€5	
BUS/METRO	Terravision Fiumicino (tel 06 6595 8646, www.terravision.it) To Stazione Termini—about every two hours from 8.30am to 8.30pm. From Stazione Termini—about every two hours from 6.30am to 6.30pm. One hour 10 minutes, €9 single, €15 return	25-minute bus journey to Anagnina metro station (line A)—€1, plus standard BIT metro ticket—€1 Terravision Ciampino (tel 06 7949 4572, www.terravision.it). To Stazione Termini—regularly from 8.40am to 0.20am. From Stazione Termini—regularly from 4.30am to 7.30pm. 40 minutes, €8 single, €13.50 return

RETURNING HOME
Fiumicino

The Leonardo Express takes about 30 minutes to reach the airport. The ticket costs €9.50, and the service runs from 5.52am to 11.52pm. If you are using the stopping train from Tiburtina, Tuscolana, Ostiense or Trastevere, the journey time is approximately 50 minutes, and trains run from 5.36am until 11.36pm. A one-way ticket costs €5. When arriving by train, allow at least an extra quarter of an hour to get from the station to the check-in desk.

If you need to travel outside these times, the night bus runs from Tiburtina to the airport, also calling at Termini. The service runs at 12.30, 1.15, 2.30 and 3.45am, and costs €3.62 one way if you buy your ticket in advance, or €5 if you buy it on the bus.

Ciampino

The airport bus from Anagnina metro station operates between 5.20am and 11pm, and costs €1 one way. Remember to allow extra time to get to the check-in desk. If you travel outside these times, you will need to get a taxi.

For information on getting around Rome, ▷ 45–53.
For information on driving in Rome, ▷ 52–53.

TIPS
- Avoid taxi and hotel touts who will approach you at the airport. Use only licensed (yellow or white) taxis.
- Buy your return (round-trip) train ticket when you arrive at Fiumicino. The queues are much longer at Termini, and the ticket will not become valid until you stamp it on your return journey.
- You will find suitcases with wheels a godsend at Fiumicino. It is quite some distance between baggage reclaim and the exit, and for some stretches you cannot use a baggage trolley, particularly on the homeward journey.

30 minutes to 2 hours, so prices vary, but will cost upwards of €40. If you have small children or heavy luggage, it might be worth using a taxi, but there are surcharges for trips to and from the airport, for each item of luggage, on Sundays and public holidays, and between 10pm and 7am.

Ciampino is Rome's second airport and, at 16km (10 miles) to the southeast, it is closer to the city. It is primarily a military airport, but also handles charter flights and some budget airlines, such as easyJet and Ryanair. It is much smaller than Fiumicino, which means it has fewer facilities. However, there are

ATMs, a foreign currency exchange, public phones and toilets.

A bus service connects the airport to the Anagnina metro station (line A), running between 6.50am and 11.40pm. There is a machine just outside the arrivals terminal for tickets, which cost €1 one way. The metro runs every 5 to 10 minutes, and takes 25 minutes. You will need a standard BIT ticket, costing €1. For other ticket options, ▷ 46.

Once the metro stops running, a taxi is your only option. The fare will cost from €35, but there are surcharges for journeys between 10pm and 7am, on Sundays and public holidays, and for each item of luggage.

At both airports, smoking is permitted only outside the airport buildings.

Both of Rome's airports have wheelchair access to all facilities. ▷ 54 for more details.

USEFUL TELEPHONE NUMBERS AND WEBSITES
AIRPORTS
FIUMICINO
- ☎ 06 65951 (flight information)
- ☎ 06 6595 4252/6595 6777 (lost and found, *ufficio oggetti smarriti*)
- ☎ 06 892021 (railways information)
- ☎ 06 6595 3794 (taxis)
- Fax 06 6595 3000
- www.adr.it
- Tourist office (www.romaturismo.it) at International Arrivals, Terminal B. Open daily 8am–7pm

- ☎ 06 6595 3541 (left luggage, *deposito bagagli*)

CIAMPINO
- ☎ 06 794941 (flight information)
- ☎ 06 7934 8320 (airport lost and found, *ufficio oggetti smarriti*)
- ☎ 06 7949 4225 (property lost on flights)
- Fax 06 6595 3646
- www.adr.it

Arriving by Car

In the days of the empire, all roads led to Rome, but in these modern times, all roads lead to the Gran Raccordo Anulare, known as the GRA. This 70km (43-mile) road completely encircles the city, and is always busy. Its 30 exits can make the GRA seem confusing, but there are only a few intersections that you need to worry about.

From Fiumicino airport, take the Autostrada Roma Fiumicino, which leads to the GRA. If you are coming from Ciampino you will need to follow the Via Appia Nuova. From Florence or Pisa, take the A1, also known as the Autostrada del Sole. Visitors arriving from Naples should also use the A1, while those coming from Abruzzo or the Adriatic coast should follow the A24.

Wherever you join the GRA, make sure you know which exit you need; your hotel can tell you which one is best. You should make sure staff at your hotel know that you will be arriving by car so that you have somewhere to park. (See also Driving, ▷ 52–53.)

If you are arriving by car, but don't want to use your car in Rome, you can leave it in the long-term parking area (*lungo sosta parcheggio*) at Fiumicino airport and take the train into the city. Parking costs €18 for 24 hours (tel 06 6595 5175).

Arriving by Train

There are rail connections between Rome and many other European cities, most of which end at Termini station and are operated by FS (Ferrovie dello Stato), the state-run railway. Contact RailEurope for more

information (tel 1-888 382 7245 in the US or 1-800 361 7245 in Canada, or www.raileurope.com; tel 08705 302008 in the UK, or www.raileurope.co.uk).

For trips to or from smaller stations, you will need to use a *locale* train, which is a stopping service, but if you are coming from another major Italian city, your best option is a faster Intercity train. There is also a Eurostar service, which runs from Milan, Turin, Genoa, Bari, Naples, Florence and Venice. This service is faster than the Intercity, but you need to reserve your ticket in advance (www.trenitalia.com).

Termini is Rome's main station. It is a large, busy station on the edge of the *centro storico*, with a tourist office, banks and ATMs, shops, bars, a post office, telephones, newspaper shops, a pharmacy, foreign exchange and left luggage. The area is popular with pickpockets.

TIP
● If you are arriving by car and staying in central Rome, you will need a permit to drive in the city. If you are staying in a hotel, the staff can arrange this, otherwise you will need to contact STA (tel 06 5711 8333).

CAR RENTAL

All major rental firms, and some local ones, have desks at both airports and also in town. However, car rental is expensive in Italy and you can often get a better deal if you arrange it before you leave home. The minimum age for renting a car is between 21 and 25 (depending on which company you use), and you will need to have held a driver's licence for at least a year. Most firms require a credit card as a deposit. Accident rates are high in Rome, so check that you have adequate insurance cover. Most car rental contracts include breakdown cover: make sure you know who to call.

RENTAL COMPANY	AT FIUMICINO	AT CIAMPINO
Avis	199 100133	06 7934 4195
Europcar	06 6501 0879	06 7934 0387
Hertz	06 6595 4143	06 7934 0095
Italy by Car	06 6529133	
Maggiore	06 6501 0678	06 7934 0368
Sixt	06 6595 3547	06 7934 0838

Arriving by Bus

Most long-distance buses terminate at Tiburtina, to the northeast of the city. Although the station is some way out of the city, it is well served by the metro (line B) and by numerous bus services (for example, No. 492).

Eurolines runs buses from more than 100 European cities. For details of routes and tickets, see the company's website (www.eurolines.com).

GETTING AROUND

Once in the city, you will find that central Rome is quite compact—it is only 4km (2.5 miles) from Basilica di San Pietro to Termini station as the crow flies. Exploring the city on foot gives you the opportunity to cut through side streets, stop for coffee in one of the many bars and generally slow the pace. If walking is not your thing, or if the distance is too great, your best option is to make use of the city's efficient public transport service.

LA METROPOLITANA
The metro system (la metropolitana) has been designed primarily to bring commuters into the city, and is not as comprehensive as similar systems in other countries. However, its two lines can be useful for getting across town, and avoiding Rome's congested streets.

BUSES
Rome's bus service is more useful for visitors, as it can often get you closer to the sights. By using a combination of bendy buses and electric minibuses, you can get within striking distance of most of the sights in this book. Remember, you can change buses as often as you need, within the time constraints of your ticket.

TRAMS
The tram system is less comprehensive than the bus service, usually operating on the outskirts of the city.
For metro, bus and tram information, call ATAC (tel 800 431784 toll-free). Lines are open Mon–Sat 8–8. Alternatively, visit the organization's website (www.atac.roma.it).

TAXIS
Taxis are useful for late-night travel, but will not necessarily save you much time. And

remember, while you are stuck in Rome's busy streets, the meter is still running, making this an expensive way to travel.

ON TWO WHEELS
Scooters can be a good way to see the city, but only if you are already used to handling two-wheeled vehicles. Bicycles are ideal for getting around traffic-free areas, such as Villa Borghese, but traffic fumes and Rome's hilly terrain make cycling on the city's streets a less attractive prospect.

TIPS
● Peak times for public transport are roughly 7.30–9, 12.30–1.45 and 7.30–8.30.
● Beware of pickpockets on busy buses, trams and metro services, especially on the lines popular with visitors.
● Buses, trams and the metro can be uncomfortably hot during the summer.

BY CAR
The advice to anyone wishing to drive in Rome is—don't! Restricted access, busy, narrow streets, bad driving and inadequate parking can mean this is a stressful way to spend your holiday. If you really must drive, stay alert and remember that pedestrians have right of way. See pages 52–53 for more information on driving in Rome.

DISCOUNTS
Children under 10 travel free on public transport if they are accompanied by an adult; discounts are also available to students. Other discounted fares are available only to residents.

Traffic around Piazza Venezia needs a helping hand from the vigile urbano (traffic police)

Metro, Bus and Tram

Rome's public transport service, run by ATAC, is cheap, frequent and reliable. There are around 282 bus routes, 6 tram routes and 2 metro lines, but don't be daunted as you will find you only need a select few to get to where you want to go. Your first stop should be ATAC's information office, where you can pick up a transport map—*Mappa dei Trasporti Pubblici*. This is free, and gives details of buses, trams, the metro and the night buses, with transport and ticket information in English and Italian. The office (open daily 7.30–7; tel 800 431784; most staff speak English) is just outside Termini, in Piazza dei Cinquecento.

ON THE MOVE

TICKETS

Apart from on the night bus (▷ 50), you must have a ticket before boarding your chosen method of transport. There are ticket machines in the metro stations, and tickets are also sold in most tobacconists *(tabacchi)* and in some bars—look for the ATAC sticker in the window. An increasing number of bus stops now have automated ticket machines.

The cheapest ticket is the integrated time ticket *(biglietto integrato a tempo—BIT)*, usually just referred to as *un biglietto* (a ticket). It costs €1, and can be used for 75 minutes from validation for

Biglietteria/Tickets

any number of bus or tram trips, plus one metro journey.

One-day passes *(biglietto integrato giornaliero—BIG)* are also available. They are valid for unlimited use on buses, trams and the metro, and on trains operated by both Cotral—who run services to other major cities—and FS—the state-run railway—until midnight on the day they are first used, and cost €4. They are not valid on the visitor lines (▷ 220) or on the non-stop service to Fiumicino airport.

The only other type of ticket that might be useful for visitors is the seven-day pass *(carta integrata settimanale—CIS)*, which costs €16 and is valid on the same modes of transport as the BIG. You must write your name and the dates it is valid for on the front of the ticket.

VALIDATING YOUR TICKET

Whichever type of ticket you choose, it must be validated the first time you use it. At metro stations the validation machines are located just before the escalators, where you descend to the trains. Buses and trams have machines on board. If you are using a BIT ticket, you must stamp it when you use it on the metro, too. Other than this one exception, you do not need to stamp your ticket every time you change vehicles.

It is illegal to travel without a validated ticket. Ticket inspectors make regular checks, and you will be fined if your ticket doesn't have a valid stamp. The fixed-rate fine is €51 plus the price of your ticket, and ignorance is no excuse.

BUSES

Rome has two types of bus: standard, single-decker buses and small electric minibuses. Most routes are covered by the standard buses, but minibuses operate on routes 116, 117 and 119. They are

A standard bus (far left) and an electric minibus (left)

not very comfortable, even if you manage to get one of the eight hard plastic seats, but they are the only buses small enough to cope with Rome's narrow streets.

Bus Stops

At every bus stop there is a board showing the route number, the headstop (or *capitolinea*—where the route starts) and a list of the main intermediate stops for each bus that uses the stop. The stop you are at will be circled. The last journey of the day will usually start from the headstop at around midnight, after which it will be replaced by a night bus (▷ 50).

Boarding the Bus

You should usually board the bus through the rear doors (*salita*), making sure you validate your ticket on the way in. If you have already validated your ticket you may enter by the front (*entrata*) or rear doors. You should use the middle doors, marked *uscita*, to leave the bus. Always try to use the correct doors, as the Romans do, but if the bus is busy you can leave by the front or rear doors. This door etiquette doesn't apply to minibuses, which have only one door.

METRO

Rome's metro (*metropolitana*) system has two lines (A and B), which make roughly a cross shape, intersecting only at Termini. A promised third line, running northwest to southeast, has been on the drawing board for years. Its construction has been hampered by the discovery of archaeological remains, which have to be assessed before work can proceed (▷ 12).

Entrances to metro stations are marked with signs showing a large white 'M' on a red background, and there is usually more than one entrance—for example, on either side of a busy street. Just below street level are the ticket machines—remember to buy and stamp your ticket before you go down to the trains. Handy

Bus showing entrance and exit doors (top). Modern tram (above)

ROMAN BUS STOPS

Line numbers

Each bus number that runs from this stop is shown, together with selected points on the whole route. This stop (Traforo) is circled.

Bus times

The first and last bus times are shown at the bottom of the column. This is the time they leave the headstop (at the top of the list), not when they leave this stop.

boards at the bottom of the escalator show you the route direction to help you identify your platform.

Although predominantly a commuter service, the metro provides a good cross-city service, and is always very busy—there is usually standing room only. This makes it very hot, particularly in summer,

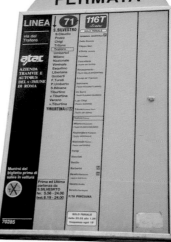

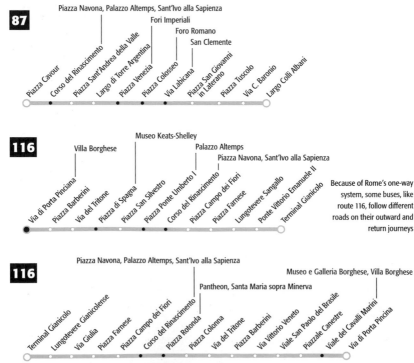

MAIN TOURIST BUS ROUTES

Certain bus routes link a number of places of interest. Below are four routes of particular interest to visitors.

ON THE MOVE

64

Palazzo Massimo alle Terme, Terme di Diocleziano

Mercati Traianei

Piazza Campo dei Fiori

Castel Sant'Angelo

Basilica di San Pietro

Termini · Piazza della Repubblica · Via Nazionale · Piazza Venezia · Largo di Torre Argentina · Piazza Sant'Andrea della Valle · Corso Vittorio Emanuele II · Lungotevere Porta · Cavalleggeri · Stazione di San Pietro

● *denotes nearest stop to place of interest*

TIPS
● To find out how to get around by public transport, contact ATAC (tel 800 431784), or visit their offices at Via Volturno 59, 00185.
● If you have access to the Internet, you can check your route online (www.atac.roma.it).

87

Piazza Navona, Palazzo Altemps, Sant'Ivo alla Sapienza

Fori Imperiali

Foro Romano

San Clemente

Piazza Cavour · Corso del Rinascimento · Piazza Sant'Andrea della Valle · Largo di Torre Argentina · Piazza Venezia · Piazza Colosseo · Via Labicana · Piazza San Giovanni in Laterano · Piazza Tuscolo · Via C. Baronio · Largo Colli Albani

116

Museo Keats-Shelley

Villa Borghese

Palazzo Altemps

Piazza Navona, Sant'Ivo alla Sapienza

Via di Porta Pinciana · Piazza Barberini · Via del Tritone · Piazza di Spagna · Piazza San Silvestro · Piazza Ponte Umberto I · Corso del Rinascimento · Piazza Campo dei Fiori · Piazza Farnese · Lungotevere Sangallo · Ponte Vittorio Emanuele II · Terminal Gianicolo

Because of Rome's one-way system, some buses, like route 116, follow different roads on their outward and return journeys

116

Piazza Navona, Palazzo Altemps, Sant'Ivo alla Sapienza

Museo e Galleria Borghese, Villa Borghese

Pantheon, Santa Maria sopra Minerva

Terminal Gianicolo · Lungotevere Gianicolense · Via Giulia · Piazza Farnese · Piazza Campo dei Fiori · Corso del Rinascimento · Piazza Rotonda · Piazza Colonna · Via del Tritone · Piazza Barberini · Via Vittorio Veneto · Viale San Paolo del Brasile · Piazzale Canestre · Viale dei Cavalli Marini · Via di Porta Pinciana

and the crowds are also a good cover for the pickpockets who operate on these trains. Look out for the route map inside the metro carriage—it shows you on which side of the carriage the doors will open at each stop, giving you a fighting chance of getting there before the train pulls away from the station. Services run between 5.30am and 11.30pm (12.30am on Saturdays), after which you

Buses can be held up by cars, pedestrians and even horses

will have to use the night bus service (▷ 50).

TRAMS
Rome's six tram routes operate mostly on the outskirts of the city and are not as useful to visitors as the buses or the metro. However, route 19 will take you to Piazza del Risorgimento, the

BUS BUSTER CHART

Use this chart to find out which buses or trams you'll need to catch to travel from one destination to another. Follow the rows of squares horizontally and vertically from the destination names until they meet. This square contains the route number. Only the most frequent services have been included. Numbers on white squares are direct. Numbers in shaded squares show that you have to change. Start out on the first route listed, then change to the second. Look at the key to find out where you must change. The W symbol indicates a walk of usually less than 1km (about half a mile).

Routes change regularly, so check an up-to-date timetable or bus map before setting out.

CHANGE AT:
- Torre Argentino
- Lungotevere Marzio
- Vittoria Colonna
- Diocleziano (to Repubblica)
- Manzioni (to Tritone)
- Termini
- San Silvestro
- Orazio (to Piazza Cavour)
- Piazza Venezia
- Fori Imperiali
- Santa Maria Maggiore
- Palazzo Esposizione
- Piazza Cavour
- Fiume
- Risorgimento
- Ferrari (to Lepanto)
- Nazionale

BASILICA DI SAN PIETRO	CASTEL SANT'ANGELO	COLOSSEO	FONTANA DI TREVI	FORI IMPERIALI	MUSEO BORGHESE	MUSEI CAPITOLINI	MUSEI VATICANI	PALAZZO ALTEMPS	PALAZZO BARBERINI	PALAZZO DORIA PAMPHILI	PALAZZO MASSIMO	PANTHEON	PIAZZA CAMPO DEI FIORI	PIAZZA NAVONA	PIAZZA DI SPAGNA	S. CLEMENTE	S. GIOVANNI IN LATERANO	S. MARIA MAGGIORE	S. MARIA IN TRASTEVERE	VILLA GIULIA
W																				
40/87	87																			
62	64	85, 850																		
40	46, 62, 63, 916	85, 87, 850, W	W																	
116	116	3, 360	52, 53	175/52																
64	46, 62, 63, 916	83, 87, 850	01, 95, 628	W	95															
W	23	87/492	492	492	490	23														
492	W	87	W	87	116	81, 628	492													
62	62	175	W	175	52, 53	95	492	116												
40	46, 62, 63, 916	175	W	W	95	W	492	W	62, 63, 95, 492											
64	64	75	175	64, 170	910	64	492/64	70	175	64, 170										
116	W	87	W	87	910/64	W	492	W	116	W	64, 70									
40	46, 62, 63, 916	87	62	64	116	46, 916	492	W	116	62, 64	64	W								
40	W	87	W	87	116	81, 628	492	W	116	W	70	W	W							
40/87	913, W	117	W	175	119	H, 64, 70, 117	913	W	11	W	64/117	W	116	W						
40/87	87	W	85, 850	85, 850	52/85	87	49/87	87	175/85	85, 850	84/117	85, 850	87	87	117					
40/70	87	85, 850	85, 850	85, 850	910/714	87	49/87	87	70/714	83, 850	714	85, 850	87	87	117	117				
64	70	75	71	84	360	70	70	70	W	70	W	70	70	70	71	W	714			
280	280	3	H	H	910/H	780	23	116	116	H	H	8	W	W	116	3	87/8	H		
19	926	87/962	52	628	52	628	19	628	52	628	78/19	628	628	628	628	87/628	87/628	360/495	23/19	19

closest public transport point to the Basilica di San Pietro and the Musei Vaticani. From here, it runs around the northern edge of Villa Borghese, close to Villa Giulia and the Museo Nazionale Etrusco, the Galleria Nazionale d'Arte Moderna and Bioparco, as does route 3. Route 3 also runs through the south of the city, ending up in Trastevere. Route 8 goes to Trastevere (and beyond), starting at Via Torre Argentina, not far from Piazza Venezia.

NIGHT BUSES

From around midnight, Rome's public transport system is replaced with night buses. The only exception to this is tram line 8, which runs until 2am. On the bus stops the night bus routes are easily

recognizable by the dark blue owl logo, and on the bus the letter 'N' will follow the route number. A night bus also follows as close as possible to each of the metro lines: Bus 55N follows line A, and bus 40N follows line B.

Night buses have conductors, and you can buy a BIT ticket on board for €1. Don't forget that if you have a BIG (one-day) ticket it will run out at midnight, so will no longer be valid.

DISCOUNTS

Children under 10 travel free if accompanied by an adult. There are no discounts for seniors (unless resident).

To qualify for discounts, students should contact their students' union to get an ISIC (International Student Identification Card) before

TIPS

● *Charta Roma: The Official City-Map* includes an up-to-date metro map. It is free from tourist information points. A free bus and tram map is available from ATAC (▷ 48).
● If the bus or tram is busy, pass your ticket through the crowd. Someone will stamp it for you and pass it back.
● Watch out for pickpockets on busy metro trains.

leaving home. Cards can also be issued by CTS (Centro Turisimo Studentesco), as can Euro<26 cards for non-students aged under 26 (contact www.cts.it in Italy, www.ctstravel.co.uk in the UK or www.ctstravelusa.com in the US).

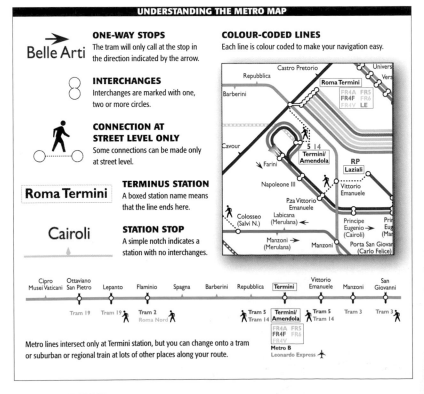

UNDERSTANDING THE METRO MAP

ONE-WAY STOPS
Belle Arti
The tram will only call at the stop in the direction indicated by the arrow.

INTERCHANGES
Interchanges are marked with one, two or more circles.

CONNECTION AT STREET LEVEL ONLY
Some connections can be made only at street level.

TERMINUS STATION
Roma Termini
A boxed station name means that the line ends here.

STATION STOP
Cairoli
A simple notch indicates a station with no interchanges.

COLOUR-CODED LINES
Each line is colour coded to make your navigation easy.

Metro lines intersect only at Termini station, but you can change onto a tram or suburban or regional train at lots of other places along your route.

Bicycles and Scooters

Seeing the city on two wheels has its advantages. Traffic jams and parking restrictions are not the problem they are for visitors in cars. However, Rome's busy streets are not for the uninitiated, and if you've never ridden a scooter or bicycle in a busy city, Rome is not the place to start. Bicycles are best reserved for exploring

the quieter parts of the city, but don't forget—Rome is built on seven hills.

To rent a scooter you must be over 21 and hold a full driver's licence. You will usually need to leave your passport and/or a credit card as a

deposit. Crash helmets are compulsory, and you should also wear gloves, shoes that enclose your feet, trousers and long sleeves.

If you are exploring the city by bicycle, helmets are not compulsory, but they are recommended. As with scooters, you will be asked to leave your passport or similar ID as a deposit. There are bicycle stands at Piazza del Popolo, Villa Borghese and Piazza Navona.

WHERE TO RENT A BICYCLE OR SCOOTER IN ROME

NEW SCOOTER FOR RENT (scooters only)
Via Quattro Novembre 96a/b
☎ 06 679 0500
🕐 Daily 8.30–8

SCOOT-A-LONG
Via Cavour 302
☎ 06 678 0206
🕐 Daily 9.30–7.30

BIKE E SCOOTER RENTAL
Via Cavour 80/a
☎ 06 481 5669
🕐 Daily 9–7

ROMA RENT
Vicolo de' Bovari 7/a
☎ 06 689 6555
🕐 Daily 8.30–7

RONCONI
Via San Leo 22
☎ 06 881 0219
🕐 Daily 9–1, 4–8

TRENO E SCOOTER
Termini station
Multiservice, platform 1
Via Marsala
☎ 06 4890 5823
🕐 Daily 9–6.30

ROMA IN SCOOTER
Corso Vittorio Emanuele II 204
☎ 06 687 6922
🕐 Daily 9.30–6.30

Vespa means 'wasp'—named after the buzzing sound made by their engines.

BICI E BACI
Via del Viminale 5
☎ 06 482 8443
🕐 Daily 8–7

SCOOTER RENT JOY RIDE
Via Cavour 199
☎ 06 481 5926
🕐 Daily 9–7

TREVI TOURIST SERVICE
(scooters only)
Via dei Lucchesi 31/32
☎ 06 6920 0799
🕐 Daily 10–10

HAPPY RENT
(scooters only)
Via Farini 3
☎ 06 481 8185
🕐 Daily 9–7

SCOOTER FOR RENT
Via della Purificazione 84
☎ 06 488 5485 (also fax)

SAFE CYCLING TIPS

● Wear bright clothing in the day, and fluorescent clothing and lights at night.
● Make other road-users aware of your movements. Indicate clearly and in advance.
● Watch out for people opening doors of stopped or parked cars.
● Don't cycle down the inside of traffic when there is a right turning ahead.
● Consider wearing a helmet. They're not compulsory, but are advisable.
● Wear gloves, and cover your knees and elbows.
● Always lock your bicycle to a fixed object when parking.

Taxis

Rome's busy streets and one-way systems mean that taxis are not the most economical way of getting from A to B, but there may be times when they are your best bet.

Always use official, licensed taxis, which are either yellow or white, and have an illuminated 'taxi' sign on the roof. You should avoid the many unlicensed taxis operating in Rome, as you have no way of knowing if they are adequately insured.

Taxis can be hailed on the street, but it is easier to get one from the *fermata dei taxi*

at Termini, Piazza Venezia, Largo di Torre Argentina, Piazza San Silvestro, Piazza di Spagna or Piazza Sonnino (in Trastevere).

If you want to be sure of a taxi, or you need to be collected from your hotel, it is best to telephone for a radio taxi. You cannot book a radio taxi in advance, so allow enough time to get to your destination. The company gives you a reference, plus the timescale within which the taxi is expected to arrive. Radio taxis start charging from the time they leave to pick you up, so the meter will not be at zero.

TIPS
● Use only licensed cabs. ● Except in radio taxis, make sure the meter is set to zero at the start of your journey. ● The meter still runs when the taxi is stationary (eg, in traffic jams).

TAXI FARES
All taxi fares are controlled by the meter, and a list of charges, in several languages, should be displayed inside the taxi. For journeys within the city, the charges are as follows: **Fixed charge:** €2.33 between 7am and 10pm (€3.36 on Sundays and public holidays between 7am and 10pm, €4.91 between 10pm and 7am). **Increments:** 11c every 141m (154yd). Stationary/slow-moving traffic: 11c every 19.2 seconds. **Surcharges for:** each item of luggage; trips to and from the airports and outside the GRA.

RADIO TAXIS

The following numbers are recommended by the tourist office for calling a radio taxi:
- ☎ 06 3570
- ☎ 06 4994
- ☎ 06 88177
- ☎ 06 5551
- ☎ 06 6645
- ☎ 06 8822
- ☎ 06 4157

Driving

What with restricted access, busy, narrow streets, bad road skills and poor parking, driving in Rome can be a stressful experience. However, if you decide you can't do without your car, here are some points to bear in mind:

Do carry your registration and insurance documents and driver's licence. You will need to produce them if you are stopped.

Don't dazzle oncoming traffic. Cars manufactured to drive on the left should adjust their headlights—kits are widely available.

Don't drive too fast. The speed limit in built-up areas is 50kph/31mph; outside built-up areas, 110kph/68mph; motorways (*autostrada*), 130kph/81mph.

Do carry a warning triangle and a fluorescent vest for emergencies, and display a nationality sticker (unless you have Euro-plates).

Do carry a first-aid kit, fire extinguisher and spare bulbs.

Don't use undipped headlights in towns or cities.

Do use dipped headlights when driving in tunnels, even if they are well lit, and at all times when driving outside built-up areas.

Don't drink and drive—penalties are severe. The legal level is below 0.05 per cent of alcohol in the bloodstream.

Don't allow children under four years old to travel without a suitable restraint system. Children under 12 years old cannot travel in the front of the car without an adapted restraint system.

Do wear a seatbelt. They are compulsory in the front and rear of the vehicle (where fitted).

Don't use a mobile phone when driving.

Don't drive in shoes that do not fully enclose the foot.

DRIVER'S LICENCES

Both UK and US driver's licences are valid in Italy, but it is recommended that you also carry a translation. In the UK, the new licences with photographs and the pink, EU-style ones include a

translation, but if you hold an older, green licence, you should either update the licence or apply for an International Driving Permit. Holders of US driver's licences should also apply for an International Driving Permit. These permits are not compulsory, but are easier to understand. They also act as another form of identification. Permits can be obtained from the Italian state tourist offices or many national motoring organizations (including the AA and AAA).

Drivers must be at least 18 years of age and hold a full driver's licence.

ACCIDENTS
If necessary, call the police (tel 112) and ask any witness to stay and make a statement. Do not admit liability. Exchange details (name, address, car details, insurance company's name and address) with other drivers.

BREAKDOWNS
If you break down, turn on your hazard warning lights, place the warning triangle 50m (164ft) behind the vehicle, and put on your fluorescent vest.

The Automobile Club d'Italia (ACI) provides a free service to foreign-registered cars. If they cannot repair your car at the roadside, they will tow you to a garage. You can contact ACI 24 hours a day (tel 116). They will

need to know where you are, your vehicle registration (license plate) number and the make of the vehicle.

FUEL
Petrol (gas) stations in Rome are small, and generally keep shop hours, closing all day Sunday. Lead-free fuel is called *benzina senza piombo* or *benzina verde*; leaded fuel is still available in some places. Some petrol (gas) stations, particularly those on the GRA, are open 24 hours.

TRAFFIC RESTRICTIONS
Most of the *centro storico* is covered by the Limited Traffic Zone, which restricts access to permit holders from 6.30am to 6pm Monday to Friday, and 2 to 6pm on Saturdays.

Electronic systems are in place to record the number of unregistered vehicles and to issue fines. If you need to drive in the restricted area, fax details of your registration number and length of stay to STA (tel 06 5711 8259). If you are staying in a hotel, the staff will usually do this for you.

PARKING

Parking in the *centro storico* is limited and expensive. Street parking is indicated by blue lines and costs €1 per hour—buy your ticket from the nearby vending machines (which only take coins) or at tobacconists or news-stands. The most convenient parking areas for the central area are:

PARKSÌ
(Villa Borghese)
Viale del Galoppatoio 33
☎ 06 322 5934
🕐 24 hours
🅿 €1.15 per hour for up to three hours, then 90c for 4th to 15th hour; €14.45 per day.

TERMINAL PARK
(Termini)
Via Marsala 30
☎ 06 444 1067
🕐 6am–1am
🅿 €5 for first two hours, then €1.50 for 3rd to 12th hour; €27 per day; €12 for second day.

PARKS
(Stazione Roma-Ostia)
Piazzale dei Partigiani
☎ 06 574 5942
🕐 6am–11pm
🅿 77c per hour; €5 per day.

TERMINAL GIANICOLO
Via di Porta Cavalleggeri
☎ 06 684 0331
🕐 7am–1.30am
🅿 €13 per hour for the first four hours, then €1 or €1.10 per hour; €113.60 per day.

PARKING DELL'AUDITORIUM,
Viale Pilsudsky 21

☎ 06 808 1646
🕐 7am–1am.
🅿 €1 per hour; €2.55 per day.

AUTOSILO VIA MANTOVA,
Via Mantova 24
☎ 06 841 3853
🕐 24 hours
🅿 €3 per hour for first hour, then €2 per hour.

PARKING LUDOVISI
Via Ludovisi 60
☎ 06 474 0632
🕐 5.30am–1.30am
🅿 €2 per hour for first five hours, then €1 per hour; €18 per day.

VISITORS WITH A DISABILITY

ON THE MOVE

Rome is a very difficult city for people with physical impairments to get around without able-bodied help. There has been a gradual improvement to accessibility in recent years, although some areas can still cause problems.

BY AIR

You should contact your airline in advance of your date of travel to let them know what assistance you will need. Both Fiumicino and Ciampino have wheelchair access to all airport services, and many signposts are in braille. At Fiumicino, there are also paths with textured surfaces to guide people with visual impairments to key places in the airport. The airports have a courtesy shuttle for visitors with disabilities that will take you to your hotel; it can be booked 24 hours ahead by contacting your airline.

BY BUS AND TRAM

Many of Rome's buses and trams have been, or are being, adapted for wheelchair access, with a view to replacing the whole network. The newer buses have lower access platforms for easier entry. For the most up-to-date information, contact ATAC's disabled services (06 4695 4001; open daily 8–2.30).

BY METRO

The metro system is also being upgraded. At the moment, most stations on line B have elevators and toilets suitable for people with disabilities. The only exceptions are Circo Massimo, Colosseo and the southbound platform of Cavour. On line A, only Cipro and Valle Aurelia have wheelchair access, but bus No. 590 follows the same route and is, on the whole, wheelchair accessible. Ten stations on line A have textured paths for people with visual impairments, although at present only Cipro is useful for sightseeing.

USEFUL CONTACTS

CO.IN SOCIALE
Via Enrico Giglioli 54a,
00172 Rome
☎ 800 271027
www.coinsociale.it
Has useful information on accessible sights in Rome and Lazio. Publishes guides, organizes guided tours, and has a minibus available for excursions and transfers.

ROMA PER TUTTI
☎ 06 5717 7094
www.romapertutti.it
Helps visitors with special needs. Organizes guided tours (booking essential), but in Italian only.

ASSOTAXI
Piazza dei Giuochi, 00194 Rome
☎ 800 980 094, fax 06 233 225 327
www.assotaxi.it
Runs taxis specially fitted with seat elevators for wheelchair access. Booking 24 hours ahead is recommended.

BY TRAIN

Some of Rome's trains have wheelchair access, and this is indicated on the timetable with a wheelchair symbol. You can also get this information from Termini station (tel 06 488 1726)—tell them where you want to start and end your journey. If you will need assistance, you should call the Ufficio Disabili 12 hours

ACROD LIMITED
PO Box 60, Curtin, ACT 2605, Australia
☎ 02 6283 3200, fax 02 6281 3488
www.acrod.org.au
The Australian organization set up to respond to the needs of people with disabilities.

HOLIDAY CARE
7th Floor, Sunley House, 4 Bedford Park, Croydon, Surrey, CR0 2AP, UK
☎ 0845 124 9971, fax 0845 124 9972
www.holidaycare.org.uk
Produces publications and information on accessibility.

SATH (SOCIETY FOR ACCESSIBLE TRAVEL AND HOSPITALITY)
347 Fifth Avenue, Suite 610, New York NY10016, USA
☎ 212-441-7284, fax 212-727-8253
www.sath.org
Lots of tips on how to travel with mobility or vision impairment.

before the start of your journey. Someone else can do this on your behalf.

BY TAXI

Most taxis can take wheelchairs, but they will need to be folded and stored in the boot (trunk).

For general information about access in Rome, ▷ 279.

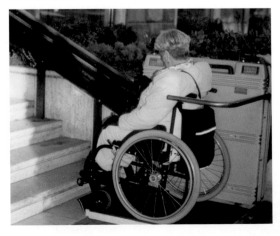

This section is divided into three parts: Sightseeing Areas guides you to the best things to see in five districts of Rome (shown on the map inside the front cover); the A–Z of Sights is an alphabetical listing of places to visit across the city, located on the maps on pages 56–59; Farther Afield describes attractions outside the city centre.

The Sights

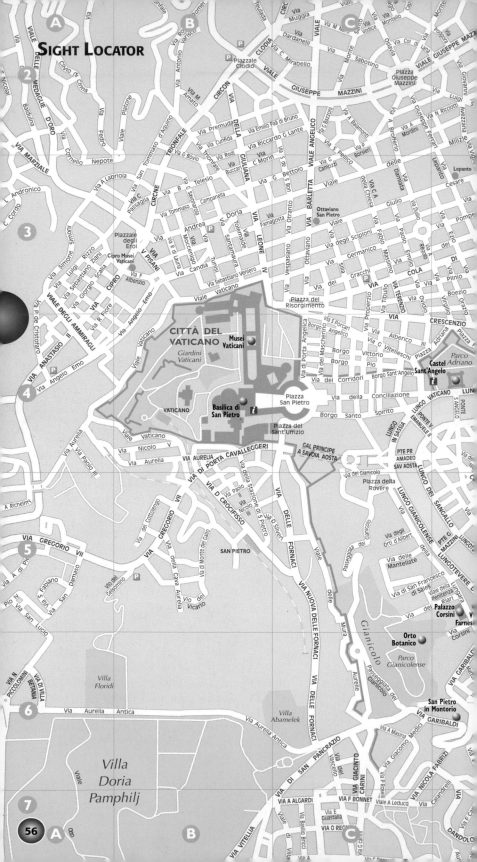

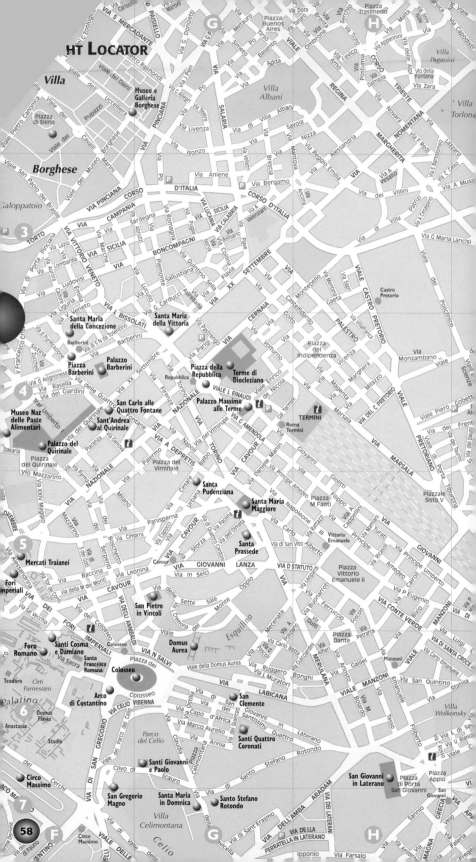

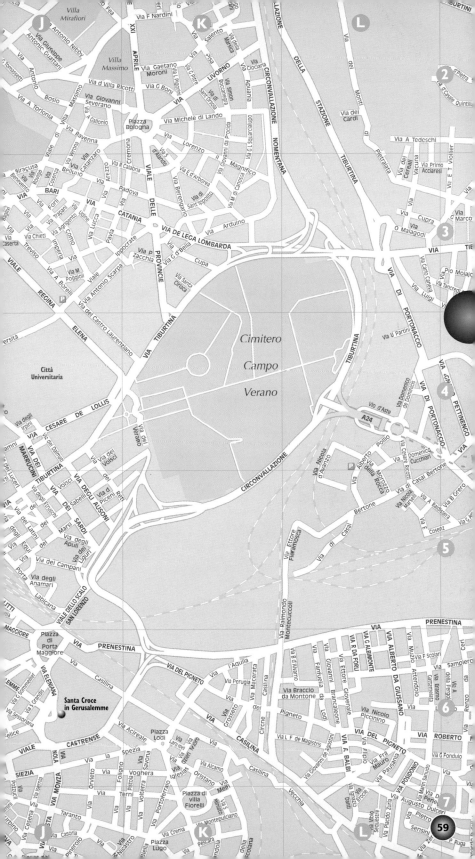

Vatican City

HOW TO GET THERE

Ⓜ Ottaviano San Pietro (for the Basilica) or Cipro Musei (for museums)
🚌 23, 32, 49, 81, 590, 982 or tram 19 to Piazza del Risorgimento; 34, 40, 62, 64 to Piazza Pio XII

It is ironic that the world's largest church, museum and piazza should all be contained within the world's smallest independent state, but the Vatican also has a lot of history to support these records.

The Vatican became the smallest independent state in 1929, with the signing of the Lateran Treaty. Until the Risorgimento (unification), Rome had been under Papal rule. With the breaching of the Vatican walls at Porta Pia on 20 September 1870, Pope Pius IX retreated to the Vatican Palace and declared himself a prisoner of the Vatican. He and subsequent popes never recognized

the now unified Italy until the signing of the Lateran Treaty nearly 60 years later.

Today, the Vatican has its own shops, postal service, banks, newspapers, radio station—even a helipad. It is still surrounded by the walls that Michelangelo built, and there are only two public entrances: Piazza San Pietro and the museums' entrance. The official language of the Vatican is Latin, but it is more usual to hear Italian.

The first time you visit Basilica di San Pietro, approach it along Via della Conciliazione so you can watch the spectacle of St. Peter's rise in front of you.

THE MAIN SIGHTS

Although, nominally, there are few sights in the Vatican, they are the highlights of most visitors' trips. It would take many years to see everything in the Vatican Museums, and the vast size of St. Peter's is awesome. For most visitors, time is short, so it pays to be selective about what you hope to see.

Capella Sistina

Although the ceiling of Michelangelo's Sistine Chapel is the most famous fresco, don't miss *The Last Judgement* on the end wall (▷ 106).

Michelangelo's *Pietà*

It's difficult to believe that Michelangelo was only 24 when he completed this sensitive portrayal of the Virgin Mary with Christ lying across her lap (▷ 68–69).

Museo Pio Clementino

Important Greek and Roman statuary, collected by Pius VI and Clement XIV (▷ 109).

Pinacoteca

The Vatican's vast collection of art, from the Middle Ages to 1800 (▷ 108–109).

St. Peter's cupola

It's a long climb to the top of the cupola, but the views are amazing (▷ 71).

Stanze di Raffaello

Julius II's suite of rooms, decorated with frescoes by Raphael (▷ 106–108).

Michelangelo's Last Judgement *in the Sistine Chapel*

WHERE TO EAT

Apart from the café in the museum, there is nowhere inside the Vatican to eat. If you are heading back towards the *centro storico*, try one of the many places around Piazza Navona. Alternatively, just to the

Get a saint's-eye view from the cupola of St. Peter's

north of the Vatican is the Prati district, where you will find the following restaurants:

DAL TOSCANO

The specialty of this family-run restaurant is its Tuscan dishes (▷ 240).

RISTORANTE-PIZZERIA PIACERE MOLISE

Good value, and just a stone's throw from the Vatican Museums (▷ 250).

ROOF GARDEN 'LES ETOILES'

A pricey alternative, but the view of St. Peter's from the roof terrace is wonderful (▷ 250).

Trastevere

HOW TO GET THERE
🚌 H, 23, 44, 280, 630, 780; tram 8

Despite growing popularity, Trastevere has managed to keep its sense of identity.
The name Trastevere means 'across the Tiber', and it is this separation that makes the area different. The Trasteverini celebrate their separateness each year in a festival called *Festa de' Noantri*, which roughly translates from Roman dialect as 'Our Own Festival'.

The narrow streets and small piazzas, the community spirit and preservation of the old ways all help to explain why the area is so popular, not just with visitors but also with Romans from the other side of the river.

Trastevere is cut in half by Viale di Trastevere. To the west is the Gianicolo—not one of the original seven hills, but it is higher and affords great views. This is also

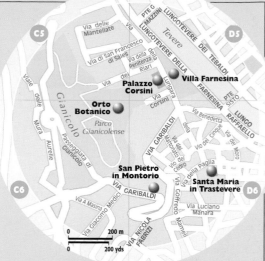

where you'll find Santa Maria in Trastevere. To the east is the bend in the river, and the Isola Tiberina (▷ 91) and Santa Cecilia in Trastevere (▷ 128).

THE MAIN SIGHTS
Trastevere itself is one of the main sights here. Spend some time sitting in Piazza Santa Maria in Trastevere, drinking coffee and people-watching. Or, on a fine summer evening, eat in one of the piazza's many restaurants with outside tables, with views of the beautifully lit church.

The beautiful courtyard of Santa Cecilia in Trastevere

Gianicolo
It's a long climb to Piazzale Giuseppe Garibaldi, but worth it for the view across the city (▷ 90).

Santa Maria in Trastevere
One of Rome's few surviving medieval churches, with beautiful apse mosaics (▷ 141).

San Pietro in Montorio
Although most famous for Bramante's Tempietto, with its perfect Classical proportions, the church itself is worth visiting for its rose window (▷ 137).

Villa Farnesina
Agostino Chigi's Renaissance suburban villa has frescoes by Raphael (▷ 146).

One of the four saints on the 18th century portico of Santa Maria in Trastevere

OTHER PLACES TO VISIT
See the orchids and palm trees at Orto Botanico (▷ 110). Palazzo Corsini (▷ 111) holds part of the national art collection, including works by Caravaggio and Van Dyck.

Da Agusto is a popular trattoria in Trastevere

WHERE TO EAT
Trastevere is overflowing with eateries, especially around Piazza Santa Maria in Trastevere.

BIBLI
A great place for Sunday brunch, or just for coffee (▷ 235).

CASETTA DÈ TRASTEVERE
The inside of this restaurant, not far from Santa Maria in Trastevere, looks like a Roman piazza (▷ 238).

DA AGUSTO
A Trastevere institution, as traditional as they come (▷ 239).

THE SIGHTS

Campo Marzio

HOW TO GET THERE

🚌 44, 46, 84, 715, 716, 780, 781, 810, 916 or tram 8 to Largo di Torre Argentina; 30, 70, 81, 87, 116, 116T, 186, 204, 492, 628 to Corso del Rinascimento; 116 also runs (west to east) through Piazza della Minerva

Is it medieval? Renaissance? Baroque? Campo Marzio is all of these and more.

Rome's liveliest area is bound to the west by the curve of the river and runs roughly as far east as the Via del Corso. It takes its name from the Roman Field of Mars (Campus Martius)—the area where the military were put through their paces. The area began to be built up after the destruction of the aqueducts, in around AD600, because the river was the only source of water. When the popes returned from Avignon, the area was further built up because of its proximity to the Vatican.

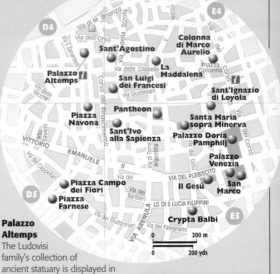

The bright flower market at Piazza Campo dei Fiori

Today, Campo Marzio is still where Romans live and work, but their numbers are swollen by the visitors who flock here, and by politicians and diplomats from Palazzo Madama, the seat of government.

THE MAIN SIGHTS

As the hub of Rome's history, there's so much to see here that you will want to make more than one visit. Lots of the sights in this area are churches, which often close during the afternoon. Make good use of this time to sit in one of the many cafés in Piazza Navona or Campo dei Fiori and watch the world go by.

Palazzo Altemps

The Ludovisi family's collection of ancient statuary is displayed in beautifully frescoed rooms (▷ 112–113).

Pantheon

Admire this ancient place of worship from the piazza before moving inside to see the vast domed ceiling (▷ 120–121).

Piazza Campo dei Fiori

Whether you go in the morning for the busy market or in the evening for a meal, this piazza is always a hive of activity (▷ 122–123).

Piazza Navona

Fountains, cafés and ice cream: Piazza Navona is always popular and there's plenty more to see nearby (▷ 124–125).

Santa Maria sopra Minerva

The interior of this rare Gothic church is a riot of blue and gold, while adults and children alike love Bernini's elephant in the piazza outside (▷ 140).

OTHER PLACES TO VISIT

Churches abound in Campo Marzio. The most impressive include Sant'Agostino (▷ 128), with Sansovino's *Madonna del Parto*, beloved of expectant mothers; Sant'Ivo alla Sapienza (▷ 133), with its spiral dome; La Maddalena (▷ 91), a baroque masterpiece just around the corner from the Pantheon; and San Luigi dei Francesi (▷ 133), home to three paintings of the life of St. Matthew by Caravaggio.

The Gothic interior of Santa Maria sopra Minerva

WHERE TO EAT

There are plenty of places to eat, drink coffee or just have an ice cream around the piazzas in the *centro storico*. Remember that you pay a premium for sitting at the outdoor tables, so only do so if you want to linger. For a quick refuel, drink your coffee standing up at the bar.

IL CONVIVIO

For a special meal, try this modern restaurant close to the Palazzo Altemps (▷ 238).

DAI TRE AMICI

For a true Roman experience, visit this popular trattoria, not far from the Pantheon (▷ 240).

DER PALLARO

Enjoy the daily fixed menu at this trattoria, just behind Sant'Andrea della Valle (▷ 241).

Northern Rome

HOW TO GET THERE

🚇 Termini, Repubblica or Barberini
🚌 52, 53, 63, 80, 95, 116, 119 to Via Veneto; H, 40, 64, 84, 86, 90, 170, 175, 492, 910 to Repubblica; H, 36, 38, 40, 64, 86, 90, 92, 105, 170, 175, 217, 310, 714, 910 or tram 5, 14 to Termini

Although not strictly speaking a district, the area between Termini station and the Via Veneto covers a wide variety of interesting places to visit.
During imperial times, the area around Via Veneto was a suburb where the wealthy had their villas. Following the sack of Rome in AD410, the area fell into disuse and reverted to open countryside. It experienced a rebirth with the building of Palazzo Barberini in the 17th century.

The Quirinale suffered a similar fate. A residential area until the Middle Ages, it had its own Renaissance when it was chosen

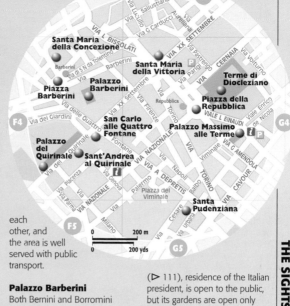

as the site for the new papal palace, Palazzo del Quirinale, in 1542. It is now home to the Italian president.

Moving up to date, Termini station is a wonderful piece of modern architecture, with a cantilevered roof over the ticket hall and taxi stand. However, this is not a good area to hang around: It's popular with pickpockets (and worse), so head straight for the church or gallery that you are interested in.

THE MAIN SIGHTS

Although slightly off the main tourist track, the sights here are still within walking distance of each other, and the area is well served with public transport.

Palazzo Barberini

Both Bernini and Borromini worked on Pope Urban VIII's palace (▷ 114).

Palazzo Massimo alle Terme

Behind the façade of this 19th-century palazzo is a wealth of coins, jewellery and ancient statuary. Don't miss the guided tour of the mosaics and frescoes (▷ 116–117).

San Carlo alle Quattro Fontane

Borromini's tiny church, with its equally small cloister, is well worth seeking out (▷ 128).

Santa Maria della Concezione

This simple church, at the bottom of the Via Veneto, hides a grizzly secret—the Capuchin monks' cemetery, decorated with their bones and skeletons (▷ 136).

Santa Maria della Vittoria

Don't miss Bernini's *Ecstasy of St. Teresa of Avila* in the Cornaro Chapel (▷ 137).

OTHER PLACES TO VISIT

Close to Piazza della Repubblica (▷ 119), famous for its Fountain of the Naiads, is Terme di Diocleziano (▷ 143), the largest baths complex ever built in Rome. Sant'Andrea al Quirinale (▷ 128), close to the Palazzo del Quirinale, was Bernini's best-loved church. The palazzo itself

(▷ 111), residence of the Italian president, is open to the public, but its gardens are open only once a year, on 2 June—the anniversary of the founding of the Italian republic.

The grand staircase at Palazzo Barberini, designed by Bernini

The ruins of Terme di Diocleziano

WHERE TO EAT

There is a wealth of restaurants along Via Veneto, but they can be pricey. For a less expensive alternative, try the side streets.

EST! EST! EST!

This pizzeria, close to San Carlino, has been in business for over 100 years (▷ 241).

PIZZARÈ

A popular pizzeria, not far off Via Veneto (▷ 248)

TRATTORIA ABRUZZESE

Close to busy Via Nazionale, with cooking from the Abruzzo region (▷ 254).

THE SIGHTS

Ancient Rome

HOW TO GET THERE

🚌 60, 75, 85, 87, 175, 810, 850 to Colosseo; 40, 60, 64, 86, 88, 492, 590, 715, 716 to Piazza Venezia

Ⓜ Colosseo

According to legend, this is where Rome began, when Romulus built his city on the Capitoline Hill in 753BC.
Since then, the area around the Capitoline Hill has remained important. The Forum was the focus of political life in ancient times, and when the city outgrew the site of what we know as Foro Romano, Julius Caesar began a new one at the nearby Fori Imperiali in 46BC, which was added to by subsequent emperors. The area is still central to political life today: Palazzo Senatorio, in Piazza del Campidoglio, is home to the city council.

For many years, the Palatine Hill was the most desirable of

The Colosseum, although now a ruin, still draws in the crowds

addresses: Augustus and Domitian both had homes here. In fact, the name Palatine gives us the word palace.

THE MAIN SIGHTS
Today, this area ranges from the historic, including Vespasian's Colosseo, through Michelangelo's Piazza del Campidoglio to the bustling Piazza Venezia and the early 20th-century Monumento a Vittorio Emanuele II. Most of it, however, is dominated by ancient ruins, and sometimes it can take a leap of imagination to make sense of it all.

Colosseo
Vespasian's amphitheatre is recognized throughout the world (▷ 74–77).

Fori Imperiali
Take the guided tour around this working archaeological site (▷ 82–83).

Foro Romano
Site of the great temples and basilicas of ancient Rome (▷ 84–89).

Musei Capitolini
Two palaces full of works of art, joined by an underground passageway and with views across the Foro Romano (▷ 98–103).

OTHER PLACES TO VISIT
If you haven't had your fill of ancient Rome, Nero's Domus Aurea (▷ 79) is next to the Colosseo, as is access to the Palatine Hill (▷ 110–111). Emperor Trajan built his shopping

complex, Mercati Traianei (▷ 91), next to the Fori Imperiali.

Santa Maria in Aracoeli (▷ 133), next to the steps leading up to Piazza del Campidoglio, is famous for its wooden statue of Christ as a child, while you can see St. Peter's chains at San Pietro in Vincoli (▷ 137).

Finally, for panoramic views over the whole city, climb to the top of Monumento a Vittorio Emanuele II in Piazza Venezia (▷ 119).

WHERE TO EAT
The area around the Fora has few restaurants. For a quick snack, you could try one of the many outlets in Piazza Venezia.

BAR CAPITOLINA
Whether or not you are visiting the museums, the café at the Musei Capitolini is a great place to refuel (▷ 234).

NERONE
Abruzzese cooking close to Colle Oppio park (▷ 245).

PASQUALINO AL COLOSSEO
Sample dishes from the Mediterranean, with just a touch of Sicily, around the corner from the Colosseo (▷ 247).

Constantine's hand, in the courtyard of the Musei Capitolini

Detail from Ara Pacis Augustae, Augustus' Altar of Peace

The Arco di Costantino, in the shadow of the Colosseo

Warhol's painting of Goethe, at the entrance to Casa di Goethe

ARA PACIS AUGUSTAE

✚ 57 E3 • Lungotevere in Augusta 00186 ☎ 06 6880 6848 ⏰ Phone for opening times 🚇 Spagna 🚌 30, 70, 81, 91, 186, 204, 224, 492, 590, 628, 913

The Altar of Peace is the best example of Augustan monumental sculpture in Rome, and is a major work from the Augustan Golden Age.

The altar, decorated with bas-reliefs carved in 9BC, was built to celebrate Augustus' triumphal return to Rome after campaigns in Spain and Gaul, and to commemorate the peace he had established throughout the Roman world. Over the centuries the altar became buried, and was lost until the first fragments were rediscovered in 1568. It was not until 1938 that the monument recovered its ancient beauty, when the Fascist regime sponsored its reconstruction.

The outside of the enclosure is decorated with mythological scenes and grand processional friezes in which life-size figures portray Augustus, the imperial family, officials and other notables. The 1930s glass pavilion is being removed, and when the altar reopens to the public it will be within a new building.

ARCO DI COSTANTINO

✚ 58 F6 • Piazza del Colosseo 00184 🆓 Free 🚇 Colosseo 🚌 60, 75, 81, 85, 117, 175, 204, 673, 810, 850

One of Rome's best-preserved imperial monuments, the Arch of Constantine stands proudly on the ancient triumphal way where victorious armies once marched.

The Senate and people of Rome built the arch in AD315 to commemorate the victory of Constantine the Great over Maxentius, the last pagan emperor of Rome, in the battle of Ponte Milvio (AD312), after which

Constantine granted freedom of worship to the Christians.

The highly decorated structure stands nearly 25m (80ft) high and consists of a large arch flanked by two smaller ones. It carries an inscription, repeated on both sides, celebrating Constantine's coming to power. Many of the arch's sculptures were actually taken from other monuments: The bas-reliefs between the statues originally showed episodes in Marcus Aurelius' life, but his features were altered to resemble those of Constantine.

AVENTINO

✚ 57 E6 • Circo Massimo 🚌 3, 44, 60, 73 to Viale Aventino, 75, 81, 95, 118, 160, 175, 204, 231, 628, 715

The Aventine is one of the most beautiful quarters of Rome. Here, the traffic and chaos of the city are left far behind, replaced by peaceful churches, charming cloisters, beautiful gardens and panoramic views over the Trastevere and St. Peter's.

This is the most southerly of Rome's seven hills. Trajan lived here before he became emperor, and his friend Licinius Sura built his private baths here. It became such an affluent area that the Visigoths destroyed it when they sacked Rome in AD410.

From the Circo Massimo (▷ 78) at the foot of the hill there is a delightful walk up to the churches of Santa Sabina (▷ 142) and Sant'Alessio.

One of the finest views of Rome can be had from the Giardino degli Aranci (Garden of Orange Trees), which extends over the site of the Savelli family's stronghold in the Middle Ages. The orange trees were planted here in 1932 to commemorate the first orange tree planted in Italy, brought from Spain by St. Dominic early in the

13th century. Legend has it that the tree can still be seen in the cloister of the Dominican monastery of Santa Sabina. **Don't miss** One of Rome's most popular 'secret' views of St. Peter's can be seen through the keyhole in the main entrance to the Priory of the Knights of Malta.

BASILICA DI SAN PIETRO

See pages 66–71.

CAPITOLINO

See page 72.

CASA DI GOETHE

✚ 57 E3 • Via del Corso 18, 00186 ☎ 06 3265 0412 ⏰ Tue–Sun 10–6 💰 Adult €3, child (under 18) €2 🚇 Flaminio 🚌 52, 53, 61, 71, 80, 85, 117, 119, 160, 590, 850 www.casadigoethe.it

Casa Moscatelli was just a small boarding house when German poet and dramatist Johann Wolfgang von Goethe lived here from 1786 to 1788, and it has changed little since that time.

In the 1990s, the second floor of the house, where Goethe spent one of the happiest and most productive periods of his life, was purchased and renovated to house the Goethe Museum, the only Goethe museum outside Germany, and it has developed into a lively cultural meeting place. The museum has a permanent exhibition, Goethe in Rome, which documents the poet's time in Italy and the influence this had on his work, and includes pictures, drawings, manuscripts, prints and books.

The German painter I. H. Tischbein, who also lived here, portrayed Goethe in a famous work known as Goethe in the Roman Countryside; you can see Andy Warhol's adaptation of it at the entrance to the exhibition.

Basilica di San Pietro

The Roman Catholic Church's principal shrine and the spiritual focus for millions of believers.
One of the world's largest churches, covering 22,067sq m (237,535sq ft)
and capable of holding a congregation of 60,000.
Incorporates architecture by the greatest High Renaissance and baroque masters.

The interior of the basilica (above left). Michelangelo's Pietà *(above middle). The colonnaded arms around the piazza (above right)*

SEEING THE BASILICA DI SAN PIETRO

The best approach to St. Peter's is by way of Via della Conciliazione. You cross into the Vatican State on entering Piazza San Pietro. It is a good idea to pause frequently while exploring the basilica and its surroundings: Everything is on a huge scale, but the proportions are so perfect that you need time to appreciate the actual size. Once inside, the best way to see St. Peter's is to start by making a circuit of the entire basilica and its artworks, then to visit the treasury, followed by the crypt. Most visitors leave the ascent to the roof and cupola till the end of the visit.

HIGHLIGHTS

PIAZZA SAN PIETRO AND THE COLONNADE

Few buildings are approached through such a superb space as that in front of St. Peter's. The elliptical piazza, folded within the curving wings of the colonnade, is considered Gian Lorenzo Bernini's architectural masterpiece. It was conceived and built between 1655 and 1667, during the pontificate of Pope Alexander VII.

The obelisk in the middle is the oldest monument. It was brought to Rome from Egypt in AD36 by the Emperor Caligula and moved to its present site in 1586; it acts as a sundial, the obelisk's shadow marking noon as it touches the white marble disc. Two beautiful fountains flank the obelisk. That on the right is the work of Carlo Maderno, dating from 1613, while the left-hand fountain, by Carlo Fontana, was erected in 1677. Between the fountains and the obelisk are two stone slabs set in the paving; stand on either one of these to see the colonnade's four rows of columns merge into one. There are 284 columns in four rows, their proportions calculated to enhance the height of the basilica's façade. Bernini designed the colonnade to enable coaches to drive through it, while the side aisles were for people on foot. The main entrance to the Vatican Palace is reached through the right-hand end of the colonnade, via the Portone di Bronzo. Look through here to get a glimpse of Bernini's famous *trompe l'oeil* Scala Regia, where columns of diminishing size are used to add greatness to what is in reality a steep and irregular staircase.

RATINGS

Historic interest	●●●●●
Photo stops	●●●●●
Value for money	●●●●●

TIPS

● St. Peter's is a working church and the dress code is strict: no shorts or bare upper arms and shoulders.
● A tour of the Scavi—the pagan cemetery and the excavations under the High Altar—adds an interesting contrast.
● Popes in good health normally give weekly Mass audiences in the Aula Paolo VI behind the left-hand colonnade. See page 68 for information on tickets. Tickets are also available in advance through your local Roman Catholic church.

The basilica seen from Via della Conciliazione (left)

Piazza San Pietro seen from the air (inset)

BASICS

www.vatican.va
This is the official website for the Vatican State and Catholic Church. It has no specific information about St. Peter's

Members of the Swiss Guard are recruited from Switzerland's four Roman Catholic cantons

THE BALDACCHINO, CONFESSIO AND CATTEDRA

The interior of St. Peter's is dominated by Bernini's great altar canopy, the Baldacchino, which stands directly above the traditional site of the tomb of St. Peter the Apostle, with the Cattedra, the great papal throne, behind. The Baldacchino's twisted bronze columns and massive lantern rise above the high altar, where only the pope may celebrate Mass. Standing 29m (95ft) high, it took over 10 years to erect and was inaugurated in 1633 by Pope Urban VIII, a member of the Barberini family—bees, their heraldic symbol, swarm among the foliage of the decoration. The Baldacchino's construction coined a famous lampoon—*quod non fecerunt barbari, fecerunt barberini* ('what the barbarians failed to do, the Barberini did')—as Urban was said to have used bronze taken from the portico of the Pantheon for the columns.

Piazza San Pietro, with the obelisk erected in 1586

In front of the Baldacchino is Carlo Maderno's sunken U-shaped Confessio—a crypt beneath the high altar—with 99 perpetually burning lamps along the balustrade and two flights of curving stairs. The kneeling statue of Pope Pius VI (1820), who is buried beneath, is by Antonio Canova. In front of this, directly beneath the papal altar and behind a grille, is the sixth-century Niche of the Pallia, a surviving relic of the first basilica and said to have given access directly to St. Peter's tomb. Excavations in the 1940s strengthened the hypothesis that there is a very early Christian tomb here, which could, indeed, be that of the saint.

Behind the Baldacchino, and designed to be viewed through it, is the extraordinary set piece known as the Cattedra. The Cattedra itself is an ancient wooden chair, said to have been St. Peter's when he was bishop of Rome, which is enclosed in a bronze throne designed by Bernini in the 1660s. This is raised above the altar of the central apse and surrounded by bronze statues of the Fathers of the Latin and Greek churches. Above this rises a great gilded metallic structure of angels, clouds and rays of light, all illuminated by the sunlight that streams through the central window in which is depicted a dove representing the Holy Spirit.

MICHELANGELO'S PIETÀ

Behind glass, in the first chapel in the right-hand aisle, gleams Michelangelo's white marble *Pietà*, a representation of the Virgin holding her dead son across her knees. It is the only work the artist ever signed and the most famous of all the treasures in St. Peter's.

This portrayal of the Virgin as a young, grieving woman is both spiritually moving and artistically groundbreaking. The young sculptor had mastered anatomy and the handling of marble drapery perfectly; he also solved the compositional problem of the two figures, one upright and one horizontal, by creating a pyramidal shape rising from the horizontal figure of Christ on his mother's lap to the Virgin's

Papal Altar, with
Confessio below

1   Door of the
    Dead, by Manzù
2   Main door, by Filarete
3   Porta Santa, by Consorti
4   *Pietà*, by Michelangelo
5   Monument to Christina of
    Sweden
6   Chapel of the Blessed Sacrament,
    by Borromini
7   Gregorian Chapel
8   Monument to Clement XIII, by
    Canova
9   Nave of the Cattedra
10 Monument to Urban VIII, by
    Bernini
11 Cattedra
12 Monument to Paul III, by della
    Porta
13 Monument to Alexander VII, by
    Bernini
14 Statue of St. Veronica, by Bernini
15 Statue of St. Helen, by Bernini
16 Statue of St. Longinus, by Bernini

17 Statue of St. Andrew, by Bernini
18 Bronze statue of St. Peter
19 Monument to Pius VII
20 Altar of the Transfiguration
21 Monument to Maria
    Clementina-Sobieski
22 Stuart Monument, by Canova
23 Baptistery
24 Equestrian statue of Constantine
25 Equestrian statue of Charlemagne
26 Sacristy
27 Treasury
28 Chapter
29 Canons' Sacristy

head at the apex. After the unveiling, Rome was astounded, and there
was talk that so young a man could never have produced such a
work. Michelangelo, furious, carved his name on the band across the
Virgin's breast, and added an 'M' in the folds of her right hand. This
pietà is the first of four that Michelangelo was to sculpt during his
long life.

BRONZE STATUE OF ST. PETER
At the base of the last pillar on the right of the nave before the
transept is enthroned a bronze statue of St. Peter holding the keys to
the Kingdom of Heaven. For many years believed to be a fifth-century
work, it is now known to date from the late 1200s and is attributed to

*The monument to Pius VII, which
stands over the door to the
sacristy*

Arnolfo di Cambio, the original designer of the Duomo (cathedral) in Florence. It is an austere and beautiful work, its simplicity emphasized by its baroque setting. Much of the right foot has been worn away by the touch of the faithful down the centuries. Kissing the foot traditionally gains an indulgence—time taken off the waiting time in Purgatory for admittance to Heaven. On major feast days the statue is bedecked with gold-encrusted robes and a tiara; you can see these in the Treasury.

THE CUPOLA AND ROOF
A gallery, 330 steps up from the roof, encloses the base of the interior of the dome, the perfect place for a bird's-eye view. At a height of 53m (174ft) above the floor of the basilica, it is from here more than anywhere else that you can appreciate the sheer size of St. Peter's;

Bernini's Baldacchino dominates the crossing (opposite). Nearby is the bronze statue of St. Peter (second right)

figures below appear minuscule. Up here you are close to the vast mosaics of Christ and the apostles, popes and saints, and angels holding the instruments of the Passion—the crown of thorns, the scourge and the nails. Designed by Cavaliere d'Arpino and executed between 1589 and 1612, the mosaics are remarkable for their size (St. Mark's pen is 1.5m/5ft long) but are hardly great works of art.

Outside, the undulating roof and breezy air make it seem as though you are on a ship at sea. Views down to the piazza below appear between the huge statues, and all around you are domes and cupolas. The main dome, with its paired columns and garlands, is true to Michelangelo's design, though probably higher than he intended. Climb the exterior of this masterpiece to its crowning lantern for breathtaking panoramas over the city.

BACKGROUND
The first basilica was built by the Emperor Constantine in AD324 on the site of a pagan cemetery, the traditional burial place of the Apostle Peter. Sumptuously decorated with marble, mosaics and gold, it was pillaged during the barbarian invasions, but held its place as the central church of Christendom. Reconstruction was planned in the 1450s, and in 1503 Pope Julius II commissioned the architect Bramante to rebuild the church; it was planned on a Greek-cross layout surmounted by a high dome, and involved the demolition of much of the original basilica. After Bramante's death in 1514, work ceased, and the next 30 years saw no progress as arguments raged about the layout. In 1547 Michelangelo, then aged 72, was appointed architect. Despite later changes, today's basilica, and particularly the ground plan, is largely inspired by Michelangelo's designs. In 1606, with building underway, the nave was once more lengthened and the façade altered by Carlo Maderno. Pope Urban VIII consecrated the new basilica in 1626. Much of the Mannerist and baroque decoration is the work of Bernini, who succeeded in unifying the various internal elements. St. Peter's is the world's most important Catholic church and is used daily for Mass, as well as for the Church's most important official religious ceremonies.

CAPITOLINO

Rome's focus of political power over the centuries.

The Capitoline Hill, the smallest of Rome's seven hills, is a good place to start an exploration of the historic city. Take in the wonderful views over the Forum from the top before exploring the rest of the hill, where you'll find one of the most interesting museums in Rome as well as the site of Michelangelo's fine trapezoidal Piazza del Campidoglio.

A PLACE IN ROMAN HISTORY
Unlike the Roman Forum, the Capitoline Hill is better known through myth than archaeology. However, there was certainly a Bronze Age settlement here, and remains of Iron Age huts from the ninth to eighth centuries BC have been unearthed. In the Middle Ages, it was called Monte Caprino (Goat Hill), suggesting that goats once grazed on the slopes.

THE HILL'S CRESTS
The hill has two crests: To the north is the Arx or citadel, and to the south, the Capitolium, a high promontory looking out over the Tiber, and now covered by the Palazzo dei Conservatori. Between the two crests is the Piazza del Campidoglio (▷ 118).

In ancient times the Arx is thought to have been a place of augury, where priests would read the omens they saw depicted in the flight of birds. The Temple of Juno Moneta (which means 'She who warns') was built here, on the top of what was thought to be the Roman mint (giving the alternative meaning of *moneta*—money). The temple had a statue of silver geese to commemorate the geese that gave the alarm when the Gauls tried to attack the city in 390BC (▷ 27). The Arx is now the site of the church of Santa Maria in Aracoeli (▷ 133).

THE HILL'S PALAZZI
The Palazzo dei Conservatori and the Palazzo Nuovo, collectively known as the Musei Capitolini (▷ 98–103), flank the Palazzo Senatorio, the seat of Rome's city council. In the sixth century BC, the Etruscan king of Rome, Tarquin the Elder, built the Temple of Jupiter Optimus Maximus (Best and Greatest), the largest of its kind ever built. The temple became the sanctuary for what is known as the Capitoline Triad, the gods Jupiter, Juno and Minerva, with statues of all three standing in the porch. Because of its height and exposed position, the temple was struck by lightning on several occasions but rebuilt each time on the same foundations.

RATINGS	
Historic interest	●●●●●
Value for money	●●●●●
Walkability	●●●●○

BASICS

✚ 57 E5 Ⓜ Colosseo 🚌 44, 46, 63, 70, 75, 81, 84, 87, 95, 715, 716, 780, 781, 810, 916 🚻 Inside the museums

www.museicapitolini.org
www.comune.roma.it

TIPS

● Special art exhibitions are held in the Palazzo Nuovo, and concerts and other events take place elsewhere on the Capitoline Hill. Check the website for information

Michelangelo's Cordonata leads to the Capitoline Hill, still the seat of government, with the city council occupying the Palazzo Senatorio, in the background (top).
Marforio, the river god, in the courtyard of Palazzo Nuovo (inset)

CASTEL SANT'ANGELO

An excellent museum that was formerly a mausoleum and a fortress. Ten stone angels line the Ponte Sant'Angelo.

RATINGS

Good for kids	● ● ●
Photo stops	● ● ● ●
Value for money	● ● ●

BASICS

✚ 56 D4 • Lungotevere del Castello 00165 ☎ 06 681 9111. Call centre: 06 3996 7600 🕐 Tue–Sun 9–8. 🚇 Ottaviano San Pietro 🚌 23, 34, 40, 62, 64, 280, 982, stopping at Lungotevere del Castello 🎫 Adult €5, child (under 18) free 🎧 At tourist information point inside, in several languages ☕ Nice café/restaurant inside 🏛 🚻

Emperor Hadrian chose this secluded spot away from the main city as the site for his tomb. From the top of the squat structure is one of the finest views over Rome, looking out across the Tiber. Today, Castel Sant'Angelo houses part of the Museo Nazionale Romano, with an excellent collection of ceramics, weapons and Renaissance paintings.

FROM MAUSOLEUM TO FORTRESS

The mausoleum remained the burial place of the imperial family up to the reign of Caracalla in AD217. Aurelian later built the mausoleum into the city's fortifications and surrounded it with walls and towers, converting it into a fortress.

In AD590 Rome was stricken with the plague, and Pope Gregory the Great organized a procession to pray for the city's release (▷ 35). As a result of the miracle, the building was renamed Castel Sant'Angelo. In the ninth century, Leo IV linked Castel Sant'Angelo to the nearby Vatican by building a high defensive wall. The *passetto*, a later covered walkway built above the wall, was used by Clement VII in 1527 to escape from Emperor Charles V's troops.

WHAT TO SEE

The spiral ramp inside the castle dates back to the time of Hadrian's mausoleum and a part of it can still be climbed to the main courtyard, where the statue of the Archangel Michael, carved by Raffaello da Montelupo in 1544, stands. Another Archangel Michael, a huge 18th-century statue in bronze, stands at the top of the terrace along with the Bell of Mercy, which in the past pealed to announce executions. The moats and gardens are a 20th-century addition. Inside, along the spiral staircase leading to the upper floors, are the remains of some decorative mosaics.

The route to the fortified Castel Sant'Angelo is watched over by Bernini's angels (below)

There are wonderful views from the top of the castle (inset)

THE SIGHTS

Colosseo

**The largest surviving ancient Roman structure in the world.
An arena nearly 2,000 years old that held over 50,000 people.
Purpose-built venue for some of the most spectacular, and barbarous,
gladiatorial games ever held.**

SEEING THE COLOSSEUM

The Colosseo, the Roman Empire's biggest amphitheatre, lies at the west end of the Foro Romano, encircled by the Caelian, Palatine and Esquiline hills. To get a sense of the building's scale and size, approach it down Via dei Fori Imperiali. Walk round the outside before you enter to take in the exterior architectural details. The Colosseum's interior has been severely damaged over the years, so joining the guided tour, or using an audio-guide, is almost essential for understanding what you are seeing.

HIGHLIGHTS

THE EXTERIOR

Only a small part of the Colosseo survives after centuries of pillaging for building stone. What's left is still impressive, and gives a good idea of the original external architecture, although the marble facings, painted stucco and statues have all gone. The Colosseum covers about 2.5ha (6 acres). It was built on marshy ground, which had to be drained, and beneath its visible arches are others sunk in the earth on cores of concrete. The external arches, and arcades behind them, are built of travertine stone, which was hauled 27km (17 miles) from Tivoli, outside Rome. Behind the travertine facing there is a tufa infill, while the upper storeys of the arcades behind the façade are built of brick-faced concrete.

Externally, the Colosseo measures 188m by 156m (615ft by 510ft) and rises to 48.5m (158ft), with a façade of three tiers of arches and an attic level. The tiers are faced with three-quarter columns in the Classical architectural orders: Doric on the first floor, Ionic on the second and Corinthian on the third, each more elaborate than the one below. The attic has small square window openings and blank walls between Corinthian pilasters, where bronze shields once hung. At the top were 240 brackets and sockets that anchored the huge *velarium*, a shade and bad-weather canopy that could be pulled right over the interior. The holes all over the walls once housed the metal clamps that held the massive stone blocks together; these, along with huge amounts of stone, were pillaged for building in the Middle Ages and in Renaissance times.

THE ARCADES AND SEATING

Behind the façade, on the outside edge of the building, superb arcades run the whole way round the Colosseo on each floor, linking the stairways that connect the different levels. Farther in, 80 walls radiate out from the central arena and support vaults for the access passageways and the tiers of seats. Off the arcades, about 80 entrances—called *vomitoriae*—led into the arena itself, allowing vast numbers of people to pass rapidly through.

Inside, there were tiers of marble benches, some of which can still be seen, where over 50,000 people could be seated. In the later days of the empire, cushions were provided, probably much appreciated since it was normal for the games to last throughout the day. Seating was arranged by rank, with the least important members of the crowd—including women—assigned places nearest the top. Closest to

From close up, the sheer size of the Colosseo is overwhelming

RATINGS	
Good for kids	● ● ●
Historic interest	● ● ● ● ●
Photo stops	● ● ● ●
Value for money	● ● ●

TIPS

● **The Colosseo's ticket office can be very busy—buy your ticket at the Palatine to avoid waiting, or online.**
● **It's hard to work out what's what, so take the guided tour to get the most out of your visit.**
● **Viewing the outside of the Colosseo after dark, when it is floodlit, adds an extra dimension.**

In places, all four floors of the Colosseo are still intact (opposite)

✚ 58 G6 · Piazza del Colosseo 00184
☎ 06 700 5469
🕐 Apr–end Sep daily 9–7.15; Oct
Tue–Sun 9–6.30, Mon 9–2; Nov to mid-
Feb Tue–Sun 9–4.30, Mon 9–2; mid-
Feb to mid-Mar Tue–Sun 9–5, Mon 9–2;
mid-Mar to end Mar Tue–Sun 9–5.30,
Mon 9–2. Last entrance 1 hour before
closing
💶 Adult €10, child (under 18) free. For
joint ticket, ▷ 287
🚇 Colosseo (line B)
🚌 60, 75, 85, 87, 175, 810, 850
🎧 English-language tours at 9.30,
10.15, 11.15, 11.45, 12.30, 1.45 and 3:
€3.50. Audioguides available in Italian,
English, French, German, Spanish and
Japanese: €4
📖 Official guidebook in English pub-
lished by Sovrintendenza dei Beni
Culturali; unoffical guidebooks in
English available at stands all over
Rome
🏪 Two well-stocked souvenir and book
shops selling guidebooks, postcards
and souvenirs
🚻 Inside the Colosseum and outside
on the south side (open 9–6)

www.ticketclic.it

THE SIGHTS

*The most famous view of the
Colosseo (below)*

*Looking out over the wide
sweep of the arena*

the arena was a special box for the emperor, his family and the Vestal
Virgins. Senators were also allotted ringside seats, and the rest of the
tickets were distributed through the heads of families, with better-
born citizens getting the better seats.

The tickets themselves were wooden plaques, carved with the
relevant entrance, aisle number, row and seat number. Spectators
found the right entrance by looking for the numbers over the exterior
arches, and you can still see traces of these. The system was supremely
efficient, capable of moving up to 70,000 people in or out in a matter
of minutes. The design has never been bettered; in essence, the
Colosseo is the prototype for every modern sports stadium.

THE ARENA
Right in the middle of the Colosseo is a jumble of ruins, all that's left
of the labyrinthine passages beneath the arena itself. In Roman times,
this area was covered by wooden flooring, topped with a waterproof
layer of canvas and overlaid with sand—the word arena comes from
the Latin word for sand. The four principal entrances were mainly
used by the gladiators and corpse removers, but far more dramatic
entrances were made through the floor itself, and you can see
outlines of the stone rims of trapdoors among the ruins.

During the Colosseo's history, tens of thousands of animals were
slaughtered, sent to Rome from all over the empire by specialist
animal collectors. Such vast numbers were needed that elephants
disappeared from North Africa, hippos from Numibia and lions from
Mesopotamia as the Roman appetite for ever more extravagant
spectacles grew. Once in Rome, the animals were transported in
cages to the Colosseo, then harried through underground passages
onto elevators that rose up to arena level through the trapdoors. With
this in mind, the maze of ruins begins to make sense.

Not all the channels were used for men and beasts. Some were water conduits, and the arena was regularly flooded for entertainments known as *naumachia*, when criminals fought to the death in re-enactments of naval battles in scaled-down galleys. Gladiatorial games began in the morning with an elaborate procession led by the games' sponsor, the prelude to a morning of staged hunts with wild animals pitted against each other or pursued by *bestiarii*, gladiators specializing in animal slaughter. The lunch break was accompanied by executions of the worst criminals, a taster for the climax of the day—the individual gladiatorial combats.

BACKGROUND

The Flavian Amphitheatre, known since the eighth century as the Colosseo, was built by the three emperors from the Flavian family. Construction started under Vespasian in AD72, and the inaugural games, held in a partially completed building, took place during the reign of his son Titus in AD80. The Colosseo was completed by Titus' brother Domitian. It was the first permanent amphitheatre to be built in Rome and one of the first buildings to combine a vast and grandiose design with immense practicality. Games and fights were held here right up until the end of the empire, with the last recorded exhibition of wild beasts under the barbarian ruler Theodoric in the sixth century. During the Middle Ages, the Colosseo was used as a fortress, and from the 15th century as a quarry, providing the stone for some of Rome's finest palazzi. By the late 1700s the crumbling structure was a romantic and overgrown ruin, dedicated since 1750 to the Christian martyrs who had been killed in its arena. Serious conservation started in the 19th century and continues still.

The ruins of the area under the arena are complex

WHAT'S IN A NAME?

The name Colosseum first appeared in the writings of English monk, the Venerable Bede, in the eighth century. Despite the fact that Bede had never been to Rome, it was soon accepted that he derived the name either from the size of the structure, or because of the huge statue of Nero that once stood nearby. Another theory is that it may once have been called *amphitheatrum ad Colle Isaeum*—'the amphitheatre near the Iseum Hill'. Constant use would have led to the dropping of *amphitheatrum*, and as initial vowels elide in Latin the resultant word would have been very close to Colosseum. Whatever the derivation, English travellers may then have taken the name back from Rome to Bede.

The Protestant Cemetery is the final resting place of English poet John Keats

St. Paul looks out from the top of the Column of Marcus Aurelius in Piazza Colonna

CIMITERO PROTESTANTE

✚ 310 E8 • Via Caio Cestio 6, 00153
🕐 Mon–Sat 9–4.30, Sun 9–2 🎫 Free;
contribution welcome 🚇 Piramide
🚌 118 📖 Guidebook €4, in English,
Italian, German and Swedish

As an oasis of peace and quiet, Rome has nowhere better than this well-kept cemetery, last resting place of many a famous name. More than 4,000 non-Roman Catholics who have died in Rome since the late 18th century lie in the shade of cypress and pine trees.

The ashes of the Romantic poet Percy Bysshe Shelley, drowned in 1822 at the age of 29 while sailing in the Gulf of Spezia, are buried here. They were brought to Rome by his friend, Trelawny, who had been present at his cremation.

The tomb of fellow poet John Keats bears a poignant epitaph: 'This Grave contains all that was Mortal of a young English poet, who on his death bed, in the Bitterness of his Heart, at the Malicious Power of his enemies, desired these words to be engraved on his Tomb Stone: Here lies One Whose Name was writ in Water.'

A simple marble tomb marks the grave of Julius, only son of Johann Wolfgang von Goethe (▷ 65), born from the German writer's relationship with Christiane Vulpius, who later became his wife. The grave bears no name, only the inscription 'Goethe filius'.

CIRCO MASSIMO

✚ 57 F6 • Viale Aventino 00184
🚇 Circo Massimo 🚌 81, 160, 204, 628, 715

Even if there is no longer much to see, the Circo Massimo has kept its magical atmosphere and the feeling of past glories. Wandering around the huge elliptical track, now a peaceful garden (if you can ignore the noise of the traffic beyond its boundaries), it is not difficult to imagine the cheers of 300,000 spectators watching the chariot races organized for the emperors of Imperial Rome.

Nestling in a hollow between the Aventine and Palatine hills, the Great Circus was more than 600m (1,970ft) long and 140m (460ft) wide, and was probably built as early as 326BC. Mainly used for two- and four-horse chariot races, it remained in use until AD549.

Emperor Augustus erected the obelisk of the Pharaoh Rameses II (now in Piazza del Popolo) on the *spina,* the dividing wall running down the middle of the track; Constantine also put up an obelisk, later moved to Piazza di San Giovanni in Laterano. The ruins of Porta Capena were part of the circus during Trajan's period. In 1145 the circus was granted to the Frangipani family—the tower at the end towards the FAO building is what remains of their fortress. Excavation and restoration works started in the 1930s.

COLONNA DI MARCO AURELIO

✚ 57 E4 • Piazza Colonna 00186
🚇 Spagna 🚌 52, 53, 61, 85, 117, 119, 160, 175, 492, 628, 630, 850

The Column of Marcus Aurelius stands in the paved and pedestrianized Piazza Colonna, an area that has always been the hub of political power and is now home to the Italian government.

It is made from Luni marble, is 29.5m (96ft) high and 3.5m (11ft) wide, and was erected between AD180 and AD193. A frieze runs in a continuous spiral round the column, with beautiful bas-reliefs depicting significant episodes in the wars conducted by the Emperor Marcus Aurelius against various Danubian tribes in the second century AD. The frieze gives a wealth of information about military and social history for this period.

A statue of Marcus Aurelius and his wife, Faustina, once stood on top of the column, but was lost; in its place, Pope Sixtus V erected a bronze statue of St. Paul (1589) by Domenico Fontana. A spiral staircase of some 200 steps inside the shaft of the column leads up to a little terrace on the top, but it is no longer possible for visitors to go inside.

COLONNA TRAIANA

✚ 57 F5 • Via dei Fori Imperiali 00184
🚇 Colosseo 🚌 60, 84, 85, 87, 117, 175, 810, 850

Trajan's Column is one of the oldest and most intact ancient monuments in present-day Rome. It is an exquisite work of art, with over 100 bas-relief scenes of the Dacian wars (waged in the region of present-day Romania) conducted by Emperor Trajan during the second century AD. More than 2,500 figures decorate 25 great blocks of marble, each one about 3.5m (11ft) wide. These magnificent carvings were probably originally painted in brilliant hues. It stands in Trajan's Forum, part of the Fori Imperiali (▷ 82–83), where you can also see the Mercati Traianei—Trajan's Market (▷ 91).

From the base of the column, which is decorated with war trophies, there is a spiral staircase leading up. A statue of St. Peter on top, by Tommaso della Porta, replaces the original statue of Trajan, which looked out over the Forum until 1587. The inside of the column can only be visited as part of an organized tour.

The marble blocks vary in diameter from the base to the

Running in a continuous spiral, the frieze on Trajan's Column shows episodes from the wars with the Dacians

Conca's Allegory of Fame from the Galleria dell'Accademia di San Luca

top of the column. So that the 40m (130ft) column appears straight, the diameter increases gradually from about two-thirds of the way up. Look also for the windows cut in the decorative panels: Barely noticeable from the outside, they allow light to enter the staircase area.

COLOSSEO

See pages 74–77.

CRYPTA BALBI

⊞ 57 E5 • Via delle Botteghe Oscure 31, 00186 ☎ Call centre: 06 399 6700 ⏰ Tue–Sun 9–7.45 🎟 Adult €4, child (under 18) free. For joint ticket, ▷ 287 🚌 30, 40, 46, 62, 63, 64, 70, 81, 492, 628, 630, 780, 787, 916 stopping at Largo di Torre Argentina

This museum, part of the Museo Nazionale Romano, focuses on how the city has changed over the centuries, with a rich collection of objects to illustrate social, economic and urban planning changes from ancient times, through the Middle Ages up to the present day. This display is at entrance level.

Two other sections have displays of vases, glass items, mosaics, a bone chessboard and other items dating from between the fifth and eighth centuries. The museum also has ancient coins and finds from the Foro Romano, including works from Palazzo Venezia and the Musei Capitolini.

DOMUS AUREA

⊞ 58 G6 • Viale della Domus Aurea/Giardini di Colle Oppio 00184 ☎ Call centre/guided tours: 06 3996 7700 Mon–Sat 9–1.30, 2.30–5 ⏰ Wed–Mon 9–7.45 🎟 Adult €6, child (under 18) free 🚇 Colosseo 🚌 60, 64, 75, 84, 85, 87, 117, 175, 810, 850 📷 Guided tour, booked in advance: in Italian, 9.40, 10.20, 12, 1.40, 2.40, 4 and 6.40; in English, 11.20, 4.40 and 6. Audioguide €2 in English, Spanish, Italian, French and German www.ticketclic.it (to book a guided tour)

Nero's Golden House was a majestic urban villa built in the middle of the city following the great fire of Rome in AD64. It stretched over the Palatine, Caelian and Oppian hills, with pavilions and, in the area where the Colosseo now stands, an enormous artificial lake and gardens. Today, 32 out of the 140 original rooms of this well-preserved site can be visited. It is worth taking a guided tour to gain a better understanding of the structure of the ancient palace.

When trying to imagine the sheer size of this magnificent house, remember that the vestibule held a 35m (115ft) bronze sculpture of the Sun with Nero's face; this colossal statue may have provided the name for the later Colosseo (▷ 77). One of the highlights of the house is the octagonal hall, an ingenious banqueting room covered with a rotating dome; the ivory ceiling was pierced so that guests could be showered with flowers and perfume.

Following Nero's suicide in AD68, the house was used as the foundations for the baths of Titus and of Trajan. It then remained hidden until the 1490s, when the section on the Oppian Hill was discovered. Its beautiful frescoes of geometric shapes, animals, faces and landscapes influenced Renaissance artists such as Raphael, who drew inspiration for a new pictorial trend called 'grotesque' from the grotto rooms of the frescoes.

The ruins are inside Colle Oppio. This local park gives a welcome area of greenery in this otherwise monument-heavy area. However, you should avoid the park after nightfall.

FONTANA DI TREVI

See pages 80–81.

FORI IMPERIALI

See pages 82–83.

FORO ROMANO

See pages 84–89.

GALLERIA DELL'ACCADEMIA DI SAN LUCA

⊞ 57 F4 • Piazza dell'Accademia di San Luca 77, 00186 ☎ 06 679 8850 ⏰ Mon–Sat 10–12.30. Closed Jul and Aug 🎟 Free 🚇 Barberini 🚌 52, 53, 60, 61, 62, 63, 71, 80, 85, 160, 850 stopping at Piazza San Silvestro www.accademiasanluca.it

This gallery, one of Rome's most prestigious, was founded to promote the training of artists in Renaissance techniques. From 1633, every artist member of the academy had to donate a work of art, resulting in a wonderful collection that includes paintings by Raphael, Antonio Canova, Sir Anthony Van Dyck, Titian, Peter Paul Rubens, Il Guercino, Il Sassoferrato, Guido Reni and Pietro da Cortona.

When its original home was demolished in the 1930s to make way for the Via dei Fori Imperiali, the academy moved to Giacomo della Porta's 16th-century palazzo.

Works of particular interest include *Portrait of Clement IX* by Baciccia, *St. Luke Painting the Virgin*, attributed to Raphael, *Judith and Holophernes* by Piazzetta, and the *Virgin and Angels* by Van Dyck. There are almost 400 portraits of all the artists of the academy from its inception to the 20th century (although not all of them are on display). Look out for the spiral staircase leading to the upper floors, based on a design by the 17th-century architect Francesco Borromini.

Fontana di Trevi

Rome's most spectacular and popular fountain.
Nicola Salvi's baroque masterpiece.
Uses water from one of the few original Roman water canals still in use.
Immortalized in Fellini's film, *La Dolce Vita*.

THE SIGHTS

RATINGS	
Good for kids	● ● ●
Historic interest	● ●
Photo stops	● ● ●
Value for money	● ● ● ● ●

BASICS
✚ 57 F4 • Piazza di Trevi 00187
⊛ Barberini
⊟ 52, 53, 61, 62, 63, 71, 80, 116, 119, 175, 204, 492, 590, 630, 850 stopping at Piazza San Silvestro
🔛 Available in souvenir shops
⊞ Many souvenir shops

From the air, you can see the Fontana di Trevi's theatrical aspect (above)

The sculptures on the fountain are full of symbolism; for example, the agitated horse to the left of Neptune (as you face him) respresents the stormy sea, while the figure blowing into a conch on the other side is the calm sea (right)

Throwing a coin into the fountain ensures your return to Rome and helps a good cause too (right inset)

SEEING THE FONTANA DI TREVI

Not far from the busy Via del Corso, down Via del Tritone and Via della Stamperia, is the most photographed fountain in Rome, the Trevi. As you step out of the shadows of the surrounding narrow streets into the small Piazza di Trevi, you are met by an overwhelming sight: The fountain, with its theatrical setting, baroque architecture, cascading water, faded rocks and wide basin, cannot fail to impress.

HIGHLIGHTS

THE BACKDROP

The story of the fountain is told in two bas-reliefs, above the two figures flanking the large central statue of Neptune. On the right, a young girl shows Agrippa's thirsty soldiers the way to a freshwater spring (by G. B. Grossi), and on the left, a panel by Andrea Bergondi shows Agrippa approving the plans for the 19km (12-mile) aqueduct from the Salone Spring to Rome.

THE FOUNTAIN

The imposing figure of Neptune, with his fluttering mantle, sits in the middle of this compelling stage, riding in his shell-shaped chariot pulled by two spirited sea horses that are steered by giant tritons. The tall niche that he stands in gives balance and symmetry to the composition. There are various animals, both mythological and real, in the basin, which represents the sea. In the niches to the right and left are the statues of Plenty (left) and Health (right) carved by Filippo della Valle.

THE RITUAL

There is one very important ritual to complete before leaving this magnificent scene behind. Legend has it that visitors should make a wish and toss two coins over their shoulder into the fountain; one coin ensures a return to Rome and the other makes the wish come true. The huge number of coins thrown into the fountain are collected daily and given to CARITAS, an Italian religious charity.

BACKGROUND

Long before the Fontana di Trevi was built, water was brought through the aqueduct designed by Augustus' adviser and friend General Agrippa in 19BC. The water that supplies the Fontana di Trevi runs underground, and it is one of the few original Roman water canals still in use. The aqueduct worked well for many centuries until it was reduced to a trickle in the Middle Ages, mostly due to lack of maintenance. In 1732, Pope Clement XII held a competition to design a new fountain to revive the splendour of ancient Rome. Salvi emerged the winner and was given the delicate task of carrying out this ambitious project. The fountain was completed after his death and finally inaugurated in 1762 by Clement XIII. A thorough restoration project was completed in 1991, returning the fountain to its original grandeur.

Fori Imperiali

**A huge area of ruins that once embodied the power of imperial Rome.
Series of fora built by succeeding emperors as symbols
of self-aggrandizement.
One of the most exciting excavations still remaining in Rome.**

SEEING THE FORI IMPERIALI

The five colonnaded areas just down the road from the
Colosseo were once the imperial fora, built as commercial and
political meeting places by successive emperors. Plundered
remorselessly over the centuries, today's ruins seem at first
glance little more than a jumble of columns and tumbled stone,
so take time to get your bearings. Excavations here are still
ongoing, and over 15,000sq m (160,000sq ft) have been
unearthed, representing more than half the original fora—and
there's still more to discover.

HIGHLIGHTS

TRAJAN'S FORUM

After the wonderfully preserved covered markets of the Mercati
Traianei (▷ 91), the adjoining Trajan's Forum needs a leap of
imagination to visualize its original appearance, when this huge forum
was one of the wonders of the world. The last and most opulent
forum to be built, it was an enormous public space,
constructed to commemorate the conquest of Dacia
(modern Romania) in AD106. The rectangular form
is still traceable, and you can see the forest of
broken columns that was once the Basilica Ulpia.
Once the size of San Paolo fuori le Mura
(▷ 148–149), it virtually masked the
magnificent Trajan's Column (▷ 78–79),
which stands behind it.

FORUM OF NERVA

Once a monumental drain and now
used as a tunnel, the Chiavicone runs
underneath the Via dei Fori Imperiali
and leads to the long, narrow Forum
of Nerva. On emerging in the forum,
you'll be able to make out the ruined
podium of the Temple of Minerva, the
goddess of household tasks. This was
largely intact up to the 17th century,
when Pope Paul V plundered the stone
to build a fountain. It was also known as
the Forum Transitorium (Passageway Forum)
because it incorporated the Argiletum, a road
linking the old Roman forum with the Subura,
the popular district.

THE FORUM OF AUGUSTUS,
THE TEMPLUM PACIS AND THE
FORUM OF CAESAR

The Subura is adjacent to the Forum of
Augustus (2BC), site of the ruins of the
Temple of Mars Ultor, built to commemo-
rate Augustus' victory at Philippi and the

*The Fori Imperiali
(above) are made up
from fora dedicated to
the great and the good
of Rome, including Trajan
(right)*

RATINGS	
Good for kids	●●
Historic interest	●●●●
Photo stops	●●●
Walkability	●●●●

BASICS

✚ 57 F5 • Via dei Fori Imperiali 00184
☎ 06 679 7786. Visitor centre 06 679
7702 (daily 9.30–6). You can see much
of the site from the walkway above it
that runs parallel to Via dei Fori
Imperiali ⊙ Fori Imperiali is a working
archaeological site, and you can only
visit as part of a guided tour. Contact
the visitor centre for details
⊙ Colosseo 🚌 60, 75, 84, 85, 87, 117,
175, 810, 850 🚶 Guided tours at 3,
3.30, 4.30 and 5.30 on Wed, Sat
and Sun, Mar–end Oct; 3 and 3.30
only, Nov–end Feb; adult €7, child
(under 12) €1.50; 1 hour 20 mins
🎧 Available at visitor centre €18
🏛 At visitor centre 🚻 At visitor centre

www.capitolium.org

deaths of Caesar's assassins. Don't miss the African marble columns—all that remains of the Temple of Peace (AD75) in nearby Vespasian's Forum—or the three columns that were once part of Caesar's temple of Venus Genitrix in his forum. The Julia family claimed the goddess as their ancestress and Caesar adorned the temple's statue with pearls from far-off Britain.

BACKGROUND

This entire vast area was constructed between 50BC, when Julius Caesar, aware that the old Republican forum had become too small for all its activities, commenced building, and AD113, when Trojan finished his forum. Succeeding fora were built by Augustus, Vespasian, Domitian and Trajan; they all ostensibly commemorate peace and treaties, but were ultimately expressions of the individual emperors' power and prestige, envisioned as fitting monuments to their personal glory.

Foro Romano

The heart of ancient Rome—the political, economic, religious and commercial hub of the city during Republican times.
One of Rome's most evocative sites.
Buildings and ruins spanning almost a thousand years.

A view across the Forum, with the Colosseo in the background (left). The Arch of Septimius Severus in the foreground (above left). The remains of the Tempio di Saturno (above right)

SEEING THE FORO ROMANO

The ruins of the Roman Forum lie in what is still the heart of Rome, just behind the looming 'wedding cake' of the Victor Emmanuel monument in Piazza Venezia (▷ 119), and below the Capitoline and Palatine hills. There are several access points: The best is through the entrance on Via dei Fori Imperiali, which leads you straight on to the Via Sacra, the sacred way, running through the heart of the complex. It is bounded to the right by the Arco di Settimio Severo, and to the left by the Arco di Tito, with most of the interesting remains lying between these two triumphal arches. At first sight, the Forum appears little more than a jumbled collection of ruins, dotted with upright columns and a few complete buildings, so take time to get your bearings.

HIGHLIGHTS

TEMPLE AND HOUSE OF THE VESTAL VIRGINS

Overlooking the Via Sacra rise the ruins of a circular white temple. This is the Temple of Vesta, goddess of the hearth, where the Vestal Virgins tended an ever-burning fire symbolizing the perpetuity of the Roman state. A Temple of Vesta stood here from the earliest times; the existing ruin and its columns are composed of fragments of the version dating from AD191, built by Septimius Severus after a fire. It was reconstructed in the 1930s.

The cult of Vesta was one of the cornerstones of Roman belief. In primitive times, fire was of such importance it attained an almost sacred significance. Difficult to kindle, it was vital that it should not go out, so the custom evolved of keeping the communal fire in a separate hut. Young girls, with few other responsibilities, were the appointed guardians; thus through the centuries a practice that originated in good sense became imbued with religious symbolism. The temple itself was always circular, in imitation of the round huts of ancient Rome, and everything connected with Vesta and her worship was charged with archaic significance. The fire had to be kept burning at all costs, a difficult task when the winds blew and rain poured through the vent in the roof.

RATINGS					
Good for kids	● ●				
Historic interest	●	●	●	●	●
Value for money	●	●	●	●	●
Walkability	●	●	●	●	

TIPS
● Making sense of the Forum is quite a challenge—use an audioguide to get more out of your visit.
● Take something to drink with you. There are no bars in the Forum area.

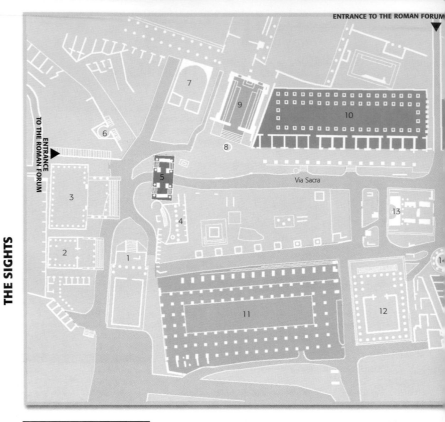

ENTRANCE TO THE ROMAN FORUM

ENTRANCE TO THE ROMAN FORUM

Via Sacra

THE SIGHTS

BASICS

✚ 57 F6 • Via dei Fori Imperiali, Via di San Teodoro, Via di San Gregorio, Piazza Santa Maria 53; Largo Romolo e Remo 5–6, 00184

☎ 06 3996 7700 or 06 6998 411

🕐 Mar–end Oct daily 9–6; Nov–end Feb 9–3.30

🎫 Free 🚇 Colosseo

🚌 75, 85, 87, 117, 175, 186, 810, 850

🎧 Tours in English at 10.30; adult €3.50, child (under 12) free. Audioguides in Italian and English, €4. Ticket office at Arco di Tito (tel 06 3996 7700)

🛈 Several on site

www.capitolium.org
Although mainly devoted to the on-going excavations in the Fori Imperiali, there's plenty of information on the Foro Romano too. Excellent virtual reconstructions of what the buildings looked like in Roman times. Easy and fast to navigate, with an English option.

www.comune.roma.it
This is a good Italian-language site about the Forum area, its archaeological history and future development. Clear maps and a virtual tour. Run by Rome City Council.

There were six Vestal Virgins, working a rota system to tend the fire. They were recruited at an early age from impeccable families and appointed for 30 years by the emperor. The first 10 years were spent learning their duties, the second practising them and the last passing on their knowledge. At the end of their service, Vestals were released from their vows and were free to marry, though few did. In return for their service, they had immense privileges (in a society where women had few rights)—wealth, land ownership, the right to pardon criminals, and access to the emperor. If they broke their vows of chastity, how-ever, the penalties were harsh—some were buried alive. The order survived into the Christian era, being finally disbanded in AD394.

Vestal Virgins lived in the Atrium Vestae, the sprawling site next to the temple. This was built, as were all patrician houses, round an elongated court, whose ruins survive. It was constructed in the second century AD, to replace an earlier building, and must have been immensely grand. Today, the central courtyard with its three pools, lined with statues of the Virgins in their long white robes, is the most striking thing to be seen. Behind lie the tumbled ruins of the Vestals' once-magnificent palace.

THE CURIA

Set back from the open space of the Forum proper is a wonderfully complete, austere, red building. This is the Curia, home to the Senate, the most important civil body during the days of the Republic. According to Roman legend, Romulus, father of Rome, summoned a hundred family heads to meet regularly for consultation. These so-called *patres* (fathers), were the first senators; their role evolved into that of decision-makers on Rome's policies at home and abroad. During the Republic, the Curia was politically the most important place in the Roman world, where famous orators and statesmen

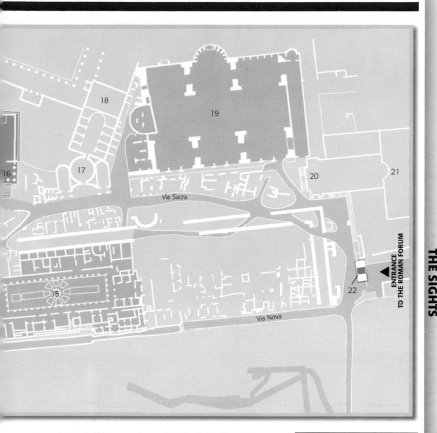

spoke, major legal affairs were disputed, and policies shaped. But as the role of the single ruler evolved, its influence waned, and by the second century AD the Senate had no control over affairs, although it continued as an institution right up to the fall of Rome.

The Curia was rebuilt several times over the centuries, and the present building was reconstructed after a fire during the reign of Diocletian (AD285–305). In AD630 it was incorporated into the church of Sant'Adriano, and thus survived to emerge virtually intact when the church was demolished in 1937. It is by no means grand or huge, being built to hold about 300 senators. The height of the Curia is half the sum of its length and breadth, a ratio prescribed by the great first-century BC architect Vitruvius as providing ideal acoustics—important in a building used for debate. Inside, three shallow tiers of marble seats face each other across the central space, with a low dais for the presiding magistrate at the far end, and a statue of a senator in the middle. Grey marble originally covered the walls—you can see

A view across the Forum, with the Temple of Antonius and Faustina in the foreground

The House of the Vestal Virgins

THE TOGA

All over the empire, free-born Romans wore the toga. It was a sign of citizenship and the privileges that went with it; it proclaimed that the wearer was protected by Roman law and could not be mistreated, flogged or crucified. The emperors issued edicts about the toga, decreeing that citizens entering the Forum or attending the games had to wear it. It was an elegant but cumbersome garment, with folds that took time to arrange; it had to be re-pleated after every wearing, and it needed constant washing. Citizens disliked putting on the toga, and avoided doing so if possible—it was difficult to do more than stroll about slowly while wearing it.

There were several types of toga: the plain white worn by ordinary citizens; a garment with a red hem for certain priests; and the *toga praetexta*, edged with purple and worn by the 600 senators. Grandest of all was the *toga picta*, woven of purple cloth, worn by the emperor on state occasions.

some surviving sections facing each side of the platform. The floor is a most beautiful example of a technique called *opus sectile*, in which large pieces of stone in different hues are fitted together in figured patterns—a harmonious blend of red, yellow, green and white marble, laid out in rosettes and cornucopias. Only the doors are replacements; the originals were removed in the 17th century, by Pope Alexander VII, to the basilica of San Giovanni in Laterano.

The senate house was a consecrated building with the status of a temple; the first act of each senator on entering was to throw incense grains on to the brazier next to the goddess of victory, whose golden statue stood on an altar at one end. Speakers addressed the Senate from their seats, and voted by division, with those in agreement moving to one side and those against to the other.

The area outside the Curia is the Comitium. Here, during the early Republic, stood the Rostra, from which orators addressed the people. Its name comes from the *rostra*—the prows or beaks—of ships captured at the Battle of Anzio in 338BC, which once decorated it. The fenced-off flat, black marble slab is the Lapis Niger, which the Romans believed marked the burial place of Romulus. A stele dating from the sixth century BC was found here; the inscription engraved on it is believed to be the earliest written form of Latin.

ARCO DI SETTIMIO SEVERO

Next to the Curia, on the triumphal route that led to the Capitoline Hill, stands the Arch of Septimius Severus, a fine example of this peculiarly Roman form of monument. It was built, in AD203, on the orders of the Senate, to commemorate the 10th anniversary of the Emperor Septimius Severus' defeat of the Parthians (in what is now Iran), and to glorify his sons, Caracalla and Geta. Being the first major architectural addition to the Forum area for 80 years, it was suitably grandiose. The central arch is flanked by two lower ones, and faced with four splendid Corinthian columns, surrounded by reliefs with reclining gods and scenes from Severus' career. Originally, it was topped with a statue of Severus and his two sons riding in a chariot drawn by six horses. This has gone, but the inscriptions along the entablature are still clear. In AD212, after he became emperor, Caracalla murdered his brother Geta, co-emperor with him, and removed his name. Look at the fourth line of the inscription and you can see the missing words *'et Gatae nobilissimo cesari'* outlined by the holes left by the clamps that once held the letters.

ARCO DI TITO

At the opposite end of the Forum from Severus' Arch, the Arch of Titus was erected in AD81 in homage to Flavian Emperor Titus and his capture of Jerusalem 11 years previously. This restrained and sober monument, heavily restored, is today most significant for its unique representations, on the inner jambs of the arch, of the sacred furnishings of the great Jewish temple in Jerusalem. On the south side is the triumphant procession entering Rome with the trophies from the temple—the silver trumpets, the sacred altar and the seven branched candlestick. On the opposite jamb is Titus, crowned with laurel by Nike (goddess of victory), standing in his horse-drawn chariot, surrounded by senators and plebs. For centuries the arch has been a symbol of shame to Jews, and even today, many refuse to pass through it.

VIA SACRA

The Via Sacra runs right through the core of the Forum, from the Palatine Hill to the Capitoline. It was the most famous street in ancient Rome, its name deriving from the sanctuaries that lined it and the victorious processions of generals and emperors that

The lone columns, fallen masonry and occasional statue in the Roman Forum give few clues to its former impressiveness

walked along it. Scholars and archaeologists have argued for years over the precise function of some of the buildings along the Via Sacra, but many are well known, as they were among the most important in the city. Just by the main entrance to the Forum site are the steps of the Regia, the house of kings, probably dating from the seventh century BC. Opposite is the best-preserved temple in the Forum, that of Antoninus and Faustina, which owes its survival to its conversion into a Christian church in the seventh century. Farther along, the huge area of broken columns was once the Basilica Aemilia, built in the second century BC to house the law courts. The Via Sacra curves left from here, with the Forum proper to the right. To the left are the long steps of the ruins of the Basilica Julia, built by Julius Caesar in the 50s BC on his return from the Gallic Wars. The romantic theory that the ruts in the stones were made by Roman chariots is unlikely to be correct, as none was allowed along the Via Sacra; they were probably gouged out by the carts of medieval builders using the Forum as a quarry.

BACKGROUND

The origins of the Forum lie in the eighth century BC when the inhabitants of what was then a small pastoral settlement began to construct a cluster of religious and civic buildings. Over the next centuries the Forum and its associated buildings became the heart of the expanding city of Rome, with ever more magnificent basilicas, temples and commercial premises. It was the venue for religious ceremonies, military triumphs, sacrifices and important funerals, the home of the law courts and banking, trading and commercial activities. It was also the city's main meeting place, fulfilling much the same purpose in Roman life as the piazza does in 21st-century Italian towns. By the second century BC the space was too constricted for Rome's ever-expanding public needs and activities, and in 54BC the first of a series of new administrative centres, the Fori Imperiali, was built by Julius Caesar. With Rome's decline, the original Forum area steadily declined, its buildings either transformed into Christian churches, or abandoned. After AD800 the Forum became little more than a convenient stone quarry for medieval and Renaissance builders. Excavation started in the 19th century, and has continued ever since.

BASILICAS

The Romans invented the architectural form of the basilica, a great hall where the central, higher space, lit by clerestory windows, was divided from the side aisles by rows of columns. Basilicas, with their exterior porticoes and colonnades, were practical buildings where crowds could gather in comfort, and they were used as meeting places for business and as law courts. They were cool and airy during stifling summer months, making it no surprise that the early Christian Church adopted the design—and the name. The Christian basilica of San Paolo fuori le Mura is a good place to get an idea of how the basilicas in the Forum must have looked in their heyday (▷ 148–149).

Baciccia's trompe l'oeil *ceiling in Il Gesù*

From Gianicolo (the Janiculum Hill), the panorama of Rome opens up before you

IL GESÙ

⊞ 57 E5 • Piazza del Gesù/Via degli Astalli 16, 00186 ☎ 06 697001 ◐ 6.30–12.30, 4–7.15 ✦ Free ⊟ 30, 40, 46, 62, 63, 64, 70, 81, 492, 628, 630, 780, 787, 916 stopping at Largo di Torre Argentina; tram 8

The inside of this church, dedicated to the Holy Name of Jesus, was undecorated when it was completed in 1584. However, at the end of the 17th century, exquisite marble decorations, stuccowork and baroque frescoes, masterpieces of illusionism, were added to make the Jesuits' principal church one of the most beautiful in Rome.

The façade of the church is divided in two: At the top, a triangular tympanum includes a large central window and two lateral niches; below is a line of pilasters with Corinthian capitals. The interior consists of a central nave with side chapels. The chapel on the left, dedicated to St. Ignatius Loyola, adorned with stuccowork, golden bronzes, sculptures and precious stones, is the work of the Jesuit architect Andrea Pozzo. Pietro da Cortona added the right-hand chapel, and on the altar there is a painting by Carlo Maratta. On the ceiling, above the central nave, a remarkable *trompe l'oeil* fresco of 1679 by Baciccia depicts the *Triumph of the Name of Jesus*: Light descends through a fake window in the sky, colossal figures representing the races and vocations of humankind float in clouds, while others, representing the cardinal sins, fall into darkness.

GHETTO AND SINAGOGA

⊞ 57 E5 ☎ Synagogue: 06 6400 0661 ◐ Mon–Thu 9–4.30, Fri 9–1.30, Sun 9–12.30 ✦ €6 ⊟ 23, 63, 280, 630, 780; tram 8 ⚑ Tours of Ghetto in English, lasting up to 1 hour, at 12.30 on Fri and Sat; €7. Meet at the Synagogue

The Ghetto is a picturesque place today, its narrow, bustling streets full of Jewish restaurants, pastry shops and workshops—despite its unhappy history, the area is still a meeting point for the Roman-Jewish community.

In 1555, Pope Paul IV created the Ghetto to segregate Rome's Jewish population. They were confined in bad sanitary conditions within the Ghetto walls, where three gates were opened in the morning and closed at dusk, and they were limited in their rights to worship and to trade. In 1888 Pope Pius IX opened the gates for the final time; the walls and houses of the Ghetto were demolished, and Rome's Jewish population were free to leave the area and given the same civil rights as they had formerly enjoyed.

The monumental Synagogue, built in 1904, overlooks the Tiber, its great dome visible from all over the city. It houses the Jewish Museum. Behind runs Via del Portico d'Ottavia, named after the ruins of the portico built in the first century BC by Augustus and his sister. Inside is the church of Sant'Angelo in Pescheria, which owes its name to the open-air fish market held nearby. The stone tablet for measuring the length of the fish is still there. This was one of the four Christian churches Jews were forced to attend every Sunday.

GIANICOLO

⊞ 56 C6 • Passeggiata del Gianicolo ⊟ 870

Although not one of Rome's original seven hills, the best view of Rome and its monuments has to be from the Janiculum Hill, especially at sunset. Its terrace is the city's largest, but there are spectacular views all the way up from the Passeggiata del Gianicolo, a fine avenue that runs all around the hill, beginning at Ponte Amedeo di Savoia. To save time and energy, take a bus to the top and return to Ponte Amedeo di Savoia on foot.

On the terrace is a huge equestrian monument to Giuseppe Garibaldi, who in 1849 fought a battle nearby to defend the Roman Republic. Eighty busts displayed along the promenade represent famous artists and heroes from Garibaldi's campaign.

The church of Sant'Onofrio has beautiful frescoes by Antoniazzo Romano and Baldassare Peruzzi, together with the remains of the 16th-century Italian poet Torquato Tasso. The adjoining convent, where Tasso spent his last years, has frescoes by Domenichino.

GIARDINO DEL PINCIO

⊞ 57 E3 ◐ Closes at sunset 🚇 Spagna or Flaminio ⊟ 88, 95, 117, 119, 204, 231, 490, 491, 495

The gardens on the Pincio Hill are Rome's first and most famous public gardens. Designed around 1810 by Giuseppe Valadier, they stretch from Trinità dei Monti to Piazza del Popolo, adjoining Villa Borghese park.

The fashionable gardens occupied part of the area where the Horti Luculliani once stood. This was the villa and terraced gardens built by the politician (and epicure) Lucullus in the first century BC, and which extended for about 20ha (50 acres) between Trinità dei Monti and Villa Medici. After the sack of Rome, in the fifth century AD, the Pincii family bought the estate, along with most of the hill, and the gardens still bear their name.

If you climb the Rampa del Pincio from Piazza del Popolo, you reach the Pincio Terrace, dedicated to Napoleon I, which

THE SIGHTS

The Synagogue, still at the heart of the Ghetto

The Giardino del Pincio gives welcome respite from the city

Boat-shaped Isola Tiberina from the air

has a spectacular view of the city. Nearby is the lovely Casina Valadier, built by Valadier between 1813 and 1817 as a coffee house. Inside are some noteworthy frescoes and tempera decorations discovered during recent restorations. A fashionable café, the building is still a meeting place for Roman aristocrats, although currently it is closed for restoration.

ISOLA TIBERINA

➕ 57 E6 🚌 23, 63, 280; tram 8

This small island in the Tiber, with its medieval buildings and Roman bridges, feels like a safe harbour, protected from the chaos of the city.

The island is erected on a volcanic rock and its shape resembles that of a ship. There are several legends about its origin, one of which concerns Esculapio, the Greek god of medicine: During the third century BC, the Romans sent a boat to Epidaurus in Greece to discover a cure for the plague. On the return journey, Esculapio left the ship in the shape of a serpent and swam to the island, indicating that a temple to the god of healing should be built there (the church of San Bartolomeo now stands where the sanctuary was erected). In the first century BC, the Romans reshaped the island with slabs of travertine to form a 'prow' and 'stern', and erected an obelisk as a mast, to commemorate Esculapio's ship. The island's tradition of healing and medicine has continued over the centuries, enhanced by the belief that the water on the island is particularly healthy. There is still a large hospital there.

Two bridges join Isola Tiberina to the riverbanks: Ponte Cestio dates back to the first century BC, and leads to Trastevere; while

Ponte Fabricio, built in 62BC, and the only Roman bridge to survive intact, joins the island to the Ghetto. The latter used to be called Ponte dei Giudei, which means the Bridge of the Jews. On the north side of the island is Ponte Rotto (Broken Bridge), the remains of a Roman wooden bridge built in 179BC.

LA MADDALENA

➕ 57 E4 • Piazza della Maddalena 53, 00184 ☎ 06 797796 🕐 Daily 7.30–12 and 5–7.30 💶 Free, audioguide €2.50 🚌 40, 46, 62, 64, 70, 81, 492, 628, 630, 780, 787, 916; tram 8 to Largo di Torre Argentina or 116 to Via della Palombella

Just a stone's throw away from the Pantheon is the church of La Maddalena, a typical example of the baroque style, sumptuously decorated and furnished according to 18th-century Roman taste.

The church is the work of various 17th- and 18th-century artists: Carlo Fontana was responsible for the dome and the vault, while Giulio Quadrio completed the church in 1699, except for the façade. The latter was finished in 1735 and influenced by the baroque master Francesco Borromini; it is made of plaster and stucco, which are more ductile and cheaper than traditional travertine.

Inside, there is a magnificent gilded wooden organ, enriched with white-stuccoed statues. In the dome and transept are frescoes by Stefano Parracel and Michelangelo Cerruti, with figures of cherubs, saints and the Doctors of the Church. There are confessionals of inlaid briarwood along the central nave. The side chapels are exquisitely decorated with 17th- and 18th-century paintings. **Don't miss** The 18th-century sacristy has six splendid marbled closets with golden edges and pictorial decorations on the vault.

MERCATI TRAIANEI

➕ 57 F5 • Via IV Novembre 94, 00184 ☎ 06 679 0048. Information and guided tours: 06 6978 0532 🕐 Mar–end Oct Tue–Sun 9–6.30; Nov–end Feb 9–4.30 💶 Adult €6.20, child (under 18) free 🚇 Colosseo 🚌 60, 84, 85, 87, 117, 175, 810, 850 🚌 Guided tour for Torre delle Milizie only (book in advance) 📖 Guidebook in English €6.45

Trajan's markets were a group of commercial buildings on six different street levels terraced up the Quirinal Hill. Today, these buildings house various exhibitions of ancient Roman art and history.

The complex was built at the beginning of the first century AD by Trajan's architect, Apollodorus of Damascus, and it remains the best example of what Roman urban architecture could achieve.

There was a covered shopping arcade with a magnificent vaulted ceiling, as well as an apartment block and some 150 shops of different shapes and types—a prototype of the modern shopping mall. It was not only a retail market, but also an administrative hub for the imperial authorities, where supplies were brought in, divided and redistributed.

The ground-floor shops were rather shallow; one has been reconstructed to show the external travertine door frames, which gave shopkeepers extra space for their goods.

Via Biberatica, with its original paving, still runs round the upper floor of the front of the complex. It may get its name from the inns that stood on the street (*bibere*, to drink), or possibly from the pepper (*piper*) and other spices sold, which could only be afforded by the wealthier citizens. The view from the upper tiers of the complex will help you to understand the layouts of Trajan's and Augustus' fora nearby (▷ 82–83).

Museo e Galleria Borghese

**Great art in a beautiful villa set amid parkland.
The best-loved museum of Romans today.**

*The Borghese's sumptuous interiors and lush gardens are the perfect backdrop for works such as
Canova's* Paolina Borghese *(right) and Bernini's* Rape of Proserpine *(opposite)*

SEEING THE MUSEO E GALLERIA BORGHESE

The Museo e Galleria Borghese is housed in a harmonious
17th-century villa standing in green parkland on the eastern
edge of the Pincio Hill. The entrance leads into the lower ground
floor, where you will find the ticket office, shop, café and other
services. The gallery and museum, a series of interconnecting
rooms set around a central hall, occupy the next two floors. The
museum's sculptural highlights are in the first rooms on the
lower floor, as are Caravaggio's paintings. The Pinacoteca, the
main picture gallery, is on the upper floor. The Borghese is
relatively small, so you are unlikely to lose your bearings or
run out of time to see everything.

HIGHLIGHTS

PAOLINA BORGHESE

Antonio Canova (1757–1822), the most famous of all neoclassical
sculptors, sculpted this portrait of Napoleon's sister Pauline in 1808.
Dominating room 1, it is acknowledged to be his masterpiece and is
certainly his most famous work. It shows the beautiful 25-year-old
reclining semi-naked on a couch, posing as Venus, with an apple in her
hand. The other hand supports her head, her hair is scooped up to
show her delicate neck and profile, and the line of her body
combines classical tranquillity with more than a hint of suggestiveness.
It was Pauline's own idea to commission this openly erotic piece from
Canova. She already had a reputation for beauty and bad conduct
when she was married off to the much older Prince Borghese, and she
visualized her elderly, dull husband using the statue to flaunt the
charms of his young wife in front of his friends. Once unveiled, *Venus*
caused an immediate scandal—how could Pauline have brought
herself to pose naked? 'There was a stove in the studio,' she replied.
Years later, separated from the prince, Pauline regretted her nudity, and
forgetting her original motives for posing, begged him to cease
exhibiting the statue to chosen friends. 'It was created only to afford
you pleasure,' she wrote. The statue is carved from finest white Carrara
marble; the sheen on the skin was achieved with candlewax.

RATINGS	
Historic interest	● ● ● ●
Value for money	● ● ● ●

TIPS

- Entrance is limited to 360
people every 2 hours, so
reserve well ahead whatever
the time of year.
- Leave plenty of time for the
Pinacoteca.
- If you're into Italian gardens,
visit the palazzo's secret
garden (tours Sat–Sun 10 and
11; free).

✚ 58 F2 • Piazzale Borghese del
Museo (entrance on Via Pinciana),
00187 ☎ 06 841 7645

🕐 Daily 9–7. Advance booking essential, ticket must be collected
30 mins before time slot
(www.ticketeria.it, tel 06
328101, fax 06 3265
1329)

💳 Adult €8.50, child
(under 18) €2

🚇 Flaminio or Spagna

🚌 52, 53, 910

🎧 Guided tours every 2 hours in
Italian and English (2 hours dura-
tion); audiotours €5, Italian,
English, Spanish, French,
German (2 hours duration)

📖 Italian, English,
French, German
guide to Galleria
Borghese €13, TCI
guidebook €19

☕ Café with bar

🏬 Shop with good selection of guides,
postcards and souvenirs

🚻 On premises

🅿 On Via Pinciana

www.galleriaborghese.it
Informative website, with English
option. There's plenty of background
detail on the museum's most important
works, full practical information and
an online booking service. The site is
clearly presented, well illustrated, fast
and easy to navigate.

The face of Bernini's David *may
be a self-portrait*

THE BERNINI SCULPTURES

Cardinal Scipione Borghese, enthused by the vitality of Gian Lorenzo
Bernini's work, commissioned three works from the sculptor: *The
Rape of Proserpine* (1621–22), *David* (1623) and *Apollo and
Daphne* (1624). With his dynamic compositions and mastery of
marble as a medium, Bernini was by far the greatest Italian exponent
of the baroque style, producing work full of drama and movement.

Apollo and Daphne is a perfect example of Bernini's genius.
The myth tells the story of how the pure and chaste
nymph Daphne was pursued by Apollo, the god of
light. Desperate to escape, Daphne implored the
other gods to save her. Her wish was granted
and she was turned into a laurel tree,
saved from Apollo's clutches by
protective bark. Bernini's life-size
sculpture shows the moment of her
change, bark creeping over her body
and her fingers sprouting leaves.
When it was in its original position,
the group was seen first from the
back left, and there is no doubt
that this is the best viewing point.
Bernini's virtuosity shines again in
the Sala degli Imperatori with
The Rape of Proserpine, another
piece inspired by pagan legend.
Proserpine, the daughter of
Ceres, goddess of the harvest,
attracted the attention of Pluto,
ruler of the underworld. He
seized the girl, taking her to
Hades, but when her mother
intervened Pluto agreed to
return her to earth for six
months of each year.
Pagans believed that
during
Proserpine's
months in Hades,
Ceres mourned,

94 MUSEO E GALLERIA BORGHESE

Canova's sculpture of Paolina Borghese (above) would once have stood on a revolving base

Bernini's Daphne and Apollo captures the moment of the nymph's metamorphosis (below)

GALLERY GUIDE

GROUND FLOOR

Entrance hall Stunning mix of marble, frescoes and sculpture

Room 1 *Paolina Borghese*

Room 2 *David*

Room 3 *Apollo and Daphne*

Room 4 Sala degli Imperatori, decorated with busts of Roman emperors and *The Rape of Proserpine*

Room 5 *Sleeping Hermaphrodite*

Room 6 *Aeneas and Anchises*

Room 7 Decorated in Egyptian style with Classical sculpture

Room 8 The Room of the Faun, with Caravaggio's paintings

THE SIGHTS

winter reigned, and the world was cold and barren. On her return, the earth welcomed Proserpine with a carpet of flowers, and crops grew once more. Bernini shows the moment of abduction: From the left we see Pluto grasping Proserpine, his fingers sinking into her flesh, while she claws at his face. Viewing the group from various angles reveals different aspects of the myth.

THE CARAVAGGIO MASTERPIECES

Michelangelo Merisi, known as Caravaggio (1573–1610), is represented by six dramatic paintings in room 8. This artist is recognized for the extraordinary realism and detail found in his work, but he is known above all for his use of *chiaroscuro*, the balance of light and shade in a painting. The device is judged by the skill with which the artist handles shadows, and the best such artists tend to paint dark pictures illuminated by brilliant shafts of light. You can see this beautifully in Caravaggio's *Madonna dei Palafreni*, painted in 1606. The Virgin holding the child Jesus stands on the left, with her mother, St. Anne, to the right. All three figures are gazing downwards, their attention riveted on a

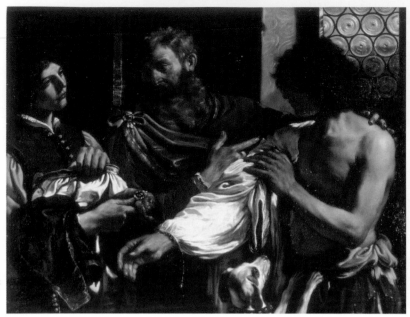

Above: The Prodigal Son *by Guercino (1591–1666)*

Opposite: The Ecstasy of St. Catherine *by Carracci (1557–1602)*

writhing snake about to strike. Jesus' foot is on the serpent, symbol of sin and heresy, as his mother teaches him how to crush it. Caravaggio painted the picture for the Confraternity of the Palafreni, who hung it in their chapel in St. Peter's basilica. It was there just a month before the reactionary Vatican clique ordered its removal on the grounds of its realism and lack of decorum. Caravaggio had his revenge when the painting was bought by Cardinal Scipione Borghese, preferred nephew of Pope Paul V, and hung in pride of place in his collection.

The artist's triumph was short-lived, for in the same year, 1606, he was accused of murder and fled Rome, eventually landing up in Malta. It was here that he painted *David with the Head of Goliath*, which he sent to the Papal Court in the hope of pardon. The subject is simple: the boy David holding the head of the slaughtered giant. It is the marvellous play of light on skin and drapery that makes the painting shine; Caravaggio portrayed himself as Goliath.

THE UMBRIAN SCHOOL

Room 9 is crammed with some of the best paintings in the gallery, mainly by Umbrian artists. Perugino and Pinturicchio are both represented, but it is the three Raphaels that shine, in particular the *Deposition*, a picture inspired as much by classical art as religion. It was commissioned in 1507 by Atalanta Baglioni, in memory of her son Grifonetto. The Baglioni were one of the most important families in Perugia, a city where feuds and power struggles were a way of life. The image of a young man's dead body was the perfect subject to commemorate the dead boy. It hung for a century in Perugia, but, with the connivance of the local priest, was spirited away in 1608 and sent to Pope Paul V, who passed it on to his nephew Scipione to adorn the Villa Borghese. Raphael used a relief on a Roman sarcophagus as his inspiration, and the whole composition echoes Michelangelo's sublime *Pietà* in St. Peter's.

TITIAN'S SACRED AND PROFANE LOVE

Of the four paintings by Titian in room 20, *Sacred and Profane Love* stands apart, transfused with warm light and soft hues. It was painted in 1514 to celebrate the marriage of the Venetians Nicolò Aurelio and Laura Baragotto. The meaning of the picture has been hotly debated down the years. It portrays two beautiful women seated on a sarcophagus, which also serves as a fountain; while one woman is clothed in white, the other is naked except for a few light draperies.

THE SIGHTS

Between them, a putto leans over the water in the fountain; behind, the tranquil landscape is washed with light. This is probably a picture about married love, the woman in white representing the bride, assisted by Venus and Cupid. Venus, with her burning flame, stands for the durability of married love. The picture's present title, coined in the late 18th century, reflects later thinking, and adds a moral dimension that was never intended. In 1899 the Rothschild family offered 4 million lire for the painting, almost half a million lire more than the total value of the rest of the collection and the villa together. The offer was promptly refused.

BACKGROUND

The Villa Borghese was built in 1612–13, designed to be the focal point of the Rome estate of the immensely rich Borghese family. Cardinal Scipione Borghese chose Flaminio Ponzio as his architect, commissioning a building modelled on the villas of ancient Rome and suitable to house his collections. Besides being a passionate and unscrupulous art collector, the Cardinal had interests ranging through music, geology and natural history, and the villa had its own farm, vineyard and zoo. The sculpture and pictures were in place by 1620 and they still form the museum's core collection. The Borgheses were forced to sell up at the end of the 19th century, and both park and villa were acquired by the Italian state in 1902. The villa underwent a lengthy restoration in the 1990s, returning both the exterior and interior to their original appearance.

CARAVAGGIO

Caravaggio's life was as dramatic as his work, full of feuds, plots and flight. In 1606 he was charged with murder and fled Rome to Naples. Pursued again, he went next to Malta, where he was made a knight of the Order of Malta. It seems he fell foul of the knights, who arrested and jailed him in 1608. He escaped and reached Sicily, from where, still in fear for his life, he moved on again to Tuscany, all the time hoping that word of his pardon would come from Rome. But no word came; he was arrested again, contracted a fever, and died on the beach at Porto Ercole.

Musei Capitolini

**The oldest museum collection in the world, with over 1,300 works.
Opulent galleries containing some of Rome's most important
Classical sculpture.
A chance to gain a fascinating insight on what lies beneath modern Rome.**

Ancient statuary, such as the remains of Constantine's giant statue (opposite), Marforio *(above left), and
a satyr (middle), and bronzes, such as the* Capitoline She-Wolf *(right), make up the collection*

SEEING THE MUSEI CAPITOLINI

Rome's civic museum collections occupy two of the three palazzi
around Michelangelo's beautiful Piazza del Campidoglio
(▷ 118). Incorporating Roman, medieval and Renaissance
elements, the complex of buildings is approached up a graceful
ramp, known as the Cordonata, just off Piazza Venezia. The
museum complex has two entrances, one on each side of the
piazza: The left-hand entrance gives access to the Palazzo Nuovo,
and that on the right to the Palazzo dei Conservatori. These two
buildings are linked by an underground gallery that runs beneath
the Palazzo Senatorio. It's best to start your visit in the Palazzo
Nuovo, although both entrances have ticket offices, cloakrooms
and bookstores. The museum shop proper is on the second floor
of the Palazzo dei Conservatori, next to the bar/restaurant.

HIGHLIGHTS

LOBBY AND COURTYARD OF THE PALAZZO NUOVO

Some of the museum's largest and most exciting pieces of
sculpture are in the lobby and courtyard of the Palazzo Nuovo.
Against the wall at one end of the lobby stands a huge
statue of the goddess Minerva, 3m (10ft) high. Probably a
product of second-century BC Greek craftsmanship and
created for a major temple, she wears a belted chiton
(tunic) and a helmet—the holes in the belt were
intended for metal ornaments that once hung from
it. The eyes are hollow, but would have been filled
with glittering metal and polished stones. At the
far end of the courtyard is *Marforio*, a sculptural
ensemble incorporated into a fountain—typical
of the practical High Renaissance approach to
ancient works of art, which was to use and adapt
them. The reclining bearded figure representing a
river god dates from the first or second century
AD, while the fountain and shells were added in
1594, producing a piece that is an amalgam of

The serene Capitoline Venus stands in splendid isolation in her own room (top).
The red marble Drunken Faun stands out against the rest of the sculptures (below)

ancient and modern. During the Renaissance, *Marforio* was used as a place to leave the satirical messages called *pasquinades*, so the figures of satyrs on either side seem appropriate. Half-man, half-goat, each balances a basket of grapes on his head; they almost certainly once supported roof beams in a loggia, probably located near the Theatre of Pompey.

A complete contrast to all this pagan revelry is seen in the magnificent and dignified gilded bronze equestrian statue of Marcus Aurelius in a glassed-off room to the right. It was once the focal point of the piazza outside, placed there on a plinth designed by Michelangelo. Threatened by modern pollution, the original has been replaced by a replica. This wonderful piece, once part of a triumphal monument, depicts the Emperor Marcus Aurelius (AD161–180) astride his horse, clad in the toga as a majestic lawgiver. Following the fall of Rome, the statue, with its outstretched hand, was believed to be that of Constantine, the first Christian emperor, and thus survived the Dark Ages when thousands of similar works were destroyed. It stood untouched outside the basilica of San Giovanni in Laterano until it was brought to the Campidoglio.

CLASSICAL SCULPTURE IN PALAZZO NUOVO

Here in the world's oldest public art collection, it is possible to gain a sense of what a museum of the 17th and 18th centuries was like, and scattered among the seemingly endless ranks of statuary in the upstairs rooms of the Palazzo Nuovo are some gems, the city's best Roman copies of Greek sculpture.

Originally, Classical statues were brightly painted and acted as focal points in buildings and public spaces. Renaissance restorers mended, replaced and polished, often substituting arms and even heads if they were damaged or missing. The *Discobolos* (discus thrower), in the Gallery, is a prime example. The original was sculpted in Greece around 460BC. Many copies were made, including the powerful torso of the figure here; the rest of the statue was reworked (not very satisfactorily) around 1700. Off the Gallery, the Hall of the Doves contains a beautiful Roman copy of a Hellenistic *Young Girl with a Dove*. The avian theme continues in the room's most famous work, the second-century AD *Mosaic of the Doves*, depicting doves drinking at a fountain, from Hadrian's Villa at Tivoli. Both marble and glass were used for the tesserae, and in the second-century *Mosaic of the Theatrical Masks*. Also off the Gallery, in a small polygonal room, is the *Capitoline Venus*, discovered in the late 17th century. Slightly larger than life-size, this is a depiction of Venus-Aphrodite, a popular theme of Classical sculptors. Beautifully modelled, this version dates from the first century BC.

In rooms IV and V are numerous portrait busts, some of which have surprisingly modern faces. Beyond here is the Great Hall with, among other full-size pieces, the *Apollo of Omphalos*, a fine Roman copy of the fifth-century BC Greek original. The masterpiece in room VII is the *Drunken Faun*, carved in red marble and, although over-restored in the 18th century, a splendid piece, full of *joie de vivre*. Beyond here, in room VIII, is the *Dying Gaul*, one of the most famous and emotive of all Classical statues. Once thought to be a dying gladiator, its true subject is clear from the warrior's weapons, his nudity and his hairstyle—all Celtic attributes.

The Dying Gaul *is a wonderful example of Classical sculpture (above).*
Mosaic of the Doves, *from Villa Adriana, gives its name to the Hall of the Doves (left)*

TABULARIUM

The remains of the Tabularium, an imposing building completed in 78BC, lie underneath the Palazzo Senatorio. In Roman times it was where the archives of the Roman State were kept, bronze *tabulae* containing the state laws and official deeds. It is reached via the underground tunnel that connects the two wings of the museum. For Classical history enthusiasts this complex is a must, but the attraction for most visitors is the view of the Forum from its arched gallery.

THE PALAZZO DEI CONSERVATORI

The Palazzo dei Conservatori's collection is much larger, spread over two floors. Many of the rooms, originally intended for official civic business, are magnificently frescoed, a fine backdrop for some stunning pieces. The central courtyard, lined with reliefs and inscriptions, contains the surviving fragments of a colossal statue of Constantine the Great, dating from AD313 and discovered in the Forum in 1486. Only the nude parts of the body would have been in marble, with the draperies in gilded bronze covering a supporting frame. Constantine appears again upstairs in the Hall of the Horatii and Curiatii as a superb bronze head. The gilded bronze *Hercules*, a Roman copy of a famous Greek fourth-century BC piece, once stood in a temple.

In room III is one of the museum's best-loved sculptures: The small bronze *Spinario* was one of the first gifts to the museum by its founder Sixtus IV in 1471, and shows a seated boy pulling a thorn from his foot. The pose is unique among ancient statues and it was popular in the Renaissance, inspiring many copies and similar works. Even more inspirational is the *Capitoline She-Wolf* in room IV, the very symbol of Rome. Part of Sixtus IV's gift, it originally stood on the

Spinario, *a first-century BC bronze, is an endearing statue*

GALLERY GUIDE

Palazzo Nuovo
I Gallery
II Hall of the Doves
III Capitoline Venus
IV Hall of the Emperors
V Hall of the Philosophers
VI Large Hall
VII Room of the Faun
VIII Hall of the Gladiator

Palazzo dei Conservatori
First floor
I Room of the Horatii
and the Curatii
II Hall of the Captains
III Hall of the Triumphs
IV Hall of the Fasti
V Hall of the Geese
VI Hall of the Eagles
VII Green Hall
VIII Yellow Hall
IX Pink Hall
X Hall of the Tapestries
XI Hall of Hannibal
XII The Chapel
XIII, XIV, XV
Hall of memorable
modern events

Second floor
I Hall 1
II Painters from Ferrara
III Painters from Venice
IV Hall 4
V Hall 5
VI Painters from Bologna
VII Hall of St. Petronilla
VIII Hall of Pietro da Cortona
IX Cini Gallery

Palazzo Senatorio
I Temple of Veiovis
II Tabularium Gallery
III Room of the
Executioner

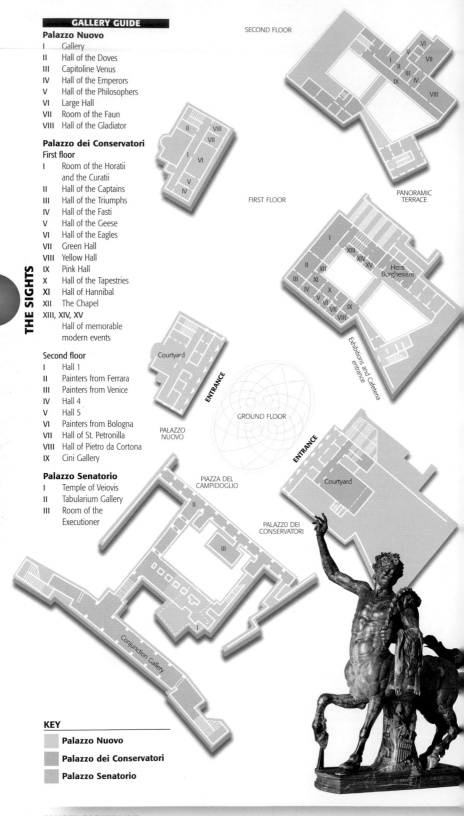

SECOND FLOOR

FIRST FLOOR

PANORAMIC TERRACE

Horti Borghesiani

Exhibitions and Cafeteria entrance

Courtyard

ENTRANCE

GROUND FLOOR

PALAZZO NUOVO

PIAZZA DEL CAMPIDOGLIO

ENTRANCE

Courtyard

PALAZZO DEI CONSERVATORI

Conjunction Gallery

KEY
Palazzo Nuovo
Palazzo dei Conservatori
Palazzo Senatorio

façade of the palazzo—without the figures of Romulus and Remus. These were added in 1509 by the Florentine sculptor Pollaiuolo, and the group was brought inside during Michelangelo's revamp of the palace. The statue is Etruscan and dates from the fifth century BC, a wonderfully intelligent portrayal of an animal once common in Italy.

PINACOTECA

The second floor of the Palazzo dei Conservatori houses the Capitoline picture gallery, founded in the 18th century by Pope Benedict XIV. There are far finer collections in Rome, but it does contain a good cross-section of Italian painting, as well as some interesting foreign works. The *Baptism of Christ* is an early Titian, its gentle piety contrasting admirably with the sensual energy of Veronese's *Rape of Europa* in the same room (III). There is a fine Correggio *Madonna* in room V, but some of the best works are in the Hall of St. Petronilla, named after the synonymous picture by Guercino (nickname of Giovanni Francesco Barbieri). Here, there are two splendid Caravaggios and a voluptuous *Romulus and Remus* by Rubens. In the Cini Gallery is *The Brothers de Wael* by another northerner, Anthony van Dyck, painted in Genoa in 1621; here also hangs a *Self-portrait* by Velázquez, painted in 1650 during his second visit to Rome.

BACKGROUND

By the 15th century, civic power in Rome was centred on the Capitoline, where the Palazzo Senatorio and Palazzo dei Conservatori were used for meetings of the magistrates who,

The mosaics in the Capitoline were made using the same processes employed today. Large sheets of glass, or thin slabs of marble, are first shattered into tiny pieces to make the mosaic tiles (tesserae). The surface on which the mosaic will be built is covered with a layer of cement, on which the outline of the image is traced. Next comes a thin layer of mortar; on this, a detailed painting of the final design is made. The pieces of glass and marble, set at fractionally different angles to refract the light, are then pressed into the wet mortar, creating an image that can endure for millennia. The smaller the tesserae, and the more varied the hue, the more expensive the mosaics.

together with the senators, governed the city. In 1471 Pope Sixtus IV presented the Roman bronzes and statues that formed the nucleus of the museum to the people of Rome, and the Capitoline thus became the world's first public museum. The buildings and piazza were restored and enlarged to Michelangelo's plans in the mid-16th century, and in 1654 Girolamo and Carlo Rainaldi designed the Palazzo Nuovo to complete the architectural ensemble.

The bronze head of Constantine dwarfs the visitors in the Hall of Horatii and Curiatii (above)

Among the exhibits of the Musei Capitolini are figures based on mythology, such as this centaur (left)

Musei Vaticani

The largest, richest, most impressive museum complex in the world, with over 1,400 rooms.
Contains sculpture, paintings and objets d'art spanning more than 3,000 years, from every corner of the Classical and modern world.

The Galleria delle Carte Geografiche is decorated with 16th-century map frescoes (above left). The giant bronze pine cone in the Cortile della Pigna (above middle). Members of the Swiss Guard (above right)

SEEING THE MUSEI VATICANI

The once horribly crowded entrance to the Musei Vaticani benefited immensely from a revamp in 2000, the Jubilee Year, although you may still have to wait in high season. The complex includes both museum and gallery complexes and parts of the papal palace, richly decorated by the world's greatest artists. The sheer size of the museum complex is in itself confusing and exhausting, so spend time planning and be aware that it is impossible to see everything in one visit. Various official routes taking in all the main attractions are suggested on leaflets available at the entrance, but these can be very crowded with tour groups, so it is a good idea to plan your own itinerary. The best way to tackle the museums is to focus on the highlights (see below), perhaps taking in one or two other collections; just walking between these will give glimpses of lots more.

HIGHLIGHTS

CAPPELLA SISTINA

The Sistine Chapel was built by Pope Sixtus IV between 1473 and 1481 to serve as both the pontiff's private chapel and as a venue for the gathering of cardinals who elect each new pope—a function it still fulfils. It is a huge structure, with a beautiful cosmatesque mosaic floor and a marble screen by Mino da Fiesole. But it is the frescoes, entirely covering the walls and ceiling, that attract up to 20,000 visitors a day. While the chapel was being built, Sixtus planned its decoration, settling on scenes from the Old and New Testaments as the subject matter, with the emphasis on the parallels between the lives of Moses and Christ. From Florence, he summoned Sandro Botticelli, together with Domenico Ghirlandaio, Cosimo Rosselli and Perugian artist Perugino. These artists, joined by Pinturicchio, Luca Signorelli and Piero di Cosimo, worked on the walls for 11 months, producing a series of glowing works that should attract thousands of visitors in their own right. The two most important scenes are Perugino's *Christ Giving the Keys to Peter* and Botticelli's *The Punishment of Korah*, each showing the Arch of Constantine in the background.

RATINGS

Good for kids	● ● ●
Historic interest	● ● ● ● ●
Value for money	● ● ● ●
Walkability	● ● ●

TIPS

● Don't try to see everything, just choose a few highlights and take breaks.
● Dress respectfully—no shorts or bare upper arms.
● Come when the museum first opens or late in the morning. Wednesday morning can be relatively peaceful as many people are in the Piazza San Pietro for the papal blessing.
● Head straight along the tourist route to what you particularly want to see—especially the Sistine Chapel before the crowds arrive—then you won't already be exhausted by the time you get there.
● Last admissions are quite early, so arrive in good time.

The impressive 1930s staircase that spirals up to the museums' entrance (opposite)

Michelangelo's masterpiece, the ceiling of the Sistine Chapel

BASICS

✚ 56 B4 • Viale Vaticano 00165

☎ 06 6988 4947

🕐 Mar–end Nov Mon–Fri 8.45–4.45 (last admission 3.20), Sat 8.45–1.45 (last admission 12.20); Dec–end Feb Mon–Sat 8.45–1.45 (last admission 12.20); closed on public and religious festivals 💶 Adult €12, child (under 15) €8, under 6 free; free entrance on last Sun of month 🚇 Cipro Musei Vaticani, Ottaviano-Vaticano

🚌 19, 32, 49, 81, 98

🎧 Two-hour guided tour €4; book on 06 6988 4466 or at museum information point. Audiotours available in Italian, English, French, German, Spanish, Japanese; €5.50. Two-hour tour of gardens on Tue, Thu and Sat at 10; €9 (book on tel 06 6988 4676, fax 06 6988 5100 or email musei@scv.va)

📖 Official guidebook to museum and Vatican State available in Italian, English, French, German, Spanish, Japanese; €7.50

☕ Café and pizzeria inside museum. Expensive, but fine for a quick refill and rest

🎫 Several shops at different points in museum well stocked with guidebooks, postcards, religious souvenirs, Vatican stamps and museum reproductions

🚻 Many throughout museum complex

www.vatican.va

The official website for the Vatican State, the Vatican Museum and Catholic Church. Lots of pictures from the collections, plus information on the Vatican.

These earlier masterpieces, however, tend to be overshadowed by Michelangelo's frescoes on the ceiling and altar wall, arguably Western art's finest achievement and certainly the largest work of painting ever planned and carried out by one man. Julius II commissioned the ceiling in 1508, and Michelangelo completed it in 1512, an artistic tour de force with narrative scenes, architectural *trompe l'oeil* effects and statuesque figures of great beauty. The central panels tell the Creation story and that of Noah; these are surrounded by a decorative scheme dominated by the figures of the prophets and sibyls and containing wonderful details, including the famous *ignudi* (nude youths).

Years later, in 1535, Michelangelo was again summoned to the chapel, this time by Paul III, to fresco the altar wall with scenes of the Last Judgement, a huge task that occupied him until 1541. The *Last Judgement* is essentially a celebration of the human body, full of power, potency and movement. Even before it was finished the amount of nudity had offended many, not least the Pope's master of ceremonies. Furious, Michelangelo depicted him in the bottom right-hand corner of Hell as Minos, the doorkeeper, complete with ass' ears and entwined in a serpent. Later, Pius IV objected to the nudity to such an extent he commissioned Daniele da Volterra to clothe the genitals—an exercise that earned him the soubriquet 'trouser-maker'. This overpainting was removed during the extensive, Japanese-funded restoration of the ceiling and *Last Judgement* during the 1980s and 1990s, a project said to have cost over $3 million.

STANZE DI RAFFAELLO

Not content with the painting of the Sistine Chapel, in 1508 Julius II embarked on a major decorative scheme in the four nearby rooms of his private apartments, today known as the Stanze di Raffaello (Raphael Rooms). The Stanza della Segnatura, the Pope's study, was Raphael's first major Roman commission, painted between 1508 and 1511. The frescoes are allegories representing the humanist ideals of theology, philosophy, poetry and justice. The *School of Athens* stresses truth acquired through reason, with the great Classical thinkers all represented, the central figures of Plato—probably a portrait of Leonardo da Vinci—and Aristotle dominating the scene. The figure on the left is said to be Michelangelo, added after Raphael had a sneak preview of his work in the Sistine Chapel. Opposite is the *Disputation of the Holy Sacrament*, while the side walls show *Parnassus*, home to the Muses, and the *Cardinal Virtues*.

Chronologically, the next room to be painted was the Stanza di Eliodoro, with its energy-charged *Expulsion of Heliodorus* and serene

Upper floor

10 Museo Gregoriano Etrusco
11 Sala della Biga
12 Galleria dei Candelabri
13 Galleria degli Arazzi
14 Galleria delle Carte Geografiche
15 Cappella di Pio V
16 Sala Sobieski
17 Sala dell'Immacolata
18 Cappella di Urbano VIII
19 Stanze di Raffaello
20 Cappella di Nicolò V
21 Loggia di Raffaello

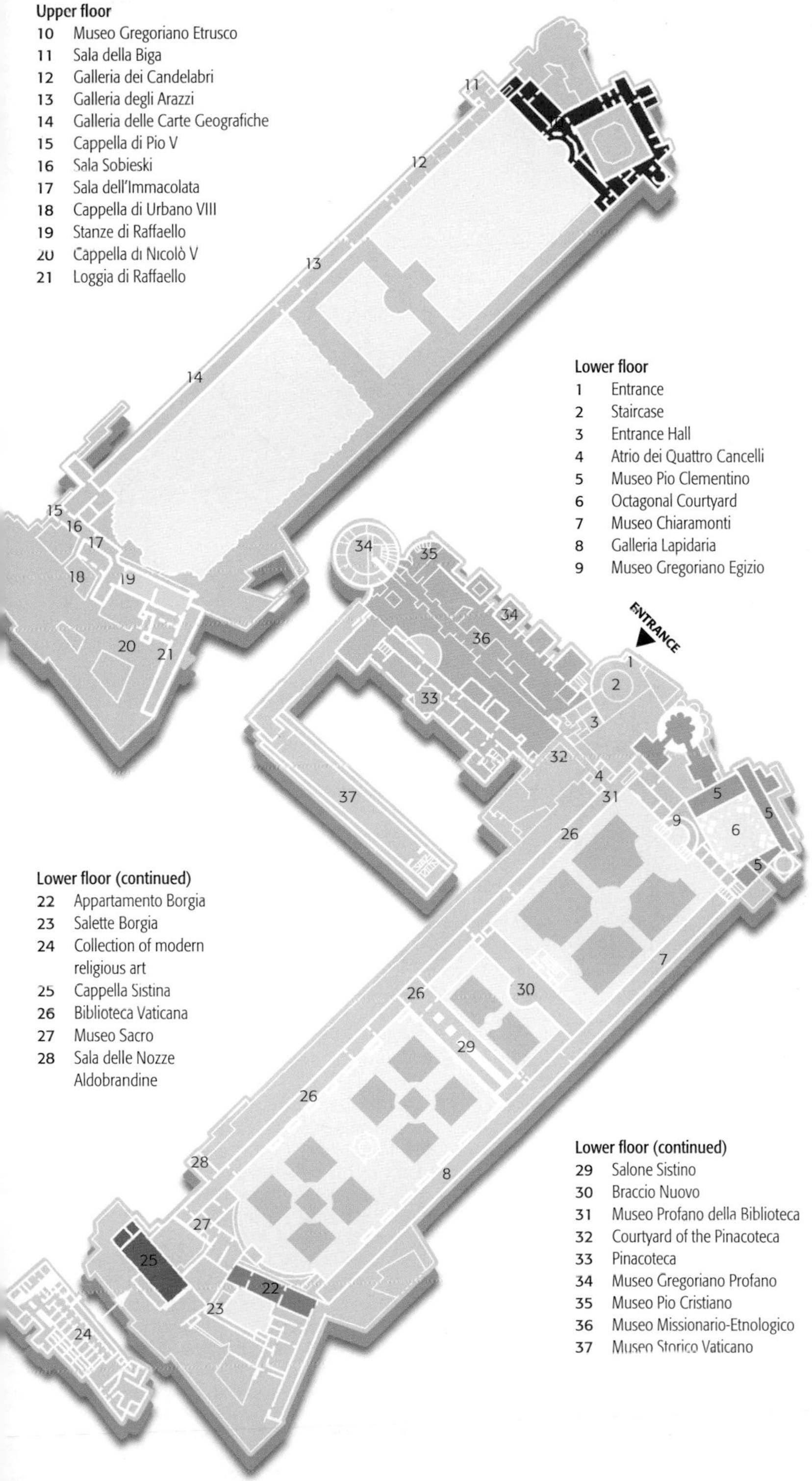

Lower floor

1 Entrance
2 Staircase
3 Entrance Hall
4 Atrio dei Quattro Cancelli
5 Museo Pio Clementino
6 Octagonal Courtyard
7 Museo Chiaramonti
8 Galleria Lapidaria
9 Museo Gregoriano Egizio

Lower floor (continued)

22 Appartamento Borgia
23 Salette Borgia
24 Collection of modern religious art
25 Cappella Sistina
26 Biblioteca Vaticana
27 Museo Sacro
28 Sala delle Nozze Aldobrandine

Lower floor (continued)

29 Salone Sistino
30 Braccio Nuovo
31 Museo Profano della Biblioteca
32 Courtyard of the Pinacoteca
33 Pinacoteca
34 Museo Gregoriano Profano
35 Museo Pio Cristiano
36 Museo Missionario-Etnologico
37 Museo Storico Vaticano

ENTRANCE

THE SIGHTS

Fresco painting is a medium in which the pigment becomes permanently part of the wall it covers, thus producing, in the right conditions, an extremely long-lasting image. The artist first draws the scene on paper, then, using a graph, expands the drawing to the desired size to make the working cartoon. The outline of the principal figures and background are then pricked out with tiny holes and the cartoon is attached to the wall surface. Renaissance artists then blew charcoal dust through the holes, leaving the outline of the picture on the wall when the cartoon was removed. As fresco pigments need to be applied to fresh, wet plaster, the artist had to assess the area he would cover that day. Once the plaster was applied, he would follow the charcoal outlines with pigment—a method still used. As the plaster dries, a chemical reaction occurs, binding the pigment and plaster and leaving a permanent image.

THE SIGHTS

The Sistine Gallery (above and right)

Miracle of Bolsena. The latter tells the story of the medieval miracle that occurred in Bolsena, when a priest who doubted the doctrine of transubstantiation (the transformation of the Eucharistic bread and wine into the actual body and blood of Christ) saw the wafer bleed during Mass. The window wall has a superb night scene, showing the *Deliverance of St. Peter from Prison*. The two final rooms were painted to Raphael's designs by his pupils after his death in 1520.

PINACOTECA VATICANA

The Pinacoteca, founded in 1816 by Pius VI, occupies a separate building, erected in 1932, within the museum complex. It is widely considered to be Rome's best picture gallery, with works from the early and High Renaissance to the 19th century. Among these are some of the most remarkable early paintings in Rome, notably Giotto's *Stefaneschi Triptych* (room II). Painted in the early 1300s for the altar of the Confessio in old St. Peter's, it shows the *Martyrdom of SS. Peter and Paul*. The deaths of both saints are shown, with St. Peter crucified upside-down, at his own request, as he felt unworthy to die the same way as Christ. Cardinal Stefaneschi, the donor, is shown on either side of the triptych. The next rooms are devoted to 15th-century Italian art. Look for Fra Angelico's lovely *Madonna and Child with Saints* in room III and the serene Umbrian pictures in room VII, especially Perugino's luminous *Madonna and Child*.

The next room (VIII) is the Pinacoteca's high point, a stunning collection of Raphael's work, including the tapestries that once hung in the Sistine Chapel, woven in Brussels from Raphael's cartoons. Dominating the room is the *Transfiguration*, a sublime work that was unfinished at the artist's death and hung above his coffin at his funeral; his pupils later completed it. The triumphant figure of the ascending Christ pulses with energy amid piercing light and lowering cloud formations, a superb contrast to the artist's *Coronation of the Virgin*, painted when he was only 20 and his first major composition. The gentle *Madonna of Foligno* was commissioned in 1512 as a votive offering, in gratitude for a lucky escape during a siege.

Leonardo da Vinci is represented in room IX by the unfinished and curiously monochrome *St. Jerome*, one of his few works where the authorship has never been disputed. Look out here, too, for the exquisite *Pietà*, by the Venetian painter Giovanni Bellini; the dead Christ lying across his mother's knees was a popular subject for Venetian artists. Venetian painting features again in room X in the shape of two canvases by Titian: a glowing *Madonna with Saints* and the subtle *Portrait of Doge Nicolò Marcello*. There are further psychological insights in Caravaggio's dramatically despairing *Deposition* in room XII, all muted tones and intense *chiaroscuro*.

MUSEO PIO CLEMENTINO

To see the cream of the Vatican's Classical sculpture collection, head for the Museo Pio Clementino and its octagonal Court of the Belvedere. The court still contains the two statues that influenced Renaissance sculptors more than any others, both acquired by Julius II: the *Laocöon* and the *Apollo Belvedere*. The *Laocöon* created a sensation on its discovery in 1506 near Nero's Golden House, when it was immediately identified from the description of the first-century Roman scholar Pliny. A Greek second-century BC group from Rhodes, it shows a Trojan priest who, having warned of the dangers of the famous wooden horse, was crushed, along with his sons, by sea serpents sent by Apollo. The *Apollo Belvedere,* a Roman copy of a fourth-century BC Greek statue, more than holds its own next to Canova's *Perseus*. Inside the museum, highlights include a beautiful Hellenistic *Sleeping Ariadne*, superb second-century AD candelabra from Hadrian's Villa at Tivoli, and fine Roman portrait busts, including a splendid one of Julius Caesar.

BACKGROUND

The Musei Vaticani form the oldest 'royal' art museum in Europe, originating as the private collections of the pope in his role as temporal ruler. Innocent III (1179–80) had made an existing palace, near the basilica of St. Peter, into the permanent seat of the papacy, and his successors enlarged and embellished it. Major work was carried out under Nicolas V in the mid-15th century, and in the 1470s Sixtus IV started to build the Sistine Chapel. Although these areas were primarily intended only for the pontiff's own use, the works of art in this part of the papal palace are today the greatest of the Vatican's treasures. It was not until the 18th century that work began on arranging the papal collections as a museum, with proper galleries being built to house sculpture, paintings and objets d'art, a process that continued into the 20th century.

The Vatican Gardens

THE VATICAN GARDENS

The Vatican Gardens date back to the early days of the Christian Church and reflect design trends through the centuries. Few visitors get to view them, but anyone can enjoy glimpses of the parterres and planting from the windows of the Vatican Museums. The overall style of the gardens is very much in the Italian tradition of formal rectangular parterres, with box hedges, cedars and stone pines, underplanted with roses and bedding plants. There are several of these parterres, linked by shady paths, with shrubs framing views of the dome of St. Peter's. Succeeding popes embellished the gardens, adding summer houses and elaborate fountains.

THE SIGHTS

Sphere with Sphere by Arnaldo Pomodoro (1990)

The Museo Keats-Shelley commemorates the British poets

Museo delle Paste Alimentari celebrates Italy's best-loved food

Ancient ruins and tranquil gardens on the Palatine Hill

THE SIGHTS

MUSEO KEATS-SHELLEY

🕀 57 E4 • Piazza di Spagna 26, 00186 ☎ 06 678 4235 🕘 Mon–Fri 9–1, 3–6, Sat 11–2, 3–6 🎫 €3 🚇 Spagna 🚌 117, 119, 530, 590 🔲 🏛
www.keats-shelley-house.org

In the delightful Casina Rossa (little red house), at the foot of the Spanish Steps, is the Keats-Shelley Memorial Foundation, which preserves letters, manuscripts and documents associated with English poets including Byron, Leigh Hunt, Shelley and Keats. In particular, it is a memorial to the last two, both of whom died in Italy.

In 1820–21, John Keats spent the last few months of his life in the Casina Rossa with his friend Joseph Severn.

In 1903, American poet Robert Underwood Johnson set about raising money to acquire the famous Casina Rossa on behalf of the Keats-Shelley Foundation. The house is now a museum documenting the life and works of the Romantic poets.
Don't miss The house has an excellent portrait of Keats painted by Severn.

MUSEO NAZIONALE DELLE PASTE ALIMENTARI

🕀 57 F4 • Piazza Scanderberg 117, 00184 ☎ 06 699 1119 🕘 Daily 9.30–5.30 🎫 €9 🚇 Barberini 🚌 52, 53, 61, 62, 63, 71, 80, 85, 160, 850 stopping at Piazza San Silvestro

Not far from the Trevi Fountain is an unusual museum dedicated to Italy's best-loved and best-known food—pasta. It traces the history and evolution of pasta and of the manufacturing processes, from early grindstones for milling the wheat to modern industrial pasta machinery. Visitors discover how pasta is made, mixed and dried. (Dried pasta goes back to the 12th century, when it was

invented to allow the food to be kept for months or even years.)

MUSEI VATICANI

See pages 104–109.

ORTO BOTANICO

🕀 56 C6 • Largo Cristina di Svezia 00153 ☎ 06 4991 7107 🕘 Apr–end Oct Tue–Sat 9.30–6.30; rest of year 9.30–5.30. Closed Sun–Mon except when there are exhibitions, on public holidays, and in Aug 🎫 Adult €3, child (under 12) €2 🚌 H, 780, 630; tram 8

In a peaceful corner of Trastevere (▷ 144–145) is the Botanical Garden, a wonderful place to escape the bustle of the area. It was the garden of the imposing Palazzo Corsini (see opposite) until 1883, and now contains a vast collection of plants, which began with the medicinal plants cultivated in the Vatican by Pope Nicholas III in the 13th century.

As you enter, a central path leads to the Tritons Fountain, built in 1570 by the architect Ferdinando Fuga and surrounded by the garden's famous palms. Farther up, on the hill, the rose garden contains species that have been cultivated in Rome since the 17th and 18th centuries. There are wonderful views of the city from the Japanese garden. Descending the slope, you will see a 400-year-old plane tree—one of the oldest in Rome—some spectacular Mediterranean conifers, pine trees, oaks, huge sequoia trees and a *ginkgo biloba* (maidenhair tree). The garden of medicinal herbs, with more than 300 species cultivated since the 15th century, is of great interest. There is an aromatic herb garden specially planted for visitors with visual impairments, and in the various greenhouses there are collections of orchids, and tropical plants.

PALATINO

🕀 57 F6 • Entrances on Via dei Fori Imperiali, Via Sacra, Via di San Teodoro and Via di San Gregorio ☎ 06 3996 7700 🕘 Apr–end Sep daily 9–7; Oct–end Mar 9–3.30 🎫 Adult €8, child (under 18) free. For joint tickets ▷ 287 🚇 Colosseo 🚌 60, 75, 81, 175, 673 to Via di San Gregorio; 60, 84, 85, 87, 117, 175, 810, 850; tram 3 to Via dei Fori Imperiali

The Palatine Hill offers a lovely walk through gardens and shaded areas, where time seems to have stood still. One of the seven hills of Rome and rich in archaeology, the Palatine is considered the cradle of the city.

Emperors preferred the Palatine for their palaces (as the site of sumptuous residences, the area in fact gave rise to the word 'palace'). Augustus set the trend by enlarging his house after it was damaged by fire; Tiberius followed (his palace is now largely beneath the Farnese Gardens), as did Nero with part of the Golden House (Domus Aurea—▷ 79). But what remains today consists mainly of Domitian's vast imperial palace.

Among the ruins on the hill are temples to Cybele, goddess of fertility, and to Apollo and Victory, and the first-century BC House of Livia. The remains of Domitian's palace include the Domus Flavia (the seat of government), the Domus Augustana (the Emperor's private quarters) and the House of the Griffins, with frescoes depicting those winged mythological beasts. The Palatine museum houses fragments of frescoes, statues, bas-reliefs and objects found in the Palatine buildings.

The Orti Farnesiani (Farnese Gardens) were designed for Cardinal Alessandro Farnese in the mid-16th century by Giacomo da Vignola and Girolamo Rainaldi. They were laid

The Palazzo del Quirinale, once a papal palace and royal residence, is now a presidential palace

Palazzo Spada is home to the Galleria Spada's collection

out on the site of the Domus Tiberiana, Emperor Tiberius' sumptuous first-century palace.

From Via Nova, the first building encountered when you enter the gardens is the Nymphaeum of Rain, decorated with Renaissance frescoes on the walls and vault. From here, two staircases with ornamental niches lead to the main gardens. At the top, Rainaldi built two pavilions, known as the Aviaries. On the eastern side is the Nymphaeum of Mirrors with beautiful mosaics on the walls, lilies, a symbol of the Farnese family, are grown here. The gardens, as planted today, are largely the work in the 19th century of the archaeologist Giacomo Boni.

PALAZZO ALTEMPS

See pages 112–113.

PALAZZO BARBERINI

See page 114.

PALAZZO CORSINI

☩ 56 D5 • Via della Lungara 10, 00153 ☎ 06 6880 2323 ⊘ Tue–Sun 8.30–7.30 ⚑ Adult €4, child (under 10) free ⊟ 630, 780; tram 8 ⊞ ⋔
www.galleriaborghese.it

This majestic 15th-century palace is in a charming corner of Trastevere, opposite Villa Farnesina and opening onto the flourishing botanical gardens (Orto Botanico—see opposite). It contains part of the Galleria Nazionale d'Arte Antica (the rest is in the Palazzo Barberini, ▷ 114) in the form of a rich collection of 16th- to 17th-century art, both Italian and international, collected since the 18th century and acquired by the Italian state in 1883. Paintings worthy of note include a triptych by Fra Angelico, a portrait of Philip II of Spain by Titian, the *Madonna della Paglia* by Van

Dyck, Rubens' *St. Sebastian* and the splendid *St. John the Baptist in the Desert* by Caravaggio. Of particular interest is the room of Queen Christina of Sweden, who died in the palace in 1689.

PALAZZO-GALLERIA DORIA PAMPHILJ

See page 115.

PALAZZO MASSIMO ALLE TERME

See pages 116–117.

PALAZZO DEL QUIRINALE

☩ 57 F4 • Piazzale del Quirinale, 00184 ☎ Segreteria Generale Presidenza della Repubblica, for guided tours: 06 46991 ⊘ Sep–end Jun Sun 8.30–12. Gardens open on Republic Day 2 June ⚑ Adult €5, child (under 18) free ⊚ Barberini ⊟ H, 40, 60, 64, 70, 71, 117, 170
www.quirinale.it

This luxurious palace looking out over the city stands on the Quirinale and is the seat of the presidency of the Italian Republic.

The palace became the popes' summer home from 1592 because of the healthier air. Later, it was used by the kings of Italy, who decorated the rooms with expensive tapestries.

The architects Domenico Fontana, Carlo Maderno and Gian Lorenzo Bernini all worked on the palace. It has a cycle of frescoes by Guido Reni in the Chapel of the Annunciation, while the Pauline Chapel, similar in size to the Sistine Chapel in the Vatican, is decorated with fine stuccowork by Martino Ferrabosco. The courtyard inside, once the reception area for heads of state, is guarded by very tall guards called Corrazzieri and leads to the magnificent staircase of honour built by Flaminio Ponzio. Across from the palace are the papal stables, recently

restored by the Italian architect Gae Aulenti, where important exhibitions are held. The palace gardens are only open to visitors on 2 June, the anniversary of the Italian Republic.

Don't miss The coffee shop has a spectacular view of the city.

PALAZZO SPADA

☩ 57 D5 • Piazza Capo di Ferro 13/ Vicolo del Polverone 00186 ☎ Call centre and ticket bookings: 06 21810 ⊘ Tue–Sun 8.30–7.30; Borromini perspective: 9.30–6.30 every hour ⚑ Adult €5, child (under 18) free ⊟ 63, 116, 630, 780; tram 8 ⊪ ⊡ ⊞ ⋔
www.galleriaborghese.it

The Spada Gallery houses the private collection of 17th-century paintings that once belonged to the wealthy Cardinal Spada, displayed in the palace he acquired in 1632. The gallery consists of four rooms, all frescoed and decorated with statues and friezes.

The collection includes many fine works of art; to get the best from your visit, use one of the information leaflets available in several languages. Look out, in particular, for Guercino Didone's painting of *Death* in room 3, with its beautiful background, and the canvases by Artemisia Gentileschi and her father Orazio, in room 4. Also in room 4 is the octagonal painting of *The Halt at the Inn* by the Flemish painter Pieter van Laer (also known as 'Il Bamboccio'), one of Cardinal Spada's best-loved artists.

The palace's courtyard is most interesting for the Borromini perspective, a corridor only 8m (26ft) long, but appearing about four times longer. The columns are not parallel, but converge towards a focal point, and the floor slopes gently upwards. The statue at the end of the corridor is smaller than it appears.

Palazzo Altemps

One of Rome's finest Renaissance buildings.
Top-class collection of Classical sculpture.
Bears witness to the key role played by Roman nobility in the
16th- and 17th-century re-appreciation of Classical culture.

The Ludovisi Throne shows the birth of Venus

RATINGS	
Cultural interest	● ● ●
Good for kids	● ● ●
Photo stops	● ● ● ●
Value for money	● ● ●

BASICS
✚ 57 D4 • Piazza Sant'Apollinare 44, 00186 ☎ 06 3996 7700 🕐 Tue–Sun 9–7 (exit 7.45) 💶 Adult €5, child (under 18) free. For joint tickets ▷ 287 🚌 70, 81, 87, 116, 186, 492, 628, 916 🎧 Audiotours: English, Italian, €4 📖 Available in museum shop: brief guide €8.20, full catalogue €49 🎫 Sells guides and souvenirs 👥

GALLERY GUIDE
Ground floor: Roman copies of ancient Greek statues; remains of ancient Roman buildings (Tower Room); portraits from the Ludovisi collection (Portrait Room); Teatro Goldini (16th-century private theatre).
Upper floor: Frescoed rooms (particularly the Painted Views Room and the Painted Loggia); Roman copies of ancient Greek statues, including the Ludovisi Throne (Tales of Moses Room), the Ludovisi Sarcophagus and *Gaul and His Wife Committing Suicide* (both in the Fireplace Salon) and *Aphrodite* bathing (Duchess' Room); Church of Sant'Aniceto; Octagonal Chapel.

SEEING PALAZZO ALTEMPS
The museum is divided between three floors around a courtyard, with statuary exhibited in arcades, loggias, courtyards and the beautifully frescoed rooms. Don't try and see everything, but concentrate on what appeals. The exhibits are stunningly lit, and the best time for a visit is as dusk falls.

HIGHLIGHTS

COURTYARD, GROUND-FLOOR ARCADES AND LOGGIA
The courtyard is probably the most handsome feature of the building. A fountain made from seashells, pumice stones and vitreous paste stands to one side; look for the Altemps coat of arms here showing lightning striking a bridge. Around the courtyard, the arcades are the perfect setting for larger-than-life-size statues, while the open space is overlooked by a loggia, its ceiling decorated with cherubs. The room behind here has *trompe l'oeil* landscapes and views covering the walls and columns, while nearby is the Sideboard Room, the scene in 1477 of Girolamo Riario's marriage to Caterina Sforza.

THE LUDOVISI THRONE
One of the most beautiful of all surviving Greek sculptures in Rome, the so-called Ludovisi Throne was thought for years to have been part of a fifth-century BC altar. More probably it was the throne for a statue of the goddess Aphrodite of Eryx, whose ancient cult is associated with Erice in Sicily. She was the patron goddess of mariners and love, revered throughout the Mediterranean. The throne portrays the birth of the goddess from the sea foam; she rises between two nymphs, her draperies clinging to her body and drops of water falling from her hair, supremely delicate, the embodiment of all that was finest in the Greek world. Find it in the Tales of Moses Room on the upper floor.

THE FIREPLACE SALON
The Roman copy of the Greek *Gaul and His Wife Committing Suicide* has been admired for centuries for its realism and pathos; it was probably commissioned by Julius Caesar as a memento of his time in Gaul. If you've seen the *Dying Gaul* in the Musei Capitolini (▷ 101), it's easy to see that these two pieces were part of a group, erected in 197–159BC to celebrate a Greek victory. The room's highlight though is the action-packed relief on the side of the so-called Ludovisi Sarcophagus. Carved from a single block of marble, it's full of life and movement, and shows Roman soldiery giving a thorough beating to some hapless barbarians.

THE CHURCH OF SANT'ANICETO
Leading off the Fireplace Salon is this highly decorated church, which was commissioned in 1603 by Giovanni Angelo Altemps to house the relics of St. Aniceto. Altemps invented a story of Aniceto's martyrdom by beheading, which mirrors his own father's death and is shown in painted cycles around the church.
Don't miss The confessio, behind the altar, has a wonderful mother of pearl-decorated ceiling.

BACKGROUND

This beautifully restored 15th-century palace was closed for many years, before being finally reopened to the public in 1997 as part of the Museo Nazionale Romano. The site of a Roman warehouse, the area of the palazzo became part of a fortification dividing two rival Roman families, the Orsinis and the Colonnas. The building as we know it today dates back to 1477 when Girolamo Riario, a nephew of Pope Sixtus IV, commissioned the palace. It was extended by the Altemps family in 1568; they added the courtyard, designed by Martino Longhi the Elder, with its portico and loggias. Between 1621 and 1623, Cardinal Ludovico Ludovisi, nephew of Pope Gregory XV, assembled his 500-piece collection, still the core of today's museum. Later owner-collectors included Cardinal Marco Sittico Altemps, who bought the palace and made it a suitable setting for his magnificent collection of books and antique sculptures. The Italian state acquired the Palazzo Altemps in 1982, and restored the building to reflect 16th- and 17th-century taste and display methods.

The Painted Loggia, on the upper floor (top)

Large statues watch over Palazzo Altemps' peaceful courtyard (above)

The Gaul and His Wife Committing Suicide (left)

BASICS

✚ 57 F4 • Via Barberini 18/Via delle Quattro Fontane 13, 00187 ☎ 06 482 4184 (for groups only) 🕐 Tue–Sun 9–7 💷 €5. Joint ticket ▷ 287 🚇 Barberini 🚌 61, 62, 175, 492, 530 to Piazza Barberini; 52, 53, 63, 80, 95 116, 119, 204, 590, 630 to Via Veneto 📖 *Capolavori Galleria Nazionale Arte Antica Palazzo Barberini* in Italian and English €12.50, available in gallery bookshop 🎧 Guided tours of apartments every 45 mins; booking recommended (tel 06 328101). Included in ticket price ☕ Beautiful café with panoramic view of Via Barberini open until 1am 📚 Arts bookshop, very well stocked. www.galleriaborghese.it 🛗

The 18th-century paintings in the Sala delle Battaglie in the Barberini apartments recall the battles of the husband of Cornelia Barberini

PALAZZO BARBERINI E GALLERIA NAZIONALE D'ARTE ANTICA

Baroque magnificence and several Renaissance masterpieces.

This imposing baroque palace bears witness to the importance of the Barberini family, and highlights the innovative genius of three great artists: Gian Lorenzo Bernini, his great rival Francesco Borromini, and the painter Pietro da Cortona. The building was commissioned in 1623 by Pope Urban VIII to provide a prestigious dwelling for his family. Carlo Maderno was the original architect, but Bernini and Borromini completed the work in 1633. The palace is now home to one of the city's principal art galleries.

INSIDE THE PALACE

On entering you see two remarkable staircases: the small, spiral staircase by Borromini on the right and a wide, monumental structure designed by Bernini on the left. Take the Bernini one to reach the gallery. You can also take a tour of the 18th-century private apartments of the Barberini family on the second floor.

GALLERIA NAZIONALE D'ARTE ANTICA

Since 1949, the palace has housed the Galleria Nazionale d'Arte Antica (National Gallery of Ancient Art; shared with the Palazzo Corsini, ▷ 111). The impressive collection of works from the 12th to 18th centuries represents private collections of some of the aristocratic families of Rome. In the small antechamber to the gallery are displayed a marble bust of Urban VIII, carved by Bernini between 1637 and 1638, and a Virgin Mary with Christ,

TIP

● While you are here, buy tickets in advance for the Borghese Gallery (▷ 93), which is always very crowded.

dating back to the second half of the 12th century. Other works to look for include the lovely *Virgin Mary with the Christ Child* by Filippo Lippi, *Narcissus* and *Judith and Holofernes*, both by Caravaggio, and Titian's *Venus and Adonis*. The gallery's best-known painting is Raphael's portrait of *La Fornarina* (*The Baker's Daughter*), believed to be the artist's mistress, painted in the year of his death.

Pietro da Cortona painted his finest work, *The Triumph of Divine Providence*, on the vault of the Gran Salone between 1633 and 1639. It is a masterpiece of baroque art, admired for its powerful portrayal of light and shade (*chiaroscuro*). The painting exalts the glory of the Barberinis; Divine Providence, holding a sceptre, stands above the clouds.

PALAZZO–GALLERIA DORIA PAMPHILJ

A magnificently decorated palace housing one of Italy's most important private art collections.

Not far from Piazza Venezia stands one of the largest palaces in Rome, Palazzo Doria Pamphilj, whose art collection is among the city's most prestigious. Owned and inhabited by the same family since the 17th century, the palace has remained untouched through the centuries; as you walk round the magnificently decorated and furnished rooms, it is like stepping back in time.

INSIDE THE PALACE

Four galleries contain a collection of 16th- to 18th-century paintings and sculptures initiated by Pope Innocent X Pamphilj in 1651. Gallery 1 contains works by Tintoretto, Titian, Raphael and Paolo Veronese, as well as Caravaggio's famous *Flight into Egypt*. This painting caused outrage in its day, since the model used for the figure of the Virgin Mary was the one Caravaggio employed for his *Mary Magdalen*, displayed in the same gallery.

Gallery 2 is dedicated to Flemish artists, with paintings by artists such as Peter Paul Rubens and Pieter Brueghel. A painting by Quentin Massys is a caricature of moneylenders, still relevant today. Also noteworthy are paintings by the Maestro della Candela (Master of the Candle), so called because he painted faces under the light of a candle. Gallery 3 is decorated with 18th-century mirrors and gilding. It contains a portrait of Innocent X—a masterpiece by the Spanish painter Diego Velázquez—and a bust of the same pope sculpted by Bernini for the Holy Year of 1650.

Gallery 4 includes two semicircular works by Annibale Carracci, part of a series of paintings for the palace chapel.

THE PRIVATE APARTMENTS

The private apartments were inhabited by the owners of the palace from the 16th to the 18th century and are now open to the public. They include the Andrea Doria Room, in memory of the great 16th-century admiral. Brussels tapestries depicting the Battle of Lepanto (a Christian victory against the Turks in 1571) decorate the walls. The Dining Room's frieze shows the various properties of the Doria Pamphilj family in the 19th century.

In the ballroom is a 17th-century harp with a double row of strings producing a unique, gentle sound.

RATINGS

Cultural interest	● ● ●
Value for money	● ● ● ●

BASICS

✚ 57 E5 • Piazza del Collegio Romano 2 ☎ 06 679 7323. Information 06 7707 2842 🕐 Daily 10–5 💶 €8, child (under 18) €5.70 🚌 30, 40, 46, 62, 63, 70, 81, 87, 116, 117, 119, 186, 204, 492, 628, 810, 916 📞 To reserve guided tour, ring 06 679 7323. Audiotours: Italian, English, French, included in price, 2 hours. Concerts (Dec and Jan only) can be booked 10 days in advance, Fri–Wed 10–4, and from 7.30 on concert days 📖 Free guide, *Breve Guida della Galleria Doria Pamphilj*, available in several languages ☕ Tea room 🚻 www.doriapamphilj.it

TIPS

● Use the audioguide, which is included in the price and helps you make sense of what you're seeing.
● The paintings are not well lit so it is better to visit during daylight hours.

The sumptuous interior of the Palazzo-Galleria Doria Pamphilj (above)

Palazzo Massimo alle Terme

**Superb national collection of Greek and Roman sculpture.
Outstanding and unique displays of ancient Roman wall paintings and mosaics.**

*Fresco from Villa Farnesina, in
Trastevere*

RATINGS

Cultural interest	●●●○
Specialist shopping	●●○
Value for money	●●●●○

BASICS

✚ 58 G4 • Largo di Villa Peretti 1,
00187 ☎ 06 3996 7700
🕐 Tue–Sun 9–7.45
💶 Adult €6, child (under 18) free. For
joint tickets ▷ 287
Ⓜ Repubblica or Termini
🚌 40, 64, 84, 86, 90, 170, 175, 492, 910
to Piazza della Repubblica;
14, 36, 38, 64, 86, 90,
92, 105, 217, 310, 714
or tram 5 to Piazza
dei Cinquecento or
Termini station
📷 Sat–Sun 10.30, 3.30 in
Italian only €3.50. Audiotours: Italian,
English €4
📖 Available from museum shop:
brief guide €8.20, full catalogue
€49
🏬 Very modern and well-
stocked bookshop open 9–7
🚻

For online reservations
www.pierreci.it

Lancellotti Discobolus

SEEING PALAZZO MASSIMO ALLE TERME

This beautifully restored and well-organized museum is part of
the Museo Nazionale Romano. The palace has four floors of
museum space, a modern library, a conference room and a
computer-based documentation area. The Classical art collection
is on the first three floors, and includes works of art from the
end of the Republican age (second–first century BC) to the late
Imperial age (fourth century AD), with some original Greek works
from the fifth century BC.

HIGHLIGHTS

GROUND FLOOR
Niobid from the Hortus Sallustiani (Room VII)
This superb Greek statue dates from 440BC, and was found on the
site of gardens once belonging to Julius Caesar; it was almost
certainly once his property. The statue portrays one of Niobe's
daughters falling as she tries to remove an arrow embedded in
her back—she and her siblings were killed by the gods Apollo and
Artemis. The piece probably came from a group decorating the
pediment of a Greek temple, later collected by Caesar.

FIRST FLOOR
The Lancellotti Discobolus (Room VI)
One of the most famous copies of the great fifth-century BC works,
this statue, discovered in the 18th century, was sent to Germany
during World War II and returned in 1948. It reproduces an original
bronze, showing an athlete throwing a discus, that was probably the
work of Myron, a Greek sculptor renowned for his portraits of athletes.
This very fine marble copy dates from the mid-second century AD.

The Sleeping Hermaphrodite (Room VII)
Dionysian cult statues were popular with both Greeks
and Romans—with the Greeks for their
religious symbolism, the Romans for
their refined sensuality. This lovely
example is a second-century AD copy of
a second-century BC Hellenistic original.
Endowed with the attributes of both sexes,
the figure reclines languidly on drapery, the slick
polished finish adding to its eroticism.

SECOND FLOOR
The House of Livia (Room II)
Crammed with realistic details, these lovely decorative wall paintings come from a villa belonging to Livia
Drusilla, wife of the Emperor Augustus. The panels,
moved from the excavations in 1951, decorated the
walls of a summer triclinium, a large and airy outside living
room, set partially below ground. Look out for the different
trees, flowers, fruit and birds, as fresh now as when they
were painted between 20 and 10BC.

The 19th-century Palazzo Massimo was a Jesuit college until 1960; it has now been lovingly restored (above)

This mosaic from Villa Maccarani shows a hippopotamus hunt by the Nile (left)

GALLERY GUIDE

The galleries are arranged thematically.

Basement Coins and jewellery.

Ground floor Power in Republican and early Imperial times. Portrait busts, full statues, mosaics, urns and basins.

First floor Development of different iconographic trends, and copies and reworkings of Hellenistic statuary. Portrait heads, sculpture and bronzes.

Second floor Wall paintings, paintings, frescoes, mosaics and stuccoes of exceptional importance and quality.

The Villa Farnesina (Gallery II, Rooms III–V)

This complete set of frescoes was discovered in 1879 near the Renaissance Villa Farnesina; they can be dated to around 20BC and may have been done to celebrate the wedding of Augustus' daughter Julia. The frescoes are immensely varied, embracing themes such as landscapes, architecture and Egyptian motifs. There are scenes portraying myths, battles and garlands of flowers and leaves: a superb example of the lavishness of upper-class Roman interior decoration.

BACKGROUND

The Palazzo Massimo, designed by Camillo Pistrucci, was built in the late 19th century by the Massimo family to replace an earlier one demolished to make way for the Termini station. In 1981 the palace was acquired by the state, and in the 1990s it was transformed into one of Rome's most attractive museums.

The monument to King Vittorio Emanuele II, Piazza Venezia

The Campidoglio (above)
Fontana delle Api (left)

PALAZZO VENEZIA

🏛 57 E5 • Via del Plebiscito 118, 00184
☎ 06 6999 4318, information 06
328101 🕐 Tue–Sun 8.30–7.30 💶 Adult
€4, child (under 18) free 🚇 Colosseo
🚌 44, 46, 84, 715, 716, 780, 781, 810,
916 🔠 ♿

The imposing palace dominating
Piazza Venezia (see opposite)
was one of the first major civil
buildings to be erected in Rome
during the Renaissance. Today, it
houses the Museo del Palazzo
Venezia, with collections of
paintings and objets d'art. Try to
time your visit to coincide with
one of the temporary art
exhibitions the palace hosts.

The Venetian Pietro Barbo
started building the palace in 1455
when he became a cardinal, and
it was enlarged when he was
elected Pope Paul II in 1464. The
palace acquired its present name
in 1564, when Pope Pius IV gave
it to the Republic of Venice as a
diplomatic residence. The popes
continued to live in a wing of the
palace until the 16th century. In
the 19th century Napoleon made
it the seat of the French
administration, and between 1930
and 1944 Mussolini established
his government here and used
the first floor of the palace for his
office.

The permanent museum dis-
plays ivory, silver and gold items,
16th- and 17th-century bronze
statues, religious works of art,
Renaissance models in plaster
and terracotta, oriental pottery
and 15th-century tapestries.

PANTHEON

See pages 120–121.

PIAZZA BARBERINI

🏛 57 F4 🚇 Barberini 🚌 61, 62, 175,
492, 630 to Piazza Barberini; 52, 53, 63,
80, 95 116, 119, 204, 590 to Via Veneto

This beautiful piazza, named after
the powerful Barberini family,

showcases the work of the
architect/artist, Gian Lorenzo
Bernini, who worked on the
family's residential palace
(▷ 114) and designed the two
fountains on the square.

In the heart of the square is
the Fontana del Tritone, commissioned in 1643 by Pope Urban
VIII: Four dolphins, tails in the air,
support a huge scallop shell on
which sits a triton blowing a jet of
water through a conch. Look for
the Barberini coat of arms (the
bees) and the papal arms (St.
Peter's keys and the papal tiara).

On the corner of Via Veneto is
the other Bernini fountain, the
Fontana delle Api. The Fountain
of the Bees was commissioned
to celebrate the 21st anniversary
in August 1644 of Urban VIII's
accession to the papacy. The fact
that Bernini finished it before
the actual date was considered
a bad omen, borne out when
the Pope died eight days before
the anniversary. In 1865, the
fountain was dismantled and
removed from its original site,
at the corner with Via Sistina. It
was reassembled in its present
position in 1916; the only
surviving original pieces are the
central part of a shell and three
bees drinking the water.

PIAZZA DEL CAMPIDOGLIO

🏛 57 E5 🚇 Colosseo 🚌 44, 46, 84,
715, 716, 780, 781, 810, 916
www.museicapitolini.org
www.comune.roma.it

The Piazza del Campidoglio is
one of the most spectacular
places in Rome, unmissable for
the superb view of the Roman
Forum and for Michelangelo's
wonderful architecture.

Michelangelo designed
the square to look out over
the city of Rome like an open
terrace, and placed on it three

magnificent buildings: the
Palazzo Senatorio, Palazzo dei
Conservatori and Palazzo Nuovo
(Musei Capitolini—▷ 98–103).
Much of the work on the palaces
was in fact carried out after
Michelangelo's death by other
architects. He also designed the
Cordonata, a monumental ramp
leading up to the square. At the
top, on either side, are Roman
statues of Castor and Pollux, the
twin sons of Jupiter by Leda,
standing beside their horses.
In the middle of the piazza's
beautiful, geometric-patterned
paving is a modern copy of the
equestrian statue of Marcus
Aurelius—the original is in the
Palazzo Nuovo (▷ 100).

Near the steps leading to the
Palazzo Senatorio (Rome's city
hall) is a fountain flanked by two
enormous bearded statues representing the Nile, represented
by a sphinx, and—on the right—
the Tiber, with the figures of
Romulus and Remus and the
she-wolf.

The Palazzo Caffarelli on the far
right of the Cordonata now hosts
temporary exhibitions.

PIAZZA CAMPO DEI FIORI

See pages 122–123.

PIAZZA FARNESE

🏛 57 D5 🚌 23, 40, 46, 62, 64, 116,
280, 916; tram 8

Just a stone's throw from Piazza
Campo dei Fiori, at the historical
heart of the Regola quarter,
Piazza Farnese is like an elegant
open-air drawing room, furnished
by the majestic Renaissance
Palazzo Farnese (now the French
Embassy) and twin fountains to
each side. The lily, emblem of
the Farnese family and symbol of
France, is the dominant theme in
the square, visible on the palace
façade and on the fountains. The
Palazzo Farnese is the high-

Relaxing in the Piazza Farnese

One of Valadier's water-spitting lions in Piazza del Popolo

Fontana delle Naiadi in Piazza della Repubblica

light of this lovely square, but unfortunately can only be visited by appointment or with a private tour. However, it is pleasant to relax and admire the splendid exterior from one of the many outdoor cafés in the square. Look up at the large central window and you may get a glimpse of frescoed walls inside.

PIAZZA NAVONA

See pages 124–125.

PIAZZA DEL POPOLO

✚ 57 E3 ⊚ Flaminio ⊟ 95, 117, 119, 491, 495, 590, 628, 926; tram 2

When approaching the square from Via del Corso, pause for a moment to admire it from a distance. Its charm lies in the complete harmony of all the distinct architectural styles within it.

Each end of the oval piazza is adorned with a fountain, with sphinxes and statues depicting the four seasons. At the end of the 16th century, Pope Sixtus V erected an Egyptian obelisk of the Pharaoh Rameses II in the middle of the square, and in 1823, Giuseppe Valadier added the rounded basins and four water-spitting marble lions to the base of the obelisk.

The 17th-century twin churches of Santa Maria dei Miracoli and Santa Maria di Monte Santo stand on either side of Via del Corso. Both churches were started by Carlo Rainaldi and completed by Carlo Fontana (work on Santa Maria di Monte Santo was supervised by Bernini). Inside Santa Maria di Monte Santo are frescoes by Baciccia and a 15th-century painting of the Virgin Mary on the high altar.

On the north side of the square is the grand entrance to the square, Porta del Popolo, erected in 1561. It was reworked by Bernini in 1655 to mark

the entry to Rome of Queen Christina of Sweden after her conversion to Roman Catholicism. The adjoining church of Santa Maria del Popolo contains exceptional works of art by Caravaggio, Raphael, Bernini and Pinturicchio, among others.

PIAZZA DELLA REPUBBLICA

✚ 58 G4 ⊚ Repubblica ⊟ H, 40, 64, 84, 86, 90, 170, 175, 492, 910

Piazza della Repubblica, one of Rome's busiest spots, has a theatrical fountain at its heart and two semicircular porticoed buildings at the sides. The huge and rather unappealing church of Santa Maria degli Angeli is the dominant building.

The square was created in the late 19th century to follow the curved line of the *exedra* (a recess with raised seating) of the nearby Terme di Diocleziano (▷ 143), hence its popular name—Piazza Esedra.

The large central fountain, the Fontana delle Naiadi (1901), gets its name from the four water nymphs that decorate it, the work of Sicilian artist Mario Rutelli. The naked naiads and the allegorical marine animals with which they are entwined represent water in various forms: rivers, lakes, oceans and underground streams. The city authorities thought the figures too erotic when they were first revealed, and ordered a fence (later removed) to be built to hide them from sight. The original central decoration of the

fountain—three tritons, a dolphin and an octopus—was nicknamed the fish fry, and was moved to the gardens of Piazza Vittorio Emanuele. The present central figure is the minor god Glaucus in combat with a fish.

PIAZZA DI SPAGNA

See pages 126–127.

PIAZZA VENEZIA

✚ 57 E5 ⊚ Colosseo ⊟ 44, 46, 84, 715, 780, 781, 810, 916

This busy traffic junction owes its name to the Palazzo Venezia (see opposite). Next to it, in fact incorporated in the palace complex, is the church of San Marco (▷ 133). With origins in the fourth century, this venerable basilica has been much altered and rebuilt over the centuries. It is worth a visit for a wonderful ninth-century mosaic in the apse. Between the palace and the church, look for *Madama Lucrezia*, one of the six 'talking statues'.

Dominating the square, however, is the white theatrical Monumento a Vittorio Emanuele II, the first king of unified Italy. Built between 1885 and 1911, 'Il Vittoriano' changed the appearance of what had been the medieval and Renaissance quarter where Michelangelo lived until his death. A convent on the Capitoline Hill and a wing of the Palazzo Venezia were among the structures that had to be demolished to make way for the vast, dazzlingly white monument. Climb to the top for superb views across the city. Since 1921 it has housed the Monument to the Unknown Soldier.

Pantheon

One of the best-preserved ancient Roman buildings anywhere.
A dome that is a magnificent feat of Roman engineering.
Last resting place of the artist Raphael.

Giacomo della Porta's fountain in Piazza della Rotonda

SEEING THE PANTHEON

From Piazza della Rotonda, a single door in the portico leads into this historically and architecturally interesting building, which has been a place of worship for over 2,000 years. If possible, visit the Pantheon during a downpour: The sight of the rain entering the building through the oculus is fascinating.

THE BUILDING

The portico is 14m (46ft) high and consists of 16 Egyptian granite columns with Corinthian capitals. The church is paved with marble and granite, and at one time the ceiling was entirely covered in bronze. When Pope Urban VIII restored the roof in the 17th century, the precious material was removed and used for the altar of St. Peter's and other works. The bronze doors are probably original. Around the interior are seven niches where statues of divinities once stood, with the statue of Jove Ultor, the Avenger, at the middle.

THE DOME

The dome, spanning 43.3m (142ft), is the largest ever built before the introduction of reinforced concrete in the 20th century; its diameter is greater than that of the dome of St. Peter's. As seen from outside, it is actually a cheat—a thick skin of brickwork over the smaller structure of the actual cupola inside. This consists of concrete, cast over a temporary framework, the material being thinner and lighter at the base of the dome than at its apex. The cupola represents the sky, while the great central unglazed opening, the oculus, stands for the sun; the oculus is the only source of natural light for the building.

THE TOMBS

Today, the Pantheon acts as the mausoleum of the royalty of Italy, accommodating the tombs of Vittorio Emanuele II, Umberto I and Queen Margherita of Savoy, and of a few notable Italians. In the first chapel on the right, next to the tomb of Vittorio Emanuele II, is a fresco of the Annunciation by Melozzo da Forlì. The third chapel contains the funerary monument by the Norwegian sculptor Thorvaldsen of Cardinal Consalvi (died 1824), and the third niche on the left holds the remains of Raphael (died 1520). Also in the chapel are a sculpture of the Madonna by Raphael's pupil Lorenzetto and an epitaph to Maria Bibbiena, Raphael's betrothed, who died three months before the artist. The tombs of King Umberto I and Queen Margherita of Savoy are beyond, followed by the tomb of the painter and architect Baldassare Peruzzi (1481–1536).

PIAZZA DELLA ROTONDA

The Pantheon faces Piazza della Rotonda, which resembles in shape the arcade thought to have surrounded the ancient Roman temple. The central fountain was designed by Giacomo della Porta in 1575. Pope Clement XI erected a 13th-century BC Egyptian obelisk dedicated to Rameses II at the centre of the basin in 1711. The granite monolith, 6.43m (21ft) tall, stood in the temple dedicated to Isis and Serapis in the nearby area of Campo Marzio before it was moved here.

BACKGROUND

The original Pantheon was built in 27BC by Augustus' general and son-in-law, Marcus Agrippa, whose name can still clearly be seen on the inscription on the façade: 'M Agrippa L.F. Cos Tertium fecit' ('Marcus Agrippa, son of Lucius, built this during his third consulate'). Built in the style of a traditional Greek pagan temple, and dedicated to all the gods, Agrippa's building was entirely destroyed in the great fire of AD80. In the early second century, Emperor Hadrian rebuilt it as we see it today, reusing the original inscription. In the sixth century, the Byzantine Emperor Phocas gave the Pantheon to Pope Boniface IV, who transformed it into a Christian church, dedicating it to St. Mary of the Martyrs. To consecrate the church, the Pope is said to have brought 28 cartloads of bones of martyrs from the Roman catacombs and buried them underneath the altar. Legend has it that during the ceremony, as the notes of the Gloria were sung, devils and malign spirits rose up and flew out of the hole in the dome.

The sun pours through the opening in the Pantheon's roof, but this church is equally impressive in the rain

TIPS

● The Pantheon is often very crowded, especially at the weekend. To make the most of a visit, go on a weekday or early in the morning.
● Relax in one of Piazza della Rotonda's cafés to enjoy the exterior view of the Pantheon and the atmosphere of the lively piazza.

Piazza Campo dei Fiori

**One of Rome's most picturesque and atmospheric squares.
The heart of a lively area.
Scene of Rome's most popular food and flower market.
A great place for people-watching.**

The Campo dei Fiori is home to one of Rome's most atmospheric markets, where the daily trade in fruit, vegetables and flowers still continues

RATINGS	
Photo stops	●●●○
Shopping	●●●●●
Value for money	●●●●●
Walkability	●●●●●

BASICS

✚ 57 D5
🚌 23, 40, 46, 62, 64, 116, 280, 870, 916; tram 8
🏠 Streetside cafés in the square
🏪 Souvenir shops in the square sell guidebooks

SEEING PIAZZA CAMPO DEI FIORI

For a slice of real Roman life, head for the Campo dei Fiori during the morning market, when the stalls are in full swing and the surrounding shops busy with people. Around lunchtime, it's a good place to pause for a snack or meal, while evenings see the piazza crowded with locals and visitors relaxing.

HIGHLIGHTS

STATUE OF GIORDANO BRUNO

This statue was erected in 1887 to replace a fountain, the Campo's original focal point. It shows the philosopher Giordano Bruno, who advocated the separation of political and religious power. In 1600, he was condemned for heresy and burned alive by the Inquisition on this very spot, the first of a series of executions here during the 17th century. Ettore Ferrari was the sculptor, and the statue soon became a meeting point for intellectuals and anti-establishment thinkers.

PALAZZO RIGHETTI AND PALAZZO DELLA CANCELLERIA

The Pio Righetti palace, at the east end of the square, was built on the site of an old palazzo, over the remains of the Theatre of Pompey. It was bought in the 18th century by the banker Righetti, from whom it takes its name. If you want to see traces of the Theatre of Pompey, on whose steps Caesar was assassinated, ask at the restaurant San Pancrazio on the east corner of the square, where there are remains of it in the cellar—you don't have to eat there to have a look. The late 15th-century Palazzo della Cancelleria is attributed to Bramante, though the interior courtyard is his sole contribution.

THE SURROUNDING STREETS

The Campo is part of the Regola district, traditionally famous for its craftsmen. Many nearby streets owe their names to the artisan workshops that once stood there: Via dei Giubbonari (jacket-makers) and Via dei Cappellari (hat-makers). These streets are still crammed with tiny shops, great trawling ground for local goods. In Via del Pellegrino look for a charming old interior courtyard—it's through a gate just round the corner of the west side of the square. Via di Monserrato,

farther on, is home to the English College, where young British men train for the priesthood.

BACKGROUND

In ancient times the square was used as grazing land for cattle, hence the name Campo dei Fiori, Field of Flowers. In those days, buildings stood on one side of the square only, with a spacious view over the Tiber on the other. By the 12th century the Palazzo Orsini, where the Palazzo Righetti now stands, dominated the scene, and the Campo became the heart of an exclusive residential and business district. It was also an important crossing point, as papal processions and pilgrims on their way to Rome's basilicas had to pass through Via del Pellegrino. Once it had been used for executions it lost its cachet, and became the heart of one of Rome's most vibrant working-class areas.

Piazza Navona

A superb baroque city space.
One of Rome's most popular meeting places.
The setting of three magnificent fountains.

Fontana del Moro

BASICS

✚ 57 D5
☎ Church of Sant'Agnese in Agone:
06 6819 2134. Domitian's Stadium:
06 6710 3819 for guided tours
◉ Church of Sant'Agnese in Agone:
Tue–Sat 9–12, 4–7, Sun 10–1, 4–8.
Domitian's Stadium: Mon–Fri 9–1, 2–5;
only open by prior arrangement.
🚌 23, 30, 62, 64, 70, 81, 87, 116, 280,
492, 628, 810, 916

The piazza is a popular place to meet for a chat

SEEING PIAZZA NAVONA

Visitors to Rome are drawn time and again to this beautiful piazza, so plan several visits to appreciate the square at different times of day. You could spend your first visit sightseeing, but be sure to return to relax, sit at a café table, take in the street performers and local worthies, or eat one of Rome's best ice creams, the wicked chocolate *tartufo* at I Tre Scalini.

HIGHLIGHTS

THE PIAZZA

Harmonious, regularly shaped Piazza Navona is one of the most remarkable examples of town planning in Rome. Notable buildings include the Palazzo Braschi, renovated by Antonio da Sangallo in 1793 and now hosting exhibitions, and the elegant Palazzo Pamphilj, the largest building in the piazza. Built between 1644 and 1650 by Girolamo Rainaldi and Francesco Borromini, the palace is now home to the Brazilian Embassy.

FONTANA DEI FIUMI

You'll be drawn at once to the famous Fountain of the Four Rivers, designed by Gian Lorenzo Bernini in 1651, which gained him the admiration and protection of Pope Innocent X. The fountain shows the main rivers of the four then known continents: the Danube in Europe, the Ganges in Asia, the Nile in Africa and the Rio de la Plata in the New World. An obelisk (from the Circus of Maxentius) rears boldly into the air surrounded by animals. Legend has it that the fountain symbolizes the rivalry between Bernini and Borromini. Innocent X asked Borromini to do the work, but Bernini obtained the commission by flattering the Pope's sister. According to popular belief, Borromini built the church of Sant'Agnese in Agone in front of Bernini's fountain out of revenge, and the statue of the Nile seems to cover its face to shield its eyes from Borromini's work. Sadly, this is purely apocryphal, since the fountain pre-dates the church—the Nile's face is covered because its source was as yet unknown.

SANT'AGNESE IN AGONE

The church of Sant'Agnese in Agone stands where, according to tradition, 12-year-old Agnes was martyred by the Emperor Diocletian. Exposed naked, the saint was miraculously covered by the prodigious growth of her own hair. Pope Innocent X commissioned the church in 1652 and Borromini took control of the project, radically changing the design of the façade and building the twin bell towers.

THE FONTANA DEL MORO AND THE FONTANA DEL NETTUNO

The Fontana del Moro at the southern end of the piazza was commissioned by Pope Gregory XIII and designed by Giacomo della Porta in 1576, with sculptures of tritons, dragons and dolphins. Bernini altered the fountain in the mid-17th century, adding the central figure of the Moor, apparently wrestling with a dolphin. At the northern end of the piazza, the 19th-century Fontana del Nettuno shows Neptune flanked by nymphs as he battles with a sea monster.

DOMITIAN'S STADIUM

To see the remains of Domitian's stadium, you can visit the building at No. 49 at the northern end of the square. A maximum of five people are allowed in at any one time, but it is well worth a visit.

BACKGROUND

The piazza was laid out in the mid-17th century on the ruins of Domitian's stadium (AD86). The stadium was originally called the Circus Agonalis (*Agones* means games in ancient Greek), but in the Middle Ages it became known as Campus Agonis, which was in turn corrupted by Roman dialect to become *n'agnona* and eventually Navona. The arena was used for festivals and sporting events, even jousting until the late 15th century, when it was paved over and transformed into a marketplace and public square.

Fontana del Nettuno (above)

The elongated piazza follows the shape of Domitian's stadium (inset)

Piazza di Spagna

**One of Rome's focal piazzas for both locals and visitors.
Site of the city's most beautiful stairway, the Spanish Steps,
and the French church, Trinità dei Monti.
Historic Anglo-Saxon links.**

SEEING PIAZZA DI SPAGNA

Start your explorations in the Piazza di Spagna itself, pausing on the far side of the fountain to take in the full sweep of the magnificent Scalinata della Trinità dei Monti (Spanish Steps). Walk all round the piazza, with its shops and buildings, before tackling the steps, pausing en route. At the top, scale the staircase leading to the church, from where there's a superb view of Rome, with the cupola of St. Peter's in the distance—wonderful at sunset.

The Fontana della Barcaccia is designed to look like a sinking boat

RATINGS	
Historic interest	●●●
Photo stops	●●●●
Value for money	●●●●

BASICS	
✚	57 E3
Ⓜ	Spagna
🚌	116, 117, 119, 590
📖	Available from souvenir shops on the square
🍴	Plenty in the area

HIGHLIGHTS

THE PIAZZA

More butterfly-shaped than square, the Piazza di Spagna contains one of Rome's most unusual fountains, the boat-shaped Fontana della Barcaccia, commissioned by Pope Urban VIII to commemorate the great flood of 1598. It was designed by father and son Bernini to represent a boat that was stranded in the piazza during the flood, and was finished in 1629. Pietro Bernini exploited the low water pressure of the Aqua Virgo at this point to achieve the 'sinking' effect.

At the piazza's southern end is a Roman column topped by a statue of the Virgin Mary, erected in 1856 to commemorate the establishment of the doctrine of the Immaculate Conception. On 8 December a procession, led by the Pope, terminates here to crown the statue with wreaths.

SCALINATA DELLA TRINITÀ DEI MONTI

The supremely elegant Spanish Steps were designed by Francesco de Sanctis and built between 1723 and 1726. Prior to this, the church was separated from the piazza by a wood, a popular hideout for criminals. There are three flights of shallow steps, 138 in all, of various widths and configurations, along with benches from which you can enjoy the increasingly lovely views. The final flight of two symmetrical staircases brings you to the Piazza della Trinità dei Monti.

THE CHURCH OF TRINITÀ DEI MONTI

King Charles VIII of France commissioned this church in 1495 on the request of St. Francis of Paola, who lived in the nearby convent. It was consecrated by Pope Sixtus V in 1585 and restored in 1816 by Louis XVIII after it was looted by Napoleon. The church of Trinità dei Monti is still owned by the French.

BACKGROUND

The Piazza di Spagna gained its name when the Spanish ambassador took up residence here, but the section towards Via del Babuino—to the left as you look up at the Trinità dei Monti—used to be called Piazza di Francia, since the French claimed the right to pass through the square to reach their church. This resulted in fierce rivalry between the two nations. You can see

Today, the steps are a popular meeting place

another sign of diplomatic strife on the steps, this time between the French and the Italians, in the confrontation of Conti eagles (from the coat of arms of Pope Innocent XIII) and the fleur-de-lys of France. During the 18th and 19th centuries, so many English visitors came to Rome and stayed in the numerous hotels and lodging houses scattered around the piazza that it eventually came to be known as the English ghetto. Poet John Keats was just one of the illustrious visitors to stay near here. He died in the Casina Rossa at the foot of the Spanish Steps on the right, now the Museo Keats-Shelley (▷ 110). Babington's English Tea Rooms, on the left-hand corner of the steps, founded in 1893 by the Misses Babington, is another sign of the square's 19th-century popularity with the English. Today, it is one of the most sophisticated, refined and expensive tea rooms in Rome.

THE SIGHTS

The Madonna del Parto *in the church of Sant'Agostino*

Bernini's best-loved church, Sant'Andrea al Quirinale

The peaceful little cloister of San Carlo alle Quattro Fontane

SANT'AGOSTINO

🕂 57 E4 • Piazza di Sant'Agostino 00186 ☎ 06 6880 1962 🕓 7.45–12, 4.30–7.30 🎟 Free 🚌 116 to Via Zanardelli; 30, 40, 46, 62, 63, 64, 70, 81, 492, 628, 630, 780, 787, 916 or tram 8 to Largo di Torre Argentina

One of the first Renaissance churches to be built in Rome, the church of Sant'Agostino still maintains its Latin-cross plan with apse, chapels and dome. Even if 19th-century additions have spoilt the church's elegance, it is still worth visiting to see the works by Caravaggio, Raphael and other fine artists.

The church was dedicated to St. Augustine of Hippo in the late 15th century and enlarged later in the same century thanks to the generosity of Cardinal d'Estouteville, Archbishop of Rouen in France.

To the left of the central portal near the main door is the *Madonna del Parto* (*Madonna of Childbirth*) by Jacopo Sansovino, a statue much revered by expectant mothers and childless couples. A fresco of the Prophet Isaiah by Raphael adorns the third pillar of the nave on the left, and below it is the sculpture *St. Anne and the Virgin Mary with the Christ Child* by Andrea Sansovino. The first chapel on the left contains Caravaggio's magnificent *Madonna di Loreto*.

SANT'ANDREA AL QUIRINALE

🕂 58 F4 • Via del Quirinale 29, 00184 ☎ 06 4890 3187 🕓 Wed–Mon 8–12, 4–7; closed Sun morning 🎟 Free 🚇 Barberini 🚌 H, 40, 60, 64, 70, 117, 170

Often called the baroque pearl, this church is one of Gian Lorenzo Bernini's best works, and was closest to his own heart. It was here that he asked to be taken towards the end of his life

to admire the effect of the light streaming through the windows, illuminating the rich and beautiful marble, gold and stucco he had used to embellish it.

The design is very unusual. The façade is on the shorter side of the building and is highlighted by elegant steps and a portico. Inside is an elliptical central hall with eight deep rectangular chapels off it, each one lit by a window over the altar. The dome above the altar is richly decorated with gilded stuccowork, marble and stucco angels and cherubs. The sacristy has a beautiful frescoed vault. In the adjacent convent are the rooms of St. Stanislaus, where the 17-year-old Jesuit novice died in 1568; the statue of the saint is by the 17th-century French sculptor Pierre Legros. Ask in the sacristy for access to these rooms.

SAN CARLO ALLE QUATTRO FONTANE

🕂 58 F4 • Via del Quirinale 00184 ☎ 06 488 3261 🕓 Mon–Fri 10–1, 3–5, Sat and Sun 10–1 🎟 Free 🚇 Barberini 🚌 H, 40, 60, 64, 70, 116, 117, 119, 170 www.sancarlino-borromini.it

This minuscule church, also known as San Carlino, is famously smaller than a single one of the piers supporting the dome of St. Peter's.

Designed in 1638, the church was the great Francesco Borromini's first work; it was also his last, as the new façade he began in 1665 was unfinished when he committed suicide two years later. The architecture of San Carlino reflects the artist's tormented and contradictory state of mind: Every curve has its counter-curve, and concave and convex sections form complicated patterns. A statue of the Counter-Reformation saint, St. Charles Borromeo, is the main focus of the curved façade.

The interior is very simple, an oval shape with stuccoed niches. The intricately designed coffered dome adds to the elegant effect the artist managed to create in such a small space.

Borromini's cloister, with two rows of Doric columns and slightly convex corners, is beautifully proportioned.

Outside are four fountains (*quattro fontane*), one on each corner of the street. They are the work of Domenico Fontana, and date from 1589.

SANTA CECILIA IN TRASTEVERE

🕂 57 E6 • Piazza di Santa Cecilia 22, 00153 ☎ 06 589 9289 🕓 Daily 9.30–12.30, 5–6.30. Cavallini fresco: Tue, Thu 10–12, Sun 11–12 🎟 Free 🚌 23, 44, 280, 780; tram 8 🎧 Audioguide in Italian, German, Spanish, French, English €1

You enter the church of Santa Cecilia through a delightful courtyard, with a portico supported by old granite columns and a lily garden with a fountain in the centre. Next, you pass an exquisite façade designed by Ferdinando Fuga in 1741.

According to legend, Cecilia, her fiancé Valeriano and his brother were persecuted and killed in AD303 because of their Christian faith. In the fifth century, a church was built over Cecilia's house, and 400 years later Pope Paschal I built a basilica on the site. In the 12th century, a Romanesque campanile and a portico were added.

A remarkable statue of St. Cecilia by Stefano Maderno is under the high altar. The sculptor was present at the opening of the saint's tomb in 1599 and made sketches of her uncorrupted body.

Splendid ninth-century apse mosaics depicting Jesus with saints Paul, Agata, Peter, Paschal,

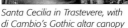
Santa Cecilia in Trastevere, with di Cambio's Gothic altar canopy

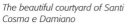
The beautiful courtyard of Santi Cosma e Damiano

The baroque façade of Santa Croce in Gerusalemme

Valeriano and Cecilia are among Santa Cecilia's treasures. Another is the beautiful fresco *Last Judgement* (1293) by Pietro Cavallini, the remains of a medieval masterpiece that once covered the walls of the central nave but was mostly lost in an 18th-century restoration of the church. The fresco was moved to the nuns' choir of the adjoining convent where it can be viewed.

SAN CLEMENTE

See pages 130–131.

SANTI COSMA E DAMIANO

🕀 57 F6 • Via dei Fori Imperiali 1, 00184 ☎ 06 699 1540 ◷ 9–1, 3–6 ▧ Free ◿ Colosseo 🚌 60, 75, 81, 175, 673 to Via di San Gregorio; 84, 85, 87, 60, 117, 175, 810, 850 to Via dei Fori Imperiali ◨ Audioguide €1 in Italian, French, English, German, Spanish

The origins of this church are rather unusual. It was formed by combining the library of Vespasian's Temple of Peace (▷ 83) and part of the Temple of Romulus in the Roman Forum, the remains of which are still visible inside. The church, the first to reuse a building in the Forum, was consecrated in AD526 by Pope Felix IV and dedicated to twin brothers, miraculous healers from Cilicia (southern Turkey).

The church took on its present form in the 17th century, under Pope Urban VIII Barberini. The original Roman church was hidden in a sort of crypt, and the present façade of the church and the cloister were erected. The 17th-century coffered ceiling is ornamented with paintings depicting the triumph of the saintly brothers, and with the Barberini coat of arms.

The sixth-century mosaics in the apse, the church's principal

treasure, were highly influential. They portray Christ against a sunset background with the apostles Peter and Paul and the saints Cosma and Damiano. The church also houses a remarkable 18th-century Neapolitan *presepio* (nativity scene).

SAN CRISOGONO

🕀 57 D6 • Viale Trastevere 00153 ☎ 06 581 8225 ◷ Open by request ▧ Church: free. Early Christian basement: €2 🚌 H, 23, 280, 780; tram 8

The simple façade of San Crisogono, one of Trastevere's great medieval basilicas, reveals little of its long history and its hidden treasures.

The original church was founded in the fifth century, and a new church was built between 1123 and 1129 over the old building. The bell tower, together with the nave, the aisles and 22 granite columns, are all that remain of the 12th-century church. Inside, there is a very fine 13th-century cosmatesque (inlaid marble) floor, and a late 13th-century mosaic in the vault of the apse, depicting the Virgin and Child with St. James and St. Crisogono, which is attributed to the school of Pietro Cavallini. The Cappella del Santissimo Sacramento is thought to have been designed by Bernini.

The overall appearance of this church, half Mannerist, half baroque, is the work of the architect Giambattista Soria, who restored the church between 1620 and 1626 on the orders of Cardinal Scipione Borghese. Soria kept the ancient pillars, rebuilding their capitals in stucco, opened up windows in the nave to let more light in, and installed a coffered ceiling with the coat of arms of Cardinal Borghese. The baldachin is also his work.

In 1907, archaeologists discovered traces of the original fifth-century Christian church 6m (20ft) below the floor. The remains, which can be visited, include a later relic chamber with eighth-century frescoes.

SANTA CROCE IN GERUSALEMME

🕀 59 J6 • Piazza di Santa Croce in Gerusalemme 12, 00183 ☎ 06 701 4769 ◷ 7–7 ▧ Free ◿ San Giovanni or Manzoni 🚌 117, 186, 218, 649, 650, 850 ◨

St. Helena, mother of Emperor Constantine, brought back to her palace in Rome a collection of relics of the Passion of Christ, which she amassed on her travels through the Holy Land. In the fourth century, part of the palace became the church of the Holy Cross in Jerusalem, built to house the fragment of the Holy Cross, a nail from the Cross, thorns from the Crown of Thorns, the original inscription over the Cross and other holy items. The church as seen today, built in the 12th century, was restored and altered in the 18th century.

Emperor Charles V's confessor, Cardinal Francesco Quiñones (died 1540) is buried in the apse; his tomb is by Jacopo Sansovino. The vault here is decorated with a Renaissance fresco depicting the discovery of the True Cross by St. Helena, attributed to Antoniazzo Romano. In the Chapel of St. Helena, reached by descending a 15th-century ramp at the end of the south aisle, are beautiful mosaics by Melozzo da Forlì and a statue of the saint adapted from a classical statue of Juno. The Holy Relics are kept in the Chapel of the Relics at the end of the north aisle. The church also contains a beautifully restored 12th-century cosmatesque (inlaid marble) floor.

San Clemente

Remains of a temple to the Persian god Mithras.
Magnificent mosaics.
Three distinct levels encapsulating the history of Rome.

The Temple of Mithras, below the church of San Clemente

RATINGS	
Good for kids	●●
Historic interest	●●●●●
Specialist shopping	●●
Value for money	●●●●

BASICS

✚ 58 G6 • Piazza San Clemente/Via di San Giovanni in Laterano 00184

☎ 06 7045 1018

🕐 Mon–Sat 9–12.30, 3-6, Sun 10–12.30, 3–6

💶 Second and third levels: €3. Upper basilica: free

🚇 Colosseo, San Giovanni

🚌 85, 87, 186, 810, 850; tram 3

📷 €3.65, all languages

🏪 Well stocked with guides and souvenirs

🚻 In courtyard

SEEING SAN CLEMENTE

In a pleasant valley between the Esquiline and Oppio hills stands one of Rome's oldest basilicas, named after St. Clement, a first-century pope. Three levels of building allow more than 2,000 years of history to be pieced together here through study of the cross-sections of the basilica. The lower—earliest—buildings are very well preserved, and although the church appears small from the outside, there is a wealth of interest within. You will be able to make more sense of San Clemente's history if you buy a map showing the outline of the three levels of building.

THE THIRD LEVEL

The best way to see the whole church is to start from the third, under-ground level. Down here is a temple of Mithras (mithraeum) and what may have been a school for initiates into Mithraism, with remains of stuccowork and frescoes. The mithraeum, the focal point of the Mithraic cult, had benches down both sides for ritual banquets and was in use until the fourth century, when the Christians probably destroyed it. The altar of Mithras is still there: On one side it shows the god cutting a bull's throat during initiation rites, and on the other a snake representing regeneration. Ironically, filling in the mithraeum to make the foundations of the first Christian church helped to preserve it. A narrow passage that was once an alley open to the sky leads to various rooms, one of which contains a source of spring water (not drinkable) that once fed an underground watercourse.

THE LOWER BASILICA

Above the temple is the apse of the lower basilica, consisting of a nave and two aisles. There are fragments of its once fine mosaic floor and some eighth-century frescoes, including one in a niche in the north wall that shows the Virgin as queen of heaven with saints. The frescoes decorating the nave show the legend of Sisinius, Prefect of Rome. Sisinius went to arrest his wife, who was attending a secret Mass held by Pope Clement. He was struck blind in the presence of the holy man, as were his servants, who carried out a column instead of the woman. What makes the Sisinius frescoes so unusual is that the accompanying inscription is written in a very early form of Italian. In the 11th–12th century, pilasters were added to reinforce earlier columns. These were decorated with frescoes showing scenes from the life and death of St. Clement and the legend of St. Alexis.

THE UPPER BASILICA

A few decades later, work began on the upper basilica. The new church preserved the plan of the previous structure: one nave and two aisles either side leading up to a triumphal arch and a semi-domed apse, a quiet courtyard, a four-sided portico with Ionic columns and architraves, and a belfry. Just before the arch is the marble-walled medieval choir, the schola cantorum, which survived from the lower basilica. But it is the apse that is the highlight of the upper basilica, decorated with a beautiful gold mosaic portraying the Crucifixion. Twelve doves symbolizing the Apostles adorn the Cross; the Virgin and St. John stand at the side, and God's hand descends from heaven bearing a crown for His son. The people arriving to drink

from the waters of life at the foot of the Cross represent followers of Christ coming for baptism. The cosmatesque (inlaid marble) floor is one of the best-preserved floors of its kind in Rome.

At the beginning of the 18th century, a radical restoration project began. New windows were added, together with the plain baroque façade, and the upper walls of the nave and ceiling were frescoed.

Don't miss In the left aisle, near the entrance, is the Cappella di Santa Caterina, the Chapel of St. Catherine, finely decorated in the 15th century with exceptional frescoes by Masolino da Panicale; these depict scenes from the life of St. Catherine.

BACKGROUND

The upper church was built by Pope Paschal II in 1108 after the earlier church was badly damaged during an attack by the Normans in 1084. He followed the original plans as closely as possible. The church on the second level has a similar layout, but is wider. Very little of the original fourth-century building still exists, aside from parts of the north and south walls and some other fragments. It was dedicated to the Christian cult in the fifth century. According to legend, St. Cyril, the apostle of the Slavs, brought St. Clement's relics from the Black Sea (where he drowned) to Rome, placing them in the church in AD869. Down on the third level are two first-century Roman buildings, divided by a narrow passage. One is a huge warehouse of the early Flavian era, built of tufa blocks, which is believed to have been the mint of ancient Rome. The second building can be dated to AD92–96. Built of brick with an underground courtyard, it was the house of a rich family. Later, it was converted to the worship of the Persian god Mithras, a religion widespread throughout the Roman Empire, with some rituals similar to Christianity. Farther down, archaeologists have found buildings that were probably destroyed in Rome's fire of AD64.

From the Mithraic temple (middle right), through the 12th-century mosaics in the apse (above and top) to the 18th-century courtyard (middle left), San Clemente's history is laid bare

Santi Giovanni e Paolo enjoys a peaceful setting on the Caelian Hill

Andrea Pozzo's trompe l'oeil cupola in Sant'Ignazio di Loyola

The spiral dome of Sant'Ivo alla Sapienza

SAN FRANCESCO A RIPA

🔢 57 D7 • Piazza San Francesco d'Assisi 00153 ☎ 06 588 1331 🕐 Mon–Sat 7–12, 4–7, Sun 7–1, 4–7.30 💶 Free 🚍 H, 23, 280, 630, 780; tram 8

The church of San Francesco a Ripa, founded in the 13th century but made thoroughly baroque 400 years later, is in the heart of Trastevere. Its two treasures are the monastic cell where St. Francis of Assisi lived when he was in Rome and a dramatic statue by Gian Lorenzo Bernini, one of his last works.

To see Bernini's masterpiece, the *Blessed Ludovica Albertoni*, go down the left aisle to the Albertoni chapel. Bernini captures perfectly Ludovica's transformation from her final agony to the ecstasy of her union with God. The paintings of St. Anne and the Virgin Mary, behind the statue, are by Baciccio.

St. Francis' cell is reached from the sacristy. It contains the saint's marble pillow and a walnut baldachin. In the convent garden is a bitter orange tree, supposedly planted by St. Francis.

SAN GIOVANNI IN LATERANO

See pages 134–135.

SANTI GIOVANNI E PAOLO

🔢 58 G6 • Piazza Santi Giovanni e Paolo 13, 00184 ☎ 06 700 5745 🕐 8.30–noon, 3.30–6.30 💶 Free 🚇 Circo Massimo 🚍 81, 117, 118, 628, 673

This church is one of the oldest Christian places of worship. It was built over a Roman house, traditionally that of two Christian martyrs, John and Paul, former soldiers who died during the reign of Julian the Apostate (AD361–363) when they rejected pagan practices. The church is

opposite Villa Celimontana and contains magnificent paintings that once embellished the Roman house beneath.

The original church was built in the fourth century by a private citizen named Pammachius. It was rebuilt by Pope Paschal II, who added a campanile and porch in the 12th century. The five arches above the remarkable porch, and the gallery, belong to the original building.

The interior mostly dates from the 18th century. Entrance to the house of John and Paul is down the steps at the end of the aisle. There are several rooms to see, some decorated with wall paintings, most notably a beautiful third-century marine fresco in the underground nymphaeum.

The apse of the church is decorated with a frieze by Pomarancio and fourth-century frescoes of the martyrdom of John and Paul.

SAN GREGORIO MAGNO

🔢 58 F7 • Piazza di San Gregorio 00184 ☎ 06 5526 1617 🕐 Daily 7–7.30 💶 Free 🚇 Circo Massimo 🚍 81, 117, 118, 628, 673

Not far from the Colosseo is the majestic church of San Gregorio Magno, set on the beautiful, quiet Caelian Hill and surrounded by tranquil gardens.

The church stands on the site of St. Andrew's monastery, founded by St. Gregory in AD575. It was restored in 1633 for Cardinal Scipione Borghese—the eagle and dragon of his coat of arms can be seen above the lower arches. A spectacular staircase and broad portico take you inside, where there are three chapels built in the early 17th century by Cardinal Cesare Baronio. In St. Barbara's chapel is a marble table supposedly used by St. Gregory to feed the poor. St. Sylvia's chapel,

dedicated to Gregory's mother, has a wonderful fresco by Guido Reni in the apse showing a concert of angels. The chapel of St. Andrew has frescoes of the *Flagellation of St. Andrew* by Domenichino and *St. Andrew's Matryrdom* also by Reni.

In the chapel at the end of the right aisle is the altar of St. Gregory the Great, decorated with bas-reliefs illustrating the saint's life. To the right, in the cell of St. Gregory, are the relics of the saint, his marble throne and the stone he used as a pillow.

SANT'IGNAZIO DI LOYOLA

🔢 57 E5 • Piazza di Sant'Ignazio 8, 00186 ☎ 06 679 4406 🕐 Daily 7.30–12.30, 3–7.30. Closed to visitors during Sun morning Mass 💶 Free 🚍 116 to Via del Seminario; 30, 40, 46, 62, 63, 64, 70, 81, 492, 628, 630, 780, 787, 916 to Largo di Torre Argentina

St. Ignatius of Loyola, founder of the Jesuit order and of the nearby Roman College, is the dedicatee of this lavishly decorated church, designed by the Jesuit architect Orazio Grassi.

The church was completed in 1685 without a cupola, but another Jesuit, the painter Andrea Pozzo, remedied this by painting a remarkable *trompe l'oeil* dome above the crossing, imitating the lighting and depth of a cupola. Pozzo's work dominates the interior. The corners of the crossing glorify the Jesuits' missionary activities, with paintings showing the Glory of St. Ignatius in each of the four known continents. In the middle of the nave Pozzo used the same technique to give a three-dimensional effect to the figures in the fresco of St. Ignatius bathed in divine light. Stand on the disc in the centre of the nave and then move towards the transept to get the best view.

THE SIGHTS

The basilica of San Marco was named after both St. Mark the Evangelist and Pope Mark

Over 122 marble steps lead to the austere façade of Santa Maria in Aracoeli

SANT'IVO ALLA SAPIENZA

➕ 57 E5 • Corso del Rinascimento 40, 00186 ☎ 06 686 4987 🕐 Mon–Fri 8.30–2.30, Sat 10–1, Sun 9–12 🎫 Free 🚌 23, 30, 40, 46, 62, 64, 70, 81, 87, 116, 280, 492, 628, 916; tram 8

The domed church of Sant'Ivo alla Sapienza is one of Francesco Borromini's masterpieces. Built in the grounds of the Palazzo alla Sapienza (Palace of Wisdom), which was the University of Rome until 1935, this church is worth visiting for its extraordinary spiral dome surmounted by a crown of flames. It is dedicated to St. Ives, patron saint of lawyers, who gave his services free to the poor.

The façade is baroque, and has two rows of arches running along the side walls. The unusual hexagonal plan suggests a honeycomb, an allusion to the Barberini bee emblem (Barberini Pope Urban VIII gave Borromini the commission).

The culmination is the extravagant dome with its spiral crown, possibly inspired by the architect's collection of shells.

SAN LUIGI DEI FRANCESI

➕ 57 E4 • Piazza San Luigi dei Francesi 00186 ☎ 06 688 271 🕐 Fri–Wed 8–12.30, 3.30–7, Thu 8–12.30 🎫 Free 🚌 23, 30, 40, 46, 62, 64, 70, 81, 87, 116, 280, 492, 628, 916; tram 8

San Luigi dei Francesi, the national church of the French in Rome, is essential viewing for lovers of Caravaggio's work—it contains no less than three canvases by him.

The church was begun in 1518 by Cardinal Giulio de' Medici, the future Pope Clement VII, and was finally completed in 1589 by Domenico Fontana, with money from France provided by Henri II, Henri III and Catherine de Médicis. On the broad travertine façade, by Giacomo della Porta,

is the salamander emblem of François I of France. The French theme continues with statues of Charlemagne and St. Louis in the lower part of the façade, and St. Clotilde and St. Joan of Valois in the upper part.

The church received much embellishment in the baroque period, with marble, paintings, gilding and stucco. Restoration work is currently under way.

There are frescoes by Domenichino in the chapel of St. Cecilia, but the church's main draw—the Caravaggio paintings—are in St. Matthew's chapel. They are dramatic depictions of three episodes from the saint's life: *St. Matthew and the Angel*, *The Calling of St. Matthew* and *The Martyrdom of St. Matthew*.

SAN MARCO

➕ 57 E5 • Piazza di San Marco 00186 ☎ 06 679 5205 🕐 Daily 7.30–7.30 🎫 Free 🚇 Colosseo 🚌 44, 46, 84, 715, 716, 780, 781, 810, 916

San Marco is well worth visiting for its ninth-century mosaic. It was founded by Pope Mark in AD336, and is dedicated to St. Mark the Evangelist, who is believed to have written his gospel in Rome.

Pope Gregory IV rebuilt the church in the ninth century, and the crypt, which contains the relics of the Persian saints Abdon and Senna, dates from the same period. Inside the porch, look for the 16th-century funerary plaque of Vanozza Catanei, who was the mistress of Pope Alexander VI and mother of Cesare and Lucrezia Borgia. The elegant Renaissance façade, with its double row of arches, is attributed to Leon Battista Alberti, who reused materials from the Colosseo and the Theatre of Marcellus.

The interior of the church is a mixture of styles. In the 15th century, a coffered ceiling showing

the coat of arms of Pope Paul II was added, and there were baroque additions in the 18th century. The real gem is the gorgeous ninth-century mosaic in the apse, which shows Christ as the central figure, his hand raised in blessing, surrounded by saints. Pope Mark (or St. Gregory) holds a model of the church.

SANTA MARIA IN ARACOELI

➕ 57 F5 • Piazza d'Aracoeli 00186 ☎ 06 679 8155 🕐 May–end Sep daily 9–12.30, 2.30–6.30; Oct–end Apr 9–12.30, 2.30–5.20 🎫 Free 🚇 Colosseo 🚌 44, 46, 84, 715, 716, 780, 781, 810, 916

There has been a church on this site since at least the sixth century, and in the eighth century it was part of a monastery. However, much of what you see today dates from the end of the 13th century.

Inside, the badly worn tomb of Archdeacon Giovanni Crivelli, carved by the Florentine sculptor Donatello in 1432, stands to the right of the entrance. Another tomb (1465), that of Cardinal d'Albret, is one of Andrea Bregno's best works. The decorative frescoes in the chapel of St. Bernardino of Siena are by Pinturicchio and depict the life and death of the saint. The left transept leads to a little chapel dedicated to the Santo Bambino (Holy Child). The jewelled wooden statue of the Christ Child is a modern replica of the 15th-century original—said to have been carved out of olive wood from the Garden of Gethsemane—which was stolen in the 1990s.

From the top of the Scalinata d'Aracoeli on the Capitolino (▷ 72) there is a great view of the city. Allow time to take this in before passing behind the austere brick façade.

THE SIGHTS

San Giovanni in Laterano

The cathedral of the city of Rome.
Grandiose basilica rich in interior decoration.
Site of the Scala Santa (Holy Staircase), one of Catholicism's most sacred relics.

Vast size is a visitor's first impression of the interior of San Giovanni

SEEING SAN GIOVANNI IN LATERANO

This solemn, peaceful basilica is best approached from the splendid piazza, named—like San Giovanni itself—after the Laterani family, who once owned this land. Inside, take time to appreciate the overall scale before focusing on the individual treasures. The baptistery is near the exit on the left and you can access the cloister from the left aisle. The Scala Santa entrance is outside.

RATINGS

Historic interest	● ● ●
Value for money	● ● ● ● ●
Specialist shopping	● ●

BASICS

➕ 58 H6 • Piazza di San Giovanni in Laterano 4, 00185
☎ 06 6988 6433, group tours only. Vatican History Museum: 06 6988 6376
◉ Basilica: daily 7–7. Cloister: daily 9–6. Baptistery: daily 7–12.30, 4–7.30. Scala Santa: daily 9–12, 3–6. Cappella Santa Santorum: only open by appointment with custodian, tel 06 772 6641, €3.50. Vatican History Museum: 9–12
🎫 Basilica, Scala Santa and baptistery: free. Cloister: €2. Cappella Santa Santorum: €3.50. Vatican History Museum: €4
🚇 San Giovanni
🚌 16, 85, 87, 117, 186, 218, 650, 850
☎ Guided tours for groups only: 9–15 people, €5.50 per person; 16 or more, €3 per person. Tel 320 096 0993, email materetcaput@yahoo.it. Audiotours: basilica and cloister €5.50 all languages
📖 Guidebook in English €3.30
🎁 Souvenir shop inside the basilica (open 9–6)
🚻 Inside complex

HIGHLIGHTS

EXTERIOR
The severe baroque east façade built by Alessandro Galilei in 1735 supports a balustrade with 15 gigantic statues representing Christ, the two St. Johns, and the Doctors of the Church. The portico in front of the church, inspired by that of St. Peter's (▷ 66–71), has antique bronze doors from the Senate House in the Foro Romano (▷ 84–89) and a huge statue of Constantine, discovered in the Baths of Constantine on the Quirinale. The last door on the right is the Holy Door, opened most recently in 2000 by Pope John Paul II to mark the start of a Holy Year, a once-every-25-years occurrence.

THE NAVE
The present interior of the church was commissioned by Pope Innocent X in 1646 and is mainly the work of Francesco Borromini. He's responsible for the nave and four aisles, while the ornate ceiling is probably by Piero Ligorio. Statues of the 12 Apostles flank the nave, each in its own separate niche and surmounted by bas-reliefs depicting stories from the Bible. On the left-hand pillar in the right aisle, its fragility protected by glass, is a restored fragment of a Giotto fresco of Boniface VIII declaring the Holy Year of 1300, while the Corsini Chapel, designed by Alessandro Galilei, is on the left.

THE TRANSEPT AND APSE
In contrast to the nave, the transept, a fine example of Mannerist decoration, is elaborately detailed in style. Nebbia, Pomarancio and Cavaliere d'Arpino were responsible for the frescoes; the ornate ceiling, showing Clement VIII's coat of arms, is by Taddeo Landini.
   The apse mosaic is a 19th-century restoration of Jacopo Torriti's 13th-century masterpiece. Torriti added figures of the Virgin, Pope Nicholas IV and major saints. The small figure of St. Francis on the left was probably included because Torriti was a Franciscan monk.

THE PAPAL ALTAR
At the heart of the basilica is the Papal Altar, at which only the pope may officiate; it contains a wooden table said to have been used by St. Peter, although it probably dates from the fourth century. Above rises a fine 14th-century Gothic canopy, made of precious marble and

decorated with mosaics. Here, too, are copies of the 15th-century reliquaries containing the relics of St. Peter and St. Paul, housed in a tabernacle frescoed with the Good Shepherd, the Crucifixion, the Virgin and various saints. Beneath the altar of the Confessio (the crypt below the Papal Altar) is the tomb slab of Pope Martin V (died 1431).

THE CLOISTERS

The exquisite cloisters, built between 1215 and 1232, are the work of Jacopo and Pietro Vassalletto, two of the most famous artists of the cosmatesque style of mosaic. The sparkling, multihued twisted and plain columns have splendid capitals, and the marble mosaic frieze is decorated with bizarre birds and beasts; stand by the ninth-century well in the middle of the garden for the best view. Fragments of the medieval basilica are displayed around the cloister walls.

The statues on top of the entrance façade can be seen from afar (far left)

The 13th-century cloisters with close-up of a pillar (middle left)

One of the majestic statues inside the church (left)

THE BAPTISTERY

The octagonal baptistery, originally built during the reign of Constantine, has four chapels containing early mosaics. The green basalt urn in the middle is the baptismal font.

THE SCALA SANTA

The Scala Santa (Holy Staircase) is supposedly from the house of Pontius Pilate in Jerusalem, ascended by Christ before his Crucifixion. The 28 marble steps—which believers climb on their knees to earn an indulgence— have covers to protect stains said to be traces of Christ's blood. The staircase leads to the Santa Santorum, once the pope's private chapel and adorned with fine mosaics.

The octagonal baptistery of St. John behind the church dates from the fifth century, though it has been much restored (above)

BACKGROUND

Originally dedicated to Christ the Saviour, and only later to St. John the Evangelist and St. John the Baptist, San Giovanni in Laterano dates from the fourth century. Following his victory over Maxentius in AD312 and the establishment of Christianity as the imperial religion, Constantine built a basilica here on the site of his rival's imperial guard's barracks. This early church represented the victory of Christianity over paganism, and was designated Mother and Head of all churches of the city and the world. In AD314 Pope Sylvester I took up residence in the group of Lateran buildings, which included a palace, a basilica and a baptistery. This became the official papal residence until the popes moved to Avignon in France in the 14th century. After various repairs and rebuildings over the centuries, the church was radically restored in the baroque style in the 17th and 18th centuries.

TIPS

● Be sure to arrive by 11am to see the Scala Santa before the crowds arrive.
● If you visit in the morning, take time to check out Via Sannio, scene of one of Rome's best-known markets (▷ 174).

The Capuchin monks' crypt in Santa Maria della Concezione

Santa Maria in Cosmedin has beautiful cosmatesque floors

The Assumption of the Virgin, in Santa Maria del Popolo

SANTA MARIA DELLA CONCEZIONE

🔲 57 F4 ✉ Via Vittorio Veneto 27, 00187 ☎ 06 487 1185 🕐 Fri–Wed 9–12, 3–6 🎟 Free (donation for cemetery) 🚇 Barberini 🚌 52, 53, 63, 80, 95, 116, 119 **www.cappucciniviaveneto.it**

The original setting of this majestic structure, the church of a Capuchin convent, has been spoiled by the construction of Via Veneto, but even so it attracts many visitors. The church's rather austere exterior gives no clue to the extraordinary sight it contains within—its macabre Capuchin cemetery.

The church was built around 1626, commissioned by Cardinal Antonio Barberini (brother of Pope Urban VIII). His tombstone is on the floor in front of the main altar, with the inscription: *'Hic jacet pulvis, cinis et nihil'* ('Here lie dust, ashes and nothing more').

On the right-hand side of the front steps is the entrance to the cemetery in the crypt. Here, the walls and ceilings of five chapels are decorated with the skeletons (some of them clothed) and loose bones of about 4,000 Capuchin monks who died between 1528 and 1870. The floor is scattered with earth brought from the holy sites in Palestine.

SANTA MARIA IN COSMEDIN

🔲 57 E6 • Via Bocca della Verità 00184 ☎ 06 678 1419 🕐 May–end Oct 9–6.30; Nov–end Apr 9–5 🎟 Free 🚇 Circo Massimo 🚌 81, 160, 628, 715

The church of Santa Maria in Cosmedin is best known for the Bocca della Verità (Mouth of Truth) and its associated super-stition, rather than for anything inside. But venture in and you will find a rare Roman medieval church that has been stripped of its later baroque additions.

There were Classical temples on the site of the present church, and in the sixth century a deaconry was established here to provide aid for the poor. The church that existed by the eighth century was given to Greek refugees from Byzantium, which was when the word Cosmedin (from the Greek for 'decorated') became part of its name. The church retains its Greek connec-tions; a Greek Orthodox Mass is celebrated here every week.

Inside the church, the 12th-century cosmatesque floors are particularly good, and the frescoes in the apse and the mosaic fragment in the sacristy are well worth a look. The Corinthian columns probably came from the preceding pagan temple.

The Bocca della Verità is a large stone disk carved with the face of a man, found just inside the church porch. According to medieval tradition, a liar risks having his hand bitten off if he dares to put it in the mouth of the image. In fact, the stone was probably nothing more sinister than a Roman drain cover, but it's a popular myth.

SANTA MARIA IN DOMNICA

🔲 58 G7 • Via della Navicella 10, 00184 ☎ 06 700 1519 🕐 9–12, 3.30–6 🎟 Free 🚇 Circo Massimo 🚌 81, 117, 673

The setting of the church of Santa Maria in Domnica, near Villa Celimontana, makes it a popular choice for weddings. It is also known as Santa Maria della Navicella ('little boat'), after the 16th-century fountain incorporating a Roman stone boat in front of the stylish church porch.

Santa Maria in Domnica was built in the ninth century by Pope Paschal I on the site of an earlier house of worship called a *dominicum*. Pope Leo X restored the church in the 16th century, and you can see his emblem—the lion—on the keystones.

The interior of the church remains much as it was in the ninth century, with a nave and two aisles separated by ancient columns of grey granite. Beautiful Byzantine mosaics decorate the triumphal arch and apse. The artist has represented the reli-gious scenes with great realism, giving the impression that there is a breeze stirring the angels' clothes. A mosaic at the middle of the vault shows Pope Paschal kneeling before the Virgin; note the square halo, known as a nimbus, indicating that the Pope was still alive at the time.

SANTA MARIA MAGGIORE

See pages 138–139.

SANTA MARIA SOPRA MINERVA

See page 140.

SANTA MARIA DEL POPOLO

🔲 57 E3 • Piazza del Popolo 12, 00186 ☎ 06 361 0836 🕐 Mon–Sat 7–12, 4–7, Sun 8–1.30, 4.30–7.30 🎟 Free 🚇 Flaminio or Spagna 🚌 117, 119, 628, 926 🎧 Audioguide €1 in Italian, English, German, French and Spanish

The church of Santa Maria del Popolo is a must for art lovers, with works by some of the great names from the 16th and 17th centuries, including Raphael, Caravaggio and Bernini.

According to legend, Nero's tomb once stood under a walnut tree on the site of this church, and the notorious emperor's ghost used to haunt the place. Pope Paschal II had the tree cut down and built a small chapel in its place. The name, St. Mary of

Bernini's *Ecstasy of St. Teresa of Avila, in the Cornaro Chapel of Santa Maria della Vittoria*

Michelangleo's *imposing statue of Moses, San Pietro in Vincoli*

the People, recalls the fact that the Pope asked the people of Rome to pay for the building of the chapel. In 1472, Sixtus IV commissioned the present church to be built by Andrea Bregno. It was later reworked in the baroque style, largely by Gian Lorenzo Bernini.

The sumptuously decorated Chigi Chapel in the left aisle was designed by Raphael for the banker Agostino Chigi, its plain exterior a sharp contrast to the rich interior; Bernini completed the chapel after Raphael's death. The bright red travertine marble Cerasi Chapel, at the end of the same aisle, contains two of Caravaggio's masterpieces: *The Conversion of St. Paul* and *The Crucifixion of St. Peter*.

SANTA MARIA IN TRASTEVERE

See page 141.

SANTA MARIA DELLA VITTORIA

✚ 58 G4 • Largo di Santa Susanna 17, 00184 ☎ 06 4274 0571 🕐 Daily 8.30–12, 3.30–7 🎟 Free 🚇 Repubblica or Barberini 🚌 60, 61, 62, 84, 90, 175, 492

This church is a monument to the baroque style in all its richness, beauty and harmony. Among its treasures is Bernini's superb *Ecstasy of St. Teresa of Avila*.

Cardinal Scipione Borghese commissioned the church to celebrate the victory of the Catholics over the Protestants at the Battle of the White Mountain near Prague in 1620, which was attributed to the chaplain taking an image of the Virgin Mary into battle. The St. Mary of Victory over the altar is a copy of the one that survived the battle—the original was destroyed by fire in 1833.

The vault is painted with *trompe l'oeil* frescoes of the *Triumph of the Virgin Mary over*

Heresies by Andrea and Giuseppe Orazi; Perugino frescoed the ceiling. On the altar is *The Most Holy Trinity* by Giovanni Francesco Barbieri (known as Il Guercino), while in the Chapel of St. Francis of Assisi is *The Virgin Offering the Child to St. Francis* by Domenichino.

The star attraction, however, is Bernini's Cornaro Chapel, the last chapel on the left-hand side. Designed in 1646 for Cardinal Cornaro of Venice, it has carvings of members of his family in side balconies, like a theatre audience, gazing at St. Teresa in her ecstasy. Bernini captures the moment that St. Teresa is pierced by a golden arrow, an experience she described in her autobiography.

SAN PIETRO IN MONTORIO AND TEMPIETTO DEL BRAMANTE

✚ 56 D6 • Piazza di San Pietro in Montorio 00153 ☎ 06 581 3940 🕐 7.30–12, 4–6. Tempietto: Nov–end Apr Tue–Sun 9.30–12.30, 2–4; May–end Oct 9.30–12.30, 4–6 🎟 Free 🚌 870

In a quiet, picturesque corner on the Janiculum Hill stands the church of San Pietro in Montorio, with a splendid view over the city of Rome. It is best known for the tiny circular building by Donato Bramante in the adjoining cloister, the much admired Tempietto.

Although there may have been an earlier church on this site, the present building dates back only to the end of the 15th century, when the Catholic Monarchs of Spain, Ferdinand and Isabella, commissioned Baccio Pontelli to build it. It was dedicated to St. Peter, who, it was believed, was crucified here.

The church is essentially Renaissance, but has a remarkable Gothic rose window in the façade. The Peruzzi

Chapel, the second on the left, was designed by Bernini.

In the middle of the cloister adjoining the church, on what was once thought to be the exact spot of St. Peter's crucifixion, stands one of Rome's most attractive Renaissance buildings. Bramante designed the beautiful Tempietto in around 1500. Its style and perfect proportions hark back to Classical temples such as the Temple of Vesta at Tivoli.

SAN PIETRO IN VINCOLI

✚ 58 G5 • Piazza San Pietro in Vincoli 4, 00184 ☎ 06 488 2865 🕐 Aug and Sep daily 7–12.30, 1.30–7; Oct–end Feb 7.30–12.30, 3.30–6; Mar–end Jul 7–12.30, 3.30–7. Closed to visitors during Mass (Sun at 11) 🎟 Free 🚇 Colosseo 🚌 60, 75, 84, 85, 87, 117, 175, 810, 850 🎧 Audioguide €1 in English, French, German, Spanish and Italian

The name of this church, St. Peter in Chains, gives a clue to one of its treasures: the chains that bound St. Peter in prison, which can be seen in a gilt bronze urn under the high altar.

The ceiling of the church is decorated with a fresco showing the miracle of the chains. According to the legend, two sets of chains that were used to bind St. Peter—in Jerusalem and in the Mamertine prison in Rome—miraculously fused together when placed side by side.

The church's main attraction, however, is Michelangelo's tremendous statue of Moses, which was one of the 40 figures that were intended to adorn the mausoleum of Pope Julius II in St. Peter's basilica. The original project was abandoned after Julius' death. The huge seated figure of Moses is sculpted from Carrara marble, and the figures in the niches are Jacob's wives, Leah and Rachel.

Santa Maria Maggiore

One of the four Roman basilicas that belong to the Vatican, and the only surviving example of the four to retain its Classical interior. Contains the city's highest bell tower.

Restoration hides a much earlier church (above and right)

RATINGS	
Historic interest	●●●○
Photo stops	●●●○
Value for money	●●●○

BASICS

✚ 58 G5 • Piazza Santa Maria Maggiore 00184 ☎ 06 483195
◉ Basilica: daily 7–7. Cappella Sforza: Mon–Fri 9–5. Museum: daily 9.30–6.30. Sacristy: daily 7–12.30, 3–6.30
▨ Basilica and Cappella Sforza: free. Museum: Adult €4, child (under 18) €2
◉ Cavour, Termini or Vittorio Emanuele
▣ 16, 71, 70, 75, 105, 204, 360, 590, 649, 714
▰ Guided tours of Loggia delle Benedizioni (€2.60) and Presepe di Arnolfo di Cambio (€1.50): Mon–Sat 9.30–1, 4–6 (loggia afternoons only). Ask in the museum. Audiotours: €4. For guided tours contact Patrizia Riccitelli (tel 06 483058 or www.prtour.it)
▤ €2.80 in English, Italian, German, Spanish.
▦ Bookshop inside basilica
👫

SEEING SANTA MARIA MAGGIORE

Spend a moment admiring the 18th-century façade of the basilica, with Rome's tallest campanile rising behind. You may then want to visit the Museum of the Patriarcale Basilica di Santa Maria Maggiore, next to the basilica. If timings are right, visit the Loggia delle Benedizione for the view over the piazza and the 13th-century mosaics by Filippo Rusuti. Pass through the portico, with a bronze statue of Philip IV and the great Holy Door, and, once inside, spend a few moments absorbing everything before you start your tour.

HIGHLIGHTS

THE NAVE AND AISLES CHANCEL

The interior of this immense church is dominated by the long nave, flanked with 40 ancient Roman columns. Above, 36 fifth-century mosaic panels tell Old Testament stories; they're high and hard to see, but perseverance pays off. Higher still, the superb Renaissance coffered ceiling is said to be decorated with the first gold to have been brought from the New World, a gift from Ferdinand and Isabella of Spain. The coats of arms are those of popes Calixtus III and Alexander V. Beneath your feet stretches a beautiful cosmatesque marble pavement, dating from the 12th century.

THE CHANCEL AND APSE

The fifth-century Byzantine-style mosaics glitter from the triumphal arch, whose four sections depict the Annunciation, the Epiphany and other scenes from the early life of Christ. The apse mosaic is later, created in 1295 by Jacopo Torriti; it shows the Coronation of the Virgin, attended by Pope Nicholas IV and Cardinal Iacopo Colonna.

The baldachino, made up of porphyry columns with bronze foliage, is by Ferdinando Fuga. It stands above the *confessio*, the most sacred spot in the basilica, which contains a silver urn by Giuseppe Valadier supposedly containing fragments of the Christ child's wooden crib.

THE CHAPELS

The Cappella Sistina, to the right of the nave, was commissioned by Pope Sixtus V and built by Domenico Fontana (1585) on a Greek-cross plan, reusing marble from a Classical Roman building. The vast chapel, with its dome, frescoes, marbles and monumental tombs, is as large as many churches. Beneath it are the remnants of the Presepio, with exquisite Nativity-scene figures by the sculptor Arnolfo di Cambio that once accompanied the holy crib (see above).

The Cappella Paolina, just off the north aisle, mirrors the Sistine Chapel, and is perhaps even more beautiful, with mosaics by Cavaliere d'Arpino, frescoes by Guido Reni and an incredibly sumptuous bejewelled altar. It is also known as the Borghese Chapel after the family name of the commissioning Pope Paul V. Nearby, off the left aisle, the Cappella Sforza was probably built by Giacomo della Porta from drawings by Michelangelo.

On the right wall at the end of the nave is the magnificent inlaid marble tomb of Cardinal Consalvo Rodriguez (died 1299), a contrast to the simple, humble tomb of the Bernini family nearby.

THE BAPTISTERY

The baptistery is baroque, the work of Flaminio Ponzio. The porphyry font was decorated by Giuseppe Valadier; the high-relief *Assumption* on the altar is by Pietro Bernini, father of the famous Gian Lorenzo.

BACKGROUND

Legend, sadly now disproved, associates the founding of the original church with Pope Liberius in the fourth century. He dreamed the Virgin instructed him to build it wherever snow fell that night—5 August, the height of summer. In the morning, snow dusted the Equiline Hill, and so here the church was built. The present church was built by Sixtus III in AD432–440. Considerable changes were made in the 12th and 13th centuries, and the chapels were added in the 16th century. The present façade, with its triple-arched loggia, was designed around the original mosaics by Ferdinando Fuga in 1746.

TIPS
● If you want to see everything properly, call in advance to book a guided tour.
● The area near the basilica, around Termini station, is not one of the safest; watch your belongings.
● Bring binoculars if you're really interested in seeing the mosaics.

Ferdinando Fuga's 18th-century façade

THE SIGHTS

THE SIGHTS

SANTA MARIA SOPRA MINERVA

A touch of Gothic amid Rome's prevailing Renaissance and baroque.

Behind its Renaissance façade, Santa Maria sopra Minerva is a rarity in being Rome's only Gothic church (although much restored in the 19th century). Some of the most prominent Italian families called upon the celebrated artists of their time to embellish their chapels, so there is plenty inside to interest art lovers.

THE TEMPLE OF MINERVA

The first church was built in the eighth or ninth century on top of (sopra) a temple of the pagan goddess Minerva. In 1280, two Dominican friars, Sisto and Ristoro, began reconstructing the church in Gothic style, apparently on the model of Santa Maria Novella in Florence, of which they were also the architects. In the 16th and 17th centuries, the interior was redecorated in baroque style, and in the 1840s, restorers indulged their taste for the Gothic style.

THE CHURCH'S INTERIOR

The interior, divided into a nave and two aisles, has chapels on either side. In the right transept is the splendid Capella Carafa, built and decorated by order of Cardinal Carafa in honour of the philosopher-saint Thomas Aquinas (1224–74). Filippino Lippi frescoed the walls of this chapel in the 1480s with scenes from the life of St. Thomas Aquinas and a beautiful *Assumption of the Virgin*. The tomb of Pope Paul IV (died 1559) is also here.

Near the high altar in the choir is a statue of the *Risen Christ with the Cross* by Michelangelo. The remains of St. Catherine of Siena, one of the patron saints of Italy, lie under the altar. In the apse are the tombs of the Medici popes Leo X and Clement VII, the work of Antonio Sangallo the Younger.

BERNINI'S ELEPHANT

Outside, in Piazza della Minerva, is one of Rome's best-loved oddities: a sixth-century BC Egyptian obelisk on the back of a marble elephant. The work was designed by Bernini and sculpted by his pupil Ercole Ferrata in 1667. The inscription on the base, by Pope Alexander VII, reads: 'A strong mind is necessary to support solid wisdom'—meaning that the obelisk represents the wisdom that grows from, and is supported by, the strong mind of the elephant.

The tomb of St. Catherine of Siena lies under the main altar (above)

The soaring Gothic arches and gilded interior (right)

The apse mosaics are one of the highlights of this medieval church

SANTA MARIA IN TRASTEVERE

A rare medieval church.

On the right bank of the Tiber lies the picturesque quarter of Trastevere (▷ 144–145), at the heart of which is the first church to be dedicated to the veneration of the Virgin Mary, Santa Maria in Trastevere. One of the finest medieval churches in Rome, Santa Maria in Trastevere remains a local church, attended by the inhabitants of the quarter.

BUILDING THE CHURCH
Legend has it that in 38BC (or alternatively on the day of Jesus' birth) a fountain of oil suddenly started flowing to announce the coming of God's son. Pope Calixtus (AD217–222) built a sanctuary on this spot, called the Taberna Meritoria, to commemorate the miracle and encourage the worship of the Virgin Mary. The present basilica was built in the 12th century during the pontificate of Innocent II, using material from the Baths of Caracalla.

THE APSE MOSAICS
The mosaics in the apse, which date from the 12th century, illustrate St. Calixtus and Pope Innocent II offering his church to Mary. The Virgin, adorned with gold, is shown in the Byzantine style with a certain oriental rigidity. At the top of the mosaic is *Paradise,* showing the hand of God crowning Jesus. The city of Jerusalem and town of Bethlehem are shown, and the lambs represent the 12 Apostles.

Another set of mosaics between the windows, a masterpiece by Pietro Cavallini, represents scenes from the life of the Virgin, including her birth, the Annunciation, the Nativity, the Epiphany, the Presentation in the Temple and the Dormition. The medallion above the throne shows the Virgin and Child between saints Peter and Paul, along with Cardinal Bertoldo Stefaneschi, who commissioned the work in 1290.

THE ALTEMPS CHAPEL
The Altemps Chapel contains the sixth-century Byzantine painting of *Our Lady of Mercy,* one of the oldest images of the Virgin in existence. The late 16th-century mosaics in this chapel demonstrate the re-emerging interest in religious art during the Counter-Reformation. To the left of the nave is the Avila Chapel, with a cupola by Antonio Gherardi decorated in a baroque *trompe l'oeil* effect.

EXTERIOR
The 12th-century bell tower has a 17th-century mosaic of the *Virgin and Child,* while on the façade there is a beautiful 12th- to 13th-century mosaic showing the Virgin Mary enthroned, with processions of women approaching from both sides. The statues of saints above the porch on the balustrade in front of the façade have stood there since the 17th century.

RATINGS				
Good for kids	●	●		
Historic interest	●	●	●	
Value for money	●	●	●	●	●

BASICS
✚ 57 D6 • Piazza di Santa Maria in Trastevere 00153 ☎ 06 589 7332
🕔 Daily 7.30–9
🚌 H, 23, 280, 630, 780
📖 *Pilgrims in the Heart of Rome: a Journey to Trastevere,* published by the nearby Community of Sant'Egidio, €12.91 🏪 Small bookshop selling general guides (open 9–5)

Twenty-two columns from ancient monuments divide the nave from the aisles

TIP
● Visit in the evening, then have a drink in one of the outdoor cafés, from where you can appreciate the beautifully lit piazza and basilica.

The mosaic of Christ surrounded by angels in Santa Prassede

The fourth-century Santa Pudenziana

Santa Sabina is lit by ninth-century windows, glazed with the mineral selenite

SANTA PRASSEDE

➕ 58 G5 • Via di Santa Prassede 9/A, 00184 ☎ 06 488 2456 ⦿ Daily 7.30–12, 3–6.30. Closed Aug 👣 Free ⦿ Cavour, Termini or Vittorio Emanuele 🚌 16, 70, 71, 360, 649

An unimposing entrance through an arch supported by pillars leads into the atrium of the church of St. Prassede, worth visiting for its bright Byzantine mosaics, notably those in the Capella di San Zeno, the most important examples in Rome.

A house of worship has stood on this spot since AD489. The present building, with its brick façade, was built in AD822 by Pope Paschal I, who enlarged it to store relics of martyrs from the catacombs. It has been rebuilt and restored many times since.

In the right aisle is the tomb of Bishop Giovanni Battista Santoni, the first work by Gian Lorenzo Bernini. Remarkable ninth-century mosaics embellish the apse and the triumphal arch. The coffered ceiling is a relatively recent 19th-century addition.

The Chapel of St Zeno in the right aisle contains beautiful mosaics depicting Christ, saints and the Virgin Mary, all on a brilliant gold background. It also has an excellent ornamental pavement in polychrome marble. In a room to the right of the entrance is a fragment of a column brought from Jerusalem in 1223; according to tradition, it is where Jesus was scourged.

SANTA PUDENZIANA

➕ 58 G5 • Via Urbana 60, 00184 ☎ 06 481 4622 ⦿ Daily 7–12.30, 3.30–7. Closed to visitors during Mass 👣 Free ⦿ Cavour, Termini or Vittorio Emanuele 🚌 16, 70, 71, 360, 649

This church is said to be on the site of the house of Senator Pudens, father of saints Prassede and Pudenziana, who welcomed St. Peter as a guest. The building was transformed into a church in the late fourth century, making it one of the oldest sites of Christian worship in Rome.

The bell tower dates from the 12th century, as does the elegant door with its fluted columns. The dome was added in the 16th century and the façade was restored in 1870.

The interior of the church was transformed into one nave in 1588 by Francesco da Volterra. He also designed the dome, which was frescoed by Nicolò Circignani.

The apse mosaic, which probably dates from the papacy of Innocent I in the fifth century, portrays Christ sitting on a throne surrounded by the Apostles and two female figures, who may be Pudenziana and Prassede, or may represent the Church of the Jews and the Church of the Gentiles.

SANTI QUATTRO CORONATI

➕ 58 G6 • Via dei Santi Quattro Coronati 00184 ☎ 06 7047 5427 ⦿ Basilica: Mon–Sat 6.15–8, Sun 6.45–12.30, 3–7.30. Cappella di S. Silvestro: Mon–Sat 9.30–12, 4.30–6, Sun 9–10.40, 4–6. 👣 Free ⦿ San Giovanni 🚌 117, 186, 218, 650, 850

Like all the churches built on the Caelian Hill, Santi Quattro Coronati (Four Crowned Saints), at the end of a steep, quiet road, is a little gem.

This picturesque church and the adjoining convent are dedicated to four Christian Roman soldiers (or possibly sculptors), martyred because they refused to worship (or make a statue of) the Greek demigod of healing, Esculapio. An earlier church was completely demolished during the sack of Rome of 1084, and 20 years later a new, fortified church was built on the site by Pope Paschal II. This had a larger central nave and a spacious courtyard at the entrance; the aisles were pulled down to make way for the lovely cloister and a dining hall.

Above the entrance is a tower-like belfry. Inside, there is an unusual *matroneum*, or women's gallery. The large apse is beautifully decorated with baroque frescoes illustrating the lives of the Quattro Coronati. **Don't miss** The adjoining cloister and the crypt just below the altar are well worth a look.

SANTA SABINA

➕ 57 E7 • Via di Santa Sabina 2, 00158 ☎ 06 5794 0660. Ask sacristan to visit Pope Pius V's room and St. Dominic's cell ⦿ Daily 7–12.30, 3.30–7 👣 Free Medieval cloister: €1 ⦿ Circo Massimo 🚌 60, 73, 75, 118, 175, 715; tram 3 to Viale Aventino

The lovely basilica of Santa Sabina, on the Aventine Hill, has kept its original fifth-century early Christian plan almost intact. Next to the church is a beautiful medieval cloister where St. Dominic is said to have planted the first orange tree in Rome, the descendants of which still perfume the monks' garden.

A church dedicated to the martyred Roman matron St. Sabina has stood on this spot on the Aventine Hill since AD425. The basilica has seen many changes over the centuries: It was turned into a fortress in the 10th century, incongruously restored in the 16th century by Domenico Fontana, and restored again in the 19th century, when all its baroque elements were removed and the church was returned to its original plan.

At the entrance, behind a front portico, is one of the church's main treasures. The entrance doors are divided into wooden panels, many of them survivors from the fifth-century church, carved with scenes from the Old

THE SIGHTS

The simple exterior of Santo Stefano Rotondo

The ruins of the finest baths ever built in Rome—Terme di Caracalla

Terme di Diocleziano

and New Testaments. The Crucifixion can be seen high up on the left.

Inside, the church is well proportioned, with light entering through the beautiful ninth-century windows, now restored to their original brilliance.

SANTO STEFANO ROTONDO

⊞ 58 G7 • Via di Santo Stefano Rotondo 7, 00184 ☎ 06 7049 3717 ◷ 9–1, 3.30 6 ⍾ Free ⊜ Colosseo, San Giovanni 🚌 81, 117, 673, 714, 850

Santo Stefano, set in a beautiful private park on the Caelian Hill, is one of the oldest and largest round churches anywhere, and has plenty to interest lovers of both art and history.

The church was built in the late fifth century by Pope Simplicius and dedicated to St. Stephen, the first Christian martyr, whose relics are here, and later also to St. Stephen of Hungary. Long before that, there was a sanctuary to the pagan god Mithras on this site. A gold-covered head from a statue was found during excavations below the church.

The walls are frescoed with 34 scenes of Christian martyrs painted by Pomarancio and Antonio Tempesta in the 16th century. The harrowing scenes have inscriptions explaining the action and giving the names of the emperors who ordered the executions. They are not for the faint-hearted.

The church's mosaics and marble decorations, once the most opulent in Rome, date from AD523–530. One shows two fourth-century martyrs, Primus and Felician, with a jewelled cross. Their relics were brought here by Pope Theodore I in the seventh century.

There is ongoing restoration work to the floor, but the church can still be visited.

TERME DI CARACALLA

⊞ 311 G7 • Viale delle Terme di Caracalla 52, 00153 ☎ 06 575 8626 ◷ Tue–Sun 9 to 1 hour before sunset, Mon 9–2 ⍾ Adult €5, child (under 18) free. For joint tickets ▷ 287 ⊜ Circo Massimo 🚌 67, 90, 118, 160, 613, 714, 715 🖪 www.beniculturali.it

The Baths of Caracalla were the most luxurious of the imperial baths, and are among the most impressive, monumental complexes to have survived from ancient Rome. Designed not only for the care of the body but as a cultural and local meeting place, they also included flourishing gardens.

The baths were opened in AD217 under Emperor Caracalla, but were completed by his successors Elegabalus and Alexander Severus. They remained in use until the wars with the Goths, when soldiers destroyed part of the aqueducts supplying water to the baths in AD537 as part of their strategy to conquer Rome.

The complex included pools, rooms for cold, hot and warm baths, porticoes, gymnasiums, halls, fine statues, libraries and even a stadium. There was capacity for 600 people at a time to bathe here. All the rooms were finely decorated with alabaster and granite, with magnificent ceilings and wall mosaics, many of them still intact.

Recent excavations have uncovered an underground mithraeum, a temple dedicated to the cult of the pagan god Mithras (see Basilica di San Clemente, ▷ 130 131).

TERME DI DIOCLEZIANO

⊞ 58 G4 • Piazza dei Cinquecento 78, 00184 ☎ 06 4782 6152. Call centre 06 3996 7700 ◷ Museum: Tue–Sun 9–7.45. Octagonal Hall: closed for restoration ⍾ Museum: adult €5, child

(under 18) free. Audioguide €4 in English and Italian. For joint tickets ▷ 287 ⊜ Termini 🚌 H, 5, 14, 36, 38, 40, 64, 86, 90, 170, 175, 217, 310, 714

This grand baths complex was the largest to be built in Rome—it could accommodate 3,000 people. Today, it incorporates the church of Santa Maria degli Angeli and part of the Museo Nazionale Romano, and is the underlying structure of Piazza della Repubblica (▷ 119).

The Emperor Diocletian never came to Rome, but in AD298 he commissioned Maximian, who ruled the Western Empire under him, to build the most luxurious baths in the city. At the height of their popularity they included libraries, concert halls, gardens, galleries, and exercise rooms. Like the Terme di Caracalla, Diocletian's were abandoned in the sixth century when the aqueducts were destroyed.

In the 16th century, Pius IV commissioned Michelangelo, then aged 86, to convert the grand central hall of the baths into a church, Santa Maria degli Angeli. His adaptation was not particularly successful and was not improved, after his death, by alterations to the design by Luigi Vanvitelli. In the early 20th century the façade was removed to reveal the unadorned curved wall of the caldarium (hot room) of the baths, while the present atrium of the church corresponds to the tepidarium (warm room). Part of the baths complex next to the church contains some of the collection of the Museo Nazionale Romano, including sarcophagi, decorations from the Aurelian temple. There is also a cloister by Michelangelo, enclosed by a portico of 100 columns and 100 arcades.

TRASTEVERE

See pages 144–145.

Trastevere

**Rome's answer to Paris' Rive Gauche.
A genuine working area with lively atmosphere.
A great place for eating and drinking in the evening.**

RATINGS

Good for food	●●●●●
Historic interest	●●●
Shopping	●●●●
Walkability	●●●●

BASICS

✚ 57 D6

🚌 H, 23, 44, 280, 780, 630; tram 8

SEEING TRASTEVERE

The main bridge from Rome proper into Trastevere is the Ponte Garibaldi, which runs into the Viale di Trastevere, a main drag that divides the area neatly into north and south zones. Use this road to keep your bearings while you explore the whole of Trastevere; in particular, don't miss the superb church of Santa Maria in Trastevere (▷ 141). Alternatively, approach over the lovely Ponte Sisto footbridge, which brings you into the area south of the *viale*. Allow half a day for the visit, and aim on eating lunch or dinner at one of the excellent *trattorie* here.

HIGHLIGHTS

SOUTH OF VIALE DI TRASTEVERE

The Torre dell'Anguillara, opposite the Isola Tiberina, is a medieval tower, the sole survivor of the many family-owned fortress-towers that once crowded Trastevere. Alongside is a fountain with a statue of Gioacchino Belli, a popular Roman dialect poet in the 19th century.

Il Chiostro dei Genovesi (Genoan Cloister) stands next to the church of Santa Maria dell'Orto. This flower-filled cloister, with its central well, was part of a 15th-century hospice for Genoan sailors.

NORTH OF VIALE DI TRASTEVERE

The Gianicolo has breathtaking views over the whole city and is home to the Orto Botanico.

The Via della Lungara, which runs parallel to the river, was built by Sixtus V to link Trastevere with the Vatican City. Halfway along stands the imposing Regina Coeli prison, named after a church that once stood here. At the end of the street, coming back towards Trastevere, is Villa Farnesina, a sumptuous residence commissioned by banker Agostino Chigi in the early 16th century and decorated with frescoes by Raphael and Giulio Romano, among others (▷ 146).

The Porta Settimiana takes you to Via della Scala, with its wine bars, pubs and cafés, leading up to the heart of the area. The Casa della Fornarina stands just inside the Porta Settimiana, at Via di Santa Dorotea 20. This 15th-century house is believed to have been the home of Margherita la Fornarina (the Baker's Daughter), the great love of the painter Raphael's life. Piazza San Callisto has an ancient arch, and is a popular meeting place for young people in the evening.

The Fontana della Botte stands at the corner of Piazza San Callisto and Via della Cisterna. Built in 1927, this curious fountain shows a barrel between two wine measures in celebration of the many popular *osterie* (inns) of the area. The Museo di Roma in Trastevere is in the former monastery of Sant'Egidio. The Municipality of Rome acquired the building in 1875, and it now holds a collection of paintings and drawings of Roman life in the 18th and 19th centuries, along with items that belonged to the Roman dialect poet Trilussa (Carlo Salustri, died 1950).

BACKGROUND

The name Trastevere comes from the Latin expression *trans Tiberim*—'on the other side of the Tiber'—and the area was initially populated by immigrants and freed slaves who had come to Rome from all over the empire. During the imperial age, this was an agricultural area, packed with farms and vineyards, and home to country villas and splendid gardens. In the Middle Ages, Trastevere's port of Ripa Grande was used by popes when they journeyed by water, and a shipyard was built there for the construction of the pontifical navy. Strategically positioned for trade, the port was used by ships coming from Ostia on the coast. Syrian and Jewish communities thrived here before they moved across the Tiber to the Ghetto area. In 1870, embankments were built for flood prevention and the port vanished. Trastevere remained a solid working-class area under papal rule, a role that continued well after unification. Today, there's more than a touch of gentrification in evidence, witnessed by the wine bars and expensive restaurants, and by climbing property prices. It still retains much of its charm, and is still a place where you'll hear the native dialect of Rome spoken by its traditional inhabitants, the Trasteverini.

Piazza di Santa Maria in Trastevere is a popular place to stop for a snack; at night the church is floodlit and people congregate on the fountain steps

TIPS

● Trastevere is a popular meeting place for young people, but some restaurants can be quite expensive, so check the prices before you go in.
● If you're in Rome at the end of July, take in the traditional and popular *Festa dei Noiantri* (Our Own Festival), celebrated with games and street stands.

Trastevere is still an area where everyday life goes on much as usual (opposite and above)

The Via Appia Antica—the most important of ancient roads

The Temple of Esculapio, in the Villa Borghese

Agostino Chigi's sumptuous Villa Farnesina

VIA APPIA ANTICA

312 H9 Circo Massimo 118, 160, 628

The Appian Way was the first and most important of the roads built in the fourth century BC. It followed an existing track from Rome south to Capua, a distance of 212km (132 miles). The road was paved with *basoli*—basalt rock stones of polygonal shape—which survive almost intact. Walking along this ancient surface, with the monuments of the Roman dead at the side of the road and the catacombs of the early Christian martyrs nearby, brings the distant past very close.

The Via Appia proper begins at Porta San Sebastiano; just before the ancient gateway, inserted in a modern wall, is the ancient column that marked the first (Roman) mile. Take the bus as far as this in order to avoid the unpleasant section of the road that runs through the city outskirts. Via Appia Antica is closed to cars on Sundays, when it is particularly popular.

At the corner with Via Ardeatina is the church of Domine Quo Vadis ('Lord, where are you going?'), where Jesus is supposed to have shamed Peter into returning to execution in Rome when he was fleeing Nero's persecution. Farther along the road are the basilica and catacombs of San Sebastiano. The catacombs are an atmospheric network of underground tunnels, used as burial places between the second and fifth centuries AD. Because they are so extensive, they can only be visited with a guide.

VILLA BORGHESE

57 F2 Sunrise–sunset Flaminio or Spagna 52, 53, 88, 95, 116, 117, 119, 490, 491, 495, 910

In the early 17th century, Cardinal Scipione Borghese decided to create a country estate, the Villa Borghese. The extensive grounds now form one of Rome's most important parks. The Cardinal kept his rich art collection in the imposing Villa Pinciana or Casino Borghese (now Museo e Galleria Borghese, ▷ 92–97), but there is much else to see in this park, including the Casino della Meridiana and the aviary. The most romantic part is the artificial lake, with a little island in the middle dominated by the temple to Esculapio, erected in the 18th century in Ionian style and adorned with a statue of the Greek god of medicine.

The Piazza di Siena is where Rome's International Horse Show takes place every May. Prince Camillo Borghese allowed people to gather here for the Festa delle Ottobrate, celebrated during October with music and dancing. There is also a zoo, Bioparco, which was set up in 1911 (▷ 194).

VILLA FARNESINA

56 D5 • Via della Lungara 230, 00186 06 6802 7268 Mon–Sat 9–1 Adult €5, child (14–18) €3.50 23, 280, 870 www.francopanini.it

If you are in Trastevere during the morning, it is well worth visiting the beautiful Renaissance Villa Farnesina for its lovely interior or for a walk in the gardens.

In 1508, Agostino Chigi, a wealthy banker from Siena, commissioned Baldassare Peruzzi to build him a suburban villa. Here, Chigi entertained artists, princes and cardinals. His banquets were memorable: After the meal, Chigi would have the gold and silver dishes thrown into the Tiber to impress his guests with his wealth. What they did not know was that the plates were caught by safety nets and returned to the kitchens. In 1580, the villa was bought by the Farnese family, and it has been known as Villa Farnesina ever since.

On the ground floor are the Loggia of Galatea, with a much admired fresco by Raphael of the *Triumph of Galatea*, and the Loggia of Cupid and Psyche, frescoed to Raphael's designs by some of his pupils. On the upper floor is the beautiful Salone delle Prospettive, with a fresco by Baldassare Peruzzi of a *trompe l'oeil* colonnade through which can be seen rural landscapes, villages and a town.

VILLA MEDICI

57 E3 • Viale Trinità dei Monti 1, 00187 06 67611 Gardens only: Sat–Sun 10.30–11.30. Closed Jul–end Aug €5 Spagna 116, 119, 590 www.villamedici.it

The grounds of the Villa Medici are one of the best examples of an Italian Renaissance garden, with rare plants growing amid the pine trees, and elegantly placed fountains and sculptures. The house is not open to the public.

In 1576, Cardinal Ferdinando Medici (later Grand Duke of Tuscany) bought the existing building as a villa-museum, incorporating ancient Roman bas-reliefs in the façade, which has recently been restored.

Look out, too, for the round fountain, topped with a cannon-ball fired, so the legend goes, from Castel Sant'Angelo by eccentric 17th-century Swedish queen Christina to announce to her hosts that she would be arriving for dinner.

Between 1961 and 1977, the French painter Balthus restored the villa to its past glory: Statues were placed in the gardens, excavation works unveiled 16th-century frescoes, and an exhibition space was created.

THE SIGHTS

VILLA GIULIA E MUSEO NAZIONALE ETRUSCO

Splendidly housed in the 16th-century Villa Giulia is the National Etruscan Museum, an ideal setting in which to introduce the way of life—and death—of the mysterious Etruscan civilization.

THE VILLA
Commissioned by Pope Julius III, the villa was built between 1551 and 1555 after a design by Giacomo da Vignola. It is set among a series of courtyards, with a beautiful loggia by Bartolomeo Ammannati, and is surrounded by pleasant gardens. The courtyard leads down to an enchanting nymphaeum with false grottoes and a Vasari fountain. The Etruscan museum was founded here in 1889.

THE SARCOPHOGUS OF THE SPOUSES
The most famous piece of Etruscan art is kept in the halls displaying the finds from Cerveteri. The terracotta Sarcophagus of the Spouses represents a husband and wife reclining in an affectionate pose, and vividly demonstrates that the Etruscans believed in the afterlife. It has become an emblem of the Etruscan civilization.

THE COLLECTION
Among the rest of the collection, the Tomb of the Warrior, dating from the sixth century BC, is of particular interest. A reconstruction beneath hall 5 shows what the funeral chambers of the tombs in Cerveteri would have looked like.

Halls 11 to 18 contain a rich collection of domestic objects made from bronze and terracotta, including mirrors, statuettes, candelabra, cinerary urns and, in particular, the bronze Chigi Vase, an exquisitely decorated wine pitcher dating from around 640–625BC (hall 15). In this room is another vase dating from the sixth century BC, decorated with the Etruscan alphabet, revealing its Latin and Greek influences and helping experts to unravel further the Etruscan language.

AN ENIGMATIC PEOPLE
The origins of the Etruscan people are shrouded in mystery. They arrived in Italy in the eighth century BC—from where, nobody knows, although there are several theories—and settled in Etruria (the area of present-day Tuscany and parts of Umbria and Lazio). They were rulers of Italy, with an empire extending from Corsica in the west to the Adriatic, and from Bologna in the north to Capua in the south, until they were conquered by the Romans in the first century BC. Little trace of the Etruscan civilization remains, except for what has been found and pieced together from the tombs.

The semicircular portico at the back of Vignola's gracious villa

RATINGS	
Cultural interest	●●●●○
Value for money	●●●●○

BASICS
✚ 57 E2 • Piazzale Villa Giulia 9, 00187
☎ 06 322 6571. Reservations:
06 824529 ⏰ Tue–Sun 8.30–7.30
🎫 Adult €4, child (under 18) free
Ⓜ Flaminio 🚋 Tram 19
🎧 Audioguide €3 📖 Available in the bookshop, *Museo Etrusco Villa Giulia* in English and Italian, €13 ☕ Caffè dell'Aranceria: beautiful café in the Giardino dell'Aranceria 🏛 Art bookshop, well stocked
www.ticketeria.it
www.beniculturali.it

TIPS
● Stroll among the orange trees in the Giardino dell'Aranceria, and pause for a coffee in the cafeteria.
● Combine the Villa Giulia with the nearby Galleria d'Arte Moderna, worth visiting for the quality of art it displays in a magnificent setting.

San Paolo fuori le Mura

Burial place of St. Paul the Apostle.
Grand 19th-century structure containing some fine medieval art.
The farthest flung of the Vatican-ruled basilicas.

San Paolo's 19th-century façade (above left) was built after the fire of 1823, but some of its older treasures, such as the 13th-century Paschal Candlestick (above right), were saved

RATINGS				
Historic interest	●	●	●	○
Specialist shopping	●	●	●	
Value for money	●	●	●	●	●

BASICS

⊞ Off 310 E9 • Piazzale San Paolo 1C, 00146

☎ 06 541 0341

🕐 Daily 7–7. Cosmatesque cloister: 9–1, 3–6

💷 Free

🚇 Basilica di San Paolo

🚌 23, 128, 761, 769, 770; tram 4

🎧 Audiotours: church—German, Italian, English and Spanish €1, 20 mins; cloister—same languages €1

📖 Many guides in several languages

🏪 Souvenirs, religious objects and guides. Beautiful art gallery, selling books, religious engravings, and herbalist products made by Benedictine friars

🚻 Clean toilets inside and outside

TIP

● Visit in the morning, as the light in the basilica is better.

SEEING SAN PAOLO FUORI LE MURA

Allow plenty of time for a visit, as the basilica is some distance from the city—the name literally means 'St. Paul Outside the Walls'. Once there, bear in mind that the present building is only 150 years old and you'll have to track down its medieval treasures. Take time to take in the sheer size of the building before starting your tour.

HIGHLIGHTS

THE FAÇADE

Size and bright hues will be your first impression of the façade, with its 10 huge columns, each 10m (32ft) tall, soaring up towards the glittering mosaic entablature. It's fronted by a portico with a covered arcade, in front of which is a huge 19th-century statue of St. Paul brandishing a sword. Another statue, this time of St. Luke, stands on the right-hand corner of the portico near the Holy Door. Above the portico on the façade is a somewhat garish mosaic showing Christ Giving Benediction between Peter and Paul, the Lamb of God and the Prophets. Statues of saints Peter and Paul guard the central entrance to the church, and silver and bronze doors portray the lives of the two saints. The bronze Holy Door, to the right of the main entrance, survived the 1823 fire; it dates from the 11th century.

THE NAVE, AISLES AND TRANSEPT

Eighty granite columns divide the church into a wide nave and four aisles, the forest of columns and shadowy spaces giving a vivid impression of what the ancient Roman basilicas must have looked like. Above soars the magnificent white and gold coffered ceiling, while light filters through screens of alabaster.

The triumphal arch leading to the chancel has inscriptions recording that the emperors Theodosius and Honorius built the original basilica. It is embellished with a mosaic funded by Galla Placidia, the daughter of Theodosius, which was transferred from the original arch after the fire in the 19th century. The Byzantine-style apse mosaics behind here were made around 1120 by craftsmen specially summoned from Venice by Pope Honorius III. The altars at the head of each arm of the transept are faced with malachite and lapis lazuli, a gift from the Tsar of Russia, Nicholas I, after the 1823 fire, while running around the nave is a mosaic frieze with portraits of all the popes.

THE CIBORIO, PASCHAL CANDLESTICK AND APSE

The triumphal arch frames the beautiful Gothic ciborium, made by Arnolfo di Cambio and Pietri Cavallino in 1285. The canopy is supported by four porphyry columns with gold capitals, while a marble plaque marks the spot where the St. Paul's relics are buried beneath the altar. To the right of the ciborium is the Paschal Candlestick by Nicola di Angelo and Pietro Vasselletto (12th century), a remarkable masterpiece of Romanesque art. Its base depicts monsters, while the shaft has scenes from the life of Jesus. In the Chapel of the Holy Sacrament to the left of the apse are a 14th-century wooden crucifix attributed to Pietro Cavallini, who is buried here, a statue of St. Bridget kneeling, by Stefano Maderno, and a wooden statue of St. Paul. To the right between the apse and the Greek-cross baptistery is a decorated stoop sculpted by Pietro Galli in the 19th century, which shows a child threatening a terrified demon with holy water.

THE CLOISTERS

The cloisters are an outstanding example of cosmatesque work by the Vassalletto family, constructed in the first quarter of the 13th century. Richer and better preserved than those of San Giovanni in Laterano (▷ 134–135), they're full of charming detail, sparkling with gold, and are exquisitely worked. It's worth spending time studying the incredible variety of the columns, some straight, some twisted, and some so richly decorated with mosaics that the base stone is invisible.

The picture gallery, to one side of the cloisters, displays paintings from the 13th to 19th centuries. The Chapel of Relics next door contains a 15th-century silver reliquary cross.

BACKGROUND

The first church here was built by Constantine over the tomb of the Apostle Paul, and was concentrated in AD324. From AD395 it was extended, so that until the construction of St. Peter's, it was the largest church in

Christendom. In the ninth century, Pope John VIII built fortifications to protect the basilica from Lombard raiders, and a village—called Giovannipoli after the Pope—grew up around it, only to fall derelict as malaria took its toll. Disaster struck on the night of 15 July 1823, when the great basilica, one of the least changed since ancient times, was practically destroyed by fire. Work immediately began on an even more magnificent replacement, based on the original plan and funded by contributions from all over the world. The new San Paolo fuori le Mura was finally completed in 1854 and, in the presence of 185 bishops, was consecrated by Pope Pius IX.

The bronze Holy Door (top left) and the beautiful 13th-century cloisters (top right) survived the 1823 fire, as did the inscription on the triumphal arch (above), which was incorporated into the new church, along with its restored fifth-century mosaics

Palazzo dei Congressi (left), in the EUR complex

EUR AND ITS MUSEUMS

🔲 Off 311 G9 🚇 EUR Fermi 🚌 703, 714, 717, 764, 765, 780, 791

The Esposizione Universale di Roma (EUR) was begun in 1936 as an emphatic statement about Fascist ambitions. The construction of this new quarter was interrupted by the outbreak of World War II, and it was not until 1951 that it was completed. Today, the EUR is a focus for a variety of events and art exhibitions, and many shops, cinemas and clubs have opened up. For visitors the main attractions are three excellent museums.

MUSEO DELLA CIVILTÀ ROMANA

Piazza Giovanni Agnelli 10, 00144 ☎ 06 592 6041 🕐 Tue–Sat 9–6, Sun 9–2 💶 €6.20, child (under 18) free
www.comune.roma.it/museociviltaromana

The Museum of Roman Culture traces the history of the city of Rome through models and reconstructions. There's a scale model of ancient Rome, showing all the buildings that stood within the Aurelian Walls in the fourth century. There are also moulds taken from Trajan's Column (▷ 78–79), giving you a chance to study the carvings close up.

MUSEO NAZIONALE DELLE ARTI E TRADIZIONI POPOLARI

Piazza Guglielmo Marconi 8/10, 00144 ☎ 06 592 6148 🕐 Tue–Sun 9–8 💶 Adult €4, child (under 18) free 🚻 👫
www.popolari.arti.beniculturali.it

The collection of the National Museum of Arts and Popular Traditions has objects relating to everyday life from the 18th century to the present day. It was put together in 1911 to celebrate the 50th anniversary of Italian unity, and moved here in 1956.

MUSEO NAZIONALE PREISTORICO ETNOGRAFICO

Piazza Guglielmo Marconi 8/10, 00144 ☎ 06 549521 🕐 Daily 9–8 💶 Adult €4, child (under 18) free
www.pigorini.arti.beniculturali.it

This internationally important ethnographic museum has collections from Africa, Oceania and America. The African display includes around 250 weapons, ivory tools from Nigeria, fabrics, and 17th-century wooden sculptures from the Congo. Inuit, pre-Columbian and Amazonian items make up the American collections. The prehistoric section covers the Stone, Bronze and Iron Ages with displays of archaeological finds, largely from Italy.

Palazzo della Civiltà del Lavoro, known as the Square Colosseum (above), contains the Museo della Civiltà Romana

SANT'AGNESE FUORI LE MURA AND MAUSOLEO DI SANTA COSTANZA

🔲 307 J1 • Via Nomentana 00162
☎ 06 861 0840 🕐 Church: daily 7.30–12, 4–6. Catacombs and mausoleum: Tue–Sat 9–12, 4–6 💶 €5
🚌 30, 60, 84, 90, 93, 168 🎫 Guided tour of catacombs included in the ticket

Although it is a little out of the way, don't miss the beautiful group of buildings consisting of Sant'Agnese fuori le Mura, the Catacombs of Sant'Agnese, the remains of a basilica from the time of Constantine and the circular Mausoleum of St. Constantia.

The catacombs were developed between the third and fourth centuries, and hold the remains of the martyred St. Agnes (▷ 124). The church above, dedicated to her, was built by Pope Honorius I in the seventh century and is one of the best-preserved Byzantine basilicas in Rome. On the apse is a seventh-century mosaic of St. Agnes with the popes Honorius I and Symmachus, the latter holding a model of the basilica.

Nearby are the huge walls of another basilica, built between AD337 and AD350 by Constantia, daughter of the Emperor Constantine. The Mausoleum of St. Constantia was erected against one side, built by Constantia for herself and her sister. Inside is a beautiful colonnade with 12 pairs of granite columns, above which are 12 windows reaching up into the frescoed dome. The barrel-vaulted ceiling of the corridor has beautiful fourth-century mosaics. One of the central panels shows Constantia and her husband Annibaliano. In a niche at the rear of the mausoleum is a copy of Constantia's red porphyry sarcophagus; the original is in the Vatican.

THE SIGHTS

FARTHER AFIELD

This chapter gives information on things to do in Rome, other than sightseeing.
Shops and entertainment venues are shown on the maps at the beginning of each section.

What to Do

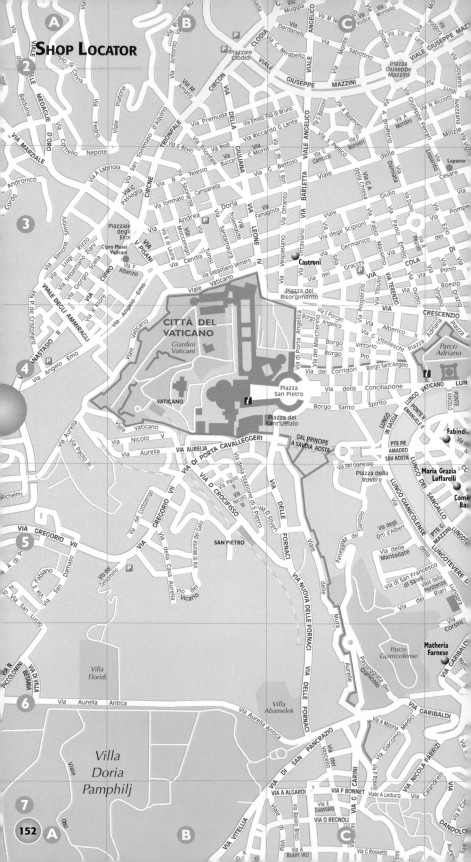

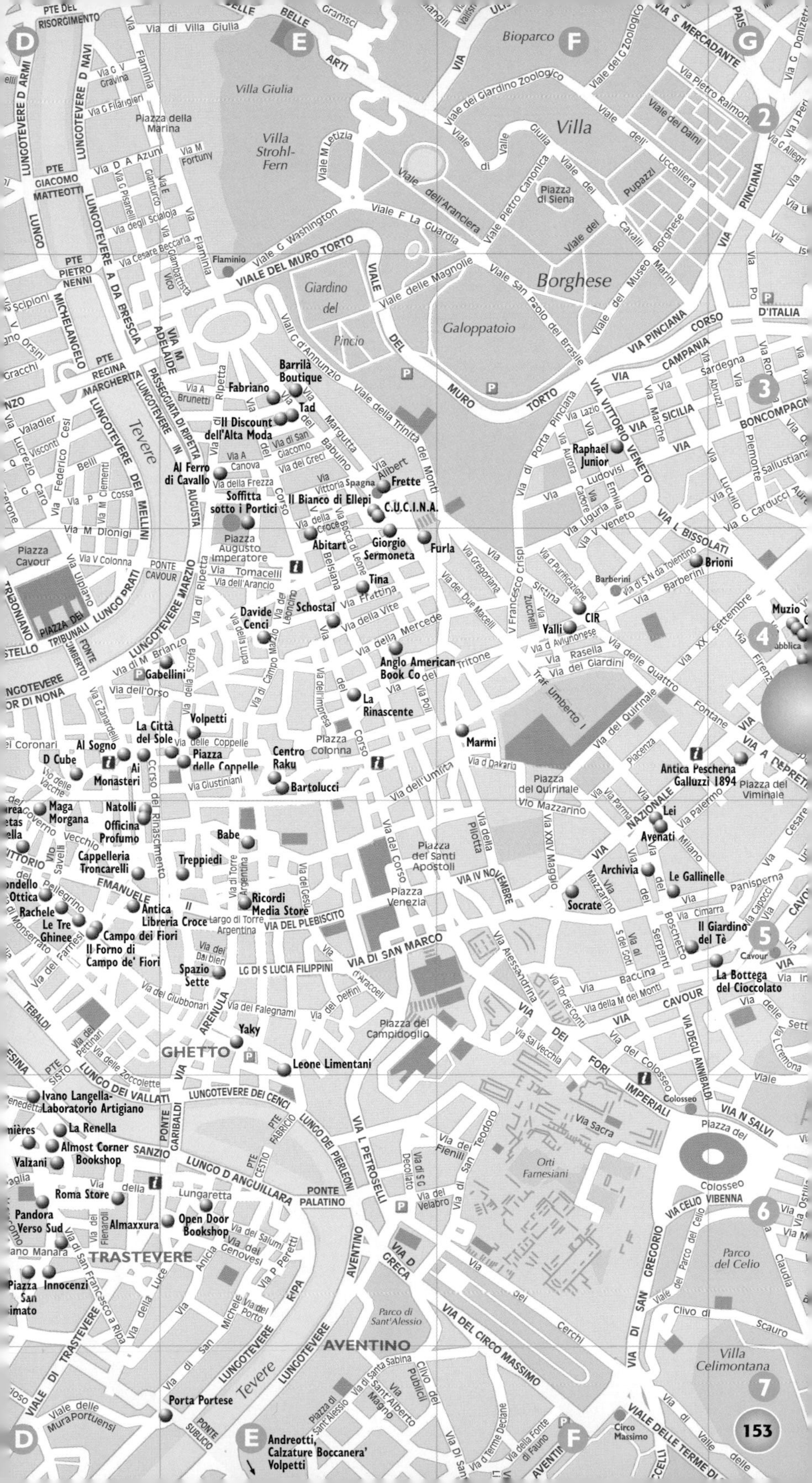
D
E
F
G
2
3
4
5
6
7
Villa Giulia
Villa Strohl-Fern
Bioparco
Villa Borghese
Piazza di Siena
Giardino del Pincio
Galoppatoio
Viale del Muro Torto
Flaminio
Piazza della Marina
Piazza Augusto Imperatore
Piazza Cavour
Tevere
Barrilà Boutique
Fabriano
Tad
Il Discount dell'Alta Moda
Al Ferro di Cavallo
Soffitta sotto i Portici
Frette
Il Bianco di Ellepi
C.U.C.I.N.A.
Abitart
Giorgio Sermoneta
Furla
Raphael Junior
Brioni
Barberini
CIR
Valli
Muzio
Tina
Schostal
Davide Cenci
Anglo American Book Co
Gabellini
La Rinascente
Marmi
Volpetti
La Città del Sole
Al Sogno
D Cube
Ai Monasteri
Piazza delle Coppelle
Centro Raku
Bartolucci
Piazza Colonna
Antica Pescheria Galluzzi 1894
Piazza del Viminale
Piazza del Quirinale
Maga Morgana
Natolli
Officina Profumo
Babe
Cappelleria Troncarelli
Treppiedi
Lei
Avenati
Archivia
Le Gallinelle
Socrate
Piazza dei Santi Apostoli
Piazza Venezia
Ottica
Rachele
Le Tre Ghinee
Antica Libreria Croce
Campo dei Fiori
Il Forno di Campo de' Fiori
Ricordi Media Store
Largo di Torre Argentina
Spazio Sette
Il Giardino del Tè
Cavour
La Bottega del Cioccolato
Yaky
GHETTO
Leone Limentani
Piazza del Campidoglio
Ivano Langella-Laboratorio Artigiano
La Renella
Almost Corner Bookshop
Valzani
Roma Store
Pandora Verso Sud
Almaxxura
Open Door Bookshop
TRASTEVERE
Innocenzi
Orti Farnesiani
Colosseo
Parco del Celio
Parco di Sant'Alessio
AVENTINO
Villa Celimontana
Porta Portese
Circo Massimo
Andreotti, Calzature Boccanera' Volpetti

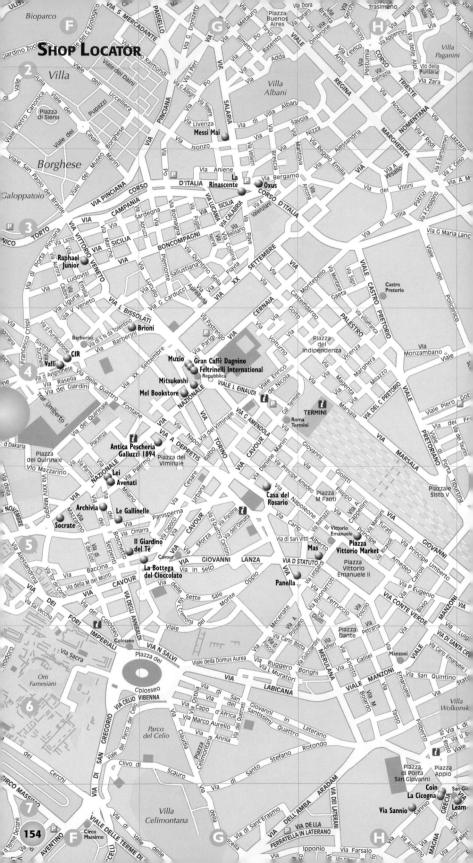

SHOP LOCATOR

SHOPPING

In the Eternal City you can almost literally shop till you drop. More and more shops are now open all day from 9.30am to 8pm. Many are also open on Sunday, often from 11am to 1pm and 4pm to 7.30pm.

Traditionally, shops have closed for the sacrosanct lunch and siesta from 1pm to 4pm, but this is becoming less common. During winter, they tend to open earlier in the afternoon, while in summer to avoid the heat (and enjoy a long lunch) 5pm is more usual. We have indicated where shops open outside these standard hours.

August is holiday time in Rome, when many small businesses take their two-week

There is no shortage of shops selling stylish accessories

annual break, and almost everything closes around Ferragosto, the public holiday on 15 August. Many shops are also closed on Monday mornings, and food stores tend to close on Saturday afternoons in summer and Thursday afternoons in winter.

CREDIT CARDS
Although Italy is traditionally a cash society, credit cards are widely accepted in Rome, with the main exceptions of small grocery shops and delicatessens. You should always get a receipt (*ricevuta fiscale*) as the law requires all

shopkeepers and restaurateurs to provide this, and they (and you) can be fined if they don't. In practice, this is rare, but it's useful if you have bought high-value goods and need proof for customs—or if you need to make an insurance claim.

SMALL IS BEAUTIFUL
Shopping malls and department stores are in their infancy in Rome, although there are exceptions such as the Cinecittà Due (▷ 164) and the popular La Rinascente (▷ 164). Small, specialized shops are the way to a Roman heart and when in Rome…!

Different areas tend to specialize in different goods. The most famous designers have taken over the streets around the Piazza di Spagna, especially along the very chic Via dei Condotti, where starry names such as Gucci, Bulgari and Prada are clustered. Here the Italian art form of *la bella figura* is at its height. Near Piazza Navona, the Via del Governo Vecchio has less expensive independent designer boutiques, while the Via dei Giubbonari, near Campo dei Fiori, has inexpensive fashion. In stylish Rome, even inexpensive clothes tend to be good quality and well-cut.

The roads down from Via dei Condotti have some gorgeous shoes, bags, belts and every other kind of accessory, while Via Nazionale, Via del Tritone and Via del Corso are good places to seek out beautiful, reasonably priced must-haves.

The Via Margutta is full of artists' studios, while Via dei Coronari showcases some of Rome's finest antiques. Trastevere is full of artisan

workshops selling handmade jewellery and ceramics.

Near the Vatican, the Via Cola di Rienzo is fashion central, with some of the big names and all the mid-market chains, as well as newcomers from overseas, such as Mango. This is also a good place to visit some of Rome's popular delis, where you'll be in gourmet heaven.

SOUVENIRS
Pasta in every shape and size, the greenest extra virgin olive oil, *funghi porcini* (dried mushrooms), truffle oil and spices all make durable food buys. Handmade ceramics,

Abitart is one of many very individual fashion stores

kitchen gadgets, espresso coffee pots and individually designed cups, kettles, salt and pepper grinders—especially those with the Alessi mark—are all Italian style at their best. There is a long tradition of artisan silver- and goldsmithing in Rome. Herbalists and shops specializing in lotions and potions have tempting arrays of fragrant delicacies.

The souvenir shops around the Vatican do a healthy trade in Catholic paraphernalia. Around the tourist honeypots are plenty of souvenirs, from figures of gladiators to models of the Colosseo.

Tridente and Via del Corso

HOW TO GET THERE
🚇 Spagna
🚌 62, 63, 116, 117, 119, 492, 590

The area around Piazza di Spagna (known as the Tridente after the trio of roads built off Piazza del Popolo to relieve congestion in the 16th century) is the smartest and most expensive shopping area in Rome, while Via del Corso sells cheaper versions of the latest styles.

VIA DEI CONDOTTI

Rome's version of Bond Street or 5th Avenue is Via dei Condotti. Start here for the best in Italian fashion: **Gucci** (No. 8), **Valentino** (No. 13), **Max Mara** (No. 17–19a), **Trussardi** (No. 49–50), **Dolce & Gabbana** (No. 51–52), **Armani** (No. 77) and **Prada** (No. 95). You will find the **Versace** store for women on Via Bocca di Leone (No. 26–27), a

The great fashion houses on Via dei Condotti—Gucci at No. 8...

street that intersects with Via dei Condotti. Just to the south, the quieter Via Borgognona runs parallel to Via dei Condotti and holds just as much to tempt the fashion-crazed: **Gianfranco Ferré** (No. 6), **Roberto Cavalli** (No. 7a), **Moschino** (No. 32a), **Fendi** store (No. 36–37), **Laura Biagiotti** (No. 43–44), **Tod's** (No. 45) and **Hogan** (No. 46). For edgier fashions try **Galassia** on Via Frattina (No. 20–21).

VIA DEL BABUINO

For a welcome respite from the hordes of Prada-hungry tourists on Via dei Condotti try Via del Babuino with its fashion options

(**Armani Jeans** at No. 70a; **Etro** at No. 102), antique collectors, jewellers and trendy specialist shops. Down towards Piazza del Popolo on the left is **Tad** (No. 155a), a so-called concept store with a fabulous selection of clothing and shoes, the Aussie Aesop range of cosmetics, a hairdresser, a flower shop and a fabrics and furniture section. It even has its own café. A few doors farther down is **Fabriano** (No. 173), a pen and stationery shop to die for with writing paper, photo albums, wallets and travel diaries. The streets that connect Via del Babuino and Via del Corso are well worth exploring too. On one of the most animated, Via della Croce, you will find some good delis and one-off clothing boutiques like that of Rome designer Vanessa Foglia, **abitart** (No. 46–47), whose bright and flowing clothes are displayed like works of art. On Via Mario de' Fiori make a beeline for **C.u.c.i.n.a.** (No. 65), one of the best kitchenware stores in Rome for choice, with a mix of cheap and more expensive brands.

VIA DEL CORSO

Avoid the part of Via del Corso from Piazza Venezia until Largo Chigi as the cheap clothing stores and traffic are uninspiring. Start instead at one of Rome's oldest department stores, **La Rinascente** (Piazza Colonna). Heading towards Piazza del Popolo you will pass huge **Diesel** (No. 186), **Energie** (No. 510) and **Benetton** (No. 426), all big Italian mid-market success stories. Keeping in teenager and

surf dude mode try also **Energie** (No. 407–408, 486–487), which stocks brands like O'Neill, Puma, Adidas, Converse and Camper. **Messaggerie Musicali** (No. 472) sells an enormous selection of CDs and DVDs, as well as books and magazines in English.

...and Prada at No. 95

WHERE TO STOP
ANTICA ENOTECA DI VIA DELLA CROCE
Via della Croce 76b, 00187
Tel 06 679 0896
🕐 Daily 11am–1am
A delightful wine bar that also serves light meals.

AU PAIN QUOTIDIEN
Via Tomacelli 24, 00187
Tel 06 6880 7727
🕐 Tue–Sun 9am–midnight, closed Mon
Great for stone-ground bread and French-style buttery croissants and pains au chocolat. Huge garnished salads (rare in Italy), soups and quiches served all day long.

Via Nazionale and the Monti District

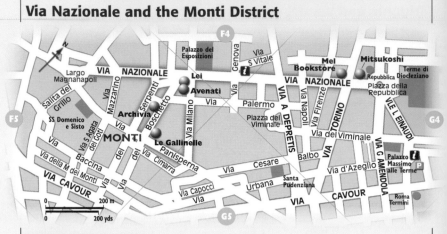

Long, wide and traffic-ridden, Via Nazionale has many affordable mainstream fashion options, a handful of genuinely cool clothing

Browsing for paintings at a street stall

boutiques and a wide selection of mid-priced shops selling handbags, luggage and footwear. Off to the southeast is the village-like Monti district, with its appealing selection of artisan shops and one-off clothing and jewellery emporia.

VIA NAZIONALE

Come out at Repubblica metro station and start walking down Via Nazionale. On your right after Mel Bookstore head in to **Fiorucci** (No. 236), a store for women who want to express their girlie side. Outfits by Dolce & Gabbana, Moschino Jeans, Kookai, Diesel, Killah and Liu Jo range from the feminine to the grungy and are undeniably fun.

Regal (No. 234) is one shop down and stocks a wide variety of mid-priced bags, umbrellas and purses. Brands vary from Eastpak to Nannini, Armani and Mandarina Duck, passing by those eminently practical, bright, foldable bags by Longchamp. Cross the street and at No. 55 (after Via Genova) you will spot **Furla** with its simple but varied range of leather bags and accessories in shades that cover the spectrum from classic to loud. By the time you've left Rome you will have seen so many branches you will start to wonder if they are a little too popular for comfort, yet the suppleness and quality of their leather, and their highly affordable prices, have assured them a huge following.

Staying on this side of Via Nazionale turn left up Via Milano for the classic looks of **Sorelle D'Italia** (No. 31), with clothes by Patrizia Pepe, Marithé & François Girbaud and Luciana Conti. The shop is cheerful and decorated with original artworks and ornaments. Back on Via Nazionale, chic women in the know come to **LEI** (No. 88). Party dresses and feminine fashions are by a mix of Belgian and British designers, patterned T-shirts are by Barcelona designer Custo; all are complemented by delicate shoes by Kallisté and Katharine Hamnett.

MONTI

Bohemian Monti's main drags are Via del Boschetto, Via Panisperna and Via dei Serpenti (which leads straight to the Colosseum); its most atmospheric piazza is Santa Madonna dei Monti (just off the map). Starting with Via del Boschetto you should make a beeline for the sheer originality of **Le Gallinelle** (No. 76), a former butcher's shop with original designs and customized vintage garments of Wilma Silvestri. On the same street you will find a selection of enticing one-off interior design and antique stores, as well as the Japanese inspired **Linn-Sui** (No. 78a) which offers so-called ecological beds and futons, slippers, rugs and tableware, as well as a range of pillows, pouffes and bags made with Designer Guild fabrics.

WHERE TO STOP

DAGNINO

Galleria Esedra
Via Vittorio Emanuele Orlando 75, 00185
Tel 06 481 8660
🕐 Mon-Sun 7.30am–10.30pm
www.pasticceriadagnino.com
Fortify yourself in this café, bar and restaurant before shopping. Dagnino's has an immaculate 1950s interior, and an incredible array of Sicilian sweets and savoury goodies.

F.I.S.H.

This minimalist restaurant serving fine fusion food actually looks and tastes the part. Great for Mediterranean-cum-Oriental cuisine, or sushi at the bar (▷ 242).

Trastevere

HOW TO GET THERE
🚌 H, 23, 280, 780; tram 8

Across the river, Trastevere feels like a city within a city. Though very touristy in parts, its shops, many of them artisan or boutiques, reflect its local atmosphere and separateness—and are open late, too.

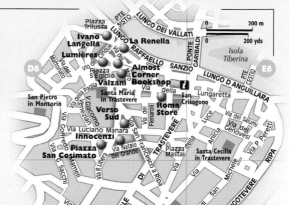

VIA DELLA LUNGARETTA AND PIAZZA SANTA MARIA IN TRASTEVERE

Enter Via della Lungaretta from Viale di Trastevere on the right-hand side and head straight for **Roma Store** (No. 63), which may not sound promising but has a vast selection of refined and hard-to-find perfumes and cosmetics from Artisan Parfumeur, L'Occitane, Acqua di Parma, Vetiver, Etro, Comptoir Sud Pacifique and Penhaligon's. Don't come here looking for

Trastevere is known for its lively markets, especially Porta Portese

J-Lo's Glow! Now walk straight into the atmospheric Piazza Santa Maria in Trastevere. **Pandora** at No. 6 is open late and is crammed with attractive and moderately priced jewellery (including some lovely glass items by the Sent sisters and other contemporary Venetian artists), and well-chosen hand-made ceramics, stoneware and glass ornaments.

VIA SAN FRANCESCO A RIPA AND VIA NATALE DEL GRANDE

Turn left out of the piazza and head to Via San Francesco a Ripa for two clothing boutiques worth

the detour: **Victory** (No. 19) and **Verso Sud** (No. 168). The former stocks dressier clothes by Marithé and François Girbaud, and Pinko, and the second stocks hip-thinking women's clothes by Isabel Marant, BP Studio, Comme des Garçons, Vivienne Westwood and Alberta Ferretti. Both have a deservedly loyal following.

Next turn right at Via Natale del Grande, a street filled with delis and stores selling fresh pasta, pastry and fish, all with a local feel and quality goods. One of the most characterful food shops in Rome is **Innocenzi** at No. 31, which stocks regional products such as olive oils, breads, pastas and sauces from all over Italy, but also the staples for Indian, Thai, Japanese and Mexican cooking. It has a good range of organic products and sells sweets loose from jars, and pulses and rice from large bags on the floor. Delightfully old-fashioned. **Piazza San Cosimato** hosts a small but lively food market every morning except Sunday.

VICOLO DEL CINQUE AND PIAZZA TRILUSSA

Walking straight ahead turn right at Piazza Sant'Egidio (where artisans sell their wares most evenings of the week) and down Vicolo del Cinque. Here you will find restaurants, artisans—whose work includes jewellery made using a glass-fusion technique—and a store dedicated to antique lamps (No. 48), as well as mad sculptural footwear creations by **Joseph Debach** (No. 19). Farther down on the left is **Jacche Calzature** (No. 24b), which sells

low-priced shoes for men and women. Amid the unexceptional there are always some finds to be had. Once in Piazza Trilussa turn left past the fountain into Via di Ponte Sisto. Here in a tiny atelier you will find the larger than life **Ivano Langella** (No. 73a) and his jewellery, with

Hat stall at Porta Portese market, held on Sunday mornings

lots of pearl, semi-precious stones, horn and chunky silver. He has counted Kylie Minogue among his clients.

WHERE TO STOP
LA RENELLA
Via del Moro 19, 00153
Tel 06 581 7265
🕐 Mon–Sun 7am–10pm
Freshly baked bread and thick, tasty slices of pizza.

TRASTÈ
An informal café where you can choose from a huge range of herbal teas, as well as *frullati* (fruit shakes) and alcoholic beverages (▷ 253).

Campo dei Fiori and Piazza Navona

HOW TO GET THERE

🚌 40, 46, 62, 64, 70, 81, 87, 571, 916

Campo dei Fiori has one of Rome's best-known local markets every morning except Sunday. In the medieval streets off it are a multitude of antique stores, artisan shops and fashionable clothing stores. The streets north of Piazza Navona attract Rome's more refined and wealthy shoppers, whereas the streets west of it are where to hunt for unique fashions, both first- and second-hand.

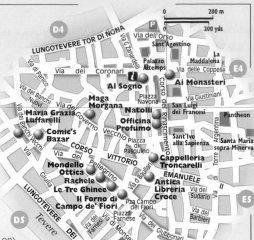

CAMPO DEI FIORI AND AROUND

Head southeast out of Campo dei Fiori along Via dei Giubbonari for a vast selection of unusual, and in some cases, cutting-edge fashions to fit all budgets. From

Tempting fruit and vegetables at Campo dei Fiori market

Levi's to hip streetwear store **Prototype**, through **Ethnic**, Italy's version of H&M, this is the place to come for trendy but original outfits. Back on Campo dei Fiori turn right down Via dei Baullari for **Loco** (No. 22) and its mad, expensive fashions for the feet. Turn right again on Piazza Pollarola for a Carrie Bradshaw slice of shoe heaven at **Nuyorica** (No. 36–37) where the latest by Marc Jacobs, Pierre Hardy and Rodolphe Menudier await you. Off the northwest of Campo dei Fiori you will find Via del Pellegrino and various potters, jewellers and the offbeat optician **Mondello Ottica**

(No. 98) with local artists' installations in the windows. Turn off briefly on to Vicolo del Bollo for delightfully patterned handmade children's dungarees, jackets and skirts by Swedish-born **Rachele** (No. 6). Back on Via del Pellegrino pop in to **Regola 71** (at the corner with Via dei Cappellari) for original fashions by Belgian and French designers that make any woman feel distinctly stylish, regardless of body shape and size. Via dei Banchi Vecchi, and the wide leafy Via Giulia to the northwest, are home to some refined antique shops and interior design stores.

PIAZZA NAVONA AND AROUND

On the northern tip of Piazza Navona is renowned toy store **Al Sogno** (No. 53), which has been going strong since 1945. Leave the piazza and turn left for Via dei Coronari, the street par excellence for antiques in Rome. Or, cross the street and walk straight until you reach Via dell'Orso and the surrounding alleys, a refined and quiet area with lots of jewellers. **Massimo Maria Melis** (No. 57) creates new jewels using ancient Roman coins in gold and silver settings. Off the southwestern end of Piazza Navona lies Via del Governo Vecchio where bazaar-like second-hand clothing shops and high fashion temples dedicated to foreign and local *stilisti* (designers) reign supreme. Running parallel to the east of Piazza Navona is Corso del Rinascimento where a branch of Florence's famous **Officina di**

Santa Maria Novella (No. 47) sells creams and perfumes from original recipes by Dominican friars. In the same vein, **Ai Monasteri** at No. 72 sells teas, honeys, liqueurs, and potions made by monks from all over Italy.

Come to Via dei Coronari to browse the antique shops

WHERE TO STOP

CAFFÈ NOVECENTO
Via del Governo Vecchio 12, 00186
Tel 06 686 5242
🕐 Summer Mon–Thu 11.30am–8.30pm, Fri, Sat 11.30-8.30pm; rest of year Wed–Sun 12.30pm–12.30am, Mon 12.30pm–8.30pm
Vegetarian brunches, light meals and salads, and an array of teas, fruit juices, *frullati* (fruit shakes) and home-made cakes.

WINE TIME
This vibrant spot is just the place for a light snack (pasta, salads, veggie and meat burgers). The kitchen is open all day (▷ 255).

Shopping Directory

This selection of retail outlets, arranged by theme, covers some of Rome's top fashion stores, plus markets and shops selling gifts, food, books and art.
- ▷ 152–155 for shopping locator maps
- ▷ 172–173 for chain stores chart
- ▷ 278 for clothing sizes

ACCESSORIES

BARRILÀ BOUTIQUE
Map 153 E3
Via del Babuino 33a, 00187
Tel 06 3600 1726
Women's shoes and boots in an unchanged 1960s interior. In the best Italian tradition, all are classic in style. Not the most up-to-date models, but each is available in at least 26 colours—something to match any bag, which you can also buy here. Prices range from €50 to €150.
⏰ Mon–Sat 9.30–8, Sun 10–7.30
🚇 Popolo or Spagna 🚌 117

BORSE SCULTURA
Map 155 J5
Largo degli Osci 67a, 00185
Tel 06 446 9284
Exquisitely handcrafted and hand-stitched bags adorned with spirals, lips, and feminine curves and shapes. Briefcases with a keyhole or mouth shape cut out of one side stand cheek by jowl with bags of more classic form. As good to look at on the arm as off. Prices start at €110.
⏰ Tue–Sat 10–1, 4–8, Mon 4–8 🚌 71, 492 to stop nearest Largo degli Osci; tram 3, 19

CALZATURE BOCCANERA
Map off 153 E7
Via Luca della Robbia 36, 00153
Tel 06 575 6804
This place is a Roman classic for wearable designer shoes. Brands such as Camper, Hogan, Tod's, Prada and Sergio Rossi are all packed together under one roof at uninflated prices. The good service is a bonus.
⏰ Mon–Sat 9–1, 3.30–7.30
🚇 Piramide 🚌 23, 30, 60, 75, 280, 716, or any bus to Piramide or Via Marmorata; tram 3

CAPPELLERIA TRONCARELLI
Map 153 D5
Via della Cuccagna 15, 00186

A cornucopia of boots and bags at Barrilà Boutique

Tel 06 687 9320
www.troncarelli.it
This family-run hat shop close to Piazza Navona, catering predominantly to men, is a pleasant throwback to a bygone age. Every conceivable hat is here, from panamas and Florentine straw hats to trilbies (felt hats with an indented crown) and flat caps, all handcrafted and to suit every occasion. Prices range from €50 to €180.
⏰ Tue–Fri 9.30–1, 3–7.30, Sat 9.30–7.30, Mon 3–7.30
🚌 46, 62, 64, 70, 87, 116, 492

FABINDIA
Map 152 D4
Via del Banco di Santo Spirito 40, 00186
Tel 06 6889 1230
www.fabindia.it
Facing the Ponte Sant'Angelo is this delightful emporium selling Indian fabrics, scarves and garments, all hand-woven and made in Indian villages. The company is devoted to developing fair and equitable relationships with the producers. The style is both traditional and more contemporary. Also stocks bags, pillows and photograph albums, made with, or covered in, Indian cottons and silks.
⏰ Tue–Sat 10–1.30, 3–7.30, Mon 3–7.30 🚌 40, 64, 116, 492, 571, or any bus to Corso Vittorio Emanuele II

FURLA
Map 153 E4
Piazza di Spagna 22, 00187
Tel 06 6920 0363
www.furla.it
Purveyors of chic bags and practical totes in cheerful tones, along with scarves, shoes and jewellery. Prices are moderate compared with other big-name accessory designers. Wild combinations and original touches add a twist. The company has several other branches in Rome.
⏰ Mon–Sat 10–8, Sun 10.30–8
🚇 Spagna 🚌 116, 117, 119, 590

GIORGIO SERMONETA
Map 153 E3
Piazza di Spagna 61, 00187
Tel 06 679 1960
www.sermonetagloves.com
The shop front is fairly small and it may feel cramped, but there's a surprise in store— just look up. The gloves are the real decor of this shop, literally thousands of them, women's and men's, in a terrific array of shades and styles. Top quality. Price range €25–€120.
⏰ Mon–Sat 9.30–8 🚇 Spagna 🚌 116, 117

MONDELLO OTTICA

Map 153 D5
Via del Pellegrino 98, 00186
Tel 06 686 1955

Eyewear with a difference:
This minimalist boutique has
regular installations by local
artists. Prices may be higher
than average, but the glasses
are superlative in quality and
sheer chic. All have that little
extra something special that
makes the price worth paying.
Friendly owners will provide
repairs with a smile whenever
they are required.

🕐 Tue–Sat 9.30–1, 4–7.30 🚌 46, 62,
64, 116, 492, 571, or any bus to Corso
Vittorio Emanuele II

OXUS

Map 154 G3
Via Bergamo 14, 00198
Tel 06 8535 6310

Milan-based designer of
striking, hand-sewn bags,
some inspired by artists such
as Catalan Joan Mirò. Also
makes items under licence for
designers, including Sonia
Rykiel, Laura Biagiotti and the
eccentrically brilliant
Castelbajac. All bags are well
finished, with inspired touches,
such as internal pockets for
mobile phones, and zips that
button shut once closed.

🕐 Mon–Fri 9.30–7.30, Sat 9.30–1,
3.30–7.30 🚌 38, 53, 63, 86, 92, 217,
360, 630, or any bus to Piazza Fiume

ART AND ANTIQUES

COMIC'S BAZAR

Map 152 D5
Via dei Banchi Vecchi 127–128, 00186
Tel 06 6880 2923

A veritable Aladdin's cave
specializing in early 20th-
century Viennese Thonet
lamps, and furniture from
the 1800s to the 1920s.
One of two entrances is just
beyond Via Sforza Cesarini,
on your left going towards
Campo dei Fiori, while the
other is a little farther down.
Their more contemporary
and ethnically inspired
store is close by at Via Giulia
140e.

🕐 Tue–Sat 9.30–7.30, Mon 3–7.30
🚌 46, 62, 64, 116, 492, 571, or any bus
to Corso Vittorio Emanuele II

LUMIÈRES

Map 153 D6
Vicolo del Cinque 48, 00153
Tel 06 580 3614

Unassuming shop crammed
with goods. If an interesting
lamp from the French art deco
or Italian Liberty periods is
what you're after, this is the
place to come. Choose from
dozens of antique lamps, all
fully restored. Or bring your
own lamp to be restored by
an artisan.

🕐 Mon–Sat 10–1, 4–8.30 🚌 H, 780;
tram 8

*Vibrant works of art at Maria
Grazia Luffarelli*

MARIA GRAZIA LUFFARELLI

Map 152 D5
Via dei Banchi Vecchi 29, 00186
Tel 06 683 2494
www.mgluffarelli.com

Bright watercolour landscapes
of hills, sea and sun. Prices
range from very low to
moderate for original works
by the eponymous artist.
Also on sale is a beautiful
range of Rome watercolour
reproductions in postcard
format, as well as prints of
Luffarelli's work mounted on
brightly painted tables.

🕐 Mon–Sat 12–8 🚌 40, 64, 116, 492,
571, or any bus to Corso Vittorio
Emanuele II

MATHERIA FARNESE

Map 152 D6
Via G. Garibaldi 53–55a, 00153
Tel 06 581 7566
www.farnese.it

This is the showroom of a
renowned group of architects
and artisans who create
stunning ceramic floor tiles
inspired by Roman villas and
18th-century patrician houses.
They also restore antique tiles,
plates and jugs. This kind of
craftsmanship comes at a
price, however.

🕐 Mon–Fri 10–2, 3–7, Sat–Sun by
appointment only 🚌 23, 280

NATOLLI

Map 153 D5
Corso del Rinascimento 55, 00186
Tel 06 6830 1170
www.muranopiumadeinitaly.com

Natolli is on a street parallel
with Piazza Navona and sells
exquisitely crafted Murano
glass, with items ranging from
chandeliers to mirrors, glasses
and even sculptures. All items
are sold with a certificate of
authenticity and signed in
limited editions. Up the road,
at No. 43, is another shop
selling smaller items. Shipping
is possible worldwide.

🕐 Mon–Sat 9–8, Sun 10–7 🚌 64, 87,
116, 492

LE TERRE DI AT

Map 155 J5
Via degli Ausoni 13, 00185
Tel 06 491748

The Sicilian-born potter who
sells her work here likes to
give an innovative, often
ethnic, twist to her ceramics.
She produces tableware, mugs
and vases, as well as exquisite
jewellery, which she plates
with gold and platinum.

🕐 Tue–Sat 10–1, 4–8, Mon 4–8 🚌 71,
492; tram 3, 19

LE TRE GHINEE

Map 153 D5
Via del Pellegrino 53a, 00186
Tel 06 687 2739

A mother and daughter design
team making jewellery and
objets d'art using Tiffany glass

and pottery techniques. The mother deals in glass and the daughter is a pottery wizard. Items range from expensive vases to very reasonable cups and goblets. Pottery Nativity scenes are on sale at Christmas. Evening classes offered.

🕐 Mon–Sat 10–8 🚌 46, 62, 64, 116, 492, 571, or any bus to Corso Vittorio Emanuele II

BOOKS

AL FERRO DI CAVALLO
Map 153 E3
Via Ripetta 67, 00186
Tel 06 322 7303
www.ferrodicavallo.com
A large collection of books on art, photography, architecture and graphic design is to be found here, mostly in English. Very helpful and friendly staff are on hand to help, but no one will bother you if you just want to browse in peace.
🕐 Mon–Sat 9.30–7.30 🚇 Flaminio 🚌 224, 590, 913

ALMOST CORNER BOOKSHOP
Map 153 D6
Via del Moro 45, 00153
Tel 06 583 6942
Interesting and unusual selection of books, especially considering the shop's small size. Competitively priced and particularly good on biography and history, with a strong emphasis on Rome and Italy. Extensive children's section, from toddlers to teenagers. Special orders at no extra charge. Over 5,000 titles on display. Helpful and knowledgeable owner.
🕐 Mon–Sat 10.30–1.30, 3.30–8, Sun 11–1.30, 3.30–8; closed Sun in Aug 🚌 H, 8, 23, 280 to Trastevere; tram 8

ANGLO AMERICAN BOOK CO
Map 153 E4
Via della Vite 102, 00187
Tel 06 679 5222
www.aab.it
This is one of the better English bookshops in the

city in a 19th-century building, a short distance from the Spanish Steps. The excellent selection includes music, cinema, philosophy, religion and science, as well as fiction and children's books. It also sells a wide range of travel guides.
🕐 Sep–end Jun Tue–Sun 10–7.30, Mon 3.30–7.30; Jul–end Aug Mon–Fri 10–7.30, Sat 10–2 🚌 40, 62, 64, 116

ANTICA LIBRERIA CROCE
Map 153 D5
Corso Vittorio Emanuele II 156, 00186
Tel 06 6880 2269
This primarily Italian bookshop, with some titles in English, specializes in books

Rome has many places where you can browse a good book

on all aspects of classical and contemporary art and photography. It has an extensive selection on two floors, and from time to time art exhibitions are held here.
🕐 Mon–Sat 10–8, Sun 10–1.30, 4–8.30 🚌 40, 62, 64, 116

FELTRINELLI INTERNATIONAL
Map 154 G4
Via V. E. Orlando 84, 00184
Tel 06 482 7870
www.lafeltrinelli.it
Come here for novels and books in English, French, Spanish, Portuguese, German and Japanese, including probably the widest selection of travel guides

in English. There's also a good section dedicated to learning Italian. Feltrinelli has more than 100,000 books, at generally more competitive prices than most other bookstores selling foreign books.
🕐 Mon–Sat 9–8, Sun 10–1.30, 4–7.30 🚇 Repubblica 🚌 H, 40, 64, 170

MEL BOOKSTORE
Map 154 G4
Via Nazionale 254–255, 00184
Tel 06 488 5405
www.melbookstore.it
Mel Bookstore takes up two floors of an appealingly spacious art deco interior with wide marble staircases. Sofas are dotted everywhere, allowing you to peruse before purchase in comfort. Other highlights include a small but interesting selection of second-hand books and CDs, a good number of English paperbacks, guides relating to current and recent art exhibitions in Rome, and a café.
🕐 Mon–Sat 9–8, Sun 10–1.30, 4–8 🚇 Repubblica 🚌 H, 40, 60, 64, 70, 117, 170

OPEN DOOR BOOKSHOP
Map 153 E6
Via della Lungaretta 23, 00153
Tel 06 589 6478
www.books-in-italy.com
An eccentric little bookshop that is a real find. The building dates from the 16th century, while the shop started life in 1965. The American owner stocks mainly second-hand books, including rare and out-of-print volumes. He also publishes his own satirical political review on current events in Italy and the world, which is well worth browsing through.
🕐 Tue–Sat 11–3, 5–8, Mon 4.30–8 🚌 Tram 8

CHILDREN'S CLOTHES

LA CICOGNA
Map 154 H7
Piazzale Appio 2, 00183
Tel 06 7049 2554
Just along from San Giovanni in Laterano, this shop is part of a chain dealing exclusively in children's clothes and fancy dress, up to the age of 14. The clothes are well made and the prices moderate. They also have a good selection of toddlers' shoes.
Tue–Sat 9.30–1, 4–7.30, Mon 4–8.30
San Giovanni

MESSI MAI
Map 154 G2
Via Salaria 91, 00198
Tel 06 8424 1541
With its memorabilia and posters on the walls, the Messi Mai feels like an American sports bar. It has an exceptional mix of new and good-condition second-hand clothes for kids. Used jeans by Levi and dungarees by OshKosh B'Gosh look brand new. New clothes and shoes from Abercrombie, Converse, Gap, Kookai and more.
Tue–Sat 9.30–1, 3.30–7, Mon 3.30–7.30 38, 53, 63, 86, 92, 217, 360, 630, or any bus to Piazza Fiume or Via Salaria

RACHELE
Map 153 D5
Vicolo del Bollo 6–7, 00186
Tel 06 686 4975
Delightful shop tucked down a side alley close to Campo dei Fiori. Clothes, from classic and retro to the latest kids' fashions, are all handmade by the Swedish owner in high-quality, durable cottons and wools. Stock items are for children up to age 6; special orders up to age 12. There is a good line of amusing accessories, including a range of hats inspired by animals and fruits.
Tue–Sat 10.30–2, 3.30–7.30 46, 62, 64, 116, 492, 571, or any bus to Corso Vittorio Emanuele II

RAPHAEL JUNIOR
Map 153 F3
Via Veneto 96–98, 00187
Tel 06 488 5692
Children's clothing by over 40 Italian designer names. Helpful and knowledgeable staff will show you all the latest trends in garments and shoes for little ones by the likes of Armani, Versace, Byblos, Les Copains and Blumarine. Customers are the sort who don't bat an eyelid at the price tag.
Mon–Sat 10–7.30 Barberini 52, 53, 63, 95, 116, 119, 204, 630

Top-flight fashions and accessories at La Rinascente

DEPARTMENT STORES AND SHOPPING CENTRES

CINECITTÀ DUE
Map 155 J7
Via Palmiro Togliatti 2, 00173
Tel 06 722 0910
www.cinecittadue.com
You can't actually tour the studios of 'Hollywood on the Tiber', where all those spaghetti westerns were filmed, but you can shop with the stars in the Cinecittà Due shopping mall. All the shops you might need under one roof, plus good parking facilities.
Mar–end Oct daily 10–8; Nov–end Feb Mon–Sat 10–8 Subagutsa 341, 409, 451

COIN
Map 154 H7
Piazzale Appio 7, 00183
Tel 06 708 0020
www.coin.it
One of Rome's most popular department stores is close to San Giovanni in Laterano. A modern, bright, mainly glass building with cosmetics, home furnishings, kitchenware, toys and fashions. The top floor is dedicated to home exhibitions. Prices are higher than in the average store; there is a snack bar on the fourth floor.
Daily 9.30–8 San Giovanni

MAS
Map 154 H5
Via dello Statuto 11, 00185
Tel 06 446 8078
Rome's first department store opened its doors in 1882. Its five floors, totalling 8,000sq m (85,000sq ft), are filled floor to ceiling with clothing, shoes and houseware. The discounted branded goods help to compensate for the lack of glamour.
Daily 9–1, 4–8 Vittorio

MITSUKOSHI
Map 154 G4
Via Nazionale 259, 00184
Tel 06 482 7828
Prices are given in euros and yen, and most of the customers here are Japanese: You may wonder if you are still in Rome, but all the goods are Italian. Accessories and some clothes from the major Italian names, plus, in the bazaar-style basement, food, wine and kitchenware.
Tue–Sat 10.30–7.30, Mon 12–7.30 Repubblica H, 40, 60, 64, 70, 117, 170

LA RINASCENTE
Map 154 G3
Piazza Fiume, 00198
Tel 06 767 9691
www.rinascente.it
More modern and with a better selection than the original Via del Corso store.

Six floors with upmarket
cosmestics and accessories,
some of the better diffusion
lines (a designer's second
and less expensive range)
such as Versace Classic
and Trussardi Sport, and
mid-range brands like Esprit,
Diesel and Calvin Klein.
It also has a good line for
teenagers. Top-floor
restaurant/café and
hairdresser.
🕐 Mon–Sat 9.30–8, Sun 10.30–8
🚌 38, 53, 63, 86, 92, 217, 360, 630, or
any bus to Piazza Fiume

TAD
Map 153 E3
Via del Babuino 155a, 00187
Tel 06 3269 5122
www.taditaly.com
Very smart store selling a
bit of anything as long
as it's cool, exotic and
expensive. Beautiful flowers,
including orchids, plus
magazines and books,
fabrics, candles, furniture,
tableware, clothing,
shoes, cosmetics—you
name it and (if it's the
latest thing) it's here.
Also, an exclusive hair
salon and café/restaurant.
🕐 Tue–Fri 10.30–7.30, Mon 12–7.30,
Sat 10.30–8, Sun 10–8 🚇 Spagna or
Flaminio 🚌 81, 117, 119, 590, 628

FASHION AND LINGERIE
ABITART
Map 153 E4
Via della Croce 46–47, 00187
Tel 06 6992 4077
www.abitartworld.com
Rome designer Vanessa
Foglia makes vivid, flowing
separates and dresses,
which look like works of
art both on and off the
body. Unusual shapes,
forms and combinations
of patterns and hues,
combined with some
quirky accessories, ensure
an individual look.
🕐 Daily 10–8 🚇 Spagna 🚌 81, 117,
119, 590, 628

BRIONI
Map 154 F4
Via Barberini 79, 00187
Tel 06 484517
www.brioniroma.com
Brioni has dressed royalty and
celebrities since 1945, and has
a well-deserved reputation as
one of Italy's top tailors. Leave
your measurements and you
can call up for a suit anytime,
anywhere. This, the oldest and
largest Brioni store, also stocks
women's ready-to-wear items.
Others branches are at Via dei
Condotti 21a and Via Vittorio
Veneto 129.
🕐 Mon–Sat 10–1.30, 3.30–7.30
🚇 Barberini 🚌 63, 116, 175, 492,
590, 630

*TAD stocks everything from
orchids to ornaments*

DAVIDE CENCI
Map 153 E4
Via di Campo Marzio 1–7, 00186
Tel 06 699 0681
Calm and sophisticated
preserve of those who prefer
old-fashioned class over
ephemeral fashion. The names
to be found here include
Burberry, Ralph Lauren, Tod's,
Hogan, Ballantyne, Brooks
Brothers and Church's.
Everything required to dress
both men and women for work
and play, with an emphasis on
timeless, unprovocative style.
🕐 Mon–Sat 9.30–1.30, 3.30–7.30
🚌 116, or any bus to Largo di
Argentina

IL DISCOUNT DELL'ALTA
MODA
Map 153 F3
Via Gesù e Maria 14 and 16a, 00187
Tel 06 361 3796
These two shops, standing side
by side, are tucked away in a
little side street opposite
Rome's Anglican church.
One sells menswear, the
other women's clothes. They
both have a good selection of
top designer labels (end of
stock) at knock-down prices.
They don't exactly advertise
themselves, but the shops are
bright, neat and compact inside.
🕐 Tue–Sat 10–7.30, Mon 2.30–7.30
🚇 Spagna or Popolo

LE GALLINELLE
Map 154 F5
Via del Boschetto 76, 00184
Tel 06 488 1017
www.legallinelle.it
Tiny and unusual boutique in a
former butcher's shop. Vintage,
ethnic and contemporary
fabrics are transformed into
inspired retro clothing with a
modern twist. There is also a
great selection of vintage
accessories and garments.
Prices are reasonable and
there's a small men's section,
with trousers and overcoats.
🕐 Tue–Sat 10–1, 3.30–8, Mon 3.30–8
🚌 H, 40, 60, 64, 70, 117, 170

LEAM
Map 154 H7
Via Appia Nuova 26, 00183
Tel 06 7720 7204
www.leam.com
Near San Giovanni in Laterano,
Leam has two stores within a
few doors of each other,
selling top designer fashion
and accessories for both sexes.
It has the best of Italian
design: Armani, Gucci, Prada,
Dolce & Gabbana and even
Philippe Starck dresses. Shop
assistants can be over-
attentive, which is a common
complaint in Rome. There is a
roof terrace and bar in the
women's store.
🕐 Tue–Sat 9.30–7.30, Mon 3.30–7.30
🚇 San Giovanni 🚌 87, 360

LEI
Map 154 F5
Via Nazionale 88, 00184
Tel 06 482 1700
The name on the shop window is understated in small letters, but it's well known to young Rome-based socialites and women of fashion. They come here for their D&G staples, Romeo Gigli ready-to-wear, and a dazzling selection of party dresses and delicate slip-on shoes by French designers such as Stephane Kélian.
⊙ Mon–Sat 10–7.30 (also Jul, Dec Sun 10–2, 4–7.30) 🚌 H, 40, 60, 64, 70, 117, 170

MAGA MORGANA
Map 153 D5
Via del Governo Vecchio 27 and 98, 00186
Tel 06 687 9995
Two shops selling clothes by designer Luciana Iannace. The shop at No. 27 has mostly hand-knitted jumpers, skirts and dresses. At No. 98 (on the other side of the road), delve into designs for the evening or for special occasions, even weddings. Prices are high, but you can still pick up a bargain.
⊙ Mon–Sat 10–8 🚌 40, 64, 116, 492, 571, or any bus to Corso Vittorio Emanuele II

SCHOSTAL
Map 153 E4
Via del Corso 158, 00186
Tel 06 679 1240
A shop with a long tradition of selling good-quality lingerie. You can also find shirts, ties and socks for both sexes. It is family-run, friendly and reasonably priced. The shop is remembered for giving every client a free shirt when it reopened after World War II, and photographs from its long history adorn the walls.
⊙ Sep–end Jun Mon–Sat 9.30–6.30, Sun 10–7; Jul–end Aug Mon–Fri 9.30–6.30, Sat 9.30–1 Ⓜ Spagna or Popolo

SOCRATE
Map 153 F5
Via Nazionale 89, 00187
Tel 06 484530
A kaleidoscope of brightly coloured shirts, sweaters and ties catches your eye in this men's shop. High fashion is represented by many designer names and the clothes are made of beautiful fabrics. Inside you will find more sombre suits as well as the dazzling collection of sportswear. Helpful assistants speak English too.
⊙ Tue–Sat 9.30–1, 3.30–7.30, Mon 3.30–7.30 Ⓜ Repubblica 🚌 H, 40, 60, 64, 70, 170, 117

Affordable sophistication at Verso Sud

TINA
Map 153 E4
Via Bocca del Leone 9, 00187
Tel 06 678 4076
All you can dream of in luscious silks, laces and embroidery for special nightdresses or underclothes. There are also exquisite children's and baby clothes, all made in Italy. Special orders can be made as well.
⊙ Tue–Sat 10–7.30, Mon 3.30–7.30 Ⓜ Spagna 🚌 62, 63, 81, 85, 95, 175, 204

TREPPIEDI
Map 153 E5
Via del Teatro Valle 55d, 00186
Tel 06 6880 6268
Two minutes from Piazza Navona, this quaintly old-fashioned shop has been famous for years in Rome for its women's lingerie and made-to-measure swimwear. Prices are high but so is the quality. Large sizes are kept in stock.
⊙ Tue–Sat 9.30–1, 4–7.30 🚌 40, 62, 64, 116

VALLI
Map 153 F4
Via del Tritone 126, 00187
Tel 06 488 2931
Famous throughout Italy, Valli's Rome shop displays beautiful materials used by all the big names in French and Italian fashion, from Armani to Valentino. Sale times offer incredible bargains.
⊙ Oct–end Nov Mon–Sat 9.30–6.30; Dec Mon–Sun 9.30–6.30; Jan–end Jun Mon–Sat 9.30–6.30; Jul–end Sep Mon–Fri 9.30–6.30, Sat 9.30–1 Ⓜ Barberini 🚌 71, 117

VERSO SUD
Map 153 D6
Via di S. Francesco a Ripa 168, 00153
Tel 06 5833 3668
On first sight Verso Sud looks minimalist and forbidding, with limited stock and a stark layout. In fact, it is a really informal place where you can feel comfortable looking without buying. Clothes range from the expensive but still affordable (Comme des Garçons) to the affordable and fashionable (Diesel Style Lab).
⊙ Mon–Sat 10–2, 4–8 🚌 H, 780; tram 8

FOOD AND DRINK
ANDREOTTI
Map off 153 E7
Via Ostiense 54b, 00154
Tel 06 575 0773
Just along from the white marble pyramid at Ostiense is this patisserie-cum-café. Try one of their delectable

choux pastries filled with a *limoncello* or rum cream, accompanied by a cappuccino. There are many other pastries, ice creams and a few savouries, too.

🕐 Daily 7.30am–9pm
Ⓜ Piramide

ANTICA PESCHERIA GALLUZZI 1894
Map 154 G4
Via Venezia 26/28, 00184
Tel 06 474 4444
This most noble of fishmongers has been supplying Romans for well over 100 years. In a lovely old palace with brick arches you'll find quality fish and shellfish caught from all over the Mediterranean. Their anchovies are said to be the best in town.

🕐 Tue–Sat 7–1.30; closed last 2 weeks in Aug Ⓜ Repubblica 🚌 64, 70

AVENATI
Map 154 F5
Via Milano 44, 00184
Tel 06 488 2681
Like most delicatessens in Rome, this one is satisfyingly old-fashioned and guaranteed to make your mouth water. Packed with traditional Italian foods not found in the local markets: quality salamis, olive oils from Tuscany, Umbria and Puglia, special pastas, wines and cheeses, including handmade, buffalo-milk mozzarella.

🕐 Mon–Sat 8–8; closed 2nd half of Aug Ⓜ Repubblica 🚌 40, 64, 71, 75, 117

LA BOTTEGA DEL CIOCCOLATO
Map 154 G5
Via Leonina 82, 00184
Tel 06 482 1473
A blissful little Italian chocolate shop. Most goodies are produced from a 19th-century Piedmont recipe; others are 'secrets of old masters'. Period cupboards and shelves, and a large mirror reflecting the chocolate creations along the walls

and in jars behind the counter. The pralines are made on the premises, and a selection of special chocolates for all festive occasions is sold. From €7 per 100g (4oz).

🕐 Mon–Sat 9.30–7.30; closed mid-Jun to end Aug Ⓜ Cavour 🚌 117

CASTRONI
Map 152 C3
Via Ottaviano 55, 00192
Tel 06 3972 3279
This deli brings a slice of the 1950s—the date the shop first started trading—to modern-day Rome. All manner of produce from Italy and the world over. Particularly impressive

Salami and cheese are just two of the culinary delights on offer

selection of jams, boiled sweets and coffee beans. It's a treat for the eyes and palate, with a beautiful wood-panelled interior stocked from floor to ceiling with goodies. The assistants in red jackets are ready to lend a hand. Espresso bar also on site.

🕐 Daily 7.30am–8pm Ⓜ Ottaviano 🚌 70, 81, 492

IL FORNO DI CAMPO DE' FIORI
Map 153 D5
Campo dei Fiori 22/22a, 00186
Tel 06 6880 6662
www.campodefiori.com
This tiny bakery has been on the Campo dei Fiori since

1850 and is always packed. There is no discernible order in which people are served, but hang on in there—all is forgiven with one bite of their *pizza bianca*, fresh from the oven, with a hint of rosemary, olive oil and sea salt, served as bread. Also home-made biscuits and cakes. Credit cards are not accepted.

🕐 Mon–Sat 7.30–2.30, 4.30–8 🚌 46, 64, 116

IL GIARDINO DEL TÈ
Map 154 F5
Via del Boschetto 112, 00184
Tel 06 474 6888
www.ilgiardinodelte.it
There is no garden, but there are over 100 teas from all over the world. Soothing classical music helps you select from a staggering collection, neatly packaged in cellophane bags with instructions attached. The teas conjure up whole other worlds, with names like Jasmine Dragon Eyes. Biscuits, jams and spiced coffees are also on sale. Tea starts at €3 per 100g (4oz).

🕐 Mon–Fri 8.30–2.30, 4–7.30, Sat 8.30–1.30, 4–7.30; closed Aug Ⓜ Cavour 🚌 117

GRAN CAFFÈ DAGNINO
Map 154 G4
Via V. E. Orlando 75 (Galleria Esedra), 00185
Tel 06 481 8660
www.pasticceriadagnino.com
Restaurant, café and bar in the unremarkable Galleria Esedra. However, once inside this Sicilian emporium of all things gastronomic, all else will be forgotten: mouth-watering ricotta, candied fruit-filled Sicilian sweets and succulent savoury delicacies. Also plenty of attractive foodstuffs you can take with you, from jams and cakes to wines, sauces and preserves.

🕐 Daily 7am–11pm Ⓜ Repubblica 🚌 H, 40, 60, 64, 70, 117, 170 to last stop on Via Nazionale

INNOCENZI

Map 153 D6
Via Natale del Grande 31, 00153
Tel 06 581 2725
Old-fashioned store in a street known for its food, with sweets in open jars, and rice and pulses spilling out of sacks on the floor. Foods from all over the world and some of Italy's best regional items can be bought, such as breads from Sardinia and honey biscuits from Calabria, as well as organic products. Credit cards are not accepted.
🕐 Mon–Wed, Fri–Sat 7–1.30, 2.30–8, Thu 7–1.30 🚌 H, 780; tram 8

PANELLA

Map 154 G5
Via Merulana 54–55, 00185
Tel 06 487 2344
For over a century, Panella has sold dozens of varieties of bread and cakes, and it has the largest selection of home-made *grissini* (breadsticks) in Rome. The three back rooms are packed with hard-to-find ingredients and spices, plus organic pastas, flours, honeys, jams and pulses.
🕐 Mon–Sat 8–2, 5–8, Sun 8–2
🚇 Vittorio Emanuele 🚌 16, 204, 714, 850; tram 3

LA RENELLA

Map 153 D6
Via del Moro 15, 00153
Tel 06 581 7265
Wonderfully fresh bread and pizza all day, every day. This also means it is crowded at all hours. Try freshly baked, thick, unctuous slices of simple *pizza bianca,* topped with olive oil and rosemary, or opt for a number of different fresh toppings. They also make excellent cakes.
🕐 Daily 7am–10pm 🚌 H, 780; tram 8

VALZANI

Map 153 D6
Via del Moro 37b, 00153
Tel 06 580 3792
Going strong since the mid-1920s, this *pasticceria* (cake shop) is an institution in the

Trastevere district. One of the best German-style cakes, *torrone* (a kind of nougat), chocolates and spicy Roman *pangiallo* fruitcake (called *panpepato* when covered in chocolate) are all made on the premises. *Diavoletti al peperoncino,* chocolates laced with chilli, will make your tongue tingle. Credit cards are not accepted.
🕐 Daily 9–8; closed Jun–15 Sep
🚌 H, 630; tram 8

VOLPETTI

Map off 153 E7
Via Marmorata 47, 00153
Tel 06 574 2352
www.volpetti.com

Your mouth will water as soon as you step inside Volpetti

Probably the best (though not the cheapest) deli in Rome. Astounding variety of breads, cheeses, hams, salamis, fresh pasta and ready-made dishes. Service is professional and cheerful. Staff let you sample the cheese to help you decide. Whatever happens, you will not come out empty-handed. It is also a good place for gifts.
🕐 Mon–Sat 8–2, 5–8 🚇 Piramide
🚌 23, 30, 60, 75, 280, 716, or any bus to Piramide or Via Marmorata; tram 3

VOLPETTI

Map 153 E4
Via della Scrofa 21/32, 00186
Tel 06 6880 6335
www.volpetti.com
Related to the more famous branch in Testaccio (▷ left). Prices are high, but quality is higher. Delicacies include truffles, 100 varieties of cheese, home-made salamis and pâtés, and a good selection of wines, all under a 16th-century copper ceiling. Try their sliced *porchetta* (roast suckling pig), which is among the best in the world.
🕐 Mon–Sat 8–8 🚌 62, 64, 87, 116, 492 to Piazza Navona

GIFTS AND SOUVENIRS

ALMAXXURA

Map 153 E6
Viale di Trastevere 83, 00153
Tel 06 580 6303
A treasure trove of objects is to be found here, all chosen with the greatest care, and of the finest quality. Everything is made in Italy, and some famous names are represented, such as Capodimonte, Marzi and Murano. There is china, porcelain and glass, as well as collector's dolls, model cars and many other delightful ideas for the perfect present.
🕐 Tue–Sat 10–8
🚌 44, 780

CASA DEL ROSARIO

Map 154 G5
Via Esquilino 33–34, 00185
Tel 06 486991
Large, rambling emporium of religious memorabilia. It needs renovating, but don't let that put you off. Covers the spectrum from tacky to serious: candles, rosaries, certificates of papal blessing and kitsch souvenirs all abound. Inexplicably, there is also a roomful of reasonably priced suitcases.
🕐 Mon–Fri 9–1, 3–7.30, Sat 9–1
🚇 Termini or Cavour 🚌 75, 84, 105, 204, 360, 590, 714; tram 5, 14

CENTRO RAKU
Map 153 E4
Via dei Pastini 20, 00186
Tel 06 678 7682
www.raku.it
The raku ceramic technique of glazed earthenware originated in 16th-century Japan, where it is mainly reserved for the tea ceremony. The word raku means 'to celebrate the day', or 'to live in harmony'. Here, in one of the most beautiful areas of Rome, near the Pantheon, are hundreds of handmade raku clocks (from €25 to €100).
🕐 Daily 10.30–8 🚌 116

D CUBE
Map 153 D4
Via della Pace 38, 00186
Tel 06 686 1218
D Cube is packed with design objects from around the planet, each labelled with its country of provenance. The range includes everything from tableware, kitchenware, candles and bags to quirkier items such as ecological radios, either clockwork or powered by solar energy. What's on offer is very original, with something for every budget. There's another branch at Via Salaria 23.
🕐 Daily 11–10 🚌 40, 64, 116, 492, 571, or any bus to Corso Vittorio Emanuele II

FABRIANO
Map 153 E3
Via del Babuino 173, 00187
Tel 06 3260 0361
Minimalist in design, this store sells stacks of paper goods and stationery such as notepads and address books, laid out tantalizingly from the brightest to the most muted. The paper, of the highest quality, has been made by the same technique for 800 years, and prices are high. Pens and briefcases are also sold.
🕐 Mon–Sat 10–7.30 🚇 Spagna or Flaminio 🚌 81, 117, 119, 590, 628

GABELLINI
Map 153 E4
Via di Monte Brianzo 76–77, 00186
Tel 06 686 1075
Fine-quality hand-painted pottery and porcelain are on display as you enter and in the room behind you see a cheerful group of artisans at work. In summer they sit in the shady courtyard at the back. They are delighted to take special orders, and goods can be shipped worldwide. They also run courses on pottery-making and painting.
🕐 Mon–Fri 9.30–6.30 🚇 Spagna 🚌 70, 87, 492

Japanese-inspired elegance at Centro Raku

MARMI
Map 153 F4
Via del Lavatore 28, 00187
Tel 06 678 6347
They've been carving things in different colours and types of stone for over 2,000 years, and the floor is done in mosaics as in ancient Rome. Inviting trays of fruit are actually made of painted alabaster. Traventine and onyx are used too for bowls, boxes and chess sets. They can arrange shipping worldwide.
🕐 April–end Oct daily 10–midnight; Nov–end Mar 10–8 🚇 Barberini 🚌 62, 63, 81, 85, 95, 175, 204

PANDORA
Map 153 D6
Piazza Santa Maria in Trastevere 6, 00153
Tel 06 581 7145
This is an unusual but tasteful store, with a great selection of contemporary Venetian glass items, Italian handmade ceramics, ethnic and handmade jewellery, small antique pieces, and accessories such as scarves and bags.
🕐 Daily 10–10
🚌 H, 780; tram 8

HEALTH AND BEAUTY

AI MONASTERI
Map 153 D4
Corso del Rinascimento 72, 00186
Tel 06 6880 2783
www.monasteri.it
This late 19th-century pharmacy has a fascinating array of edible goods (chocolate, honeys and jams) and cosmetics, made in monasteries throughout Italy to traditional recipes. For ladies of a certain age, there's *olio alla trigonella* (fenugreek oil) to firm up the bust and smooth neck wrinkles.
🕐 Mon–Sat 10–1, 2.30–7.30 🚌 40, 64, 116, 492, 571, or any bus that goes along Corso Vittorio Emanuele II, or 30, 70, 81, 87, 186, 628 to Corso del Rinascimento

MUZIO
Map 154 G4
Via Vittorio Emanuele Orlando 77, 00185
Tel 06 488 3529
Every kind of shaving implement, manicure set, mirror, hair accessory and penknife under the sun can be found in this traditional store with old-fashioned service. The goods are of high quality, and they stock lesser-known aftershaves, shaving creams, toothpastes and soaps. There is another branch at Via del Tritone 50.
🕐 Mon–Sat 9.30–8 🚇 Repubblica 🚌 H, 40, 60, 64, 70, 117, 170 to last stop on Via Nazionale

OFFICINA PROFUMO—FARMACEUTICA DI SANTA MARIA NOVELLA
Map 153 D5
Corso del Rinascimento 47, 00186
Tel 06 687 9608
www.smnovella.com
This elegant branch of the pharmacy in Florence's Via della Scala, founded in 1612, sells creams, soaps and perfumes from original recipes by Dominican friars. Some of the recipes go back to medieval times. Their signature and extremely fragrant pot-pourri is made with herbs from the Florentine hills.
🕐 Mon–Sat 10–7.30 🚌 40, 64, 116, 492, 571 to Corso Vittorio Emanuele II, or 30, 70, 81, 87, 186, 628 to Corso Rinascimento

ROMA STORE
Map 153 D6
Via della Lungaretta 63, 00153
Tel 06 581 8789
Despite the unpromising name, this Trastevere shop stocks an incredibly tantalizing selection of hard-to-find and sophisticated British and French perfumes, including L'Artisan Parfumeur, Creed, Etro, Penhaligon's, L'Occitane, Vetiver and Comptoir Sud Pacifique. Creams and imported US and UK brands of soap and toothpaste complete the almost infinite stock.
🕐 Daily 10–8 🚌 H, 780; tram 8

HOME AND SOFT FURNISHINGS

ARCHIVIA
Map 154 F5
Via del Boschetto 15a, 00184
Tel 06 474 1503
A profusion of beautiful glass and furnishings. Reasonably priced gifts, from signed handmade glasses to vases, Italian pottery, unusually framed mirrors, rugs, cushions and gorgeous curtains in natural materials and a vast array of hues. It will come as no surprise that the owner is an interior designer.
🕐 Tue–Sun 10–2.30, 3.30–7.30, Mon

3.30–7.30; closed Aug 🚇 Repubblica
🚌 40, 64, 71, 75, 117

IL BIANCO DI ELLEPI
Map 153 E3
Via della Croce 3/4, 00187
Tel 06 679 6835
Delightful shop in a 16th-century building on the north side of Piazza di Spagna, just across from the Spanish Steps. You will find all sorts of towels, bathrobes and bathmats, which can be personalized. A shipping service is available to anywhere in the world. Prices start at €15.
🕐 Mon–Sat 9.30–7.30 🚇 Spagna
🚌 116, 117

Even Rome's pharmacies can be strikingly stylish

CIR
Map 153 F4
Piazza Barberini 11, 00187
Tel 06 488 3433
Beautifully hand-embroidered table and bed linens are the specialty here, some appliquéd and others with drawn thread work—truly heirloom pieces. There are also some embroidered silk women's blouses and smocked children's clothes.
🕐 Tue–Sat 9.30–7.30, Mon 3.30–7.30
🚇 Barberini 🚌 61, 62, 175

C.U.C.I.N.A.
Map 153 E3
Via Mario de' Fiori 65, 00187
Tel 06 679 1275
www.cucinastore.com
This is still the place to come for the most complete selection (more than 20,000 items) of kitchen utensils in steel, porcelain and wood. Prices to suit all budgets. Culinary heaven for cooks of all levels.
🕐 Tue–Sat 10.30–7.30, Mon 3.30–7.30
🚇 Spagna 🚌 81, 117, 119, 590, 628

FRETTE
Map 153 E3
Piazza di Spagna 11, 00187
Tel 06 679 0673
www.frette.it
Beautiful sleepwear and household linens in stylish prints are what Frette is all about. You'll find only the best fabrics—cottons, linens, cashmeres and silks—as well as a range of beautiful accessories and some shoes and clothing. Old-style glamour, but in step with modern design. There is another branch at Via Nazionale 84.
🕐 Tue–Sat 10–7.30, Mon 1.30–7.30
🚇 Spagna 🚌 116, 117, 119, 590

LEONE LIMENTANI
Map 153 E5
Via del Portico d'Ottavia 47, 00186
Tel 06 6880 6686
Every possible cooking utensil, plus the finest porcelain and crystal, are to be found in this rambling, basement warehouse-style store. Everything is 10–20 per cent less expensive than in smarter stores in the city. Take a numbered wooden plaque at the entrance, and wait for an assistant.
🕐 Tue–Fri 9–1, 3.30–7.30, Mon 3.30–7.30, Sat 9.30–7.30 🚌 H, 23, 63, 280, 630, 780 to Lungotevere dei Cenci, or any bus to Largo di Torre Argentina or Piazza Venezia, then walk

SPAZIO SETTE

Map 153 E5
Via dei Barbieri 7, 00186
Tel 06 6880 4261

Housed in a 17th-century cardinal's palace, this is one of the few stores in Rome that will make even the most hardened shopper salivate over furnishings for the kitchen, living room and bathroom. The range includes vases, lamps and various other ornaments from the biggest names in Italian and international design.

🕐 Tue–Sat 9.30–1, 3.30–7.30, Mon 3.30–7.30 🚌 30, 40, 46, 62, 64, 81, 87, 186, 492, 628, 916; tram 8 to terminus

YAKY

Map 153 E5
Via S. Maria del Pianto 55, 00186
Tel 06 6880 7724
www.yaky.it

Real collectors' items can be found in this treasure trove of beautifully handmade Chinese furniture and household items of the finest quality. Dark polished wooden objects contrast with bright, shimmering silks and polished lamps, creating a rich interior. Willing, friendly staff are there to help make your choice and arrange shipping worldwide.

🕐 Mon–Sat 10–8, Sun 10.30–7.30 🚇 Spagna 🚌 63, 271, 630

JEWELLERY

AUREA AETAS VALLICELLA

Map 153 D5
Vicolo del Governo Vecchio 53, 00186
Tel 06 686 1840

Under the arch in a side street off Corso Vittorio Emanuele II are two linked shops, the workshops of three master goldsmiths. Pieces are designed to your specifications, or you can choose from the catalogue. Good value for money. Orders can be made by email, and worldwide shipping is possible. Items from €80. English spoken. Credit cards are not accepted in the shop.

🕐 Mon–Sat 9.30–5.30 🚌 40, 62, 64

LA GRANDE OFFICINA

Map 155 J5
Via dei Sabelli 165b, 00185
Tel 06 445 0348

Husband and wife set precious and semi-precious stones and pearls to maximum effect, using inventive mountings—for example, ball bearings studded with diamonds, old Balinese coins or a large black pearl on a simple gold band. Items for all budgets.

🕐 Tue–Fri 10–7.30, Mon 12–7.30, Sat 10–1.30; closed Aug 🚌 71, 492; tram 3, 19

IVANO LANGELLA–LABORATORIO ARTIGIANO

Map 153 D6

The market at Campo dei Fiori lives up to its name

Via di Ponte Sisto 73a, 00153
Tel 333 420 9100

Ivano Langella makes intricate jewellery, fashioning silver, gold and bronze with pearl, horn and even plants, to create eye-catching rings and necklaces. Custom-made pieces will be ready in 3–5 days. Credit cards are not accepted.

🕐 Mon–Sat 10.30–1, 4–10 🚌 H, 780; tram 8

MARKETS

CAMPO DEI FIORI

Map 153 D5
Campo dei Fiori, 00186

This 'field of flowers' hosts Rome's liveliest produce market. Traders hawk vibrant

vegetables, seafood, meat, household goods and flowers. Order small items by the *etto* (100g/4oz). Art fair on Sun. Credit cards are not accepted.

🕐 Mon–Sat am 🚌 46, 62, 64, 87, 116, 492

PIAZZA DELLE COPPELLE

Map 153 E4
Piazza delle Coppelle

This tiny but very scenic food market wedged in among the cars and tourists just north of the Pantheon makes a welcome respite from a tiring morning's sightseeing. There are fresh flowers as well as food. Credit cards are not accepted.

🕐 Mon–Sat 7–1 🚌 23, 30, 75, 280, 716 or buses to Via Marmorata; tram 3

PIAZZA SAN COSIMATO

Map 153 D6
Piazza San Cosimato

Trastevere's liveliest food and produce market, which, despite the area's tourist attraction, is still mainly visited by local people. All types of produce are on sale but the cheeses are especially good.

🕐 Mon–Sat 7–1 🚌 H, 23, 280, 780; tram 8

PIAZZA VITTORIO MARKET

Map 154 H5
Via Principe Amadeo, 00185

The former Piazza Vittorio market has moved indoors, and has been officially renamed Nuovo Mercato Esquilino, but most still refer to it by its old name. The move has not dented its popularity and it continues to attract thousands of Romans every day. The area has a large Asian population, which is reflected in the produce sold. You'll find everything from exotic fruits to clothing and suitcases—all at least a third less expensive than anywhere else. Credit cards are not accepted.

🕐 Mon–Thu 7am–5pm, Fri–Sat 7am–4pm 🚇 Vittorio

CHAIN STORES

NAME	Menswear	Womenswear	For children	Shoes	Cosmetics and toiletries	Sports equipment and clothes	Accessories	Household	Books, music and DVDs	Perfume	HEAD OFFICE
Beauty Point					✓					✓	06 904 0631
Benetton	✓	✓	✓								0422 519111
BluNauta	✓	✓					✓				06 696421
Brioni	✓	✓									06 462 0161
Calzedonia						✓	✓				06 6992 5490
Camper				✓							06 6992 5678
Cisalfa						✓					06 7696 7210
Coin	✓	✓	✓	✓	✓		✓	✓		✓	041 2398000
Confalone								✓			06 6500 3137
C.u.c.i.n.a.								✓			06 679 1275
D Cube								✓			06 678 9054
Diesel	✓	✓	✓				✓				06 678 3933
Energie	✓	✓		✓							0871 5891
Etam	✓	✓	✓				✓				06 4891 6926
Ethic		✓									06 4120 0621
Expensive		✓									800 311678
Feltrinelli									✓		02 725721
Foot Locker				✓		✓					06 8740 6040
Frette		✓						✓			039 60461
Furla				✓			✓				051 6202711
Gente	✓	✓					✓				06 320 7671
Geox				✓							0423 282529
Intimissimi	✓	✓									06 6830 1784
Laltramoda		✓									06 882991
Mandarina Duck							✓				51 764411
Mariella Burani		✓									0522 373131
Miss Sixty		✓									0871 5891
Officina Profumo Farmaceutica di Santa Maria Novella					✓					✓	055 216276
Onyx	✓	✓	✓				✓				06 4050 1243
Oviesse	✓	✓	✓	✓	✓	✓	✓	✓		✓	041 2398000
Pandemonium	✓	✓									06 686 8061
Prénatal			✓								039 651638
Pro Fumum					✓					✓	06 679 5982
Replay	✓	✓	✓								0423 9251
Ricordi Media Store									✓		02 725721
La Rinascente	✓	✓	✓	✓	✓	✓	✓	✓		✓	06 679 7691
Sephora					✓					✓	06 4782 3445
Sisley	✓	✓									0422 519111
Stefanel		✓									0422 8191
Upim	✓	✓	✓	✓	✓	✓	✓	✓		✓	06 446 5579

Rome is a great city for shopping. As well as a wide range of individual specialist stores, it has its share of chain stores, including a number of internationally known names, such as Italy's greatest export, Benetton. The numbers of stores shown in the table below are those in Rome, but you will usually find branches in other Italian cities too.

NUMBER OF STORES	DESCRIPTION	SHOP WEBSITE
45	Glossy cosmetics store, selling all the best-known brands at bargain prices.	www.beautypoint.it
20	Some of the best and most affordable casualwear in Italy.	www.benetton.com
11	Simple designs, quality fabrics and good all-round value.	www.blunauta.it
3	Classic cuts and designer fabrics—popular with the stars.	www.brioni.it
32	Swimwear and anything that goes on your feet and legs.	www.calzedonia.it
1	Unconventional footwear from Spain that is made to last.	www.camper.com
15	All the well-known brands of sportswear, sports equipment and trainers.	www.cisalfa.com
4	A department store selling mid-range to elegant stock.	www.coin.it
6	Beautiful handmade furniture and sofas.	none
3	Everything you need in the kitchen, and much more.	www.cucinastore.com
3	Innovative and sleek-looking gifts and souvenirs at this design store.	none
3	Urban trendsetters who embrace innovative fabrics and bright shades.	www.diesel.com
5	Store selling the hippest brands for surf dudes and beach babes.	www.energie.it
16	French version of H&M; less hip, but affordable and imaginative.	www.etam.com
11	Cool, cheap and original, with a focus on vintage looks and ethnic fabrics.	www.ethic.it
8	Not expensive as the name suggests, but affordable and wearable.	www.expensive-fashion.it
4	One of the best bookshops in Italy, with regular guest writer appearances.	www.lafeltrinelli.it
8	All the trainers you could ever want under one roof.	www.footlocker-europe.com
4	Beautifully crafted linens for the home, plus enticing nightwear.	www.frette.it
13	Handcrafted leather bags and footwear with an ultra-modern twist.	www.furla.it
4	Accessories, denim, dresses and eveningwear by hip designers.	www.genteboutique.it
5	Modern styles with soles that keep water out, but let your feet breathe.	www.geox.com
31	Cute and glamorous underwear at affordable prices.	www.intimissimi.it
3	Well-made versatile and stylish clothes that won't break the bank.	www.laltramoda.it
5	Functional, high-tech leather bags and leisurewear.	www.mandarinaduck.com
1	Well-tailored womenswear—from romantic and retro to sexy and revealing.	www.mariellaburani.it
4	Casualwear and jeans for funky teens and twentysomethings.	www.misssixty.com
1	Founded by monks in the early 17th century, this store sells beautifully packaged soaps, perfumes and creams made from plants and herbs.	www.smnovella.com
4	A teenager's dream come true; a vast selection of bright trendy gear.	www.onyx.it
25	Low-end to medium-priced clothes (including swimwear) and homewares.	www.oviesse.it
2	Sassy streetwear that mixes Dolce & Gabanna with Calvin Klein.	www.pandemonium.it
11	Everything for your baby or toddler in one store.	www.prenatal.it
3	An exclusive store selling harder-to-find ranges such as Kiehl's and Aesop.	none
3	The place to come for jeans and funky accessories.	www.replay.it
5	Established and reasonably priced music store that sells concert tickets.	
2	Jewellery, cosmetics, accessories and designer clothes (also in larger sizes).	www.larinascente.it
2	A minimalist, glossy cosmetics superstore with its own affordable range.	www.sephora.com
12	Cool and up-to-date fashions.	www.sisley.com
14	Affordable but modern styles for women that stand the test of time.	www.stefanel.it
16	Department store selling cheap but sturdy fashions and household items.	www.upim.it

PORTA PORTESE

Map 153 E7

Piazza Porta Portese and around, 00153

Rome's most famous flea market is home to nearly 2km (1 mile) of bargains. The whole of Via Portuense from the Porta Portese to Trastevere station is flanked by stands and teeming with people—and there's more in the side streets. Fashionable clothes to antiques and downright junk. Be early for the best buys and beware of pickpockets. Credit cards are not accepted.

🕐 Sun 6.30–1 🚇 Porta Portese 🚊 Tram 3

SOFFITTA SOTTO I PORTICI

Map 153 E3

Piazza Augusto Imperatore, 00186

Tel 06 3600 5345

Approximately 100 stands where anybody can come once a month to sell all the curious heirlooms and other objects hidden in their attic. The focus is on antiques and rare items, and the setting—under the porticoes around the piazza—is very pleasant, especially in the summer. Credit cards are not accepted.

🕐 3rd Sun of month 9–8; closed Aug 🚌 71, 81, 117, 119, 224, 913

VIA SANNIO

Map 154 H7

Via Sannio, 00183

The market, based in one street and with an indoor section, starts at the side of the Coin department store. Saturday has the most stalls and the best atmosphere. All sorts of clothes, new and second-hand, in a wide range of styles for both sexes. Credit cards are not accepted.

🕐 Mon–Fri 8am–2pm, Sat 8am–5pm 🚇 San Giovanni

RICORDI MEDIA STORE

Map 153 E5

Largo di Torre Argentina 6, 00186

Tel 06 6866 3001

www.lafeltrinelli.it

This attractively designed music store is in a building that once housed the Verdi archives. It has the largest classical DVD/CD collection in Rome, plus an extensive selection of Italian music, sheet music and musical instruments. Other outlets are at Termini, Viale Guilio Cesare, Galleria Colonna and Via del Corso.

🕐 Mon–Sat 9am–10pm, Sun 4–8; Jul–end Aug closed Sun 🚌 40, 62, 64, 117 to Piazza Venezia

You could spend hours scouring Porta Portese market for bargains

AL SOGNO

Map 153 D4

Piazza Navona 53, 00186

Tel 06 686 4198

www.alsogno.com

This veritable box of treats will enthrall adults and children alike. It's packed with beautifully made toy animals, from miniature to life size, exquisite Italian handmade dolls and wooden Pinocchios, and Venetian masks and handcrafted chess sets.

🕐 Daily 10–8 🚌 64, 87, 116, 492

BABE

Map 153 E5

Via della Palombella 22, 00186

Tel 06 6830 1875

The idea in this inspired store, just behind the Pantheon, is that anything kids up to 12 will like goes: toys, gadgets, drawing pens, soft toys, bags, party decorations and some clothing items. They also organize children's birthday parties in a special room downstairs, and the staff are very friendly.

🕐 Oct–end May Mon–Sat 10–2, 3–7.30; Jun–end Sep Mon–Sat 10–8 🚌 116 to Pantheon, or 30, 40, 64, 492, 916 (plus several others) to Largo di Torre Argentina

BARTOLUCCI

Map 153 E4

Via dei Pastini 98, 00186

Tel 06 6919 0894

www.bartolucci.com

Not far from the Pantheon is this master craftsman's workshop—all articles are handmade, the result of the most skilled and patient work.

More than a hundred different animal clocks with moving eyes, wooden marionettes, horses and much more. Prices start at just a few euros.

🕐 Daily 9am–11pm 🚌 116

LA CITTÀ DEL SOLE

Map 153 E4

Via della Scrofa 65, 00186

Tel 06 6880 3805

www.cittadelsole.com

Between Piazza Navona and the Pantheon. This is a toy store for the progressive parent, crammed with educational toys, puzzles, games and books. Divided into sections for children aged 0–14, with a focus on creative playing and learning. All the best toys in safe plastics and wood.

🕐 Tue–Sat 10–7.30, Mon 3.30–7.30 🚌 116

WHAT TO DO

ENTERTAINMENT

Rome is often likened to an outdoor theatre and its 'actors' have an innate sense of style. A night at the opera, a concert or the theatre is a showcase for visual display and it would be almost a sin not to dress suitably for the occasion. So, don your finery in the certainty you will not be overdressed! Note that smoking is no longer allowed in any public venue.

CLASSICAL MUSIC

For classical music, the Accademia Nazionale di Santa Cecilia (▷ 180) is the jewel in the crown. Founded in the 16th century, it attracts some of the world's best-known conductors. The winter season is held at the giant Auditorium, Parco della Musica (▷ 181).

Other main companies include the Accademia Filarmonica

There is a wide selection of classical music on offer

Romana (tel 06 320 1752; www.filarmonica romana.org), which can claim Verdi, Donizetti, Paganini and Rossini among its founders. Its varied offerings include chamber music, opera, ballet and ancient music. This Accademia uses the Teatro Olimpico (▷ 182) for its Thursday concerts and also acts as a venue for many of the events in the trendy RomaEuropa Festival (▷ 182).

In the listings, the opening times refer to the box office and the dates to when the season runs. Credit cards are accepted at most venues; we have stated only when they are

not. Smoking is usually allowed at outdoor events.

THEATRE

The main theatres include Teatro di Roma-Argentina (▷ 185). The little Teatro Valle (▷ 185), in the remains of the Teatro di Pompei, is a theatrical jewel and is managed by the Italian Drama Board—the Ente Teatrale Italiano (ETI). Also managed by the ETI, the Teatro Quirino (Via Mario Minghetti, tel 06 679 4585) stages productions by well-known playwrights. There are around 80 theatres in and around the city, and there are many experimental performances to see as well as classical offerings.

The Teatro dell'Opera (▷ 182) has almost perfect acoustics. The season runs from November to June and during the summer, at different open-air venues. The resident ballet company, Corpo di Ballo, also performs at the Teatro dell'Opera and in the summer at other venues (www.opera. roma.it). For contemporary ballet and modern dance try the Teatro Olimpico, Teatro Vascello (▷ 182) or Teatro Greco (Via R. Leoncavallo 16, tel 06 860 7513; www.teatrogreco.it).

CINEMA

Cinema is flourishing in Rome. Although foreign films tend to be dubbed into Italian there are more and more cinemas showing them in their *versione originale* (original version). The Nuovo Olimpia (▷ 180) often dedicates one of its screens to original-language films. The Cineporto has become one of

the most popular summer festivals. Generally credit cards are not accepted.

CONCERTS

The new Auditorium Parco della Musica is Rome's long-awaited venue for classical, rock and pop concerts. There are also some stunning venues that play host to international stars—such as the Villa Borghese and Ostia Antica's Roman theatre. Most smaller venues do not take credit cards.

WHAT'S ON

For listings of what's on where, the weekly *Roma C'è* has an English-language section. *Trovaroma* appears on Thursdays (free with *La*

The Teatro dell'Opera is one of Italy's finest venues

Repubblica); it covers the week's cultural events, and has an English-language section. The monthly *WHERE Rome* is available from any APT tourist information point.

TICKETS

The following agencies are useful. They usually charge a commission of about 10 per cent:

● Orbis (Piazza dell'Esquino 37, tel 06 482 7403).
● Hello Ticket (tel 06 808 8352 or freephone 800 907080).
● Chartanet is an online booking service (www.chartanet.it).

ENTERTAINMENT LOCATOR

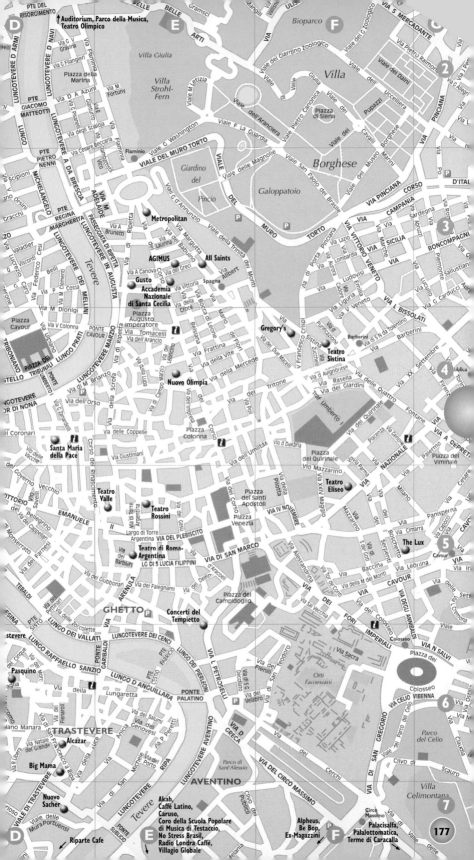

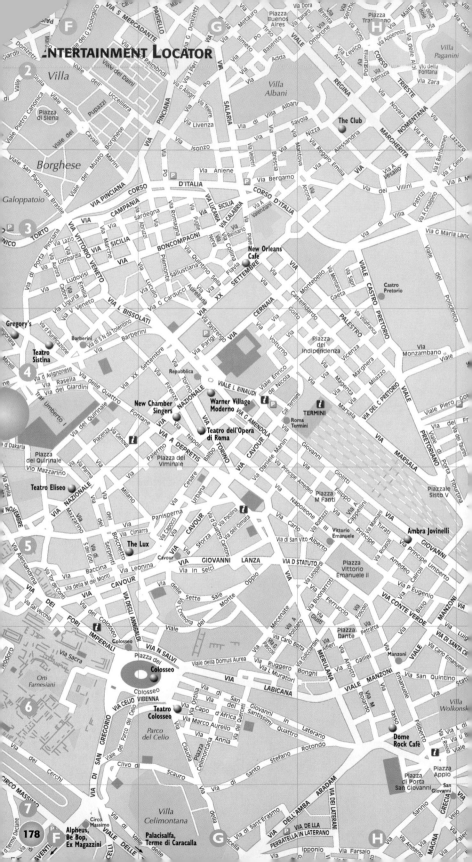

ENTERTAINMENT LOCATOR

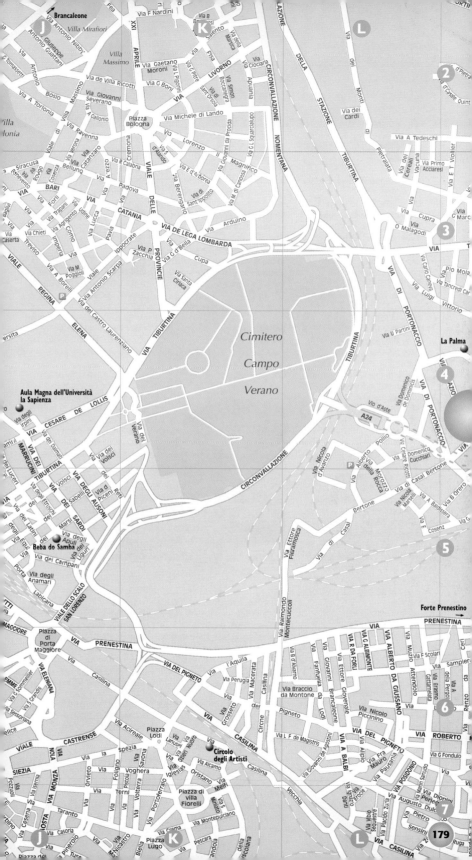

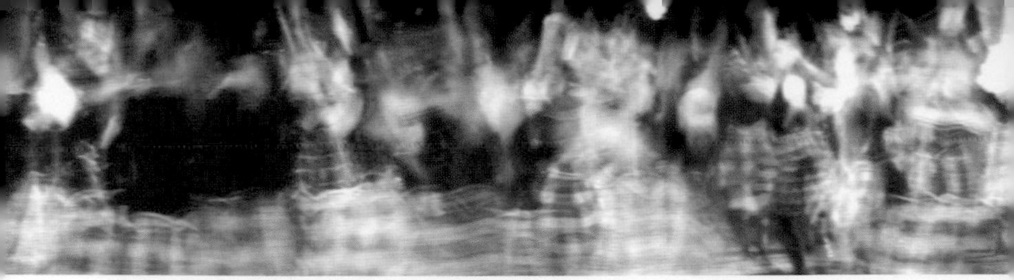

ALCAZAR
Map 177 D6
Via Cardinale Merry del Val 14, 00153
Tel 06 588 0099
One of the first to show blockbusters in their original language (Mon only), with a decadent velvet interior. Frequented by students and expatriates. Bar with coffee and popcorn.
🕐 Daily 👟 €5–€7 🚌 H, 23, 44, 56, 75, 280 to Viale Trastevere; tram 8

INTRASTEVERE
Map 177 D6
Vicolo Moroni 3a, 00153
Tel 06 588 4230
Housed in a 17th-century building, this is Rome's most celebrated independent cinema.
🕐 Daily, 3 screenings 👟 €4.50–€7 🚌 H, 23, 44, 56, 75, 280 to Viale Trastevere; tram 8

METROPOLITAN
Map 177 E3
Via del Corso 7, 00187
Tel 06 320 0933
Four screens and maximum comfort in a cinema with bar, air-conditioning, and ticket machines where you can pay by credit card. One screen is dedicated to original-version films from September to June.
🕐 Daily screenings from 4pm 👟 €5 and €7.50 🚇 Spagna 🚌 81, 117, 119, 590, 628

NUOVO OLIMPIA
Map 177 E4
Via in Lucina 16b, 00186
Tel 06 686 1068
A two-screen cinema with an interesting choice of art-house and more mainstream Italian and foreign films, most of which are not dubbed. Often the only cinema in town to screen certain films.
🕐 Daily; closed Aug 👟 €5–€7 🚌 81, 628 to Via del Corso

NUOVO SACHER
Map 177 D7
Largo Ascianghi 1, 00153
Tel 06 581 8116
Trastevere cinema owned by iconic Italian film director Nanni Moretti. It screens a number of independent films from abroad. Films are shown in their original language on Monday. In the summer, there is also an open-air screen. Large snack bar with drinks and food.
🕐 Daily 👟 €4.50–€7 🚌 H, 23, 44, 56, 75, 280 to Viale Trastevere; tram 8

PASQUINO
Map 177 D6
Piazza Sant'Egidio 10, 00158
Tel 06 581 5208

Rome has a number of excellent outdoor venues

A Roman institution near Santa Maria in Trastevere, with three screens. Films are in their original language. Crowded espresso bar before screenings.
🕐 Daily; closed Jun–end Sep 👟 €4.15 and €6.20 🚌 H, 23, 44, 56, 75, 280 to Viale Trastevere; tram 8

WARNER VILLAGE MODERNO
Map 178 G4
Piazza della Repubblica 45, 00184
Tel 06 477 791
www.warnervillage.it
A recent addition to the Roman cinema scene, this venue is large, airy and hi-tech. Decent popcorn and comfortable seats with plenty of leg room make it a pleasant experience all round. The schedule is commercial, but one of the five screens shows blockbusters and big romantic comedies in their original language.
🕐 Daily screenings from 2.30pm 👟 €7.50, €5.50 before 6pm and Wed 🚇 Repubblica 🚌 H, 40, 64, 170, 492

ACCADEMIA NAZIONALE DI SANTA CECILIA
Map 177 E3
Via Vittoria 6, 00187. Tel 06 328171. Box office: Biglietteria Auditorium, Parco della Musica, Viale Pietro de Coubertin 15.
Tel 06 8024 2355
www.santacecilia.it
The Music Academy of Rome attracts the best professors and students. A beautifully put together menu of musical events is staged in different locations throughout the city. The offical season means that it is closed in July, but the Accademia stages a number of outdoor concerts. Check the website for more details.
🕐 Oct–end Jun Thu–Tue 11–6 👟 €16–€46 🚌 Bus to Piazza del Popolo

AGIMUS (ASSOCIAZIONE GIOVANILE MUSICALE)
Map 177 E3
Via dei Greci 18, 00187
Tel 06 3211 1001
www.agimus.it
Organized by the Associazione Giovanile Musicale, Rome's biggest youth choir stages performances at venues such as churches and parks.
🕐 Sep–end Jul Mon–Sat 3–7 👟 €10 🚇 Termini 🚌 53, 217, 231, 910

ASSOCIAZIONE MUSICALE ROMANA ALL'ORTO BOTANICO
Map 176 D5
Via dei Banchi Vecchi 61, 00186 Botanical gardens: Largo Cristina di Svezia 23b, 00186
Tel 06 686 8441
www.uniroma.it
Rome's botanical gardens provide a much-loved venue

WHAT TO DO

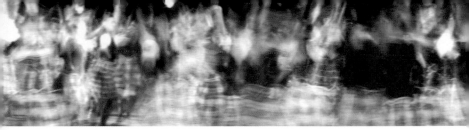

for music events, mainly hosted by the Roman Music Association. From Gershwin to classical, plus a harpsichord festival.

🕐 Box office open 1 hour before concert, no advance tickets. Season: Mar–Sep 🚇 €10–€25 🚌 H, 630, 780

AUDITORIO CONCILIAZIONE

Map 176 C4
Via della Conciliazione 4, 00186
This venue, formerly the Auditorio Pio, holds a range of classical concerts and operas.

🕐 Daily 10.30–1.30, 3–6. Season: Oct–Jun 🚇 €10–€50 🚌 23, 40, 62, 64

AUDITORIUM, PARCO DELLA MUSICA

Map off 177 D2
Viale Pietro de Coubertin 30, 00197
Tel 06 802411
www.musicaperroma.it
Architect Renzo Piano has finally given Rome the concert hall it deserves. Opened in 2002 near Stadio Flaminio, this three-auditorium complex is the city's biggest music venue, with a capacity for 4,600.

🕐 Daily 11–6, 8–start of performance 🚇 From €8 🚇 Flaminio, then tram 2 🚌 53, 217, 231, 910 to Auditorio

AULA MAGNA DELL'UNIVERSITÀ LA SAPIENZA

Map 179 J4
Piazzale Aldo Moro 5, 00185. Box office: Lungotevere Flaminio 50, 00185
Tel 06 361 0051
www.concertiiuc.it
This is the concert hall of the University of Rome, playing mostly classical music but occasionally some jazz, too. It is always packed with student audiences. A great venue, with some of Rome's best futuristic architecture.

🕐 Mon, Tue, Thu and Fri 10–5, Wed and Sat 10–noon, Oct–end Apr 🚇 €12–€33 🚇 Policlinico 🚌 Trams 3, 19

CONCERTI DEL TEMPIETTO

Map 177 E6
Teatro di Marcello, Via del Teatro di Marcello 44, 00186. Box office: Via Rodolfo Morandi 3, 00139
Tel 06 8713 1590
www.tempietto.it
In winter, the Associazione Musicale 'Il Tempietto' stages concerts at the Sala Baldini in Piazza Campitelli and in the Basilica di San Nicola. In summer, the music is performed alfresco in the stunning, ancient Teatro di Marcello.

🕐 Season: Jun–end Sep 🚇 €15 🚌 81, 160, 204, 628 to Via del Teatro di Marcello, or 40, 64, 87, 628 to Piazza Venezia, then walk

Rome attracts many of the world's top conductors

CORO ROMANI CANTORES

Via Franco Sacchetti 78, 00137
Tel 06 8713 9264
www.spmtestaccio.it
This choir specializes in early Renaissance music, which is often played on period and antique instruments. Performances take place in various venues around the city, the most impressive of which is Santa Maria Maggiore.

🕐 Season: Sep–end Jun 🚇 Free

CORO DELLA SCUOLA POPOLARE DI MUSICA DI TESTACCIO

Map off 177 E7
Via Monte Testaccio 91, 00153
Tel 06 575 0376
www.scuolamusicatestaccio.it
The choir of Testaccio's well-known music school is based in Rome's charming Testaccio district. Patrons benefit from a series of concerts and choral events. The school also has a brass band.

🕐 Season: Sep–Jun 🚇 Free 🚌 75, 280

NEW CHAMBER SINGERS

Map 177 E3
All Saints Church, Via del Babuino 153, 00187
Tel 06 3600 1881
This amateur choir, previously directed by members of Rome's Episcopalian church, is now in the hands of the Anglican church, All Saints.

🕐 All year 🚇 Free 🚇 Repubblica 🚌 H, 40, 64, 70, 71, 170

OPERA ALLA TERME DI CARACALLA

Map off 178 G7
Terme di Caracalla. Box office: Teatro dell'Opera, Via Firenze 72, 00184
Tel 06 481601. Booking office tel 06 481 7003
Lavish productions with real elephants used to take place here, but the practice ended in 1995 when archaeologists decreed that the shows endangered the monuments. Smaller music concerts are still held here in the summer: Bring a cushion to sit on.

🕐 4 Jul–15 Aug Tue–Sat 9–5, Sun 9–1.30 🚇 €20–€50 🚇 Circo Massimo 🚌 67, 90, 118, 160, 714, 715

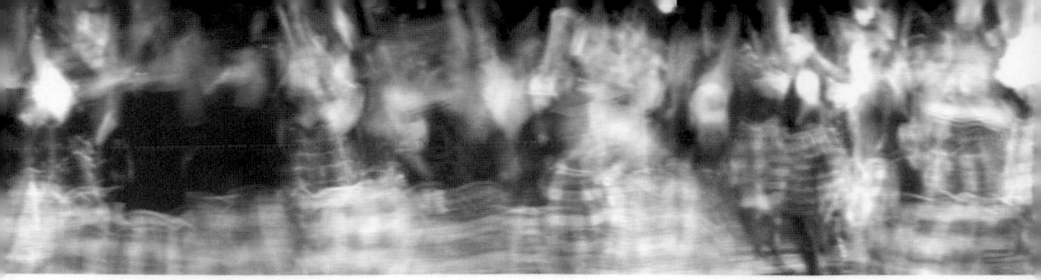

ORATORIUM IL GONFALONE
Map 176 D5
Via del Gonfalone 32a, 00186. Box office: Vicolo della Scimmia 1b, 00186
Tel 06 687 5952
Specializing in chamber music, Il Gonfalone hosts excellent groups from around the world. Events are held in the 16th-century Oratorio del Gonfalone, complete with frescoes and a gilded ceiling.
🎫 Oct–end May Mon–Fri 9.30–4 💶 €8–€13 🚌 116, or 46, 62, 64, 87, 492 to Campo dei Fiori, then walk

ROMAEUROPA FESTIVAL
Via XX Settembre 3, 00186
(box office at Via del Teatro Valle 21)
Tel 06 4229 6300 or 800-795525 (free)
www.romaeuropa.net
A series of concerts in spectacular theatre settings, all close to the city. Organized in collaboration with the French Academy at Villa Medici, the German Academy at Villa Massimo and the Rome International Cultural Centre.
🎫 20 Sep–30 Nov Mon–Fri 10–1, 2–6 💶 €12–€46

SANTA MARIA DELLA PACE
Map 177 D4
Box office: Chiostro del Bramante, Vicolo della Pace 2
Tel 06 780 7695
www.millenunanote.org
Piano recitals and ensembles take place in the church in summer on various days. Adjacent to the famous Bar della Pace, the perfect place for a post-concert espresso.
🎫 Aug 💶 €11–€15 🚌 46, 62, 64, 87, 116, 492 to Piazza Navona

TEATRO GHIONE
Map 176 C4
Via delle Fornaci 37, 00186
Tel 06 637 2294
www.ghione.it
Close to Piazza San Pietro, Teatro Ghione is dedicated to up-and-coming stars, big-name pianists and other soloists. The lively audience gives the place a more relaxed feel.

🎫 Mon–Fri 10–1, 4–8 💶 €16–€21 🚌 46, 64, 571, 916

TEATRO OLIMPICO
Map off 177 D2
Piazza Gentile da Fabriano 17, 00196
Tel 06 326 5991
www.teatroolimpico.it
Very comfortable venue for music lovers, although upstaged of late by the new Auditorium (▷ 181). Owned by the Accademia Filarmonica. Acoustics and concerts are always excellent.
🎫 Mon–Fri 10–1, 3–5.30, or after 8 for same-day tickets, Sep–end May 💶 €20–€35 🚌 32, 168, 186, 280, or any bus to Piazza Mancini then cross river; tram 2

The RomaEuropa Festival features spectacular concerts

TEATRO DELL'OPERA DI ROMA
Map 178 G4
Via Firenze 72, 00186
Tel 06 481 7517
www.opera.roma.it
One of Italy's top opera houses and also an official venue for ballet. The interior of the theatre is adorned with all the trimmings expected of a true opera house, including velvet boxes. When closed over the summer, performances are run through Opera alla Terme di Caracalla (▷ 181).
🎫 Nov–end May Mon–Fri 9.30–2 💶 €8–€120 🚌 30X, 64

TEATRO VASCELLO
Map 176 C7
Via Giacinto Carini 72, 00165
Tel 06 588 1021
www.teatrovascello.it
On the edge of Trastevere, this is a small but good venue for experimental dance and some classic ballet. Also organizes workshops and conferences dedicated to the arts.
🎫 Sep–end Jun Tue–Sat 5.30–9, Sun 3–5 💶 €12 🚌 44, 75, 115, 710, 870

CONTEMPORARY LIVE MUSIC
AKAB
See Clubs, ▷ 189

ALPHEUS
Map off 177 F7
Via del Commercio 36, 00153
Tel 06 574 7826
Many huge rooms for large music events and live bands, with dancing to close the night. You can hop from room to room, changing musical genre as you please.
🎫 Sun–Fri 10pm–4am, Sat 4pm–3am 💶 €7 🚇 Piramide 🚌 60, 95, 118, 175, 280, 719

BE BOP
Map off 177 F7
Via Giulietti 14, 00153
Tel 06 5728 8959
www.bebopmusicclub.it
Large, comfortable 100-seat venue playing exclusively jazz and blues. The live acts are mainly Italian, although international guests are often invited.
🎫 Tue–Sun 10.30–2am 💶 Free; €4 to join club as one-off payment 🚇 Piramide 🚌 30

BEBA DO SAMBA
Map 179 J5
Piazza dei Campani 12, 00185
Tel 339 878 5214
www.bebadosamba.it
African and Central American sounds predominate at this popular two-room venue in the studenty San Lorenzo district, but there is room for anything as long as it

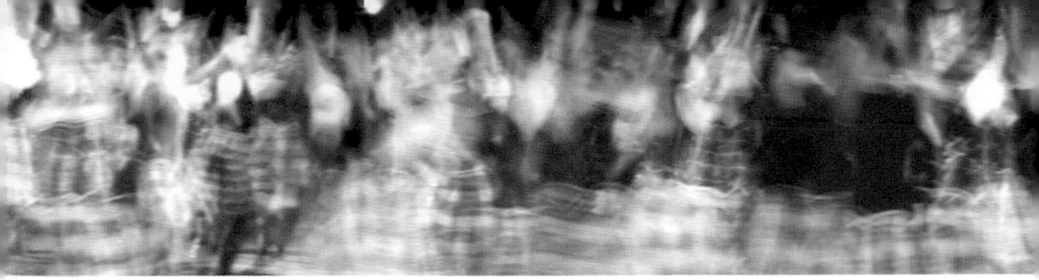

is not mainstream. There are sofas and cushions in one room, and stage and bar in the other.

🎵 Daily 9pm–2.30am 🎫 Compulsory annual membership €3

🚌 71, 491; tram 3, 19

BIG MAMA
Map 177 D6
Vicolo San Francesco a Ripa 18, 00158
Tel 06 581 2551
www.bigmama.it

Trastevere jazz joint where local and international bands play in a cavernous, smoke-filled underground room. The audience sits close to the band and dancing on tabletops is not uncommon.

🎵 Nov–end Jun 9pm–1.30am
🎫 €6–€13 🚌 H, 23, 44, 56, 75, 280 to Viale Trastevere, or any bus to Piazza Mastai; tram 8

BRANCALEONE
Map 179 J2
Via Levanna 11, 00162
Tel 06 8200 0959
www.brancaleone.it

Italy is flooded with *centri sociali*, unofficial underground youth centres. Brancaleone, however, has been authorized by the town hall because of its socially useful activities. This non-profit group is one of Rome's best *centri sociali*, holding live concerts and serving draught beer.

🎵 Thu–Sun 10.30pm–5am
🎫 €5 donation 🚌 60, 211, 311, 343

CAFFÈ LATINO
Map off 177 E7
Via Monte Testaccio 96, 00153
Tel 06 5728 8556

Once *the* place for live music, this place still draws a crowd in a city that loves Latin and jazz. Live acts Monday to Wednesday, followed by dancing. Sunday is gay night.

🎵 Daily 11pm–3am 🎫 €5–€10
🚇 Piramide 🚌 75, 280

CARUSO/CAFÈ DE ORIENTE
Map off 177 E7
Via Monte Testaccio 36, 00153
Tel 06 574 5919

Best bet for Latin sounds, ranging from salsa to hip hop. Mix of live bands and Rome's best DJs. Always packed, especially on Sunday, which is disco night. Arabic music nights, too.

🎵 Daily 11am–4pm 🎫 €8–€10
🚇 Piramide 🚌 75, 280

CIRCOLO DEGLI ARTISTI
See Clubs, ▷ 190

THE CLUB
Map 178 H2
Via Cagliari 25, 00186

Head to Big Mama for cool jazz

Tel 06 9760 3944
www.theclubnet.it

A corner of New York in the centre of Rome, with excellent young musical talent in elegant surroundings. Feast on an unsurpassed range of bar food with delicious combinations in either the cocktail bar or at your table—otherwise visit the restaurant, with a selection of dishes from a creative Italian repertoire.

🎵 Tue–Sun 8pm–2am 🚌 84, 90; tram 3, 19

DOME ROCK CAFÈ
Map 178 H6
Via D. Fontana 18, 00185
Tel 06 7045 2436

This recent addition to Rome's music scene has become very popular in a short space of time, thanks to good beer and great dance music.

🎵 Daily 6pm–3am 🎫 Free 🚌 87, 117, 218 to Piazza San Giovanni

EX-MAGAZZINI
Map off 177 F7
Via dei Magazzini Generali 8, 00153
Tel 06 575 8040

A Rome classic in the Testaccio/Ostiense area. Live music and dancing inside a former greengrocer's premises. The acts come from Rome's underground music scene and range from Italian rap to jazz. It also holds art exhibitions.

🎵 Tue–Sun 9pm–4.30am 🎫 €8, incl one drink 🚇 Piramide 🚌 60, 95, 118, 175, 280, 719

FONCLEA
Map 176 C3
Via Crescenzio 82a, 00197
Tel 06 689 6302

This is a restaurant and pub that also hosts a mixture of funk, Latin and other live music acts. The food and drink (including 200 different cocktails) are great. This audience is always ready to move to the music.

🎵 Daily 12–3, 8.30pm–2am 🎫 Free; except Sat, €5 🚇 Ottaviano 🚌 23, 271, 280, 492, 990

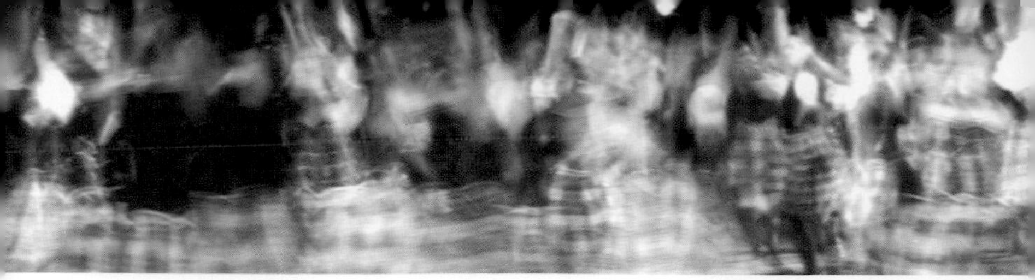

FORTE PRENESTINO

Map off 179 M5
Via Federico Delpino, 00175
Tel 06 2180 7855
www.forteprenestino.net
This *centro sociale* (underground youth centre) lies outside the city in a 15th-century fortress complete with moat and underground tunnels. Students, hippies and political activists screen films and hold parties. There are also a number of live band performances, but for specific details please call ahead.
🕐 Daily, usually 11pm–late 💶 €5 donation 🚋 Tram 5 or 19 to Via Prenestina, or take a taxi

GREGORY'S

Map 177 F4
Via Gregoriana 54d, 00186
Tel 06 679 6386
www.gregorysjazzclub.com
John Bull and Guinness are washed down to the sound of live jazz at this nightspot. There is a jam session every Wednesday and the fans who come here take their jazz very seriously.
🕐 Tue–Sun 8pm–3.30am; closed Aug 💶 Free 🚇 Barberini 🚌 52, 53, 61, 62, 63, 80, 95, 116, 117

GUSTO

See Restaurants, ▷ 244

THE LUX

Map 177 F5
Salita del Grillo 7, 00184
Tel 06 678 1799
www.thelux.it
Located just behind Trajan's Markets not far from the Forums, this is a wonderful blend of wine bar, music venue and cocktail bar, with a resident DJ and two floors divided into four separate areas. Happy hour is from 7 to 10pm. The DJ takes a break twice a week when local artists provide live entertainment.
🕐 Tue–Sat 7pm–2am 🚇 Cavour 🚌 H, 40, 60, 64, 70, 117, 170

NEW ORLEANS CAFE

Map 178 G3
Via XX Settembre 52, 00186
Tel 06 4201 4785
The only place in Rome where you can enjoy the soothing tones of traditional jazz from the 1920s and 1930s every night. Traditional Italian fare at a reasonable price adds to the enjoyment. Music starts at 10pm.
🕐 Mon–Sat 8pm–1am 🚇 Repubblica 🚌 910

NO STRESS BRASIL

Map 177 E7
Via degli Stradivari 35, 00153
Tel 06 5833 5015
www.nostressbrasil.net

Serious jazz is on tap at Gregory's

This is actually a *churrascaria*, where you can eat some of the best steak in town imported directly from Argentina and Brazil. Live music by Brazilian bands and blues concerts accompany you every evening and are followed by DJ sets and partying till dawn.
🕐 Daily 8.30pm–3.30am 💶 Free Mon–Thu and Sun, €10 Fri–Sat 🚇 Piramide G23, 30, 75, 280, 673, 716, 719; tram 3

PALACISALFA

Map off 178 G7
Viale dell'Oceano Atlantico 271, 00144
Tel 06 5728 8018
www.palacisalfa.com

When music fans complained that the Palalottomatica (see below) was not ideal for smaller concerts, city officials built the Palacisalfa. It is a more friendly venue with good sound quality and atmosphere.
🕐 Performances usually at 8pm 💶 €12–€40 🚇 EUR Fermi 🚌 706, 779

PALALOTTOMATICA

Map off 177 F7
Piazzale dello Sport, Viale dell'Umanesimo, 00144
Tel 06 540901
www.palalottomatica (schedule)
www.ticketweb.it (tickets)
The biggest venue in the city hosts all the top international acts—everyone from Sting to the Rolling Stones has played in this sports stadium-turned-concert hall.
🕐 Performances usually at 8pm 💶 €20–€40 🚇 EUR Palasport

THE PLACE

Map 176 C4
Via Alberico II 27/29, 00193
Tel 06 6830 7137
www.theplace.it
Just behind Castel Sant'Angelo is this new jazz club, hosting performances from acclaimed Italian and international artists. It's open throughout the year, excluding the usual August month-long siesta. You can enjoy typical Italian cuisine before you settle down to some excellent music.
🕐 Daily from 8pm for buffet supper, music from 10.30pm 💶 €10–€30 🚇 Lepanto 🚌 81, 492

RADIO LONDRA CAFFÈ

Map off 177 E7
Via Monte Testaccio 65b, 00153
Tel 06 575 0044
At the heart of clubbers' row in Testaccio, this is the place to go for classic rock, 80s music, good dancing and live bands. It serves beer and snacks, and has a laid-back attitude.
🕐 Mon–Sat 9pm–3am 💶 €10 inc drink 🚇 Piramide 🚌 75, 280

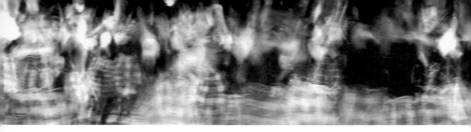

RIPARTE CAFE
Map off 177 D7
Via Degli Orti Di Trastevere 7, 00153
Tel 06 586 1816
Two elegantly furnished, stylish and high-tech rooms with a minimalist flair. Soft candlelight and traditional cooking as well as more creative dishes with an oriental twist are complemented by an extensive wine list. This cocktail bar has a lively, bubbly atmosphere and the live music on Friday and Saturday evenings should not be missed.
🔵 Mon–Thu 7pm–1am, Fri and Sat 7pm–2am 🚌 H; tram 8

VILLAGGIO GLOBALE
Map off 177 E7
Lungotevere Testaccio, 00153
Tel 06 575 7233
Rome's most popular music venue is in a former slaughterhouse (the Mattatoio). Huge outdoor courtyard for concerts and dancing. During larger events, food stands are set up inside.
🔵 Varies, usually 6pm–3am
💶 Maximum €10 🚌 75, 280, or bus to Lungotevere Testaccio

THEATRE
AMBRA JOVINELLI
Map 178 H5
Via Guglielmo Pepe 43–7, 00185
Tel 06 4434 0262
www.ambrajovinelli.com
Built at the turn of the 20th century, this was once Rome's foremost variety venue but was almost knocked down in the 1990s after a period of steady decline. It was entirely renovated and reopened in January 2001 and now pulls in some of the best comic actors in Italy, and also puts on some of the best comic plays and one-man shows. It also hosts jazz concerts.
🔵 Sep–end May, with one-off events in Jun and Jul. Box office Oct–end Jun Mon–Sat 10–7, Sun 11–1.30; Jul, Sep Mon–Sat 10–1, 2–6; closed Aug
💶 €11.50–€27.50 🚇 Termini 🚌 70, 71; tram 5, 14

TEATRO COLOSSEO
Map 178 G6
Via Capo d'Africa 5, 00184
Tel 06 700 4932
In the shadow of the mighty Colosseo, this venue is a rarity for Rome—a theatre staging English-language plays. It is a good showcase for young directors and actors, and the small stage suits one-man shows.
🔵 Sep–end Jun Mon–Sat 10–1, 3–7
💶 €10–€20 🚇 Colosseo 🚌 30

TEATRO ELISEO
Map 177 F5
Via Nazionale 183, 00184
Tel 06 488 2114
www.teatroeliseo.it

Checking out the evening's entertainment

Large, modern and popular, the Eliseo puts on plays by major and established Italian and international playwrights, while the smaller Piccolo Eliseo next door pays more attention to contemporary and fringe theatre.
🔵 Sep–end May. Box office Mon–Sat 9.30–2.30, 3.30–7; closed Aug, and Sat in Jun and Jul 💶 €8–€27 🚌 40, 64, 70, 71, 170

TEATRO DI ROMA— ARGENTINA
Map 177 E5
Largo Argentina 52, 00186
Tel 06 6840 0345
www.teatrodiroma.net
One of Rome's most historic theatres, a leading venue for beautifully staged productions. A performance here is a night out and the audience dresses up accordingly. There is a cocktail bar.
🔵 Box office: Mon–Sat 10–2, 3–7
💶 €12–€27 🚌 64, 87, 492 to Largo Argentina; tram 8

TEATRO ROSSINI
Map 177 E5
Piazza Santa Chiara 14, 00186
Tel 06 683 2281
www.alfieroalfieri.com
Run by Alfiero Alfieri, with performances dedicated to comedy, local dialect and the traditional characters of popular and traditional Roman theatre.
🔵 Daily 10am–8pm 💶 €15–€18
🚌 64, 87, 492 to Largo Argentina; tram 8

TEATRO SISTINA
Map 177 F4
Via Sistina 129, 00186
Tel 06 420 0711
www.ilsistina.com
This theatre stages largely dramatic productions and some musicals, including international extravaganzas. The informal atmosphere draws a young audience, which tends to participate vocally.
🔵 Oct–end May daily 10–7
💶 €20–€40 🚇 Spagna

TEATRO VALLE
Map 177 E5
Via del Teatro Valle 21a, 00186
Tel 06 6880 3794
www.teatrovalle.it
Charming little theatre with excellent dramatic performances, including the classics, all produced with great attention to detail. This also makes it popular with students.
🔵 Tue–Sat 10–7 💶 €11–€29
🚇 Barberini 🚌 64, 87, 492 to Largo Argentina, or any bus to Corso Vittorio Emanuele; tram 8

NIGHTLIFE

Whether it's a quiet drink in an atmospheric *enoteca* or dancing until dawn in a smoke-filled club, there's something for everyone in Rome. Choose from lounge, house, retro, electronica, cheesy Euro sounds, hip hop, R&B, cigar rooms, speed-dating, high tech, cool sounds with attitude, hot South American, reggae—the list is endless. Most clubs don't get going until around 1am, so a visit to a couple of bars and a late pizza is the Roman way to kick off proceedings.

WHERE TO GO
The Campo dei Fiori is the place for posing and pubs, Trastevere bristles with buzzing bars, and the university quarter, San Lorenzo, is always a happening scene with lots of cheap bars and pubs. But the heart of hip Roman life is Testaccio. This hilly area just

The Campo dei Fiori is one of the hubs of the city's nightlife

south of the Aventine Hill is out of the *centro storico*.

If you're using public transport, there is a *servizio notturno* (night bus service), identified by the letter N. It covers most of the city from midnight to 5.30am, after which normal daytime service is resumed. But traditionally, all-night revellers round off a night on the tiles with a cappuccino and fresh *cornetti caldi* (hot croissants) at one of the bars, such as the Bar del Mattatolo in Testaccio.

There are plenty of alternative and gay hang-outs—especially in Testaccio. The Alibi was one of the first scene-setters to put Testaccio on the club map and it's still just as popular today.

PRICES
Clubs and discobars can be expensive. In addition to the entrance fee, they often make you pay for a membership card *(tessera)*. Admission often includes one free drink, but

from then on you pay full price. Prepare to wait for entry to the hottest clubs. It pays to dress up. Cool clothes, vampire garb, black leather goth style, scanty and flimsy—any number of variations are de rigueur in the hippest spots.

GAY AND LESBIAN
For more on the gay scene, pick up a copy of *Babilonia*, a monthly magazine which has comprehensive listings for the whole of Italy (€5.20 at news-stands), or log on to www.arcigay.it, Italy's foremost gay and lesbian network (Italian and English), or www.mariomieli.org, a

Trastevere is full of lively bars

Rome-based gay and lesbian group (Italian only).

BARS AND PUBS

ALIBI
Via Monte Testaccio 69, 00153
Tel 06 574 3448
This cellar was dug into an old Roman rubbish dump, Monte Testaccio, a hill made of broken pottery. Today, its vaulted arches throb with music. Popular with the gay crowd in summer, when the large terrace comes into use, the bar is more mixed in the winter. No credit cards.
🕐 Wed–Sun 10pm–5am 💶 €10–€15
🚇 Piramide 🚌 75, 280

ANTICA BIRRERIA
Via di San Marcello 19, 00187
Tel 06 679 5310
Art nouveau beer hall near Piazza Venezia. German beer is served in big steins. Inexpensive and brimming with alcohol-fuelled cheer.
🕐 Mon–Sat noon–midnight 💶 Free
🚌 40, 46, 62, 64, 916

ANTICA ENOTECA DI VIA DELLA CROCE
Via della Croce 76b, 00187
Tel 06 679 0896
Old-fashioned style at its most

enticing, with frescoed walls and wooden ceilings. Good wine, plus cheese and light snacks. Some outdoor seating is available in summer.
🕐 Daily 11am–1am 💶 Free
🚇 Spagna 🚌 116, 117, 119

ANTICO CAFFÈ DELLA PACE
See Restaurants, ▷ 233

ASSIZE OF ALE
Via della Vite 96, 00187
Tel 06 6920 2391
www.assizeofale.it
Wine and cocktail bar in an

ancient building not far from Piazza di Spagna. The theme is medieval and yet the feel is of an exclusive men's club. Food is available, and the happy hour is usually 6–7pm.

🕐 Daily 11am–2am 🎟 Free
🚇 Spagna

BARTARUGA

Piazza Mattei 7, 00186
Tel 06 689 2299

This retro kitsch venue has it all: a grand piano, Murano crystal, comfortable sofas and suffused lighting. In summer, it spills out onto one of the most beautiful little piazzas in Rome. Occasional live music and cabaret nights. No credit cards.

🕐 Mon–Sat 3pm–2am 🎟 Free
🚇 Largo Argentina

LA BOTTICELLA

Via Tor Millina 32, 00186

A small bar with dark wood surroundings, close to Piazza Navona. The bar has a comfortable atmosphere with excellent cocktails, simple platters of cheese and salami, and an excellent selection of Italian wine. The background music doesn't interfere with the conversation. Friendly English-speaking service and reasonable prices.

🕐 Daily 5.30pm–12.30am 🚌 46, 62, 64, 87, 116, 492

CAFFÈ EMPORIO

Piazza dell'Emporio 1, 00153
Tel 06 575 4532

Large, spacious and relaxing bar with comfy sofas and armchairs arranged around tables in chic surroundings. Renowned for its simple but delicious *aperitivi*, the bar is very busy, especially towards the end of the week. Happy hour is 5.30–6.30pm.

🕐 Daily 5pm–1am
🚇 Piramide 🚌 23, 30, 75, 716; tram 3

IL CENTRALE

Via Celsa 6, 00186
Tel 06 678 0501
www.centraleristotheatre.it
Il Centrale is a *ristotheatre*,

taking its name from the fact that it is in a former theatre from the 1920s. It has a bar with a DJ, a lounge area and a restaurant where you can eat while watching a live cabaret or music show. *Aperitivo* time is 7–10pm, and for €8 you can have a drink and all you can eat from a buffet of pasta salads.

🕐 Thu–Sun 7pm–3am; closed Jun to mid-Sep 🎟 From €8 🚌 30, 40, 46, 64 or any bus to Piazza Venezia or Largo Argentina

CHARITY CAFÉ

Via Panisperna 68, 00184
Tel 06 4782 5881
www.charitycafe.it
Intimate bar playing live jazz and

There is no shortage of cocktail bars in the city

blues at night, when it serves wine, cheese and salami. In the afternoon, it becomes a tea room offering 25 types of herbal tea. Happy hour is 4–10pm. Membership required (free).

🕐 Daily 4pm–3am 🎟 Free
🚇 Colosseo

CITTA DEL GUSTO

Via Enrico Fermi 161, 00144
Tel 06 551 1221

This converted warehouse is now the up-and-coming venue for food and wine. With terraces overlooking the Tiber, you can find great food in the restaurant, or just relax in the cocktail bar after a long day of exploring the Eternal City.

🕐 Demonstrations and wine-tasting: Tue–Sat 7.30am–midnight. Restaurant and shop: Tue–Fri 9am–11.30pm, Mon 9am–4pm

COMING OUT

Via San Giovanni in Laterano 8, 00184
Tel 06 700 9871
www.comingout.it

Look for the rainbow flag over the door and the crowds spilling out into the street. Central Rome's most happening gay bar has a warm, orange interior, good bar food, a message night on Tuesday, karaoke on Wednesday and live music on Thursday.

🕐 From 7pm; events from 10.30pm
🚇 Colosseo 🚌 60, 75, 87, 117, 175; tram 3

CUL DE SAC

See Restaurants, ▷ 239

EDOARDO II

See Restaurants, ▷ 241

ENOTECA TRASTEVERE

Via della Lungaretta 86, 00153
Tel 06 588 5659

Tavern-like wine bar with more than 900 wines, in addition to salads, soups and home-made desserts. During weekends, a pianist plays soft jazz and swing. Outdoor tables in summer make for great people-watching.

🕐 Thu–Tue 6pm–2am 🎟 Entry free; Dinner €20, Wine €15 🚌 H, 175; tram 8 to Piazza Sonnino

ESCOPAZZO

Via d'Aracoeli 41, 00186
Tel 06 6920 0422
www.escopazzo.it

This wine and cocktail bar, very near Piazza Venezia, Rome's central hub, is an intimate place perfect for a romantic soirée. The music is live most days, the atmosphere relaxed and relaxing. No credit cards.

🕐 Tue–Sun 10pm–3am 🎟 Free
🚌 40, 64, 170, 175 to Piazza Venezia

FRIENDS ART CAFÉ

See Restaurants, ▷ 242

GARBO

Vicolo Santa Margherita 1a, 00153
Tel 06 5832 0782
www.garbobar.com
For those who prefer quiet
conversation and a chance to
speak to some locals about
the gay scene. Small, candlelit
bar tucked on a side street in
Trastevere. Tasteful and
elegant. No credit cards.
🕐 Tue–Sun 10pm–3am 💷 Free, but
Arcigay membership is required (€7)
🚌 H; tram 8 to Piazza Sonnino

HABANA CAFE

Via dei Pastini 120, 00186
Tel 06 678 1983
www.habanaroma.it
A small, chaotic cocktail bar
with live music and snacks.
There is a real buzz here, and
some potentially mind-
blowing combinations–their
mojito has to be tried to be
believed. This is the place
to be if you like to be in the
thick of it. Happy hour is from
9–11pm.
🕐 Tue–Sun 9pm–3.30am 🚌 62, 64,
70, 81, 571; tram 8

HANGAR

Via in Selci 69, 00184
Tel 06 488 1397
Rome's oldest gay bar is an
American-style pick-up bar for
men. Layout is long, narrow and
crowded, with music videos
playing on either side of a
central corridor. No credit cards.
🕐 Wed–Mon 10.30pm–2.30am; closed
Aug 💷 Free; Arcigay membership
required (€7) 🚇 Colosseo 🚌 75, 84
to Via Cavour

JONATHAN'S ANGELS

Via della Fossa 16, 00186
Tel 06 689 3426
This popular haunt is a must
for both casual visitors and
hardened night-owls. The
music is cheesy (bad Italian or
French retro), which matches
the quirky decoration. No
credit cards.
🕐 Daily 8pm–3.30am 💷 Free 🚌 46,
62, 64, 492 to Corso Vittorio Emanuele
II (ask for Campo dei Fiori); 116 to
Campo dei Fiori

MAD JACK'S

Via Arenula 20, 00186
Tel 06 6880 8223
www.madjacks.com
This Irish pub will suit those
looking for a festive place in
which to pass the night hours.
The music is loud and drinks
are flowing.
🕐 Daily 11.30am–3am 💷 Free 🚌 40,
64 to Largo Argentina; tram 8

MAX'S BAR

Via A. Grandi 7a, 00185
Tel 06 7030 1599
www.maxbar.net
Very popular gay bar for men
of all ages, not far from
Termini station. It is literally
underground, so can become

*Ombre Rosse is a fashionable
choice, night and day*

quite hot and crowded. It has
two bars, a dance floor, and a
large sitting/socializing area.
No credit cards.
🕐 Thu–Mon 10.30am–3.30am
💷 Thu–Sun €7–10, includes one drink;
Mon free 🚇 Manzoni

OMBRE ROSSE

Piazza Sant'Egidio 12, 00153
Tel 06 588 4155
www.ombrerosse.com
In Trastevere, next door to
the popular Pasquino English-
language cinema (▷ 180).
Everything from full breakfast
to afternoon tea, and from
aperitifs to nightcaps. Live jazz
or blues on Thursday or
Sunday nights.

🕐 Mon–Sat 7.30am–2am, Sun
6pm–2am 💷 Free 🚌 H, 23, 44, 56,
75, 280 to Viale Trastevere; tram 8 to
Piazza Sonnino

OPPIO CAFFÈ

Via delle Terme di Tito 72, 00184
Tel 06 474 5262
www.oppiocaffe.it
High-tech meets ancient
history: glass and steel bar
fixtures, Plexiglas seats and
plasma video screens, all
underneath imperial Roman
brickwork. There is an amazing
view of the Colosseo from the
terrace. Live music Thursday
and Friday.
🕐 Tue–Sat 7am–2am, Sun–Mon
7am–8pm 💷 Free 🚇 Colosseo

IL POSTO DELLE FRAGOLE

Via Carlo Botta 51, 00184
Tel 06 4782 4868
www.ilpostodellefragole.org
This bar/club promotes
Scandinavian culture in Rome.
Nightly events include films
and live music, from
Scandinavian to blues. No
credit cards.
🕐 Tue–Sun 5pm–2am; closed Jun–Sep
💷 Varies depending on events held;
membership required (free) 🚇 Vittorio
Emanuele 🚌 85, 87, 810

SHAKI

Via Mario de' Fiori 29a, 00187
Tel 06 679 1694
This ultra-cool bar, with a
faintly oriental, minimalist
design, is in the chic
Tridente area. The food is
tantalizingly fresh, the wine
expensive.
🕐 Daily 10am–midnight 💷 Free
🚇 Spagna 🚌 116, 117, 119

SIDE MEETING POINT

Via Labicana 50, 00184
Tel 348 692 9472
This popular gay bar with
retro-kitsch interior is one
of the few exclusively gay
nightspots in Rome. It spills
out onto the street in
summer.
🕐 Daily noon–2am 💷 Free
🚇 Colosseo

STARDUST LOUNGE
Vicolo de' Renzi 4, 00153
Tel 06 5832 0875
Small, smoky club in
Trastevere full of atmosphere.
Although it no longer has
live music, the setting retains
a jazz club feel in a soulful
way rare in Rome. No credit
cards.
ⓒ Mon–Sat 7pm–2am, Sun
noon–2am 🕮 Free 🚌 H, 175; tram 8
to Piazza Sonnino

LA TAVERNA DEL CAMPO
Campo dei Fiori 16, 00186
Tel 06 687 4402
www.pierluigi.it
This tavern is always full, both
inside and out, and has
reasonably priced food and
loud music. There are tables
on the piazza.
ⓒ Apr–end Oct daily 9am–2am;
Nov–end Mar Tue–Sun 9am–2am
🕮 Free 🚌 46, 62, 64, 87, 116, 492

TRASTE'
Via della Lungaretta 76, 00153
Tel 06 589 4430
www.traste.it
Casual bar in the heart of
Trastevere, popular with a
younger crowd. Simple
setting, with large cushions
and trendy design. Very
wide drinks selection, both
alcoholic and non-alcoholic.
No credit cards.
ⓒ Daily 5pm–2am 🕮 Free 🚌 H, 175;
tram 8 to Piazza Sonnino

TRINITY COLLEGE
Via del Collegio Romano 6, 00186
Tel 06 678 6472
www.trinity-rome.com
This Gothic-looking building
houses one of Rome's most
reliable Irish pubs, in the well-
heeled area between the
Pantheon and Via del Corso.
ⓒ Daily noon–3am 🕮 Free
🚌 62, 63, 81, 85, 95, 117, 119, 175

TUMBLER
Via degli Equi 22, 00185
Tel 338 2431856
www.actumbler.com
Some of the best cocktails in
town, excellent snacks, and

live music on Wednesday,
Thursday and Friday. A great
atmosphere and friendly
staff.
ⓒ Tue–Sun from 7pm 🚌 491, 71;
tram 3, 19

IL VINAIETTO DI MARIO E GIANCARLO
Via Monte della Farina 38, 00186
Tel 06 6880 6989
Just off the crowded and
expensive Campo dei Fiori.
Somewhat flexible opening
hours, but some of the best
prices for a good glass of wine
in the city. No credit cards.
ⓒ Mon–Sat 8.30–2, 6.30–9 🕮 Free
🚌 40, 46, 62, 64, 492, 630; tram 8

*Dance till the early hours in one
of Rome's many clubs*

WINE TIME
See Restaurants, ▷ 255

CLUBS

AKAB – CAVE
Via Monte Testaccio 69, 00153
Tel 06 578 2390
One of Rome's oldest
nightclubs, but still very much
in style. The theme changes
throughout the week to cover
electronica, hip hop, R&B, pop
and house. Hosts international
DJs, rock bands and even
occasional cabaret acts.
Two floors with a secluded
courtyard. No credit cards.
ⓒ Tue, Thu–Sun 11pm–4.30am
🕮 €10; Fri–Sat €20 Ⓜ Piramide
🚌 75, 280

ALIEN
Via Velletri 13–19, 00198
Tel 06 841 2212
www.aliendisco.it
Large disco with three dance
floors: black and white for the
Rock Room, carpets and
incense for the India Room, and
deep blues for the Main Room.
ⓒ Tue–Sun 11pm–5am 🕮 €10; Sat
€18; Sun free 🚌 490, 495 to Piazza
Fiume

BAJA
Lungotevere Arnaldo da Brescia, 00196
Tel 06 3260 0118
This moored boat near Piazza
del Popolo features a judicious
mix of high-tech and ethnic
design. Cool dub, house and
lounge sounds downstairs.
The cocktails are fantastic,
and food is served upstairs.
ⓒ Tue–Sun 8pm–3am 🕮 Restaurant
free; piano bar €10 for men, €5 for
women Ⓜ Flaminio 🚌 95, 117, 119,
491, 590, 926; tram 2

BLOOM
Via del Teatro Pace 29–30, 00186
Tel 06 6880 2029
Sushi upstairs and cool
sounds in a futuristic setting
downstairs. It is the trendiest
of the Roman *fashionista*
hang-outs, so you may well
have trouble getting in—but
it's worth a go.
ⓒ Mon–Sat 7pm–3am; closed Jul–end
Aug 🕮 Free 🚌 46, 62, 64, 87, 116, 916

CAFFÈ LATINO
See Contemporary Live Music,
▷ 183

CIRCOLO DEGLI ARTISTI
Via Casilina Vecchia 42, 00182
Tel 06 7030 5684
www.circoloartisti.it
This large venue is more of
a meeting place than a
nightclub. Two dance floors
plus a large outdoor area,
including bars, food stands,
and even a cinema. Live music
from acid jazz and funk to
reggae-rap. Friday is gay night.
No credit cards.
ⓒ Tue–Sun 7.30pm–4am 🕮 €6
🚌 105

CLASSICO VILLAGE
Via G. Libetta 3, 00154
Tel 06 574 3364
www.classico.it
The coolest of Rome's many once-a-week gay dance events. The crowd, of both sexes, typifies *la bella figura*—cutting a fine figure on the dance floor. Warehouse-style premises, with three dance floors and two courtyards. No credit cards.
🕐 Daily 9.30pm–3am 🍷 €15
🚇 Garbatella 🚌 23, 702 to Via Ostiense

CLUB PICASSO
Via Monte Testaccio, 00153
Tel 06 574975
A dance spot with two levels: upstairs for dining, drinking and conversation, with a karaoke piano-bar in the background; downstairs for high-energy dancing.
🕐 Tue–Sun 8pm–4am 🍷 Free
🚇 Piramide 🚌 23, 30, 75, 716

GILDA
Via Mario de' Fiori 97, 00187
Tel 06 678 4838
www.gildabar.it
The place to see and be seen: It's all about attitude and who you know. A night here is a must if you want to see Rome's people of the moment. Live music on weekends.
🕐 Oct–end May daily 11.30pm–4.30am 🍷 €15 🚇 Spagna

GOA
Via G. Libetta 3, 00154
Tel 06 574 8277
Chic club that attracts a stylish, but not too pretentious, crowd. One large room in a bright ethnic/industrial style consists of various nooks for dancing, drinking or just hanging out. No credit cards.
🕐 Tue–Sun 11pm–3am 🍷 €20, depending on artist 🚌 23, 702 to Via Ostiense

JUNGLE CLUB ROMA
Via di Monte Testaccio 95, 00153
Tel 333 720 8694
www.jungleclubroma.com
This dark, gloomy and popular Goth venue is embellished with decoration reminiscent of Central America and industrial lighting effects. One room is for drinking and the other for dancing. The music ranges from live to DJ sets that cater especially for the Italian 'dark' scene: post-punk, Goth, industrial and heavy metal sounds. You'll need plenty of black eyeliner.
🕐 Tue–Sun 10.30pm–4am 🍷 €5, free

Everything from hip hop to house is played in Rome's clubs

before 11pm 🚇 Piramide 🚌 30, 118, 160, 175, 280; tram 3

LA MAISON
Vicolo dei Granari 4, 00186
Tel 06 683 3312
Fashionable, multi-room venue where TV and film stars mingle with more humble beings. The interior design is opulent with chandeliers and comfortable divans, and the music is varied.
🕐 Tue–Sun 10.30pm–4am
🍷 €10–€15 🚌 40, 46, 62, 64 to Corso Vittorio Emanuele II, or 30, 70, 81, 204, 628 to Corso Rinascimento

PIPER CLUB
Via Tagliamento 9, 00198
Tel 06 841 4459
www.piperclub.it
One of Rome's first discos and still very popular. High-tech effects complement the playlist. Many intimate seating areas allow you to see but not be seen. Well north of central Rome.
🕐 Thu, Fri–Sun 11pm–3am, Sat 4pm–3am 🍷 Sat €18, Sun varies
🚌 53, 63, 86, 92, 168, 630; tram 3, 19

QUBE
Via di Portonaccio 212, 00159
Tel 06 4385 4450
www.qube-disco.it
Young bodies dance till they drop in Rome's biggest underground disco. Friday is Muccassassina night, which is now more straight and mainstream than gay and alternative.
🕐 Thu–Sat 11pm–4am 🍷 Varies
🚌 168, 204, 409, 545, 649, or 71, 492 to Tiburtina station, then walk

SIENA ART CAFÉ
Viale del Galoppatoio 33, 00197
Tel 06 3600 6578
A vast, minimalist New York-style venue under Villa Borghese, which has quickly become a must for trend-seekers. Celebrity-spotters will be happy, too.
🕐 Tue–Sat: restaurant 9–1am; disco 11.30pm–4am 🍷 €20–€25 🚌 116

SPEEDY GONZALEZ
Via G. Libetta 13, 00154
Tel 06 5728 7338
Whimsical re-creation of a Mexican village in the Ostiense district. It serves a large selection of South American cocktails as well as typical Mexican dishes. Noisy and fun atmosphere, with music ranging from 70s to the latest hits. No credit cards.
🕐 Daily 10.30am–3am; closed Aug 🍷 Sat €14 men, €9 women; free all other nights 🚌 23, 702 to Via Ostiense

SPORTS AND ACTIVITIES

Generally Romans prefer to watch rather than participate in sport, and there are plenty of sporting options all over the city if you want to experience the buzz of watching a live event. Highlights of the Roman sporting calendar include the Rome City Marathon in March and the Italian Open in May, one of Europe's major tennis tournaments. Italy's national rugby team plays at the Stadio Flaminio. Participatory sports are not high on most people's agenda during a visit to the Eternal City, but if you do want to sweat off some of those calories head to Villa Borghese for cycling, boating and rollerblading. The city also has some excellent swimming pools.

SOCCER

The great national passion is soccer, and Rome's two teams, Lazio and Roma, are hero-worshipped. Lazio play in blue and white with an eagle as the mascot, while Roma wear red

Soccer is more than just a game in Rome

and yellow with a wolf. One team plays at home almost every Sunday from September until June at the Stadio Olimpico. Tickets for big matches tend to sell out quickly, and you should expect to pay prices up to around €85. Tickets are also available from ticket agencies such as Orbis (tel 06 4620 4310).

OTHER SPORTS

There are few tennis courts in the city, but the Italian Open tennis tournament in May is a very popular, stylish event, held at the Foro Italico. The International Horse Show comes to town in April and May at the Villa Borghese, and other equestrian events, including flat racing, steeplechases and show jumping, take place at the Ippodromo delle Capanelle (Via Appia Nuova, tel 06 718 8750). Should you want to

experience Rome on horseback you could try the Centro Ippico di Villa Borghese (Vicolo del Galoppatoio 23, tel 06 320 1667) or the Cavalieri dell'Appia Antica (Via dei Cerceni 15, tel 06 780 1214).

OTHER ACTIVITIES

As kitsch as it might sound, a stroll around the edge of the Forum, a cool drink overlooking the Colosseo, or a visit to the Fontana di Trevi, especially at moonlight, is magical. Don't forget to toss your coins over your shoulder to

The Circolo del Golf di Roma is surrounded by ancient ruins

ensure your return to the Eternal City.

EQUESTRIAN

CONCORSO IPPICO INTERNAZIONALE
Piazza di Siena, Villa Borghese 00186
Tel 06 3685 8321
www.piazzadisiena.com
It is not well known that Rome is host to an important annual equestrian event, with show-jumping at the heart of the action.
🗓 End Apr–early May 🎟 Adult €10–€44, child €6–€7
🚌 116, 231, 491, 495

GOLF

CIRCOLO DEL GOLF DI ROMA
Via Appia Nuova 716a, 00178
Tel 06 780 3407
www.golfroma.it
This lovely 18-hole course is surrounded by umbrella pines and Roman ruins. Non-members may play on summer weekends if there is no competition taking place. There is a great restaurant.
🗓 Tue–Sun 8am–sunset 🎟 Green fees €77 🚇 Colli Albani, then a taxi

GREEN SPACES

GIANICOLO HILL
Piazzale Aurelio, 00152
Join families and lovers strolling the ridge overlooking Rome. There is a bar, carousel, puppet show and summer evening theatre, plus miniature pony rides on weekends. The nearby Villa Doria Pamphilj is the city's largest park.
🎟 Free 🚌 44 to corner Via Giacinto Carini and Via Fratelli Bonnet, or 31, 791, 982

VILLA BORGHESE
Villa Borghese, 00186
Rome's green oasis is all about renting rollerblades and bicycles, or rowing boats on the tree-lined lake. A very popular park with locals at weekends.
🕐 Daily 24 hours 🎫 Free 🚌 95, 116, 119, 204, 490, 491, 495

VILLA DORIA PAMPHILJ
Villa Doria Pamphilj, 00152
One of the most beautiful parks in Rome, with villas, ponds and green woods. City officials have installed workout stations for stretching and muscle toning.
🕐 Daily dawn–dusk 🎫 Free 🚌 Tram 8

MARATHON
ROME CITY MARATHON
Via dei Fori Imperiali, 00186
Tel 06 406 5064
www.maratonadiroma.it
Each spring runners flock to participate in this event, which is slowly achieving the status of the marathons in London and New York. It starts and finishes on the Via dei Fori Imperiali.
🕐 3rd Sun in Mar 🚇 Colosseo 🚌 60, 75, 85, 117, 175, 186, 271, 571, 810, 850

ROMAN EXPERIENCES
CLIMBING THE MONUMENTO VITTORIO EMANUELE
Piazza Venezia, 00187
Tel 06 699 1718
Mussolini built this much-ridiculed monument—often called the Wedding Cake—in homage to Italian unification. The white marble edifice dominates the area, but the view from the top is superb.
🕐 Daily 9–6; last entrance Apr–end Oct 5.30, Nov–end Mar 4.30 🎫 Free 🚇 Colosseo 🚌 44, 46, 84, 715, 716, 780, 781, 810, 916

RUGBY
STADIO FLAMINIO
Stadio Flaminio, Viale Tiziano, 00196
Tel 06 3685 7832
www.federugby.it
Don't think that Italians only go mad for soccer. The national rugby team competes in the

---

Six Nations tournament (with England, France, Ireland, Scotland and Wales). The country has 24 rugby clubs, and the best games are in the capital when RDS Roma hits the field. Credit cards are not accepted.
🕐 Season: Oct–end May 🎫 €10–€30 🚌 204, 231, 910; tram 2

SOCCER
STADIO OLIMPICO
Viale dello Stadio Olimpico, 00194
Tel 06 36851
www.stadioolimpico.it
No spectator sport is more important to Romans than soccer. The city has two rival teams that share the stadium

You can work off some calories at the Roman Sports Center

and play at home on alternate Sundays. When Roma fans are in, they sit on the south side of the stadium; when Lazio is playing, their fans sit on the north side.
🕐 End Aug–early Jun Sun 🎫 €15–€85 🚌 32, 168, 186, 280 to Piazza Mancini, then cross river

SPORTS VENUES
ROMAN SPORTS CENTER
Villa Borghese, Viale del Galoppatoio 33, 00186
Tel 06 320 1667/06 321 8096
Rome's smartest sports venue is just a stone's throw from the Spanish Steps. This facility has three aerobics rooms, saunas, two weights rooms and an

---

Olympic-sized swimming pool. Day membership is available.
🕐 Mon–Sat 8am–10pm, Sun 9–3 🎫 Daily pass €26 🚌 95, 116, 119, 204, 490, 491, 495

SWIMMING
CAVALIERI HILTON
Via Cadlolo 101, 00136
Tel 06 3509 2950
www.cavalierihilton.it
The pool at this hotel in the northwest of the city is part of an impressive suite of spa facilities. It is among Rome's cleanest and least crowded. There is a good restaurant and bar on site.
🕐 May–end Sep daily 9–7 🎫 Mon–Fri €45, Sat–Sun €65 (for all spa facilities) 🚌 46, 912

PISCINA DELLE ROSE
Viale America 20, 00144
Tel 06 592 6717
Rome's largest open-air pool, at the heart of the ultra-sleek Palasport sports facility built by Mussolini. A great place to bring the kids on weekends. Credit cards are not accepted.
🕐 May–end Sep daily 9am–10pm 🎫 €10 🚇 EUR Palasport

TENNIS
CAMPIONATO INTERNAZIONALE DI TENNIS
Foro Italico, Viale dei Gladiatori, 00194
Tel 06 321 7213
Every May, Rome hosts the Italian Open tennis tournament, Europe's most important tennis event outside the Grand Slam. There are events for both men and women.
🕐 1–15 May 🎫 €8–€55 🚌 32, 168, 186, 280 to Piazza Mancini, then cross river

CIRCOLO DELLA STAMPA
Piazza Mancini 19, 00196
Tel 06 323 2452
Owned by the professional body for Italian journalists, this tennis club has both clay and synthetic-grass courts for rent at reasonable prices. There is a friendly atmosphere, with tennis lessons available for all skill levels.

Mon–Fri 8am–11pm, Sat–Sun 8–7
€12 per hour 48, 53, 231, 280, 910; tram 2

THE BRUNSWICK
Lungotevere dell'Acqua Acetosa 10, 00196
Tel 06 808 6147
The Brunswick has bowling lanes, games rooms and mini-

golf. On special occasions the bowling balls are fluorescent and disco lights shine overhead. Credit cards are not accepted.
Daily 10am–2am €2 before 2pm, €6 after 2pm 231

HEALTH AND BEAUTY

If the pressures of exploring the Eternal City start to take their toll, there are a number of options available to visitors for relaxing tired feet and indulging in some well earned pampering.

AVEDA SALON
Rampa Mignanelli 9, 00187
Tel 06 6992 4886
www.avedaroma.com

Unwind after a hard day's sightseeing

This is the salon of Aveda, Europe's leading potions and lotions brand. You can try plant steam inhalation, skin hydration or mild aromatherapy, plus facial treatments, manicures, pedicures and waxing. Aveda beauty products are on sale.
Tue–Sat 10–8, Mon 3.30–7.30
Manicure: €25, facial: €80
Spagna

BOSCOLO GRAND HOTEL
Via Vittorio Veneto 70, 00187
Tel 06 478719
A wealth of pampering services can be had at the Boscolo's Dibi Beauty Centre.

There's a beautiful swimming pool, plus solarium, a giant Turkish bath and a Jacuzzi. Massages last for over an hour. There's also a manicure salon and fitness centre.
Aug Tue–Fri 11–7; Sep–end Jul Mon–Sat 10–8 Massage: €65, facial: €60 Barberini

ELLEFFE HAIR
Via di San Calisto 6–6a, 00153
Tel 06 5833 3875
Fabio and Luce run this rather trendy-looking hair salon just off the main square in Trastevere. Up-to-date cuts, colours and styles are Fabio's domain, skilfully meeting your demands with his natural talent, while Luce takes care of the beauty treatments such as manicure, pedicure, peeling, waxing and massage.
Tue, Wed, Fri, Sat 10–7, Thu 10am–11pm H, 23, 44, 75, 280; tram 8

GRAND HOTEL TIBERIO
51 Via Lattanzio, 00136
Tel 06 399629
www.ghtiberio.com
If you're a guest at this four-star hotel, you can relax in the intense heat of its sauna, or tone up your muscles in its gym by purchasing a reasonably priced day pass. Within walking distance of Vatican City.
Daily 7.30am–9.30pm
All-day use of sauna and fitness centre: €17 Proba Petronia-Appiano

HOTEL DE RUSSIE
9 Via del Babuino, 00187
Tel 06 328881
Top hotel with a huge range of holistic techniques including shiatsu, reflexology and aromatherapy, as well as massage, saunas and facials. Masks, body wraps and personal training are also available.

A soothing massage in one of Rome's luxurious salons

Daily 9–8 Aromatherapy session: €90 Spagna

TERME DEI PAPI
12 Strada Bagni, 01100 Viterbo
Tel 0761 3501
www.termedeipapi.it
In the province of Lazio, 75km (45 miles) north of Rome, this spa is in beautiful grounds. There are mud baths, herbal inhalations, facials, organic treatments and a sumptuous wooden-decked swimming pool. There's also pleasant walking in the nearby hills. Advance booking is advised.
Mon–Sat 7–7, Sun 9–7 Mud bath: €25–€90 Take the Orte exit

CHILDREN'S ROME

There are few attractions specifically aimed at children in Rome, but there are also few other destinations where they can act out fantasies of chariot races, clamber over ruins or relive the stage set of *Gladiator*. And, if all else fails, there's always a delicious ice cream—the Italians are still the masters of glorious *gelato*.

FOOD

Children's menus don't really exist in Rome, but pizza and pasta are aplenty and, in all but the smartest establishments, restaurateurs will generally give children a warm welcome; menus are easily adaptable. Rome is also the perfect place for picnics. Stock up on goodies at the Campo dei Fiori

and take your picnic to the Villa Borghese gardens; on the northern side is the recently renovated Bioparco zoo, always very popular. Or picnic on the Palatine Hill, the legendary birthplace of Rome. Here the cooler air is refreshing and the views over the Forum and Colosseo are superb.

WHAT TO SEE

The Colosseo is free for under-18s, and is probably the top attraction. Your family can pose with a Roman centurion for memorable photographs (for a price). Visit the Circo Massimo, the oldest and largest ancient arena where chariot races were held, as seen in *Ben Hur*. The city is positively awash with fountains—there are over 4,000—always popular with kids. Encourage them to toss a coin into the Trevi Fountain, but don't let them take a dip as this will incur a hefty fine.

A gelato is guaranteed to go down well

EXPLORA—IL MUSEO DEI BAMBINI

Via Flaminia 82, 00192
Tel 06 361 3776
www.mdbr.it
Rome's first and only children's museum, particularly good for children aged up to eight. Themes are humankind, the environment, communications and society. There is an on-site restaurant. Reservations required; tours last 1 hour 45 mins.
🕐 Mon–Fri 9.30, 11.30, 1 and 3 and 5, Sat and Sun 10, 12, 3 and 5; closed 2 weeks in mid-Aug 🎟 Adult €6, child (3–12) €7, under-3s free 🚇 Flaminio 🚌 95, 117, 119, 204, 231, 490, 495, 618, 916; tram 2, 3, 19

LUNEUR PARK

Via delle Tre Fontane, 00144
Tel 06 592 5933
www.luneur.it
Built in 1953, the oldest fun park in Italy has kept up with the times. Activities and rides range from the traditional to the adrenalin-pumping, with a puppet theatre, several haunted houses, bumper cars, a lake with motor boats and rides with names like Flipper, Thriller and Space Kickers. Suitable for children and teenagers.
🕐 Apr–end Nov daily 4pm–midnight; Dec–end Mar Mon–Fri 3–8, Sat 3–2am, Sun 10–10 🎟 Rides €1–3 🚇 Magliana, Palasport or EUR Fermi 🚌 706, 707, 714, 717, 765, 771

MUSEO CRIMINOLOGICO DI ROMA

Via del Gonfalone 29, 00186
Tel 06 6830 0234
www.museocriminologico.it
A criminological museum covering the history of the Italian prison system, the solving of crimes and the punishment of criminals. Instruments of torture and engravings depicting various forms of punishment may interest older kids. No credit cards.
🕐 Tue–Sat 9–1 (also Tue, Thu

Children love posing with a real Roman centurion

2.30–6.30) 🎟 Adult €2, under-18s free 🚌 40, 46, 62, 64, 517 to Chiesa Nuova on Corso Vittorio Emanuele II

VILLA BORGHESE

Porta Pinciana
Tel 06 3600 4399
Rambling park extending for 6.5km (4 miles) through the heart of the city. Rent bikes or a boat, ride a trolley train, hop on an old-fashioned carousel or visit the Bioparco zoo.
🕐 Bioparco: Apr–end Sep daily 9.30–7; Oct–end Mar 9.30–5 🎟 Park: free. Bioparco: adult €8.50, child (6–12) €6.50 🚇 Flaminio or Spagna 🚌 95, 116, 119, 204, 495 🚊 🚲

FESTIVALS AND EVENTS

Today's celebrations are less extravagant than they were in the days of ancient Rome, but there are still many festivals and exhibitions held in the city throughout the year.

JANUARY

SAN SILVESTRO AND CAPODANNO

31 December–1 January
Crowds throng to Piazza del Popolo to see out the old year and welcome in the new with a free disco, concert and spectacular firework display. New Year's Day is a public holiday.
Piazza del Popolo
🚇 Flaminio 🚌 88, 95, 117, 119, 490, 491, 495; tram 2

The Rome City Marathon takes place every March

EPIFANIA–LA BEFANA

6 January (public holiday)
The Feast of the Epiphany is celebrated in a Mass said by the Pope at St. Peter's. The Romans know Epiphany better as *La Befana*—the old witch—who, according to legend, gave presents to good children and lumps of coal to bad ones. Piazza Navona is full of market stalls from mid-December to Epiphany; *La Befana* arrives in the piazza late on 5 January.
Basilica di San Pietro, Piazza San Pietro
🚇 Ottaviano 🚌 46, 64, 98, 916, 982
Piazza Navona
🚌 23, 30, 62, 64, 70, 81, 87, 116, 280, 492, 628, 810, 916

SANT'EUSEBIO ANIMAL BLESSING

17 January
The congregation of the little church of Sant'Eusebio all'Esquilino consists of animals with their doting owners, keen to get them blessed.
Via Napoleone 111
🚇 Vittorio 🚌 70, 71, 105; tram 5, 14

FEBRUARY–MARCH

CARNEVALE

February–March (the week before Lent)
There are street celebrations and masked revellers throughout the city during the traditional pagan festival of Carnevale ('farewell to meat').

MARCH

FESTA DI SANTA FRANCESCA ROMANA

9 March
Santa Francesca Romana is the patron saint of motorists. Drivers bring their cars to her church to be blessed.
Eastern (Colosseo) end of the Foro Romano
🚇 Colosseo 🚌 60, 75, 85, 87, 117, 175, 810, 850

MARCH–APRIL

SETTIMANA SANTA E PASQUA

Mid-March to mid-April (date varies)
Holy Week starts with an open-air Mass in St. Peter's Square on the Saturday before Palm Sunday. On Good Friday, the Pope's Stations of the Cross (*Via Crucis*) and Mass take place at the Colosseo late in the evening. On Easter Sunday there is a papal blessing at St. Peter's. Easter Monday is a public holiday.
Piazza del Colosseo
🚇 Colosseo 🚌 60, 75, 85, 87, 117, 175, 810, 850
Vatican
🚌 34, 46, 64, 98, 881, 916, 982

APRIL

NATALE DI ROMA

21 April
Celebrations of Rome's official birthday focus on the torchlit Campidoglio, with spectacular firework displays.
Piazza del Campidoglio
🚌 44, 46, 84, 715, 780, 781, 810, 916

APRIL–MAY

FIERA D'ARTE DI VIA MARGUTTA

Late April–May (also in October/November)
The street is full of art galleries that burst into life during these two open-air exhibitions.

Superb fireworks mark Rome's official birthday in April

Via Margutta
☎ 06 812 3340
🚇 Spagna 🚌 88, 95, 117, 119, 628, 926; tram 2

MAY

MOSTRA DELL'ANTIQUARIATO

May (also late October)
During the two-week-long fair, held in Via de'Coronari—the heart of the antiques trade—the street is lit with candles and shops stay open late.
Via de'Coronari
☎ 06 361 2322/06 6880 6052
🚌 30, 40, 46, 70, 81, 87, 116
www.assviadeicoronari.it

JUNE

FESTA DI SAN GIOVANNI
24 June
The Festival of St. John involves much consumption of snails *(lumache in umido)* and roast suckling pig *(porchetta)*, plus a fair and a fireworks display in the Piazza di San Giovanni in Laterano. A candlelit procession at night is usually led by the Pope to the church.
San Giovanni in Laterano, Piazza di San Giovanni in Laterano
San Giovanni 16, 85, 87, 117, 218, 650, 850

JUNE–SEPTEMBER

ESTATE ROMANA
21 June–September
Outdoor film screenings, music, ballet and theatre are among hundreds of events throughout the Roman Summer Festival in venues from parks to *palazzi.*
www.estateromana.it

FESTA DI SANTI PIETRO E PAOLO
29 June
Rome's patron saints, Peter and Paul, are honoured in this annual festival. At St. Peter's there is a Mass, while at St. Paul's there is an all-night street fair outside the church.
Basilica di San Pietro, Piazza San Pietro
Ottaviano 34, 46, 64, 98, 881, 916, 982
San Paolo fuori le Mura, Piazzale San Paolo 1c
Basilica di San Paolo 4, 23, 128, 761, 769, 770

JULY–AUGUST

CINEPORTO
July–August
Two large screens showing dubbed films have made this into a hugely popular summer festival in the park. In between screenings there are frequent live concerts.
Parco della Farnesina, north suburbs by the Stadio Olimpico
06 3600 5556
www.cineporto.com

TEATRO ROMANO DI OSTIA ANTICA
Mid-July to mid-August
Concerts and Greek and Roman classics are performed in this beautifully preserved open-air theatre, southwest of the city. Take a cushion.
Scavi di Ostia Antica, Viale dei Romagnoli 117
06 5635 8099

FESTIVAL EUROMEDITERRANEO
July–August
The stunning Villa Adriana is the setting for a wide range of events, from opera to drama and flamenco dancing—all with a Mediterranean feel.

Flamenco is one of the delights of the Festival Euromediterraneo

Villa Adriana, Via di Villa Adriana
06 6880 9107/8/9/10
Cotral bus from Metro Ponte Mammolo.

AUGUST

FESTA DELLA MADONNA DELLA NEVE
5 August
To commemorate the legend of snow falling on the Esquiline Hill on this day in AD352, petals are showered onto the congregation attending Mass in the basilica.
Basilica di Santa Maria Maggiore, Piazza Santa Maria Maggiore
06 483195
16, 70, 71, 75, 105, 204, 360, 590, 649, 714; tram 5, 14

FERRAGOSTO
15 August (public holiday)
This is the main midsummer holiday, when just about everything closes down.

SEPTEMBER–NOVEMBER

ROMAEUROPA FESTIVAL
September–November
This is Rome's major arts festival, with something for every taste offered by performers of international calibre. The venues include some of Rome's most glorious monuments.
Festival Office: Via XX Settembre 3
06 4890 4024 (information line); 06 474 2308 (booking line)
www.romaeuropa.net

NOVEMBER

OGNISSANTI
1 November (public holiday)
All Saints' Day, also known as Day of the Dead, is marked by Romans visiting family graves and a Mass celebrated by the Pope at the Verano cemetery.
Cimitero del Verano, Piazzale del Verano
71, 163, 492; tram 3, 19

DECEMBER

FESTA DELL'IMMACOLATA CONCEZIONE
8 December (public holiday)
Religious service in the piazza to celebrate the Festival of the Immaculate Conception, where the focal point is the statue of the Madonna, decorated with flowers.
Piazza di Spagna
Spagna 116, 117, 119, 590

NATALE & SANTO STEFANO
25–26 December (public holidays)
During the Christmas period, ornate cribs *(presepi)* decorate many of Rome's churches—the largest is in St. Peter's Square along with a towering Christmas tree. If you want to attend Midnight Mass in St. Peter's, put your request in months in advance.
Prefettura Office: Piazza San Pietro
06 6988 3273
34, 46, 64, 98, 881, 916, 982

Rome is compact enough to explore on foot, and this section describes six walks that take in some of the most interesting parts of the city. The areas covered by the walks are marked on the map on the inside front cover of the book. This chapter also gives suggestions for excursions outside the city (▷ 210).

Out and About

GHETTO TO TRASTEVERE

This walk passes through two of Rome's less explored areas, the Ghetto and the Isola Tiberina, before crossing the Tiber to the popular but unspoilt Trastevere quarter.

THE WALK

Distance: 4.25km (2.5 miles)

Allow: 3 hours minimum

Start at Piazza del Campidoglio

End at Campo dei Fiori

HOW TO GET THERE

For Piazza del Campidoglio, the nearest metro station is Colosseo (line B). Alternatively, several buses will take you nearby: Nos. 44, 46, 84, 715, 716, 780, 781, 810 and 916.

From Piazza del Campidoglio, with the Palazzo Senatorio straight in front of you, take the lane on the right-hand side, which leads towards the Foro Romano, but stay on Via di Monte Tarpei. At the bottom, turn right onto Via della Consolazione, cross the piazza and turn down Via di San Giovanni Decollato, turning left into Via del Velabro to find San Giorgio in Velabro.

1 San Giorgio in Velabro is named after the area where Rome's founding twins, Romulus and Remus, were discovered. The interior of the church is beautifully simple, and reuses marble and granite columns from ancient buildings. The façade of the church was severely damaged in a bomb blast in 1993, but sympathetic renovation has restored it to its former glory.

Retrace your steps past two ancient arches: Arco degli Argentari (Arch of the Moneychangers) adjoins the church, while the second, Arco di Giano, is on the opposite side of the road. Continue to the large Piazza della Bocca della Verità. On your right, look for two surprisingly well-preserved second-century BC temples, the circular Tempio di Vesta and the rectangular Tempio di Fortuna Virilis. Across the

piazza on the left-hand side is the 12th-century church of Santa Maria in Cosmedin **2** (▷ 136)—look for the large stone face called Bocca della Verità (Mouth of Truth) in the porch. According to legend, the mouth clamps shut on the hands of liars. With your back to the church, walk straight across the square, up the stepped ramp, and then right to join Lungotevere dei Pierleoni. Pass through Piazza Monte Savello, where the road becomes Lungotevere dei Cenci. Just ahead of you is the synagogue. Turn right onto Via del Portico d'Ottavia, leading to the Portico d'Ottavia.

3 The Portico d'Ottavia is a fragment of a Roman building begun in 146BC and dedicated to Octavia, Augustus' sister. It now forms part of the 12th-century Sant'Angelo in Pescheria (Angel of the Fishmarket), a reminder of the area's long fishing history in the nearby river. It's currently closed for restoration.

Turn left at the top of the street, onto Via dei Funari, which leads to Piazza Mattei and the heart of the old Ghetto **4** (▷ 90). Although the walls have long been demolished, many Jewish families and businesses are still based in the area. The piazza is best known for the Fontana delle Tartarughe (Fountain of the Tortoises), one of the most charming in the city. Turn left onto Via della Reginella, which leads back to Via Portico d'Ottavia. Turn right then left through Piazza delle Cinque Scole to rejoin Lungotevere dei Cenci. Turn left, passing the synagogue,

Put your hand in the Mouth of Truth

then right onto the Ponte Fabricio, Rome's oldest bridge, which crosses the Tiber to the Isola Tiberina **5** (▷ 91).

The island has a tradition of healing, begun in 291BC when a temple was dedicated to Esculapio, the god of healing, and today much of the island is given over to a hospital.

Leave the island, on the opposite side, by Ponte Cestio. This leads you directly into Trastevere (▷ 144–145), another district well worth exploring. Cross the busy Lungotevere dell'Anguillara and carry straight on to Piazza in Piscinula. Turn right onto Via della Lungaretta. Continue straight on until you come to Piazza di Santa Maria in Trastevere and the church of the same name (▷ 141). Facing the church, take the right-hand road out of the piazza: Via della Paglia. Continue to Piazza di San Egidio, then turn right across the piazza and take the left-hand road, Via della Scala. When you reach the junction with Via Garibaldi, turn right onto Via di San Dorotea, which leads to Piazza Trilussa, a small piazza right beside the Tiber. From here, cross the river by the traffic-free Ponte Sisto. Turn left, and follow the right fork into Via Giulia, through a pretty archway draped with vines.

6 Via Giulia, one of Rome's most elegant streets, was laid out for Pope Julius II in 1508 and formed the main approach to St. Peter's. There are now many interesting buildings lining this street, including the church of Santa Maria dell'Orazione e Morte **7**, ghoulishly decorated with skulls.

As Via Giulia opens out onto a piazza, turn right onto Vicolo della Moretta, which soon leads on to Via del Pellegrino. Take the first right onto Via dei Cappellari, with its traditional artisans' workshops. At the end of the street is Campo dei Fiori **8** (▷ 122–123).

OUT AND ABOUT

Palazzo Senatorio, in Michelangelo's Piazza del Campidoglio (left)

The Mattei family commissioned the Tortoise Fountain for 'their' square (above)

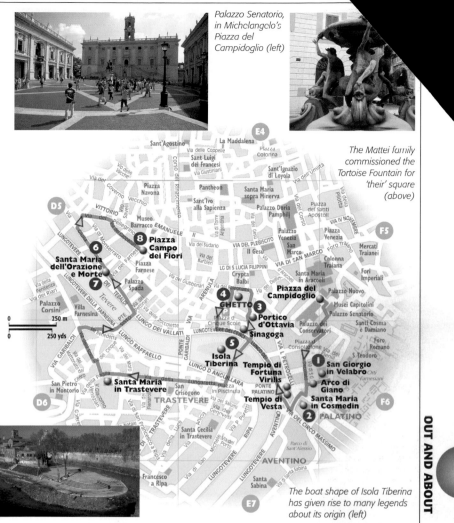

E4

Sant'Agostino

La Maddalena

Piazza Colonna

Sant'Luigi dei Francesi

Santa Maria sopra Minerva

Sant'Ignazio di Loyola

Piazza Navona

Pantheon

Sant'Ivo alla Sapienza

Palazzo Doria Pamphilj

Palazzo dei Santi Apostoli

D5

Museo Barracco

Il Gesù

Palazzo Venezia

Piazza Venezia

F5

8 Piazza Campo dei Fiori

VIA DEL PLEBISCITO

San Marco

Mercati Traianei

6

Santa Maria dell'Orazione e Morte

Piazza Farnese

VIA DI SAN MARCO

Colonna Traiana

Fori Imperiali

7

Palazzo Spada

Crypta Balbi

Santa Maria in Aracoeli

Palazzo Nuovo

Palazzo Corsini

Villa Farnesina

4 GHETTO

Piazza del Campidoglio

Musei Capitolini

Palazzo Senatorio

0   250 m
0   250 yds

3 Portico d'Ottavia

Sinagoga

Palazzo dei Conservatori

Santi Cosma e Damiano

Foro Romano

5

Isola Tiberina

Tempio di Fortuna Virilis

1 San Giorgio in Velabro

S. Teodoro

Santa Maria in Trastevere

Tempio di Vesta

Arco di Giano

Santa Maria in Cosmedin

F6

San Pietro in Montorio

D6

TRASTEVERE

PALATINO

2

Santa Cecilia in Trastevere

AVENTINO

Francesco a Ripa

Santa Sabina

The boat shape of Isola Tiberina has given rise to many legends about its origin (left)

E7

OUT AND ABOUT

WHEN TO GO

Any time, but remember that many churches will be closed during the afternoon.

WHERE TO EAT

There are many restaurants and cafés in Trastevere and Campo dei Fiori, or for traditional Jewish fare, try Giggetto al Portico d'Ottavia (▷ 242).

PLACES TO VISIT

San Giorgio in Velabro
Via del Velabro 19, 00186
☎ 06 6920 4534
🕐 Daily 10–12.30, 4–6.30

The church of Santa Maria in Trastevere dominates the piazza that shares its name (above)

Bramante's Via Giulia cuts a straight line through Rome's winding medieval streets (left)

ROUND PIAZZA NAVONA

m Piazza Navona to Piazza di Spagna and back, via the
vi, this walk takes in some of Rome's best-known sights.

Start at Piazza Navona
End at Piazza Navona

HOW TO GET THERE
Take a bus to Piazza Navona: Nos. 23, 46, 64, 87, 119 and others all pass nearby.

Leave Piazza Navona from the northern end (near the Fontana del Nettuno—pictured below). From Via Agonale, turn right onto Piazza Sant' Agostino. On your left is the church of Sant'Agostino (▷ 128).

❶ **Sant'Agostino** is known for its works of art, including Caravaggio's *Madonna di Loreto* (or Madonna of the Pilgrims, 1605) in the first chapel off the left aisle. The painting caused a scandal when it was first unveiled because of its realism— the Virgin was depicted with dirty feet and some of the pilgrims shown as old and sick.

Having crossed the piazza, bear left on Via della Scrofa, which becomes Via di Ripetta, until you reach Via Tomacelli. Turn right onto Via Tomacelli and then bear left onto Piazza Augusto Imperatore. Cross the piazza, then turn right onto Via dei Pontefici. At the end of the street is the Accademia Nazionale di Santa Cecilia (▷ 180).

❷ **L'Accademia Nazionale di Santa Cecilia** is the national school of music, founded in 1585. It has an orchestra of 90 members and has performed more than 14,000 concerts.

Turn right onto Via del Corso, a busy street, lined with shops. A short way along the street, turn left onto Via della Croce, renowned for its food shops and cafés; at No. 76 is Antica Enoteca, an old wine bar. Follow the road until it opens out into lively Piazza di Spagna ❸ (▷ 126–127). Turn right to reach the bottom of the Spanish Steps, usually busy with both locals and visitors chatting or simply taking in the atmosphere and the view. With your back to the steps, cross the piazza onto Via dei Condotti. Spend some time window-shopping along this, one of Rome's most exclusive shopping streets before bearing left onto Via Belsiana just before you reach Via del Corso again. Continue as far as Piazza San Silvestro, crossing Via Frattina and Via della Vite, and go diagonally across the square to turn down a little street called Via del Pozzetto. Take the first right, Via Poli, which crosses Via del Tritone and takes you to Piazza di Trevi and Nicola Salvi's theatrical Fontana di Trevi (▷ 80–81).

❹ **Opposite the Trevi Fountain** is the church of Santi Vincenzo e Anastasio, notable for its grisly relics: Between 1590 and 1903, the hearts and lungs of 22 popes, preserved in urns, were interred in the crypt.

Facing the Trevi Fountain, take the traffic-free street to the left, Via delle Muratte, which leads back to Via del Corso. Turn right onto the Corso, towards Piazza Colonna, named after Marcus Aurelius' column, which stands in the middle of the square. Erected between AD180 and 193, the monument illustrates victorious episodes in the Emperor's war campaigns. With your back to the Corso, take Via dei Bergamaschi, the narrow street in the far

left-hand corner of the piazza, which leads to Piazza di Pietra.

❺ **On the right-hand side of** the Piazza di Pietra, you can see the last remaining columns of Hadrian's temple, now incorporated into the 17th-century Borsa, the stock exchange. These 15m (50ft) columns formed part of a temple built and dedicated to the Emperor Hadrian in AD145 by his successor Antoninus Pius.

Carry straight on along Via de' Burro to reach the rococo Piazza di Sant'Ignazio, with its beautiful church (▷ 132). Step inside to admire the magnificent *trompe l'oeil* dome by the Jesuit architect Andrea Pozzo. Continue down Via di Sant'Ignazio—the Jesuit Collegio Romano is on your left— until you emerge onto Piazza del Collegio Romano. Turn right onto Via Piè di Marmo, which leads to Piazza della Minerva and the church of Santa Maria sopra Minerva ❻ (▷ 140), with Bernini's delightful statue of an elephant outside. On the right-hand side of the church's façade are several plaques showing the water levels when the Tiber flooded between 1598 and 1870.

With the church on your right, continue down Via della Minerva to Piazza della Rotonda and the Pantheon ❼ (▷ 120–121), one of Rome's best-preserved ancient monuments. Facing the Pantheon, take Via della Rotonda, the road that runs up the right-hand side of the building, then take the first right, Via della Palombella, which leads onto Piazza Sant'Eustachio. Here you will find Sant'Eustachio il Caffè where, some say, they serve the best coffee in Rome (▷ 251). Leave the square on the opposite side, down Via dei Staderari. This takes you along the side of the church of Sant'Ivo alla Sapienza ❽ (entrance on Corso del Rinascimento; ▷ 133). Via dei Sediari, opposite the church's entrance, will take you back to Piazza Navona.

OUT AND ABOUT

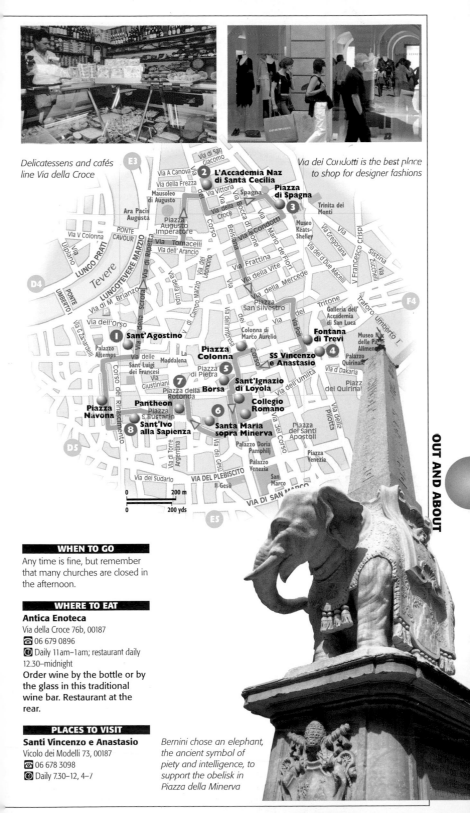

Delicatessens and cafés line Via della Croce

Via dei Condotti is the best place to shop for designer fashions

E3

Via di San Giacomo

Via A Canova

2 L'Accademia Naz di Santa Cecilia

Via della Frezza

Via Vittoria

Spagna

Piazza di Spagna

3

Mausoleo di Augusto

Ara Pacis Augusta

Piazza Augusto Imperatore

Via della Croce

Via di Bocca di Leone

Trinita dei Monti

Museo Keats-Shelley

PONTE CAVOUR

Via V Colonna

LUNGOTEVERE MARZIO

Via Tomacelli

Via dell'Arancio

Via del Corso

Belsiana

Via Mario de'Fiori

Via de'Condotti

Via Frattina

Via della Vite

Via Gregoriana

Via del d Due Macelli

V Francesco Crispi

Sistina

Via Zucchelli

D4

Tevere

Via di M. Brianzo

Via della Scrofa

Via di Ripetta

Via della Lupa

Via di Campo Marzio

Via del Leoncino

Via della Mercede

Piazza San Silvestro

Tritone

Galleria dell' Accademia di San Luca

Traforo Umberto I

F4

Via C Cardelli

Via dell'Orso

1 Sant'Agostino

Palazzo Altemps

Via delle Coppelle

La Maddalena

Via Giustiniani

Sant'Luigi dei Francesi

7

Piazza della Rotonda

Pantheon

Piazza S. Eustachio

Colonna di Marco Aurelio

Piazza Colonna

Piazza di Pietra

5

Borsa

Sant'Ignazio di Loyola

SS Vincenzo e Anastasio

Fontana di Trevi

4

Via di Dataria

Palazzo Quirinale

Piazz del Quirinal

Via dell'Umiltà

Via dei Pastini

Museo N delle Pas Aliment

Piazza Navona

8 Sant'Ivo alla Sapienza

Via di Torre Argentina

Corso del Rinascimento

6

Santa Maria sopra Minerva

Collegio Romano

Palazzo Doria Pamphilj

Palazzo Venezia

Via del Gesù

Via del Corso

Piazza dei Santi Apostoli

Piazza Venezia

San Marco

Piazza della Pilotta

D5

Via del Sudario

VIA DEL PLEBISCITO

Il Gesù

VIA DI SAN MARCO

0   200 m

0   200 yds

E5

OUT AND ABOUT

WHEN TO GO

Any time is fine, but remember that many churches are closed in the afternoon.

WHERE TO EAT

Antica Enoteca
Via della Croce 76b, 00187
☎ 06 679 0896
🕐 Daily 11am–1am; restaurant daily 12.30–midnight
Order wine by the bottle or by the glass in this traditional wine bar. Restaurant at the rear.

PLACES TO VISIT

Santi Vincenzo e Anastasio
Vicolo dei Modelli 73, 00187
☎ 06 678 3098
🕐 Daily 7.30–12, 4–7

Bernini chose an elephant, the ancient symbol of piety and intelligence, to support the obelisk in Piazza della Minerva

IN THE FOOTSTEPS OF THE ANCIENT ROMANS

From Michelangelo's Piazza del Campidoglio, you plunge down into the pedestrian lanes of the Foro Romano to lose yourself in the ancient ruins of imperial Rome.

THE WALK

Distance: 2km (1.2 miles)	
Allow: 2 hours	
Start at Piazza del Campidoglio	
End at Piazza del Campidoglio	

HOW TO GET THERE

For Piazza del Campidoglio, the nearest metro station is Colosseo. Alternatively, several buses will take you nearby: Nos. 44, 46, 84, 715, 716, 780, 781, 810 and 916.

From Piazza del Campidoglio

take the lane to the left of Palazzo Senatorio, the middle palace. Look up at the corner of the building to see a statue of the legendary she-wolf with Romulus and Remus, the twins credited with the foundation of Rome. At the back of the building, the whole of the Foro Romano ❶ (▷ 84–89) opens up in front of you. Take in the view from this elevated position before descending the steps to the Forum.

Before passing through the Arco di Settimio Severo, look to your right. The columns here belong to the Tempio di Saturno.

❷ The Tempio di Saturno is one of the oldest buildings in the Forum, dating from 479BC, although what remains today is from reconstructions in 42BC and AD284. As the god of agriculture, Saturn was extremely important. The Saturnalia, a festival in his honour that took place in December, lasted a whole week, during which time slaves were given temporary liberty and a huge public banquet took place in the Forum.

Pass through the Arch of Septimius Severus, with the red-brick Curia ❸ on your left. Continue along the Via Sacra, the main route through the Forum, passing the Basilica Aemilia on your left, until you come to the area covered by a green roof. This is the Tempio di Cesare ❹.

Despite laws banning burials in the Forum, Mark Antony appealed to the Romans to allow Caesar's body to be cremated here. Augustus built a temple in Caesar's honour in 29BC, and a column marks the place where he was cremated.

With the temple on your left, look straight ahead. What you see is the temple of the twin brothers of Helen of Troy, Castor and Pollux, the Dioscuri, whose statues stand in the Piazza del Campidoglio. To the left of the temple is the Basilica Giulia. Although very little remains, it is clear that this was a large and important building. It was built as a courthouse and a meeting place for the city's civic tribunals. Rejoin the Via Sacra. The next building on your left, surprisingly intact, is the Tempio di Antonino e Faustina ❺.

Built by Emperor Antoninus Pius in AD141, the temple was dedicated to his wife Faustina, in honour of her virtue. However, the contemporary gossip was that the emperor was the only one who did not know about his wife's numerous affairs. The building was converted to a church in the 11th century, which ensured its survival.

Next to the temple is the church of Santi Cosma and Damiano ❻ (▷ 129), whose entrance is on Via dei Fori Imperiali. The small, round building on the Forum side of the church is the fourth-century AD Tempio de Divo Romolo, dedicated to the son of Emperor Maxentius rather than the mythical founder of Rome. With your back to the temple, the large complex ahead of you is the Atrium Vestae, the house of the Vestal Virgins ❼. Continue along the Via Sacra; the vast, triple-arched building on the left is the Basilica di Massenzio ❽.

The basilica was begun during the reign of Maxentius in AD306 and continued by his successor, Constantine. The building was designed as a hub for business and justice. Maxentius designed the building to be entered from the right-hand, shorter side, with a nave and aisles running its 100m (330ft) length. Constantine moved the entrance to the longer side (facing you), which produced three shorter (65m/215ft), broader aisles, each ending in the barrel-vaulted room that is seen today.

The next building along the Via Sacra is the Tempio di Venere e Roma. There is no public access, but you get a good view of the building as you leave the Forum. Walk through the Arco di Tito, and leave the Forum along the last stretch of the Via Sacra. At the end is the Meta Sudans, the remains of a large fountain built at the same time as the Colosseo. Turn right to walk around the Arco di Costantino (▷ 65), then go around the outside of the Colosseo (▷ 74–77; the entrance is on the northwest side of the amphitheatre).

Walk up Via dei Fori Imperiali towards the Fori Imperiali (▷ 82–83) before turning right onto the traffic-free Via del Foro di Traiano. On the right is the Foro di Augusto, of which very little remains. On the left, on the opposite side of Via dei Fori Imperiali, is the Foro di Cesare, the first to be built outside the old Forum. The greater part of these forums is buried under Via dei Fori Imperiali, built by Mussolini in 1932. At the end of the traffic-free street, turn right, and then left onto Via Alessandrina. This road leads you to Mercati Traianei (▷ 91, entrance on Via Quattro Novembre) on the right and, on the left, Foro Traiano. The broken columns do little to suggest that this was once one of the city's finest monuments, but Colonna Traiana (▷ 78–79), at the top of the site, remains largely intact (although the statue of Trajan on top was replaced in the 16th century with one of St. Peter). Follow the road around to the left to arrive at Piazza Venezia, just around the corner from Piazza del Campidoglio.

OUT AND ABOUT

Rome's founding twins, Romulus and Remus, were suckled by a she-wolf

Take in an elevated view of the Foro Romano before you descend the steps

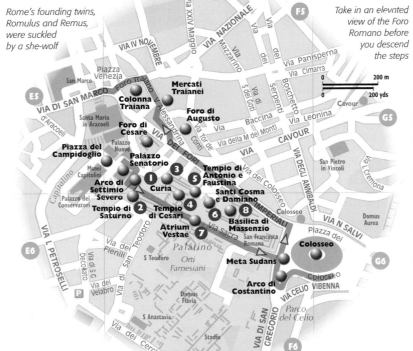

Via XXIV Maggio
VIA IV NOVEMBRE
VIA NAZIONALE
Via Mazzarino
Via del Serpenti
Via Panisperna
Via Cimarra
Via del Boschetto
F5

Piazza Venezia
San Marco
E5
VIA DI SAN MARCO
Foro Traiano
Mercati Traianei
Via Baccina
Via Leonina
CAVOUR
Cavour
G5

d'Aracoeli
Santa Maria in Aracoeli
Colonna Traiana
Foro di Cesare
Via Alessandrina
VIA DEI FORI
Foro di Augusto
Via Tor de' Conti
Via della M dei Monti
VIA

Piazza del Campidoglio
Palazzo Nuovo
Musei Capitolini
Palazzo Senatorio
❸
Tempio di Antonio e Faustina
❺
VIA DEI FORI IMPERIALI
San Pietro in Vincoli
Via L Cremona
Capitolino
Palazzo dei Conservatori
Arco di Settimio Severo
❶
Curia
Santi Cosma e Damiano
Colosseo
VIA N SALVI
Tempio di Saturno
❷
Tempio di Cesari
❹
❻
Basilica di Massenzio
VIA DECII ANNIBALDI
Domus Aurea

VIA L PETROSELLI
E6
Atrium Vestae
❼
Via sacra
San Francesca Romana
Colosseo
Piazza del Colosseo
Domus Aurea

Via dei Fienili
Via del Decorato
Via di S Teodoro
Palatino
S Teodoro
Orti Farnesiani
Meta Sudans
Colosseo
G6

P
Via del Velabro
Via di S G Decorato
Domus Flavia
Arco di Costantino
VIA CELIO VIBENNA
Parco del Celio

S Anastasia
VIA DI SAN GREGORIO
Via del Cerchi
Stadio
F6

0 ___ 200 m
0 ___ 200 yds

OUT AND ABOUT

WHEN TO GO

Any time is suitable, but in summer the outside of the Colosseo is floodlit after dark. The fora close at dusk.

WHERE TO EAT

Although there is nowhere to eat in the Forum, there are many places nearby, such as Gran Caffè Martini e Rossi (▷ 243) or the Musei Capitolini's Bar Capitolina (▷ 234).

The Arch of Septimius Severus on the old triumphal route to the Capitoline

IN THE FOOTSTEPS OF THE ANCIENT ROMANS 203

PIAZZA DI SPAGNA TO PIAZZA SAN PIETRO

Some of Rome's best shopping streets form the route to one of the city's main attractions, the Basilica di San Pietro.

THE WALK

Distance: 2.5km (1.5 miles)	
Allow: 3 hours	
Start at Piazza di Spagna	
End at Piazza San Pietro	

HOW TO GET THERE

For Piazza di Spagna, take the metro to Spagna.

Allow some time to look at the many shops in the grid of streets surrounding Piazza di Spagna ❶ (▷ 126–127) before taking Via Frattina (to the left if you have your back to the Spanish Steps). This is a great place to shop for designer labels. On emerging onto Via del Corso, cross the road into Piazza San Lorenzo in Lucina, a charming square with outdoor cafés, and a church of the same name.

❷ San Lorenzo in Lucina is one of Rome's earliest churches, but was rebuilt in 1112. The columns in its façade were recycled from ancient buildings. Inside is a 19th-century memorial to the French painter Nicolas Poussin (died 1665), who is buried in the church.

Cross the square and take Via del Leone on the right. This leads to Largo Fontanella Borghese, which

Look through the archways of Palazzo Borghese to glimpse the grandeur within

takes its name from the elegant Palazzo Borghese ❸ on the right, once the city residence of the Borghese, one of Rome's most powerful families.

Both Cardinal Scipione Borghese, whose art collection is housed in the Museo e Galleria Borghese, and Napoleon's sister Paolina Borghese, the subject of one of the museum's best-known sculptures, lived here. The

palace is closed to the public, but a glance into the courtyard gives an idea of its elegance.

Cross the square, and leave it by Via del Clementino, passing through Piazza Nicosia and along Via di Monte Brianzo. Take the last small lane on your left, Via dei Soldati, then go left onto Via dell'Orso, lined with charming shops. Turn right at the church of Sant'Antonio dei Portoghesi onto Via dei Pianellari which leads to Piazza Sant'Apollinare, where you will see Palazzo Altemps ❹ (▷ 112–113).

With your back to the museum, Piazza Navona ❺ (▷ 124–125) is straight ahead. Midway down, on the right-hand side, take Via di Sant'Agnese in Agone. On the corner of Via della Pace is Antica Caffè della Pace, a great place for a drink. Turn right to find the church of Santa Maria della Pace.

Legend has it that, during a 15th-century war with Florence, a painting of the Virgin bled when it was pierced by a soldier's sword. Pope Sixtus IV made a vow that he would build a church if the Virgin interceded to bring peace. She obliged, and Santa Maria della Pace was begun

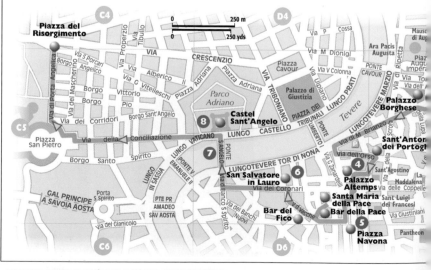

Fishing in the shadow of Bernini's 'Breezy Maniacs' on the Ponte Sant'Angelo

around 1480. The Cappella Chigi contains frescoes by Raphael, and the adjacent cloister is by Bramante—his first work in Rome.

Return to Antica Caffè della Pace, turn right and then go straight on along Vicolo delle Vacche and Vicolo della Vetrina. On your left is a charming café, Bar del Fico, in a square of the same name. From Vicolo della Vetrina turn left onto Via dei Coronari, where there are a great number of antique and furniture shops. The church of San Salvatore in Lauro **6** is on your right. Continue straight on, down the small Vicolo del Curato, as far as Via del Banco di Santo Spirito. Turn right and head straight for Ponte Sant'Angelo **7**.

There has been a bridge here since AD134, when it was built to connect with Hadrian's mausoleum (now within Castel Sant'Angelo). Bernini's stone angels line the bridge, watching over the traditional pilgrims' route to San Pietro. With their flowing robes and outstretched wings, they appear to be struggling to keep their balance in the wind, which has earned them the nickname 'Breezy Maniacs'.

Cross the bridge to Castel Sant'Angelo **8** (▷ 73). Turn left onto Via della Conciliazione, which leads you straight to Bernini's majestic Piazza San Pietro. Facing the basilica, follow the right-hand colonnade to Via di Porta Angelica, which leads up to Piazza del Risorgimento. From here frequent buses run back to the city centre.

OUT AND ABOUT

WHEN TO GO
Go in the morning or late afternoon to catch the churches open. Sunset from Ponte Sant'Angelo is a spectacular sight.

WHERE TO EAT
In addition to the bars mentioned here, there are plenty of restaurants and cafés around Piazza Navona. Try Antico Caffè della Pace (▷ 233), Il Capriccio (▷ 237) or Da Francesco (▷ 239).

Antica Caffè della Pace
Via della Pace 3–7, 00186
☎ 06 686 1216
🕐 Daily 8am–2am (Mon from 4pm)
Popular with locals and visitors alike. The bar also owns the pizzeria next door.

PLACES TO VISIT
San Lorenzo in Lucina
Via in Lucina 16a, 00186
☎ 06 687 1494
🕐 Daily 8–8; cloister Tue–Sun 10–7

Santa Maria della Pace
Vicolo dell'Arco della Pace 5, 00186
☎ 06 686 1156
🕐 Daily 10–12.45, Tue and Sat also 4.30–6

ROME'S CHURCHES

In busy squares redolent of history, or dreaming peacefully in quiet, romantic little streets, the churches that punctuate this walk offer both interest and variety.

Distance: 2km (1.2 miles)
Allow: 2.5 hours
Start at Piazza di Santa Maria Maggiore
End at Piazza di Santa Maria Maggiore

The nearest metro stations for Piazza di Santa Maria Maggiore are Cavour (line B) and Vittorio Emanuele (line A). Bus Nos. 16, 70, 71, 360 and 649 also stop nearby.

With your back to the basilica of Santa Maria Maggiore (▷ 138–139), take Via Merulana, a major thoroughfare on the right. Take the first narrow street on the right to visit the church of Santa Prassede ❶ (▷ 142) and its beautiful mosaics. Follow the road around to the left to rejoin Via Merulana, lined with lively shops. Cross Viale Manzoni and climb up to Piazza di Porta San Giovanni in Laterano ❷ (▷ 134–135). The entrance to the church is on the opposite side of the building from here. Take time to admire the basilica, the Lateran Palace, and the Egyptian obelisk, which was originally erected in Thebes during the 15th century BC. Almost opposite the entrance to San Giovanni is the Scala Santa.

❸ This Holy Staircase is said to be the steps from Pilate's palace in Jerusalem climbed by Jesus at his trial. They were brought to Rome by St. Helena, mother of the Emperor Constantine. Wood now protects the marble steps, and glass panels show what are claimed to be Christ's bloodstains. The devout climb the steps on their knees to earn indulgences (remission from temporal sins).

After returning to the square, leave by Via di San Giovanni in Laterano, then take the road on the left, Via di Santo Stefano Rotondo, which runs alongside the Ospedale San Giovanni. Almost at the end of the road on your left is the church of Santo Stefano Rotondo ❹ (▷ 143), with its beautiful circular plan.

This obelisk, near Santa Maria Maggiore, was erected in 1587 as a landmark for visiting pilgrims

At the end of the road, turn right onto Via della Navicella, right again to Piazza Celimontana past the Ospedale del Celio, and then another sharp right onto Via Annia. Carry straight on, turning left near the end onto Via dei Querceti. Walk down the steps and you'll see the back of the church of Santi Quattro Coronati ❺ (▷ 142). The entrance is in the next street, the charming and quiet Via dei Santi Quattro Coronati.

The Santi Quattro Coronati is named after four early Christians, possibly soldiers, who refused to worship pagan idols. They were killed by having an iron crown (corona), driven into their heads.

At the end of Via dei Querceti, bear left onto Via di San Giovanni in Laterano; the basilica of San Clemente ❻ (▷ 130–131) is in front of you. This 12th-century church hides a much older history, having been built over a fourth-century AD church and a much earlier pagan temple. Just past the basilica, turn right onto Via Celimontana. At the junction with Via Labicana, cross the road and turn left, heading towards the Colosseo. Keeping on the right-hand side of the road, climb up to Via Nicola Salvi, which leads to the Colle Oppio. Turn right onto Via delle Terme di Tito, left onto Largo della Polveriera, then right and left onto Via Eudossiana, passing the entrance gate to Colle Oppio.

❼ Colle Oppio, on the slopes of the Esquiline Hill, is a charming mix of grass, trees and archaeological ruins. It is popular with Romans, but should be avoided after dark.

Follow Via Eudossiana down past the University School of Engineering until you reach Piazza San Pietro in Vincoli ❽. Allow some time to visit the church (▷ 137), which contains Michelangelo's mighty sculpture of Moses. Facing the church, there is a tiny passageway on your left; go down the steps and you'll find yourself on Via Cavour. Head towards the right, then, at Largo Visconti Venosta, take Via Urbana, which leads to the church of Santa Pudenziana ❾ (▷ 142). At the end of the road, turn right and cross Piazza d'Esquilino to return to Santa Maria Maggiore.

OUT AND ABOUT

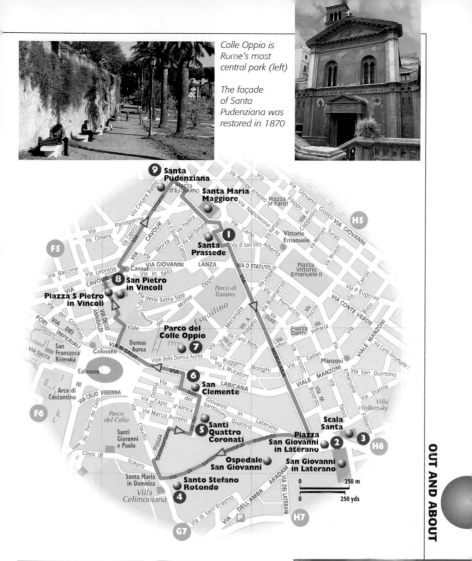

Colle Oppio is Rome's most central park (left)

The façade of Santa Pudenziana was restored in 1870

WHEN TO GO

Morning is best, as many churches close in the afternoon. Try to get to San Giovanni in Laterano by 11am, to visit the Scala Santa before the church shuts at noon. Avoid Colle Oppio after dark.

WHERE TO EAT

There are plenty of eateries to choose from along Via Cavour and Via di San Giovanni in Laterano.

PLACES TO VISIT

Scala Santa
Piazza di San Giovanni in Laterano 14, 00185
☎ 06 6988 6433
🕐 Daily 9–12, 3–6

Surrounded by decorative leaves, this macabre skull is set into the plaster of the wall at the Church of Santa Prassede

San Giovanni in Laterano is the cathedral of the city of Rome

VILLA BORGHESE

A walk through this popular park, once the private estate of Cardinal Scipione Borghese, is the perfect antidote to the turmoil of Rome's busy streets.

THE WALK

Distance: 2km (1.2 miles)

Allow: 2 hours

Start at Piazza del Popolo

End at Piazzale Flaminio

HOW TO GET THERE

The most convenient metro stations are Flaminio or Spagna. Alternatively, take a bus: Nos. 117, 119, 628 and 926 all serve the area.

Piazza del Popolo was the city's northern focal point (▷ 119). Two important Roman roads, Via Cassia and Via Flaminia, entered the city through the Porta del Popolo before making their way to the Capitolini and the fora. Today's traffic-free square is the site of two almost identical churches, Santa Maria dei Miracoli and Santa Maria di Monte Santo ❶, which stand on the corners of Via di Ripetta and Via del Babuino.

These two churches were designed by Carlo Rainaldi (and others) in 1679. His brief was to build identical churches, but the land available was not of equal size. What he built is an optical illusion: When viewed from the piazza, the churches appear the same, but Santa Maria di Monte Santo, on the left, has an oval dome while that of Santa Maria dei Miracoli, on the right, is round.

With your back to the churches, take Viale G. d'Annunzio, on the right-hand side of the square. Follow the road as it snakes up, turning left onto Viale Mickievicz for the last leg into the Giardino del Pincio ❷ (▷ 90). Continue to Piazzale Napoleone I for a panoramic view over the *centro storico*. Retrace your steps as far as Viale dell'Obelisco and turn left. Don't miss the Casina Valadier, an elegant coffee house and restaurant on your right. Carry straight on, crossing Viale dell'Orologio, with its fascinating water-clock, and passing the bar/restaurant La Casina dell' Orologio, until you reach Piazzale dei Martiri and the entrance to

An Egyptian obelisk surrounded by marble lions spouting water dominates Piazza del Popolo

the Villa Borghese park (▷ 146). Keep walking straight on, along Viale delle Magnolie, until you reach Via de Casina di Raffaello, the first right after busy Piazza delle Canestre. Just ahead is a small house, said to have belonged to Raphael ❸. Follow this road up to the Tempietto di Diana ❹.

This 18th-century Classical temple is dedicated to Diana, goddess of hunting. The ceiling is decorated with blue medallions: The central motif is of Diana, accompanied by one of her hunting dogs; the rest are all hunting motifs.

Turn left at the temple, onto Viale dei Pupazzi. From here there is a good view, to the left, of the stadium-shaped Piazza di Siena, where Rome's International Horse Show is held in May ❺. When you reach Piazzale dei Cavalli Marini, continue straight on to the end of the path. To your right is the Museo e Galleria Borghese ❻ (▷ 92–97). Turn to your left and head towards Piazzale del Giardino Zoologico and the entrance to Bioparco ❼.

There has been a zoo on this site since 1911, but it was updated in 1997 and now concentrates on conservation. The zoo arranges many activities for children.

Keep left, walking down Viale del Giardino Zoologico until you reach Largo P. Picasso. Climb the steps up to the Tempio di Esculapio, which is almost surrounded by a lake where rowing boats can be hired. Take the next lane on the right (at the side of the temple) to emerge onto Piazza Paolina Borghese. From here it is just a short walk to the Galleria Nazionale d'Arte Moderna, where you could stop for a coffee in the Café degli Arti.

❽ **The Galleria Nazionale d'Arte Moderna displays work by Italian and foreign artists, from 1800 to the present day. It is also used for major exhibitions. Alternatively, farther along Viale delle Belle Arti is the Museo Nazionale Etrusco ❾ (▷ 147).**

To leave the park, retrace your steps to Piazza Paolina Borghese and take the road in front of you, Via Bernadotte, which leads you down to Piazzale Fiocco and the Esculapio Fountain. Continue straight down to Viale Washington, which ends with the spectacular gate in Piazzale Flaminio. On your left is the gate leading back to the busy Piazza del Popolo.

OUT AND ABOUT

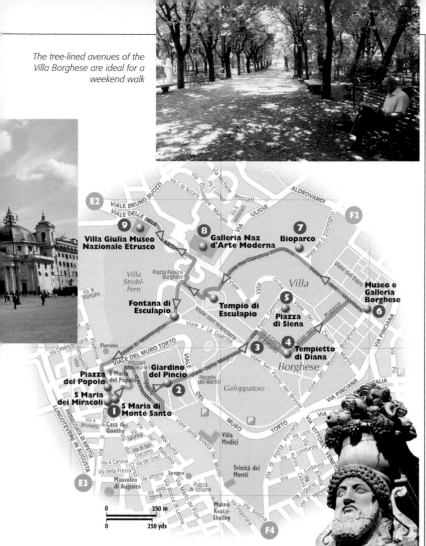

The tree-lined avenues of the Villa Borghese are ideal for a weekend walk

Map labels:

E2
VIALE BRUNO BUOZZI
VIALE DELLE BELLE

9 **Villa Giulia Museo Nazionale Etrusco**

8 **Galleria Naz d'Arte Moderna**

7 **Bioparco**

F2

ALDROVANDI
ULISSE

Villa Strohl-Fern

Piazza Paolina Borghese

Villa

Fontana di Esculapio

Tempio di Esculapio

5 **Piazza di Siena**

Museo e **Galleria Borghese** 6

Flaminio

Piazza del Popolo S Maria del Popolo

Giardino del Pincio

3

4 **Tempietto di Diana**

Borghese

S Maria dei Miracoli

S Maria di Monte Santo 1

2

Galoppatoio

Casa di Goethe

Villa Medici

Mausoleo di Augusto

Trinità dei Monti

Piazza di Spagna

E3

F4

Museo Keats-Shelley

0   250 m
0   250 yds

OUT AND ABOUT

WHEN TO GO

Villa Borghese is open from dawn to dusk, so visit at any time during the day. It is popular with Roman families on Saturdays and Sundays.

WHERE TO EAT

Recently reopened after extensive renovations are the Casina Valadier, which has one of the best views in Rome and is ideal for light refreshments or for splashing out on a special meal, and the bar of La Casina dell'Orologio.

Casina Valadier
Piazza Bucharest 00187
☎ 06 6992 4640
⊙ Bar: Mar–end Nov Tue–Sat 11.30–11, Sun 11.30–2.30; restaurant: Mar–end Nov Tue–Sat 12–2.30, 8–10.30, Sun 12–2.30

La Casina dell'Orologio
Viale dei Bambini 00187
☎ 06 679 8515
⊙ Thu–Tue 8–8

PLACES TO VISIT

Bioparco
Viale del Giardino Zoologico, 00187
☎ 06 360 8211 ⊙ Apr–end Oct Mon–Fri 9.30–6, Sat and Sun 9.30–7; Nov–end Mar daily 9.30–5

Galleria Nazionale d'Arte Moderna
Viale delle Belle Arti 131, 00187
☎ 06 322981
⊙ Tue–Sun 8.30–7.30. Closed 1 May
www.gnam.arti.beniculturali.it

Bioparco, in Villa Borghese, is a popular zoo where the main emphasis is on conservation

EXCURSIONS

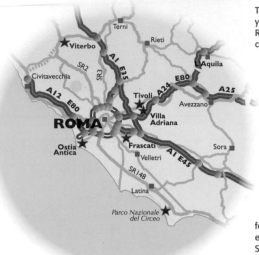

There may come a point in your stay when you tire of Rome's endless museums and churches, particularly if you visit during the oppressively hot summer months. The countryside of Lazio and beyond is a refreshing change from the city's heat, and much of it is accessible by public transport, making it an easy day's escape. Whenever possible, avoid visiting on Saturday and Sunday: The Romans enjoy getting out of the city, too, and the popular places will be crowded. Plan your visit for a weekday and you might even have the place to yourself. So why not do as the Romans do: Pack up a picnic and head for *la campagna*.

1. EXCURSION

VITERBO

Lazio's most historic town, with fine medieval and Renaissance buildings, an unspoilt atmosphere and the bonus of a world-class 16th-century garden nearby.

OUT AND ABOUT

BASICS

Tourist Information Office
Piazza San Carluccio 5, 01100
☎ 0761 304795

Museo Nazionale Archeologico
Rocca Albornoz, Piazza della Rocca, 00110
☎ 0761 325929
🕐 Tue–Sun 8.30–7.30

Museo Civico
Piazza F. Crispi, 00110
☎ 0761 340810
🕐 Apr–end Oct Tue–Sun 9–7; Nov–end Mar 9–6

Villa Lante
Via Iacopo Barozzi 71, 00110
Bagnaia
☎ 0761 288008
🕐 Apr–end Oct Tue–Sun 8.30–7.30; Nov–end Mar 8.30–5.30
🎟 Adult €2, child (under 18) free

www.viterboonline.com
Excellent multi-language site covering Viterbo and the surrounding area, with full information on everything there is to see, as well as good listings, travel hints, and information about what's on. Good links, an efficient search facility and plenty of maps and photos.

HOW TO GET THERE

Train: every 20 minutes from Termini, Roma Ostiense or Stazione Flaminio; journey time approximately 1.5–2 hours. The town is a 10–15-minute walk

Cotral bus: from Saxa Rubra (Via Flaminia) every 30 minutes; journey time approximately 1.5 hours

By car: take A1 (E35) north to GRA, then exit at Orte onto S204 signed to Viterbo (110km/68 miles); journey time 1.5 hours

Villa Lante is 5km (3 miles) east of Viterbo. Bus No. 6 hourly from Piazza Martini dei Ungheria; by car, east of town at Bagnaia, follow signs off S204

OVERVIEW

The largest town in northern Lazio and a quietly prosperous provincial capital, Viterbo has a long history. It's this legacy of the past, in the shape of intact medieval walls, a maze of narrow streets and its stately palazzi, that gives the town its appeal today. Viterbo was originally an Etruscan settlement, absorbed by Rome in AD310. Its heyday was the Middle Ages, when a succession of popes scuttled here to live away from trouble in Rome, making it their capital in 1257. It was during this period that the magnificent walls went up, civic buildings and churches were constructed and the town took on its present form.

THE HEART OF TOWN

After the decidedly unattractive approach to the town, it's a relief to see the battlemented walls that encircle the old town. Once inside, spend time getting your bearings in the Piazza del Plebiscito, a fine square surrounded by 15th- and 16th-century palaces, still home to the town's council. The main, arcaded building is the

Renaissance Mannerist gardens. The villa is easily reached from Viterbo, and you should certainly leave time to fit in a visit.

Spreading over a series of five terraces, the gardens are perfectly proportioned and richly detailed, the planting enhancing the importance of water in the overall design. It's a lovely place on a hot summer's day.

Don't Miss Walk up the Via San Pellegrino to the Piazza San Pellegrino; it's Viterbo's main street and has an example of just about everything that makes the area special.
Villa Lante has 16th-century water jokes—ask the guide to activate them.

15th-century Palazzo dei Priori, decorated, like many others, with lions and palm trees, symbols of Viterbo. The palazzo's council chamber, reached through a lovely courtyard overlooking the river valley, is decorated with a series of murals telling the town's history. From here, head down Via San Lorenzo to the Romanesque church of Santa Maria Nuova—where St. Thomas Aquinas preached for peace in 1266—before heading through a couple of pretty piazzas to the Quartiere San Pellegrino, Viterbo's oldest area. Its tangle of narrow alleys is picturesque, with outside staircases, fountains and flower-drenched balconies.

The loggia of Palazzo Papale (top).
San Pellegrino quarter (above).
The gardens of Villa Lante (right).
Piazza del Plebiscito (far left)

PIAZZA SAN LORENZO

For a bit more culture, retrack to the Piazza del Plebiscito and head in the opposite direction, towards Piazza San Lorenzo. The square was built on the original Etruscan town and is flanked by the 13th-century Palazzo Papale and the Duomo. The Great Hall in the Papal Palace was once the scene of half a dozen or so papal elections, but for most visitors it's the view from the open Gothic loggia to the green gorge that slices into central Viterbo that's truly memorable. Memorable, too, is the serene beauty of the Romanesque Duomo, with its elegant striped cosmatesque floor and stately campanile.

CHURCHES AND MUSEUMS

Santa Maria Nuova, built in 1080, and the Duomo are the pick of the town's churches, but it's worth tracking down the 19th-century building dedicated to Santa Rosa, at the far end of Corso Italia. Inside a chapel in the south aisle is the saint's body, still dressed in nun's clothing; macabre, but fascinating.

The Museo Nazionale Archeologico, up the hill in Piazza della Rocca, focuses on archaeological finds from the Stone Age to the Middle Ages, with the emphasis firmly on the Etruscan finds from the area around Viterbo. There are more local treasures in the Museo Civico, outside the walls and next to the 12th-century church of Santa Maria della Verità, including Roman sarcophagi found nearby, but it's the paintings on the upper floors that shine.

THE VILLA LANTE

To the east of Viterbo is the small town of Bagnaia, completely dominated by the 16th-century palace of the Villa Lante, whose gardens are considered one of the finest of all the existing

WHERE TO EAT

Ristorante Il Portico
Via Cardinal La Fontaine 28, 00110
Tel 0761 328021
🕐 Tue–Sun
In summer you can eat outside this charming restaurant, close to Santa Maria Nuova, which serves local dishes and seafood.

Enoteca la Torre
Via della Torre 5, 00110
Tel 0761 226467
🕐 Mon–Sat 1–2.30, 7.30–10.30
Right in the heart of town, this *enoteca* has an excellent choice of wines and food.

OSTIA ANTICA

Ancient Rome's port is one of the top three best-preserved Roman towns in Italy, and is a haven of romantic ruins and soothing greenery.

BASICS

Ostia Antica
Viale dei Romagnoli 717, 00170
☎ 06 5635 8099
🕐 Apr–end Oct Tue–Sun 8.30–7.30;
Nov–end Mar Tue–Sun 8.30–5.30
💶 Adult €4, child (under 18) free.
Includes entry to Museo Ostiense nearby
🍴 🛈 Both on site
📖 Bookshop with guidebooks
(guidebook in English €6.50), maps
and plans, postcards and souvenirs
🅿 available (fee)

Borgo
🕐 Castello: Tue–Sun 9–1

www.ostia-antica.org
This superlative English-language site is
aimed at visitors and academics alike, so
there's an immense range of information
at every level. Lots of plans, photos, 3-D
reconstructions, practical advice and links
to a huge number of related sites.

www.ostiaantica.net
An enthusiastic site crammed with
history, information and photos. You
can take a virtual tour to help you
decide what you want to see. Only
the main headings are in English, so
you'll need to read Italian to get the
most out of it.

HOW TO GET THERE

Train: from Stazione Ostiense to Ostia
Antica (metro to Piramide); journey time
30 minutes. Metro from Termini; journey
time 30 minutes

By car: 35–40 minutes if the traffic's not
bad; take Via del Mare (SS8) from Porta
San Paolo

OVERVIEW

Roman legend puts Ostia's
founding in the seventh century
BC; factual dating of the ruins
points to the fourth century BC.
From then, a small port and
trading community established
itself, getting a boost from its
military role during the First
Punic War. The second century
BC was boom time, with the
commercial port growing in
importance as Rome flourished
and Ostia's own population
reached half a million. The port
was soon a victim of its own
success, unable to handle the
vast quantity of trade generated

by the empire and, initiated by
Claudius, a second port—close
to the modern airport—was
constructed in the first to second
centuries AD. This Portus Romae
attracted more and more
shipping, and Ostia became
largely a residential town.
By the fifth century and the fall of
Rome, it was largely abandoned,
the sea retreated and the port
silted up. Malaria and pirates did
the rest, and by the 17th century,
Ostia Antica was all but forgotten.

EXCAVATIONS

Archaeological excavations began
in the 19th century, and today
about half the town has been
uncovered, with some low-key
excavations still continuing. For
visitors, Ostia is a quintessentially
romantic Classical ruin, complete
with elegant umbrella pines,
grassy slopes and spreads of

wildflowers. These certainly
contribute to its evocative
allure, but they make its
preservation a nightmare,
damaging walls and
foundations: It's the old Italian
story of too much to preserve
and not enough money to do it.

DECUMANUS MAXIMUS

Like all Roman towns, Ostia was
bisected by a dead-straight main
street, the Decumanus Maximus,
and its cobbled length is the first
thing you see as you enter the
site through the Porta Romana.
On either side of this there's a
confusing jumble of streets and
ruins, admittedly evocative, but
you'll need a plan to make sense
of it all. A city this size needed
civic buildings, temples,
administrative offices,
entertainment complexes and
shops, as well as housing for a
population covering the full social
spectrum. Some of these you
should certainly track down, so
head down the Decumanus
towards the town. The first big
building on the right is the Terme
di Nettuno, the public baths, built
by Hadrian and wonderfully
decorated with mosaics aptly
showing Neptune himself and his
wife Amphitrite, goddess of the
sea. Next to the baths is the
amphitheatre, a semicircular
building that went up in AD196;
its tiers of seats for 4,000 have
been restored and it is used for
summer concerts. Ostian citizens
could move through the back of
the theatre directly into the
Piazzale delle Corporazioni.

PIAZZALE DELLE
CORPORAZIONI

This is the mercantile heart of the
city. Here, the shipping agents
had their offices, many of them
identified by the black and white
mosaics in front of their doors—
chandlers, grain-merchants,
rope-makers and others. Their
warehouses, known as *horrea*,
are scattered all over Ostia.

*Follow the Decumanus Maximus
to see the sights of Ostia Antica*

To get some idea of the scale of commerce in ancient times, spend a few moments simply taking in the sheer number of these *horrea* and their impressive proportions.

Near the piazzale, there are a couple of private houses you should see: the Casa di Apulius and the Casa di Diana. The former's owner splashed out on an atrium and mosaic-decorated rooms, interior design that was unusual this far north—you're more likely to see it in Pompeii. He was a devotee of the slightly sinister god Mithras, and there's a Mithraic temple next to the house. The owners of the nearby Casa di Diana worshipped the

Fragment of wall decoration (top).
Terme di Nettuno (above).
The amphitheatre (left)

same god and had a mithraeum at the back of their grand house, with its central courtyard.

THE INSULAE AND FORUM

Not all Ostians lived in villas, and it's the blocks of workers' flats that really speak to us across the centuries. These *insulae* (islands) rose to four or five floors, had running water, heating and plumbing and often shared a communal garden—the Casa di Giardino is a fine example. Citizens of all classes flocked to the Forum, with its Capitol, baths and basilicas, but just as many doubtless spent time in the Thermopolium, near the Casa di Diana. This ancient café, with its high counter, outside seats, display shelves and wall paintings of the day's special, tells us more about the Romans than a thousand broken columns.

To flesh out the bones of what you've seen, head for the museum, which is devoted to

finds from the site. There's a fine statue of Mithras killing a bull (the god's symbol), sarcophagi from all over the town and wall paintings with touching scenes of everyday life.

THE BORGO

It's worth a detour across the road to the Borgo, Ostia's medieval village. It's dominated by the Castello, built for Pope Julius II in 1483–86 by Pontelli. Once the customs house for ships sailing up the Tiber to Rome, it lost its usefulness when the river changed course in 1587.

Don't miss The size and scale of Ostia are more impressive by far than the capital's Forum, and it gives a far better idea of ancient Roman life.
The combination of pine trees, greenery and spring wildflowers within the ruins themselves make a lovely picture.

TIPS
● Allow a whole day for the site; perhaps bring a picnic.
● In summer, take water with you, and rest in the shade during the early afternoon.
● Buy a plan of the site (available at the museum shop) and spend time when you arrive planning your visit.

WHERE TO EAT
Ristorante il Monumento
Piazza Umberto I 8, 00170
Tel 06 565 0021
◉ Tue–Sun 12.30–3, 7.30–10.30
At the entrance to the beautiful medieval Borgo you can enjoy reasonably priced local dishes on the veranda here.

There are plenty of seafood restaurants in Ostia Lido along the Lungomare. Take a train or metro to Ostia Lido C. Colombo (the last stop on the line you arrived on).

TIVOLI

A hill town that's home to one of Europe's greatest Renaissance water gardens, a gorge complete with crashing waterfalls, and tempting restaurants for alfresco dining.

Cardinal d'Este's 16th-century gardens descend in a series of terraces

OUT AND ABOUT

BASICS

Tourist Information Office
Piazza Garibaldi, 00011
☎ 0774 311249

Villa d'Este
Piazza Trento, 00011
☎ 0774 333404
🕐 Apr–end Sep Tue–Sun 8.30–6.30;
Mar Tue–Sun 8.30–5; Oct–end Feb
Tue–Sun 8.30–4
💶 Adult €6.50, child (under 18) free
📖 Guidebook €6 and €5
▢ ▣ ⚇

Villa Gregoriana
This is currently closed for restoration,
but is planned to reopen in 2006.
Contact the tourist information office for
more details.

HOW TO GET THERE

Train: from Stazione Tiburtina; journey
time approximately 35–60 minutes
Cotral bus: from Ponte Mammolo
(Via Prenestina) every 15 minutes;
journey time 1 hour
By car: take A24 northeast, then Tivoli
exit; allow about 1 hour

OVERVIEW

Perched among olive groves on a ridge of the Monti Tiburtini, Tivoli has always been an escape for Romans from the heat of the city—it's amazing what a bit of height can do to the freshness of the air. In Classical times it was a retirement town and summer retreat for wealthy Romans, including the emperor—Hadrian's enormous Villa Adriana is just outside the town (▷ 216–217). Later, Renaissance nobility built country villas throughout the town and surrounding area. The most famous of these is the Villa d'Este, whose world-famous gardens are a symphony of lush greenery and thundering water.

The town has other delights. It's enfolded in an oxbow formed by the River Aniene, and retains its picturesque medieval streets, fine churches and a general air of prosperity, wealth derived from the travertine stone quarries you'll see lining the road on the way into town.

THE VILLA D'ESTE

Tivoli's main draw is the Villa d'Este and its stunning landscaped garden, where cascading water is combined with lush cool greenery. The Renaissance villa was converted from a former Benedictine convent by Pirro Ligorio for Cardinal Ippolito d'Este in 1550. The cardinal was the son of Lucrezia Borgia and the Duke of Ferrara, and had grown up in a rich and sophisticated court, a background that is reflected in both the villa and gardens. Ten rooms on the ground floor of the villa have been restored; these are vividly frescoed with scenes from mythology and the history of Tivoli by Girolamo Muziano and Federico Zuccari. The frescoes were executed between 1550 and 1560. There's a great view over the garden's symmetrical terraces from the loggia.

The Villa's Gardens
Below the villa stretch the gardens, some of the most spectacular and theatrical ever designed. They represent the full flowering of Renaissance culture and had a huge influence on garden design throughout Europe. Laid out around a central axis, the design is strictly formal, based on the combination of static lines of greenery, sculpture and statuary with living water. It's this contrast between the sombre planting and the exuberance of the myriad fountains and water features that gives the Villa d'Este gardens their appeal.

The Fountains
Fountain-wise, the stupendous Organ Fountain takes top prize. Fully restored, it sends millions of litres of water thundering into the air against a spectacular decorative stone background. Visitors have always loved the Viale delle Cento Fontane, a wooded walkway flanked by a hundred cooling spouts of water, whose focal point is the splendid Fontana dei Draghi (its builder Pope Gregory XIII's emblem featured a *drago*, or dragon). The Fontana dell'Ovata is fringed with statues and set against a shadowy arcade, and the great Gian Lorenzo Bernini was responsible for the graceful shell-shaped Fontana del Bicchierone. Another stunner is the Fontana della Rometta, little Rome, with reproductions of Rome's main Classical monuments.

These set-pieces are scattered throughout the gardens, but wherever you go you'll be surrounded by the sound of water and find a surprise round every corner. Originally, the surprises included the watery jokes found in every great Renaissance garden—jets that drenched visitors at the touch of a hidden button, benches that flooded when sat upon, curtains of water to trap the unwary, owls

that whistled and chirruped during the day. These no longer work, but remember that such conceits were as much part of the gardens as the beauty of the fountains and cascades.

VILLA GREGORIANA
Tivoli's other garden, the Villa Gregoriana, was created much later. The River Aniene was prone to flood the town, and in 1831 Pope Gregory XVI solved the problem by diverting the flow of water over an artificial waterfall, the Cascata Grande. Bernini had a hand in the plan, designing a

Tivoli's watery gardens were designed to provide respite from the city's heat, and they continue to do so today

smaller cascade at the neck of the 60m-deep (200ft) gorge. The park and gorge are a wonderfully luxuriant habitat, overgrown and wild, and a good contrast to the formal style of the Villa d'Este.

The Waterfalls
From the deafening vantage point overlooking the Cascata Grande, there's a path, noisy and cool with the rush of water, zigzagging down to the bottom of the gorge. It passes two smaller waterfalls before retracking to the main falls and continuing past two grottoes; water rushes straight down past the Grotto della Sirena, and the Grotta di Nettuno is heavily and picturesquely covered with

mineral deposits. It's a steep climb back up the other side, but worth it for the views from the top and the close-up of the little Tempio di Vesta. The temple is in the grounds of a restaurant, but you can go in and peer out from the belvedere.

THE TOWN
It's worth a quick wander round the town, particularly along the Via del Duomo, where there's a high percentage of late-medieval houses. Fans of the Romanesque should take in some of the churches: San Pietro alla Carità has a lovely façade and Classical columns. The Duomo, founded in the fifth century, has a Romanesque campanile, though its portico dates from 1650. To see an earlier portico, head for San Silvestro—its columns are Roman, and there are 13th-century frescoes in the apse.

WHERE TO EAT

Antica Hostaria de' Carrettieri
Via D. Giuliami 65, 00011
Tel 0774 330159
🕐 Thu–Tue 12.30–3, 7.30–10.30
The Sardinian owner serves dishes from home in a warm, friendly atmosphere. Close to the medieval heart of town.

Ristorante Sibilla
Via della Sibilla 50, 00011
Tel 0774 335281
🕐 Tue–Sun 12.30–3, 7.30–10.30
An enviable location, with tables set around the temples of Vesta and Sibilla, overlooking the famous cascades of Villa Gregoriana.

VILLA ADRIANA

The epitome of a romantic ruin, the remains of the largest and most elaborate villa ever constructed during the Roman Empire, set in a peaceful and beautiful landscape.

BASICS

Tourist Information Office
Piazza Garibaldi, 00011
Tivoli
☎ 0774 311249

Villa Adriana
☎ 0774 382733
🕐 Mar–end Oct daily 9–6; Nov–end Feb 9–3.30
💶 Adult €6.50, child (under 18) free
▢ ▢ ▢

HOW TO GET THERE

Train: from Stazione Tiburtina to Tivoli; journey time approximately 30 minutes
Cotral bus: from Ponte Mammolo (Via Prenestina) to Tivoli; journey time 50 minutes. From Tivoli, take bus No. 4/4X from Piazza Garibaldi out to Villa Adriana
By car: take A24 northeast, then Tivoli exit; Villa Adriana is signed from here. Allow about 1 hour

OVERVIEW

The Villa Adriana, just outside Tivoli, was built by Hadrian, emperor from AD 118 to 138. As a provincial, Hadrian was viewed with suspicion by both the Senate and the aristocracy. It was partly for this reason that Hadrian made this grandiose villa his main residence when he was in Rome, rather than taking over one of the existing imperial palaces. He also kept away from the power struggles in Rome by travelling throughout the empire, and probably hoped eventually to make this sumptuous villa his

retirement home. Sadly, ill health forced him south and he only had a few years to enjoy the completed villa. His travels had played a large part in the planning; an enthusiastic sight-seer, Hadrian dotted his creation with reconstructions of buildings that had impressed him throughout the Roman world—a sort of second-century theme park. Building started in AD 125 and continued for 10 years. Tivoli, with its famous travertine quarries and abundant water, was an ideal place for such a vast project, as there was plenty of tufa and lime available to mix the tonnes of cement needed.

The villa eventually covered more than 100ha (250 acres), with over 30 buildings, some of which have still to be excavated. After Hadrian's death, the

complex fell rapidly into disrepair, was plundered and forgotten, until early Renaissance enthusiasts rediscovered it in 1450.

WHAT TO SEE

You'll need plenty of imagination to visualize the ancient glory of the site; all the upper parts of the buildings are gone, making the complex seem much more open than it was originally. What now appear to be open spaces were once covered walkways connecting the various buildings, which were several floors high, embellished with domes and faced with marble and other precious stones. It must once have looked like an enclosed city—it's worth remembering that the villa covered an area as large as the area of imperial Rome itself. Archaeologists still haven't discovered the original purpose of many of the structures, so it makes sense to concentrate on the best and save some energy to soak up the atmosphere.

THE PECILE

Kick off at the Pecile, the huge colonnade near the entrance. Once surrounded by gardens, its focus point is the central pool. Hadrian based its design on the

The subterranean Cryptoportico (left).
Hadrian's Teatro Marittimo (below)

OUT AND ABOUT

Once flanked with statues, the Canopus is the highlight of a visit to Villa Adriana

Stoa Poikile of Athens, which he admired on his travels. It was probably used as a gymnasium and it's thought it also served as an after-dinner promenade during the summer. Along the west side you'll see the Cento Camerelle, a warren of small rooms probably used as storage space and slave quarters.

TEATRO MARITTIMO

In the northeast corner of the Pecile there's access through the ruins of a large hall (the niches once held statues of Greek philosophers) to the Teatro Marittimo, one of the villa's highlights and one of the few places where there's a real impression of the original appearance. An Ionic-columned portico rings a circular canal, once crossed by movable bridges leading to a little round island. This was Hadrian's own retreat, where he withdrew to read, paint and relax in the miniature *domus*, complete with peristyle, that stood on the islet.

THE BATHS

Just south of here is a modestly sized set of baths, with a *heliocaminus*, a round pool used for sunbathing where you baked before bravely plunging into the nearby *frigidarium*, the cold-water pool. Far grander are the *terme* proper, a vast bath complex with open-air pools, hot baths heated by an elaborate system and courtyards for relaxing. By contrast to this hedonism, there's a bit of cultural stimulus near here in the shape of the Canopus, modelled on an Egyptian site that had much

impressed the emperor. It's a replica of the Temple of Serapis at Canopus, which was linked to the Nile by a canal; here, an artificial waterway runs down a man-made valley to the temple replica—it's fringed with statues and fragments of columns, including four serene caryatids. It must have been a wonderful backdrop for late-night dining, which was probably its purpose. Have a look at the nearby Pretorio, the barracks, then visit the underground portico, deliciously cool and shady, where the emperor took his summertime strolls.

PALAZZO IMPERIALE

Winter would have seen Hadrian making full use of the Palazzo Imperiale itself, a complex that covered 50,000sq m (180,000sq ft) and came complete with an efficient underground heating system. The palace was made up of three complexes set round their own peristyles, which housed both residential and official rooms. The Piazza d'Oro, in the southeast, has yielded some

fabulous archaeological treasures; like so much else from here, they're now dispersed to museums in Rome and all over the world. The library building is another thought-provoking area—two originally multi-floor buildings that housed works in Greek and Latin. One side of the library courtyard was occupied by 10 guest rooms, perhaps for visiting scholars, paved with black and white mosaic floors and complete with three sleeping niches in each room.

There's much more besides, best enjoyed as part of the overall scene. There's also an entire underground series of roads, passages and storerooms, from where the infrastructure needed to run this huge palace operated. The small museum has some statues, portraits and mosaics (though all the best are elsewhere), and is also the place to see the latest discoveries, sometimes exhibited here.

OUT AND ABOUT

PARCO NAZIONALE DEL CIRCEO

A national park with a wide variety of wildlife habitats, wonderful coastal scenery, great beaches and a couple of pretty villages.

BASICS

Centro d'Informazione Parco Nazionale del Circeo
Via Carlo Alberto 107
Sabaudia 04014
☎ 0773 511386
Main park information centre with exhibitions, audio-visual show, natural history museum and picnic area

Tourist Information Office
Sabaudia 04014
☎ 0773 515046

Tourist Information Office
San Felice Circeo 04014
☎ 0773 547770

www.parks.it/parco.nazionale.circeo
This wonderful site, beautifully laid out and packed with information and photographs, tells you everything you'll want to know about Circeo and its habitats, flora and fauna. There's practical information, news of what's happening and links to all of Italy's national and regional parks. In English.

HOW TO GET THERE

Cotral bus: from Laurentina to San Felice Circeo/Sabaudia; journey time 2.25 hours
By car: take S148 south via Latina, then follow signs east to Sabaudia; journey time 1.5–2 hours

OVERVIEW

South of Rome, the Pontine Marshes, malaria-ridden, unproductive and unhealthy, once stretched along the coast below Anzio. In 1928 Mussolini embarked on a massive drainage project, transforming the region into a productive agricultural area, complete with the new towns of Latina and Sabaudia. As early as the late 1920s, conservationists realized the threat the scheme might cause to this sensitive and classic coastal environment, and in 1934 the Parco Nazionale del Circeo was founded. Covering an area of 8,500ha (21,000 acres), it's the smallest of Italy's national parks, but despite its diminutive size, the park embraces a superb variety of natural environments, ranging from dunes, wetlands, sea caves and beaches to thick deciduous woods and limestone

maquis. Roads, tracks and paths thread through the park and link the different zones, making the whole area accessible and enjoyable to every type of visitor. Circeo is the perfect antidote to the noise and heat of Rome, a green oasis with immensely varied scenery and a mixed flora and fauna that's unique in this part of Italy.

WHAT TO SEE

Circeo has superb woods of deciduous oaks, holm and cork oaks, but it's the dunes, maquis and wetlands that draw naturalists and birdwatchers to the park. The dunes are backed by four lakes, drawing a wide variety of both resident and migratory birds, so there should be no problem spotting something interesting—over 230 species have been recorded. You may see the turned-over earth that signals wild boar, or get a glimpse of fallow and roe deer, foxes or even a pine marten. Wildflower lovers will find spring the best time to come, when the maquis—the typical scrubby Mediterranean habitat—is at its best, burgeoning with brilliant cistus, rosemary and broom. The park has man-made attractions, too, in the shape of a rich archaeological heritage—Domitian's Villa is the best known.

EXPLORING THE PARK

Explore the park by heading south from Sabaudia, taking in the dunes and wetlands on the way to Monte Circeo, at 541m (1,775ft) the highest point. The drive south covers the quintessential Mediterranean

coastline of the promontory—white-sand beaches, rocky coves and aromatic pines running down to the sea. From Monte Circeo there are fabulous views north over the beaches and lagoons. Monte Circeo is the legendary island of Circe mentioned in Homer's *Odyssey*, and the whole promontory resembles the sorceress' reclining figure. From the top, the road exits the park into the picturesque, and distinctly trendy, coastal village of San Felice Circeo. In summer, it's crowded with flashy cars and yachts, but any other time should be high on the sightseeing list.

Don't miss The view over the dunes from the summit of Monte Circeo is superb—and you can drive up to the top.
If you're here during spring or autumn migration, try birdwatching in the wetlands.

TIPS

● Spend time at the visitor centre in Sabaudia to learn about the park.
● Take a boat trip around the lagoon from Sabaudia, or up and down the coast or to Circe's grotto from San Felice Circeo.
● If you want to stay the night, try one of the moderately priced hotels in San Felice, which are busy only in high season.

WHERE TO EAT

Il Grottino
Piazza Vittorio Veneto 3, San Felice Circeo, 04014
Tel 0773 548446
This seafood restaurant, just outside the old town, has a panoramic terrace overlooking the attractive Golfo di San Felice.

Ristorante Lo Scolglio
Via Caterattino 38, Sabaudia, 04014
Tel 0773 515581
Enjoy excellent seafood and wines, set off by the view of the beach from the terrace.

FRASCATI

The loveliest of the Castelli Romani towns of the Colli Albani hills, famous for its wine and dominated by a majestic villa and its gardens.

BASICS

Tourist Information Office
Piazza Marconi 1, 00044
☎ 06 942 0331

Villa Aldobrandini
Via Cardinale Massaia 12, 00044
🄲 Garden only: Apr–end Nov Mon–Fri 9–1, 3–6; Dec–end Mar Mon–Fri 9–1, 3–4

For *cantine* visits, ask at the tourist information office or enjoy a tour and tasting at one of the local restaurants

HOW TO GET THERE

Train: from Stazione Termini every 15–30 minutes; journey time approximately 30 minutes
Cotral bus: from Anagnina metro station to all the Castelli Romani towns; journey time approximately 30 minutes
By car: take S215 south (exit Tuscalano on GRA), then S216 to Frascati; journey time approximately 50 minutes

OVERVIEW

South of Rome stretches a ridge of volcanic hills, the Colli Albani, famed for the light and aromatic white wines produced from the rich soil. The hills are home to a group of 13 towns, the Castelli Romani, so called because they developed around the feudal castles built by the popes and the Roman aristocracy. Despite the sprawling post-World War II development around them, each has its own charm, with Frascati leading the field.

WHAT TO SEE

The grandest of Frascati's villas is the Villa Aldobrandini, designed by Giacomo della Porta in 1598 for Cardinal Aldobrandini, a 'nephew' (a tactful euphemism for an illegitimate son) of Pope Clement VII. The vast palace, all faded majesty, dominates the town, and is surrounded by a superb example of an early baroque garden, laid out between 1598 and 1603. Head first for the terrace with its fabulous views towards Rome, then explore the other

The view back towards Rome (above).
Villa Aldobrandini (bottom)

terraces, avenues and follies, including the water theatre.

The town is scattered with other gently decaying palaces, like the Villa Falconieri and the Villa Mondragone. Villa Torlonia, among the grandest, was destroyed during World War II, but its gardens are now the town's park—don't miss the fountain, designed by Carlo Maderno.

The baroque cathedral is worth a look, as are some of the other churches, particularly Il Gesù, but do leave time to get to grips with the wine. Made here since the third century BC, Frascati is a worldwide hot seller, and it's a revelation to drink it in its birthplace. Light, floral and aromatic, it's made from

both Trebbiano and Malvasio grapes, two varieties that thrive in the porous volcanic soils.

Don't miss Sip a glass of the famous wine in the place it's made.
Come in late afternoon for the best views across the Campagna towards Rome.

TIPS

● Avoid weekends, when Frascati is packed with Romans out for the day, so it's hard to get a trattoria table.
● The fountains in the gardens of the Villa Aldobrandini are often switched off, so be prepared.
● You can pick up a *panino* from one of the *porchetta* (whole roast suckling pig) stands on Piazza del Mercato and eat it in one of the *cantine* while you sample the wine.

WHERE TO EAT

Al Fico
Via Anagnina 86, 00044
Tel 06 9431 5390
The local dishes are excellent in this central restaurant. Sit outside, on the terrace or in the garden, or go downstairs for wine tasting in the cellar.

Ristorante Cacciani
Via Diaz 15, 00044
Tel 06 942 0378
Enjoy excellent local cuisine on the terrace of this elegant restaurant. There's a great wine list, too.

OUT AND ABOUT

There are many organized tours in and around Rome and beyond. Choices range from escorted walking tours around the city's streets and museums to personalized tours with your own guide. Most tours are available in a number of languages.

GUIDED WALKS

Walking tours are a great way of getting into the heart of the city. There are lots of companies offering walking tours of Rome, so you are sure to find something that appeals.

ENJOY ROME

Via Marghera 8a, 00187
Tel 06 445 1843/06 4938 2724
www.enjoyrome.com
A wide selection of city itineraries (in English only), including special tours of Bernini's Rome or Fascist Rome. Most tours cost €21, or €15 for under-26s, and last for 3 hours. They run every day except Christmas Day and 6 January.

THROUGH ETERNITY

Tel 06 700 9336
www.througheternity.com
Archaeologists, art historians and other experts on ancient Rome offer the usual popular tours, plus an interactive one, where audience participation is essential. Prices vary according to the length of time, but start at €20 for a 2.5-hour tour.

SELF-GUIDED WALKS

If you prefer to go your own way, why not use an audioguide?

ROMEWALKS

www.audiowalks.com
These tapes can be ordered through the above website. They cost around £11.50 ($18.99) for two 90-minute cassettes.

CYCLING TOURS

ENJOY ROME

Via Marghera 8a, 00187
Tel 06 445 1843/06 4938 2724
www.enjoyrome.com
Three-and-a-half-hour cycling

tours of the city for €25 (€20 for under-26s), which includes bicycle rental.

BUS TOURS

There are many companies providing a range of bus tours of Rome and beyond.

ATAC

Via Gaeta 78, 00185
Tel 06 4695 2252, 800 431784
www.atac.roma.it,
www.trambusopen.com
Rome's public transport company runs the 110 City Tour, which leaves from Termini station. You can buy a Stop and Go ticket for €13, which allows you to hop on and off the bus all day. The service runs daily at 15-minute intervals from 8.40am to 8.25pm, and makes 10 stops. You can book in advance at the ticket office, or buy your tickets on the bus or at any of the stops.

ATAC also runs **Archeobus**, which departs every hour daily from 9.45am to 4.45pm. It has 16 stops at the treasures of the Via Appia Antica (▷ 146). The journey takes 2 hours 20 mins and costs €8. A joint ticket for the 110 City Tour and Archeobus costs €20 and lasts 2 days.

Other bus companies run tours around the city and to popular places farther afield, such as Tivoli and Ostia Antica. These include **Appian Line** (Piazza Esquilino 6/7, ▷ 06 487861), **Green Line Tours** (Via Farini 5a, 00185, tel 06 483787, www.greenlinetours.com) and **Stop 'n' go** (tel 06 4890 5729, www.romecitytours.com).

BOAT TOURS

BATTELLI DI ROMA

Tel 06 678 9361
www.battellidiroma.it
Cruises along the Tiber, with a commentary, leaving from Ponte Castel Sant'Angelo. Tickets can be bought in advance from the Hotel Reservations desk at Termini station or on board the boat. Daytime cruises cost from €10 and leave at 9am, 10.30am, 3.30pm and 5pm. Evening cruises, at 8pm, include dinner and cost €43.

FLIGHTS

CITYFLY SPA

Rome Urbe Airport
Via Salaria 825, 00138
Tel 06 88333
www.cityfly.com
Get a bird's-eye view of Rome in a nine-seater, two-engine plane. This 20-minute tour costs €80 per person (minimum two people), with a 30 per cent discount for children under 10.

PERSONAL GUIDES

CAST

Via Cavour 184, 00184
Tel 06 482 5698
www.cast-turismo.it
Provides guides for groups of up to 20 people. Three-hour tours cost €113.

OUT AND ABOUT

Eating and Staying

EATING OUT IN ROME

In Rome, prepare yourself for rich, sun-drenched tastes. More than 5,000 eateries cater for every budget and provide every kind of dining experience. The feasts of ancient Rome may have long since disappeared, but eating is so much a social way of life that it is far from uncommon to spend hours over a meal. Traditionally, many establishments are family-run, the owners priding themselves on offering fresh, home-made delicacies.

Pasta, salami and locally produced wine all help to create a memorable meal

CUCINA ROMANA

The fertile countryside around Rome in the Lazio region is rich in herbs, exquisite vegetables and pungent garlic and onions. Tender, plump globe artichokes, fried whole in olive oil until crispy, are served to perfection by the Romans. Known as *carciofi alla giudia,* this is a typical and delicious dish of the atmospheric Ghetto area, whose origins date back over 400 years and are reflected in Roman cuisine, *cucina romana,* and Jewish dishes in the local restaurants.

Fishy delights are plentiful, too, with a bountiful harvest of seafood from the shores just 24km (15 miles) from the city. Many of the city's starriest restaurants are temples to the best of seafood, including Alberto Ciarla (▷ 232), Quinzi e Gabrieli (▷ 249) and La Rosetta (▷ 251).

As in other Italian regions, pasta is still the mainstay of the Roman meal. *Spaghetti alle vongole* (with clams and tomatoes) is one of the best-known Roman pasta dishes, while *spaghetti alla carbonara,* made with cured bacon, egg yolk and cheese, is equally famous and Roman to the core. The ever-popular pizza comes in every variety, from the authentic thin, crisp *pizza romana* to the thicker, puffier Neapolitan version.

Traditional *cucina romana* uses the often discarded parts of animals and originates from the area of Testaccio, near the old slaughterhouse where many locals once worked. The butchers were paid partly in cash, partly in offal—known as the fifth quarter—including liver, heart, intestines and brains. Slow cooking with herbs and spices transformed these cuts into high-protein, low-cost dishes that can still be found in many of Rome's top restaurants today. *Coda alla vaccinara,* literally 'tail in the style of the slaughterhouse worker', is a famous signature dish of braised oxtail that was created at Rome's oldest and most famous restaurant in Testaccio, Checchino dal 1887 (▷ 238).

WHEN TO EAT

If you are eating breakfast in a bar, as many Romans do, you will find that most of them open at around 7–7.30am for cappuccino and a *cornetto* (croissant). In hotels, breakfast usually starts at 8am, and includes cereal, cold meat and cheeses.

Restaurants open for lunch at 12.30 or 1pm, and serve until around 3pm. Romans generally eat dinner late, so many establishments don't open for evening meals until 8pm, although you will find those that open earlier. Some places, especially cafés and bars, stay open all day.

WHERE TO EAT

Perhaps confusingly, there are several different types of eating establishment in Rome. A *ristorante* tends to be the most expensive, with pristine table linen and equally pristine waiters. The *trattoria* is less formal, less expensive and often still family-run. An *osteria* or *hostaria* can be basic, sometimes with paper tablecloths and no written menu, but can often serve some of the best food in the city. Interestingly, some of Rome's trendiest and most glamorous establishments have adopted the name *osteria,* echoing the shabby chic fashion. A *rosticceria* or *tavola calda* is a fast-food outlet serving mostly cold foods that you can eat then and there or take away for a picnic. A take-out pizzeria is advertised as *pizzeria rustica* or *a taglio* (by the slice). If you want to sit down to enjoy your pizza, always look for the sign *pizzeria forno a legno* to make sure that it is traditionally cooked in a wood-fired brick oven.

EATING

WHAT'S ON THE MENU

A traditional full meal begins with *antipasti* (starters/hors d'oeuvres). This is followed by *primi*—the first, pasta course. This could be *spaghetti alle vongole*, which is best on Tuesdays and Fridays when the clams are guaranteed to be fresh, or *gnocchi alla romana*, little dumplings made in the traditional Roman way in different sauces—Thursday is gnocchi day. The second course, *secondo*, is usually a meat, fish or vegetarian dish, accompanied by *contorni*—

and night, getting their quick fix of caffeine. It is also normal to drink the heady brew standing up, even in the most famous cafés, such as the Sant'Eustachio Il Caffè (▷ 251), which, many say, serves the best espresso in Rome.

The line between café and bar is very blurred, but generally a bar is good for a quick drink, while a café is where you sit and people-watch while enjoying your coffee, or meal, or long, cool drink—or all three. You will certainly pay at least double if

Pizza, ice cream and an espresso are Rome's version of fast food; waiter service adds to the cost

vegetables, which are served as side dishes. Finally, you come to the *formaggio* (cheese) and/or *dolci* (puddings), the espresso and perhaps a drink to aid digestion—*digestivo*. If this quantity of food seems daunting, do not despair. Locals rarely eat such gargantuan meals and pick and mix their courses. However, while it may be acceptable to order *antipasti* alone for lunch, it is not the done thing for dinner and, should you miss out the pasta course, you may be given a sad-eyed look—not for nothing is it known as *il primo*. Very smart restaurants will sometimes offer a *gourmet menu degustazione*, not to be confused with a *menu turistico*. With the latter you usually pay for quantity rather than quality and it is unlikely to give you an authentic Roman dining experience. If you see yellowing photographs of various dishes displayed outside a restaurant, just don't even go there!

PRICE MATTERS/IL CONTO

Although in theory restaurants are no longer allowed to add a bread and cover (*pane e coperto*) charge, many feign oblivion to this and just charge for the bread anyway, usually between €1—€2 per head. Normally, service is not included, although a minority do still add it as a fixed item. In everyday establishments, a tip of 5 per cent is perfectly adequate, but in *ristoranti*, if the service has been good, 10 per cent would be acceptable. You should always be given a receipt (*ricevuta fiscale*) after paying the bill (*il conto*) as, theoretically, the restaurant could be fined if they don't issue one.

CAFFÈ SOCIETY

Drinking coffee is a ritual in Rome—some would say it is an addiction. It is quite normal to see people at the bar counter at every time of day

you elect to be waited upon rather than consume your drink at the bar.

The type of coffee you drink is also important. Romans wouldn't dream of drinking milky cappuccinos after noon, opting instead for the quick caffeine fix of an espresso or a caffè macchiato, with just a drop of milk.

Another variation on the theme is the *enoteca*, or wine bar. These are extremely popular and keep popping up all over the city. Some are self-consciously chic, others are dark and atmospheric, yet others serve excellent food, but all are united in their love of their carefully selected wine. You can drink by the glass or bottle, usually with cold and hot snacks.

GELATERIE

The *gelato* is an indispensable part of Roman life. Some view it as an art form, such as Il Gelato di San Crispino (▷ 242), just behind the Trevi Fountain, which many regard as the best ice cream maker in town. Here, the choices are distinctively seasonal, ranging from summer raspberry to nougat, *tiramisù* and countless others. Glorious *gelato* is almost a fashion accessory during the evening *passeggiata* and, even if you don't want to take time to sit and enjoy it, there are kiosks at the corner of almost every street. Look out for the sign *produzione artiginale*, meaning that it is home-made, and avoid the most lurid, which probably means it contains synthetic additives. Other variations include a *gratachecca*, a water ice grated by hand and topped with fruit syrup.

But for the truly sublime, do try a *tartufo* ice cream. Named after its resemblance to the shape of an exotic truffle, this chocolate-studded ice cream is utterly delicious, expensive and not a little decadent.

Eating is one of Rome's great pleasures. To appreciate its cuisine fully you will need an adventurous spirit and at least a smattering of Italian. If you don't speak the language, menus can be a daunting prospect, but knowledge of a few key words will help you to work out what's on offer, order what you want and avoid any embarrassing blunders. This menu reader is designed to help you translate common words and familiarize yourself with dishes that you are likely to come across on a Roman menu.

Cured hams and salami, lemons, chillis and aubergines (eggplants)

Piatti–Courses
antipasti starters
stuzzichini appetizers
primi piatti first courses
secondi piatti main courses
contorni vegetables/side dishes
dolci desserts
spuntini snacks

Carne–Meat
agnello lamb
cacciagione game
coniglio rabbit
cuore heart
fegato liver
maiale pork
manzo beef
pancetta bacon
pollame poultry
pollo chicken
prosciutto Parma ham
prosciutto cotto cooked ham
rognoni kidneys
salsiccia sausage
tacchino turkey
vitello veal

Pesce–Fish
alici anchovies
baccalà dried salt cod
branzino sea bass
dorate bream
fritto misto mixed fried fish
merluzzo cod
pesce spada swordfish
sarde sardines
sogliola sole
tonno tuna

triglia mullet
trota trout

Frutti di Mare–Seafood
aragoste lobster
calamari squid
canestrelli scallops
cozze mussels
gamberetti prawns
granceola spiny spider crab
molluschi shellfish
ostriche oysters
seppia cuttlefish
vongole clams

Verdure–Vegetables
asparagi asparagus
carciofo artichoke
carote carrots
cavolfiore cauliflower
cavolo cabbage
cetriolino gherkin
cetriolo cucumber
cicoria chicory
cipolla onion
fagioli beans
fagiolini green beans
fave broad beans
finocchio fennel
lattuga lettuce
melanzane aubergines (eggplant)
patate potatoes
peperone red/green pepper (capsicum)
piselli peas
pomodori tomatoes
spinaci spinach

verdure cotte cooked greens
zucchini courgettes (zucchinis)

Metodi di Cucina–Cooking Methods
affumicato smoked
al forno baked
alla griglia grilled
arrosto roasted
bollito boiled
casalingo home-made
crudo raw
fritto fried
frulatto whisked
ripieno stuffed
stufato stewed

La Pasta–Pasta
cannelloni baked meat- or cheese-filled tubes
conchiglie shell shapes
farfalle butterfly shapes
fettucine wide strips
fusilli spiral shapes
lasagne sheets of pasta, layered with meat sauce and béchamel sauce to make *lasagne al forno*
linguine thin strips
pappardelle rippled strips
penne quill shapes
ravioli pasta cushions filled with meat, cheese or spinach
rigatoni short, fat tubes
tagliatelle thin ribbons or strips
tortellini little 'hats' with meat or cheese filling
trenette long narrow strips

EATING

Salsi/Sugi–Sauces

amatriciana bacon, tomato and onion
arrabbiata tomato and hot chilli
cacciatore sauce for meat: tomato, onion, garlic, wine
carbonara smoked bacon, egg, cream and black pepper
passata sieved tomatoes
pesto basil, garlic, pine nuts, olive oil and pecorino cheese
puttanesca tomato, garlic, hot chilli, anchovies, capers
ragù minced meat, tomato

brodo broth
frittata omelette
gnocchi small dumplings made from potato and flour or semolina
minestra vegetable soup
risotto rice cooked in stock
risotto ai funghi mushroom risotto
risotto alla Milanese risotto with saffron
strufolone rolled pizza
uovo egg
zuppa soup

Bevande–Drinks

acqua minerale mineral water (*gassata*, sparkling; *naturale*, still)
birra beer
caffè corretto coffee with liqueur/spirit
caffè freddo iced coffee
caffè latte milky coffee
caffè lungo weak coffee
caffè macchiato coffee with a drop of milk
caffè ristretto strong coffee
digestivo after-dinner liqueur
dolce sweet

Wild mushrooms, olive oil, fresh fish and yellow peppers

and garlic
salsa di pomodoro tomato
salsa verde piquant/ vinaigrette

Specialità–Special Dishes

carpaccio thin-sliced raw beef served with a cold vinaigrette
coda alla vaccinara oxtail stew
osso bucco veal stewed with tomatoes, onions and garlic
pastiera Neapolitan Easter grain pie, filled with ricotta and flavoured with orange
peperonata sweet pepper (capsicum) and tomato stew
polpetti meatballs
saltimbocca veal escalopes with ham, sage and white wine
scaloppini thinly sliced veal cooked in white wine
stracotto beef stew
timballo baked meat and vegetable pie

Contorni–Side Dishes

insalata mista mixed salad
insalata tricolore mozzarella, tomato and fresh basil
insalata verde green salad
pane bread
patate fritte chips (french fries)
polenta maize-meal dish
riso rice

Altri Piatti–Other Dishes

antipasto misto mixed cold meats: salami, ham etc.
brodetto fish soup

Dolci–Cakes/Desserts

cassata Sicilian fruit ice cream
cioccolata chocolate
crema custard
macedonia fruit salad
panna cream
una pasta a cake/pastry
semifreddo chilled dessert made with ice cream
tiramisù chocolate/coffee sponge dessert
torta tart
zabaglione egg, sugar and Marsala dessert
zabaione di Verduzzo custard pudding with Friuli wine
zuccotto ice-cream sponge
zuppa inglese trifle

Frutti–Fruits

arancia orange
fragola strawberry
lampone raspberry
mela apple
melone melon
pera pear
pesca peach
pesca noci nectarine
uve grapes

Formagi–Cheeses

formaggio di capra goat's cheese
formaggio dolce mild cheese
formaggio nostrano local cheese
parmigiano Parmesan
pecorino Roman hard cheese, like Parmesan

ghiaccio ice
liquore liqueur
porto port wine
secco dry
spumante sparkling wine
succo di arancia orange juice
té tea
té al latte freddo tea with milk
té freddo iced tea
vini pregiati quality wines
vino bianco white wine
vino rosato rosé wine
vino rosso red wine
vino di tavola house wine

Condimenti–Seasonings

aceto vinegar
aglio garlic
aromatiche herbs
basilico basil
capperi capers
pepe pepper
peperoncino chilli
prezzemolo parsley
rosemarino rosemary
sale salt
salvia sage
senape mustard
timo thyme
zucchero sugar

Il Conto–The Bill

coperto cover charge
IVA value-added tax (sales tax)
servizio compreso service charge included
servizio non compreso service charge not included

	LOCATION
Bruschetterie	
Bruschetteria degli Angeli	Campo dei Fiori
Bruschetteria Nonna Papera	Trevi
Cafés	
Antico Caffè della Pace	Piazza Navona
Antico Caffè Greco	Piazza di Spagna
Babington's Tea Rooms	Piazza di Spagna
Bar Capitolina	Campidoglio
Bar Gianicolo	Monteverde
Bar San Calisto	Trastevere
Bibli	Trastevere
Café Café	Colosseo
Café dell'Arancia	Trastevere
Café di Marzio	Trastevere
Café Renault	Via Nazionale
Da Benito	Ghetto
Friends Art Café	Trastevere
Non Solo Bevi	Colonna
Open Music Café	Via Latina
Le Pain Quotidien	Augusto Imperatore
Sant'Eustachio il Caffè	Pantheon
Tazza d'Oro	Pantheon
Trastè	Trastevere

Enoteche	
The Albert	Trevi
Antica Locanda	Monti
La Barrique	Via Nazionale
Cul de Sac	Piazza Navona
Il Goccetto	Campo dei Fiori
Pane Vino e San Daniele	Musei Capitolini
Il Piccolo	Piazza Navona
Trimani 'Il Winebar'	Termini

Vineria Reggio (above)	Campo dei Fiori
Wine Time	Corso Vittorio

Fish Restaurants	
Alberto Ciarla	Trastevere
La Caraffa	Appio-Latina
F.I.S.H.	Monti
Grotte del Teatro di Pompeo	Campo dei Fiori
Pierluigi	Campo dei Fiori
Quinzi e Gabrieli	Piazza Navona
Ristorante Consolini	Aventino
Taverna Angelica	Vatican

Gelaterie	
Fassi–Palazzo del Freddo	Piazza Vittorio
Gelateria della Palma	Pantheon
Il Gelato di San Crispino	Trevi
Giolitti	Montecitorio
Tre Scalini	Piazza Navona
Vitti	Augusto Imperatore

	LOCATION
Jewish/Kosher	
Da Paris	Trastevere
Giggetto al Portico d'Ottavia	Ghetto
La Taverna del Ghetto	Ghetto
Roman	
Agata e Romeo	S. Maria Maggiore
Al 34 (Trentaquattro)	Piazza di Spagna

Antonio al Pantheon (above)	Pantheon
Casetta de Trastevere	Trastevere
Checchino dal 1887	Testaccio
Otello alla Concordia	Via del Corso
Pasqualino al Colosseo	Colosseo
Renato e Luisa	Campo dei Fiori
Ristorante Il Matriciano	Vatican
Silvio alla Subarra	S. Maria Maggiore
Sora Lella	Isola Tiberina
Taverna 'Da Giovanni'	Castel S. Angelo
Taverna Parione	Piazza Navona
Tram Tram	San Lorenzo

Pizzerie	
Acqua, Farina e…	Trieste
Almacrì	Trastevere
Il Capriccio	Piazza Navona
Ciccia Bomba	Piazza Navona
Corallo	Piazza Navona
Da Baffetto	Piazza Navona
Da Vittorio	Trastevere
Dar Poeta	Trastevere
Est! Est! Est!	Quirinale/Viminale
Good Good	San Giovanni
Gran Caffè Martini e Rossi	Colosseo
Ivo a Trastevere	Trastevere
Panattoni (I Marmi) (below)	Trastevere
Pizza Ciro	Piazza S. Silvestro
Pizza Forum	Colosseo
Pizzarè	Via Veneto
Pizzeria La Montecarlo	Piazza Navona
Pizzeria Popi Popi	Trastevere
San Clemente	Colosseo

EATING

	LOCATION				LOCATION
San Marino	Trieste	**Mediterranean**			
Taverna de'Mercanti	Trastevere	La Terrazza			Via Veneto
Il Tulipano Nero	Trastevere				
		Salads			
Italian		Insalata Ricca			Campo dei Fiori
Al Bric	Campo dei Fiori				
Al Ceppo	Parioli	**Spaghetterie**			
Alfredo a Via Gabi	San Giovanni	L'Archetto			Trevi
Ambasciata d'Abruzzo	Parioli	T-Bone Station			Piazza Barberini,
Antico Arco	Monteverde				Piazza di Spagna
L'Archeologia	Via Appia Antica				
Il Bacaro	Pantheon	**Trattorie**			
Il Boom	Trastevere	I Buoni Amici			San Giovanni
Borgo Nuovo	Vatican				
Bramante	Piazza Navona				
Il Brillo Parlante	Popolo				
Il Convivio	Piazza Navona				
Il Cortile	Monteverde				
Da Agusto	Trastevere				
Da Settimio	Pantheon				
Dal Toscano	Vatican				
Edoardo II	Piazza Venezia				
El Toulà	Augusto Imperatore				
Evangelista	Ghetto				
Gusto	Augusto Imperatore				

Roof Garden 'Les Etoiles'

Lumière di Sicilia	Monteverde		
Maccheroni	Pantheon		
Myosotis	Pantheon		
Navona Notte	Piazza Navona		
Nerone	Colosseo		
Obika	Augusto Imperatore	Da Francesco	Piazza Navona
Osteria dell'Anima	Piazza Navona	Da Giovanni	Trastevere
Il Pomodorino	Via Veneto	Dai Tre Amici	Pantheon
La Proposta	Giovanni	Der Pallaro	Campo dei Fiori
Ristorante Giovanni	Via Veneto	Ditirambo	Campo dei Fiori
Ristorante Nuova Stella	S. Maria Maggiore	Fiaschetteria Beltramme	Piazza di Spagna
Ristorante-Pizzeria		Grappolo d'Oro/Zampanò	Castel Sant'Angelo
Piacere Molise	Prati	Osteria "Ar Galletto"	Campo dei Fiori
Romolo 'Nel Giardino di		Osteria del Campidoglio	Campidoglio
Raffaello e della Fornarina'	Trastevere	Perilli a Testaccio	Testaccio
Roof Garden 'Les Etoiles'	Prati		
La Rosetta	Pantheon	**Vegetarian**	
Siciliainbocca	Vatican	Il Margutta	Popolo
Trattoria Abruzzese	Equilino/Viminale	Il Tiepolo	Flaminio
Trattoria da Nazzareno	Termini		
Vecchia Roma	Musei Capitolini		

EATING

International	LOCATION	TYPE
Hard Rock Café (left)	Via Veneto	American
Baires	Piazza Navona	Argentinian
Ketumbar	Testaccio	Asian
Lowenhaus	Popolo	Bavarian
Antico Bottaro	Popolo	French
Un Cochon dans Mon Jardin	Parioli	French
L'Eau Vive	Piazza Navona	French
Charly's Saucière	San Giovanni	French
Ouzerie	Trastevere	Greek
Il Guru	Monti	Indian
Sitar	Colosseo	Indian
Osaka	San Giovanni	Japanese
Zen Sushi	Vatican	Japanese
Tapa Loca	Piazza Navona	Spanish
Thai Inn	Monteverde	Thai

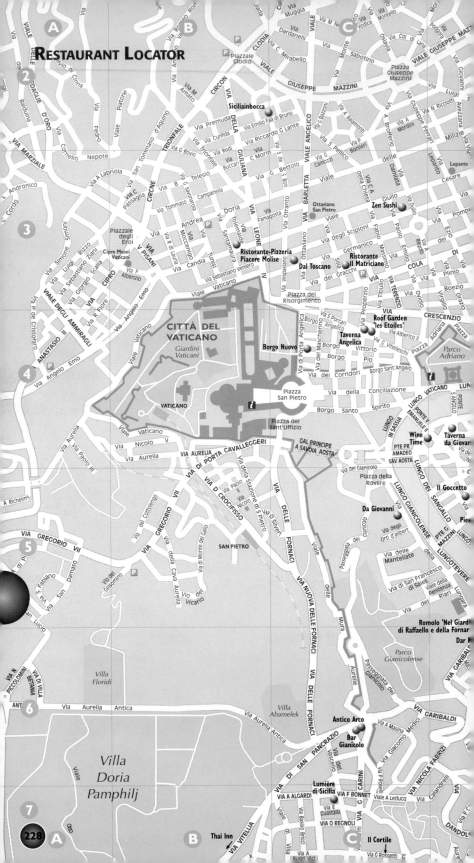

Restaurants

The prices given are for a two-course lunch (L) for one person and a three-course dinner (D) for one person, without drinks. The wine price is the starting price for a bottle of wine. Note that smoking is no longer allowed in any restaurant.

ACQUA, FARINA E...

Map off 231 J2
Via Tripolitania 105–109, 00198
Tel 06 8632 4853
The specialty of this pizzeria is *strufoloni*—rolled pizza with traditional fillings, including mozzarella, courgette (zucchini) flowers and anchovies. Mozzarella with fried chicory is also superb. For dessert try *strufolone* spread with chocolate and sprinkled with coconut. It's outside central Rome, but the bus connections are good.
🕐 Daily 7.30pm–11.30pm; closed 8–25 Aug
🖐 D €12, Wine €11
🚌 38, 60X to Viale Libia

AGATA E ROMEO

Map 230 H5
Via Carlo Alberto 45, 00185
Tel 06 446 6115
Enjoy Roman and southern Italian dishes in this intimate and elegant restaurant. *Baccalà* (salt cod), smoked and cooked with an orange sauce, is just one of the delights on the menu, and is best accompanied by an Italian wine from their great wine list. Reservations essential.
🕐 Mon–Fri 1–2.30, 8–10.30; closed Aug and 2 weeks in Jan
🖐 L €40, D €80, Wine €25
Ⓜ Vittorio Emanuele
🚌 4, 70, 71, 614

AL 34 (TRENTAQUATTRO)

Map 229 E3
Via Mario de'Fiori 34, 00187
Tel 06 679 5091
This comfortable, intimate restaurant produces Roman and southern Italian meat and fish dishes using seasonal vegetables and herbs. The service is fast and efficient— great for those in a hurry. Al 34 is very popular, which means that reservations are essential.
🕐 Tue–Sun 12.30–3, 7.30–11; closed Aug
🖐 L €12, D €30, Wine €12.50
Ⓜ Spagna
🚌 116, 119

AL BRIC

Map 229 D5
Via del Pellegrino 51, 00186
Tel 06 687 9533
Very stylish *osteria* and wine bar with many small tables in a large room overlooking Via del Pellegrino, near Campo dei Fiori. The wine list is huge, with more than a thousand labels. The menu has a wide selection of creative dishes matched perfectly with wine suggestions. Try spaghetti with anchovies and pecorino cheese or pears with Gorgonzola cheese and the home-made bread. Among the desserts, don't miss the strudel with cinnamon ice cream.
🕐 Jun–end Sep Tue–Sat 7.30pm–11.30pm, Sun 12.30–2.30; Oct–end May daily 7.30pm–11.30pm
🖐 D €50, Wine €10
🚌 64, 87, 492 to Largo Argentina; tram 8

AL CEPPO

Map off 230 G2
Via Panama 2/4, 00198
Tel 06 841 9696
www.ristorantealceppo.it
In the residential Parioli district a few kilometres from central Rome is this fine restaurant specializing in grilled foods. There are three rooms, one of which is a lounge for your *aperitivo*. Dining rooms are furnished with chestnut benches, tasteful linen and lights made of Murano glass. The menu, which changes daily, places a special emphasis on the Marches region of Italy, although fish is served on Tue and Fri. The chargrilled rib-eye steak with juniper berries, bay leaves and oregano is a real treat. Extensive wine cellar.
🕐 Tue–Sun 1–3, 8–11; closed Aug
🖐 L €20, D €50, Wine €13
🚌 53, 360; tram 3, 19 to Piazza Ungheria

THE ALBERT

Map 229 F4
Via del Traforo 132, 00187
Tel 06 481 8795
This well-established English pub between the Spanish

ALBERTO CIARLA

Map 229 D6
Piazza San Cosimato 40, 00153
Tel 06 581 8668
www.albertociarla.com

Internationally reputed fish restaurant on the market piazza of San Cosimato in the district of Trastevere. Its rather retro and formal red-and-black, mirrored interior is being transformed into something more minimalist in style, but the innovative menu and supreme skills of master chef Alberto Ciarla remain. Bean soup with seafood, and lentils from Ponza with lobster are but two pearls in this sea. Six different tasting menus are available if you simply can't choose. Vast wine cellar.
🕐 Mon–Sat 8pm–12.30am
🖐 D €65, Wine €14
🚌 H to Piazza Santa Maria in Trastevere, 115; tram 3, 8

Steps and the Trevi Fountain is ideal for a break from sightseeing. Family run and with friendly service, it provides a step back in time: The furniture is Victorian, and there is a fireplace and stained-glass ceilings. Well worth the stop for a proper pint or a lunch buffet at good prices. Afternoon tea, too. Credit cards are not accepted.

EATING

- Daily 12pm–2am
- Salad bar €6, pint €5, spirits €4.50
- Barberini
- 71, 116, 117 or any bus to Piazza San Silvestro

ALFREDO A VIA GABI
Map off 230 H7
Via Gabi 36/38, 00183
Tel 06 7720 6792
www.alfredoaviagabi.it
It is well worth venturing out of the *centro storico* for this one. Only 1.5km (1 mile) from the basilica of San Giovanni in Laterano, it's the perfect retreat after a day of looking around churches. It retains a smart 1950s ambience: handsome, dark wood panelling and carved screens, crisp white linen, brass candelabras and a profusion of fresh flowers. The Italian cuisine is refreshingly original, such as pasta with wild mushroom sauce, a baked dish of anchovy and artichoke, and zabaglione mousse.
- Wed–Mon 12–3, 7.30–11; closed Aug
- L €20, D €30, Wine €12
- Re di Roma
- 87, 360

ALMACRÌ
Map off 229 D7
Via F. Benaglia 3, 00153
Tel 06 589 5651
Don't be misled by its stylish furniture and popularity—this Trastevere restaurant is excellent value whether you choose pizza, pasta or meat. Pizzas are huge, with traditional or creative toppings. The *tagliata di pollo* (grilled chicken) served with salad and cherry tomatoes is recommended. Roast potatoes are rich on garlic, salads vast and crisp, and the desserts good. The wine list is negligible—it's better to choose from the 26 bottled beers. Reservations are essential.
- Tue–Sun 7.30pm–11pm
- D €15, Wine €4
- H, 23, 44, 56, 75, 280; tram 8 to Viale Trastevere

AMBASCIATA D'ABRUZZO
Map off 230 G2
Via Pietro Tacchini 26, 00197
Tel 06 807 8256
www.ambasciatadabruzzo.com
This restaurant in the smart Parioli district is well known for its dishes from the Abruzzo.

The region (east of Lazio) is renowned for its hams and cheeses, hence the astounding antipasti here, a meal in itself: salamis, fresh sheep's milk ricotta, buffalo mozzarella, a plate of Abruzzo cured ham, fried vegetables, a soufflé of potatoes, and jellied veal's head. They also do a sampler of practically everything on the menu for €30. Seating available outside in summer.
- Daily 12–2.30, 7–midnight
- L €10, D €22, Wine €7
- 56, 910 to Via Antonelli and Viale Bruno Buozzi, 926

ANTICA LOCANDA
Map 229 F5
Via del Boschetto 85, 00184
Tel 06 4788 1729
www.antica-locanda.com
Brick walls, oak beams and candlelight make this a delightful place in which to

spend an evening sampling fine wines from all over Italy. It's just a 10-minute walk from the Forum in the heart of one of the city's oldest quarters. There's a limited but good selection of food: pasta, mixed vegetables and daily specials. Two good Chardonnays to try are the Tenuta Santa Anna and the Prinè Chardonnay Barrique. For reds, try the Cabernet Bosco del Merlo. Wines are sold by the glass or bottle.
- Tue–Sun 10am–1am
- L €10, D €22, Wine €12
- Cavor
- 117, or any bus to Via Nazionale

ANTICO ARCO
Map 228 C6
Piazzale Aurelio 7, 00152
Tel 06 581 5274
Sample modern cuisine inside an 18th-century palazzo on the Gianicolo Hill. Antico Arco attracts international accolades for dishes such as

ANTICO CAFFÈ DELLA PACE
Map 229 D4
Via della Pace 3/7, 00186
Tel 06 686 1216
www.caffedellapace.it
A real Roman institution just off Piazza Navona—a Liberty-style (art nouveau) café, with marble interior and wrought-

iron tables under an ivy cascade outside. Attracts the showbiz crowd when they are in Rome, including Robert De Niro, Mel Gibson, Sophia Loren and Madonna. Possibly the last stronghold of *la dolce vita*. Good for light meals or an *aperitivo*. Credit cards are not accepted.
- Tue–Sun 8am–2am, Mon 4pm–2am
- Cocktails from €10, sandwiches from €7
- 46, 62, 64, 87, 116, 492 to Piazza Navona

pheasant breast with truffles on a potato tart, spaghetti with cheese, pepper and courgette (zucchini) flowers, and Sicilian cassata made from ricotta cheese. The extensive wine list contains over 400 labels.
- Mon–Sat 7.30pm–midnight; closed 2 weeks in Aug.
- D €35, Wine €12
- 44, 870

EATING

ANTICO BOTTARO

Map 229 E3
Passeggiata di Ripetta 15, 00186
Tel/Fax 06 323 6763
www.anticobottaro.it

This sophisticated restaurant near Piazza del Popolo is popular with gourmets looking for creative cuisine with a distinctly French twist. The baroque décor contributes to the atmosphere of refined elegance, and although it is very formal the staff are friendly. It also has one of Rome's best selections of Italian and international wine.

🕐 Tue–Sun 8pm–11.30pm
🍴 D €75, Wine €20
Ⓜ Flaminio
🚌 95, 117, 119

ANTICO CAFFÈ GRECO

Map 229 E4
Via dei Condotti 86, 00186
Tel 06 679 1700

This famous old café was founded in 1767 by a Greek, hence the name. It has always been popular with the rich and famous, and numbered Keats, Byron and Goethe among its clientele. Look for pictures of some of the café's well-known past customers in the back room.

🕐 Daily 8–8
🍴 Coffee from €4.75, cake €6.20 (table service only)
Ⓜ Spagna
🚌 119 to Piazza di Spagna, or 52, 58, 61, 71, 85, 160 to Piazza San Silvestro

ANTONIO AL PANTHEON

Map 229 E4
Via dei Pastini 12, 00186
Tel 06 679 0798

Family-run restaurant in a pedestrian street near the Pantheon. Large, brick-vaulted room with 1960s paintings adorning the walls. The food is quintessentially Roman and the clientele local. Try the fresh fettuccine with creamy walnut sauce and, for a main course, the calves' liver cooked in

chilli, olive oil and wine. The portions are very generous and the service is a joy.

🕐 Mon–Sat 12–3, 7–11; closed 3 weeks in Aug
🍴 L €12, D €20, Wine €16
🚌 40, 62, 64, or any bus to Piazza Navona and Corso Vittorio Emanuele II

L'ARCHEOLOGIA

Map off 230 G7
Via Appia Antica 139, 00179
Tel 06 788 0494
www.larcheologia.it

Near the catacombs on the Appian Way, this elegant restaurant has three dining

rooms and a garden full of ancient statues. Open fires and warm hues make for a luxuriant setting. Dishes from the Lazio region are served: roast veal stuffed with pancetta and a black truffle sauce, and *fettuccine alla catullo* (seafood pasta) are two winners. Try the Virtu Romane white wine—at €15 it's worth twice the price. Finish off with a visit to the medieval wine cellar.

🕐 Wed–Mon 12.30–3, 7.30–11
🍴 L €60, D €80, Wine €6
🚌 218 to Catacombe di San Callisto

L'ARCHETTO

Map 229 E4
Via dell'Archetto 26, 00186
Tel 06 678 9064

Serves pizza and grilled meat, but, most of all, spaghetti—there are more than 100 different kinds to choose from and portions are always generous. Dishes range from traditional recipes such as carbonara and *spaghetti alle vongole* (with clams) to more creative incarnations: The lemon spaghetti is especially good. There are a few tables outside, plus vaulted ceilings and arches inside. Excellent fruit salad.

🕐 Daily 12–3, 7–1
🍴 L €12, D €22, Wine €5.50

BAR CAPITOLINA

Map 229 E5
Piazzale Caffarelli 4, 00186
Tel 06 6919 0564

What many don't know is that you can access the bar of the Musei Capitolini without actually visiting the museum. It's worth having a drink or lunch here because, apart from reasonable prices, it has a large terrace with stunning views of the Tarpeian Rock and ancient Rome. Guests with disabilities should ask for lift access, as it is quite a climb up. The way in to the bar is via the museum exit on Piazzale Caffarelli (look carefully as there are no signs outside).

🕐 Tue–Sun 9–8
🍴 Roll, sandwich and salad €19 (terrace €28), Wine €7.75, Coffee €1.30 (terrace €4)
🚌 40, 64, 87, 628 to Piazza Venezia, or 40, 62, 63, 64, 492, 571, 628, 916 to Teatro di Marcello

Ⓜ Baberini
🚌 117, 119, or any bus to Piazza Venezia or Via del Corso

BABINGTON'S TEA ROOMS

Map 229 E3
Piazza di Spagna 23, 00186
Tel 06 678 6027

The area around the Spanish Steps has been a magnet for British visitors since the days of the Grand Tour. This very British tea room was opened by two spinsters in 1896 to cater for homesick visitors. Today, you can still enjoy a pot of Earl Grey with your afternoon tea, but you will also see American food, such as pancakes and maple syrup. Brunch is served all day.

🕐 Wed–Mon 9–8.15
🍴 Brunch €34
Ⓜ Spagna
🚌 116, 119

EATING

IL BACARO

Map 229 E4
Via degli Spagnoli 27, 00186
Tel 06 686 2554

Near the Pantheon, this restaurant is ideal for a romantic dinner, especially in

summer when you can dine outdoors under a roof of ivy vines. The creative cuisine is strongly based on seasonal products, including rigatoni pasta with blue Stilton and Brussels sprouts, and beef fillet cooked with Merlot wine. Among the home-made pastries, the flaky, creamy *millefoglie sbriciolato con crema pasticcera* (millefolglie crumble with a creamy sauce) is sublime. Excellent wine and cheese lists. Reservations recommended.

⏰ Mon–Fri 1–3.30, 7.30–11.30, Sat 7.30–11.30; closed 1 week in Aug
🖐 L €12, D €30, Wine €14
🚌 64, 87, 492 to Largo Argentina; tram 8

BAIRES

Map 229 E5
Corso Rinascimento 1, 00186
Tel 06 686 1293
www.baires.it

The bright walls and floors, as well as the sounds of tango, create a South American atmosphere just behind Piazza Navona. Argentinian grilled meat served with various sauces form the menu. Starters include marinated chicken (*pollo all'escabeche*), and

there's a wide choice of salads and soups. Unsurprisingly, the wine list focuses on Argentina; the house red and white are organic.

⏰ Daily 12–3.30, 7.30–midnight
🖐 L €12, D €25, Wine €8
🚇 Colosseo
🚌 87, 116, 492

BAR GIANICOLO

Map 228 C6
Piazzale Aurelio 5, 00152
Tel 06 580 6275

This coffee shop is a Roman institution. Families flock here after weekend excursions in the Gianicolo park. At night, young people buzz in and out, but visitors may feel more welcome in the afternoon than later on. The menu includes fresh apple and carrot juice, small pizzas and light sandwiches. Opt for bar service if you're in a hurry. Credit cards are not accepted.

⏰ Tue–Sun 6am–1am
🖐 Espresso 75c, Fresh juice €2.50
🚌 44

BAR SAN CALISTO

Map 229 D6
Piazza San Calisto 3, 00153
Tel 06 583 5869

Join the rowdy night-time crowd in Piazza San Calisto and sample Bar San Calisto's famous *affogato* (ice cream drizzled with liqueur). The vodka-lemon sorbet is especially sought after. The scene is calmer during the day. The bar, nicknamed Marcello's, serves inexpensive coffee, beer and ice cream from cramped, utilitarian premises. It's glamorous in a gritty way: a true slice of old Trastevere. Credit cards are not accepted.

⏰ Mon–Sat 7am–2am
🖐 Coffee 80c, ice cream €1–€2
🚌 H, 63, 75

LA BARRIQUE

Map 230 F5
Via del Boschetto 41b, 00184
Tel 06 4782 5953

A wine bar, particularly loved by theatregoers, just off Via Nazionale. Ideal for a light but sophisticated dinner; for a romantic evening, reserve the tiny mezzanine floor with the sofa. Creative cooking, with every dish designed for a perfectly matched wine. Desserts change daily, but

the mousses are always mouth-watering. The ample wine list includes a good choice of wine by the glass.

⏰ Mon–Fri 1–3, 6–2, Sat 6pm–2am
🖐 L €8, D €15, Wine €3 (by the glass)
🚇 Repubblica or Cavour
🚌 30X, 64

BIBLI

Map 229 D6
Via dei Fienaroli 28, 00153
Tel 06 588 4097
www.bibli.it

This Trastevere bookshop-cum-cafeteria is particularly popular for Sunday brunch. A selection

of pastas, quiches, couscous with vegetables and other vegetarian dishes are served buffet style. Among the home-made cakes, poppy seed is very popular. The wine list is limited, but the choice of teas and herbal infusions is so vast as to make this a perfect place for an afternoon reviver. There is also a tiny courtyard for hot summer nights.

⏰ Daily 11am–midnight; Mon 5.30–11.30 buffet-style dinner
🖐 Brunch €15, D €30, tea €2
🚌 H, 23, 44, 56, 75, 280; tram 8 to Viale Trastevere or Piazza Sonnino

IL BOOM

Map 229 D6
Via dei Fienaroli 30a, 00153
Tel 06 589 7196
www.ilboom.it

Italian 1960s atmosphere, with an original jukebox and photos of *la dolce vita* celebrities hanging on the walls of this Trastevere *ristorante*. The *granmisto* is a selection of different starters, from fried vegetables to creative *bruschette* (toasted bread). *Gnocchetti sardi pasta* with rocket (arugula) and ricotta is a specialty. The wine list focuses on southern Italy, but there are also Passiti and Malvasie to complement the home-made desserts.

🕐 Daily 7.30–midnight
🍴 D €25, Wine €9
🚌 H, 44, 780; tram 3, 8

BORGO NUOVO

Map 228 C4
Borgo Pio 104, 00197
Tel 06 689 2852
www.borgonuovo.org

This place is ideal if you have just visited the Basilica di San Pietro or the Vatican museums and need a quiet sit down and some tasty, freshly prepared Italian food. The portions are generous, the service friendly and efficient, and the menu easy to follow. It's open all day, and there's a good range of vegetarian, meat and fish options.

🕐 Wed–Mon 12–10
🍴 L €16, D €30, Wine €10
🚇 Ottaviano (Piazza del Risorgimento)
🚌 81

BRAMANTE

Map 229 D4
Via della Pace 25, 00186
Tel 06 6880 3916

The setting of this chic bar/restaurant, complete with an art nouveau window, could scarcely be bettered: It's on one of the city's most prestigious and beautiful baroque squares, Piazza Navona. Inside, you could be in a Tuscan-style villa, softly lit with oil lamps; the walls are frescoed with local scenes and classical music plays. Unfortunately, the cuisine is not the most imaginative, especially for the above-average prices. However, the service is first class.

🕐 Mon–Sat 6.30pm–2am, Sun 12.30–2pm
🍴 L €25, D €30, Wine €25
🚌 46, 62, 64, 87, 116, 492 to Piazza Navona

IL BRILLO PARLANTE

Map 229 E3
Via della Fontanella 12, 00187
Tel 06 324 3334
www.ilbrilloparlante.com

Wine bar with a selection of cheeses and salami served on the wood counter upstairs, and restaurant with vaulted ceilings and five small rooms below.

Popular among the locals. Excellent grilled Danish meat and also fish. The pizzas are good but not memorable. Among the home-made desserts, the chocolate tart and tiramisu are great, but it's worth coming for the pear mousse alone. Excellent wine list—a choice of 300 for every budget. Tables outside during the summer.

🕐 Tue–Sun 12.30–3.30, 7.30–1, Mon 7.30pm–1am; closed 1 week in Aug
🍴 L €12, D €25, Wine €16
🚇 Flaminio
🚌 117, 119

BRUSCHETTERIA DEGLI ANGELI

Map 229 E5
Piazza B. Cairoli 2a, 00186
Tel 06 6880 5789

Just behind Campo dei Fiori, this eatery offers an alternative to pizza. Huge *bruschette* (toasted breads) are served with over 50 different

toppings, from tomatoes and rocket (arugula) salad to Asiago cheese and *speck* (bacon), plus pasta and meat dishes and huge salads. The international beer list is ample. Tables are available outside during the summer. Paper tablecloths and warm wooden furniture contribute to the rustic image.

🕐 Sep–end Jun Mon–Sat 12–3, 7–1, Sun 7pm–1am; Jul–end Aug daily 7pm–1am
🍴 *Bruschette* from €8, Beer from €4
🚌 64, 87, 492 to Largo Argentina; tram 8

BRUSCHETTERIA NONNA PAPERA

Map 229 F4
Via dei Modelli 60, 00186
Tel 06 678 3510

In a tiny alley behind the Trevi Fountain is this eatery, with country-style wooden furniture, cherry tomatoes hanging from the ceiling, and

ceramic decorative tiles. Huge *bruschette* with all sorts of toppings, including a lovely version with ham and chicory, plus savoury crêpes with artichoke cream or salmon: A good idea for a light lunch.

🕐 Wed–Mon 12–3, 7–10
🍴 *Bruschette* €6.50, D €30, Wine €11
🚌 40, 64, 87, 628 to Piazza Venezia, or any bus through Via del Corso

I BUONI AMICI

Map 230 H6
Via Aleardo Aleardi 4, 00185
Tel 06 7049 1993

This trattoria near San Giovanni in Laterano is one of

CAFÉ DI MARZIO
Map 229 D6
Piazza Santa Maria in Trastevere 15, 00153
Tel 06 581 6095

Sip exquisite coffee or hot chocolate facing the golden façade of Santa Maria in Trastevere. Of course, the see-and-be-seen outdoor tables are costly; visitors on a budget should go inside and enjoy an espresso at the bar, then soak in the view from the fountain steps. Di Marzio is also popular enough to be able to accept large notes (bills)—a lifesaver here in the land of correct change.

🕐 Feb–end Nov 7am–2am
☕ Coffee from 80c inside (€1.60 outside)
🚌 H, 63, 75 to Via Trastevere

the best-value restaurants in Rome, despite its celebrity clientele. Traditional interior design, with red-and-white checked tablecloths. Delicious antipasti include aubergines (eggplant), courgettes (zucchini), spinach and squid salad. Try the fresh pasta with lobster and some chargrilled fish to follow, or the roast lamb. Leave room for the home-made tiramisu and *pannacotta*. The Cannonau red from Sardinia is a bargain at only €8 a bottle.

🕐 Mon–Sat 12.30–3, 7.30–11
🍴 L €11, D €25, Wine €7
Ⓜ Manzoni
🚌 16, 81, 87, 117, 714

CAFÉ CAFÉ
Map 230 G6
Via dei SS. Quattro 44, 00184
Tel 06 700 8743
Escape the tourist traps encircling the Colosseum and relax in bohemian elegance at this café/restaurant. The

Swedish owner serves up coffee, cakes, fresh juice, home-made ice cream and light Italian fare. Expect hand-lettered menus, bright walls and soft jazz. The tiny place fills up quickly for Sun brunch, a €4 buffet of crunchy salads, *bruschette*, cheese and prosciutto. Highly recommended for vegetarians and vegans, plus for visitors on their own, who will delight in the generous pile of newspapers.

🕐 Mar–end Jul, Sep–end Oct daily 10am–2am; Nov–end Feb, Aug Thu–Tue 10am–2am
🍴 L €4, D €10, Wine €13
Ⓜ Colosseo

CAFÉ DELL'ARANCIA
Map 229 D6
Piazza Santa Maria in Trastevere 2, 00153
Tel 338 110 8064
There's a good reason this café/*gelateria*/cocktail bar is called the café of oranges:

Sitting out under the canopy, you are surrounded by baskets of the fruit. It's the perfect place to pass an hour or two people-watching in the Piazza di Santa Maria in Trastevere, and what better way to enjoy the square than with the house special, a Campari citrus cocktail served in a giant crystal flute? A range of citrus cocktails, as well as coffee and ice cream are available. Credit cards are not accepted.

🕐 Fri–Wed 10am–1.30am; closed Dec–end Jan
🍴 Cocktails €8, ice cream €8
🚌 23; tram 8

CAFÉ RENAULT
Map 229 F5
Via Nazionale 183b, 00184
Tel 06 4782 4452
www.cafe-renault.it
A vast, high-tech café right in front of Banca d'Italia on Via Nazionale, with metal chairs,

leather sofas and holograms on the tabletops. Self-service cafeteria with light lunches during the day and great cocktails (their mojito is made with mint, lime, rum and tonic water) and also a full restaurant menu in the evenings. Occasional live music (especially lounge-style) and multimedia events connected with the car manufacturer that gives the café its name.

🕐 Mon 8–8, Tue–Fri 8am–2am, Sat 12pm–2am, Sun 4pm–1am
🍴 L €12, D €30, Wine €4
Ⓜ Repubblica or Termini
🚌 30X, 64

IL CAPRICCIO
Map 229 D5
Via della Pace 27a, 00186
Tel 06 6880 4458
Pizza a taglio (cut pizza) to go is a Roman institution. This establishment is just along from Piazza Navona. You

decide how much they should slice off the large rectangular tray-baked pizzas and then pay by weight—no slice is too small. Other tasty morsels are the olives *ascolane* (large green olives, stuffed with meat and herbs and deep fried) or *suppli* (deep-fried tomato risotto and cheese balls). Credit cards are not accepted.

🕐 Tue–Sun 9am–4am; closed 2 weeks in Feb, end Aug
🍕 Pizza slice approx. €1.10 per 100g/4oz, Beer €3
🚌 46, 62, 64, 87, 116, 492 to Piazza Navona

EATING

LA CARAFFA
Map off 231 J7
Via Giovanni Villani 44, 00179
Tel 06 786513
This fish restaurant bordering the archaeological park of the Appian Way is one of Rome's best-kept secrets. People come to sample its simple, inexpensive but excellent fish dishes, served in two dining rooms and on a covered terrace. The huge seafood and vegetable buffet immediately catches the eye. The restaurant is best known for its *spaghetti alla scogliera*, a mountain of seafood on a bed of spaghetti, served on a silver platter— easily enough for two. Visa only accepted.
🕐 Daily 12.30–3, 7–11; closed 3 weeks in Aug
🍴 L €10, D €22, Wine €6
Ⓜ Furio Camillo
🚌 87, 628

CASETTA DE' TRASTEVERE
Map 229 D6
Piazza Dé Renzi 31a–32, 00153
Tel 06 580 0158
www.casettaditrastevere.com
Enter this ordinary-looking restaurant on a quiet little piazza, and inside is another piazza bright with red-and-white checked tablecloths and washing hanging from lines—a life-size re-creation of a Roman square. It's on two levels—you can sit in the house balconies and watch the piazza below. Unsurprising but remarkably inexpensive menu: *Rigatoni della casetta* is nicely al dente and incorporates porcini mushrooms, sausage and cheese. Vegetarian dishes are available. There are tables outside on the real piazza, too.
🕐 Daily 12–3, 7–12
🍴 L €12, D €25, Wine €6
🚌 H, 23, 280, 780 to Lungotevere Ponte Sisto; tram 8

CHARLY'S SAUCIÈRE
Map 230 H6
Via di San Giovanni in Laterano 270, 00184
Tel 06 7049 5666
This well-established restaurant specializes in French and Swiss cuisine, which is served by professional, attentive staff. As you might expect, French wine is prominent on the carefully selected wine list.

IL CONVIVIO
Map 229 D4
Vicolo dei Soldati 31, 00186
Tel 06 686 9432
www.ilconviviotroiani.com

The interior of this restaurant, down a narrow cobbled street behind Palazzo Altemps in the heart of Rome, is high-tech and gloriously spacious. Service is excellent. The *degustazione* (tasting) menu includes a bit of everything, while the creative regional menu changes frequently. If available, try the courgette (zucchini) flowers filled with porcini mushrooms and goat's cheese, or the rabbit stuffed with olives and sausage with a fennel sauce. Choice wine list—more than 2,000 different bottles.
🕐 Mon–Sat 8pm–10.30pm
🍴 D €70, Wine €24
🚌 46, 62, 64, 87, 116, 492 to Piazza Navona

🕐 Mon–Sat 12.45–2.15, 8–midnight; closed 2 weeks in Aug
🍴 L €14, D €30, Wine €12
Ⓜ Mazzini
🚌 85, 117, 850

CHECCHINO DAL 1887
Map off 229 E7
Via di Monte Testaccio 30, 00153
Tel 06 574 6318
www.checchino-dal-1887.com
Although it lies outside central Rome, the Checchino dal 1887 is well worth the trip. In the cool, vaulted restaurant you can sample traditional Roman cuisine, including *bue garofolato*, a rustic dish of beef, which is exclusive to this establishment. All this can be accompanied by a choice from Rome's best wine list. Reservations are essential.
🕐 Tue–Sat 12.30–3, 8–midnight; closed 1 week in Aug

🍴 L €20, D €35, Wine €14
Ⓜ Piramide
🚌 23, 75, 280, 716 to Piramide or Via Marmorata

CICCIA BOMBA
Map 229 D5
Via del Governo Vecchio 76, 00186
Tel 06 6880 2108
Just round the corner from Piazza Navona, this tiny, cosy place serves excellent pizzas and has its wood-burning oven in full view. Try some of the antipasti with grilled and marinaded vegetables, with some freshly baked focaccia with rosemary. Air conditioned in summer.
🕐 Thu–Tue 12.30–3, 7.30–midnight; no pizza Mon lunchtime
🍴 L/D €25, Wine €10
🚌 62, 64, 81, 571

UN COCHON DANS MON JARDIN
Map off 230 G2
Via G. Antonelli 30, 00197
Tel 06 807 3968
www.uncochon.it
The two floors of this restaurant in the Parioli district are decorated with frescoes of country life, but in spite of the name, no French cuisine is served. Starters are creative and delicious, such as fried artichokes with potatoes. Grilled Argentinian meat is the specialty. The pasta and rice are also very good, especially risotto with chicory and Barolo red wine. Excellent wine list but the house wines are good.
🕐 Daily 12.30–3, 7–midnight
🍴 L €8, D €25, Wine €10
🚌 56, 910 to Piazza Euclide

CORALLO
Map 229 D4
Via del Corallo 10, 00186
Tel 06 6830 7703
This restaurant/pizzeria is divided into different rooms, all with a maritime theme and a quiet atmosphere ideal for a calm meal. Very thin pizza baked in a wood oven is the house special, and the focaccia is very popular. The beef filet is also delicious and perfectly cooked, and there's fresh fish on Tuesday and Friday. Reservations advised. Tables outside in summer.
🕐 Daily 7.30pm–1am, Sat–Sun also 12–4pm
🍴 L €20, D €25, Wine €8
🚌 64, 87, 492 to Largo Argentina; tram 8

EATING

DA AGUSTO
Map 229 D6
Piazza de' Renzi 15, 00153
Tel 06 580 3798

This is what cheap and cheerful Roman dining is all about. Sit outside in summer at folding wooden tables with paper tablecloths, on which your bill will be scribbled at the end of the evening. Inside is rather cramped and a little chilly in winter. Spontaneous singing often breaks out and a carafe of the house wine aids appreciation. The *pasta e fagioli* (thick borlotti bean soup with pasta) and gnocchi are well worth crossing the Tiber for. Credit cards are not accepted.

🕐 Mon–Fri 12.30–3, 8–11, Sat 12.30–3; closed mid-Aug to mid-Sep
🍴 L €8, D €13, Wine €5
🚌 H, 23, 280, 780 to Lungotevere Ponte Sisto; tram 8

IL CORTILE
Map off 228 C7
Via Felice Cavallotti 46, 00152
Tel 06 580 3455
The antipasto buffet here is legendary: Plump button mushrooms, marinated bell peppers, grilled aubergines (eggplant), bean salad, caramelized onions and breaded courgette (zucchini) strips are just a few of the delights. The first and second courses don't compare, so load up on starters and skip to the desserts. The atmosphere is elegant yet congenial, especially at the candlelit outdoor tables of this Monteverde restaurant.

🕐 Tue–Sat 12–3, 8–11, Sun 12–3; closed Aug
🍴 L €18, D €35, Wine €8
🚌 44

CUL DE SAC
Map 229 D5
Piazza Pasquino 73, 00186
Tel 06 6880 1094
Very close to Piazza Navona, Cul de Sac was originally just a wine bar, but it's gradually built a reputation for food as well. It's well known for its pâtés—such as the sweet and sour wild boar pâté—served with

toasted bread (€8). The interior is reminiscent of a 1950s train, furnished in beautiful solid white wood. Thirty-five wines are available by the glass and over 1,400 are in stock.
🕐 Daily 12–4, 8–12.30
🍴 L €10, D €15, Wine €15
🚌 46, 62, 64, 87, 116, 492 to Piazza Navona

DA BAFFETTO
Map 229 D5
Via del Governo Vecchio 114, 00186
Tel 06 686 1617
Eat early, or if you come later be prepared to wait like a Roman, joining the exuberant mob outside one of Rome's

best pizzerias. Sixties radicals headed here; now the whole world vies for a seat. Don't miss the savoury *bruschetta al pomodoro* (toasted bread topped with tomato, basil and olive oil). Be prepared for more genial jostling at the outdoor tables, and long waits for the superb pizzas. No credit cards.
🕐 Daily 6.30pm–1am
🍴 D €10, Wine €10
🚌 46, 62, 64, 87, 116, 492 to Campo dei Fiori

DA BENITO
Map 229 E5
Via dei Falegnami 14, 00186
Tel 06 686 1508
Very friendly, family-run spot in a quiet, cobblestone side street near Largo Argentina. Serves hot and cold food

cafeteria style; just choose and point, then take it to your table. When you've finished, simply tell the cashier what you had. There are always a couple of fresh specials of the day, including home-made pasta. A plateful of assorted mixed vegetables with olive oil dribbled over, together with *polpette* (meatballs), makes a perfect quick lunch. Credit cards are not accepted.
🕐 Mon–Sat 7am–7.30pm
🍴 L €8, D €10, Wine €5
Ⓜ Cavour
🚌 64, 87, 492 to Largo Argentina; tram 8

DA FRANCESCO
Map 229 D4
Piazza del Fico 29, 00186
Tel 06 686 4009
Set on a jewel of a square just a few minutes from Piazza Navona, this trattoria is very popular with locals (expect to wait if you come after 8pm). With paper tablecloths and no frills, the best tables are outside. Try their fantastic focaccia with Parma ham, which is served alongside the vegetable and fish buffet. Shellfish pastas are good (Tuesday and Friday), as is the porcini mushroom pasta. Pizzas are available evenings only (from €5). Good draught beer and house wine. Credit cards are not accepted.
🕐 Wed–Mon 12–3, 7–1, Tue 7pm–1am
🍴 L €30, D €60, Wine €7
🚌 46, 62, 64, 87, 116, 492 to Piazza Navona

EATING

DA GIOVANNI
Map 228 C5
Via della Lungara 41a, 00165
Tel 06 686 1514

Artists' hang-out on the edge of Trastevere. Prices are unbelievably low and the cooking is good, plain Roman fare. It's tiny and you can't make reservations, so come as close to opening time as possible. The menu changes daily but *fettuccine al sugo* (pasta with tomato sauce) is always there. Try the pasta with chickpeas or borlotti beans if you can. House wine doesn't cost much more than bottled water.

⏰ Mon–Sat noon–3, 7–10; closed Aug
🍴 L €8, D €12, Wine €8
🚌 23, 280 to Ponte Mazzini

DA PARIS
Map 229 D6
Piazza San Callisto 7a, 00153
Tel 06 581 5378

This great restaurant serving Jewish food near Santa Maria in Trastevere is known for its fish and pasta, and particularly for the traditional Roman dish of *trippa alla romana* (tripe in the Roman style). All this is accompanied by an excellent wine list. There is a small terrace in front, where meals are served in warm weather. Reservations are essential.

⏰ Tue–Sat 1–3, 7.30–11, Sun 12–3
🍴 L €25, D €40, Wine €10
🚌 75; tram 8

DA SETTIMIO
Map 229 E4
Via delle Colonnelle 14, 00186
Tel 06 678 9651

Wrought-iron flourishes and sprawling piles of fruit greet you at this vivid gem of a restaurant by the Pantheon. Graffiti covers the walls, old beams and terracotta tiles. The fare is simple but spot on, including the best *penne all'arrabiata* (pasta with fiery chilli, tomato and garlic sauce)

DAI TRE AMICI
Map 229 E5
Via della Rotonda 8, 00186
Tel 06 687 5239

An unpretentious trattoria in a 16th-century building just behind the magnificent Pantheon that epitomizes the Roman spirit of dining—lots of noise and organized chaos. Waiters weave their way through the packed tables with dishes such as *farfalle alla calabrese* (pasta with garlic, butter and cheese) followed by wafer-thin beef with porcini mushrooms. Beamed ceilings, wicker chairs and simple wooden tables. The antipasto buffet is extensive and great for vegetarians. Fresh fish Tue and Fri. Best to make a reservation or go before 8pm.

⏰ Daily 12–3, 7–midnight
🍴 L €10, D €24, Wine €8
🚌 116, or any bus to Largo Argentina, such as 64, 87, 492

in town, and superb truffles and game dishes. Reserve a table for dinner, as both tiny rooms quickly overflow with cheerful customers.

⏰ Tue–Sat 12.30–3, 7.30–11.30; closed Aug
🍴 L €12, D €30, Wine €8
🚌 116, or any bus to Largo Argentina, such as 64, 87, 492

DA VITTORIO
Map 229 D6
Via di San Cosimato 14, 00153
Tel 06 580 0353

This pizzeria serves endearingly heart-shaped and incredibly tasty Neapolitan pizzas. Start with the mixed antipasti and oil-drenched crust called *pizza bianca*. Many dishes have this as a base, sprinkled only with mozzarella, but Vittorio will also indulge customers craving a sauce, as with the festive

---

bouquet of rocket (arugula) and cherry tomatoes on the pizza Margherita. Reservations are crucial, as the tiny, blue-lit nook fills quickly. Credit cards are not accepted.

⏰ Mon–Sat 7.30–midnight
🍴 D €14, Wine €4
🚌 H, 63, 75

DAL TOSCANO
Map 228 C3
Via Germanico 56, 00192
Tel 06 3972 5717
www.ristorantedaltoscano.it

This family-run restaurant serves Tuscan cuisine. It offers efficient service in a pleasant, vaulted room with traditional wooden furniture; and a shaded terrace in summer. The *pappardelle* pasta with wild boar sauce is a Tuscan treat, as are the huge chargrilled Fiorentina steaks or the thinly sliced beef cooked with wine and salad leaves. Accompany it all with a glass of superb Chianti.

⏰ Tue–Sun 12.30–3, 8–11; closed 2 weeks in Aug
🍴 L €20, D €35, Wine €13
🚇 Ottaviano

DAR POETA
Map 229 D6
Vicolo del Bologna 45, 00153
Tel 06 588 0516

Be sure to maintain your place in line at this casual pizzeria, undisputedly one of the city's best. It serves up traditional

toppings, as well as eccentric combinations such as apple and Grand Marnier. The chefs shun the typical Roman thin crust, preferring soft, dripping pizza on a slow-risen base. Dar Poeta skips the frills (no reservations, and the bill is scrawled on the tablecloth) and concentrates on a jovial atmosphere and great food.

⏰ Daily 7.30pm–midnight
🍴 D €10, Wine €8
🚌 H, 23, 280, 780 to Lungotevere Ponte Sisto; tram 8

DER PALLARO

Map 229 D5
Largo der Pallaro 15, 00186
Tel 06 6880 1488

Traditional Roman cooking in a timeless trattoria right behind Campo dei Fiori. No need to choose from a menu, as the waiter will bring you everything that's on that day, from starter to dessert, for the price of €20, including house wine. The cooking is simple but good, and the portions generous. Excellent choice for late dinners. In summer you can eat outside in the square. Credit cards are not accepted.

🕐 Tue–Sun 12–4, 7.30–1; closed 2 weeks in Aug
✋ L €20, D €20 (includes house wine)
🚌 64, 87, 492 to Largo Argentina; tram 8

DITIRAMBO

Map 229 D5
Piazza della Cancelleria 74, 00186
Tel 06 687 1626
www.ristoranteditirambo.it

Downtown trattoria (one block south of Corso Vittorio Emanuele) that far transcends the tourist menu, even

satisfying the difficult-to-please *bel mondo* of Rome. The kitchen uses organic ingredients, and produces home-made bread (often with olives or pumpkin seeds),

pasta (including its showcase dish with zucchini flowers) and desserts. Furnishings lean towards country chic. The wine list is legendary. Reservations are essential.

🕐 Tue–Sun 1–3, 7.30–11.30, Mon 8pm–11.30pm; closed Aug
✋ L €20, D €32, Wine €12
🚌 46, 62, 64, 87, 116, 492 to Campo dei Fiori

L'EAU VIVE

Map 229 E5
Via Monterone 85, 00186
Tel 06 6880 2101/06 6880 1095

Unusual restaurant run by an international sisterhood of nuns, in a Renaissance building with frescoed vaulted ceilings. Cuisine is international, mainly French, and includes soups, main courses and desserts. Classical music plays in the background. Excellent wine list. The restaurant helps the nuns raise funds for missions to developing countries. You can join the sisters for evening prayers at 10pm.

🕐 Mon–Sat 12.30–2.30, 7.30–11; closed Aug
✋ L €12, D €15, Wine €9
🚌 64, 87, 492 to Largo Argentina; tram 8

EDOARDO II

Map 229 E5
Vícolo Margana 14, 00187
Tel 06 6994 2419
www.edoardosecondo.it

Sophisticated gay restaurant very close to the Jewish quarter and Piazza Venezia. Candles and soft lighting complement pale stucco walls with modern paintings and photographs. It has been transformed from one of Rome's most popular gay bars into a comfortable place to dine as well. Mainly Mediterranean cuisine—meat and fish, plus delicious vegetable pies and a vast assortment of cakes and pastries. Good selection of more than 100 wines.

🕐 Wed–Mon 7.30pm–midnight; closed 1 week in Aug
✋ D €25, Wine €8
🚌 40, 64, 87, 628 to Piazza Venezia

EL TOULÀ

Map 229 E4
Via della Lupa 29b, 00186
Tel 06 687 3498
www.toula.it

Considered to be one of Rome's best restaurants, El Toulà is a great place to look

for the rich and famous. The service is exceptional, the Venetian and international cuisine divine and the wine list superb.

🕐 Tue–Fri 1–3, 8–11, Sat, Mon 8pm–11pm; closed Aug
✋ L €50, D €70, Wine €6
🚇 Spagna
🚌 81, 117, 119, 492 to Via del Corso or Largo Carlo Goldini

EST! EST! EST!

Map 230 G4
Via Genova 32, 00185
Tel 06 488 1107

At 100 years old, this is one of Rome's longest-established pizzerias. It stays with the tried and tested combination of excellent pizza and Italian wines, served in a simple room with wooden tables.

🕐 Tue–Sun 7pm–midnight
✋ Pizza €6, Wine €10
🚇 Repubblica
🚌 H, 64, 170

EVANGELISTA

Map 229 D6
Via delle Zoccolette 11a, 00186
Tel 06 687 5810

In this genteel restaurant near the Tiber, ideal for long, intimate meals, the stars of the rich menu are its artichoke dishes. Try them *alla giudia*

(Roman-Jewish style, fried whole in batter) or *al mattone* (crushed between two bricks, then baked). Also recommended is the pasta with aubergines (eggplant), almonds and ricotta. The interior design is elegant and the service gracious.

🕐 Mon–Sat 7.30pm–11.30pm; closed Aug
✋ D €50, Wine €15
🚌 H, 23, 280, 780 to Lungotevere Ponte Sisto; tram 8

FASSI–PALAZZO DEL FREDDO

Map 230 H5
Via Principe Eugenio 65, 00179
Tel 06 446 4740

One of the very best ice-cream shops in Rome. The location, close to the Basilica of Santa Maria Maggiore and Termini station, is not one of the most salubrious these days, but it's fine during the day, and the ice cream makes it all worthwhile. You can sit inside and be impressed by the incredibly high ceilings, or in a little internal garden. Credit cards are not accepted.

🕐 Tue–Sun 12–12
🍨 Ice creams from €1.30
Ⓜ Vittorio

FIASCHETTERIA BELTRAMME

Map 229 E3
Via della Croce 39, 00187

Known to locals as Cesaretto, and very easy to miss in the narrow Via della Croce, this traditional trattoria is wonderfully understated. Locals, artists and shop-keepers, together with a few visitors in the know, sit down to simple but well-prepared food, including pasta and salads. They do not accept bookings—there's no telephone, anyway—so arrive early for the chance of a shared table in this popular eatery. Credit cards are not accepted.

🕐 Mon–Sat 12–3, 7.30–10.30
🍽 L €16, D €25, Wine €8
Ⓜ Spagna
🚌 117, 119

F.I.S.H.

Map 230 F5
Via dei Serpenti 16, 00184
Tel 06 4782 4962
www.f-i-s-h.it

Australian-inspired sushi restaurant near the Colosseo that recalls the Sydney waterfront. After an *aperitivo* with oysters at the bar, head into the restaurant. The back

room has a view of the cooking area. Oak wood is alternated with glass and iron seats and tables. Select from three menus: Mediterranean, oriental and Antipodean. Finish with the crème brûlée with coconut and dates or a sashimi of exotic fruits.

🕐 Tue–Sun 1–3, 8–2; closed 2 weeks in Aug
🍽 L €20, D €32, Wine €4
Ⓜ Cavour or Colosseo
🚌 117

FRIENDS ART CAFÉ

Map 229 D6
Piazza Trilussa 34, 00154
Tel 06 581 6111

Excellent place near the Tiber for an *aperitivo*; great value. Snacks set out on the counter are included in the price of a drink. Behind the bar there's a dining area decorated with modern paintings that serves salads, vegetable pies and a small selection of pastas and meat dishes, plus desserts.

🕐 Mon–Sat 7am–2am, Sun 6pm–2am
🍽 L €15, cocktails €6
🚌 23; tram 8

GELATERIA DELLA PALMA

Map 229 E4
Via della Maddalena 20, 00186
Tel 06 6880 6752

Close to the Pantheon, this ice cream shop offers a huge

variety, including no less than 20 different kinds of chocolate, plus mousses and ice cream with meringues. For those who prefer the taste of fruit, the raspberry is simply unforgettable. There are two wooden benches inside, but the place gets extremely crowded. The best idea is to buy your ice cream, then stroll down to Piazza della Rotonda in front of the Pantheon. Credit cards are not accepted.

🕐 Daily 8am–1am
🍨 Ice creams from €1.80
🚌 64, 87, 492 to Largo Argentina; tram 8

IL GELATO DI SAN CRISPINO

Map 229 F4
Via della Panetteria 42, 00187
Tel 06 679 3924
www.ilgelatodisancrispino.com

This has to be the best ice cream shop in Rome—its attention to detail makes others pale in comparison.

The ice creams are rich, creamy and additive-free, and the signature *gelato di San Crispino* is made with wild Sardinian honey. It can be hard to find as it has a very discreet entrance without a real sign. Facing the Trevi Fountain, head right down Via Lavatore, then take the second left down Via Panetteria; San Crispino is halfway down on your right.

🕐 Mon, Wed–Thu, Sun 12pm–12.30am, Fri–Sat 12pm–1.30am
🍨 Ice cream €1.70–€6 per cup
🚌 61, 62, 116, 175, 492, 630

GIGGETTO AL PORTICO D'OTTAVIA

Map 229 E5
Via del Portico d'Ottavia 21a, 00186
Tel 06 686 1105
www.giggettoalportico.com

Family-run restaurant in the heart of the Ghetto. For more than 80 years, it has specialized in traditional Roman-Jewish cuisine. Original brick-vaulted ceilings and beams decorated with strings of garlic, chillies and laurel. Without a doubt the pièce de résistance is the *carciofi alla giudia* (Jewish artichoke), and you should try the unusual salad featuring wild chicory shoots with an anchovy dressing—all prepared to perfection. Wine cellar with over 500 labels, and exceptional desserts, too.

🕐 Tue–Sun 12.30–3, 7.30–11
🍽 L €14, D €50, Wine €12
🚌 62, 64, 87, 492, 628 to Largo Argentina

EATING

GIOLITTI

Map 229 E4
Via degli Uffici del Vicario 40, 00186
Tel 06 699 1243
www.giolitti.it
This family-run *gelateria* has been making delicious ice creams since 1900. Ever popular with Roman families, the Liberty-style (art nouveau) room, with olive-green ceilings and marble floors, is the perfect setting in which to linger over an ice cream (over 60 varieties), or a home-made pastry with a cup of tea. For pure indulgence, ask for *panna* (whipped cream) on top of your ice cream. There is also a takeaway counter.
🕐 Daily 7am–1am
🍦 Ice creams €4.80–€9 (to take away €1.80–3)
🚌 52, 53, 61, 71, 80, 85, 160, 850

IL GOCCETTO

Map 228 D5
Via dei Banchi Vecchi 14, 00186
Tel 06 686 4268
Wine bar in a medieval bishop's house between Corso Vittorio Emanuele and the Tiber. Frescoes on the walls, and bottles and glasses stored on the shelves and in open cupboards, create a relaxed atmosphere. Not only is there a vast wine list (800 different labels), but there's also an extensive cheese list and other regional delicacies, including various kinds of salami and ham.
🕐 Mon–Sat 11.30–2, 6.30–9
🍷 Selection of salami/cheese from €8, desserts from €5, Wine €3 (by the glass)
🚌 64, 87, 492 to Largo Argentina; tram 8

GOOD GOOD

Map off 231 J7
Via Latina 103, 00179
Tel 06 780 0855
Restaurant-pizzeria serving some of the best pizzas in town. Experience the hustle and bustle of Roman family life, especially on Sundays, traditionally pizza night. Make a reservation or you could be in for a long wait. Good antipasto table and 40 varieties of pizza. For the finishing touch, accompany your meal with excellent draught beer or a carafe of the sparkling house wine.
🕐 Tue–Sun 7–midnight; closed 2nd half of Aug
🍕 Pizza €14, Wine €6
🚇 Furio Camillo
🚌 87, 628

GRAN CAFFÈ MARTINI E ROSSI

Map 230 G6
Piazza del Colosseo 3a, 00184
Tel 06 700 4431

Bar/restaurant/pizzeria popular with locals, and what better location could it have than looking across to the Palatine Hill, with the Colosseo just across the road? Friendly staff and an early 1900s feel to the interior. Food is served all day and there's an extensive wine cellar. There are good-value all-inclusive menus, plus vegetarian dishes and pizzas, or if a snack is all you want, try one of the *panini* (hot or cold filled rolls) on offer. Pizzas from €7.
🕐 Daily 8am–1am
🍷 L €10, D €25, Wine €20
🚇 Colosseo
🚌 85, 87, 117; tram 3

GRAPPOLO D'ORO/ ZAMPANÒ

Map 229 D5
Piazza della Cancelleria 80, 00186
Tel 06 689 7080
One of the best-priced places near Campo dei Fiori, this unspoiled trattoria has remained unchanged for years. Traditional Italian dishes are always good here, and the *ravioli alla Gorgonzola* is divine. This place is popular with locals, so arrive early to be sure of a table.
🕐 Daily 12.30–2.30, 7.30–11; closed Tue lunch
🍷 L €12, D €25, Wine €12
🚌 46, 62, 64 to Corso Vittorio Emanuele II

GROTTE DEL TEATRO DI POMPEO

Map 229 D5
Via del Biscione 73, 00186
Tel 06 6880 3606
www.ristorantidiroma.com/grotteteatropompeo.it
The back rooms of this restaurant, which is just behind the spot where Julius Caesar was assassinated, are carved out of the first stone theatre in Roman history. Some of the best fish dishes around are served here: Spaghetti with seafood, oven-baked turbot with potatoes, or grilled scampi are all excellent. Good wine list. In summer, sit outside and try the Prosecco Mionetto (€14), a sparkling wine perfect with fish.
🕐 Tue–Sun 12–3, 7–11; closed Aug
🍷 L €12, D €22, Wine €6
🚌 64, 87, 492 to Largo Argentina; tram 8

IL GURU

Map 230 F5
Via Cimarra 456, 00184
Tel 06 474 4110
Excellent Indian food in the heart of Rione Monti, near the Colosseo. Every detail of

the ethnic interior is designed to re-create a little corner of India in Rome. House specials are tandooris and curries of varying strengths. You can choose one of three fixed menus—vegetarian, meat or fish—or order à la carte. Traditional desserts and Indian beer. Welcoming staff.
🕐 Daily 8pm–1am
🍷 D €25, Wine €6
🚇 Cavour
🚌 68

EATING

GUSTO

Map 229 E3

Piazza Augusto Imperatore 9, 00186

Tel 06 322 6273

www.gusto.it

Very trendy, state-of-the-art restaurant, pizzeria and wine bar behind the Mausoleum of Augustus. Exposed brickwork, industrial lighting and

somewhat inflated prices, so you won't find many locals here. Pizzas (from €6) and salads are decent. A slight twist is given to some traditional recipes. However, this place is about ambience and there's plenty of that. Live jazz on Tue and Thu at 11pm. There's also a kitchen shop.

🕐 Daily 12.45–3, 7.30–12

🍽 L €8 (buffet), D €14, Wine €18

🚇 Spagna

🚌 81, 116, 117, 628, 913

HARD ROCK CAFÉ

Map 229 F3

Via Vittorio Veneto 62a, 00187

Tel 06 420 3051

www.hardrock.com

Yes, there's one in Rome, and on the exclusive Via Veneto. The interior is standard Hard Rock: wooden floors and a litter of 1950s paraphernalia, the only

exception being the frescoed angels on the ceiling. It seats over 260, with lots of nooks and crannies to hide in. The menu is the same as always, with burgers and chips. And there's a shop where you can add another Hard Rock t-shirt to your collection.

🕐 Daily 12pm–2am

🍽 L €28, D €48, Wine €9

🚇 Barberini

🚌 52, 53, 56, 58b, 95, 116

INSALATA RICCA

Map 229 D5

Largo de' Chiavari 85, 00186

Tel 06 6880 3656

This Italian chain concentrates on salads and *bruschette* (toasted bread with toppings) to marvellous effect. Start with artichoke pâté or sesame goat's cheese on seared bread. Then tuck into a massive salad, ranging from mozzarella and tomato to greens drizzled in honey, and topped with walnuts and slivers of Parmesan. The interior incorporates exposed brick and sponge-painted walls, but most prefer the crowded outdoor tables. Its bilingual staff are famous for making visitors welcome.

🕐 Daily 12.30–3.30, 7–12

🍽 L €8, D €12, Wine €4

🚌 46, 62, 64, 87, 116, 492 to Campo dei Fiori

IVO A TRASTEVERE

Map 229 D6

Via di San Francesco a Ripa 158

Tel 06 581 7082

A Roman institution. The classic pizza is always good, but the owners also come up with interesting and unusual

toppings. It's busy and bustling, so arrive early or be prepared to wait for a table. However, the turnover is quick and the service efficient.

🕐 Wed–Mon 6pm–2am

🍽 Pizza €6, Wine €5.78

🚌 8, 44, 75, 780 to Viale Trastevere

KETUMBAR

Map off 229 E7

Via Galvani 24, 00154

Tel 06 5730 5338

Ethnic food is very belatedly beginning to make its mark in Rome. The name of this very stylish Asian restaurant/bar, with sleek Indonesian furnishings and vaulted ceilings, means coriander (cilantro) in Malay. There's a fusion of Asian influences in the kitchen. Sushi is their special—and it's very good. So, too, is the *nasi goreng* (Indonesian fried rice). Try the triple chocolate dessert to finish. All a bit pricey, but worth it.

🕐 Daily 8pm–3am

🍽 D €50, Wine €20

🚇 Piramide

LOWENHAUS

Map 229 E3

Via della Fontanella 168, 00186

Tel 06 323 0410

Why eat Bavarian food in Rome? For the answer, try Lowenhaus' superb *stinco di maiale al forno* (roast pork shin with roast potatoes and cabbage). Also a great place if you have a taste for good German beer; the list is endless and includes some very idiosyncratic ones. Also serves cakes such as strudel and *Sachertorte* (chocolate cake). The restaurant is divided into several rooms, and there are tables outside in summer.

🕐 Daily 11am–2am

🍽 L €10, D €25, Wine €10

🚇 Flaminio

🚌 116, 117

LUMIÈRE DI SICILIA

Map 228 C7

Via Fratelli Bonnet 41, 00152

Tel 06 581 3287

Popular local restaurant serving up the best Sicilian cuisine north of Palermo. Start with the mixed antipasti

or *caponata*, an aromatic mélange of aubergine (eggplant), bell pepper, basil and pine nuts. First courses include mouth-watering pistachio pesto, ravioli crammed with orange and ricotta, and squid-ink risotto. The staff are courteous, humorous and warm, even if your children get underfoot. Worth straying off the beaten track for (it's out towards Villa Doria Pamphilj).

🕐 Tue–Sun 8pm–11pm, Fri–Sun also 1pm–3pm
🍴 D €40, Wine €11
🚌 44

MACCHERONI
Map 229 E4
Piazza delle Coppelle 44, 00186
Tel 06 6830 7895
This is a funky place, which is popular more for its lively atmosphere and young staff than its food. The pasta dishes are very good, but the rest is average.

🕐 Daily 1–3, 7.30–12
🍴 €10, Wine €7
🚌 23, 30, 75, 280, 716 or any bus to Via Marmorata; tram 3

IL MARGUTTA
Map 229 E3
Via Margutta 118, 00187
Tel 06 3265 0577
www.ilmargutta.it
The only real vegetarian restaurant in the city is in this famous artists' street from the film *Roman Holiday*. Large, futuristic space with traditional touches, with art exhibited on the walls. There is a buffet at lunchtime,

but it is more intimate in the evening. Over 40 vegetarian dishes (mostly organic) available. There are 120 wines on offer, some organic, all at reasonable prices. Very good dessert wine list, too.

🕐 Daily 12.30–3.30, 7.30–11; closed 2 weeks in Aug
🍴 L €18, D €35, Wine €15
🚇 Flaminio or Spagna
🚌 116, 117

MYOSOTIS
Map 229 E4
Vicolo della Vaccarella 3–5, 00186
Tel 06 686 5554
www.myosotis.it
Despite being so near to the Pantheon, lively Myosotis is great value for money. The chef uses only the freshest ingredients to make sure that everything on the menu is of the highest standard. The fresh pasta dishes are particularly good; try the carbonara or seafood sauces.

🕐 Mon–Sat 12.30–3, 7.30–11.30; closed Aug and first week in Jan
🍴 L €18, D €40, Wine €7
🚇 Spagna
🚌 30, 40, 64, 70

NAVONA NOTTE
Map 229 D5
Via del Teatro Pace 44, 00186
Tel 06 686 9278
This pizzeria/restaurant near Piazza Navona is one of the few in the *centro storico* that offers a tourist menu. For €5, you can have mussels with

focaccia, followed by either spaghetti, such as *spaghetti alla amatriciana,* or a pizza and a glass of wine. The typical Roman thin-crust pizzas are made in a wood-burning oven. Good honest fare and simple style. Get a seat outside if you can, and enjoy the buzz and bustle in the heart of Rome.

🕐 Wed–Mon 5.30–12; closed Jan
🍴 D €12, Wine €5
🚌 62, 64, 87, 116, 492

NERONE
Map 230 G6
Via delle Terme di Tito 96, 00184
Tel 06 481 7952
This small, friendly trattoria, close to the Colosseo, is famous for its Abruzzese cooking—the antipasti buffet is particularly good. In warm weather there are tables

outside, opposite the Colle Oppio.

🕐 Mon–Sat 12–3, 7–11; closed Aug
🍴 L €15, D €30, Wine €8
🚌 30b, 75, 85, 87, 117, 175, 196 to Piazza del Colosseo
🚇 Colosseo

NON SOLO BEVI
Map 229 E4
Piazza di Pietra 64, 00186
www.nonsolobevi.it
The name means 'not just drinks', which is true enough as this trendy cafeteria serves a vast assortment of salads. The Brunello di Montalcino salad (named after the fine red wine from Tuscany) heaps on rocket (arugula), cherry tomatoes, Gorgonzola, Brie and *stracchino* (soft) cheese, Indian corn, olives, courgettes (zucchini) and mozzarella. Have a seat outside or try the vaulted cellar. Great location just a few steps from the Temple of Hadrian.

🕐 Apr–end Nov daily 7.30am–1am; Dec–end Mar 7am–9pm
🍴 Salads €9, Wine €20, Beer €5.30
🚇 Spagna
🚌 116

OBIKA
Map 229 E4
Piazza di Firenze, Angolo Via dei Prefetti 00186
Tel 06 683 2630
Traditional ingredients contrast with the cool, minimalist décor in this bustling wine bar. The young staff care passionately

about sourcing the best suppliers to create intensively flavoured dishes. Their specialty is *mozzarella di buffalo* (so fresh the milk runs out) served in a variety of ways, as well as organic salads and pasta. Get there early to get a table outside in the little square.

🕐 Daily 10am–12am
🍴 L €15, D €30, Wine €8
🚌 116

OPEN MUSIC CAFÉ
Map off 230 H7
Piazza Galeria 14, 00179
Tel 06 7049 2512

Very popular 24-hour café, but with limited indoor seating. Rock and pop music is bearably loud in the evening, but outside seating is also available. The interior design is sleek—stainless steel, glass and mirrored walls, mosaic floors, TV monitors and a wavy bar. Most evenings, at about 7pm, they dish out free snacks, such as prawns, salmon and olives, and even pizza and pasta. Credit cards are not accepted.

🕐 Daily 24 hours
🍴 L €50, Wine €20
🚌 360 to Termini station

OSAKA
Map 230 H6
Viale Carlo Felice 29–31, 00185
Tel 06 700 1821

Japanese restaurant in front of the basilica of San Giovanni in Laterano. Lovely interior in black and dark red, with low tatami-covered tables furnishing half the room. The freshly prepared sushi is very good, but if you don't know what to choose, try one of their very reasonably priced fixed menus, either the snake bento (€15) or the sashimi bento (€13). Included in both menus are soup, rice, sushi and fruit. Individual sushi from €1.75.

🕐 Tue–Sun 1–3, 7–midnight; Mon 7–midnight
🍴 L €15, D €25, Wine €8.50
🚇 San Giovanni
🚌 87, 117, 218

OSTERIA "AR GALLETTO"
Map 229 D5
Vicolo del Gallo 1, Piazza Farnese 102, 00186
Tel 06 686 1714

This family-run trattoria, with tables spilling outside into the corner of Piazza Farnese, has one of the most soothing views in Rome. It offers a fine array of largely vegetarian antipasti, excellent home-made ravioli and pasta, grilled lamb or beef, and classic *dolci*. It gets very busy, and is not a place to come if you are in a hurry.

🕐 Mon–Sat 12.30–3, 7.30–11
🍴 L €25, D €40, Wine €12
🚌 117

OSTERIA DEL CAMPIDOGLIO
Map 229 E6
Via dei Fienili 56, 00186
Tel 06 678 0250

This small trattoria tucked between the Palatine and Capitoline hills, just a few minutes' walk from the Foro Romano, has tables outside in the summer overlooking the baroque façade of Santa Maria della Consolazione. It offers Roman and Tuscan cuisine, with a range of fish and meat dishes, home-made *dolci* and good house wine.

🕐 Mon–Sat 11.30–3.30, 7.30–11.30
🍴 L €25, D €35, Wine €6
🚌 81, 85, 170, 628 (bus stop on Via Petroselli)

OSTERIA DELL'ANIMA
Map 229 D4
Via Santa Maria dell'Anima 8, 00186
Tel 06 686 4661

Refined restaurant behind Piazza Navona, with a refreshingly different look (seascape frescoes in pastel

tones). With seasonal menus, the young chef invests a great deal of thought in the cuisine and its presentation. Prices are surprisingly reasonable. Try the ravioli filled with scampi and artichokes in a tomato and cream sauce, or thinly sliced beef alternated with *caciotta* (ewe's milk) cheese, tomatoes from Pachinio

and salad leaves. All the bread is home-baked. Over 150 wines, many from Tuscany.

🕐 Daily 10am–2am
🍴 L €12, D €25, Wine €13
🚌 40, 62, 64, or any other bus to Piazza Navona or Corso Vittorio Emanuele II

OTELLO ALLA CONCORDIA
Map 229 E3
Via della Croce 81, 00187
Tel 06 679 1178

Take refuge from the shopping madness of Via del Corso in this magnificent 18th-century courtyard, laden with plants, fruit, amphorae, hanging vines and an ancient bath fountain. Family-run for over 50 years, the restaurant serves typically Roman fare. The antipasto of meats and salamis is a nice varied selection to start with, and the baked aubergine (eggplant) *parmigiana* is divine. Try a local Castelli Romani (Frascati) wine with your meal.

🕐 Mon–Sat 12.30–3, 7.30–11; closed 3 weeks in Jan
🍴 L €11, D €23, Wine €16
🚇 Spagna
🚌 116, 117, 492

OUZERIE
Map 229 E6
Via dei Salumi 2, 00153
Tel 06 581 6378
www.clubgrecia.bbk.org

This restaurant/club in Trastevere is practically the only place in Rome where you can find Greek food and be spontaneously entertained. Authentic taverna setting with fishing nets and bouzoukis, serving taramasalata, calamari,

Greek salads, prawns baked with feta cheese and tomato, delicious kebabs, baklava, and yogurts with a variety of

toppings. Live entertainment Friday and Saturday (reservations essential at weekends). Nominal membership (€1.50) payable on your first visit. Credit cards are not accepted.

🕐 Mon–Sat 8.30pm–2am; closed 2 weeks in Aug
🍴 D €18, Wine €10
🚌 H to Viale Trastevere or Piazza Mastai; tram 3, 8

LE PAIN QUOTIDIEN
Map 229 E4
Via Tomacelli 24–25, 00186
Tel 06 6880 7727
Rustic wooden tables and contemporary paintings on the ochre-coloured walls make a pleasing setting for a light lunch or coffee break, with a selection of salads, sandwiches and cakes. Sit round a large table, either inside or on the roof terrace. Brunch Saturday and Sunday.

🕐 Mon–Sat 9am–midnight, Sun 9am–11pm
🍴 L €18
Ⓜ Spagna
🚌 95, 117, 119

PANATTONI (I MARMI)
Map 229 D6
Viale Trastevere 53–59, 00153
Tel 06 580 0919
Huge marble-slab tables earn this classic Trastevere pizzeria two nicknames: *I Marmi* (The Marbles) and the less appetizing *l'Obitorio*

(The Morgue). Somehow the grim association doesn't succeed in scaring off customers. Vast pizzas and chilled Peroni beer are de rigueur. Stark and cranky, but endearing. Credit cards are not accepted.

🕐 Thu–Tue 6.30pm–2.30am; closed 2 weeks in Aug
🍴 D €12, Wine €11.50
🚌 H, 63, 75

PANE VINO E SAN DANIELE
Map 229 E5
Piazza Mattei 16, 00186
Tel 06 687 7147
In one of the most charming little piazzas in Rome, this homely wine bar serves wine by the glass—including good full-bodied reds from the Fantinel vineyards—and dishes from Friuli. It offers generous platters of prosciutto, salami and cheese, and a selection of salads and soups; try the polenta with

mushrooms, or wild boar followed by a slice of home-made ricotta cake or fruit salad.

🕐 Mon–Sat 11am–2pm
🍴 L/D €20, Wine €15
🚌 60, 64, 70, 170, 571 (Largo Argentina)

PASQUALINO AL COLOSSEO
Map 230 G6
Via SS. Quattro 66, 00184
Tel 06 700 4576
In view of the Colosseo, on a quiet side street, is this trattoria with dining on two levels. Downstairs is wonderfully 1960s, with mock-wood lino walls and huge rotating fans, while the upper level is more classic in style. The cuisine is essentially Mediterranean (fresh fish daily) with a touch of Sicilian. Pasta with mushrooms, peas and sausage, and *carpaccio* (thinly sliced raw, dressed fish) of sea bass and tuna are both exceptional. Swordfish steak with capers and olives is nicely original and the tiramisu is first class.

🕐 Tue–Sun 12–3, 7–11
🍴 L €18, D €40, Wine €8
Ⓜ Colosseo
🚌 85, 87, 117; tram 3

PERILLI A TESTACCIO
Map off 229 F7
Via Marmorata 39, 00153
Tel 06 574 2415
This classic Roman trattoria in Testaccio between the Piramide and the Tiber is always busy with regulars enjoying large portions of robust pasta, roast lamb, ox tail, *carciofi* or *puntarelle* with anchovy dressing, followed by bowls of *fragoline* (wild strawberries). The service is efficient and the atmosphere informal and lively.

🕐 Thu–Tue 1–3, 8–11; closed Aug
🍴 L €25, D €45, Wine €10
Ⓜ Piramide
🚌 60, 75, 95; tram 3

IL PICCOLO
Map 229 D5
Via del Governo Vecchio 74, 00186
Tel 06 6880 1746
A lovely wine bar near the beginning of Via del Governo Vecchio where bottles of wine are stored up to the ceiling. A few tables outside,

plus just a couple inside that add to the intimate atmosphere. The ample wine list includes white *fragolino* (a sweet wine with strawberry aroma) and blackberry and raspberry sangria. There's a selection of different cheeses and meats: Try the *bresaola*— dried fillet of beef—or delicious sun-dried tomatoes from Calabria. Credit cards are not accepted.

🕐 Daily 12pm–2am
🍴 L €14 (selection of salami/cheeses from €7), Wine €3 (by the glass)
🚌 87, 492 to Largo Argentina; tram 8

PIERLUIGI

Map 229 D5
Piazza dei Ricci 144, 00186
Tel 06 686 1302
www.pierluigi.it

Fish restaurant par excellence, and reasonably priced considering its setting and quality. It's on a gem of a piazza, with plenty of tables outside. Inside, cool terracotta floors, brick arches and chunky medieval beams are beautifully spotlit. Scampi risotto is a good choice, as is the *carpaccio* (thinly sliced raw, dressed fish) of tuna or swordfish. Fresh fish of the day is displayed in a glass cabinet. Ask to see the wine cellar. Good service.

🕐 Tue–Sun 12.30–3, 7.30–midnight
🍴 L €22, D €30, Wine €14
🚌 46, 62, 64, 87, 116, 492 to Campo dei Fiori

PIZZA CIRO

Map 229 E4
Via della Mercede 43–45, 00186
Tel 06 678 6015
Pizzeria behind Piazza San Silvestro and not too far from

Piazza Navona. The checked tablecloths may be a little banal, but the patio at the back is just perfect on a warm summer night. Serves Neapolitan-style pizzas (large and thick), but you can also ask for a thinner Roman one. The starters are exceptional, especially the *antipasto*

PIZZERIA LA MONTECARLO

Map 229 D5
Vicolo Savelli 11A–12–13, 00186
Tel 06 686 1877

Typical Roman pizzeria in a medieval quarter near Piazza Navona, with simple, unfussy food and service. Arrive before 8.30pm. The walls are totally covered with photographs of more or less famous diners. Thirty different types of pizza are baked in wood ovens. The house special is the *pizza montecarlo*: tomato, mozzarella, mushrooms, artichokes, sausage, eggs, peppers, onion and olives. One pizza is made with seasonal vegetables. Credit cards are not accepted.

🕐 Tue–Sat 12–3, 6.30–1; closed 2 weeks in Aug
🍴 Pizza €6, L €6, D €18, Wine €11
🚌 40, 62, 64, or any other bus to Piazza Navona or Corso Vittorrio Emanuele II

---

sfizioso of typical Neapolitan fried savouries. *Pizza bufalina doc,* with buffalo mozzarella, is the most popular.

🕐 Daily 10am–2.30am
🍴 Pizza €7.50, L €11, D €20, Wine €14
🚌 117, 119, 175, 492, or any bus to Piazza San Silvestro

PIZZA FORUM

Map 230 G6
Via di San Giovanni in Laterano 34–38, 00184
Tel 06 700 2515
www.pizzaforum.it
Large pizzeria behind the Colosseo. An entrance hall with Roman cobblestones brings you alongside the pizza ovens and invites you to enter the spacious dining room, which is furnished with stained glass. Possibly the best pizzeria in Rome

---

PIZZERIA POPI POPI

Map 229 D6
Via delle Fratte di Trastevere 45, 00153
Tel 06 589 5167

On one of the little alleys that join Viale Trastevere to the basilica of Santa Maria in Trastevere, Popi Popi is excellent for both its pizzas and its prices. Very popular with young Romans, especially in summer, when you can sit outside and enjoy Trastevere's bustle. There's a selection of traditional dishes in addition to pizzas.

🕐 Fri–Wed 7pm–1am
🍴 Pizza €5.40, D €15, Wine €5
🚌 H, 23, 44, 56, 75, 280 to Viale Trastevere; tram 8

---

serving proper Neapolitan pizza (thicker than Roman pizza). Choice of over

35 pizzas and excellent salads. Service is neat and friendly. Pizzas from €5.

🕐 Daily 12–3, 7.30–midnight
🍴 L €8, D €12, Wine €9
🚇 Colosseo
🚌 85, 87, 117; tram 3

PIZZARÈ

Map 230 G3
Via Lucullo 22, 00199
Tel 06 4201 3075
In a 1920s-style building surrounded by palm trees, just a short walk from Via Veneto, this is probably the most popular pizzeria in the heart of Rome. Real Neapolitan pizza with buffalo mozzarella, bought fresh daily. Try *ripieno fritto*, a folded and fried pizza with a tomato, mozzarella, ham and ricotta filling, or *pizza re*, with tomato sauce, fresh Sicilian cherry tomatoes and buffalo mozzarella. Also home-made traditional Neapolitan cakes, including

---

the famous *pastiera* (filled with ricotta, egg yolks and candied peel). Reservations are essential.

🕐 Daily 12.30–3.30, 7.30–1am
🖐 L €7.50, D €12, Wine €6; special lunch meals for €7.50
🚇 Barberini

IL POMODORINO

Map 230 F3
Via Campania 45, 00187
Tel 06 4201 1356

Pizzeria/*ristorante* with the best value available in the extortionately priced Via Veneto. Indoor and outdoor seating for up to 400 people. Inside is Neapolitan terracotta with a white, beamed ceiling, pastel walls and red-and-white table linen. Huge central buffet, packed with vegetables. Pizza chefs work on one side

of the room, and the 13 other chefs in the open kitchen. A superb dish is the veal *millefoglie*, a mountain of thinly sliced meat layered with crisply fried artichokes.

🕐 Daily 12.30–3, 7.30–midnight, Sat 7.30–midnight
🖐 Pizza €7, L €8, D €20, Wine €10
🚇 Veneto
🚌 52, 53, 56, 58, 58b, 95, 116

LA PROPOSTA

Map 231 J7
Via Terni 13, 00182
Tel 06 701 5615

A 10-minute walk from the basilica of San Giovanni in Laterano. Low-ceilinged vaulted room, painted in shades of ochre and white, with waist-high partitions separating the tables. Chef's recommendations are faultless, such as *fettuccine alla carlofortina* (pasta in a red pesto sauce), or stuffed rabbit with a blueberry sauce. The wine recommendations are excellent, too, with the vast majority under €25.

Such harmonious suggestions are difficult to refuse.

🕐 Mon–Sat 7.30pm–midnight; closed Aug
🖐 D €25, Wine €10
🚇 Re di Roma
🚌 16, 85, 87, 117; tram 3, 19

QUINZI E GABRIELI

Map 229 E4
Via delle Coppelle 5, 00186
Tel 06 687 9389

Well-established, if pricey, fish restaurant in a splendid 15th-century palazzo not far

from Piazza Navona. Three wonderfully camp dining rooms with murals of exotic beaches, stone columns and a wooden canopy (a cross between *South Pacific* and *Carousel*) created by a filmset designer. Service is efficient, with Italian flair. A house special is the raw fish platter, with bass, crayfish, tuna and squid. Try the spaghetti with lobster, which is the best in Rome and well worth splurging on.

🕐 Mon–Sat 7.30pm–11.30pm
🖐 D €100, Wine €25
🚌 116, 492

RENATO E LUISA

Map 229 E5
Via dei Barbieri 25, 00186
Tel 06 686 9660

Tiny restaurant (only 10–15 tables) behind Largo di Torre Argentina. Traditional Roman cuisine with a touch of creativity. Starters include mozzarella cheese with pesto

or truffles, grilled or au gratin vegetables and focaccia (pizza crust with olive oil). Among the pastas, the special is fettuccine with cherry tomatoes and ricotta cheese. Good house wine.

🕐 Tue–Sun 8.30pm–midnight
🖐 D €30, Wine €7
🚌 64, 492 to Largo Argentina; tram 8

RISTORANTE CONSOLINI

Map 229 E7
Via Marmorata 28, 00153
Tel 06 5730 0148

This place is located at the foot of the Aventine hill over ancient Roman warehouses near the Tiber, with an elegant spacious terrace on two levels, which makes an ideal setting. The spread of antipasti is delightful, and the menu has delicate risotto and fish dishes as well as traditional Roman fare.

🕐 Tue–Sun 12.30–3, 7.30–11
🖐 L €35, D €50, Wine €9
🚌 44, 75, 95; tram 3

RISTORANTE GIOVANNI

Map 229 F3
Via Marche 64, 00187
Tel 06 482 1834

Family-run restaurant close to Via Veneto. The dining room has terracotta floor tiles, beams, pristine white walls and traditional wooden chairs. Home-made gnocchi with pheasant sauce is a satisfying, if heavy, starter.

The *osso buco* (veal stew in tomato sauce) with rice is a house recommendation, as is the fresh squid cooked on an open fire. The wine cellar contains 175 labels to choose from; the house wine is a crisp white Verdicchio from the Marche region.

🕐 Sun–Thu 12.30–3, 7.30–11, Fri 12.30pm–3pm; closed Aug
🖐 L €15, D €35, Wine €12
🚇 Veneto
🚌 52, 53, 56, 58, 58b, 95, 116

RISTORANTE IL MATRICIANO
Map 228 C3
Via dei Gracchi 55, 00192
Tel 06 321 2327
The family-run Il Matriciano has a devoted following and is not far from St. Peter's. The food is good, uncomplicated country fare. Try the classic *bucatini matriciana*, richly flavoured with bacon, tomatoes and basil, or opt for the creamy ricotta ravioli or vegetable soup, or the *abbacchio* (suckling lamb) *al forno*, offering you a chance to sample Roman cooking in all its rustic simplicity. In the summer there are tables under a shady canopy outside.

🕐 Thu–Tue 12.30–3, 8–11.30; closed Aug
🖐 L €25, D €40, Wine €9
🚇 Ottaviano
🚌 81

RISTORANTE NUOVA STELLA
Map 230 G4
Via Manin 54, 00184
Tel 06 487 5390
www.nuovastella.it
This is an unpretentious spot between Termini and Santa Maria Maggiore. The two large dining areas have white linen tablecloths and an eye-catching buffet; fresh fish is

available Tuesday and Friday. Specials include spaghetti with prawn, courgettes (zucchini) and tomato sauce, fettuccine with hare, and the classic

saltimbocca romana (veal with ham, cooked in white wine and butter), served with delicious rosemary roast potatoes. In warmer weather the tables spill out onto the pavement.

🕐 Mon–Sat 12–3, 6.30–11
🖐 L €15, D €20, Wine €10
🚇 Termini
🚌 40, 64

RISTORANTE-PIZZERIA PIACERE MOLISE
Map 228 B3
Via Candia 60, 00195
Tel 06 3974 3553
Fresh flowers, damask linen and pale walls create an

intimate setting in this elegant family-run restaurant, in a shopping street just minutes away from the Musei Vaticani. Pasta with aubergines (eggplant), tomatoes and olives, and roast lamb cutlets with rosemary potatoes are dishes to savour. There's a good selection of fresh fish and decent house wine. A bottle of Banfi-Brunello di Montalcino is cheaper to buy here than in the shops.

🕐 Daily 12–3, 7–midnight
🖐 L €12, D €25, Wine €10
🚇 Cipro Musei Vaticani
🚌 23, 70, 99, 492

ROMOLO 'NEL GIARDINO DI RAFFAELLO E DELLA FORNARINA'
Map 228 D5
Via di Porta Settimiana 8, 00153
Tel 06 581 8284
Next to the ancient gateway of Settimiano, this is where Raphael's lover, 'La Fornarina', once lived, and where the popular poet Trilussa used to wine and dine. Divided into four rustic dining rooms, it has wonderful oak-beamed ceilings, stone floors and an original fireplace. However, the garden is the place to be. For starters, try the fried

ROOF GARDEN 'LES ETOILES'
Map 228 C4
Via dei Bastioni 1, 00193
Tel 06 687 3233
www.atlantehotels.com

For unparalleled views of St. Peter's, and food to match, this roof-terrace restaurant is a must if you can afford it—the dining room is one level down. It offers high-backed upholstered dining chairs, candlelit tables and views of St. Peter's illuminated beyond. Sumptuous Mediterranean cuisine includes a raw tuna and tomato pasta, and château filet with foie gras and sliced truffle. Imaginative wine list that includes one of Umbria's best-kept secrets—the Sagrantino di Montefalco red.

🕐 Daily 12.30–2.30, 7.30–10.30
🖐 L €40, D €85, Wine €15
🚇 Ottaviano
🚌 70, 492

mozzarella rolled with Parma ham and a hint of anchovy. As a main course, how about chicken breast with mozzarella and Parma ham, artichoke and a creamy tomato sauce?

🕐 Tue–Sun 12.30–3, 7–11; closed Aug
🖐 L €20, D €35, Wine €10
🚌 23 to Ponte Sisto or Viale di Trastevere; tram 8

EATING

LA ROSETTA

Map 229 E4

Via della Rosetta 8–9

Tel 06 686 1002/06 6830 8841

www.larosetta.com

Wonderful fish and seafood, brought in daily from Sicily, form the basis of La Rosetta's menu. Cooked in the simplest ways to enhance its quality, it is best accompanied by a Sicilian white wine. The restaurant is always popular, so reservations are essential.

🕐 Mon–Sat 1–3, 8–11.30; closed 3 weeks in Aug

🍴 L €50, D €135, Wine €35

🚌 119 to Piazza della Rotonda, or 70, 81, 87, 90 to Corso del Rinascimento

SAN CLEMENTE

Map 230 G6

Via di San Giovanni in Laterano 124, 00184

Tel 06 7045 0944

www.sanclemente.it

This bar/pizzeria/pub is a great place to refuel between the Colosseo and the basilica of San Giovanni in Laterano. It has three vaulted rooms and

a terrace, 15 different beers and decent, inexpensive food. The tourist menu, available for lunch and dinner, consists of cannelloni followed by roast chicken and potatoes, with wine or beer, plus coffee, and all for €11.90—with a free lithograph of the Colosseo thrown in.

🕐 Daily 7am–1am

🍴 L €10, D €15, Wine €8

🚇 Colosseo or San Giovanni

🚌 85, 87, 117; tram 3

SAN MARINO

Map off 231 K2

Via San Marino 52, 00198

Tel 06 855 8439

This lively pizzeria, well off the tourist trail, is particularly popular with students, but not too chaotic. Among the starters, the *bruschetta* with tomatoes is unforgettable, and

SPECIAL

SANT'EUSTACHIO IL CAFFÈ

Map 229 E5

Piazza Sant'Eustachio 82, 00186

Tel 06 6880 2048

www.santeustachioilcaffe.it

The scent of pure Arabian coffee hangs in the air here, in a square with a view of the church of Sant'Eustachio and the Senate buildings. Connoisseurs come from far and wide to this café, which has been here since 1938 (the mosaic floor dates from the 1930s), to try what is generally regarded as the best coffee there is. All the blends are roasted on the premises in wood-fired ovens—hence the glorious aroma. Credit cards are not accepted.

🕐 Daily 8.30am–1am

☕ Coffee from 80c

🚌 40, 62, 64, 85, 87, 117, 492 to Corso Rinascimento

the fried courgette (zucchini) flowers and *suppli* (fried rice balls with tomato sauce and mozzarella) are very good. Ample choice of thin-crust pizzas, including sausage, mushroom and mozzarella, and cherry tomato. Place your order by drawing a cross on the menu. Credit cards are not accepted.

🕐 Mon–Sat 7pm–midnight

🍴 D €15, Wine €5.50

🚌 38, 60X to Piazza Istria

SICILIAINBOCCA

Map 228 C2

Via E Faà di Bruno 26, 00192

Tel 06 3751 2485

For a slice of Sicilian sunshine and hospitality in Rome, try this fish restaurant with a good array of antipasti, some favourites like *maccheroni alla Norma* with aubergines or pasta with sardines, grilled swordfish, stuffed calamari or baked anchovies, and superb desserts. The wine list is predominantly Sicilian.

🕐 Tue–Sat 12–2.30, 7–11

🍴 L €30, D €45, Wine €15

🚇 Ottaviano

🚌 30

SILVIO ALLA SUBURRA

Map 230 G5

Via Urbana 67–69, 00184

Tel 06 486531

This old-fashioned, traditional trattoria with no frills, house wine, delicious home-made pasta, and tasty meat dishes cooked with wine and herbs is the sort of place you would expect to find in a village in the hills. Simple and timeless, with nothing happening in a hurry, there are a few tables outside on the narrow street in the summer.

🕐 Daily 12.30–3, 7–11

🍴 L €20, D €35, Wine €7

🚇 Cavour

SITAR

Map 230 G5

Via Cavour 256a, 00184

Tel 06 488 4004

This oasis of tranquillity on busy Via Cavour combines superior Indian cuisine from the northern regions of the country with excellent service and presentation. The interior design is subtle and welcoming, with vaulted bricked ceilings, tiled floors and the eponymous sitar hanging on the wall. The friendly owner is on hand to help you decide, but the chicken tikka followed by butter chicken is recommended; as for dessert, try *gulab jamun* (fried dough balls in a delicate syrup). The Indian wine is a revelation, full-bodied and with a great bouquet.

🕐 Daily 12–3, 7–11.30

🍴 L €12, D €20, Wine €8

🚇 Cavour

🚌 75, 84

EATING

SORA LELLA

Map 229 E6
Via di Ponte Quattro Capi 16, 00153
Tel 06 686 1601

A family-run restaurant established in 1943 by the sister of the then famous actor Aldo Fabrizi. It is on Isola Tiberina, in the Tiber, near Trastevere—arguably one of the most special locations in Rome. Roman cuisine is at its best here, and if you're lucky enough to sit near the

window, you'll have a river view. All the typical dishes are on offer, from oxtail with cinnamon, cloves, raisins and pine nuts to some memorable *carciofi alla giudia* (Jewish artichokes). There is an ample wine list. Reservations are recommended.

🕐 Mon–Sat 12.45–2.30, 8–11; closed Aug
🍽 L €20, D €35, Wine €16
🚌 23; tram 8

TAPA LOCA

Map 229 D4
Via di Tor Millina 4–5, 00186
Tel 06 683 2266

Between Piazza Navona and the beautiful Piazza della Pace is a real rarity: a Spanish restaurant in Rome. The comfortable, large dining area, with chunky tables and chairs, lies within a 16th-century palazzo. Four different paellas, including vegetarian, and a wide variety of meat, fish and vegetarian tapas. There is also a good selection of Torres wines.

🕐 Daily 6.30pm–2am
🍽 D €25, Wine €11.50
🚌 46, 64, 87, 116, 492 to Piazza Navona

TAVERNA ANGELICA

Map 228 C4
Piazza Amerigo Capponi 6, 00193
Tel 06 687 4514

This popular restaurant is the best mid-priced option near

TAZZA D'ORO

Map 228 E4
Via degli Orfani 84, 00186
Tel 06 678 9792
www.torrefazionetazzadoro.com

This bustling bar/coffee shop near the Pantheon sparks major arguments: Is it the city's best coffee or merely a contender? The standard blend is creamy and fragrant, but the Jamaican Blue Mountain provides the smoothest buzz. Seasonal choices include *granita di caffè* (coffee sorbet) and *cioccolata calda con panna* (hot chocolate with whipped cream). Take home a bag of beans or Aroma di Roma coffee liqueur from the gift shop. Bar service only, no seating.

🕐 Mon–Sat 7am–8pm
🍽 Coffee from 75c, *granita* €1.30
🚌 40, 62, 64, or any bus to Piazza Navona or Corso Vittorio Emanuele II

the Vatican. Don't be misled by the name—the interior is minimalist and the cooking delicate and innovative. Most of the dishes are fish- or seafood-based, and there is a carefully selected wine list. Reservations are essential.

🕐 Mon–Sat 7–midnight, Sun 12.30–2.30, 7.30–midnight. Closed 2 weeks in Aug
🍽 L €12, D €30, Wine €8
🚌 19, 23, 34, 51, 64, 81, 492, 982
Ⓜ Ottaviano

TAVERNA DA GIOVANNI

Map 228 D4
Via Banco Santo Spirito 58, 00186
Tel 06 686 4116

This restaurant serves good, no-frills Roman food across the river from the Castel Sant'Angelo. It's better to dine

here than on the overpriced St. Peter's side of the river. It has three rooms and a terrace, the walls are covered with canvases, and copper pots hang from the 15th-century wooden ceiling. There is an extremely good-value three-course menu with wine and bottled water for €15, and an upgraded version with a large antipasto and coffee added for €19. The pasta starters are very generous.

🕐 Tue–Sun 12–2.30, 7–11
🍽 L €15, D €19, Wine €11
🚌 46, 62, 64, 98, 280

LA TAVERNA DEL GHETTO

Map 229 E5
Via del Portico d'Ottavia 8, 00186
Tel 06 6880 9771
www.latavernadelghetto.com

A kosher restaurant just along the street from the Portico d'Ottavia in the heart of the

Ghetto district. The dining area, within a 14th-century building, is an attractive brick-pointed room with an arched Gothic ceiling. The kosher kitchen serves Roman-Jewish dishes, and the menu changes every 2 weeks. Chicory and anchovy pie and baked salted cod with pine nuts, raisins and cherry tomatoes are two typical dishes. There's a good wine list, including Israeli selections.

🕐 Sun–Thu 12–3, 7–11; Fri noon–3; Sat 7–11
🍽 L €18, D €40, Wine €21
🚌 62, 64, 87, 628, or any other bus to Largo Argentina

EATING

TAVERNA DE'MERCANTI
Map 229 E6
Piazza de'Mercanti 3a, 00153
Tel 06 588 1693
Tucked away in a tiny piazza near Porta Portese, there is a medieval atmosphere to this pizzeria as you climb the torch-lit staircase to the dining area on the first floor. Once an inn, the large room with wooden beams, the red-and-white tablecloths, and the bustle of activity make this informal venue popular with Romans looking for a simple, affordable meal. There is a choice of grilled meats as well as pizza.
🕐 Daily 7pm–10.30pm
🍴 Pizza €25, D €45, Wine €12
🚊 Tram 3

TAVERNA PARIONE
Map 229 D5
Via dei Parione 38–39
Tel 06 686 9545
There has been a restaurant in this 15th-century palazzo, near Piazza Navona, for over 60 years. This spacious, simple

place, with artwork on the walls, serves wholesome Roman food, including pizzas, accompanied by wine from its own cellar. Popular with local celebrities—look for their pictures on the photo board. There are tables outside in warm weather.
🕐 Daily 12–3, 7–midnight
🍴 L €10, D €18, Wine €15
🚇 Spagna
🚌 46, 64

T-BONE STATION
Map 229 F4
Via Francesco Crispi 29–31, 00186
Tel 06 678 7650
Between Piazza di Spagna and Piazza Barberini is the trendiest steakhouse in Rome. The theme is based around black-and-white movie stills and high-tech

design. Steaks are the obvious choice, but the salads are huge and appetizing, especially the fresh crispy spinach and the classic chicken Caesar with parmesan topping (make sure the cheese is slivered, *a scaglie*, not grated). The cocktails are also excellent.
🕐 Daily 7pm–1am
🍴 D €52, Wine €12
🚇 Barberini
🚌 52, 53, 61, 62, 63, 80, 95, 116, 117, 119, 175, 492, 590

LA TERRAZZA
Map 229 F3
Via Ludovisi 49, 00187
Tel 06 478121
The formal atmosphere of the Hotel Eden's Michelin-starred restaurant is a good excuse to dress up. The food is predominantly modern Mediterranean, and is always excellent—try smoked scallops with asparagus, or sea bass with black olives and oregano. And as if this wasn't enough, the view is fantastic.
🕐 Daily 12.30–3, 7.45–10.30
🍴 L €45, D €100, Wine €30
🚇 Spagna or Barberini
🚌 116, 119

THAI INN
Map off 228 B7
Via Federico Ozanam 94, 00152
Tel 06 5820 3145
Fairy lights, blue lanterns, bamboo matting, fake flowers and butterflies create a tranquil Asian atmosphere in the Monteverde district of the city. The waiters—who generally speak better English than Italian—are attentive, and the Thai chefs would make a name for

themselves in any city. The menu includes vast coconut soups, grilled fish with banana leaves, '18 Buddhist

Warriors' (delicately steamed vegetables), and crisp Thai beer.
🕐 Tue–Sun 7.30pm–11.30pm
🍴 D €20, Wine €8
🚌 44

IL TIEPOLO
Map off 228 D2
Via G. B. Tiepolo 3, 00199
Tel 06 322 7449
Between Stadio Flaminio and the Tiber, this little bistro serves light meals—mostly vegetarian dishes, including rich salads, pastas and pies—and the menu changes daily. Stuffed potatoes are the house special, and fillings range from artichokes to truffles and Gorgonzola. Reservations are advised as the place is tiny, but there are tables outside in the summer.
🕐 Daily 1–3, 7.30–midnight; closed 1 week in Aug
🍴 L €12, D €20, Wine €8
🚇 Flaminio
🚊 Tram 2

TRAM TRAM
Map 231 J5
Via dei Reti 44, 00185
Tel 06 490416
This restaurant, in the heart of San Lorenzo (one of the liveliest districts of Rome, near the university), serves

a mixture of Apulian and Roman cuisine. There's also a choice of vegetarian dishes, including delicious vegetable lasagne. There are tables outside in summer, next to the tram tracks that give the restaurant its name. The wine list is excellent. Reservations are advised.
🕐 Tue–Sun 12.30–3, 8–midnight; closed 1 week in Aug
🍴 L €12, D €25, Wine €10
🚌 492

TRASTÈ
Map 229 D6
Via della Lungaretta 76, 00153
Tel 06 589 4430
By day, a chic but informal café in Trastevere where you can choose from a huge range of herbal teas, as well as *frullati* (fruit shakes), milkshakes and alcoholic drinks. In the evening, it becomes a pub.
🕐 Daily 5pm–2am
🍴 Panino €4, Crepes €4.50, Wine €3 (by the glass)
🚌 780; tram 8

TRATTORIA ABRUZZESE
Map 230 G4
Via Napoli 4, 00184
Tel 06 482 5556
After passing through an entrance shrouded with plants, you find yourself in this welcoming trattoria spread over four rooms. Photographs of rich and famous patrons cover the walls. It specializes in the cuisine of Abruzzo, the mountainous region to the east of Lazio, which is famous for its wild boar and rich, heavy pasta. Try the *pasta alla amatriciana* (with bacon, tomato and onion) or one of their divine chargrilled veal chops.
🕐 Mon–Sat 12–3, 7–11.30
🍴 L €9, D €18, Wine €6
🚇 Repubblica
🚌 64, 70, 117

TRATTORIA DA NAZZARENO
Map 230 H4
Via Magenta 35, 00185
Tel 06 495 7782
This great-value restaurant in the busy Termini station area offers an especially good antipasto buffet for vegetarians, and a fish buffet as well. The interior, dominated by the enticing central buffet table, is large, with white walls, stone floors and wooden chairs. *Bucatini* pasta with tomatoes and

pancetta, and *osso buco* (veal stew in tomato sauce) are popular with the locals. Try the local Castelli Romani house wine.
🕐 Thu–Tue 12–3.30, 6.30–11
🍴 L €12, D €16, Wine €7
🚇 Termini
🚌 40, 64

TRE SCALINI
Map 229 D4
Piazza Navona 28–32, 00100
Tel 06 6880 1996
You cannot visit Piazza Navona without sampling Tre Scalini's tartufo ice cream. There are tables outside where you can sit and enjoy your *gelato*, but at a premium. Why not take your ice cream away to eat in the piazza in the shade of Bernini's fountain?
🕐 Sun–Fri 10am–12, Sat 10am–3am
🍴 €2.50 (small ice cream to take away)
🚌 63, 492 or any bus to Largo Argentina

TRIMANI 'IL WINEBAR'
Map 230 G3
Via Cernaia 37b, 00185
Tel 06 446 9630
www.trimani.com
This great wine bar/restaurant is just along from Termini station in a leafy piazza. The original, 120-year-old Carrara

marble counter has survived renovations, and the plain wooden tables and striking basaltic slab floor harmonize perfectly with the bottles lining the walls. All dishes include a wine suggestion—for instance, the wine recommended to accompany *bresaola* (thinly sliced dried fillet of beef) with Gorgonzola, walnuts and pear, or pâté de foie gras, is the Schiaffo Colacicci Anagni 2000, one of more than 600 wines, all of which are served by the glass. The platter of Italian cheeses is easily shared.

The bar is open all day.
🕐 Mon–Sat 11.30–3, 7–midnight
🍴 L €40, D €58, Wine €10
🚇 Repubblica or Castro Pretorio

IL TULIPANO NERO
Map 229 D6
Via Roma Libera 15, 00153
Tel 06 581 8309
This small pizzeria is a rarity in Rome, as it serves gluten-free pizza for gluten-intolerants as well as a variety of well-prepared, tasty pasta and main dishes. It also has a good choice of salads and homemade *dolci*. It is a friendly spot and not expensive.
🕐 Daily 12–12
🍴 L €12, D €25
🚌 44, 175; tram 3 or 8

VECCHIA ROMA
Map 229 E5
Piazza Campitelli 18, 00186
Tel 06 686 4604
A great restaurant, which has remained unspoiled despite its popularity. In summer, salads can be eaten outside in the pretty piazza, while in winter diners move to the 18th-century interior for more substantial meals, based around polenta. Reservations are recommended.
🕐 Mon–Tue, Thu–Sun 1–3, 8–11
🍴 L €10, D €17, Wine €8
🚌 44, 46, 56, 60, 75, 85, 87, 95

EATING

VINERIA REGGIO

Map 229 D5
Piazza Campo dei Fiori 15, 00186
Tel 06 6880 3268

Wine bar on the market square of Campo dei Fiori in an original 16th-century building, with exposed beams, terracotta floors and a marble bar. Have a light lunch and a glass of wine among locals after a visit to the market. The wine selection is vast, with fine choices from all

over Italy. In the evening, the atmosphere is vibrant, with people spilling out onto the piazza. Wines per glass start at €1.30 and go up to €10.50.

🕒 Mon–Sat 8.30am–2am, Sun 4pm–2am; closed 2 weeks in Aug
🍽 L €8, Wine €4
🚌 46, 62, 64, 87, 116, 492 to Campo dei Fiori

VITTI

Map 229 E4
Piazza S. Lorenzo in Lucina 33, 00186
Tel 06 687 6304

They've been making ice creams here since 1898 to special Sicilian recipes,

and now they have extended their range to include mouthwatering cakes and pastries. The bar

inside is finished in warm dark wood, or when it's fine weather you can enjoy a refreshing break sitting outside in the charming square.

🕒 Apr–end Sep daily 7am–2am; Oct–end Mar 7am–10pm
🍦 Ice cream €1.60–€3 takeaway, €7 at table
🚇 Spagna
🚌 81, 117, 119, 590, 628

WINE TIME

Map 228 C4
Piazza Pasquale Paoli 15, 00186
Tel 06 687 5706
www.winetime.it

This wine bar offers panoramic views of Castel Sant'Angelo, and an ample wine list of about 300 labels, mainly Italian. Glossy wood tables, open cupboards displaying bottles and glasses, and a 10m (33ft) wooden counter running through the main room give a stylish yet warm touch. All dishes are coupled with a suitable wine, from

the creative starters (roasted Piedmont cheese, smoked ham with vegetables) to the salads and meat dishes. Reservations are advised.

🕒 Mon–Fri 10am–2 am, Sat 4pm–2am
🍽 L €9, D €16, Wine €9.50
🚌 40, 64 to Corso Vittorio Emanuele II

ZEN SUSHI

Map 228 C3
Via degli Scipioni 243, 00192
Tel 06 321 3420
www.zenworld.it

This minimalist, modern Japanese restaurant invites you to sit at the bar and select tempting dishes from a constantly replenished conveyer belt. The colour-coded plates indicate the price. Sashimi is prepared on request, as are hot dishes like tempura and *yakiniku*. Japanese beer, sake and Italian wine are all available. Temporary exhibitions by contemporary artists line the walls.

🕒 Tue–Fri 1–3, 8.30–11
🍽 L €18–35, D €45
🚇 Lepanto
🚌 30

STAYING IN ROME

Following Rome's renaissance in the wake of the Jubilee Year in 2000, there are now more luxury hotels than ever. Previously crumbling palazzi have been restored and many of the longer-established hotels have been completely renovated. The number of five-star hotels in the city is now 20—almost double what it was before the millennium celebrations.

LOCATION, LOCATION

As in any city, Rome has a wide range of accommodation types, from small, low-budget *pensioni* around Termini to grand, five-star luxury hotels on the Via Veneto. What to expect, in terms of price and quality, depends largely on whereabouts your hotel is in the city (see table top right).

Staying in the *centro storico* means that you are close to all of Rome's sights, but also to its sounds. Rome is a noisy city that goes to bed late and gets up early. Narrow streets and tall buildings tend to amplify the sounds of traffic and late-night revellers. Quiet places can be found, on the edge of the popular areas or in hotels with double or even triple glazing. Some of the more expensive hotels have soundproofing. When booking a hotel, ask for a quiet room, which will either be at the back of the building or overlooking a central courtyard.

If you really value your sleep, book a hotel in the quieter Aventino, Celio or Prati districts. The disadvantage here is that you will have to spend time on buses or trams, commuting into the *centro storico*. However, public transport is inexpensive and reliable, and hotels here are often cheaper than similarly rated establishments in the heart of the city.

WHAT YOU GET FOR YOUR EUROS

The familiar star system operates in Italy, with five stars denoting the highest standard of comfort, luxury and facilities. A one-star hotel or *pensione* has few facilities and frequently does not include a private bathroom. Normally both television and telephone will be downstairs in the lobby. These establishments tend to have an early curfew, do not accept credit cards and do not have a 24-hour desk service. You should expect to pay up to around €110 for a double room per night, although some are substantially cheaper.

Prices in a two-star rise to around €160 for a double room. Three stars go from about €80 to €310, four stars from €220 to around €620, while five-star de luxe properties start at around €420 and keep on soaring upwards.

Some hotels charge extra for breakfast and, as a general rule of thumb, the more expensive the establishment, the less likely it is that breakfast is included. In the listings that follow, breakfast is included unless stated otherwise. In the more moderately priced hotels, most rooms will have telephones and a mini-bar, and prices here tend to include breakfast, tax and service charges. The smaller boutique hotels are extremely popular and tend to be in lovely, old historic buildings tucked away from the main streets. These do not come cheap, but offer many services and usually include breakfast, tax and service. The larger, de luxe hotels usually have full business facilities and access to the internet, as well as health spas and pools. The cost of a stay here is usually exclusive of both breakfast and service.

RESERVATIONS

As Rome is an eternally popular destination, it pays to reserve well in advance, especially if your stay is over the peak periods, which, nowadays, tend to be the greater part of the year. However, January to March and August are the least popular months of the tourist calendar and you should be able to find some good deals at this time. Do consult hotels' websites for details of special offers, and remember that specialist tour operators usually have a fixed allocation in some of the best hotels and can include your flights and transfers at very competitive prices for an all-in package. If you arrive without a reservation, do ask to see the room first before you commit yourself. Information and accommodation agencies are always a useful resource.

Il Tridente The chic shopping area around the Piazza di Spagna has traditional hotels in the upper price range

Via Veneto Rome's top-end hotels are here, although it is no longer the heart of *la dolce vita*

The Pantheon and Piazza Navona High- to mid-price hotels in an area buzzing with life

The Ghetto and Campo dei Fiori Low- to medium-price hotels with bags of character

Monti and Esquillino Traditionally an area of low-budget accommodation

Prati, Aventino and Celio Peaceful, quietly charming mid- to high-price hotels, away from the activity of the *centro storico*

Trastevere Better known for its bars and nightlife, but has added to its quota of accommodation

The Vatican From spartan pilgrim hostels to comfortable hotels in bustling medieval lanes

ACCOMMODATION SERVICES

The APT (Azienda di Promozione Turistica di Roma) tourist office at Via Parigi 5, Esquilino (tel 06 3600 4399, www.romaturismo.com) provides an independent list of accommodation, although you are responsible for making your own reservation. The office is open Mon–Sat 9–7, while the phoneline is open daily 9–7.30. There is also a branch at Fiumicino airport (tel 06 3600 4399). Also at Rome's Fiumicino airport, **Hotel Reservation Service** (arrivals halls, Terminals A, B and C; open daily from around 7.30am to 10.30pm—times do vary) has English operators and can provide details of availability of accommodation in every price range. The service also has branches at Ciampino airport Apr–Nov and at Termini (platform heads 2–3 and 20). The telephone number for the Hotel Reservation Service is 06 699 1000, www.hotelreservation.it.

Termini—the area around the station—is full of 'officials' who are keen to direct you to a hotel. Some are appointed by the tourist office, others are impostors, so be wary. To avoid any misunderstanding it is always better to go direct to the tourist information point (PIT—Punti Informativi Turistici, instantly recognizable by the green-painted kiosk) at Termini (daily 8am–9pm). There are other information points around the city.

A very useful service is run by **Enjoy Rome**, which is a private English-speaking agency that can give helpful advice and also provides a free accommodation booking service. Its main office is just by Termini station (take the north exit from the station at Via Marsala, walk straight along for three blocks and it is on the left) at Via Marghera 8a (tel 06 445 1843, www.enjoyrome.com). It is open Mar–end Oct Mon–Fri 8.30–7, Sat 8.30–2; Nov–end Feb Mon–Fri 9–6.30, Sat 8.30–2. Credit cards are not accepted.

OTHER OPTIONS

Camping The Touring Club Italiano publishes an annual directory, *Campeggi in Italia*, which covers sites throughout the country and is available in bookstores (around €12).

Bed-and-Breakfast Bed-and-breakfast is a relatively new concept in Rome, but it is booming. More than a thousand are now registered, from spare bedrooms in out-of-town family flats to rooms in opulent palazzi. They are the new shabby chic trend and some are a great deal more chic than shabby.

The **Bed and Breakfast Italia** agency (Palazzo Sforza Cesarini, Corso Vittorio Emanuele 284, tel 06 687 8618, www.bbitalia.it) lists around 250 properties, including luxury four-crown accommodation in palazzi. Prices start from around €60 per room in this category, descending to around €25 in a two-crown establishment.

Rent an apartment If you want to rent an apartment, the peak times for availability tend to be in July, August and December, when the owners traditionally take their own holidays. Agencies specializing in apartment and villa rentals include:

Homes International, Via L. Bissolati 20, tel 06 488 1800. The service covers short- and long-term rentals for apartments and villas, and English is spoken. The office is open Mon–Fri 9–1, 2–7, Sat 9–1.

Rome Property Network, Via dei Gesù e Maria 25 (near Piazza del Popolo), tel 06 321 2341, www.romeproperty.com. English is also spoken at this agency, where they specialize in apartments and villas in the *centro storico* and Trastevere. It is open Mon–Fri 9–6.

Useful websites include www.flatinrome.com and www.romeguide.it.

STAYING

HOTEL LOCATOR

CITTÀ DEL VATICANO

Giardini Vaticani

Villa Doria Pamphilj

Villa Floridi

Villa Abamelek

Parco Gianicolense

Parco Adriano

Nova Domus

Alimandi

Bbroma

Atlante Star

Adriatic

Holiday Inn Rome West

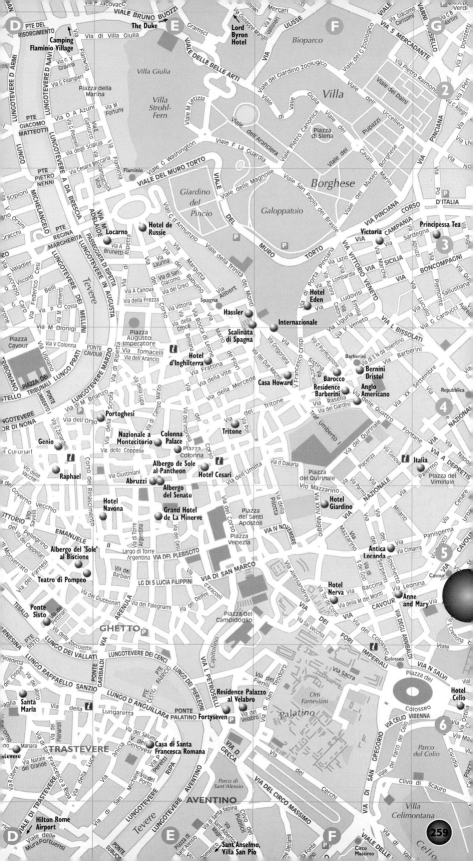

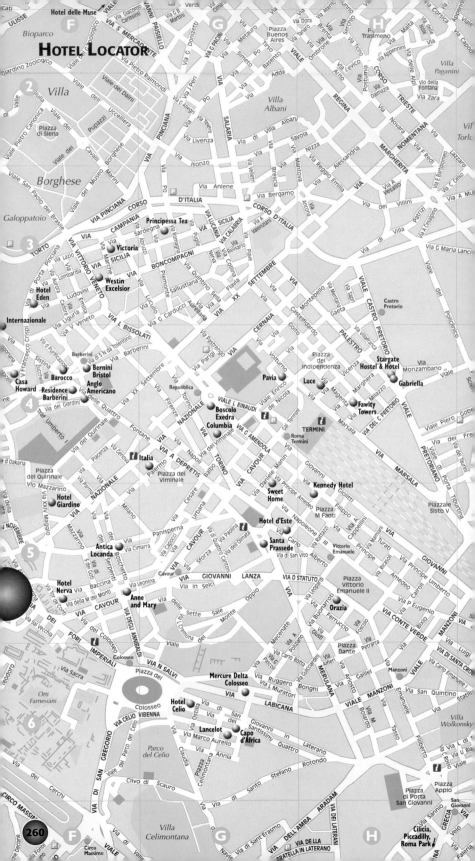

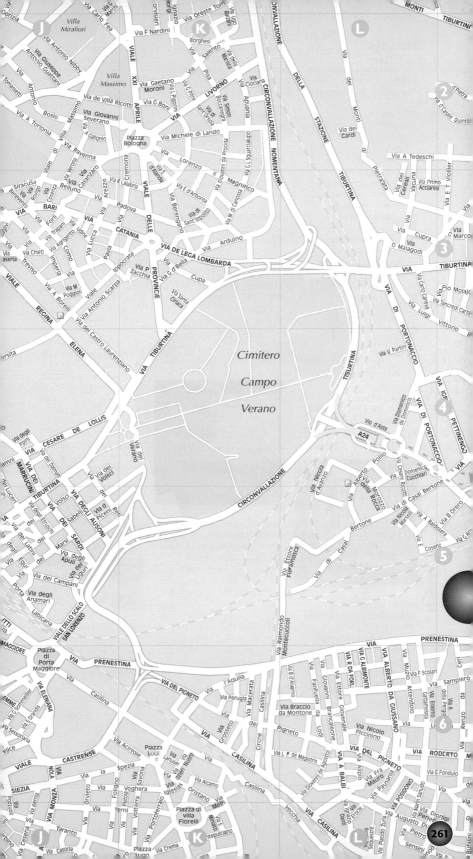

Hotels

The hotels below are listed alphabetically and cover a range of budgets. The prices given are for a double room for one night and include breakfast, unless otherwise stated.

ABRUZZI
Map 259 E4
Piazza della Rotonda 69, 00186
Tel 06 679 2021
www.hotelabruzzi.it
Although its prices have increased in recent years, this hotel still represents one of the best deals in the city, considering what you get: The most dramatic view of the Pantheon that Rome has to offer. Most rooms have private bathrooms, and all have double glazing and air conditioning.
€160–€195
25
116

ADRIATIC
Map 258 C4
Via G. Vitelleschi 25, 00193
Tel 06 6880 8080
www.adriatichotel.com
A family-run hotel, just three blocks from St. Peter's. The reception has a pleasant interior of reds and golds,

plus an old-style wooden desk. Rooms are moderately spacious with patterned carpets and reproduction furniture. Not all guest rooms have private bathrooms, but they do have satellite TV and air conditioning (€15 extra per day).
€75–€105, excluding breakfast
42
Ottaviano San Pietro
40, 62, 64, 81

ALBERGO DEL SENATO
Map 259 E4
Piazza della Rotonda 73, 00186
Tel 06 678 4343
www.albergodelsenato.it
An elegant Renaissance palace houses this recently refurnished hotel with spectacular views of the Pantheon and its square. The roof terrace makes an ideal setting for relaxing and enjoying being in the heart of old Rome. Rooms are very comfortable and the service is efficient and welcoming.
€198–€301
57

ALBERGO DEL 'SOLE' AL BISCIONE
Map 259 D5
Via del Biscione 76, 00186
Tel 06 6880 6873
www.solealbiscione.it
In a little side street just off bustling Campo dei Fiori,

this competitively priced hotel is in the heart of medieval Rome. Rooms are clean, if on the small side, with old furniture. All have TV and bathroom with shower. Staff are friendly and there is a gem of a roof terrace for viewing the surrounding skyline. There is no access for visitors in a wheelchair. Paid parking, but credit cards are not accepted.
€110–€140, excluding breakfast
60
20 rooms
40, 62, 64, 87, 116, 492

ALBERGO DE SOLE AL PANTHEON
Map 259 E4
Piazza della Rotonda 63, 00186
Tel 06 678 0441
www.hotelsolealpantheon.com
This chic hotel claims to be the oldest in Rome, and with a history stretching back to 1467 it could be right. It has an enviable location in the same square as the Pantheon, with stunning views from the windows at the front of the building. Some rooms have painted ceilings or tiled floors, and more than half have a jacuzzi; all have satellite TV. In warm weather, breakfast is served in the attractive courtyard.
€240–€360
30

Spagna
119 to Piazza della Rotonda, 70, 81, 87 to Corso del Rinascimento, or any bus to Largo di Torre Argentina

ALIMANDI
Map 258 B3
Via Tunisi 8, 00192
Tel 06 3972 3948
www.alimandi.it
Superior three-star, family-run hotel that is very good value for money. The 19th-century building, close to the Vatican Museums, retains some original features, including elegant Venetian stuccowork. Rooms are spacious, with modern furnishings and pastel shades; all have satellite and pay TV, and roomy bathrooms with hairdryers. There is an internet computer point for guests

to use, and a free airport shuttle, plus parking. The Continental buffet breakfast is served on the roof terrace or in the dining room.
Closed 10 Jan–10 Feb
€130–€185
35

Cipro Musei Vaticani or Ottaviano San Pietro
81, 492, 495

STAYING

ANGLO AMERICANO

Map 259 F4
Via delle Quattro Fontane 12, 00184
Tel 06 472941
www.hotelangloamericano.it
This distinguished hotel has
a genteel, belle époque
atmosphere, from the cool,
blue-and-white striped
wallpaper in the lounge to
the solemn busts guarding
the door. The 18th-century
palazzo has well-ordered and
well-appointed rooms, all with
private bath, hairdryer, satellite
TV and internet connection.
The hotel is near the Piazza
di Spagna, Trevi Fountain,
Via Veneto and Parliament, so
it's popular with politicians.
💶 €150–€180
🛏 120
♿
🚇 Spagna

ANNE AND MARY

Map 260 F5
Via Cavour 325, 00184
Tel 06 6994 1187
www.anne-mary.com
This welcoming bed-and-
breakfast occupies an elegant
19th-century building near
the Colosseo. Rooms are
simple but dramatic, with
clean lines and swooping
curtains. Each has a small
private bathroom with
enclosed shower, TV and
safe. The wood parquetry on
the hall floors is especially
handsome. Via Cavour is a
large, somewhat frantic
artery, but the convenience
for sights and shops is worth
the muted noise.
💶 €100–€130
🛏 6 (all non-smoking)
♿
🚇 Cavour
🚌 75, 81, 85, 87, 116, 117

ANTICA LOCANDA

Map 260 F5
Via del Boschetto 84, 00184
Tel 06 4788 1729
www.antica-locanda.com

In the oldest part of Rome,
not far from the Colosseo, is
this quaint, inexpensive,
family-run hotel. Check in at
the 15th-century wine bar of
the same name next door.
There is no elevator up to the
four floors, but a porter service
is provided. Rooms have
beamed ceilings, wooden
floors with rugs, and Italian
reproduction furniture, plus
TV, minibar, shower and
hairdryer. There is a large
flower-filled roof terrace
(and on request the use of a
barbecue) overlooking this
medieval part of the city.
The Continental breakfast is
served in the wine bar.
💶 €104–€180
🛏 10
♿
🚇 Cavour
🚌 117, or any bus to Via Nazionale

ATLANTE STAR

Map 258 C4
Via G. Vitelleschi 34, 00193
Tel 06 687 3233
www.atlantehotels.com
This luxury hotel between
Vatican City and the Castel
Sant'Angelo exudes class

and elegance. Richly
upholstered sofas, heavy
drapes, stuccoed ceilings
and plush carpets, all in
gold, reds and blues, plus
antiques and 18th-century
paintings. The rooms are
equally lush and spacious;
half have whirlpool baths.
There is a bar and a renowned
gourmet restaurant, plus a
free airport shuttle. There
are astounding views of
St. Peter's from the breakfast
room.
💶 €160–€350
🛏 70
♿
🚇 Ottaviano San Pietro
🚌 32, 81, 492

BAROCCO

Map 259 F4
Via della Purificazione 4, 00187
Tel 06 487 2001
www.hotelbarocco.com
Three historic buildings have
been merged to form this
intimate, elegant hotel. The
newer wing has jacuzzi tubs
in some rooms, while the
older part is rich with cherry-
wood-framed mirrors, opulent
drapes and precious marble.
Although it overlooks Piazza
Barberini, the hotel is well
soundproofed, muting Rome's
constant roar. Visitors praise
the Barocco's fresh flowers,
extra towels, courtesy kits
and efficient staff. Guests in
the suites also get dressing
gowns.
💶 €190–€280
🛏 37 rooms (all non-smoking),
5 suites
♿
🚇 Barberini

BBROMA

Map 258 B3
Via Sebastiano Veniero 78, 00192
Tel 06 6821 0776
www.bbroma.com
This is a collection of bed-and-
breakfasts put together on a
website by a group of friends.

Some of these rooms are near
the Vatican, and reservations
are handled centrally by
Signora Erminia Pascucci.
Rooms are generally spacious
and nicely furnished, mostly in
a late 19th-century style. All
have telephone, TV and
bathroom. The organization
also arranges for stays in
rooms in houses with
communal kitchens and in
apartments. Be sure to check
the website for conditions.
Credit cards are not accepted.
💶 €75–€90
🛏 4 near the Vatican, plus 50 more
around the city
🚇 Cipro Musei Vaticani
🚌 19, 23, 70, 492, 495

BERNINI BRISTOL

Map 259 F4
Piazza Barberini 23, 00187
Tel 06 488 3051
www.berninibristol.com
This grande dame has always been popular with aristocrats and royalty. The 1874 palazzo is refurbished, but antiques and vintage tapestries maintain the tone. Both restaurants are renowned, especially the rooftop panorama of L'Olimpo, with its impressive views. Once the heart of *la dolce vita*, the Bernini's nightclub and lounges remain chic. Facilities include babysitting, car rental, valet parking, private garage, secretarial service, sauna and hot tub. Pets are welcome.

€480, excluding breakfast
127 (100 non-smoking)
Barberini
61, 62, 116, 119, 175, 492, 590

BOSCOLO EXEDRA

Map 260 G4
Piazza della Repubblica 47, 00185
Tel 06 489381
www.boscolohotels.com

True luxury, built over the remains of Diocletian's third-century baths, on Piazza della Repubblica. Carrara marble and Venetian glass are used to stunning effect in the lobby. The two restaurants were created by architect Adam Tihany. Guest rooms are equally lush, in Regency style with marble bathrooms, satellite TV and safe. There is contemporary artwork throughout. This hotel also has a solarium, spa, and roof terrace with swimming pool and bar.

€275–€383, excluding breakfast
240 (96 non-smoking)
Repubblica
40, 64 to Via Nazionale

CAMPING FLAMINIO VILLAGE DI VITTORIO CANTELLA E FIGLI SRL

Map off 259 D1
Via Flaminia Nuova 821, 00189
Tel 06 333 2604
www.villageflaminio.com
Only a few kilometres from the city, these bungalows are well served by public transport. They are also well furnished with bath, shower and private garden. Many have kitchens and living rooms, plus satellite TV, garden furniture, barbecue and parking, and a weekly maid service. There is also a shaded campsite in the peaceful urban oasis of Parco di Veio. Services here include pool, laundry, restaurant/bar/pizzeria, safe deposit and internet. A riverside cycle path leads all the way into the city. Car and scooter rental is available.

Bungalows €65–€71, campsite €29–€34 including tent
48 bungalows, 300 tent plots
200 from Piazza Mancini
Flaminio to Due Ponti

CAPO D'AFRICA

Map 260 G6
Via Capo d'Africa 54, 00184
Tel 06 772801
www.hotelcapodafrica.com
Handsome 19th-century building close to the Colosseo in a fashionable district. It is a fusion of contemporary and classic, with a hint of Japanese

design. The beautiful rooms are in warm ochre and saffron tones, and the perfectly fitted bathrooms are in marble and wood. The American buffet breakfast is served on the roof with views of the Colosseo. There is also a large, well-equipped gym and solarium.

€290
54 (20 non-smoking)
Colosseo
81, 85, 87, 117; tram 3

CASA HOWARD

Map 259 F4
Via Capo le Case 18, 00187
Tel: 06 6992 4555
www.casahoward.com
Staying in this very central little hotel feels like staying as a guest in a private apartment. Care has been taken with the decorations and furnishings to create a warm, soft ambience, and each room is unique. It is on the first floor, reached either by a marble staircase or an elevator. Breakfast can be served in your room on request.

€160–€210, excluding breakfast
5, plus 5 in nearby annexe

Spagna, Barberini
52, 53, 63, 95, 116, 204

CASA DI SANTA FRANCESCA ROMANA

Map 259 E6
Via dei Vascellari 61, 00153
Tel/Fax 06 581 2125
www.sfromana.it
Tucked away in Trastevere, an unprepossessing entrance leads to a spacious reception area and onto a charming courtyard with orange trees. This was a grand family house until the 16th century, when it became a convent; the chapel is on the first floor. It now offers guests simply furnished rooms.

€150
37
Circo Massimo
23, 44, 280

CILICIA

Map off 260 H7
Via Cilicia 7, 00179
Tel 06 700 5554
www.hotelcilicia.com
This 1950s-built hotel is just a five-minute walk from the city end of the Via Appia. The interiors have an old-world feel, with an austere cherry-wood reception desk and Austrian blinds. The lounge has a studded-leather bar counter, and the dining room has some grandeur, but is comfortable enough. The ample-sized rooms all have bath, satellite TV, minibar and electronic safe. Parking is available.

€135–€155
62 (5 non-smoking)
San Giovanni
360

COLONNA PALACE
Map 259 E4
Piazza Montecitorio 12, 00186
Tel 06 675191
www.itihotels.it
Overlooking the Parliament buildings in the hub of 16th-century Rome, the Colonna is a superb base for discovering

the Eternal City. It is fairly chintzy throughout—pink walls, bright floral upholstered chairs and drapes, and neo-Grecian columns. Rooms are spacious, with bathroom, TV and minibar. The breakfast room, serving a Continental buffet breakfast, overlooks the Presidential Palace. There is also a roof terrace bar and a solarium.

€249–€350

102

46, 62, 116

COLUMBIA
Map 260 G4
Via del Viminale 15, 00184
Tel 06 474 4289
www.hotelcolumbia.com
This charming hotel is just a stone's throw away from Termini station, just around the corner from Teatro dell'Opera, and its friendly, efficient staff are always happy to help. All the rooms are simply furnished and have satellite TV. Breakfast is served on the roof terrace—a great way to start the day—and as the day wears on, you can relax in the bar or lounge. Ask for a quiet room, as those near the road can be noisy.

€133–€149

45

Termini

40, 64 or any bus to Termini

THE DUKE
Map off 259 E1
Via Archimede 69, 00197
Tel 06 367221
www.thedukehotel.com

In the heart of the well-heeled Parioli district, between the parks of the Villa Borghese and the Villa Gloria, this hotel boasts beautiful English country-house interiors with a classical influence. There is a delightful art nouveau glass cupola in the Polo Lounge. The guest rooms are luxurious and intimate, spacious and light, in warm hues, with fresh flowers, minibar, safe, satellite TV and games console. There are also large marble bathrooms. Children get a welcome pack and free tickets to the zoo.

€320–€430

78

Flaminio

52, 53, 168, 217, 230, 231, 910

FAWLTY TOWERS HOTEL AND HOSTEL
Map 260 H4
Via Magenta 39, 00187
Tel 06 445 0374
www.fawltytowers.org
Decent inexpensive hotel/hostel accommodation near Termini station, with both private and shared rooms. When you arrive, take the elevator up to the fifth floor. This certainly isn't dormitory bunk-bed accommodation; instead, you get a bed for the night in a four-person room. The place has a clubby feel; there are wood floors and a theme of cheerful orange and zany stripes, with bouquets of sunflowers and an odd papier-mâché puppet head. It is slightly eccentric in a fun and functional way. There is a communal kitchen and free internet access, and no curfew. Credit cards are not accepted.

€55–€89, excluding breakfast

16 (all non-smoking)

6 rooms

Termini

40, 64 or any bus to Termini

FORTYSEVEN
Map 259 E6
Via Petroselli 47, 00186
Tel 06 678 7816
www.fortysevenhotel.com
A team of young designers has created a cool minimalist hotel within ancient Rome, overlooking the Temple of Vesta. A spectacular roof terrace restaurant offers magnificent views, while the hotel is fully equipped with the latest technology, with computers in every room. There is also an inside courtyard and a fitness centre with a sauna. The staff are particularly friendly and helpful.

€300

61

Circo Massimo

H, 30, 44, 63, 81, 95, 170

GABRIELLA
Map 260 H4
Via Palestro 88, 00185
Tel 06 445 0120
www.gabriellahotel.com
This first-floor hotel with elevator is near Termini station and the main bus terminal. There is a

comfortable feel about the place: It has a welcoming lobby and small reading/TV lounge with sofas and coffee tables. The medium-sized rooms have ceramic floors, Tuscan-style matching coverlets and curtains, double-glazed windows, safe, minibar and satellite TV. The white-tiled bathrooms have showers (some have baths) and hairdryers. There is a spacious breakfast room/bar serving a Continental breakfast, and the staff speak English.

€70–€150

23 (all non-smoking)

Castro Pretorio

492, or any bus to Termini

GRAND HOTEL DE LA MINERVE

Map 259 E5
Piazza della Minerva 69, 00186
Tel 06 695201
www.hotel-invest.com

This historic 17th-century hotel is close to the Pantheon. The classically furnished lobby has Roman statues, palm trees, marble flooring and an art nouveau glass cupola. Guest rooms are elegantly furnished and painted in soft pastel blues and ochre; some have exposed beams or frescoed ceilings. All have marble bathrooms, satellite/pay TV, coffee-maker, trouser press, safe and internet access. Amenities include restaurant, bar, roof garden, sauna and fitness facilities. The staff are always ready to help.

🖐 €348–€455, excluding breakfast
🛈 135
🅂 🆈
🚌 116, or any bus to Via del Corso

GENIO

Map 259 D4
Via Zanardelli 28, 00186
Tel 06 683 2191
www.leonardihotels.com
This hotel has a nice touch of the old world about it. Antique furniture and rich red carpets throughout give

HASSLER

Map 259 E3
Piazza Trinità dei Monti 6, 00187
Tel 06 699340
www.hotelhasslerroma.com
The *bel mondo* gather at the Hassler to be cosseted by Roberto Wirth (of the Swiss hotel dynasty) and his impeccable staff. The hotel sits at the top of the Spanish Steps, surveying St. Peter's, the Villa Medici and the Vittorio Emanuele monument. The interior is lavish, rich with marble, frescoed walls, hand-painted tiles, fringed curtains and a glass-roofed lounge. Big spenders prefer the penthouse, though corner room 403 is also coveted. Facilities include a restaurant, bar, hair salon, massage, babysitting, laundry, room service, tennis court and the use of bicycles free of charge.

🖐 €396–€650, excluding breakfast
🛈 100 rooms, 15 suites
🅂
🚇 Spagna

it a regal air. It has good-sized, high-ceilinged rooms with embroidered armchairs and marble-fitted bathrooms. Bar and roof terrace have fine views of nearby St. Peter's and Castel Sant'Angelo. It is a wonderful base for exploring the Renaissance quarter of Rome and is just seconds away from Piazza Navona. A free airport shuttle service is available, as is private parking.

🖐 €120–€220
🛈 66
🅂
🚌 70, 81, 87, 116, 492

HILTON ROME AIRPORT

Map off 259 D7
Via Arturo Ferrarin 2, 00050 Fiumicino
Tel 06 65258
www.hilton.com
The Hilton is the only hotel on or near the airport grounds, right in front of the departure hall. The rooms are spacious and the hotel has a number of comforts, such as all-day dining in the buffet-style restaurant, as well as a café with pizza and pasta. Other amenities include fitness

facilities with indoor pool, gym, two outdoor floodlit tennis courts, sauna, steam room and massage—plenty to help guests get over jet lag. You can take a train or the free shuttle to the city, 35 minutes away.

🖐 €160–€235
🛈 517 (204 non-smoking)
🅂 🆒 🆈
✈ Fiumicino Airport

HOLIDAY INN ROME WEST

Map off 258 A6
Via Aurelia, km 8,400, 00163
Tel 06 6641 1200
www.alliancealberghi.com
If Rome's chaos and excitement become overwhelming, you can retreat to the Holiday Inn 8km (5 miles) west of the city, on the Via Aurelia highway. It is ideal for frazzled executives, with 14 meeting rooms, secretarial and translation services, and private limousine hire, plus a gym and pool to unwind. There is also free internet access, a restaurant, cocktail lounge, garden, snooker tables and children's playground. Pets cost an extra €6 per night. Park free or in the guarded lot (€5). There is a free shuttle service to the city from the hotel.

🖐 €104–€250, excluding breakfast
🛈 196 rooms (102 non-smoking), 8 suites
🅂 🆒 🆈
🚇 Cornelia, then bus 246

HOTEL CELIO

Map 260 G6
Via dei Santi Quattro 35c, 00184
Tel 06 7049 5333
www.hotelcelio.com
The simple façade of this elegant hotel, just a short walk from the Colosseo, belies its stunning interior. All bedrooms have frescoes, inspired by Renaissance painters, and include satellite TV and VCRs with a selection of films in English and Italian. Rooms on the upper floors have jacuzzis.

🖐 €150–€290
🛈 20
🅂 🆈
🚇 Colosseo
🚌 116, 117

STAYING

HOTEL CESARI

Map 259 E4
Via di Pietra 89a, 00186
Tel 06 674 9701
www.albergocesari.it

The quiet but central position of this charming, friendly hotel means that it has a loyal client base, and so early booking is recommended. Built in 1787, close to the Pantheon, the building includes 11 pillars from the second-century AD Temple of Hadrian. Its large rooms all have satellite TV.

€185–€220
47 (21 non-smoking)

60, 62, 85, 117, 119, 160 to Via del Corso

HOTEL D'ESTE

Map 260 G5
Via Carlo Alberto 4b, 00135
Tel 06 446 5607
www.hotel-deste.com

This early 19th-century hotel is in a tree-lined street, directly across from the basilica of Santa Maria Maggiore and a

few minutes away from Termini station. There is a charming reception hall with a cobbled floor and beamed ceiling. The bar and restaurant are on the first floor, making the hotel unsuitable for wheelchair users. Guest rooms are simple, clean and spacious, with parquet floors and reproduction furniture. All have TV and bathroom with hairdryer. There is alfresco dining in summer.

€80–€130
37

Vittorio
70, 360

HOTEL GIARDINO

Map 259 F5
Via XXIV Maggio 51, 00187
Tel: 06 679 4981
www.hotel-giardino-roma.com

The English owner Katie offers

SPECIAL
HOTEL DE RUSSIE

Map 259 E3
Via del Babuino 9, 00187
Tel 06 328881
www.hotelderussie.it

Near Piazza del Popolo in the heart of the city, amid all the top designer shops, this is arguably Rome's top hotel. It is a historic palazzo, where the contemporary and classic are blended. Guest rooms have high ceilings and are lovingly furnished, and the bathrooms are works of art. Amenities include spa with hydropool, sauna, Turkish baths and beauty treatments. The first-class restaurant is elegant and, when its doors are opened onto the gardens, the most romantic spot in Rome.

€440–€770, excluding breakfast
129 (37 non-smoking)

Flaminio
117

her guests a warm welcome, and free tea and coffee are always available to revive weary sightseers. Her rooms are decorated in soft pastels and comfortably furnished. Ask for a room on the road side for views up to the Palazzo del Quirinale—double glazing shuts out the traffic noise.

€90–€140
11

Cavour, Barberini
H, 40, 60, 64, 70, 117, 170

HOTEL D'INGHILTERRA

Map 259 E4
Via Bocca di Leone 14, 00187
Tel 06 69981
www.royaldemeure.com

The wealthy Torlonia family built this palazzo, now a sumptuous hotel, near the

boutique-lined Via Condotti. Outside it has an imposing golden façade, supported by arches, while beyond the entrance a black-and-white carpet runs through the lobby, punctuated by delicate antiques and plump red sofas. The guest rooms, though less dramatic, are pleasant, with thick carpeting, carved bed frames, and carefully chosen paintings and prints. There is 24-hour room service.

€315–€511, excluding breakfast
98 (20 non-smoking)

Spagna

HOTEL DELLE MUSE

Map off 260 F1
Via T. Salvini 18, 00197
Tel 06 808 8333
www.hoteldellemuse.com

Hilltop Parioli is one of Rome's most elite areas, and a cool oasis in summer months. It is worth tracking down this pleasant hotel, particularly if you have special requirements. The management is sensitive towards vegetarian, kosher and halal diets. They also have family discounts and an internet booking discount of 5 per cent, and pets are welcome. There is free email and internet access, a restaurant, bar and outdoor garden. Tours depart from the hotel.

€83–€160
60

360 to Piazza delle Muse

HOTEL EDEN

Map 259 F3
Via Ludovisi 49, 00187
Tel 06 478121
www.hotel-eden.it

Just off the Via Veneto is the Eden, one of Rome's top hotels. Its relaxed, old-fashioned luxury makes it a popular choice with visiting celebrities and royalty. All the rooms are tastefully furnished with antiques, and have marble bathrooms, satellite TV and internet access. After dinner in La Terrazza restaurant, relax in the piano bar.

€350–€520, excluding breakfast
121

Barberini
63, 116 or any bus to Via Veneto

STAYING

HOTEL NAVONA

Map 259 E5
Via dei Sediari 8, 00186
Tel 06 686 4203
www.hotelnavona.com

The Italo-Australian owners create a friendly atmosphere in this hotel, close to the Piazza Navona and Pantheon in a quiet side street, which makes it very popular. Some parts of the building date from the first century AD, and were built over the Baths of Aggripa; Keats and Shelley once stayed on the top floor. The rooms are basic and simple, most have bathrooms, and air conditioning is available at a €15 supplement. The breakfast isn't the best, but there are plenty of places to eat nearby. Credit cards are not accepted.

💶 €100–€145
🛏 35
♿ 31 rooms
🚇 30, 70, 86, 87, 116

HOTEL NERVA

Map 259 F5
Via Tor de'Conti 3, 00184
Tel 06 678 1835
www.hotelnerva.com

Tucked behind the walls of the Fori Imperiali, this hotel is in a quiet street and could hardly be more central. It was recently totally refurnished to a comfortable standard, with modern bathrooms, fully equipped soundproofed rooms and a garage. Staff are very friendly and helpful, and breakfast is served in the frescoed bar downstairs.

💶 €130–€220
🛏 22
♿
🚇 Cavour
🚌 60, 75, 84, 85, 87, 175, 186, 271

INTERNAZIONALE

Map 259 F4
Via Sistina 79, 00187
Tel 06 6994 1823
www.hotelinternazionale.com

Wisteria winds up the front of this palazzo—a faint echo perhaps of the ancient Roman gardens that once stood here. The building evolved over the years, serving as a convent in the 16th and 17th centuries. Today, the breakfast lounge is in soothing pastel blues and purples, and this tranquil scheme continues throughout, from the cupids in the cupola

to the silk wall coverings in the bedrooms. There is 24-hour room service, a bar, currency exchange, babysitting and parking, and pets are welcome.

💶 €150–€210
🛏 42
♿
🚇 Spagna
🚌 62

ITALIA

Map 259 G4
Via Venezia 18, 00184
Tel 06 487 0919
www.hotelitaliaroma.com

Inexpensive, friendly, family-run hotel in a 19th-century building just off Via Nazionale,

the second-largest shopping street in the city. Reception is on the first floor, and there is a small elevator. Both public and guest rooms are very clean and simple throughout, and the guest rooms have TV, minibar, air conditioning (€8 extra per day), bathroom, hairdryers and safes. All are spacious, with parquet floors, functional furniture and cream walls. The hotel has a bar and a safe at reception.

💶 €75–€114
🛏 32 (15 non-smoking)
♿ 21 rooms
🚇 Repubblica
🚌 64

KENNEDY HOTEL

Map 260 H5
Via Filippo Turati 62–64, 00185
Tel 06 446 5373
www.hotelkennedy.net

This three-star hotel is between Termini station and the basilica of Santa Maria Maggiore. Half of the guest rooms overlook the archaeological park of the Roman Aquarium. Rooms are spacious, with fitted wardrobes, double-glazed windows, satellite TV, and small but well-equipped bathrooms. The public areas

LORD BYRON HOTEL

Map off 259 E1
Via Giuseppe de Notaris 5, 00197
Tel 06 322 0404
www.lordbyronhotel.com

In the leafy Parioli district, overlooking the Villa Borghese, is the Lord Byron, which, true to its name, is a romantic hideaway. The art deco villa has scarlet sofas, lacquered furniture, gilded mirrors and marble bathrooms. There is a piano bar for relaxation, where servings of port and petits fours can lull you to sleep each night. The hotel's restaurant, Sapori del Lord Byron, is considered one of Italy's finest. Ask for room 503, 602 or 603, as they have spectacular views. Parking is available.

💶 €335–€445
🛏 36 (6 non-smoking)
♿
🚇 Flaminio
🚌 117

are warmly lit, and there is a small reading room with some books and guides in English. The three small breakfast rooms with a bar serve a buffet breakfast.

💶 €80–€160
🛏 51
♿
🚇 Termini
🚌 40, 64, 70

LANCELOT

Map 260 G6
Via Capo d'Africa 47, 00184
Tel 06 7045 0615
www.lancelothotel.com
This welcoming, family-run hotel is just around the corner from the Colosseo. The entrance hall and

restaurant have period furniture and Murano glass chandeliers. Other public spaces are the bar, the library and a delightful courtyard. Rooms are spacious, and most have wooden floors, pastel walls and individual charm. All have a safe, satellite TV and bathroom with shower. Some guest rooms have their own terraces, but there's also a lovely roof terrace.
🖐 €150–€189
🛏 60
🆓
📍 Colosseo or Manzoni
🚌 81, 85, 87, 117; tram 3

LOCARNO

Map 259 E3
Via della Penna 22, 00186
Tel 06 361 0841
www.hotellocarno.com
Artists and intellectuals, including Umberto Eco (author of *The Name of the Rose*), opt for this art deco refuge on a sleepy street near Piazza del Popolo. The 1925 building retains original features, including a cast-iron elevator. The interiors have been skilfully designed, using period lamps and furnishings, and each room is individually decorated. Guests have free use of the business and internet facilities, and vintage bicycles.
🖐 €190–€310
🛏 66 (6 non-smoking)
🆓
📍 Flaminio
🚌 117

LUCE

Map 260 H4
Via Magenta 34, 00185
Tel 06 446 9277
www.sebraeli.it
This modern, light, three-star hotel is close to Termini station and the shops. All public areas have attractive

inlaid marble floors and comfortable sofas. The breakfast room is elegant, with upholstered spoon-back chairs and gold-braided tablecloths. Guest rooms are stylish and spacious, with draped curtains, fitted wooden furniture and good spot lighting. All rooms have bathroom, TV and minibar. Parking is available.
🖐 €104
🛏 68
🆓
📍 Termini
🚌 40, 64

MERCURE DELTA COLOSSEO

Map 260 G6
Via Labicana 144, 00184
Tel 06 770021
www.mercure.com
One of the last developments (1975) allowed in this part of the old city, the Mercure is in view of the Colosseo and beside Nero's Domus

Aurea (Golden House). It has a beautifully marbled, spacious reception with internet access, a high-tech minimalist bar and a piano

bar. Medium-sized rooms with marble bath, comfortable sofas, satellite and pay TV, safe and minibar. There is also a bar on the roof with a 360-degree view of the city.
🖐 €110–€274
🛏 160 (40 non-smoking)
🆓 🏊 Outdoor
📍 Colosseo or Manzoni
🚌 87, 117; tram 3

NAZIONALE A MONTECITORIO

Map 259 E4
Piazza Montecitorio 131, 00186
Tel 06 695001
www.nazionaleroma.it
Next to the Parliament buildings, and close to the Trevi Fountain and Piazza di Spagna, this charming hotel has an old-world feel,

with dark wood panelling, marble floors and columns in the lobby. The medium-sized rooms have high ceilings and period furniture, and are decorated in gold and brown tones; all have bathroom, satellite/pay TV, minibar and safe. The old-fashioned bar and restaurant has marble floors and a wooden Renaissance-style ceiling; Italian and Continental cuisine is served.
🖐 €242–€352
🛏 92
🆓
🚌 46, 62, 116

NOVA DOMUS
Map 258 B3
Via G. Savonarola 38, 00195
Tel 06 399511
www.novadomushotel.it
In a quiet location near
St. Peter's, this four-star
hotel has a distinct touch

of the 1950s. Good-sized,
traditionally furnished rooms
in warm hues, with satellite
TV and private bathroom.
The good restaurant
compensates for a notable
lack of eating places in the
area. The staff are friendly
and knowledgeable, and
exceptional private city
guides are provided at a
modest price.

✋ €130–€370
ℹ 117 (40 non-smoking)
🔁
🚇 Cipro Musei Vaticani
🚌 492

ORAZIA
Map 260 H5
Via Buonarroti 51, 00185
Tel 06 446 7202
www.hoteloraziaroma.it
The Orazia is on the fifth
floor of a building on the
Colle Esquilino, just one
street away from the
Colosseo. Guest rooms
are furnished in classic
Italian 19th-century style,
including marble floors.
All have private bath or

shower, hairdryer, telephone,
minibar and satellite TV.
The same Italian style is

found in the breakfast room,
where evening meals can
be served on request.

✋ €90–€200
ℹ 38
🔁
🚇 Vittorio Emanuele
🚌 70, 360

PAVIA
Map 260 G4
Via Gaeta 83, 00185
Tel 06 488 0379
www.hotelpavia.it
Small, simple three-star
hotel in the Termini station
area, overlooking the
ancient remains of Terme
di Diocleziano. The interior
design of the rooms is
not exciting and there is
functional plywood furniture.
However, the rooms do
have satellite/pay TV,
minibar, electronic safe,
internet access points

and basic showers. There
is a pleasant bar/lounge
area open 24 hours. The
hotel is based on two floors,
but there is no elevator.

✋ €70–€160
ℹ 20
🔁 €13 extra
🚇 Castro Pretorio
🚌 492, 495

PICCADILLY
Map off 260 H7
Via Magna Grecia 122, 00183
Tel 06 7047 4858, 06 7046 4859
www.bestwestern.it
Part of the Best Western
chain and extremely good
value for money. It is south
of the city, near the basilica
of San Giovanni, in a busy
shopping street. Elegant,
modern, first-floor lobby, and
light, quiet and moderately
spacious guest rooms. All
have TV, minibar and safe.
The bathrooms are on the
small side, but are fitted with
showers and hairdryers.
There are panoramic views

from the breakfast room
on the ninth floor, which
has red marble floors and
leather sofas.

✋ €75–€165
ℹ 55 (20 non-smoking)
🔁
🚇 San Giovanni or Re di Roma
🚌 87, 360

PONTE SISTO
Map 259 D5
Via dei Pettinari 64, 00186
Tel 06 686310
www.hotelpontesisto.it
This grand hotel is in Rome's
famed jewellers' row, just
along from the Tiber and
the bridge from which it

takes its name. The interior is
truly splendid: marble floors,
glass foyers and ample
reception space, with a fine
courtyard decked with
contemporary wrought-iron
furniture and palm trees,
creating an oasis for its
guests. The guest rooms
are tastefully furnished with
cherrywood suites and all-
marble bathrooms; satellite
TV with the option of internet
access is also available. The
roof terrace has a breathtaking
360-degree view of baroque
Rome.

✋ €310
ℹ 103 (50 non-smoking)
🔁
🚌 116, 280

STAYING

PORTOGHESI

Map 259 E4
Via dei Portoghesi 1, 00186
Tel 06 686 4231
www.hotelportoghesiroma.com

A gem of a hotel, tucked into the labyrinth of the Tor di Nona area, north of Piazza Navona. This is a far cry from tourist Rome—you can feel the city's heartbeat, as mopeds sputter and passers-by chatter. It's easy to miss the unassuming entrance, flanked by potted evergreens: Keep an eye out for the row of dainty flags. Highlights include the breakfast solarium and inevitable roof terrace, which overflows with flowers.

🖐 €150–€185
🛏 28
🔄
🚇 Spagna
🚌 116, 280

PRINCIPESSA TEA

Map 260 G3
Via Sardegna 149, 00187
Tel 06 474 4243
www.hoteltea.com

The Principessa Tea presides over the Via Veneto and Villa Borghese. This is true old-world elegance—traditional and elaborate without being fussy. Oriental carpets, gilt mirrors and mauve upholstery add to the genteel atmosphere. The Ludovici Group deserves high praise for preserving the style of this grande dame hotel. There is an American bar, traditional trattoria and four suites, plus indoor parking on request.

🖐 €70–€160
🛏 38
🔄
🚇 Spagna

REAL ROME

Office: Via delle Cese, 00040 Ariccia
Tel 339 827 1285
www.realrome.com

Why not do the real Roman thing and stay in a stylish apartment in the *centro storico*? Browse the selection of apartments online, then contact this friendly agency. The coordinator is Tim Pearson; most owners speak English. Don't be surprised if the kitchen—well stocked with staples such as olive oil and coffee—also comes with a gift of fresh pastries. Highly

RAPHAEL

Map 259 D4
Largo Febo 2, 00186
Tel 06 682831
www.raphaelhotel.com

Day or night, the ivy-covered façade of this hotel, a few steps away from Piazza Navona, always looks a dream. There is a period feel to the antique-filled lobby, with its golden velvet sofas and gilt tables. The guest rooms are littered with objets d'art and are beautifully furnished, mixing patterns and faux-marble. Facilities in the rooms include satellite TV, safe and minibar. The restaurant is of international repute and the roof terrace has unparalleled views of the city. There are also fitness facilities.

🖐 €390–€420, excluding breakfast
🛏 47 (5 non-smoking)
🔄 🎿
🚌 40, 62, 64, 87, 116, 492, 628 to Piazza Navona

recommended for those craving privacy and a slightly different experience of the Eternal City. There is a three-day minimum stay, and credit cards are not accepted.

🖐 €70–€110
🛏 54 apartments
🔄 40 apartments

RESIDENCE BARBERINI

Map 259 F4
Via Quattro Fontane 171–172, 00184
Tel 06 420 3341
www.residencebarberini.com

These sleek suites are packed with modern gadgets: All have a king-sized bed, marble bathroom, TV with DVD, personal computer, internet access, printer, webcam, fax, microwave

oven and refrigerator. The penthouse includes a large roof garden with wicker loungers, dining table and pavilion. Furnishings are simple and elegant, including snowy-white quilts and wrought-iron bed frames. Breakfasts are served in the guest rooms or on the terrace. Contemporary art is exhibited in the communal areas.

🖐 €250–€340, excluding breakfast
🛏 11 suites (6 non-smoking)
🔄
🚇 Barberini

RESIDENCE PALAZZO AL VELABRO

Map 259 E6
Via del Velabro 16, 00186
Tel 06 679 2758, 06 679 2985
www.velabro.it

Surrounded by ancient monuments and just across from the Tiber, this is self-

sufficiency in a dream setting. The apartments are light and very spacious, with a living/dining room with folding door concealing a gallery kitchen, plus bedroom and bathroom. Lemon walls, satellite TV and comfortable sofa beds all make for a relaxed atmosphere. There is a bar and two terraces for enjoying the stunning views. Ideal for families.

🖐 €166–€202, excluding breakfast
🛏 35
🔄
🚌 81, 160, 204, 628, then 15-min walk

ROMA PARK

Map off 260 H7
Via della Caffarelletta 114, 00179
Tel 06 7835 9552
www.romapark.com
Originally a villa, this hotel
in a leafy suburb, overlooking
the archaeological park of
Caffarella, maintains the
atmosphere of a large country
house. Rooms have a light,
spacious feel, pastel walls
and cherry-wood furnishings.
All have bathroom and satellite
TV. The cheerful breakfast
room, furnished in bamboo,
serves a buffet breakfast,
while the adjoining roof
garden is the perfect spot for
an evening *aperitivo*. There is
private parking, and some very
good inexpensive trattorias
nearby.

€110–€130
42
Furio Camillo
628

SANT'ANSELMO

Map off 259 E7
Piazza S. Anselmo 2, 00153
Tel 06 578 3214
www.aventinohotels.com
This hotel has a serene setting
high on the Aventine Hill, and
is just minutes from the Circo
Massimo. The predominant
style is 19th-century, but the
furnishings have overtones
of Napoleonic grandeur.
The extremely elegant

rooms have marble floors,
embroidered bedspreads and
gilt-edged furniture, plus
satellite TV, electronic safes
and stylish bathrooms.
A Continental breakfast
is served in a garden
shaded by orange trees
in summer, and there is
a roof terrace.

€104–€166
46
23, 75, 175, 715, 716; tram 3

SANTA MARIA

Map 259 D6
Vicolo del Piede 2, 00153
Tel 06 589 4626, 06 589 5474
www.hotelsantamaria.com
In the heart of Trastevere, and
close to the church of the
same name, is this charming
little hotel. The former 15th-
century cloister is now a
private, tranquil garden with
orange trees, and all the rooms
bar one open onto it. The
guest rooms are large, and all
have satellite TV, safe, minibar
and hairdryer, plus internet
connection. There is also
private parking.

€155–€210
20
H, 780; tram 8

SANTA PRASSEDE

Map 260 G5
Via di Santa Prassede 25, 00184
Tel 06 481 4850
www.hotelsantaprassede.it
The street and hotel take their
name from the church of Santa
Prassede, known for its early

Christian mosaics; Santa Maria
Maggiore is just around the
corner. The 27 quiet guest
rooms, all in typically Roman
shades and with dark wooden
floors, have private bathroom,
central heating and safe
deposit box. There is a bar and
a TV lounge as part of the
communal areas. Laundry
service available.

€80–€145
25
Termini or Cavour
64, 70, 71

SCALINATA DI SPAGNA

Map 259 F3
Piazza Trinità dei Monti 17, 00187
Tel 06 679 3006
www.hotelscalinata.com
You need to reserve months—if
not years—in advance at this
boutique hotel at the top of

the Spanish Steps. La
Scalinata's 16 rooms are
highly coveted (especially
those with the best views).
The breakfast terrace,
overlooking the red-tiled
roofs and cupolas, has
wrought-iron chairs and
riots of blossom. Active
visitors enjoy jogging in the
nearby Villa Borghese park.
The less active can plug in a
laptop, or use the free
internet TV with email
service.

€160–€250
16 (5 non-smoking)
Spagna
116

STARGATE HOSTEL AND HOTEL

Map 260 H4
Via Palestra 88, 00185
Tel 06 445 7164
www.stargatehotels.com
Very clean and efficient hostel/
hotel near Termini station, and
it's extremely good value. The
first option is to stay at the
hostel, which has dormitory
rooms sleeping four to six
people. These are spacious,
with bunk-beds, desks, chairs,
wardrobe, washbasin, TV and
internet access. The hostel
also has its own internet
lounge and kitchen. Some
rooms come with own shower,
and there is a communal
shower on each floor. Towels
and linen are provided and
there's a launderette. No
curfew is imposed. The hotel

rooms are similar but more private, catering for one or two people. An Italian breakfast of coffee and brioche is included.

🖐 Hostel €50–€80, hotel €40–€90
ⓘ Hostel 20, hotel 20
⑤ €15 extra
🚇 Castro Pretorio or Termini
🚌 492

SWEET HOME
Map 260 G4
Via Principe Amedeo 47, 00185
Tel 06 488 0954
www.hotelsweethome.it
Near Termini station, Sweet Home is a two-star hotel with a late 19th-century feel to it.

It has high ceilings and spacious rooms with simple, painted wooden tables, TV, comfortable sofas and bright design; half the rooms have a bath, half a shower. The breakfast room has a bar, which is open throughout the day, and there is a charming, private room with chandelier available for meetings. There's also an internet access point. Hotel staff are friendly and helpful.

🖐 €56–€95
ⓘ 18
🚇 Termini
🚌 40, 64, 70

TEATRO DI POMPEO
Map 259 D5
Largo del Pallaro 8, 00186
Tel 06 6830 0170
www.hotelteatrodipompeo.it
The Theatre of Pompey—site of Caesar's assassination in 44BC—was absorbed into a medieval palazzo, where this boutique hotel can now be found. It is just steps away from the Campo dei Fiori, but insulated from its noise. Breakfast is taken in an archaeological site, a cavern dotted with palms. All rooms are double or twin, with private bath and simple

interiors: turquoise coverlets, terracotta tiles and wood-beam ceilings stained dark with age. Avoid the less charming annexe. Other facilities include room service, babysitting and laundry.

🖐 €170–€190
ⓘ 12
⑤
🚌 46, 62, 64, 87, 116, 492 to Campo dei Fiori

TRASTEVERE
Map 259 D6
Via Luciano Manara 24, 00153
Tel 06 581 4713
www.hoteltrastevere.net
Very small, family-run hotel overlooking the lively market of San Cosimato and just a few minutes from

Piazza di Santa Maria in Trastevere. The charming entrance hall is painted in pastels, with the occasional garland adorning the walls. Rooms are plainly furnished in light tones, have bath and hairdryer, and all look out onto the delightful square. The Continental buffet breakfast is served on the ground floor next to the entrance hall. An elevator is available.

🖐 €80–€105
ⓘ 23
⑤ 10
🚌 H, 44, 780 rooms; tram 3, 8

TRITONE
Map 259 E4
Via del Tritone 210, 00187
Tel 06 6992 2575
www.travelroma.com
This hotel has a great location, just 100m (110yd) from the Trevi Fountain, making it ideal for exploring the centro storico of the city. Breakfast is served on the roof terrace, from which there are fabulous views. The rooms are clean

and simply furnished, and all are soundproofed.

🖐 €150–€228
ⓘ 43
⑤
🚇 Barberini
🚌 175, 204, 492, 590

VICTORIA
Map 260 F3
Via Campania 41, 00187
Tel 06 473931
www.hotelvictoriaroma.com
Efficiently run by its Swiss management, the Victoria is just inside the Aurelian Walls, at the top of Via Veneto and within striking distance of the area's restaurants. The bedrooms are large, as are the bathrooms, and all rooms have satellite TV. In the summer months, the buffet breakfast is served in the roof garden. The hotel also has a bar and restaurant, and private parking is available.

🖐 €120–€280
ⓘ 113
⑤
🚇 Spagna
🚌 95, 116, 116T, 119, 204

VILLA SAN PIO
Map off 259 E7
Via S. Melania 19, 00153
Tel 06 574 5174
www.aventinohotels.com
This hotel is in a peaceful location on the exclusive Aventine Hill. The entrance hall is bright with an inlaid marble floor, and antiques are scattered throughout the hotel. Guest rooms are sumptuously furnished in late 18th-century style—elaborate bed furnishings, parquet floors, rich gold and red hues—and come with satellite TV and an electronic safe. The bathrooms are luxurious; some come with whirlpool baths and power showers. There are helpful staff and a 24-hour bar.

🖐 €140–€240
ⓘ 76
⑤
🚇 Piramide
🚌 23, 30, 60, 75, 673, 716; tram 3

HOTEL CHAINS

Name of hotel chain	Description	Hotels in Rome	Website and phone number
Best Western	The world's largest group, with 4,000 independently owned hotels in 80 countries.	8	www.bestwestern.it
Boscolo Hotels	Seventeen luxury hotels in some of the most sophisticated cities in Italy and beyond.	3	www.boscolohotels.com
Charming Hotels	The Charming Hotels group was founded only in 1995, but it already has 60 luxury hotels worldwide.	5	www.thecharminghotels.it
The Giannetti Hotels Group	Italian chain of stylish three- and four-star hotels.	1	www.thegiannettihotelsgroup.com
Golden Tulip (inc. Tulip Inns)	This Netherlands-based company has around 440 hotels in 51 countries, branded as either Golden Tulip (four-star hotels) or Tulip Inns (three stars).	5	www.goldentulip.com
Hilton	This American-based chain of top-class hotels has almost 500 branches throughout the world.	1	www.hilton.com
Ibis	Part of the French Accor group, Ibis is a fast-growing chain, with more than 670 hotels worldwide.	1	www.ibishotel.com
ITI Hotels	A group of 30 hotels, mostly in Sardinia, but also in Rome, South, Central and North America.	1	www.itihotels.it
Jolly Hotels	Jolly has been running hotels in Italy since 1949 and now has establishments in 26 cities there.	4	www.jollyhotels.it
Mercure	Part of the French group Accor, Mercure has 715 hotels in 45 countries, at various price levels.	3	www.mercure.com
Le Meridien	Le Meridien is a global hotel group with over 135 luxury hotels in 56 countries.	1	www.lemeridien.com
Novotel	Part of the French group Accor, Novotel has 373 hotels in 63 countries.	1	www.novotel.com
Quality Inns/ Comfort Inns	Quality Inns offer mid-priced accommodation, while Comfort Inns is a limited-service chain.	1 1	www.choicehotels.com
Rocco Forte Hotels	Rocco Forte Hotels is a collection of nine individual, luxury hotels in key locations around the world.	1	www.roccofortehotels.com
Roscioli Hotels	A family-owned chain of prestigious four-star hotels, all in the heart of Rome.	4	www.rosciolihotels.it
Sina Hotels	Founded by the Bocca family in 1959, Sina Hotels now has six four- and five-star hotels in key Italian cities.	1	www.sinahotels.it
Sofitel	Part of the French group Accor, Sofitel is the company's premium brand, with 160 hotels worldwide.	1	www.sofitel.com
Sol Meliá	Spain's leading hotel company has over 350 hotels in 30 countries.	1	www.solmelia.com
Starwood Hotels	Starwood is the name behind such prestigious hotel chains as Sheraton, Westin and St. Regis, owning, leasing or managing almost 750 hotels in 79 countries.	5	www.starwood.com

STAYING

Planning

CLIMATE

Rome's weather can be unpredictable. Rainfall can be high, even in the warmer, summer months but, equally, you can experience bright, clear, cold days in winter. The charts below show what you are likely to find, but it best to pack for all eventualities.

WHEN TO GO

The best time to visit Rome is in spring or autumn (fall), when the temperature should be pleasantly warm. There is less risk of rain than in the winter months, but you might still catch the occasional shower. The downside of visiting at this time of year is that everyone else does too. Easter, especially, is popular, with high numbers of tourists swollen by visiting pilgrims to the Holy City. The summer, particularly July and August, can be oppressively hot, with temperatures of up to 40°C (105°F) broken by sudden and dramatic thunderstorms. Many Romans take their holidays in

August, and it is not unusual for shops and restaurants to be closed for between two weeks and a month. Winters are generally mild and damp, and snow is rare.

WEATHER REPORTS

Weather reports are given during most news bulletins on Italian channels, as well as on English-language channels shown on satellite TV, such as CNN and BBC World.

You can also check the website of your local news network station, such as the BBC (www.bbc.co.uk) or CNN (www.cnn.com), or a specialist website like the Weather Channel (www.weather.com).

WHAT TO TAKE

La bella figura is alive and well, and living in Rome. Romans tend to dress smartly at all times, and anyone appearing scruffy is likely to be stared at—although you won't be refused admission to most places.
- Most importantly, bring comfortable shoes. You will probably do a lot of walking, either through the streets or around museums or archaeological sites—very tiring on the feet.
- Bring clothes that cover your shoulders and knees for visiting churches. A lightweight raincoat is useful for summer showers, as is a folding umbrella.
- A small bag is handy for daily use, such as a shoulder bag that can be worn across the body, or a money belt.
- Bring your address book, for emergency contacts or postcards, and photocopies of all important documents, such as your passport and insurance details.
- A torch (flashlight) is useful for viewing works of art in dark churches. You may also find binoculars useful for a closer look.

Italy is on Central European Time (CET), one hour ahead of GMT (Greenwich Mean Time, measured from London) during the winter. At the end of March, the clocks are put forward by one hour, and then put back again at the end of October.

CITY	TIME DIFFERENCE	TIME AT 12 NOON IN ITALY
Amsterdam	0	noon
Auckland	+11	11pm
Berlin	0	noon
Brussels	0	noon
Chicago	-7	5am
Dublin	-1	11am
Johannesburg	+1	1pm
London	-1	11am
Madrid	0	noon
Montréal	-6	6am
New York	-6	6am
Paris	0	noon
Perth, Australia	+7	7pm
San Francisco	-9	3am
Sydney	+9	9pm
Tokyo	+8	8pm

- Bring a first-aid kit, including plasters (Band Aids), antiseptic cream, painkillers and any prescription medicine.
- Don't forget an Italian phrasebook. Although most people you meet will speak English, any attempt at Italian is always appreciated.
- Earplugs are useful if you are a light sleeper, or if your hotel doesn't have double glazing. Rome is a noisy city.

PASSPORTS

British citizens need a passport to enter Italy. Visitors from other EU countries should contact the Italian embassy in their home country for details of the documentation required. Non-EU visitors will need a passport,

TEMPERATURE

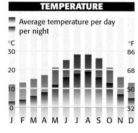

Average temperature per day
per night

°C 30 20 10 0
°F 86 68 50 32

J F M A M J J A S O N D

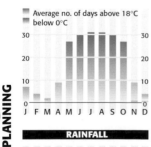

Average no. of days above 18°C
below 0°C

30 20 10 0

J F M A M J J A S O N D

RAINFALL

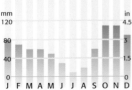

Average rainfall

mm 120 80 40 0
in 4.5 3 1.5 0

J F M A M J J A S O N D

PLANNING

which should be valid for at least six months from the date of entry.

If you intend to work or study in Italy, make sure your passport is stamped with your date of entry. You will need it to apply for a *Permesso di Soggiorno*.

VISAS

If you are an EU national, or are from Australia, Canada, New Zealand or the United States, you do not need a visa for stays of up to 90 days. To extend your visit for a further 90 days, you can, one time only, apply to any police station. This extension cannot be used for studying or employment, and you must prove that you can support yourself financially.

If you are a citizen of a country not mentioned above, you should contact the Italian embassy in your home country to check visa requirements.

Visa and passport regulations differ depending on your nationality and are subject to change. Check prior to a visit and follow news events that may affect the situation.

DUTY-FREE AND DUTY-PAID GUIDELINES

Anything that is clearly for personal use can be taken into Italy free of duty. However, it is worth carrying receipts in case you need to prove on your return home that they weren't bought while you were in Italy.

For the most up-to-date information on duty-free and duty-paid allowance, see either the US Department of Homeland Security's website (www.customs.treas.gov) or that of HM Customs and Excise (www.hmce.gov.uk). You cannot buy goods duty-free if you are journeying within the EU.

Whatever your entitlement, you cannot bring home goods for payment (including payment in kind) or for resale. These goods are considered for commercial use, and duty is payable.

CUSTOMS

Importing wildlife souvenirs from rare or endangered species may be either illegal or require a special permit. Check customs regulations before you buy.

HEALTH ISSUES

No vaccinations are necessary, unless you are coming from an

DUTY-FREE AND DUTY-PAID GUIDELINES

Duty-paid guidelines for non-EU citizens

US citizens can bring home up to $800 of duty-paid goods, provided they have been out of the country for at least 48 hours and haven't made another international trip in the past 30 days. This limit applies to all members of the family, regardless of age, and exemptions may be pooled.

- 200 cigarettes; or
- 100 cigarillos; or
- 50 cigars; or
- 250g smoking tobacco

- 1 litre of spirits or strong liquors
- 2 litres of still table wine
- 2 litres of fortified wine, sparkling wine or other liquors
- 60cc/ml of perfume
- 250cc/ml of toilet water

Duty-paid guidelines for EU citizens

European Union citizens can take home unlimited amounts of duty-paid goods, as long as they are for personal use. In the UK, HM Customs and Excise consider anything over the following guidelines as for commercial use:

- 3200 cigarettes; or
- 400 cigarillos; or
- 200 cigars; or
- 3kg of tobacco
- 110 litres of beer

- 10 litres of spirits
- 90 litres of wine (of which only 60 litres can be sparkling wine)
- 20 litres of fortified wine (such as port or sherry)

ITALIAN EMBASSIES ABROAD

Australia
12 Grey Street, Deakin,
ACT 2600
Tel 02 6273 3333
www.ambitalia.org.au

Canada
275 Slater Street,
21st Floor, Ottawa, Ontario
K1P 5H9
Tel 613 232 2401
www.italyincanada.com

Ireland
63/65 Northumberland
Road, Dublin 4
Tel 01 6601744
www.italianembassy.ie

New Zealand
34–38 Grant Road,
P. O. Box 463, Thorndon,
Wellington
Tel 04 4735 339
www.italy-embassy.org.nz

South Africa
796 George Avenue,
Arcadia 0083 Pretoria
Tel 430 5541/2/3/4
www.ambital.org.za

UK
14 Three Kings Yard,
London W1K 4EH
Tel 020 7312 2200
www.embitaly.org.uk

USA
3000 Whitehaven Street
NW, Washington DC 20008
Tel 202 612 4400
www.italyemb.org

infected area. If you have any doubts, contact your doctor before your trip. Take out your insurance as soon as you book your journey. If you leave it too close to your departure date you may not be covered for delays.

Make sure your insurance policy is valid for the duration of your visit. Most policies cover cancellation, medical expenses, accident compensation, personal liability, and personal belongings (including money). Your policy should cover the cost of getting you home in a medical emergency.

If you have private medical cover, check your policy, as you may be covered while you are away. Also, check your home contents insurance: It may cover

loss of money and personal belongings away from home.

As well as health insurance, European citizens should carry a European Health Insurance Card (EHIC; formerly the E111 form), available from post offices, health centres and social security offices. This entitles you to free or reduced-cost healthcare. Health insurance often doesn't cover treatment you can obtain with this card. Each person travelling needs their own EHIC, and needs to get it stamped in their home country.

For up-to-date information, see the Department of Health's website on www.doh.gov.uk (in the UK), or the National Center for Infectious Diseases on www.cdc.gov/travel in the US.

PRACTICALITIES

ELECTRICITY
- The power supply is 240 volts.
- Plugs have two (or sometimes three) round pins. It is a good idea to bring an adaptor with you, although these are readily available in the city.
- Visitors from North America should also bring a transformer for appliances operating on 110/120 volts; again, you can find these in Rome.

LAUNDRY
Most visitors trust their laundry to their hotel, where your clothes are returned to your room and the charge (usually high) added to your bill. However, there are alternatives:
- Rome's old-style cleaners (*tintorie*) are still plentiful in the city. Charges start at around €2, but check the rate for any additional services, such as pressing pleats. A *tintoria* will also provide a dry-cleaning service. There are plenty of modern laundries (*lavanderie*) in the city, too.
- Self-service launderettes are few and far between. One of the most central is Punto Blu at Via Cavour 168, tel 06 481 7857 (open daily 8am–10pm).

MEASUREMENTS
- Italy uses the metric system, with all foodstuffs sold by the kilogram or litre. Italians also use the *ettogramme* (hectogram—100g or just under 4oz), usually abbreviated to *etto*.
- Fuel is sold by the litre, and distances are measured in kilometres.

TOILETS
- You will find public toilets at railway stations and in larger museums, but otherwise they are few and far between. There are toilets in Piazza San Pietro, either side of the square, and others at the Colosseo.
- In other parts of Rome you will need to use the toilet in a bar or café. Although they are obliged to let you use their facilities, staff prefer you to buy something.
- Facilities can be basic, to say the least. Toilet paper may or may not be provided, and sometimes there is only one toilet for both men and women.

CONVERSION CHART

FROM	TO	MULTIPLY BY
Inches	Centimetres	2.54
Centimetres	Inches	0.3937
Feet	Metres	0.3048
Metres	Feet	3.2810
Yards	Metres	0.9144
Metres	Yards	1.0940
Miles	Kilometres	1.6090
Kilometres	Miles	0.6214
Acres	Hectares	0.4047
Hectares	Acres	2.4710
Gallons	Litres	4.5460
Litres	Gallons	0.2200
Ounces	Grams	28.35
Grams	Ounces	0.0353
Pounds	Grams	453.6
Grams	Pounds	0.0022
Pounds	Kilograms	0.4536
Kilograms	Pounds	2.205
Tons	Tonnes	1.0160
Tonnes	Tons	0.9842

- In some places there will be a dish for gratuities—you should tip around 25c.
- Where separate facilities exist, make sure you recognize the difference between *signori* (men) and *signore* (women).

SMOKING
- Smoking is still very popular in Italy. However, a new law prohibiting smoking in all public areas—including bars and restaurants—is now in force. It also covers public transport, airport buildings and public offices, such as post offices and police stations.
- Cigarettes and other tobacco products can only legally be sold in *tabacchi* (tobacconists) and only to those over 16. The stand-alone *tabacchi* are only open during normal shop hours (usually 8–1, 3.30–8), but others are attached to bars, so stay open longer.

CLOTHING SIZES

Clothing sizes in Italy are in metric. Use the chart below to convert the size you use at home.

UK	Metric	US	
36	46	36	SUITS
38	48	38	
40	50	40	
42	52	42	
44	54	44	
46	56	46	
48	58	48	
7	41	8	SHOES
7.5	42	8.5	
8.5	43	9.5	
9.5	44	10.5	
10.5	45	11.5	
11	46	12	
14.5	37	14.5	SHIRTS
15	38	15	
15.5	39/40	15.5	
16	41	16	
16.5	42	16.5	
17	43	17	
8	36	6	DRESSES
10	38	8	
12	40	10	
14	42	12	
16	44	14	
18	46	16	
20	46	18	
4.5	37.5	6	SHOES
5	38	6.5	
5.5	38.5	7	
6	39	7.5	
6.5	40	8	
7	41	8.5	

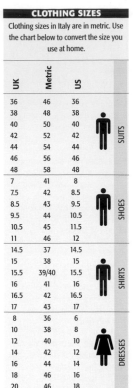

LOCAL WAYS
- A few words of Italian will always go down well (▷ 291–296), even if you can only manage hello and goodbye.
- Italians tend to use please and thank you less frequently than other nationalities.
- Use *buongiorno* up to midday, and *buonasera* in the afternoon and evening.

Italian is as much about gestures as it is about words

- Show respect and dress appropriately when visiting places of worship. Cover your shoulders and knees. St. Peter's in particular has a strict dress and conduct code.
- Don't intrude on religious services unless you wish to take part.
- Always check before taking photographs in churches and museums, and never use flash on pictures, frescoes or mosaics.
- Italians tend to drink only with meals, and public drunkenness is frowned upon.
- In cafés, never pay bar prices then attempt to use the tables.
- If you only want a one-course meal, eat in a pizzeria. It's considered bad form to eat fewer than two courses in a restaurant.
- Be polite but assertive when waiting to be served. Although it may look disorganized, everyone knows who is in front of them (▷ 13).

VISITING ROME WITH CHILDREN

- Children are welcomed at most restaurants. Although children's menus are rare, most places will serve up small portions, and will often produce simple meals of pasta in tomato sauce or pizza.
- Disposable nappies (diapers) and baby foods are available in many food shops, but changing facilties are hard to find. Museums and restaurants with the most modern facilities are your best option.

- A lack of public toilets, most of which will not be as clean as you'd like (see opposite), can make things difficult for people with very young children. Always carry tissues or wipes, as not all establishments will supply toilet paper.
- Rome has few attractions specifically aimed at children, many of whom will get bored visiting museums and galleries. As a compromise, look out for things that will interest your child, such as animals in paintings or as part of sculptures.
- Admission to most of Rome's museums and galleries is free for under-18s. Where there is a charge, it is usually reduced for children.
- Children under age 10 travel free on Rome's public transport system. Some of Rome's metro stations are not accessible with prams (baby carriages).
- ▷ 194 for suggested attractions for children.

VISITORS WITH DISABILITIES

- Wheelchair access in Rome is improving, but very slowly. It is always worth checking with individual establishments what their access is like. The narrow, cobbled streets and lack of pavements can prove difficult for people with mobility issues.
- All the major hotels, as well as the newer ones, should have wheelchair access. In older buildings, it is not always possible to make the changes needed, and you should contact the

USEFUL CONTACTS FOR VISITORS WITH DISABILITIES

CO.IN Sociale Via Enrico Giglioli 54a, Rome, tel 800 271027, www.coinsociale.it (in English and Italian)
Useful information on accessible sights. Publishes guides, organizes guided tours; minibus available for excursions and transfers.
Holiday Care 7th Floor, Sunley House, 4 Bedford Park, Croydon, Surrey CR0 2AP, tel 0845 124 9971, fax 0845 124 9972, www.holidaycare.org.uk Publications and information on accessibility.
SATH (Society for Accessible Travel and Hospitality), 347 Fifth Avenue, Suite 610, New York NY10016, tel 212-441-7284, fax 212-727-8253, www.sath.org
Lots of tips on how to travel with mobility or visual impairment.

individual hotels to ask about your specific needs.
- Rome's public transport system has improved in recent years, and around half the stations are accessible by wheelchairs. Most new buses have ramps that can be lowered for access.
- ▷ 54 for more information.

PLACES OF WORSHIP

The majority of Rome's churches are Catholic, and Basilica di San Pietro is the most important. The Catholic churches below have services in English on Sundays.
Other religions are well represented: If your faith is not shown below, contact the tourist information office for details of your nearest place of worship.

Catholic	San Silvestro, Piazza San Silvestro 1, tel 06 679 7775. Santa Suzanna, Piazza San Bernardo, tel 06 488 2748
Jewish	Sinagoga (Synagogue), Lungotevere Cenci, tel 06 6840 0661
Muslim	Moschea di Roma, Viale della Moschea, tel 06 808 2167
Protestant	St. Paul's Episcopal, Chiesa Americana di San Paolo, Via Napoli 58, tel 06 488 3339 Anglican Church of England, All Saints', Via del Babuino 153b, tel 06 3600 1881 Presbyterian Church of Scotland, Chiesa di Scozia, Via XX Settembre 7, tel 06 482 7627
Orthodox	Chiesa Ortodossa Copta, Via Sante Bargellini 13, tel 06 4173 4446

PLANNING

Italy is one of 12 European countries that have adopted the euro as their official currency. Euro notes and coins were introduced in January 2002, replacing the former currency, the lira.

BEFORE YOU GO
● It's advisable to use a combination of cash, travellers' cheques and credit cards, rather than relying on one means of payment during your trip.
● Check with your bank and/or credit card company that you can withdraw cash from ATMs. You should also check what fee will be charged and what number you should call if your card is lost or stolen.
● Notify your credit card company that you will be using your card abroad. Some place blocks on use overseas for security reasons.
● Remember to keep a separate note of your travellers' cheque numbers, with a note of the number to call if they are stolen.

LOST/STOLEN CREDIT CARDS
American Express
06 7228 0371
Diners Club
800 864064
CartaSi including MasterCard and Visa
800 151616
MasterCard
800 870866
Visa
800 877232

EXCHANGE RATES
● The euro exchange rate for visitors is subject to daily fluctuation. For up-to-date rates for a wide range of currencies, visit www.oanda.com.

CREDIT CARDS
● Italians have traditionally used cash, but this is changing and credit and debit cards are now more widely accepted, but not for small sums. Look for the credit card symbols in the shop window or check with the staff.

● Food bills are usually paid for in cash. Market traders and smaller establishments will often only take cash.

TRAVELLERS' CHEQUES
● Travellers' cheques are accepted almost everywhere. For the best exchange rates, take travellers' cheques in euros, pounds sterling or US dollars.
● There is a branch of Thomas Cook at Piazza Barberini, and a branch of American Express in Piazza di Spagna. They will cash travellers' cheques issued by their company without charging commission.

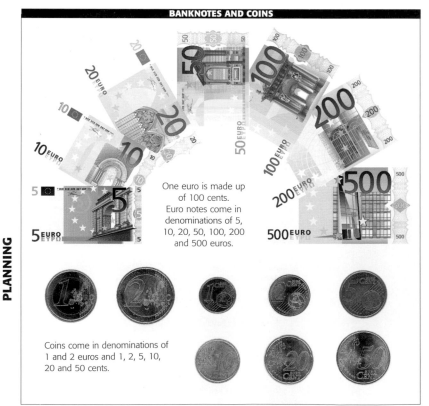

BANKNOTES AND COINS

One euro is made up of 100 cents. Euro notes come in denominations of 5, 10, 20, 50, 100, 200 and 500 euros.

Coins come in denominations of 1 and 2 euros and 1, 2, 5, 10, 20 and 50 cents.

PLANNING

LOST AND STOLEN CARDS AND TRAVELLERS' CHEQUES

● If your credit card or bank card is stolen, report it to the police and the appropriate emergency number. All are open 24 hours a day and have English-speaking staff.
● If your travellers' cheques are stolen, notify the police, then follow the instructions given with the cheques. You can contact the Rome office of American Express or Thomas Cook, or telephone the following toll-free numbers:
– For American Express travellers' cheques, call 800 872000
– For Thomas Cook travellers' cheques, call 800 872050

ATMS

● Cash machines, called Bancomats in Italy, are plentiful in Rome, and many are accessible 24 hours a day.
● Most have instructions in English (and other languages) as well as Italian.
● Check with your bank before leaving home that you will be able to access your account from Italy.

BANKS

● There is no shortage of banks in Rome, most of which have cash machines and exchange facilities, although there are often long queues for this as they offer the best rates.
● Banks are usually open from 8.30 until 1 or 1.30, and again for an hour or so in the afternoon. Some now open on Saturdays.

BUREAUX DE CHANGE

● There are bureaux de change (cambio) all over the city, usually open throughout the day until around 7.30. They often offer 'commission-free' exchange, but the exchange rates are not usually as good as those from banks.

DISCOUNTS

● EU citizens who are over 65 can often get discounted admission charges to museums and galleries—use your passport or driver's licence as proof of age.
● Children's admission charges are usually available up to 18 years of age, and reductions on the full adult rate are sometimes made for 18–26 year olds.
● Students sometimes qualify for discounts. You should apply for a Student Identity Card from the ISIC (▷ 50).
● Sometimes these discounts are only available for European citizens.

WIRING MONEY

● Wiring money is a lengthy process and the bureaucracy involved means that it is probably not worthwhile unless you are planning to be in Rome for a while.
● Ask your bank at home for a list of affiliated banks. You can get money wired to any bank from home, but if your bank already has a connection with certain banks in Italy, it will make the process a lot easier.
● If you have a bank account in Italy and at home, you can transfer money directly if both banks are part of the Swift system of international transfers. Again, it takes about 5–7 days, if not longer.

● Always ask for a separate letter, telex or fax to be sent to Swift, confirming that the money has been sent. It can take up to a week for the money to transfer.
● American Express, Moneygram and Western Union Money Transfers are faster from the US, but more expensive. Citibank has a service where you can transfer money for a flat fee of $10 to anywhere in the world.

TAX REFUNDS

● Sales tax, known as IVA, is added to all goods and services in Italy.
● Visitors from non-EU countries are entitled to reimbursement of the tax paid on major purchases.
● The store must provide a properly completed invoice (una fattura), itemizing all goods, the price paid for them and the tax charged, as well as full address details of both the vendor and the purchaser.
● The goods must be taken out of the EU within three months of the date of purchase.
● When leaving Italy, present the fattura to customs for stamping. You may need to show the goods, so make sure they are easy to reach.
● When you get home, send the stamped receipt to the shop. Your refund will either be made by cheque or directly back to your credit card account.

TIPPING

Italians do not tip heavily. Service is often included in your hotel or restaurant bill, although a little extra is appreciated, if the service has been good. The following is a general guide:

Pizzerias/trattorias: round up to the nearest euro
Smart restaurants: 10%
Bar service: up to 25c, or 5–10% for table service
Taxis: round up to nearest 50c
Porters: 50c–€1 per bag
Chambermaids: 50c–€1 per day
Cloakroom attendants: 50c
Toilets: 25c

10 EVERYDAY ITEMS AND HOW MUCH THEY COST	
Takeaway sandwich	€3
Bottle of water	75c
Cup of coffee (outside/inside)	80c/€3.50
Beer–half a litre (outside/inside)	€3.50/€7
Glass of house wine (outside/inside)	€1/€5
Daily newspaper (Italian)	€1.20
Roll of camera film	€5
20 cigarettes	€3.50
Ice cream (takeaway)	€3.50
Litre of petrol (gasoline)	€1.15

Visitors from many countries are entitled to free or reduced-cost emergency health treatment through Italy's national health system, both from doctors and hospitals.

BEFORE YOU GO

● No vaccinations are required, but it is a good idea to check when you last had a tetanus injection and, if more than 10 years ago, have a booster before you travel.

● Italy has a standard agreement with other EU countries entitling EU citizens to a certain amount of free health care, including hospital treatment. In the UK, you should ask for a European Health Insurance Card (EHIC) before you leave home (▷ 277).

● If you will need treatment for a pre-existing condition while you are away, such as injections, you should apply to your department of health for an E112.

● Despite this reciprical arrangement, you are strongly advised to take out travel insurance. For non-EU visitors this is essential.

● Vistors from the US and Canada may find that their existing health policy covers them while they are abroad. Check with your insurance company before you travel, and remember to bring your policy identification card.

● Check with your doctor or pharmacist for the chemical name of any prescription drugs you need, in case you have to replace them while you are away. The brand name will often change from country to country.

● It is a good idea to take photocopies of all important documentation, such as travel insurance and your EHIC (for EU citizens), which should be kept separate from the originals. You could scan the photocopies, and send them to an email address that can be accessed anywhere in the world.

HOW TO GET A DOCTOR (UN MEDICO)

● To get in touch with a doctor, it's best to ask at your hotel reception. There is also a group of American doctors practising at Via Ludovisi 36, 00187 (tel 06 488 4143).

HEALTHY FLYING

● Visitors to Italy from as far as the US, Australia or New Zealand may be concerned about the effect of long-haul flights on their health. The most widely publicized concern is deep vein thrombosis, or DVT. Misleadingly called 'economy class syndrome', DVT is the forming of a blood clot in the body's deep veins, particularly in the legs. The clot can move around the bloodstream and could be fatal.

● Those most at risk include the elderly, pregnant women and those using the contraceptive pill, smokers and the overweight. If you are at increased risk of DVT see your doctor before departing. Flying increases the likelihood of DVT because passengers are often seated in a cramped position for long periods of time and may become dehydrated.

To minimize risk:
Drink water (not alcohol)
Don't stay immobile for hours at a time
Stretch and exercise your legs periodically
Do wear elastic flight socks, which support veins and reduce the chances of a clot forming

EXERCISES

1 ANKLE ROTATIONS	2 CALF STRETCHES	3 KNEE LIFTS

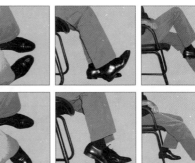

Lift feet off the floor. Draw a circle with the toes, moving one foot clockwise and the other counterclockwise | Start with heel on the floor and point foot upward as high as you can. Then lift heels high, keeping balls of feet on the floor | Lift leg with knee bent while contracting your thigh muscle. Then straighten leg, pressing foot flat to the floor

Other health hazards for flyers are airborne diseases and bugs spread by the plane's air-conditioning system. These are largely unavoidable but if you have a serious medical condition seek advice from a doctor before flying.

HOW TO GET TREATMENT WITH YOUR EHIC

● If you are taken ill while you are away, take your EHIC to the Unità Sanitaria Locale (USL) office (ask your hotel reception or consult the *Pagine Gialle*, Yellow Pages), who will give you a certificate of entitlement. Take this to any doctor or dentist on the USL list for free treatment.

● If you are referred to a hospital, you will be given a certificate that entitles you to free treatment. If you go to hospital without being referred by a doctor, you should give the EHIC to the hospital.

● If you do not have a USL certificate, you will have to pay for treatment and may have difficulty getting the money back afterwards, and then probably only a partial refund.

● If you are charged in full for medicines, keep the price tags—you will not get a refund without them.

● It is advisable to carry a photocopy of your EHIC, as some doctors and hospitals keep the form. If they do, you can pick up another form when you get home.

PLANNING

• In addition to your EHIC, make sure you have adequate medical cover as part of your travel insurance.

HOW TO GET TREATMENT WITH TRAVEL INSURANCE

• Take copies of your travel insurance documents to the doctor or hospital—they may be able to bill your insurance company direct.
• If you pay for treatment, keep all your receipts as you won't be able to make an insurance claim without them.

DENTISTS (DENTISTI)

• For emergency dental treatment with an EHIC, contact the USL, as above.
• If you do not have an EHIC, you should contact a private dentist (ask at your hotel reception). Again, take a copy of your insurance details, and keep your receipts.

PHARMACIES (FARMACIE)

• Rome's pharmacies sell toiletries as well as a wide range of over-the-counter medicines.
• Pharmacists are well trained and can give advice or deal with minor ailments.
• Most pharmacies are open from 8.30 to 1 and again from 4 until 8, but they operate a rota system so that there is at least one open at all times—there will be a list displayed in the window or published in the newspaper.
• If the pharmacy does not have the medicine that you need, try the pharmacy at the Vatican.

OPTICIANS (OTTICHI)

• Opticians can usually carry out minor repairs to your glasses, such as replacing screws, on the spot, for little or no charge.
• Lenses can often be replaced overnight.
• If you really cannot survive without your glasses or contact lenses, bring a copy of your prescription with you so that

Not your average pharmacy—the elegant Officino Profumo

you can have replacements made up. Better still, bring spares.

ALTERNATIVE TREATMENTS

• You can buy homeopathic remedies at most pharmacies.
• For information on homeopathic doctors and treatments (including acupuncture), contact S. Ano, Piazza Navona 49, 00186 Rome, tel 06 687 9030 (closed Mon and Wed morning).

TAP WATER

• Yes, you can drink the water. Rome's tap water is completely safe, as is the water in the city's drinking fountains.
• However, you should look out for signs that say *acqua non*

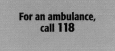

For an ambulance, call 118

potabile, indicating that the water is not drinkable.

SUMMER HAZARDS

• The sun can be strong between May and September, and a high-factor sun block is recommended. Your sunglasses will make a stylish accessory.
• There are few biting insects as such in Rome, but if you plan to visit the surrounding area, you might like to take an insect repellant, although insect bites are more irritating than dangerous.

PLANNING

COMMUNICATION

TELEPHONES
CALL CHARGES
● There are two call bands for telephone charges. Peak time is Mon–Fri 8am–6.30pm, and Sat 8am–1pm; all other times are off peak. The same call bands now apply for international calls.

PAYING FOR CALLS
Public telephones
● Most payphones now take phonecards, rather than cash. You can buy cards for calls within Italy in denominations of €5 and €10 at tobacconists, news-stands and some bars. You need to tear off the top right-hand corner of the card before you use it.
● For overseas calls, buy an Interglobal Card 5 (€5), which can be used with public, private and mobile phones. Like scratch cards, they have a hidden number.

Telefono a scatti
● There are now a number of places around Rome where you can make a metered call from a soundproofed booth, such as Fiumicino airport and Termini station. At the end of the call, you pay the cashier.
● There is no additional charge for this service, but you will find that most of them are not open late enough to take advantage of the cheaper rates in the evening. The only exception is the Palazzo delle Poste at Piazza San Silvestro, which is open 24 hours.

SPECIAL PREFIXES
● The area code for Rome is 06, and you need to dial this as part

of the telephone number, even if you are calling from within Rome.
● Numbers beginning 800 are free, known as *numeri verdi*, and those that start with 840 or 848 will be charged at only one unit.
● Italian mobile phone numbers start with 3, although you might still see them written as 03, their old format (drop the zero and dial the rest of the number).

MOBILE PHONES
● British, Australian and New Zealand mobile phones can be used in

Remember you need to tear off the corner of your phonecard

Italy without any problems. You may need to unbar your telephone for use overseas: Contact your service operator for details.
● American mobile phones can be used only if they are triband, because of the different frequency.
 ● It can be very expensive to use your mobile phone abroad, as

you will often be charged to receive calls as well as to make them. If you travel frequently, consider swapping your SIM card for one from an alternative provider—either a network based in Italy or a dedicated provider of international mobile phone services. You can buy these at mobile phone stores before you leave home or when you are in Rome.

• Another alternative is to rent a mobile phone while you are in Rome. Phones can be rented from HLC Via Bettolo 6, 00195; Tel 06 372 0700, congiunti2@yahoo.it. The shop is open Mon–Sat 9–6, and rental charges are €9 per day or €50 per week, plus the cost of calls.

• Text messages are often a cheaper alternative to voice calls, but check the charges with your service provider.

• Remember to add the international dialling code to the numbers you wish to call at home. Add + and the international code (see panel opposite).

INTERNET ACCESS
• The internet is a great way of

keeping in touch while you are away from home. Increasing numbers of hotels are offering internet access, and internet cafés are springing up all over the city.

• One of the biggest venues is EasyEverything (Via Barberini 2, tel 06 4290 3388; www.easyeverything.com), with 250 terminals. It is open 24 hours a day, seven days a week.

• Thenetgate (www.thenetgate. it) currently has five branches in Rome: Piazza Firenze 25, Via delle Grazie 4, inside the drugstore at Termini, Hotel Palatino in Via Cavour, and Via Cluniacensi 26–30 in Tiburtina.

• The netcafe.com (www. netcafe.com/countries.italy.htm) has an impressive searchable directory of internet cafés in Rome, and indeed the rest of the world.

• In stations and airports there are now public internet points,

which you can pay for with a normal phonecard.

POST OFFICES
• The main post office is the Ufficio Postale Centrale at Piazza San Silvestro, 00187 (tel 80 31 60,

www.poste.it). It is open Mon–Fri 9–6 and Sat 9–2.

• The city's other post offices open Mon–Fri 8.25–2 or 2.30 and Sat 8.25–noon. The central offices have a currency exchange, which is sometimes

are sent by *Raccomandata*. The cost varies considerably, depending on the size and weight of the package.

• Post boxes are red and have two slots: *Per la città* is for Rome, and *Tutte le altre destinazione* for everywhere else, including international destinations.

• The Vatican operates its own

The Vatican's Swiss-run postal service uses blue or yellow mailboxes (left and middle) in contrast to the red boxes elsewhere in the city

open throughout the day until 6.30.

MAIL
Postage rates (national and international)
• Rome's notoriously bad postal service has greatly improved. Letters can now be sent by *posta prioritaria*, similar to first-class post in the UK.

• The postage rate for Europe is slightly higher than that for letters sent within Italy.

• You can buy postage stamps (*francobolli*) from post offices, although they are always very busy. You can also buy them from tobacconists, where there will be less of a wait.

• Registered letters or parcels

postal service, which is more efficient than the Roman one. There is a post office outside Basilica di San Pietro, in Piazza San Pietro, where you can buy stamps, and there is a post box outside. Both are on the left as you face the basilica.

• Italian stamps are not valid in Vatican City, and vice versa.

POSTCARDS
• These are classed as low priority post. However, you can send your postcard by *prioritaria*. This faster service should only take around three days, and is similarly priced (see table below). Otherwise delivery can be slow. It helps if you put your postcard in an envelope.

POSTAGE RATES			
Airmail (via aerea)	**Letter (20g)**		**Delivery time**
Europe	65c		up to 2 weeks
US and rest of world	70c		up to 2 weeks
Posta Prioritaria	**Letter (under 50g)**	**Letter (50–100g)**	**Delivery time**
Europe	62c	€1.80	3 days
US and rest of world	€1	€2	4–8 days

PLANNING

PERSONAL SECURITY

Rome is basically a safe city and instances of serious crime against visitors are rare. The main problems for visitors are likely to be pickpockets or bag snatchers. By taking a few sensible precautions, you can minimize the risk of becoming a victim.

● Never carry money or valuables in your back pocket—always keep them secure in a money belt, pouch or similar.

● Don't flaunt your valuables.

● Never put your camera or bag down on a café table, where it could be snatched.

● Beware of groups of children who have perfected a scam where they show you a piece of cardboard and while you try to read what is written on it they steal from your pocket or handbag.

● Carry bags or cameras on your side that is away from the road, to minimize the risk from bag snatchers on scooters.

● Keep a close eye on your possessions while on crowded buses or metros, particularly in areas popular with visitors.

● Leave valuable jewellery in the hotel safe.

● Women should note how the Roman women wear their handbags—across their bodies,

EMERGENCY NUMBERS	
Police	
113	
Carabinieri 112	
Ambulance 118	
Fire brigade 115	
Red Cross 06 5510	
Police HQ (Questura)	
06 46861	
Samaritans	
(English-speaking volunteers available 1–10pm)	
06 7045 4444	

rather than just over one shoulder where they could be easily snatched.

● If you have a codeable safe in your hotel room, don't use your date of birth as the code. It is on your passport and your hotel registration.

● After dark, avoid parks, the area around Termini and the edge of Trastevere.

● You should report any theft to a police station, where you will need to make a statement. Although it is unlikely that you will get your belongings back, you will need the statement (denuncia) to make a claim on your insurance. The main police station is Questura, Via San Vitale 15 (tel 06 46861).

LOST PROPERTY

● The ATAC lost property office (Ufficio Oggetti Rinvenuti) is at Via Niccolò Bettoni 1 (open Mon–Wed, Fri 8.30–1, Tue also 3–5, Thu 8.30–5, Aug morning only; tel 06 581 6040).

● For anything lost on any FS trains, try the office on platform 24 of Termini (open daily 7am–midnight, tel 06 4782 5543).

● If you will be making an insurance claim, you will need to report the loss to the police to get a statement (denuncia).

● If your passport is lost or stolen, report it to the police and your embassy (see below).

● If your credit card or travellers' cheques are stolen, report them to the issuing company (▷ 280).

WHAT TO DO IF YOU ARE ARRESTED

If you are taken into custody by the police, you could be held for up to 48 hours without appearing before a magistrate. You can also be interviewed without a lawyer present. You do, however, have the right to contact your consul, who is based at your country's embassy.

Your consul will not be able to get you out of prison, but they can put you in touch with English-speaking lawyers and interpreters, and contact your family on your behalf.

WHAT TO DO IF YOU LOSE YOUR PASSPORT

If you lose your passport, contact your embassy in Rome. It helps if you have a note of your passport number, so either keep a note of it or carry a photocopy of the information page separately from your passport. Alternatively, you could scan the page and email it to a web-based account that can be accessed anywhere.

POLICE

There are three branches of the police in Italy, any of whom should be able to help you if you are in difficulty.

● The carabinieri are military police, easily recognizable by the white sash they wear across their bodies. They deal with general crime, including drug control.

● The polizia is the state police force, who wear blue uniforms. They, too, deal with general crime, and if you are unfortunate enough to be robbed (or worse), they are the ones you will need to see.

● The vigili urbani, in dark blue uniforms and white hats, are traffic police.

CONTACTING YOUR EMBASSY	
American Embassy	Via Vittorio Veneto 119a, 00187, tel 06 46741, www.usis.it
Australian Embassy	Via Antonio Bosio 5, 00161, tel 06 852721, www.italy.embassy.gov.au
British Embassy	Via XX Settembre 80a, 00187, tel 06 4220 0001, www.fco.gov.uk
Canadian Embassy	Via G.B. de Rossi 27, 00161, tel 06 445981, www.canada.it
Irish Embassy	Piazza di Campitelli 3, 00186, tel 06 697 9121, www.europeanirish.com
New Zealand Embassy	Via Zara 28, 00198, tel 06 441 7171, www.nzembassy.com
South African Embassy	Via Tanaro 14, 00198, tel 06 852541, www.sudafrica.it

PLANNING

OPENING TIMES AND TICKETS

PUBLIC HOLIDAYS

Shops and banks generally close on public holidays, and roads and railways are usually very busy. However, with the exception of Labour Day, Assumption and Christmas Day, most bars and restaurants will still be open. There is a limited public transport service on Labour Day and the afternoon of Christmas Day.

If a public holiday falls on a weekend, it is not celebrated on the next working day, as it is in the UK and the US. However, if the holiday falls on a Tuesday or Thursday, many people take the Monday or Friday off to make a *ponte* (bridge) to the weekend.

ROMAN HOLIDAYS	
1 Jan	New Year's Day
6 Jan	Epiphany
Mar/Apr	Easter Monday
25 Apr	Liberation Day
1 May	Labour Day
2 Jun	Republic Day
29 Jun	St. Peter and St. Paul Day (or St. Peter's Day)
15 Aug	Assumption of the Virgin (Ferragosto)
1 Nov	All Saints' Day
8 Dec	Feast of the Immaculate Conception
25 Dec	Christmas Day
26 Dec	Santo Stefano

SHOPS

Traditionally, shops open between 8 and 9, closing for lunch at around 1. They reopen at 3.30 or 4 and close at 8. Most are closed all day Sunday plus Monday morning.

However, Rome's shops are increasingly staying open all day—look for the sign *orario continuato*.

BANKS

These open Mon–Fri 8.30–1.30. Some larger branches might open on Saturday.

POST OFFICES

These open Mon–Fri 8.15–2, Sat 8.15–noon or 2.

DOCTORS AND PHARMACISTS

Pharmacists are usually open the same hours as shops, but take it in turns to stay open during the afternoon and late into the evening. Look for the list posted in the window for the nearest pharmacy that will be open.

TICKETS

Generally in Rome you will find that most churches do not charge admission (although often a donation is expected). There is sometimes a charge made at churches where there is a special architectural feature or work of art.

Most Roman establishments operate separately, each charging their own admission fee. The exceptions are the Roma Archeologica Card, which is valid for seven days and gives admission to eight different places of interest (Colosseo, Palatino, Terme di Caracalla, Terme di Diocleziano, Palazzo Altemps, Palazzo Massimo alle Terme, Villa dei Quintili and the tomb of Cecilia Metella), and the Museum Card, which is valid for three days and covers Palazzo Altemps, Palazzo Massimo alle Terme, Crypta Balbi and Terme di Diocleziano. The cards cost €23.50 and €8.50 respectively, and are available from any of the participating sights.

Tickets for popular museums and galleries can be booked in advance through a number of agencies, who charge a booking fee on top of the normal admission price.

TICKET AGENCIES
Ticketclic (www.ticketclic.it)
Colosseo
Crypta Balbi
Domus Aurea
Musei Capitolini
Palazzo Altemps
Palazzo Massimo alle Terme
Terme di Caracalla
Terme di Diocleziano
Villa Adriana (Tivoli)
Ticketeria (www.ticketeria.it)
Galleria Borghese
Galleria Corsini
Galleria Spada
Museo Etrusco (at Tarquinia)
Museo Nazionale Etrusco
Necropoli dei Monterozzi (at Tarquinia)
Palazzo Barberini
Palazzo-Galleria Doria Pamphilj
Palazzo Venezia
Villa Giulia

MUSEUMS AND GALLERIES

The opening times for museums and galleries vary greatly. Some are open all day, while others close at lunchtime. Many close one day each week, usually Monday. Check the Sights section of this book (▷ 65–150) or contact the museum or gallery concerned for the most up-to-date information.

CHURCHES

Most churches open early in the morning for Mass, often around 7. They close at lunchtime, opening again at around 4 and closing at 7. Some of the larger churches are open all day, and some are closed to non-worshippers during services. Check the Sights section of this book (▷ 65–150) or contact the church to check.

Many restaurants are open late for alfresco summer eating

CAFÉS AND BARS

The hours kept by Rome's cafés and bars vary considerably from establishment to establishment and according to season. Some are open for breakfast, others open in time for lunch and some are only open in the evenings. Wine bars usually close at midnight or later.

RESTAURANTS

Restaurants that serve lunch open at around 12.30 and usually close during the afternoon. They reopen, along with those that only serve dinner, sometime after 7 and stay open late. Pizzerias are usually only open in the evening.

Many restaurants close for the whole of August—look for the sign *chiuso per ferie*.

PLANNING

TOURIST OFFICES

The main tourist office in Rome is at Via Parigi 5, near Terme di Diocleziano (06 48891, open daily 9–7.30). The best number for tourist information is 06 3600 4399, where they speak good English. There are smaller, information points (open daily 9.30–7.30) in green pagodas, dotted around the city, which can supply you with maps and other information (in English).

- Aeroporto Leonardo da Vinci (in arrivals, Terminal B)
- Stazione Termini, platform 4
- Largo Goldoni, Via del Corso
- Piazza San Giovanni in Laterano
- Palazzo delle Esposizioni, Via Nazionale
- Piazza delle Cinque Lune, near Piazza Navona
- Piazza Pia, near Castel Sant'Angelo
- Piazza del Tempio della Pace, near Fori Imperiali
- Piazza Sonnino, Trastevere
- Via dell'Olmata, near Santa Maria Maggiore
- Piazza dei Cinquecento, outside Termini
- Via Marco Minghetti, near Trevi Fountain
- Via San Pietro (left-hand side of Basilica's façade, for information on St. Peter's; tel 06 6988 2019)

ITALIAN GOVERNMENT TOURIST OFFICES

AUSTRALIA	CANADA	UK	US
Level 26, 44 Market Street, NSW 2000 Sydney, tel: 92 621666	175 Bloor Street East, Suite 907 South Tower, Toronto, Ontario M4W 3R8, tel: 416 925-4882, fax: 416 925-4799; www.italiantourism.com	1 Princes Street, London W1B 2AY, tel: 020 7489 1254/020 7355 1557, fax: 020 7499 3567; www.enit.it	630 Fifth Avenue, Suite 1565, New York NY 10111, tel: 212 245-5618/245-4822, fax 212 586-9249; www.italiantourism.com Also offices in Chicago and Los Angeles

WEBSITES

TOURISM

www.romaturismo.it
The city of Rome's official website is packed with useful information, such as hotel and restaurant listings, suggested itineraries and events. You can also request brochures. In English and Italian.

www.enjoyrome.com
This independent website, staffed by English-speakers, is great for organized tours, accommodation and information on life in Rome. In English only.

www.vatican.va
Information on the Vatican state, including the museums, but not much on St. Peter's. In six languages, including English.

www.comune.roma.it
The city council's website, with details of tourism and events. In English.

www.romaclick.com
This English-language website is good for booking online accommodation.

www.romeguide.it
Information on exhibitions and attractions, plus online ticket-booking. In English.

TRANSPORT

www.atac.roma.it
Details of routes, fares and tickets for buses, trams and the metro. In English and Italian.

www.trenitalia.it
Information on getting around the country by Italy's train service. In English and Italian.

www.adr.it
Covers both of Rome's airports. Includes airport services and flight information.

NEWS

www.bbc.co.uk
For UK, regional and world news, plus weather reports. You can also listen to BBC radio stations via the website.

www.cnn.com
For US and world news, plus weather reports.

www.ilmessaggero.it
Rome's newspaper online, with news, sport and events. In Italian only.

KEY SIGHTS QUICK WEBSITE FINDER

SIGHT	WEBSITE	PAGE
Basilica di San Pietro	www.vatican.it	66–71
Casa di Goethe	www.casadigoethe.it	65
Colosseo	www.ticketclic.it	74–77
Fori Imperiali	www.capitolium.org	82–83
Foro Romano	www.capitolium.org	84–89
Galleria Borghese	www.galleriaborghese.it	93–97
Musei Capitolini	www.museicapitolini.org	98–103
Musei Vaticani	www.vatican.va	104–109
Palazzo Barberini	www.galleriaborghese.it	114
Palazzo Corsini	www.galleriaborghese.it	111
Palazzo-Galleria Doria Pamphilj	www.doriapamphilj.it	115
Palazzo Quirinale	www.quirinale.it	111
Palazzo Spada	www.galleriaborghese.it	111
San Carlo alle Quattro Fontane	www.sancarlino-borromini.it	128
Santa Maria della Concezione	www.cappucciniviaveneto.it	136
Santa Maria sopra Minerva	www.basilicaminerva.it	140
Villa Farnesina	www.francopanini.it	146
Villa Medici	www.villamedici.it	146

PLANNING

MEDIA

TELEVISION
- Italy has three state-run television stations (RAI-1, -2 and -3), three stations run by Berlusconi's Mediaset group (Italia Uno, Rete Quattro and Canale Cinque), plus a number of local channels. RAI-3 has an international news programme, which includes an English-language section. It starts at 1.15am.
- Italian television shows are almost always accompanied by scantily-clad women. Moves are underway to change this, with a view to portraying a more respectful image of women, but with the role of 'game show girl' as popular as ever, how successful this will be remains to be seen.
- Most hotels, from mid-range upwards, have satellite television, which means you can keep up to date with the news on BBC World or CNN.

RADIO
- RAI Radio 1, 2 and 3 (89.7FM, 91.7FM and 93.7FM respectively), the state-run stations, have a mixture of light music, chat shows and news – all in Italian.
- Radio Vaticano (93.3FM) broadcasts news in a number of languages. There are English-language broadcasts daily at 5.00am, 4.15pm and 7.50pm.
- Some of the local radio stations play American and British music, so if you are feeling homesick, try Radio Centro Suono (101.3FM) for music from the 1960s up to the present day. Radio Antenna 1 (107.1FM) plays American and British hits from the 1970s, 80s and early 90s. For light classical music, try 100.3FM, or if Latin-American is your thing, tune into Radio Mambo (106.85FM).
- The BBC World Service frequencies for Rome are MHz 6.195, 9.410, 12.095, 15.485 and 17.640. Check www.bbc.co.uk/worldservice for schedules. You can also listen to programmes directly via the website.

NEWSPAPERS
English-language newspapers
- You can often buy major

international newspapers on the day of publication, from about 2pm, at larger news-stands. Titles include *The Times, The Guardian, The Financial Times, The New York Times, The Wall Street Journal* and the *International Herald Tribune.*

Italian-language newspapers
- *Il Messaggero* is the local paper, popular with Romans. *La Repubblica, Corriere della Sera, La Stampa* and *Il Sole/24 Ore* are the main national dailies. *La Repubblica* and *Corriere della Sera* both have local editions for Rome. *La Repubblica* has a good what's-on section on Thursdays and a glossy magazine supplement on Saturdays called *La Repubblica delle Donne*, with excellent articles reflecting all aspects of Italian life and society.
- There are two daily sports papers published in Italy: *La*

Search out the English-language magazines at news-stands

Gazzetta dello Sport and the *Corriere dello Sport* are mainly dominated by soccer and motor sport news. *La Gazzetta dello Sport* also publishes a supplement on Saturdays called *Sport Week*, which tends to cover a wider range of sports, and contains excellent colour photos and features on the week's events.

MAGAZINES
- English-speakers will see many familiar-looking magazines on the news-stands. Italian versions of well-known publications such as *Vogue* and *Marie Claire* are very popular.
- Many Italian magazines on sale in Rome are adorned with pictures of scantily-clad women, but this isn't necessarily a reflection of their content (although it can be).
- English-language magazines are few and far between, but if you read a little Italian, magazines such as *Panorama* and *L'Espresso* are good for news, while *Sette* (Thursdays) and *Venerdì* (Fridays) are colour supplements with lots of pictures.
- *Roma C'è* (Fridays) has an English-language section. *Wanted in Rome* is aimed at resident English-speakers, but also has what's-on listings (every other Tuesday).

Relaxing in the Giardino del Pincio with a good book

From scholarly works to the more light-hearted, there has been plenty written about ancient Rome

BOOKS

There are any number of books dealing with Rome's long and eventful history. By far the most in-depth is Edward Gibbon's 19th-century *The History of the Decline and Fall of the Roman Empire*, published in six volumes (although abridged versions are available from publishers such as Penguin). *The Battle for Rome*, by Robert Katz, recounts the German occupation of Rome and the fall of Mussolini.

For history in novel form, try *I, Claudius*, by Robert Graves, or Irvine Stone's *The Agony and the Ecstasy*. More light-hearted is Lindsey Davis' series of detective stories, based around the Roman Empire, but mostly set in Rome.

Anyone interested in Italian politics should read *The Dark Heart of Italy* by Tobias Jones, which discusses Berlusconi's administration (▷ 18).

John Varriano's *Rome: A Literary Companion* is full of quotes from major writers who spent time in Rome. Another good companion is *City Secrets Rome*, by Robert Kahn, which gives you an insight into how modern-day Romans see their city.

For younger readers, *The Rotten Romans*, part of the popular Horrible Histories series, takes a more light-hearted look at this facinating period of history. It is aimed at 9–12-year olds.

FILMS

Mussolini's Cinecittà studios didn't really come into their own until after World War II, when they began to make neo-realist films, like *Ladri di Biciclette* (Bicycle Thieves—1948). A winner of both a BAFTA and a Golden Globe, it was shot entirely in Rome, using non-actors.

The 1950s saw a resurgence in film-making in Rome, with the much-acclaimed *Roman Holiday* (1953), which thrust Audrey Hepburn into the limelight. You'll recognize many of the landmarks she and Gregory Peck visit, including the Bocca della Verità (▷ 136). *Three Coins in a Fountain* (1954) followed closely behind, and although the storyline now seems old-fashioned, it's still a great travelog for Rome. Probably the most famous image of Rome is Anita Ekberg's dip in the Trevi Fountain in *La Dolce Vita* (1960), which was also filmed in Tivoli and Viterbo (▷ 214 and 210).

The Agony and the Ecstasy (1965) is one of a great number of historical epics set in Rome, with Charlton Heston as a tortured Michelangelo painting the Sistine Chapel's ceiling for Julius II (Rex Harrison).

Roma (1972) is a typical piece of Felliniesque film-making. This plotless film shows Fellini's Rome, which he voices over in the English-language version.

More recently, *The Talented Mr. Ripley* (1999) was filmed all over Italy, including Rome, and *Gladiator* (2000) is set, in part, in Rome, although much of it was filmed elsewhere.

MAPS

There is a central street map at the back of this guide (▷ 298–313) and a metro and tram map in the inside back cover. All the tourist information points have free street maps if you want to pick up something else while you are out there. There are free metro and bus maps available from the information office at Termini (▷ 46).

ITALIAN WORDS AND PHRASES

Once you have mastered a few basic rules, Italian is an easy language to speak: It is phonetic and, unlike English, particular combinations of letters are always pronounced the same way. The stress is usually on the penultimate syllable, but if the word has an accent, this is where the stress falls.

Vowels are pronounced as follows:

a	casa	as in	mat short 'a'
e	vero	as in	base
e	sette	as in	vet short 'e'
i	vino	as in	mean
o	dove	as in	bowl
o	otto	as in	not
u	uva	as in	book

Consonants as in English except:
c before **i** or **e** becomes **ch** as in **ch**urch
ch before **i** or **e** becomes **c** as in **c**at
g before **i** or **e** becomes **j** as in **J**ulia
gh before **i** or **e** becomes **g** as in **g**ood
gn as in on**i**on
gli as in mil**li**on
h is rare in Italian words, and is always silent
r usually rolled
z is pronounced **tz** when it falls in the middle of a word

All Italian nouns are either masculine (usually ending in **o** when singular or **i** when plural) or feminine (usually ending in **a** when singular or **e** when plural). Some nouns, which may be masculine or feminine, end in **e** (which changes to **i** when plural). An adjective's ending changes to match the ending of the noun.

CONVERSATION

What is the time?
Che ore sono?

When do you open/close?
A che ora apre/chiude?

I don't speak Italian
Non parlo italiano

I only speak a little Italian
Parlo solo un poco italiano

Do you speak English?
Parla inglese?

I don't understand
Non capisco

Please repeat that
Può ripetere?

Please speak more slowly
Può parlare più lentamente?

What does this mean?
Cosa significa questo?

Write that down for me, please
Lo scriva, per piacere

Please spell that
Come si scrive?

I'll look that up
Lo cerco

My name is
Mi chiamo

What's your name?
Come si chiama?

Hello, pleased to meet you
Piacere

This is my friend
Le presento il mio amico/la mia amica

This is my wife/husband/daughter/son
Le presento mia moglie/mio marito/mia figlia/mio figlio

Where do you live?
Dove abiti?

I live in…
Vivo in…

I'm here on holiday
Sono qui in vacanza

Good morning
Buongiorno

Good afternoon/evening
Buonasera

Goodbye
Arrivederci

See you later
A più tardi

See you tomorrow
A domani

See you soon
A presto

How are you?
Come sta?

Fine, thank you
Bene, grazie

I'm sorry
Mi dispiace

That's alright
Si figuri

USEFUL WORDS

yes	thank you	where	when	why
sì	**grazie**	**dove**	**quando**	**perchè**
no	you're welcome	here	now	who
no	**prego**	**qui**	**adesso**	**chi**
please	excuse me!	there	later	may I/can I
per piacere	**scusi!**	**là**	**più tardi**	**posso**

Could you help me, please? **Può aiutarmi, per favore?**	I'll take this **Prendo questo**	Do you have shoes to match this? **Ha delle scarpe che vadano con questo?**
How much is this? **Quanto costa questo?**	Do you have anything less expensive/smaller/larger? **Ha qualcosa di meno caro/più piccolo/più grande?**	This is the right size **Questa è la taglia (misura–for shoes) giusta**
I'm looking for… **Cerco…**		
Where can I buy…? **Dove posso comprare…?**	Are the instructions included? **Ci sono anche le istruzioni?**	Can you measure me please? **Può prendermi la misura, per favore?**
How much is this/that? **Quanto costa questo/quello?**	Do you have a bag for this? **Può darmi una busta?**	
When does the shop open/close? **Quando apre/chiude il negozio?**	I'm looking for a present **Cerco un regalo**	This doesn't suit me **Questo non mi sta bene**
	Can you gift-wrap this please? **Può farmi un pacco regalo?**	Do you have this in…? **Avete questo in…?**
I'm just looking, thank you **Sto solo dando un'occhiata**	Do you accept credit cards? **Accettate carte di credito?**	Should this be dry-cleaned? **Questo è da lavare a secco?**
This isn't what I want **Non è quel che cerco**	I'd like a kilo of… **Vorrei un chilo di…**	Is there a market? **C'è un mercato?**

0 zero	6 sei	12 dodici	18 diciotto	40 quaranta	100 cento
1 uno	7 sette	13 tredici	19 diciannove	50 cinquanta	1000 mille
2 due	8 otto	14 quattordici	20 venti	60 sessanta	million milione
3 tre	9 nove	15 quindici	21 ventuno	70 settanta	quarter quarto
4 quattro	10 dieci	16 sedici	22 ventidue	80 ottanta	half mezza
5 cinque	11 undici	17 diciassette	30 trenta	90 novanta	three quarters tre quarti

MONEY

Is there a bank/currency exchange office nearby?
C'è una banca/un ufficio di cambio qui vicino?

Can I cash this here?
Posso incassare questo?

I'd like to change sterling/dollars into euros
Vorrei cambiare sterline/dollari in euro

Can I use my credit card to withdraw cash?
Posso usare la mia carta di credito per prelevare contanti?

What is the exchange rate today?
Quant'è il cambio oggi?

I'd like to cash this travellers' cheque
Vorrei incassare questo travellers cheque

POST AND TELEPHONE

Where is the nearest post office/mail box?
Dov'è l'ufficio postale più vicino/la cassetta delle lettere più vicina?

What is the postage to…?
Quando costa spedire una lettera a…?

One stamp, please
Un francobollo, per favore

I'd like to send this by air mail/registered mail
Vorrei spedire questo per posta aerea/posta raccomandata

Can you direct me to a public phone?
Dov'è il telefono pubblico più vicino?

What is the charge per minute?
Quanto si paga al minuto?

Can I dial direct to…?
Posso chiamare… in teleselezione?

Do I need to dial 0 first?
Devo comporre prima lo zero?

Where can I find a phone directory?
Dove posso trovare un elenco telefonico?

Where can I buy a phone card?
Dove posso comprare una carta telefonica?

What is the number for directory enquiries?
Qual è il numero del servizio informazioni?

Please put me through to…
Mi passi…

Have there been any calls for me?
Ci sono state telefonate per me?

Hello, this is…
Pronto, sono…

Who is this speaking please?
Con chi parlo?

I'd like to speak to…
Vorrei parlare con…

Extension…please
Interno…per piacere

Please ask him/her to call me back
Puo dirgli/dirle di richiamarmi?

COLOURS

black	light blue
nero	**celeste**
brown	sky blue
marrone	**azzuro**
pink	purple
rosa	**viola**
red	white
rosso	**bianco**
orange	gold
arancia	**oro**
yellow	silver
giallo	**argento**
green	grey
verde	**grigio**
blue	turquoise
blu	**turchese**

SHOPS

Baker's	Fishmonger's	Lingerie shop
Panetteria or **Forno**	**Pescheria**	**Biancheria intima**
	Florist	Newsagent's
Bookshop	**Fiorista**	**Giornalaio**
Libreria		
	Gift shop	Perfume shop
Butcher's	**Regali**	**Profumeria**
Macelleria		
	Grocer's	Photographic shop
Cake shop	**Alimentare**	**Fotografo**
Pasticceria		
	Hairdresser's	Shoe shop
Clothes shop	**Parrucchiere**	**Calzature**
Abbigliamento		
	Jeweller's	Sports shop
Delicatessen	**Gioielleria**	**Articoli sportivi**
Salumeria		
	Launderette	Tobacconist's
Dry-cleaner's	**Lavanderia** or	**Tabaccheria**
Lavasecco	**Tintoria**	

GETTING AROUND

Where is the train/bus station?
Dov'è la stazione ferroviaria/ degli autobus (dei pullman— long distance)?

Does this train/bus go to…?
È questo il treno/l'autobus (il pullman—long distance) per…?

Does this train/bus stop at…?
Questo treno/autobus (pullman—long distance) ferma a…?

Please stop at the next stop
La prossima fermata, per favore

Where are we?
Dove siamo?

Do I have to get off here?
Devo scendere qui?

Where can I buy a ticket?
Dove si comprano i biglietti?

Is this seat taken?
È occupato?

Where can I reserve a seat?
Dove si prenotano i posti?

Please can I have a single/ return ticket to…
Un biglietto di andata/andata e ritorno per…

When is the first/last bus to…?
Quando c'è il primo/l'ultimo autobus per…?

I would like a standard/first class ticket to…
Un biglietto di seconda/ prima classe per…

Where is the information desk?
Dov'è il banco informazioni?

Where is the timetable?
Dov'è l'orario?

Do you have a subway/bus map?
Ha una piantina della metropolitana/degli autobus?

Where can I find a taxi?
Dove sono i tassi?

Please take me to…
Per favore, mi porti a…

How much is the journey?
Quanto costerà il viaggio?

Please turn on the meter
Accenda il tassametro, per favore

I'd like to get out here please
Vorrei scendere qui, per favore

Could you wait for me please?
Mi può aspettare, per favore?

Is this the way to…?
È questa la strada per…?

Excuse me, I think I am lost
Mi scusi, penso di essermi perduto/a

Monday **lunedì**	morning **mattina**	today **oggi**	May **maggio**	December **dicembre**	Epiphany **Epifania**
Tuesday **martedì**	afternoon **pomeriggio**	yesterday **ieri**	June **giugno**	spring **primavera**	Easter **Pasqua**
Wednesday **mercoledì**	evening **sera**	tomorrow **domani**	July **luglio**	summer **estate**	Assumption **Ferragosto**
Thursday **giovedì**	night **notte**	January **gennaio**	August **agosto**	autumn **autunno**	All Saints' Day **Ognissanti**
Friday **venerdì**	day **giorno**	February **febbraio**	September **settembre**	winter **inverno**	Christmas **Natale**
Saturday **sabato**	month **mese**	March **marzo**	October **ottobre**	New Year's Day **Capodanno**	26 December **Santo Stefano**
Sunday **domenica**	year **anno**	April **aprile**	November **novembre**		New Year's Eve **San Silvestro**

IN TROUBLE

Help!
Aiuto!

Stop, thief!
Al ladro!

Can you help me, please?
Può aiutarmi, per favore?

Call the fire brigade/police/an ambulance
Chiami i pompieri/la polizia/un'ambulanza

I have lost my passport/wallet/purse/handbag
Ho perso il passaporto/il portafogllio/il borsellino/la borsa

Is there a lost property office?
C'è un ufficio oggetti smarriti?

Where is the police station?
Dov'è il commissariato?

I have been robbed
Sono stato/a derubato/a

I have had an accident
Ho avuto un incidente

Here is my name and address
Ecco il mio nome e indirizzo

Did you see the accident?
Ho visto l'incidente?

Are you insured?
È assicurato/a?

Please can I have your name and address?
Mi dà il suo nome e indirizzo?

I need information for my insurance company
Ho bisogno d'informazioni per la mia compagnia d'assicurazione

ILLNESS

I don't feel well
Non mi sento bene

Could you call a doctor please
Può chiamare un medico, per favore

Is there a doctor/pharmacist on duty?
C'è un medico/farmacista di turno?

I need to see a doctor/dentist
Ho bisogno di un medico/dentista

Where is the hospital?
Dov'è l'ospedale?

When is the surgery open?
Quando apre l'ambulatorio

I need to make an emergency appointment
Ho bisogno di un appunta-mento di emergenza

Do I need to make an appointment?
Ho bisogno di un appuntamento?

I feel sick
Mi sento male

I am allergic to…
Sono allergico/a a…

I have a heart condition
Ho disturbi cardiaci

I am diabetic
Sono diabetico/a

I'm asthmatic
Ho l'asma

I've been stung by a wasp/bee
Mi ha punto una vespa/un'ape

Can I have a painkiller?
Posso avere un analgesico?

How many tablets a day should I take?
Quante pillole al giorno devo prendere?

How long will I have to stay in bed/hospital?
Per quanto tempo dovrò rimanere a letto/in ospedale?

I have bad toothache
Mi fanno molto male i denti

I have broken my tooth/crown
Mi sono rotto un dente/una corona

A filling has come out
Ho perso un'otturazione

Can you repair my dentures?
Può ripararmi la dentiera?

Waiter/waitress
Cameriere/cameriera

What time does the restaurant open?
A che ora apre il ristorante?

I'd like to reserve a table for…people at…
Vorrei prenotare un tavolo per…persone a…

A table for…, please
Un tavolo per…, per favore

We have/haven't booked
Abbiamo/non abbiamo prenotato

Could we sit there?
Possiamo sederci qui?

Is this table taken?
Questa tavola è occupata?

Are there tables outside?
Ci sono tavoli all'aperto?

Where are the toilets?
Dove sono i gabinetti?

We would like to wait for a table
Aspettiamo che si liberi un tavolo

Could you warm this up for me?
Mi può riscaldare questo, per piacere?

We'd like something to drink
Vorremo qualcosa da bere

Could we see the menu/wine list?
Possiamo vedere il menù/la lista dei vini?

Do you have a menu/wine list in English?
Avete un menù/una lista dei vini in inglese?

What do you recommend?
Cosa consiglia?

Is there a dish of the day?
C'è un piatto del giorno?

What is the house special?
Qual è la specialità della casa?

I can't eat wheat/sugar/salt/pork/beef/dairy
Non posso mangiare grano/zucchero/sale/maiale/manzo/latticini

I am a vegetarian
Sono vegetariano/a

I'd like…
Vorrei…

I ordered…
Ho ordinato…

Could I have bottled still/sparkling water?
Vorrei acqua minerale naturale/gassata

Could we have some more bread?
Può portare ancora pane?

Could we have some salt and pepper?
Può portare del sale e del pepe?

The food is cold
Il cibo è freddo

The meat is overcooked/too rare
La carne è troppo cotta/non è abbastanza cotta

This is not what I ordered
Non ho ordinato questo

Can I have the bill, please?
Il conto, per favore?

Is service included?
Il servizio è compreso?

The bill is not right
Il conto è sbagliato

We didn't have this
Non abbiamo avuto questo

How much is this dish?
Quanto costa questo piatto?

I'd like to speak to the manager, please
Vorrei parlare con il direttore

The food was excellent
Abbiamo mangiato benissimo

I have made a reservation for…nights
Ho prenotato per…notti

Do you have a room?
Avete camere libere?

How much per night?
Quanto costa una notte?

Double/single room
Camera doppia/singola

Twin room
Camera a due letti

With bath/shower
Con bagno/doccia

May I see the room?
Posso vedere la camera?

I'll take this room
Prendo questa camera

Could I have another room?
Vorrei cambiare camera

Is there a lift in the hotel?
C'è un ascensore nell'albergo?

Is the room air-conditioned/heated?
C'è aria condizionata/riscaldamento nella camera?

Is breakfast included in the price?
La colazione è compreso?

Do you have room service?
C'è servizio in camera?

When is breakfast served?
A che ora è servita la colazione?

I need an alarm call at…
Potete svegliarmi alle…

The room is too hot/too cold/dirty
La camera è troppo calda/troppo fredda/sporca

I am leaving this morning
Parto stamattina

Please can I pay my bill?
Posso pagare il conto?

Please order a taxi for me
Mi chiama un tassì, per favore

Where is the tourist information office/tourist information desk, please?
Dov'è l'ufficio turistico/il banco informazioni turistiche?

What can we visit in the area?
Che cosa c'è da vedere in questa zona?

Do you have a city map?
Avete una cartina della città?

Can you give me some information about...?
Puo darmi delle informazioni su...?

What sights/hotels/restaurants can you recommend?
Quali monumenti/alberghi/ristoranti mi consiglia?

Please could you point them out on the map?
Me li può indicare sulla cartina?

What is the admission price?
Quant'è il biglietto d'ingresso?

Is there a discount for senior citizens/students?
Ci sono riduzioni per anziani/studenti?

Are there guided tours?
Ci sono visite guidate?

Are there boat trips?
Ci sono gite in barca?

Where do they go?
Dove vanno?

Is there an English-speaking guide?
C'è una guida di lingue inglese?

Are there organized excursions?
Ci sono escursioni organizzate?

Can we make reservations here?
Possiamo prenotare qui?

What time does it open/close?
A che ora apre/chiude?

Is photography allowed?
Si possono fare fotografie?

Do you have a brochure in English?
Avete un opuscolo in inglese?

What's on at the cinema?
Cosa danno al cinema?

Where can I find a good nightclub?
Mi può consigliare un buon nightclub?

What time does the show start?
A che ora comincia lo spettacolo?

Could you reserve tickets for me?
Mi può prenotare dei biglietti?

How much is a ticket?
Quanto costa un biglietto?

Should we dress smartly?
È necessario l'abito da sera?

on/to the right **a destra**	in front of **davanti**	closed **chiuso**	town **città**	lake **lago**
on/to the left **a sinistra**	behind **dietro**	daily **giornalmente**	old town **centro storico**	bridge **ponte**
around the corner **all'angolo**	north **nord**	cathedral **cattedrale**	town hall **municipio**	no entry **vietato l'accesso**
opposite **di fronte a...**	south **sud**	church **chiesa**	boulevard **corso**	push **spingere**
at the bottom (of) **in fondo (a)**	east **est**	castle **castello**	square **piazza**	pull **tirare**
straight on **sempre dritto**	west **ovest**	museum **museo**	street **via**	entrance **ingresso**
near **vincino a**	free **gratis**	monument **monumento**	avenue **viale**	exit **uscita**
cross over **attraversi**	donation **donazione**	palace **palazzo**	island **isola**	toilets— men/women **gabinetti— uomini/donne**
	open **aperto**	gallery **galleria**	river **fiume**	

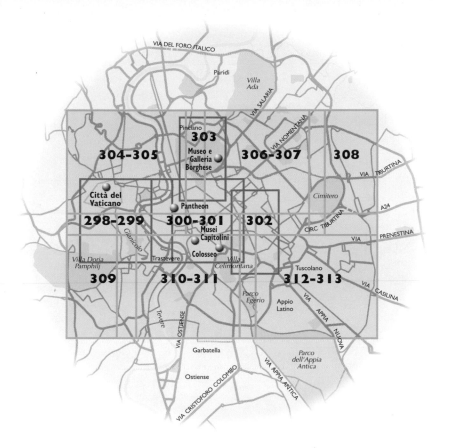

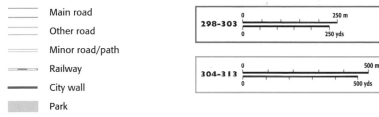

Main road

Other road

Minor road/path

Railway

City wall

Park

Important building

Featured place of interest

Tourist information office

Metro station

Railway station

P   Parking

298–303

| 0 | | 250 m |
| 0 | | 250 yds |

304–313

| 0 | | 500 m |
| 0 | | 500 yds |

Maps

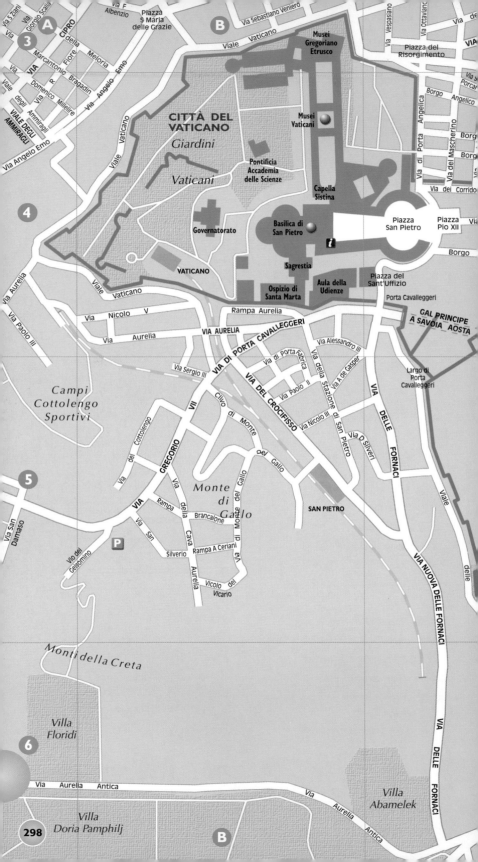

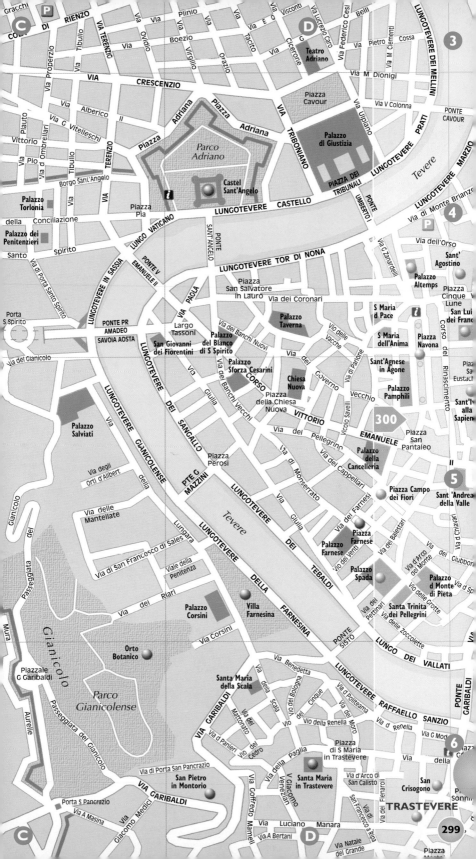

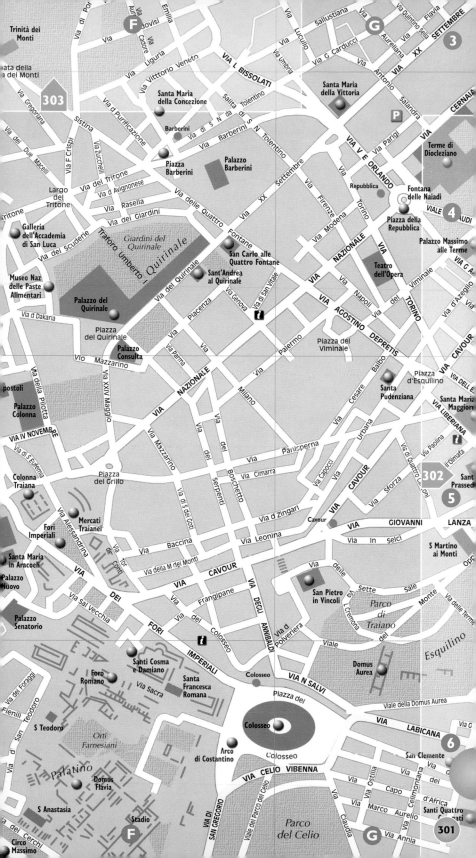

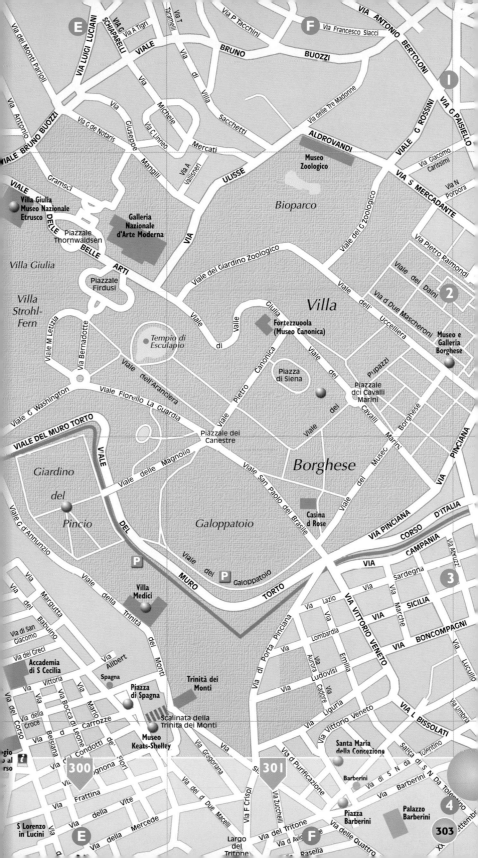

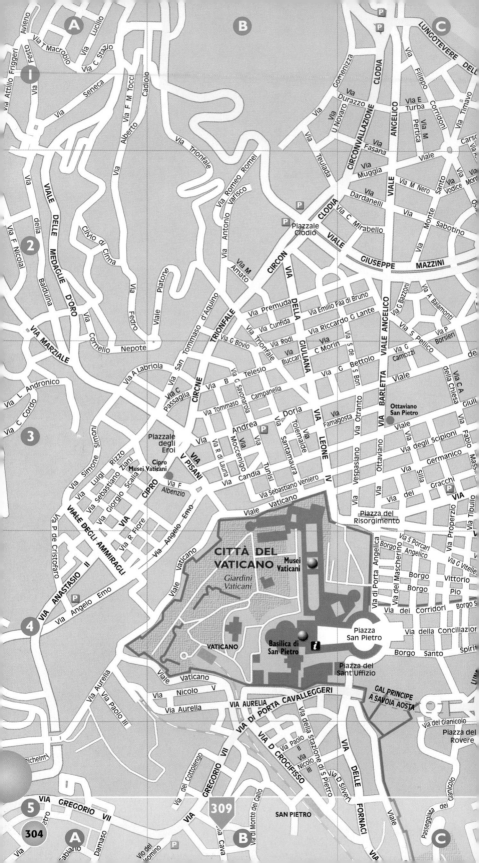

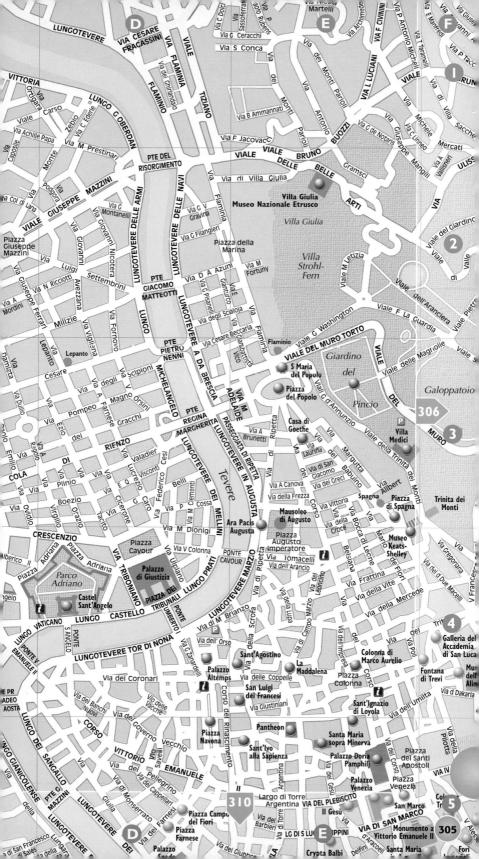

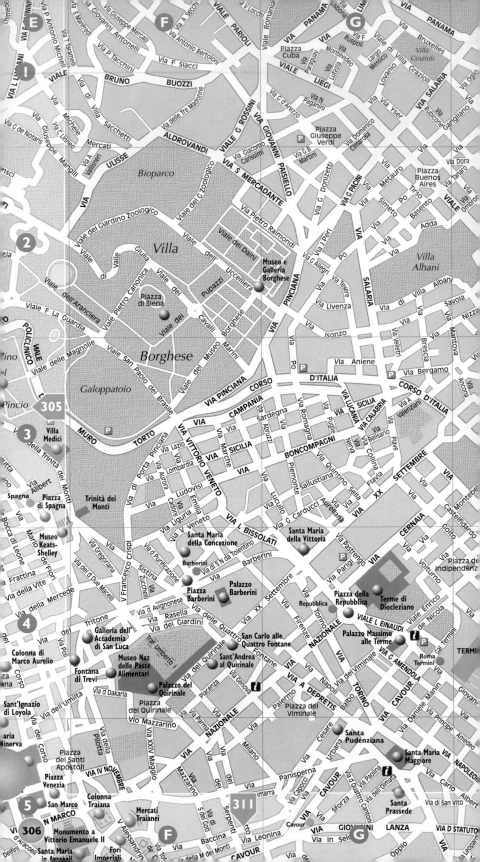

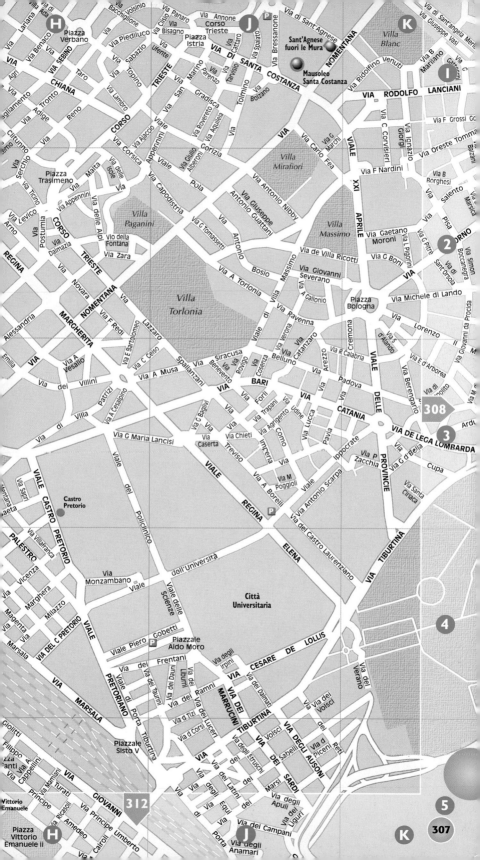

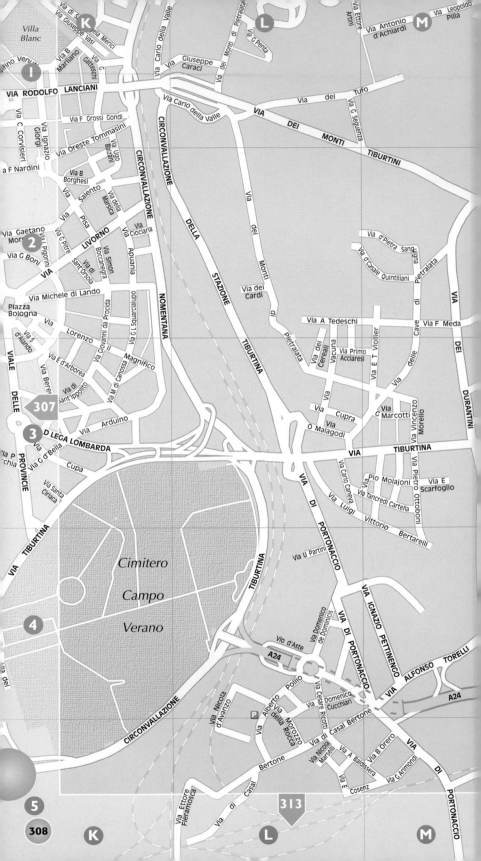

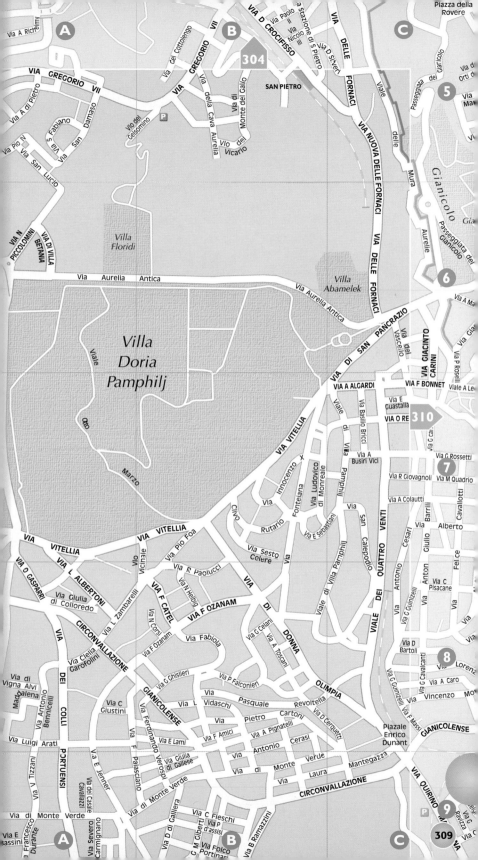

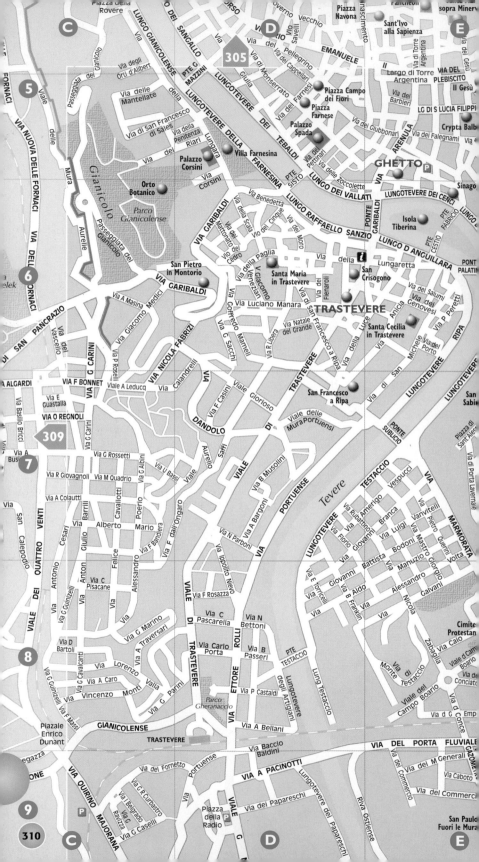

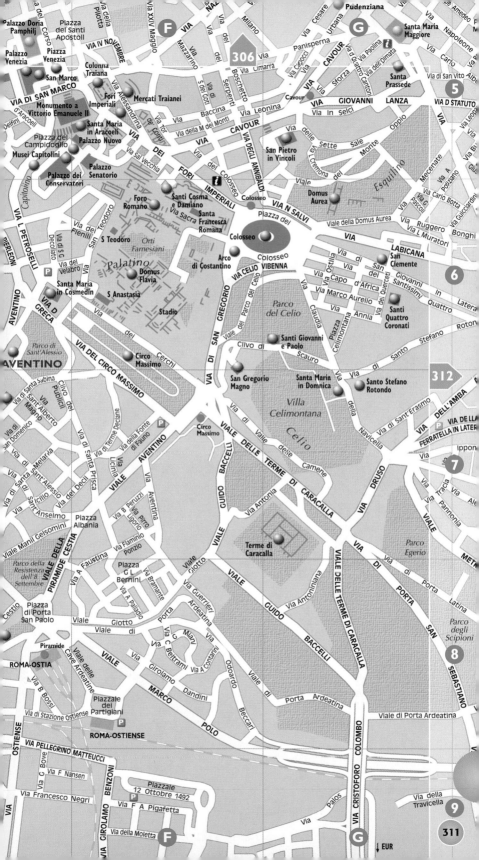

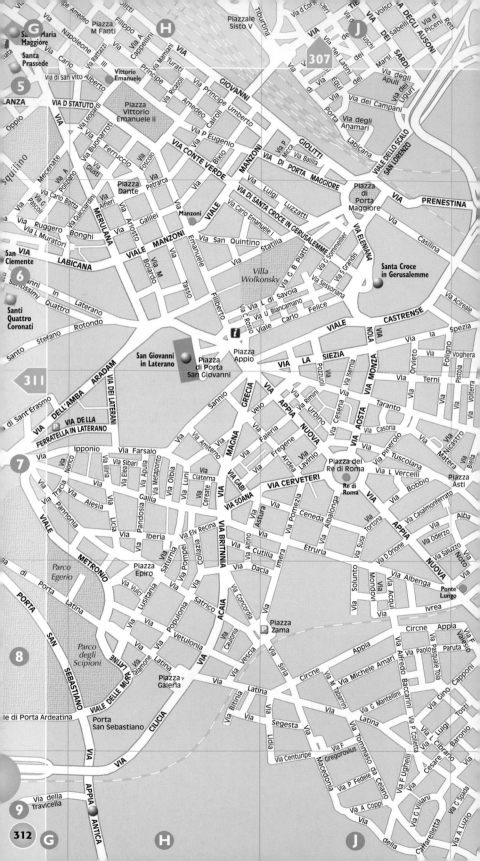

ARCHITECTURAL GLOSSARY

Aisle: the interior corridors of a church, running either side of the nave

Alabaster: a fine grained limestone, often red and white or yellow and white. Thinly cut, it was used to glaze church windows in the Middle Ages

Allegory: a painting, sculpture or story where the meaning is shown through symbols

Apse: the semi-circular end of a church or chapel

Arcade: a range of arches, supported by pillars

Architrave: a moulded frame around a door or window

Atrium: an inner courtyard, open to the sky

Baldacchino/baldacchin: a canopy, usually over a throne or altar

Balustrade: a series of short pillars, or balusters, supporting a rail

Baroque: architectural style popular in 17th-century Rome. It is characterized by its elaborate decoration of convex and concave curves

Basalt: dark volcanic rock

Basilica: originally, in ancient Rome, a public hall, but the building shape and the name were later used for early Christian churches. A basilica has no transepts

Bas-relief: a carving showing a three-dimensional scene, whose surface is relatively shallow

Belvedere: a small tower on the roof of a building

Byzantine: architectural style developed after AD330, when Byzantium became capital of the Eastern Empire. It is characterized by its Eastern influences and highly decorated style

Campanile: a bell tower, often separate from the main building

Cartoon: a full-size preliminary sketch for a painting, mosaic or tapestry

Caryatid: a column, sculpted as a female figure

Casina: literally 'little house', used by 18th-century gentry for dancing, entertainment and gambling

Catacomb: an underground cemetery, usually Christian

Cattedra: the bishop's throne usually in the apse of the cathedral church

Chancel: the eastern end of a church, where the high altar is found

Chiaroscuro: the treatment of light and shade in painting

Cinerary urn: used to hold ashes after cremation

Circus: in ancient Roman architecture, an elongated rectangular structure with rounded ends used for horseracing; in 18th-century architecture, a row of houses in a circular pattern

Classical: architectural style characterized by its use of elements from Ancient Greece or Rome, including finely proportioned, simple shapes, and which has its roots in the 5th century BC. Classicism has seen many revivals from the 15th century to the present day, including Renaissance in the 16th century and Neoclassicism, which was popular between the late 18th and early 19th centuries

Cloister: a courtyard, often in a monastic building, surrounded by a covered passageway with an open arcade or colonnade on the interior side

Coffering: ceiling decoration made up from patterns of recessed squares or other shapes

Colonnade: a row of columns supporting a beam

Column: an upright, usually used as a decorative support, but sometimes freestanding as a monument. The design and proportions of columns vary, depending on their order (see Orders of columns, below)

Confessio: an underground area of a church, usually below the altar, which houses relics

Cosmatesque: decorative flooring of marble, glass and stones

Crossing: the area of a church where the transepts, nave and chancel intersect

Cruciform: cross-shaped, usually refers to a church

Crypt: area below the main church, usually for graves

Cupola: a domed roof

Etruscans: a race of people who inhabited Rome from around the 8th century BC. Their architecture was similar in style to that of Greek architecture of the same period

Exedra: in ancient Rome, a recess with raised seating

Fascist era: the extreme right-wing nationalist movement of 1922–43

Flavian era: the period of rule of Emperor Vespasian and his sons, Titus and Domitian, from 69–96AD

Forum: in ancient Rome, a large open space surrounded by public buildings

Fresco: a painting made directly onto damp plaster so that the image becomes permanent

Frieze: a decorated band, often along the top of a wall

Gothic: architectural style popular between the late 12th century and the mid-16th century, recognizable by its pointed arches and ribbed vaulting on the ceiling

Greek cross: a church layout, whose ground plan resembles a cross with four equal arms (see also Latin cross)

Grotesque: style based on ancient Roman decoration found in underground ruins

Holy Door: a door in a major basilica, which is only opened in a Jubilee Year (every 25 years—the last Jubilee Year was 2000). The devout can earn an indulgence by passing through the door

Imperial age: the age of the emperors, from 27BC to 284AD

Lantern: a small roofed tower with windows all around

Lapis lazuli: a blue mineral used as a gemstone. In Renaissance Italy, it was ground to make a bright blue pigment

Latin cross: a church layout, whose ground plan resembles a cross with three short arms and one longer one

Loggia: a room or gallery that is open on one or more sides

Malachite: a bright green mineral, often used as a gemstone

Mannerism: an architectural style, popular between 1530 and 1590, characterized by breaking the rules of Classicism and using Classical forms in a way other than is traditionally be acceptable

Medallion: a round decorative panel

Medieval period: between 1000 and 1453

Nave: the long arm of a Latin cross church; the opposite end to the apse

Nymphaeum: in ancient Rome, a temple of the nymphs (semi-divine female river spirits)

Oculus: a circular opening, usually in a wall, but also at the top of a dome

Orders of columns: the style of the column. In classical architecture there are four main orders of column: Doric, Tuscan, Ionic and Corinthian. All have a base, a shaft (the main part of the column) and a capital (the decorative top part). Doric columns have fluted shafts and a simple two-part capital. Tuscan columns are similar, but with a smooth shaft. Ionic columns are usually slimmer and taller, and their capitals have two large curls (sometimes two on each face), called volutes. Corinthian columns are slimmer again, with a very elaborate capital, decorated with leaves and curls. A final order, the Composite column, has a capital similar to a Corinthian one, but topped with the volutes of an Ionic capital

Papal altar: an altar at which only the pope can say Mass

Pediment: in classical architecture, a low gable and entableture forming a triangular shape. Usually on the outside of a building, but also above doorways and fireplaces

Peristyle: columns ranged around a building or courtyard

Pier: a supporting pillar; the solid wall between two windows or other openings, or; certain types of

Gothic column that appear to be made of many shafts (when viewed in cross-section)

Pilaster: a decorative column, protruding only slightly from a wall. It will always correspond to one of the orders of column (see above)

Porphyry: a hard rock, flecked with white or red crystals

Portico: a roofed area, usually the focus of a building's façade, supported by columns and topped with a pediment (see above)

Reliquary: an elaborate container holding part of a deceased holy person's body

Renaissance (High Renaissance): a period of Classical revival, popular in 16th-century Italy, where it is sometimes called the *Rinascimento*

Republican age: from the declaration of the republic in 509BC to 27BC

Rococo: architectural style popular in the 18th century, characterized by low-relief decoration, usually in white and gold

Romanesque: an architectural style popular in the 11th–12th centuries, combining Classicism with influences from Byzantium and Islam

Rose window: large, circular window, usually in a church

Sacristy: in a church, where the vestments and sacred vessels are kept

Sarcophagus: a stone coffin

Satyr: a mythological woodland god with an animal's ears and tail

Sepulchre: a tomb cut from rock, or built from stone or brick

Stucco/stuccowork: a slow setting plaster, used to form intricate decoration

Tabernacle: in a church, an ornamental container for the consecrated host

Tempietto: literally, a small temple

Tesserae: small squares of glass, marble or stone, used to make mosaics

Transept: the short arms of a Latin cross church

Travertine stone: a white or light calcium carbonate-based rock, used for building

Triptych: a picture or carving on three panels, often used as an altarpiece

Trompe l'oeil: paintings that appear to show a room or landscape by use of perspective

Tufa: a porous rock found around mineral springs

Tympanum: between the lintel over a door and the arch above it. Also used to describe the flat area inside a pediment (see above)

Vaulting: an arched ceiling or roof

Villa: in Renaissance architecture, a country residence. Sometime used to describe the surrounding parkland

ACKNOWLEDGMENTS

Abbreviations for the credits are as follows:
AA = AA World Travel Library, t (top), b (bottom), c (centre), l (left), r (right)

UNDERSTANDING ROME

5cl AA/Alex Kouprianoff; 5c AA/Jim Holmes; 5cr AA/Peter Wilson; 8tr AA/Clive Sawyer; 8tc AA/Simon McBride; 8tcr AA/Peter Wilson; 8bcr AA/Clive Sawyer; 8br Brand X Pictures; 9tl AA/Clive Sawyer; 9cl AA/Clive Sawyer; 9bl AA/Clive Sawyer; 9br AA/Clive Sawyer; 10tr AA/Jim Holmes; 10cl AA/Clive Sawyer; 10cr AA/Simon McBride; 10bl AA/Simon McBride; 10bc AA/Jim Holmes; 10r AA/Alex Kouprianoff

LIVING ROME

11 AA/Clive Sawyer; 12/13bg AA/Clive Sawyer; 12tl AA/Jim Holmes; 12tc AA/Dario Mitidieri; 12tr AA/Clive Sawyer; 12c AA/Clive Sawyer; 12cb AA/Jim Holmes; 12b AA/Simon McBride; 13tl AA/Simon McBride; 13tc AA/Jim Holmes; 13tr AA/Clive Sawyer; 13cl AA/Clive Sawyer; 13cbl AA/Simon McBride; 13cbr AA/Clive Sawyer; 14/15bg AA/Simon McBride; 14tc AA/Jim Holmes; 14tr AA/Alex Kouprianoff; 14cl Rex Features Ltd; 14c Rex Features Ltd; 14b Rex Features Ltd; 15l AA/Alex Kouprianoff; 15tl AA/Alex Kouprianoff; 15tr Getty Images; 15c AA/Dario Mitidieri; 16/17bg AA/Clive Sawyer; 16tl AA/Clive Sawyer; 16tr AA/Dario Mitidieri; 16c AA/Max Jourdan; 16cr AA/M Siebert; 16cb AA/Jim Holmes; 16b AA/Alex Kouprianoff; 17tl AA/Jim Holmes; 17tc AA/Jim Holmes; 17tr AA/Alex Kouprianoff; 17cl AA/Jim Holmes; 18/19bg AA/Dario Mitidieri; 18tl AA/Jim Holmes; 18c AA/Jim Holmes; 18r Rex Features Ltd; 18b AA/Clive Sawyer; 19tl AA/Dario Mitidieri; 19tc AA/Clive Sawyer; 19cl AA/Dario Mitidieri; 19c AA/Clive Sawyer; 19r AA/Ken Paterson; 19b Rex Features Ltd; 20/21bg AA/Dario Mitidieri; 20tl AA/Jim Holmes; 20tc AA/Dario Mitidieri; 20r AA/Jim Holmes; 20b AA/Jim Holmes; 21tl AA/Simon McBride; 21tc AA/Martin Trelawney; 21tr AA/Terry Harris; 21c AA/Alex Kouprianoff; 21cr AA/Jim Holmes; 22/23bg Rex Features Ltd; 22tl Rex Features Ltd; 22tc Rex Features Ltd; 22cr Rex Features Ltd; 22r Rex Features Ltd; 22b Rex Features Ltd; 23tc Rex Features Ltd; 23tr Rex Features Ltd; 23cl Cinecittà Studios; 23cr Rex Features Ltd; 24bg AA/Clive Sawyer; 24tl AA/Clive Sawyer; 24tr AA/Clive Sawyer; 24cl AA/Clive Sawyer; 24c Rex Features Ltd; 24cr AA/Clive Sawyer; 24bcr AA/Clive Sawyer; 24b Rex Features Ltd

THE STORY OF ROME

25 AA/Simon McBride; 26/27bg AA; 26cl AA/Peter Wilson; 26cr AA/Jim Holmes; 26/27 AA; 27ct AA/Simon McBride; 27cl AA; 27cr AA/Peter Wilson; 27b Mary Evans Picture Library; 28/29bg AA/Simon McBride; 28ct Mary Evans Picture Library; 28c Hulton Archive/Getty Images; 28bl Mary Evans Picture Library; 28b Mary Evans Picture Library; 29c AA; 29b by courtesy of APT – Rome; 30/31bg AA/Jim Holmes; 30c AA; 30bl AA/Clive Sawyer; 30br Mary Evans Picture Library; 31l Mary Evans Picture Library; 31c AA; 31br AA/Jim Holmes; 32/33bg AA/Simon McBride; 32c AA; 32bl AA/Clive Sawyer; 32br AA/Jim Holmes; 33c AA/Jim Holmes; 33cr AA/Clive Sawyer; 33bl AA/Simon McBride; 33bc by courtesy of APT – Rome; 33br AA/Peter Wilson; 34/35bg AA/Peter Wilson; 34cr AA; 34bl Mary Evans Picture Library; 34bc AA/Peter Wilson; 34/35 AA/Jim Holmes; 35cl AA; 35cr AA/Alex Kouprianoff; 35b AA; 36/37bg AA/Dario Mitidieri; 36c AA; 36bl AA/Simon McBride; 36b AA/Peter Wilson; 36/37 AA; 37c AA/Dario Mitidieri; 37cr AA/Jim Holmes; 37b AA/Dario Mitidieri; 38/39bg AA/Peter Wilson; 38c Hulton Archive/Getty Images; 38cr AA; 38bl Mary Evans Picture Library; 38/39 Mary Evans Picture Library; 39cl Hulton Archive/Getty Images; 39bl AA/Simon McBride; 39bc AA/Peter Wilson; 40bg AA/Jim Holmes; 40c Hulton Archive/Getty Images; 40cr Rex Features Ltd; 40bl Hulton Archive/Getty Images; 40br Hulton Archive/Getty Images

ON THE MOVE

41 Digital Vision; 42t Digital Vision; 42c Digital Vision; 43t Digital Vision; 43c Digital Vision; 44t AA/Simon McBride; 44ct AA/Simon McBride; 44c AA/Martyn Adelman; 44cr AA/Simon McBride; 45t AA/Barrie Smith; 45c AA/Simon McBride; 45b AA/Simon McBride; 46t AA/Barrie Smith; 46c AA/Simon McBride; 46bl AA/Simon McBride; 46bc AA/Simon McBride; 47t AA/Barrie Smith; 47ct AA/Simon McBride; 47cb AA/Simon McBride; 47bl

AA/Max Jourdan; 47bc AA/Simon McBride; 48t AA/Barrie Smith; 48c AA/Simon McBride; 49t AA/Barrie Smith; 49c AA/Simon McBride; 50 AA/Barrie Smith; 51t AA/Clive Sawyer; 51cr AA/Jim Holmes; 51cl AA/Max Jourdan; 51b AA/Jim Holmes; 52t AA/Peter Wilson; 52c AA/Jim Holmes; 52b AA/Max Jourdan; 52/3 Digital Vision; 53t AA/Clive Sawyer; 53c AA/Simon McBride; 54t Digital Vision; 54b The picture used has been accorded by Regency San Marino srl www.accessibleitaly.com

THE SIGHTS

55 AA/Simon McBride; 60cl AA/Simon McBride; 60cr AA/Simon McBride; 61cl AA/Jim Holmes; 61cr AA/Clive Sawyer; 61b AA/Alex Kouprianoff; 62cl AA/Alex Kouprianoff; 62cr AA/Clive Sawyer; 63cl AA/Jim Holmes; 63cr AA/Simon McBride; 64c AA/Jim Holmes; 64b AA/Clive Sawyer; 65tl AA/Dario Mitidieri; 65tc AA/Simon McBride; 65tr Casa di Goethe; 66 main AA/Simon McBride; 66 inset by courtesy of APT – Rome; 67t by courtesy of APT – Rome; 67cl AA/Dario Mitidieri; 67c AA/Peter Wilson; 67cr AA/Simon McBride; 68c by courtesy of APT – Rome; 68b AA/Clive Sawyer; 70 AA/Tony Souter; 71lcl AA/Simon McBride; 71cl by courtesy of APT – Rome; 71cr AA/Dario Mitidieri; 71rcr AA/Simon McBride; 72t AA/Simon McBride; 72c AA/Jim Holmes; 73 main by courtesy of APT – Rome; 73 inset AA/Simon McBride; 74 AA/Simon McBride; 75t AA/Peter Wilson; 75c AA/Simon McBride; 76c AA/Clive Sawyer; 76b AA/Jim Holmes; 76/77 AA/A Kouprianoff; 78tl AA/Clive Sawyer; 78tc AA/Clive Sawyer; 78tr AA; 79tl AA/Dario Mitidieri; 79tr Allegory of Fame by Sebastiano Conca (1680-1764) Accademia di San Luca, Rome, Italy/Bridgeman Art Library; 80t AA/Simon McBride; 80c by courtesy of APT – Rome; 81 main AA/Clive Sawyer; 81 inset AA/Simon McBride; 82t AA/Jim Holmes; 82c by courtesy of APT – Rome; 82b AA/Simon McBride; 83t AA/Jim Holmes; 83c AA/Tony Souter; 83b AA/Jim Holmes; 84 AA/A Kouprianoff; 85t AA/Simon McBride; 86cl AA/Simon McBride; 86cr AA/Clive Sawyer; 87 by courtesy of APT – Rome; 88 AA/Alex Kouprianoff; 89cl AA/Simon McBride; 89c AA/Alex Kouprianoff; 89cr by courtesy of APT – Rome; 89b AA/Simon McBride; 90tl AA/Jim Holmes; 90tc AA/Simon McBride; 91tl AA/Alex Kouprianoff; 91tc AA/Alex Kouprianoff; 91tr by courtesy of APT – Rome; 92 AA/Dario Mitidieri; 93t AA/Kathy Gould; 93cl AA/Dario Mitidieri; 93c AA/P Wilson; 93cr AA/Dario Mitidieri; 94/95 AA/Dario Mitidieri; 94b AA/Dario Mitidieri; 95t AA/Dario Mitidieri; 95b Apollo and Daphne, 1622–25 (marble) by Giovanni Lorenzo Bernini (1598–1680) Galleria Borthese, Rome, Italy/Bridgeman Art Library (Lauros/Giraudon/Bridgeman Art Library); 96 The Prodigal Son (oil on canvas) by Guercino (Giovanni Grancesco Barbieri) (1591–1666) Galleria Borghese, Rome, Italy/Bridgeman Art Library; 97 The Ecstasy of Saint Catherine (oil on canvas) by Agostino Carracci (1557–1602) Galleria Borghese, Rome, Italy/Bridgeman Art Library; 98 AA/Clive Sawyer; 99t AA/Clive Sawyer; 99cl AA/Simon McBride; 99c AA/Simon McBride; 99cr AA/Jim Holmes; 99b AA/Jim Holmes; 100t AA/Clive Sawyer; 100b AA/Clive Sawyer; 101t AA/Clive Sawyer; 101c AA/Clive Sawyer; 101b AA/Clive Sawyer; 102 AA/Clive Sawyer; 103 AA/Clive Sawyer; 104 AA/Simon McBride; 105t AA/Clive Sawyer; 105cl AA/Simon McBride; 105c AA/Simon McBride; 105cr AA/Alex Kouprianoff; 106 AA/Simon McBride; 108t AA/Simon McBride; 108c AA/Simon McBride; 109t AA/Simon McBride; 109b AA/Jim Holmes; 110tl AA/Dario Mitidieri; 110tc AA/Clive Sawyer; 110tr AA/Alex Kouprianoff; 111tl AA/Jim Holmes; 111tr AA/Simon McBride; 112t AA/Simon McBride; 112c AA/Jim Holmes; 113t Scala; 113c AA/Simon McBride; 113b A Gaul Committing Suicide, Pergamon School, 3rd century BC (marble) (b/w photo) Palazzo Altemps, Rome, Italy/Bridgeman Art Library (Bridgeman Art Library/Alinari); 114c AA/Peter Wilson; 114b AA/Jim Holmes; 115 AA/Peter Wilson; 116t Sleeping Hermaphrodite (marble) (b/w photo) Palazzo Massimo alle Terme, Rome, Italy/Bridgeman Art Library (Bridgeman Art Library/Alinari); 116c Seated women before a statue, detail from Room B of the Villa Farnesina (fresco) (b/w photo) Palazzo Massimo alle Terme, Rome, Italy/Bridgeman Art Library (Bridgeman Art Library/Alinari); 116b The 'Lancellotti' Discus Thrower (bronze) (b/w photo) Palazzo Massimo alle Terme, Rome, Italy/Bridgeman Art Library (Bridgeman

Art Library/Alinari); 117t AA/Simon McBride; 117c Hippopotamus hunt with a view of the Nile, from Villa Maccarani (mosaic) (b/w photo) Palazzo Massimo alle Terme, Rome, Italy/Bridgeman Art Library (Bridgeman Art Library/Alinari); 118tl by courtesy of APT – Rome; 118tc AA/Dario Mitidieri; 118tr AA/Jim Holmes; 119tl AA/Jim Holmes; 119tc AA/Alex Kouprianoff; 119tr AA/Dario Mitidieri; 119b AA/Simon McBride; 120t AA/Dario Mitidieri; 120c AA/Simon McBride; 121 AA/S McBride; 122t AA/Alex Kouprianoff; 122lcl AA/Jim Holmes; 122cl AA/Alex Kouprianoff; 122cr AA/Alex Kouprianoff; 122rcr AA/Jim Holmes; 123t AA/Peter Wilson; 123b AA/Jim Holmes; 124t AA/Simon McBride; 124c AA/Tony Souter; 124b AA/Clive Sawyer; 125 main AA/Clive Sawyer; 125 inset by courtesy of APT – Rome; 126t by courtesy of APT – Rome; 126cl AA/Dario Mitidieri; 126cr AA/Jim Holmes; 127 main AA/Clive Sawyer; 127 inset AA/Dario Mitidieri; 128tl AA/Dario Mitidieri; 128tc AA/Clive Sawyer; 128tr AA/Jim Holmes; 129tl AA/Jim Holmes; 129tc AA/Jim Holmes; 129tr AA/Simon McBride; 130t AA/Dario Mitidieri; 130c AA/Clive Sawyer; 131t Corbis; 131cl AA/Simon McBride; 131cr AA/Jim Holmes; 131b AA/Jim Holmes; 132tl AA/Jim Holmes; 132tc AA/Dario Mitidieri; 132tr AA/Alex Kouprianoff; 133tl AA/Simon McBride; 133tr AA/Jim Holmes; 134t AA/Simon McBride; 134cl AA/Jim Holmes; 134cr AA/Simon McBride; 135cl AA/Peter Wilson; 135c AA/Simon McBride; 135cr AA/Peter Wilson; 135b AA/Simon McBride; 136tl AA/Dario Mitidieri; 136tc AA/Dario Mitidieri; 136tr AA/Jim Holmes; 137tl AA/Dario Mitidieri; 137tr AA/Dario Mitidieri; 138t AA/Dario Mitidieri; 138cl AA/Simon McBride; 139c AA/Dario Mitidieri; 139b AA/Simon McBride; 140bl AA/Clive Sawyer; 140br AA/Clive Sawyer; 141t AA/Simon McBride; 141b AA/Simon McBride; 142tl AA/Dario Mitidieri; 142tc AA/Jim Holmes; 142tr AA/Jim Holmes; 143tl Santa Stefano Rotondo; 143tc by courtesy of APT – Rome; 143tr AA/Simon McBride; 144t AA/Simon McBride; 144c AA/Alex Kouprianoff; 144b AA/Jim Holmes; 145t AA/Alex Kouprianoff; 145lcl AA/Alex Kouprianoff; 145cl AA/Simon McBride; 145cr AA/Jim Holmes; 145rcr AA/Simon McBride; 146tl AA/Peter Wilson; 146tc AA/Peter Wilson; 146tr AA/Jim Holmes; 147 AA/Clive Sawyer; 148t AA/Clive Sawyer; 148cl AA/Clive Sawyer; 148cr AA/Clive Sawyer; 149c AA/Clive Sawyer; 149cr AA/Clive Sawyer; 149b AA/Clive Sawyer; 150t AA/Jim Holmes; 150c AA/Clive Sawyer

Project editor
Kathy Gould

AA Travel Guides design team
David Austin, Glyn Barlow, Alan Gooch, Kate Harling, Bob Johnson,
Nick Otway, Carole Philp, Keith Russell

Picture research
Liz Allen, Chris Butler, Debbie Ireland, Charlotte Lippmann, Vivien Little, Serena Mellish, Carol Walker

Internal repro work
Susan Crowhurst, Ian Little, Michael Moody

Production
Lyn Kirby, Helen Sweeney

Mapping
Maps produced by the Cartography Department of AA Publishing

Main contributors
Sally Roy (consultant), Anton Alexander, The Content Works, Giovanna Dunmall, Adele Evans,
Tim Jepson, Simona Marchetta, Lee Marshall, Michael Nation, Frank Van den Broeke

Copy editors
Audrey Horne, Janet Tabinski

Updater
Frances Wolverton

Revision management
Cambridge Publishing Management Ltd

Published by AA Publishing, a trading name of Automobile Association Developments Limited, whose
registered office is Fanum House, Basing View, Basingstoke, RG21 4EA. Registered number 1878835.

A CIP catalogue record for this book is available from the British Library.
ISBN 10: 0-7495-4009-5
ISBN 13: 978-0-7495-4009-8

Key Guide is a registered trademark in Australia and is used under license.
Binding style with plastic section dividers by permission of AA Publishing.
Colour separation by Keenes
Printed and bound by Leo, China

Find out more about AA Publishing and the wide range of travel publications and services the AA
provides by visiting our website at www.theAA.com/bookshop

A02359
Mapping in this title produced from:
Map data © 1997–2003 Navigation Technologies BV. All rights reserved.
Mapping © GEOnext (Gruppo De Agostini) Novara
Relief map images supplied by Mountain High Maps ® Copyright © 1993 Digital Wisdom, Inc
Weather chart statistics supplied by Weatherbase © Copyright 2003 Canty and Associates, LLC

We believe the contents of this book are correct at the time of printing. However, some details,
particularly prices, opening times and telephone numbers do change. We do not accept
responsibility for any consequences arising from the use of this book. This does not affect your
statutory rights. We would be grateful if readers would advise us of any inaccuracies they may
encounter, or any suggestions they might like to make to improve the book. There is a form
provided at the back of the book for this purpose, or you can email us at Keyguides@theaa.com

COVER PICTURE CREDITS

Front Cover and Spine: AA/P Wilson Back Cover, top to bottom: AA/C Sawyer, AA/C Sawyer,
AA/D Miterdiri, AA/J Holmes

Dear Key Guide Reader

●

Thank you for buying this Key Guide. Your comments and opinions are very important to us, so please help us to improve our travel guides by taking a few minutes to complete this questionnaire.

You do not need a stamp (unless posted outside the UK). If you do not want to cut this page from your guide, then photocopy it or write your answers on a plain sheet of paper.

Send to: Key Guide Editor, AA World Travel Guides
FREEPOST SCE 4598, Basingstoke RG21 4GY

Find out more about AA Publishing and the wide range of travel publications the AA provides by visiting our website at
www.theAA.com/bookshop

ABOUT THIS GUIDE

Which Key Guide did you buy? _____

Where did you buy it?_____

When? _ _ month/ _ _ year

Why did you choose this AA Key Guide?
❏ Price ❏ AA Publication
❏ Used this series before; title _____
❏ Cover ❏ Other (please state) _____

Please let us know how helpful the following features of the guide were to you by circling the appropriate category: very helpful (**VH**), helpful (**H**) or little help (**LH**)

Size	**VH**	**H**	**LH**
Layout	**VH**	**H**	**LH**
Photos	**VH**	**H**	**LH**
Excursions	**VH**	**H**	**LH**
Entertainment	**VH**	**H**	**LH**
Hotels	**VH**	**H**	**LH**
Maps	**VH**	**H**	**LH**
Practical info	**VH**	**H**	**LH**
Restaurants	**VH**	**H**	**LH**
Shopping	**VH**	**H**	**LH**
Walks	**VH**	**H**	**LH**
Sights	**VH**	**H**	**LH**
Transport info	**VH**	**H**	**LH**

What was your favourite sight, attraction or feature listed in the guide?

Page _____ Please give your reason _____

Which features in the guide could be changed or improved? Or are there any other comments you would like to make?

ABOUT YOU

Name (*Mr/Mrs/Ms*) _____

Address _____

_____

Postcode _____ Daytime tel nos _____
Please *only* give us your mobile phone number if you wish to hear from
us about other products and services from the AA and partners by text or mms.

Which age group are you in?
Under 25 ❑   25–34 ❑   35–44 ❑   45–54 ❑   55+ ❑

How many trips do you make a year?
Less than 1 ❑   1 ❑   2 ❑   3 or more ❑

ABOUT YOUR TRIP

Are you an AA member?   Yes ❑ No ❑

When did you book?   _ _ month/_ _ year

When did you travel?   _ _ month/_ _ year

Reason for your trip?   Business ❑ Leisure ❑

How many nights did you stay? _____

How did you travel?   Individual ❑ Couple ❑ Family ❑ Group ❑

Did you buy any other travel guides for your trip? _____

If yes, which ones? _____

_____

Thank you for taking the time to complete this questionnaire. Please send it to us as
soon as possible, and remember, you do not need a stamp (*unless posted outside
the UK*).

Titles in the Key Guide series:
Australia, Barcelona, Britain, Brittany, Canada, Costa Rica, Florence and Tuscany, France, Germany,
Ireland, Italy, London, Mallorca, Mexico, New York, New Zealand, Normandy, Paris, Portugal, Prague,
Provence and the Côte d'Azur, Rome, Scotland, South Africa, Spain, Venice, Vietnam.
To be published in November 2006:
Thailand